CITY OF WORDS

CITY OF WORDS

American Fiction 1950–1970

TONY TANNER

Harper & Row, Publishers
New York · Evanston · San Francisco · London

1817

Portions of this book have appeared previously in slightly different form.
Thanks are due to the *Critical Quarterly, Novel, London Magazine, Salmagundi, Twentieth Century Studies, Partisan Review* and *TriQuarterly*.

FIRST U.S. EDITION

STANDARD BOOK NUMBER: 06-014217-0

LIBRARY OF CONGRESS CATALOG CARD NUMBER: 70-156554

Contents

6 CONTENTS

FOR MARCIA

So, at any rate, fanciful as my plea may appear, I recover the old sense — brave even the imputation of making a mere Rome of words, talking of a Rome of my own which was no Rome of reality. That comes up as exactly the point — that no Rome of reality was concerned in our experience, that the whole thing was a rare state of the imagination ...

Henry James: *William Wetmore Story*
and His Friends

Prefatory Note

This book is a study of some of the novels written in America between 1950 and 1970. Indirectly I hope it manages to say something about the novel as a form and America as a country as well. I should stress from the outset that my primary aim is to try to *understand* the American imagination as it has expressed itself in fictional forms during this period. I think such efforts of understanding addressed to contemporary literature can be helpful, and that they are quite as much a part of the critic's task as the revivification of the literature of the past. A close study of the literature of the present can help us to arrive at a clearer perception of some of the plights and privileges of our own inescapable modernity. As John Cage says—'Here we are now.' The last two decades have seen important changes and developments in American life and literature, and I felt that there was more than usual justification for a detailed consideration of a large number of works. On a more personal level, this book represents a long meditation on what America and its literature have meant to me since I first went there in 1958 and contracted an incurable interest in, and affection for, both. I would like this book to stand as a tribute, offered with admiration and gratitude, to the many good people, places and books I have encountered there.

Although I have tried to cover most of the more interesting novelists of the past two decades, there are inevitably some omissions. I have not, for instance, considered the work of William Styron, James Jones, James Baldwin, Jack Kerouac, Flannery O'Connor, Mary McCarthy, J. F. Powers, Thomas Berger, Terry Southern, Richard Stern, Paul Bowles or Jean Stafford to name only a few. I regret that I did not have the space to consider some of the more recent writers such as Joyce Carol Oates, Charles Newman, Robert Coover, Irvin Faust, Leonard Michaels, Rudolph Wurlitzer, Ishmael Reed, Alison Lurie and Gil Orlovitz. But the book is already long and I must leave my principle of selection to justify itself, or fail to, as the case may be. With any book of this kind there is the difficulty of deciding whether to assume that the reader has read the novel under discussion or needs to be told the story. I have tried to write each chapter in such a way that it will contain enough material to enable someone with no previous knowledge of the writer concerned to read it and understand what the novels are about. On the other hand I have tried

II

to avoid wearying the informed reader with plot summaries and re-capitulations. Background material which I consider to be relevant and illuminating is contained in a series of appendices which should, ideally, be read in connection with the chapters which refer to them. Considerations of length have also made me decide to keep annotation to a minimum and I have not attempted to find room to include bibliographies for so many writers. Such bibliographies already can fill whole issues of valuable magazines like *Critique* and it seems unnecessary to repeat them here.[1]

In the field of criticism there are of course forerunners to the work offered here. *Radical Innocence* by Ihab Hassan[2] and *After Alienation* by Marcus Klein,[3] for instance, are two books which I respect and whose importance I want to acknowledge. I only came across Robert Scholes's *The Fabulators*[4] when this present manuscript was substantially completed, but it is clearly an important work in this field. Leslie Fiedler's *Waiting for the End*[5] is characteristically idiosyncratic and stimulating. As my own approach is different from any of those I have encountered, I have not thought it desirable to extend the text by constantly pointing out the self-evident fact that other critics have interesting ideas and comments on the same writers. Specific debts are acknowledged in the text or notes. I would single out the work of Richard Poirier on American literature as having provided a constant stimulus (in particular his book *A World Elsewhere*[6]).

I am indebted to the universities of Northwestern, Emory and Stanford for having invited me to hold seminars on contemporary American fiction. I first tried out many of my ideas in these seminars and I have profited greatly from the discussions which followed. I would like to express my gratitude to all those students who took part in these seminars, as well as more generally to the faculty members of those universities who made our visits so interesting and pleasant. I am indebted to the Provost and Fellows of King's College for allowing me to take a year off from teaching, and to Mr Patrick Parrinder who took over my duties during that period. Without this time I could not have written this book. I would like to express my sense of indebtedness to the many friends with whom I have discussed matters which are raised in this book—Henry Nash Smith, Charles Newman, Ian Watt, Thom Gunn, Don Doody are some of them. I am grateful to Dr Robert Young for some discussions (and loan of books) concerning Behaviorism; and to Mr Renford Bambrough of St John's College, Cambridge, for some helpful correspondence clarifying a point about Wittgenstein which I make in my Conclusion. I would like to express my gratitude to Ed Victor for suggesting that I write the book in the first place, and for his subsequent valuable editorial help. I also wish to thank Annabel Whittet for her alert copy-editing, and Rina Clark for her splendidly prompt, reliable and intelligent typing.

Finally I wish to record my great indebtedness to my wife who has participated in every stage of this book. Many of the ideas in it arose out of conversations with her, and her suggestions, comments and editorial work on the text have been, quite simply, indispensable. The dedication to her is offered as a, necessarily inadequate, act of recognition.

King's College, Cambridge   TONY TANNER
January 1970

Introduction

When I started thinking about writing this book I had no pre-
conceived notions about recurrent themes by which I could group
writers, or neat categories in which I could place their work. If anything, I embarked on my readings and re-readings motivated mainly
by a sense of admiration for the wide range of individual talent which
had emerged in American fiction during the last two decades. I have
tried to preserve my respect for the individual achievement by
offering detailed consideration of a number of novels, and, for the
most part, allowing a chapter for each separate author. To some
extent these chapters are intended to be self-contained studies of the
writers concerned. At the same time, with continued intensive reading, certain recurring preoccupations, concerns, even obsessions,
began to emerge from what at first appeared to be very dissimilar
novels. I hope these recurring patterns of interest will be seen to
distinguish themselves quite naturally in the course of this book,
without any sense that a corresponding attempt has been made to
detract from the individuality of each author's work.

One or two of the more prominent preoccupations may be mentioned in this introduction as a prelude to an explanation of the title
of my book. I shall try to show that there is an abiding dream in
American literature that an unpatterned, unconditioned life is
possible, in which your movements and stillnesses, choices and
repudiations are all your own; and that there is also an abiding
American dread that someone else is patterning your life, that there
are all sorts of invisible plots afoot to rob you of your autonomy of
thought and action, that conditioning is ubiquitous. The problematical and ambiguous relationship of the self to patterns of all kinds —
social, psychological, linguistic — is an obsession among recent
American writers. It has long been recognized that there is a tenacious feeling in America that while other, older countries are ridden
by conventions, rules, all sorts of arbitrary formalities which trap
and mould the individual, in America one may still enjoy a genuine
freedom from all cultural patterning so that life is a series of unmediated spontaneities. But the social anthropologist has now told
the American individual that 'man has no direct contact with
experience *per se* but ... there is an intervening set of patterns which

channel his senses and his thoughts' (see Appendix One); the Behavioral psychologist has insisted that 'the situation we are in dominates us always' (see Appendix Two); while the linguist has asserted that 'the forms of a person's thoughts are controlled by inexorable laws of pattern of which he is unconscious' (see Appendix Three).

Such theories or assertions have certainly helped to enhance the American writer's dread of all conditioning forces to the point of paranoia which is detectable not only in the subject matter of many novels but also in their narrative devices. Narrative lines are full of hidden persuaders, hidden dimensions, plots, secret organizations, evil systems, all kinds of conspiracies against spontaneity of consciousness, even cosmic take-over. The possible nightmare of being totally controlled by unseen agencies and powers is never far away in contemporary American fiction. The unease revealed in such novels is related to a worried apprehension on the part of the author that his own consciousness may be predetermined and channelled by the language he has been born into.

Here then is the paradox for a writer. If he wants to write in any communicable form he must traffic in a language which may at every turn be limiting, directing and perhaps controlling his responses and formulations. If he feels that the given structuring of reality of the available language is imprisoning or iniquitous, he may abandon language altogether; or he may seek to use the existing language in such a way that he demonstrates to himself and other people that he does not accept nor wholly conform to the structures built into the common tongue, that he has the power to resist and perhaps disturb the particular 'rubricizing' tendency of the language he has inherited. Such an author—and I think he is an unusually common phenomenon in contemporary America—will go out of his way to show that he is using language as it has never been used before, leaving the visible marks of his idiosyncrasies on every formulation. Of course, this is not in itself a new position for the writer to find himself in. The desire or compulsion to project the shape of one's own unique consciousness against the imprisoning shapes of the external world is a crucial component of Romanticism. Saul Bellow's suspicion of 'agreed pictures', or what he also calls 'systems', is in line with epistemological dissent which goes back at least as far as Blake, who said in 'Jerusalem', 'I must Create a System or be enslav'd by another Man's.'*

---

* Long before any American writer was bemoaning the fact that we inherit the 'agreed pictures' of reality handed down by a past age, Blake had defined the process in 'Marriage of Heaven and Hell':

But there is another side to this self-preserving creation of one's own 'system', and we can go to another writer from the first part of the Romantic movement for a concise formulation of it. Thus Coleridge: 'We have imprisoned our own conceptions by the lines which we have drawn in order to exclude the conceptions of others.' That which *defines* you at the same time *confines* you. It is possible to become imprisoned in a system of your own choosing as well as in a system of another's imposing. At the same time there has to be some sort of system because you cannot have pure unstructured consciousness nor, as long as you are involved in language, can you have pure unmediated reality. (William James makes the point with characteristic vigour. 'Had we no concepts we should live simply "getting" each successive moment of experience, as the sessile sea-anemone on its rock receives whatever nourishment the wash of the waves may bring.' It is worth noting that this image suggests that without language we would return to a fluid state and go with the flow, or 'the wash of the waves'. The crucial opposition between language and 'flow' is one to which I will return in the last chapter.) Any writer has to struggle with existing language which is perpetually tending to rigidify in old formulations, and he must constantly assert his own patterning powers without at the same time becoming imprisoned in *them*.

It is my contention that many recent American writers are unusually aware of this quite fundamental and inescapable paradox: that to exist, a book, a vision, a system, like a person, has to have an outline—there can be no identity without contour. But contours signify arrest, they involve restraint and the acceptance of limits. The main villain, Urizen, in Blake's myth is named after horizon, that is to say limit or boundary, and I think many American writers share Blake's feeling. For restraint means the risk of rigidity, and rigidity,

---

The ancient Poets animated all sensible objects with Gods or Geniuses, calling them by the names and adorning them with the properties of woods, rivers, mountains, lakes, cities, nations, and whatever their enlarged and numerous senses could perceive.
    And particularly they studied the genius of each city & country, placing it under its mental deity:
    Till a system was formed, which some took advantage of, & enslav'd the vulgar by attempting to realize or abstract the mental deities from their objects: thus began Priesthood ...

And thus, to move back to our own times, began those competing image systems put out by political ideologies and mass media alike which upset so many contemporary American writers because each image system implicitly claims that it *is* reality and not an arbitrary, and often pernicious, abstraction of selected aspects of it.

so the feeling goes, is just about the beginning of *rigor mortis*. Between the non-identity of pure fluidity and the fixity involved in all definitions—in words or in life—the American writer moves, and knows he moves. This I think can be discerned in some basic similarities of plot and situation and image which recur in apparently very different novels. I suggest that this is because the plot—the situation of the character among things—is a reflection or projection of the author's sense of his own situation among words. I am advancing the idea that if we ask, what is the relation of the recent American hero to his environment? we are also asking, what is the relation of the recent American writer to his language? (A good example of what I mean would be *Lolita*. This is of course 'about' the love affair between Humbert and Lolita, but, as Nabokov himself has implied, it is also very much about the author's love affair with the English language.)

It may help to clarify the point if I give a minor example of a recurring image which appears in a number of different novels, each time applicable both to the plot situation and the author's situation. Augie March learns from Einhorn that 'in the naked form of the human jelly, one should choose or seize with force'. The unnamed narrator of *Invisible Man* describes a nightmare told to him by a girl 'in which she lay in the center of a large dark room, becoming a formless mass while her eyes ran in bilious jelly up the chimney. And so it is', he continues, 'without light I am not only invisible, but formless as well; and to be unaware of one's form is to live a death.' The narrator of *Naked Lunch* by the end can say, 'I am always somewhere *Outside* giving orders and *Inside* this straight-jacket of jelly', the jelly of the human body which is 'stamped with the seal of alien inspection'. With only a slight change in the image Rojack in *An American Dream* says of his relationship to Deborah that 'marriage to her was the armature of my ego; remove the armature and I might topple like clay.' While in *Cabot Wright Begins*, Cabot Wright comes on this crucial passage in an old book of popular science shortly before embarking on his career as a rapist: 'The animals of the open sea are conveniently divided into the active swimmers (nekton) and the more passive drifters (plankton). The swimmers include whales ... The drifters, jelly-fishes.'

Clay, jelly, jelly-fish—what this image cluster suggests is the dread of utter formlessness, of being a soft, vulnerable, endlessly manipulable blob, of not being a distinct self. The nightmare of non-identity, of no-form, is a recurrent one. On the other hand, any one adopted armature which will contain and give shape and definition to the jelly or clay is at the same time felt to be an imprisoning deathly

constriction, as Rojack's marriage is; and in the name of liberty
these armatures, or imposed outlines, or the constructions other
people build around us are to be cast off or broken through. (Wilhelm
Reich's stress on the need to 'dissolve' the 'character armor' is
relevant here, see Appendix Four.) But then there follows the risk of
a return to formlessness. In *Cabot Wright Begins* Warburton
denounces America as 'a nation of frozen jelly-fish'. This is the worst
of both worlds—a sort of rigidified shapelessness. The problem for
the author and his hero alike is how are these undesirable alternatives
to be avoided; can the binary opposition of fixity/fluidity be mediated
by some third state or term?

This problem is quite crucial when it comes to working out the
desirable relationships between self and society, and the whole
problem of 'identity' is such an obsessive one among the novelists I
shall be discussing that I have added a short appendix on various
non-fictional approaches to the problem (see Appendix Five). The
kind of paradox suggested by Walt Whitman when he celebrated
both the idea of an American society in which everyone would flow
together in a loving 'ensemble', and also the 'principle of individuality, the pride and centripetal isolation of a human being in himself
—identity—personalism', still confronts the American writer in
various forms. We may say that a central concern for the hero of
many recent American novels is this: can he find a freedom which is
not a jelly, and can he establish an identity which is not a prison? I
will be looking at this problem in chapters to come, but at this point
I would add that the dilemma and quest of the hero are often analogous to those of the author. Can he find a *stylistic* freedom which is
not simply a meaningless incoherence, and can he find a stylistic
form which will not trap him inside the existing forms of previous
literature?

Between social space and private, inner space, there is a third or
mediating area in which the writer searches for his freedom and
his form—and that of course is verbal space. To say that this space is
important for writers would be the most foolish kind of tautology,
but the peculiar importance of this space for the American writer is
something which I shall seek to demonstrate. The importance of
verbal space as being the space in which the writer can not only
arrange his perceptions of the external world in his own pattern, but
also allow his consciousness to have what Henry James called its 'fun'
('if we but allow the term its full extension') has been recognized
and described by Richard Poirier in his admirable and important
book *A World Elsewhere*, from which I wish to quote some relevant
passages.

The books which in my view constitute a distinctive American tradition within English literature are early, and often clumsy examples of a modernist impulse in fiction: they resist within their pages the forces of environment that otherwise dominate the world. Their styles have an eccentricity of defiance, even if the defiance shows sometimes as carelessness ... they both resemble and serve their heroes by trying to create an environment of 'freedom', though as writers their efforts must be wholly in language ... the greatest American authors really do try, against the perpetually greater power of reality, to create an environment that might allow some longer existence to the hero's momentary expansions of consciousness.

And, as he goes on to imply, to the author's own expansions of consciousness as well. To the extent that a writer is having what James called his 'fun' (see Appendix Six) he feels free of the conditioning and controlling forces.

In this connection I want to introduce a term which I think is useful to describe certain characteristics of contemporary American writing. In describing the style of writers like Melville, Hawthorne and James, one could say that it is a style which pays unusual attention to 'foreground'. I first found the term applied to prose in G. B. Tennyson's excellent book *Sartor Called Resartus*[1] and he in turn had taken it from the Prague school of linguists. It indicates the use of language in such a way that it draws attention to itself—often by its originality. Obviously the term is of widespread applicability in discussing literature. One could say that some writing, like that of Jane Austen, seems to have a minimum of foreground, the language inviting no lingering at the surface but directing us instantly back to its referents. While other writing, Carlyle's for instance, as Tennyson shows, is heavily foregrounded and we are compelled to submit to the turbulence, or share the delight, of the writer's mind working itself out in visible verbal performance. (Just so, a patch of paint on a canvas can be representational or function as a paint mark referring only to surface texture and design. Richard Hamilton, for instance, has shown how paint can operate both as a sign and as a thing in itself within the same frame, and I am suggesting that within the same book words can be both referential and part of a verbal display.) I have introduced the term here because I think that much contemporary American writing is foregrounded to a remarkable extent, and that it was precisely in such foregrounding that writers like Melville and James liberated and explored the potentialities of their own consciousness. Foregrounding is also a way of demonstrating one's resistance to, and liberation from, other people's notions as to how one should use language to organize reality. The environment of freedom made possible by language—particularly by foregrounding—is the 'world elsewhere' referred to in Poirier's title, neatly adapted from *Coriolanus*, and as such it is closely related to my designation of the City of Words—a title which I will now try to explain.

It was suggested by a sentence in Vladimir Nabokov's *Pale Fire*, which reads: 'In the vicinity of Lex he lost his way among steep tortuous lanes.' 'He' is the thug Gradus who, according to the narrator, assassinates the poet John Shade. He loses his way in the city of Lex (= Word) because he has no imagination, takes no delight in fictions and art, and has no sense of the possibilities afforded to consciousness by the hospitable realm of language. He is a mindless brute, the basest kind of materialist who will never be at home in the lanes of Lex. For to the extent that a man does master those lanes, he is emancipated from that impoverishment of consciousness and destructive stupidity epitomized by Gradus. On this reading, my title could obviously apply to any writers, for they all live in the city of Lex. I would seek to justify invoking it with particular reference to American writers by suggesting that they reveal an unusual degree of awareness of this City of Words. Not the sort of awareness evinced by a writer like Flaubert; rather, a general self-consciousness about the strange relationship between the provinces of words and things, and the problematical position of man, who participates in both. With Hawthorne, the American writer often seems to feel or imply—'I am a citizen of somewhere else.' I have taken the liberty of calling that 'somewhere else' the City of Words.

Consider, for instance, Melville's *Moby Dick* which, as everyone knows, is about a whaling voyage of multiple significance. If you asked someone how the book opened he would probably answer with the famous sentence—'Call me Ishmael.' But if we look again we find that the first word is 'Etymology', followed by a description of a 'late consumptive usher to a grammar school'. 'The pale Usher—threadbare in coat, heart, body, and brain; I see him now. He was ever dusting his old lexicons and grammars, with a queer handkerchief, mockingly embellished with all the gay flags of all the known nations of the world.' Some etymology is duly provided, supposedly by this usher, followed by a series of 'Extracts' from sources as various as Genesis and Darwin, covering a wide range of sacred and secular texts, 'supplied by a sub-sub-librarian'. All in all, it is a very 'bookish' beginning, reminding us comically yet seriously of documents as well as whales. It makes us aware that what we are holding is just one more document, and that Melville himself is a kind of usher or librarian handing to us his own very special kind of lexicon.

More than that, I think, it immediately opens the suggestion that the book itself will be about the relationship of language to objects, as well as the relationship of men to whales. For naming is a kind of harpooning (we speak of 'pinning things down' when we have defined them), and in giving such prominence to man's naming activities before moving on to his hunting instincts, Melville is surely making a crucial point. That first sentence of the narrative offers us another clue. 'Call me Ishmael' — not 'I am Ishmael'. This touch of vernacular casualness is more than a hint about the narrator's character. The book is about the whole 'calling' process. Ahab's ultimate error is that he believes in the identity of names and things. He calls the white whale evil, then affirms that it *is* evil. The violence with which he speaks of the whale as a wall and a mask through which he wants to smash is a manifestation of his annihilating egoism which attempts to destroy, or devour, the world to replace it by self. Just as Ahab swallows the crew, so he wants to engorge the world outside him. The attempt is of course disastrous, the world swallows him in a vortex and also sucks down the ship, which he has transformed into an extension of himself. With his ropes and harpoons he had sought to ensnare the whale; at the end he is indeed in direct contact with the whale, tied to it by his own equipment. It is a fatal attachment and offers a graphic illustration of the fate of consciousness that seeks to appropriate the reality which will lie for ever outside it.

If the book has a moral, it is the very American one that we should respect the mysterious otherness of nature and not seek to possess it. The book itself dramatizes its own meaning. By the end we know everything about what men have thought and said and written about the whale, all the versions of it they have formulated, from the religious to the utilitarian. We have seen the whale mythologized and measured. But at the end we are left only with a book, not a whale. The only whale which Ishmael actually enters — i.e. whose inwardness is reached — is a dead one. But a dead whale is mere matter; its essential reality has departed. The whale is most real when it is actually plunging through the sea, and then it can not be appropriated, only appreciated, as Melville appreciates it in some of the most beautiful prose in American literature. It is an illusion to think we can ever 'catch' reality.

Ishmael survives because he learns that things are separate and other from what we call them. When Ahab wants to project his version of the whale on to the whole crew, Ishmael finally holds back, for he recognizes the essential separateness of names and objects. He knows that man is bound to name the world, but he has a much looser and more flexible sense of how language relates to the world than anyone else. He does not strap himself tight to the whale as Ahab so literally and fatally does. He knows that there is a whale; and he knows that it is men who project meanings on to it. Call me Ishmael: call it Moby Dick. He knows that when we send out the lines and nets of language into the world all we bring back is language. In this connection we may remember the pale usher who loved to dust his old lexicons and grammars and who is, after all, the first character to appear in the book. He, we recall, embellished colourful flags on the blankness of his handkerchief. Ahab, too, is an embellisher, projecting his designs on to the blankness of the whale. But he mistakes the flags for the handkerchief. Avoiding this error enables Ishmael to survive.

The instinct to 'embellish' is a crucial factor in Hawthorne's greatest novel. The very title *The Scarlet Letter* suggests that the subject will be involved with a matter of language, alphabetical if not lexical, and the skilful needlework which Hester Prynne expended on her scarlet letter 'A' may be compared to the creative care Hawthorne lavishes on the letters which make up his book. Among many other possibilities, 'A' may be allowed to suggest 'artist', since artistry of all kinds is explored throughout the book. (The three main characters all come from Europe, bringing a different 'art' to the American continent—theological rhetoric, scientific analysis and needlework.) As in *Moby Dick*, we are not confronted immediately with the text of the narrative. In the long chapter called 'The Custom-House', Hawthorne goes into considerable detail about the source of his tale, and once again we find an American writer conjuring up a picture of a man among manuscripts and papers, 'unfolding one and another document'. Hawthorne rummaging among those 'musty papers' heaped up in the Custom-House does indeed provide us with a very apt image of the first great American novelist searching though the records of the old customs of his country in quest of an appropriate theme for his fiction. When he finally comes across a single letter 'A' one does feel that he has discovered a beginning, the primal letter which inevitably reminds us of the biblical message that the creation of a world and of the word are closely related processes. We may regard Hawthorne as an artist in search of America and say that he did indeed discover its embroidered initial. America, after all, only came into existence when somebody named it. Which is not to forget that the unnamed continent had been there since the beginning of time.

Something of this is suggested by the description of Hester Prynne's grey cloth dress: 'it had the effect of making her fade personally out of sight and outline; while, again, the scarlet letter brought her back from this twilight indistinctness.' Twilight indistinctness is what Hester has found and enjoyed in the forest (which is also the place of her lawless passion). The distinguishing 'A' was bestowed on her in the market-place which is, precisely, where phenomena are brought *into* sight ('a thousand unrelenting eyes'), dragged into language and submitted to definition. Although Hester is in fact from England, there are several suggestions in the book that she imbibes or even embodies the spirit of the American continent. The uncongenial forestland of the new world becomes her home, and everywhere else becomes 'foreign' to her (one simile compares her to a wild Indian roaming freely in the woods). The richness of her nature, signified by the fecund abundance of her hair, might fairly be seen to parallel that of the American continent. If one allows that in some way she does embody something of the fertile plenitude of the American land, then her story has some added implications. Men came to America and did, indeed, make it bear fruit, but in ways often attended by guilt. In addition they projected the outlines of their terms and distinctions, their moral categories and fantasies, on to the continent, just as they fasten a letter of moral definition on Hester. Call her Adulteress. Arguably the book is not so much symbolical as it is a study of how people compulsively symbolize the realities around them, and then act on the assumption that their symbolic interpretations are identical with those realities.[2] When Dimmesdale looks up at the night sky and sees a light in the form of an 'A' it is, comments Hawthorne, as if a man 'had extended his egotism over the whole expanse of nature, until the firmament itself should appear no more than a fitting page for his soul's history and fate.' Which points directly to that tendency in man first to write on nature what he later thinks he discovers there. We are not far from the mental world of Ahab.

But that is not the end of the story as a study in the naming process. For one thing, Hester — again like America — is too rich and potent a figure to be enclosed in a single definition. Her full reality extends beyond the letter that has been fastened on her, so that in later years people wonder if the 'A' might not mean Able, or even Angel. She has this much in common with Moby Dick, that she can mean different things to different people and is susceptible to apparently conflicting names. Finally she is of course more than the sum of letters and appellations that have been, or could be, applied to her, just as reality lies for ever outside the fixities of language. But once the letter 'A' has been attached to her it cannot really be removed. There is a most pregnant moment when, in the forest, she discards the letter and claims that with that one gesture she has annihilated the past and can ' "make it as it had never been!" ' She feels freedom flowing back to her. It is at this moment that she lets her hair down by taking off her constricting cap, and at that moment too that the sun breaks through into the dim dell. With that sudden flood of sunlight Hawthorne is making a very subtle phenomenological observation. 'The objects that had made a shadow hitherto, embodied the brightness now.' When objects are transposed into language they become shadows; when language is removed they recover their full object-identity, embodying rather than reflecting. So when Hester discards her letter, it is appropriate that it seems as though reality has been restored to the world—out of the shadows of language and back to the thing itself. But it is a temporary gesture—just as it remains an abiding American dream. It is a very important part of the book that Hester finally feels bound to return and reassume her letter. Just as once America was discovered it could never be unnamed and allowed to revert to its earlier status beyond the reach of European language and lust.

But if she cannot shed the letter, she can transform it, and this is the other aspect I wish to stress. When she comes out of prison, the onlookers are amazed (and affronted) to see the scarlet letter 'so fantastically embroidered and illuminated upon her bosom. It had the effect of a spell, taking her out of the ordinary relations with humanity, and inclosing her in a sphere by herself.' This is exactly what the American artist has often found to be the effect of his own dedication to his art, and Hester's fantastic embroidery is another example of foregrounding. Hester, then, may be seen as an analogue of America now arrived at that level of consciousness which enables it to become the artist of itself. In this way a crude imposition is transformed into a beautiful embellishment. Stigma becomes adornment; soon, the demand for Hester's beautiful needlework spreads through the community. There is a detectable implication here that the American artist will have to make up for the acts of his forefathers, the American settlers. What is clear is that Hawthorne realized that he was a 'man of letters' in a more particular way than European writers. Peculiarly aware of his activity of applying language to a body of reality which finally lies for ever outside our names for it, Hawthorne, like Melville, does not make Ahab's grievous error of mistaking the flags for the handkerchief. They both emphasize their awareness of their relation to words and things.

I would like to cite one more example from the classical, formative period of American literature. Edgar Allan Poe's 'The Narrative of Arthur Gordon Pym' is offered as a document which is meant to tease the reader who is trying to establish its status. For it purports to be the deposition of a man who, according to his own diary, vanished in a vortex or whirlpool at the South Pole but nevertheless seems to have returned to write his own Introduction in which he speaks of fact, fiction and fable, and his relations with Mr Poe, in a slightly confusing manner. The document of the narrative breaks off, and the work as a whole concludes with a note by Poe, a sort of factual-fictional editorial quite familiar in more recent fiction. The conclusion of Pym's narrative comes when the ship is about to be engulfed in a vast 'white curtain' which ranges along the whole horizon. As the ship is about to enter the 'curtain', Pym sees it as 'a shrouded human figure' with a perfectly white skin. Inevitably one thinks of the whiteness of the whale in *Moby Dick*, and the blank wall of his featureless face. And in shifting from 'curtain' to 'human figure' in his description of the terminal whiteness which lies at the end of the voyage, Pym reveals an inclination to see meaningful shapes in the unmeaning blankness which, in one form or another, is a frequent subject of study in American fiction.

In this connection Poe's final note is particularly interesting. In his narrative, Pym describes an odd series of chasms and caves he and his mates discovered on the island of Tsalal. He offers drawings of their shapes and describes the feeling he and the others experienced that they 'bore some little resemblance to alphabetical characters'. Finally he decides that this was an illusion. Poe, as editor, takes up the point with some energy and applies himself to some 'minute philological scrutiny' of the hieroglyphics of Pym's drawings. With slight amplifications or modifications, eminently justifiable in his view, he decides that the various groups of signs variously form the Ethiopian verbal root 'to be shady', the Arabic verbal root 'to be white', and the full Egyptian word meaning 'the region of the south'. Are the words really 'graven within the hills' or supplied by the heated mind of the editor? Is nature encoded or blank? The problem of whether there are significant patterns and signs to be detected in reality which obsesses so many recent American writers is here adumbrated in one of Poe's most brilliant fictional games.

Once again we are made aware of an American writer's sense of the problematical relationship between the languages we inherit and the new worlds into which we sail. And the message which the editor insists he detects adds little to the experience — definition without revelation. Pym and the crew are indeed going south and they do pass through extremes of darkness and whiteness. We may say that the implication is that, when pursued to its extreme, reality proves to be totally ambiguous. But we are made to remember that it is only ambiguous when men come along with their categories — white, black — and affix them to the surface of what they encounter. Beyond all that, reality is just what it is. In a very special sense man is indeed an editor, a philologist, a librarian, a supervisor of the house of custom — in a word, the guardian of language, the carrier of the signs by which and inside which he lives. He is also a voyager, hunter and explorer — harpoonist as well as usher. These three seminal works by such major American writers suggest that they all felt that one aspect of the American experience was a tendency to get these two activities confused so that inherited names and letters were mixed up with the new realities to be encountered. In advancing the proposition that American writers evince a heightened awareness of the separateness of words and things, I am not making the absurd suggestion that this is something new in world literature. It is rather a matter of degree which I wish to point to. Any writer starts with a sense of the interesting mixture of marriage and divorce which characterizes the relationship of language to the world. What is true is that many writers in the past have felt the possibility of putting together a verbal structure which would offer a stable model of some aspect of the reality around them. The gradual loss of that assurance is part of the history of the emergence of modern literature and has been discussed by other critics. My point is that American writers seem from the first to have felt how tenuous, arbitrary, and even illusory, are the verbal constructs which men call descriptions of reality. Again speaking of a matter of degree, the European writer usually seems to have felt more firmly embedded in his given environment than his American counterpart; to have been more sure of his language and his society, using the former to speak about the latter with more confidence and insight even if he feels alienated from the prevailing structures. If anything, it is the instability of language and society which has more often made itself felt to the American writer. This has meant that, while American writers have established an authentically realistic (at times documentary) literary tradition, there has also been from the start in American literature an intermittent sense of the futility of pretending that the putative exactitude of words can ever measure up to the actual mystery of things. Along with this has gone a suspicion that there can be something damaging in confusing names and their referents.* So while there is often an almost sportive sense of how easily language can float free from a given environment, there is sometimes a feeling that it is dangerous to get too involved in the unreal world of words. There is detectable an element of radical distrust of language among many American writers, even while paradoxically they must perforce continue to work with it to preserve the extended range of mental possibilities it makes available.†

Thus at the end of *Huckleberry Finn*, in an intuitive move to hold on to some basic innocence and integrity, Huck gives up language altogether and makes for a mythical wordless West. But Samuel Clemens continued writing. I am suggesting that many American writers have felt slightly strange about their habitation in the City of Words, a feeling which can express itself in the manifest prodigalities and profusions of James and Faulkner as well as in the wary denudations of Hemingway. On the one hand there is the suspicion that by living too much in language you may cut yourself off from direct contact with reality. (There is a profound quest for silence running right through American literature, even in its most prolix manifestations.) On the other hand there is the liberating feeling that the writer may submit his letters to as much fantastic embroidery as he pleases as a gesture of freedom from the restricted vision and impaired perspectives of the community.

This, I think, is why we find a good deal of stress on 'treatment' among American writers; in Henry James's terms, the weaving of the web, 'the ingenious use made of the material'. For it is in the weaving, the patterning power of his art, that the writer demonstrates his independence from other people's naming of things. 'That's the struggle of humanity' says Saul Bellow's Augie March, 'to recruit

* After this manuscript was completed I found the following statement in William Burroughs's most recent book, *The Job* (1970). 'There are certain formulas, word-locks, which will lock up a civilization for a thousand years ... The idea that the label is the thing leads to all sorts of verbal arguments, when you're dealing with labels, and think you're dealing with objects.' At the end of this book in a Utopian vision he imagines a machine which will 'vibrate the words loose from the body' of the human patient, who will then leave 'the old verbal garbage behind' (i.e. be freed from implanted alien patterns of perception and conception) and receive 'the baptism of silence'. He will then see things as they really are. This represents a modern formulation of an old American dream.

† A contemporary example: William Gass writes in an essay, 'That novels should be made of words, and merely words, is shocking, really. It's as though you had discovered that your wife were made of rubber'; but is soon saying, 'stories are wonderful devices for controlling the speed of the mind, for resting it after hard climbs; they give a reassuring light to a dark place, and help the reader hold, like handsome handles, heavy luggage on long trips.' 'A True Lie-Minded Man', in *The American Novel Since World War II*, edited by Marcus Klein (Fawcett Publications, New York, 1969).

others to your version of what's real.' One of the main struggles of
the American writer is to hold out against all such recruiting assaults
on his own consciousness, if only to secure space in which to
experience his own powers of mental arrangement and construction.
One can trace this suspicion of the other person's 'version of what's
real' back to earlier American writers. Thus Emerson: 'Then, though
I prize my friends, I cannot afford to talk with them and study their
visions, lest I lose my own.' Loss of communication rather than loss
of private vision is an option many American writers have preferred.
But the suspicion of other people's visions and versions, and the
attempt to resist and extrude them, seems to dominate American
fiction of the past two decades in a way which differentiates it
from the work of previous periods.

I will conclude this Introduction by juxtaposing a quotation from
Ortega y Gasset's book *History as a System*[3] and one from
Hawthorne's tale 'Wakefield'. Ortega y Gasset is discussing the
distinctive activities of man:

> In the vacuum arising after he has left behind his animal life he
> devotes himself to a series of nonbiological occupations which are
> not imposed by nature but invented by himself. This invented
> life—invented as a novel or a play is invented—man calls
> 'human life,' well-being. Human life transcends the reality of
> nature. It is not given to man as its fall is given to a stone or the
> stock of its organic acts—eating, flying, nesting—to an animal.
> He makes it himself, beginning by inventing it. Have we heard
> right? Is human life in its most human dimension a work of
> fiction? Is man a sort of novelist of himself who conceives the
> fanciful figure of a personage with its unreal occupations and
> then, for the sake of converting it into reality, does all the things
> he does—and becomes an engineer?

The notion that what we think of as peculiarly human life,
particularly social life, is a fiction, an invented superstructure which
man the engineer has erected on 'natural' reality, is not a new one.
But it is one which seems to have been entertained by American
novelists of the past two decades to an extent that makes it begin to
look like an obsession. Since the time of the Puritans, there has been
a strong tendency for Americans to regard the fictional as the false,
the made thing as the mendacious thing, at least in the realm of art
and when viewing the customs and manners of society (technological
invention falls in another category). Henry James probes this suspicion with great insight in *The Europeans*. Where another civilization might celebrate man's powers of fabrication and his ability to

supplement the given world with his own creations, there is a traditional line of American thought which suspects that these powers and abilities might be cutting man off from 'reality' — reality being whatever was there before man started heaping up his fictions on it.*

In 'Wakefield' Hawthorne tells us that he once read about a man named Wakefield who one day for absolutely no reason simply walked out of his house, leaving his wife with no explanations, and took up secret residence in the next street, living there in hiding for the next twenty years. Then one day he walked back into his original house as though he had been away for a few hours. Hawthorne, retelling the story, adds his own speculations about the moods and motives of Wakefield during his extraordinary defection and 'self-banishment'. He concludes with this moral: 'Amid the seeming confusion of our mysterious world, individuals are so nicely adjusted to a system, and systems to one another and to a whole, that, by stepping aside for a moment, a man exposes himself to a fearful risk of losing his place forever. Like Wakefield, he may become, as it were, the Outcast of the Universe.' Hawthorne sets his story in London, but both tale and moral are profoundly American. The feeling that society is an arbitrary system or fiction which one might simply step out of is one which still motivates a large number of American heroes. Outside all systems and fictions, freedom and reality may yet be found. At the same time, there has always been the concomitant dread that 'by stepping aside for a moment', one might simply step into a void. What a man can or does step into when he steps out of society, whether or not it is possible to get beyond systems and fictions, are recurrent preoccupations in the novels we will be considering.

* A good example of this attitude may be found in Saul Bellow's most recent novel, *Mr Sammler's Planet* (1969), in which Sammler, another of Bellow's compulsive self-communers who suspects all explanations of reality yet cannot stop embarking on his own explanations, speculates in the following way:

Arguments! Explanations! thought Sammler. All will explain everything to all, until the next, the new common version is ready. This version, a residue of what people for a century or so say to one another, will be, like the old, a fiction. More elements of reality perhaps will be incorporated in the new version. But the important consideration was that life should recover its plenitude, its normal contented turgidity. All the old fusty stuff had to be blown away, of course, so we might be nearer to nature.

Some pages later, however, he is bemoaning the mass and pressures of modern life which deprive the individual 'of the power to impart design'. But is not any design implicitly or explicitly a version, a fiction, an hypothetical explanation or system? The urge to shed all explanations is made ambiguous by the yearning to recover some sense of design, not only in Bellow but in much contemporary American fiction.

'Wakefield' was singled out by the Latin American author Jorge Luis Borges for special praise. He is a writer who acknowledges a great admiration for Hawthorne, Poe and Melville and who has in turn become an important influence on contemporary American writers. So, too, has Vladimir Nabokov, and it is the work of these two writers which I will be briefly considering in the opening chapter. In the following chapters I will be examining the problematical relationship of the American hero to the systems in which he finds himself and the fictions which surround him.

Chapter 1   On Lexical Playfields

Nabokov and Borges are two writers whose work is exerting a strong influence on the American fiction of the present. Whether or not Nabokov's American passport makes him an American writer is a piece of taxonomy which is of very little interest – it is probably better to say that he is a Russian writer who spent long years in Europe before continuing his exile in America. Clearly his experience of America helped to influence the final form of two of his major works, while his latest novel he describes as 'set in a dream America'. But scholars such as Andrew Field have shown that the seeds of his 'American' novels were sown and growing before he emigrated there, and it is what might be called the *example* of Nabokov that I wish to comment on here. In an interview he stated his opinion that 'Average reality begins to rot and stink as soon as the act of individual creation ceases to animate a subjectively perceived texture.'[1] These creative acts effectively maintain reality, just as – it is his comparison – electricity binds the earth together. The desire to 'animate a subjectively perceived texture' is visibly at work in many contemporary American novels and among other things it leads to that foregrounding I have referred to. A book like *Pale Fire* is nearly all foreground. Something of this is implicit in Nabokov's comment in the same interview that

> one of the functions of all my novels is to prove that the novel in general does not exist. The book I make is a subjective and specific affair. I have no purpose at all when composing the stuff except to compose it. I work hard, I work long, on a body of words until it grants me complete possession and pleasure.

Not until it mirrors some pre-selected area of external reality. This is rather like James's 'fun', but taken further. For in *Pale Fire* we cannot even be sure of what is notionally real and what is illusion or sport. Lewis Carroll is one of Nabokov's favourite writers, but we do see Alice before she passes through the mirror or falls down the hole; a boundary between differing worlds is visibly crossed. Whereas in *Pale Fire* we don't know whether mad Kinbote 'exists' and Shade is his fantasy; or whether Shade is indeed a poet and Kinbote a projection of his subconscious. We have only documents: a Foreword, a poem, a commentary, an index. Were they all written by Kinbote, by Shade? All we can be sure of is that they were all written by Nabokov. In a sense this is a banal truth about all novels, that they are the fictions of the author. But there are certain conventions for establishing the status of the referents in the book. When James says London, or Joyce says Dublin, we permit ourselves to draw on our associations from more orthodox geographies. But when Nabokov says America and Zembla and puts them together in the same frame as though belonging to the same dimensions – cohabiting on one plane – then our reading of the signs is necessarily more confused, the old associations are unsettled, and normal confidences as to the location of the 'real' are shaken. The old geographies no longer obtain. This of course is exactly what he intends and I think we can imagine the kind of delight it might give to American writers who have a suspicion of old maps. It certainly gave pleasure to Mary McCarthy, who wrote a very persuasive and appreciative eulogy on the book when it appeared.[2] She appreciated the novel just because it was such a beautiful game: 'a novel on several levels is revealed, and these "levels" are not the customary "levels of meaning" of modernist criticism but planes in fictive space ... Each plane or level in its shadow box proves to be a false bottom; there is an infinite regression, for the book is a book of mirrors.' She concluded with the assertion that the book is 'one of the very great works of art of this century.'

I am not maintaining that all American novelists responded with this degree of enthusiasm to *Pale Fire*, but McCarthy's pleasure at Nabokov's subversion of 'customary levels of meaning' and the expertise with which he conducts his games in 'fictive space' seems to be indicative of a dissatisfaction with the norms and procedures of the more conventional novel shared by many of her contemporaries. Among other things *Pale Fire* is an exhibition of the kind of freedom from inherited formulae and prescriptions which many American writers are seeking. In a book of mirrors every statement is dubious since we cannot establish the degree of refraction or indeed the reliability of the source, but Kinbote perhaps speaks for his author when he insists 'that "reality" is neither the subject nor the object of true art which creates its own special reality having nothing to do with the average "reality" perceived by the communal eye.' This is of course a king talking, whether a genuine or a fantastical one does not matter, and he reveals at the very least a regal contempt for the 'communal' models of reality.

Nabokov's work is full of individuals who experience intense isolation of consciousness. No matter what is the particular occasion of their alienation or self-imposed severance from the commonalty, they are all types of the artist, created by the man who said, 'the type of artist who is always in exile even though he may never have left the ancestral hall or the paternal parish is a well-known biographical figure with whom I feel some affinity.' There is obviously a good deal of aristocratic disdain here for the mass of ordinary people labouring heavily in more clogged and constricting versions of reality. But it is equally clear that a large number of American writers feel a great dismay or repugnance at the idea that the reality they live in should be determined by the surrounding masses and their media. Nabokov's apparently effortless gestures of self-liberation through the sheer activity of writing—he is a veritable Houdini in slipping out of the bonds of the established genres—could well make him an attractive, even heroic example to many of them. For it is not uncommon for an American writer to feel 'always in exile' while still at home. There is a minor figure mentioned in *Pale Fire* who, we are told, one day 'thought he was God and began redirecting the trains'. He is called a lunatic but Shade defends him as a fellow poet and rejects the former term. ' "That is the wrong word," he said. "One should not apply it to a person who deliberately peels off a drab and unhappy past and replaces it with a brilliant invention." ' For those seeking to 'invent' themselves rather than be content to become the third persons of other people's definitions, there is much solace to be found in this authoritative defender of 'brilliant invention'.

The insistence throughout his work is that there is no such thing as life or reality, there is only your life and what you make of it, your reality and how you shape it. Of course a majority of the people may accept the conditions and terms of reality as it is already defined for them. In some senses they may have to. Nabokov tells us that the first inspiration for *Lolita* was a story about an ape who after months of coaxing produced the first drawing by an animal; 'this sketch showed the bars of the poor creature's cage.' It is obviously a pregnant and pathetic story for a writer whose work is full of prisons of all kinds, political and psychological, social and personal—the lonely motel room, the claustrophobia of an obsession. Alfred Appel is right to say that 'his characters continually confront mirrors where they had hoped to find windows, and the attempt to transcend solipsism is one of Nabokov's major themes.'[3] But in addition his characters might find bars where they had looked for windows, and like the poor ape take these as the necessary limits of reality. Both Humbert and Kinbote are effectively in prisons while they are writing their stories or notes, but they do not limit themselves to describing the bars of the cage. If anything their bars are all but banished by the almost compulsive resourcefulness of their styles. There is a literary, as well as a metaphysical, moral in this and my contention is that American writers have not been slow to see it.

There are already many admirable critics and exegetes of Nabokov's work, such as Andrew Field, Alfred Appel, Carl Proffer, and Mary McCarthy herself. For any adequate treatment of Nabokov's work, they should be consulted. My only purpose here is to make a few points about *Pale Fire* which are relevant to the context of this study. One of the readings which the novel allows (to put it no more strongly) is that Kinbote is Shade's creation, his fantasy life, the other half of the dour New England poet who projects himself in the poem; the mad notes being, as it were, the complement of those rational and balanced Pope-like couplets. An important clue here could be Nabokov's statement in the same interview that 'John Shade in *Pale Fire* leads an intense inner existence' and in the Notes we do read of a character who reminds one 'of a slow speaking ventriloquist who is interrupted by his garrulous doll'. This fits rather well the terseness of Shade's poem, and the intrusive volubility of Kinbote's notes, thrusting in Zemblan material on the smallest pretext or no pretext at all. If we take Kinbote as someone — something — living in unwilling exile in a rather unspecific sense, something suppressed and all but totally excluded from those places into which he wishes most to be accepted, then I think it is quite possible to see him as incorporating the fantasy life of John Shade. Which is the 'real life' of John Shade, the factual or the fantastic? Nabokov's fiction is certainly not going to decide. It is quite possible that Shade has found release for his fantasy life in an imaginary world which he has constructed around the 'Zembla' he came across in Pope's poetry. In another interview Nabokov said that 'a sad and distant kingdom seems to have haunted my poetry and fiction since the twenties. It is not associated with my personal past.'[4] It seems appropriate in all sorts of ways that the last entry in the index, which is the last line in *Pale Fire*, should simply be: 'Zembla, a distant northern land.' In differing ways that land is Kinbote's, Shade's and Nabokov's.

The least contentious or digressive of Kinbote's notes is his comment on lines 557-8, 'the loveliest couplet in this canto'. The couplet reads:

> How to locate in blackness, with a gasp,
> Terra the Fair, an orbicle of jasp.

The Russian *zemlya* apparently means land, terra; and Terra the Fair could be earth or Zembla, any world you can locate which will, to go on to line 559, help you 'keep sane in spiral types of space'. It would seem that on this sentiment Shade and Kinbote are at one; as though Pope and the mad king had found a point of concurrence in Shade's poem. *Pale Fire* is Nabokov's 'orbicle' in which different orders of reality can be brought together in new relationships by the 'combinational magic' of the author. The idea of usually separate realms merging, communicating or interpenetrating is kept alive in various ways throughout the book, and crucial motifs throughout are those of the mirror and the window, the obvious meeting points of different 'spaces' or worlds. Most critics have pointed out that the first lines of Shade's poem

> I was the shadow of the waxwing slain
> By the false azure in the windowpane;

point directly to the possible confusion of realms – seeing an extension of ordinary reality in what is in fact a reflection – which is at the heart of the book. In one sense it is Nabokov's delight to conflate these realms; but there is also the warning of the bird which is dead because of its inability to perceive where one world gives way to another. This should perhaps remind us that the book is among other things a murder story, and that the physical Shade is unmistakably dead at the end, even if the royal creation of his fantasy lives on in desperate disguises.

There are several ominous breakages which seem to presage the fatal intersection of the poem and the bullet – a stained-glass window broken by a football, a TV screen smashed by a thunderbolt. The way these hard, mindless facts shatter the fragile panes of fancy simply through the force of their propulsion is an apt prefiguration of the movement of Gradus towards the last line of Shade's poem. Gradus is represented as a creature of a lower order, a 'dummy', a 'clockwork man'. He comes from that group called the Shadows dedicated to destroying the king, one of whose members 'had lost a leg in trying to make anti-matter'. Such people exist only to further the work of negation. And clearly Gradus is representative of all that is utterly inimical and hostile to art and imagination. It is worth noting that when Nabokov/Kinbote is describing the behaviour of Gradus he does so in a style which is minutely factual and detailed. By itemizing his meals, his newspaper, his bowel movements, Nabokov emphasizes the utter physicality of the man – a thing among things – and it seems clear that Nabokov is at the same time offering a low parody of realism and naturalism, as though to demonstrate that such a style is only appropriate for creatures immersed so deeply and mindlessly in the realm of fact.

The exact identity or status of Gradus/Grey I am not attempting to decide; in a book of mirrors it is proper that it should remain ambiguous. But his role in Nabokov's overall pattern is hinted at in a couple of clues which can point us to Nabokov's own attitude towards literature. Early on in his search Gradus, not for the first time, goes astray. 'In the vicinity of Lex he lost his way among tortuous lanes.' When he is finally searching for his prey on the campus it happens again, this time in the library. A library is very exactly a lexical town and what we notice here is that Gradus gets completely lost every time he approaches the realm of words and books. Shade and Kinbote on the contrary are very much at home on what Kinbote aptly calls 'lexical playfields'. To make the point even clearer, Kinbote tells us that Shade had a great fondness for 'all sorts of word games and especially for so-called word golf', and that he himself has done 'hate-love in three, lass-male in four, and live-dead in five'. On lexical playfields man enjoys a flexibility, indeed a mastery, that he cannot hope to gain in the world of material fact. The rigid categories and concepts of life and death, the great mysteries of sexual differences and emotional opposites become plastic and malleable — the deft player can turn them into their opposites. This is the artist's temporary triumph over the brute materiality and momentum incorporate in Gradus. On lexical playfields a man can be a king, even if he is a king in hiding, while Gradus is doomed for ever to get lost as he approaches the city of Lex.

Card games and chess games of course proliferate in Nabokov's work, and so does another game — literary parody ('parody is a game' he said in the second interview referred to). This game, like many games, is also a form of defence; it is a way of distancing an influence and reducing its potency. Proust said that a writer might parody another writer to become free of his spell and thus able to write his own novels. Just so we could see Nabokov keeping at bay, for example, Poe and Dostoevsky, in *Lolita*. This is of particular relevance to young writers who, with all the writers in world literature ready to impress forms on their creative minds, have found a special value in parody as a way of writing which liberates itself from the style it seems to be emulating. The game, then, is the thing: ' "Oh, my Lolita, I have only words to play with!" ' cries Humbert, but we have seen that for Nabokov that is how the game has to be played. One of the things that all games have in common is that they occupy a distinct symbolic space which is organized by fixed rules which do not apply outside the playfield. Clearly there is some very radical urge for stability, for known and familiarized territory, in the human instinct to invent games. Kinbote at one point talks of 'the fanning out of additional squares which a chess knight (that skip-space piece), standing on a marginal field, "feels" in phantom extensions beyond the board, but which have no effect whatever on his real moves, on the real play.' It is the space around the board which stimulates the sense of the need for marked squares and rules governing lines of motion.

In Shade's poem he says that the I.P.H. (Institution for Preparation for the Hereafter) among other things prepared one for possibly unpleasant surprises after death.

> What if you are tossed
> Into a boundless void, your bearings lost,
> Your spirit stripped and utterly alone,
> Your task unfinished, your despair unknown ...

Then it is that the I.P.H. taught you 'how to locate in blackness' that 'orbicle of jasp', and 'How to keep sane in spiral types of space.' The orbicle, the chessboard, the card game, the novel — these are all ways ultimately of keeping sane in space, of establishing some known and organized terra firma which can support and sustain you in the 'boundless void'. There has always been a highly developed awareness of 'space' in American writing, and the compulsion to erect a verbal world, map out a lexical playfield, to triumph over vertigo, diffusion, and victimization, which the perpetual exile Nabokov exhibits, has certainly had its effect on a generation of American writers who are not unfamiliar with those feelings in their own country.

'The fear of the crassly infinite, of mere space, of mere matter, touched Averroes for an instant. He looked at the symmetrical garden ... ' The implied opposition here between the man-made symmetry and mere space and matter is analogous to the feeling I have been trying to point to in Nabokov's work. It comes however, from a story by Jorge Luis Borges, a writer whom Nabokov admires and with whom he has much in common (even in possible influences — they both greatly admire Lewis Carroll, James Joyce, of course, and Robert Louis Stevenson, and it seems that both of them were struck by Carlyle's idea in *Sartor Resartus* of writing a commentary on an imaginary work of literature). Borges is a Latin American writer whose work has had a significant influence on recent American writers. Some of the recurrent furniture of his stories is like Nabokov's — mirrors, chess, games, labyrinths, doubles; they both share an awe for man's fiction-making powers, and help to remind us that we live in fictions anyway, that the dividing line between dream and reality is not so easily drawn. In an interview Borges rejected any idea that his work was tendentious – 'I have no intentions' – and referred to it as 'a kind of juggling', a juggling of 'just words'.[5] He also said, 'Really, nobody knows whether the world is realistic or fantastic, that is to say, whether the world is a natural process or whether it is a kind of dream, a dream that we may or may not share with others.' This feeling is partly responsible for the strange, haunting atmosphere of his short elusive parables whose ontological status often seems to be in doubt. By this I mean that most of them are offered as bits of impeccable, if arcane, erudition, but erudition conducted in such remote areas of knowledge that it is impossible for the reader to tell where erudition ends and invention begins, and he enters a realm of twilight or penumbral knowledge. From strange depths in the stories we are suddenly brought back to the surface and do not know quite what it is we have read. It may be a dream or a game or a fantasy, but why then did it move us so much?

It is the constructional power of the human mind that moves and amazes Borges. His stories are full of the strangest architecture – the Library of Babel, the City of the Immortals, the Garden of Forking Paths, as well as examples of the endless variety of lexical architecture to which man throughout history has devoted his time – philosophical theories, theological disputes, encyclopaedias, religious beliefs, critical interpretations, novels, and books of all kinds. There are also a large number of plots referred to in his stories (cosmic and criminal), and there is a comparable amount of that counter-plotting called detection. All these are ways in which man has introduced shapes into that 'mere space, mere matter' which touched the heart of his ancient philosopher with dread.

The imperatives of pattern-making, of 'building', are very clear to Borges, as are their own very equivocal results, and that is one reason why his short parables are so remote from any of the conventions of European naturalism. He admires Henry James, but prefers the stories to the novels, and the situations to the characters: it would seem that he prefers to aim for an almost diagrammatic clarity, aware that such clarity can make for the most intense sense of mystery and enigma. One of his stories, 'Funes, the Memorious', is about a young man who after an accident is able to perceive every detail of everything going on around him. In addition to this hypersensitivity of perception he is unable to forget a single perceptual or imaginary experience. This sets him the task of trying to invent new ways of classifying the constantly growing heaps of his perceptions; yet he is aware that the job is both interminable and useless. The moral would seem to point to the possible thraldom of detail.

He was the solitary and lucid spectator of a multiform world which was instantaneously and almost intolerably exact ... It was very difficult for him to sleep. To sleep is to be abstracted from the world ... I suspect, nevertheless, that he was not very capable of thought. To think is to forget a difference, to generalize, to abstract. In the overly replete world of Funes there were nothing but details, almost contiguous details.

Funes dies of pulmonary congestion. This sense of the need for abstractions to secure some removal from the welter of experience can be found in a number of the American novelists we will be discussing.

While having a deep feeling for the shaping and abstracting powers of man's mind, Borges has at the same time a profound sense of how nightmarish the resultant structures might become. The library at Babel is referred to by the narrator as the 'universe' and one can take it as a metaphysical parable of all the difficulties of deciphering man's encounters in existence. On the other hand Babel remains the most famous example of the madness in man's rage for architecture, and books are only another form of building. In this library every possible combination of letters and words is to be found, with the result that there are fragments of sense separated by 'leagues of insensate cacophony, of verbal farragos and incoherencies'. Most books are 'mere labyrinths of letters'. Since everything that language can do and express is somewhere in the library, 'the clarification of the basic mysteries of humanity ... was also expected'. The 'necessary vocabularies and grammars' must be discoverable in this lexical totality. But 'it is now four centuries since men have been wearying the hexagons ... '; the story is full of the sadness, sickness and madness of the pathetic figures who roam around the library as around a vast prison.

There is a touching little story called 'The House of Asterion' in which a voice describes with some defensiveness the house it lives in, denying that it is a prison. 'The house is the same size as the world; or rather, it is the world.' At the end we realize that the voice is that of the Minotaur describing the strange architecture of his labyrinth, and the imaginary distractions with which he fills his solitude. I don't think the point is simply that existence itself is labyrinthine (although Borges in praising Henry James and Kafka suggests that 'they both thought of the world as being at the same time complex and meaningless ... I think they both lived in a kind of maze'); the suggestion is rather that the labyrinths man builds are his varying attempts to make a statement about the labyrinths he lives in. A good example of this is what is perhaps the most haunting and odd architecture in all of Borges, the city built by the Immortals. When the narrator finally manages to find a way into the city his reaction comes in three successive responses. 'This palace is a fabrication of the gods ... The gods who built it have died ... The gods who built it were mad.' Empty and unthreatening it, is yet in some way a distillation of the dreadful. What the narrator subsequently finds out is that the troglodytes who live in miserable holes outside the city are in fact the Immortals. They built the mad city as a last symbol — an 'inversion and also temple of the irrational gods who govern the world'. Then, resolving to live in pure thought, they abandoned their final structure and took to the caves. They have receded almost completely from perception of the external world. That the last concrete work of the Immortal artists should be a mad city, which is at once intended as a parody and an image of the irrational gods felt to control the world, carries a moral which reflects on all the lesser structures which man builds or puts together in Borges's work.

The labyrinth with its multiplication of possible paths and choices is also for Borges an image of the possible proliferation of varying realities in time, as well as in space. In 'The Garden of Forking Paths' we read of a man, Ts'ui Pên, who set out to make a book and a labyrinth. His family supposed these to be two separate activities and, ignoring the chaotic manuscripts he left, they search for 'the garden of forking paths' in the outside world. Only the narrator discovers the secret. The *book* is the labyrinth. In it time keeps forking and bifurcating so that various possible futures are envisaged. The narrator realizes that this was an image of the universe as the author conceived it. 'This web of time ... embraces *every* possibility. We do not exist in most of them. In some you exist and not I, while in others, I do, and you do not, and in yet others both of us exist.' Elsewhere Borges imagines a similar phenomenon in spatial terms. 'I thought that Argos and I participated in different universes; I thought that our perceptions were the same, but that he combined them in another way and made other objects of them.' A part of the appeal that Borges has for American writers is his sense that 'reality' is an infinitely plural affair, that there are many different worlds and that the intersection points might not be so fixed as some people think, that the established ways in which we classify and order reality are as much 'fictions' as his stories. Like his imaginary writer Herbert Quain he affirms 'that of the various pleasures offered by literature, the greatest is invention'. To elevate invention over more conventional modes of 'imitation' is to demonstrate how the mind can liberate itself from its own circumstances in a way which has much more appeal for young American than young English writers. (Why this should be so is a matter to be taken up later in the book: see especially Chapter Six.)

Of particular importance in this connection is Borges's story called 'Tlön, Uqbar, Orbis Tertius' which is about the invention of a world (it is perhaps worth noting in passing the quite amazing popularity of Tolkien's *The Lord of the Rings* in America—another invented world, or worlds). The story starts with the sentence 'I owe the discovery of Uqbar to the conjunction of a mirror and an encyclopaedia,' clearly relating those physically unlocatable spaces created by those two primary reflectors of reality, mirrors and words. In its more economic way the story is as much a book of mirrors as *Pale Fire*. The narrator and his friends come across a reference to an undocumented country named Uqbar in an encyclopaedia. No other references outside this entry can be found elsewhere. In that entry the language and literature section has one notable characteristic: 'it remarked that the literature of Uqbar was fantastic in character, and that its epics and legends never referred to reality, but to the two imaginary regions of Mlejnas and Tlön.' The fantastic literature of a country which itself seems to be unreal—already the mind is beginning to lose its hold on these receding planes. Borges's stories are often like those drawings of impossible objects which seem to abrogate the dimensions of customary perception so that they are both visible yet impossible to 'read' in the ordinary way.

The narrator later comes across *A First Encyclopaedia of Tlön* which contains the inscription ORBIS TERTIUS, so he now has 'a substantial fragment of the complete history of an unknown planet, with its architecture and playing cards' and all the other details of its philosophies, games and taxonomies. From a study of this book, the narrator and his friends conclude that this 'brave new world' was 'the work of a secret society' of specialists of all disciplines in all the spheres of human knowledge, each contributing his share. And, rather like Ts'ui Pên's book, what seems at first to be a random mess turns out to be a coherent structure, a complete cosmos with carefully formulated, 'albeit provisional', laws. What is notable about the language of Tlön is that it is purely idealistic, and has no nouns. 'For them, the world is not a concurrence of objects in space, but a heterogeneous series of independent acts.' A conception of the world which does not employ nouns is rather like a story which portrays a situation without using characters: in both cases you have the idea of a diagram of energies and qualities which has dispensed with the usual separation of people and things into clearly defined identities.

It is another example of freedom from accepted reality pictures. And the metaphysicians of this country are like artists — Borgesian artists. They are not after truth, but 'a kind of amazement'; they regard metaphysics as a type of fantastic literature. The geometry of the country embraces a belief which at a certain level Borges would accept as a truth about conditions of perception. 'This system ... states that, as man moves about, he alters the forms which surround him.' In this world objects can be brought into being by suggestion and hope. Contrariwise things also tend 'to lose their detail when people forget them'. In this fantastic land it would seem that the potency of mind over matter is everywhere evident — perception precedes and determines reality, and those games of consciousness variously subsumed under imagination and dreams seem, like Nabokov's artistic electricity, to sustain the world.

All this is clearly very central to Borges's own thinking about his art. But the Postscript adds a dimension of considerable importance to the story. The mystery of Tlön is 'cleared up entirely' as the narrator says with unconscious irony. It all started in Lucerne or London in the seventeenth century when 'a benevolent secret society ... came together to invent a country.' Two centuries later this 'persecuted brotherhood' turned up in America. An American millionaire who had joined them proposed 'the invention of a whole planet' with the additional idea that the enormous project should be kept 'a secret'. What happens subsequently is that first of all the alphabet of Tlön is found on an object in this world — 'Such was the first intrusion of the fantastic world into the real one' — and later, objects from Tlön also make their appearance. Suddenly a complete set of *The First Encyclopaedia of Tlön* turns up, probably as part of a deliberate plot which the narrator describes as 'the plan of projecting a world which would not be too incompatible with the real world'. As the planted evidence mounts up the world enthusiastically accepts Tlön:

> reality gave ground on more than one point. The truth is that it hankered to give ground. Ten years ago, any symmetrical system whatsoever which gave the appearance of order — dialectical materialism, anti-Semitism, Nazism — was enough to fascinate men. Why not fall under the spell of Tlön and submit to the minute and vast evidence of an ordered planet.

The superior attraction of Tlön to that of reality is that it is a human fabrication and therefore amenable to human deciphering. Since man made it, it makes sense to man. The narrator foresees a day when all the different languages will disappear and the whole world will be

Tlön. He however vows that he will ignore this phenomenon. Instead he will shut himself up and work on a translation into Spanish of Sir Thomas Browne's *Urn Burial*.

What is important in this conclusion is the depth of Borges's vision. At the beginning Tlön seems like a delightful monument to man's power of invention and imagination, the work of a *benevolent* society. Yet the story shows how quickly a provisional system may impose its fantasy structure on the world and be taken for reality; any system, including Nazism. What at one stage might be a gesture of liberation may at a later stage become a monolithic imprisoning force, so that whole societies abandon themselves to the soothing simplicities of a construct of 'reality' which is in origin simply a man-made coherent fantasy. We hear much of man's rage for order; what Borges makes clear is that the same yearning may be responsible for our most pleasing artefacts *and* our most grotesque and hideous ideologies. Very aware of the consolations afforded man by his patterning powers and capacity for abstractions, Borges is also well aware of the related danger that at any time man may accept one of his invented systems as the definitive model of reality—and go mad. In the story of Tlön the narrator hopes to keep himself free from the prevailing and usurping fantasy by shutting out the world, or Tlön, by working in a hotel room on a revision of a translation never to be published, perhaps thereby retaining a bit of freedom by moving quietly and self-effacingly around older lexical spaces. A modest resolution, perhaps, yet in his lonely determination to extrude an imposed system this figure has a great deal of relevance for con-temporary American fiction.

The important thing is that he is aware of the possibilities of conspiracy. Borges shares this apprehension of powers which may be interfering with the given reality or imposing a world of their own. In 'The Babylon Lottery' for instance he brings into focus man's suspicion or intuition that chance events are in fact all determined by secret decrees emanating from 'the Company'. Not that the Company can be identified—'nothing is so contaminated with fiction as the history of the Company'—but speculation about it is endless. Since the Company's agents are secret it is impossible to differentiate its orders from those of impostors. Some people think that the Company is eternal; others that it is omnipotent only in certain areas. One conjecture has it that the Company simply does not exist, while another argues that it is pointless to argue whether it exists or not since Babylon is simply an infinite game of chance. You could say that this is a parable about the origin of religious belief, or a parable about paranoia. But the way it touches on man's feelings of being controlled from without by the invisible agents of some unknown conspiracy, of having his 'reality' quietly, yet constantly, tampered with, makes it a tale which seems to be echoed or paralleled by some of the more experimental writing in America today.

Borges knows that, as he puts it, 'a system is nothing more than the subordination of all the aspects of the universe to some one of them' and that a system is like a fiction in that it selects and arranges its signs and symbols, quite aware that such a thing as a total statement about reality is impossible. If systems/fictions can result in Nazism as well as *Don Quixote* then the position of the writer himself as fiction-maker is always potentially equivocal since he is introducing Tlön into the reader's world. But so far from wishing to impose any one fiction/system on to the reader, Borges keeps the fact of its fictitiousness well in the foreground. At the end of his stories we often find ourselves oddly released from the subject of the tale and returned to the spectacle of one of those enigmatic narrators inventing what he purports to be describing, making an intricate sequence of referential gestures which turn out to be 'a diagram of his mental history'. When the narrator is Borges himself the same observation holds true. By continuing to invent, he at least shows his ability to do so. This in itself is evidence that he has not been claimed or arrested by any of the other competing inventions which lay more or less subtle siege to the individual consciousness.

In this connection an article by Richard Poirier[6] is relevant, since he describes what he sees as the purpose of self-parody in modern literature, saying:

> Self-parody in Borges, as in Joyce and Nabokov, goes beyond the mere questioning of the validity of any given invention by proposing the unimpeded opportunity for making new ones. Invention creates life in literature in the sense that invention is itself the act and evidence of life. It is a way of being present, in every sense of that word.

And he concludes his article: 'Nothing we have created, in politics or literature, is necessary – that is the central aspect of the literature of self-parody which humanly matters.' This is a most rewarding way to regard this kind of literature and it gives some indication of how American writers of the present time are reading writers like Nabokov and Borges. Not that they aren't important writers by any standards, but it does seem as though they have a special appeal for the writer struggling within the American environment, trying to discover the significance and value of his own inventive power among the flowing, constantly metamorphosing fictions which make up contemporary American 'reality'.

In particular their example seems to have been an influential one for writers brought up in a period when Ortega y Gasset's idea of the death of the novel has been extended to embrace the notional mortality of language itself in Marshall McLuhan. Nabokov and Borges have shown that writers need not succumb to the exhaustion which is supposed to have afflicted the literature they are involved with. Whatever else they may be, they are great survivors, and a study of their particular techniques and approaches would reveal all manner of strategies for survival. John Barth is one American writer who has written enthusiastically about the work of Borges—'it illustrates how an artist may paradoxically turn the felt ultimacies of our time into material and means for his work.'[7] He cites *Pale Fire* and *Labyrinths* as two exemplary ways of confronting the 'felt ultimacy' of the exhaustion of narrative possibilities. Borges's work is also salutary: 'When the characters in a work of fiction become readers or authors of the fiction they're in, we're reminded of the fictitious aspect of our own existence.' Barth sees the labyrinth as a place which contains 'all possibilities of choice'. Most people get exhausted before they reach the heart of the labyrinth; it is only the hero, the 'virtuoso', who, 'confronted with baroque reality, baroque history, the baroque state of his art', has no need to explore all the possible paths in the labyrinth. 'He need only be aware of their existence or possibility, acknowledge them, and go straight through the maze to the accomplishment of his own work.' As Borges does.

The enthusiasm of McCarthy and Barth for the work of Nabokov and Borges is symptomatic of a more general admiration for their work, and what I have called their example, among American writers. I have tried to suggest some reasons for this and what there is in the achievement of these particular writers that younger American novelists might particularly value. At the same time one can fairly make the observation that one thing common to the work of both men is a certain attenuation of reality in the old sense of an empirically perceived environment. It is, as it were, distanced, or forced to recede as the author pre-empts the foreground for a display of his patterning powers. Nabokov's America is indeed at times fairly itemized, yet in such a way as to make it seem almost dreamlike and inert—secondary to the game he is playing and entirely dominated by it. As Nabokov has said of himself, he is absolute tyrant over his characters, and I think this extends to all his material. All good art necessarily requires the control of the artist; talk about characters running away from the writer is usually misleading. Still, one feels that there are shades and degrees in this matter, and Nabokov is quite willing to reduce his characters to playing cards to facilitate the impeccable progress of the perfectly conducted game. One novel is called *King, Queen, Knave*, and everywhere in his work characters are robbed of a certain dimension to fit into Nabokov's cherished patterning. As in Borges, the figures in the fictions move like chessmen – they are there mainly to reveal the brilliance of the chessplayer, and the rules of the game.

Borges seems to me the more profound writer of the two. He manages to convey a melancholy sense of the pathos of all man's makings in time – cities, beliefs, books, dreams – and distil a rare pity from the spectacle, which is kept marvellously clear by his metaphysical wit. Nabokov's cerebral conjurings are certainly extraordinarily clever, but occasionally he arouses suspicions of a fundamental hollowness under the diagrammatic brilliance of the surface. Be that as it may, in both writers the pattern of the game seems to be more important than the characters and material details serving to illustrate it. Both writers seem to have a need to elevate abstractions over perceptions; perhaps to avoid the paralysed congestion of 'Funes the Memorious', perhaps in response to some deeper fear. In this connection Wilhelm Worringer's distinction between abstraction and empathy seems to me relevant.[8]

Now what are the psychic presuppositions for the urge to abstraction? We must seek them in these peoples' feeling about the world, in their psychic attitude toward the cosmos. Whereas the precondition for the urge to empathy is a happy pantheistic relationship of confidence between men and the phenomena of the external world, the urge to abstraction is the outcome of a great inner unrest inspired in man by the phenomena of the outside world; in a religious respect it corresponds to a strongly transcendental tinge to all notions. We might describe this state as an immense spiritual dread of space.

I have tried to suggest that just such a dread of space is discernible in works by both Nabokov and Borges, but more generally I think we can take up the suggestion that the urge toward abstraction betokens in some respects a defensive attitude towards the outer world; it points to the erection of invented shapes rather than the emulation of perceived ones. Again, from one point of view, all art necessarily participates in the urge to abstraction, but we are aware of differences of degree. It seems to me that if we can discern an unusually strong tendency towards the schematic, the visibly patterned, in much contemporary American fiction, we may see it as an attempt to evoke a personal stability and clarification as a result of a marked lack of confidence in the presence and pressures of the given environment. Certainly I do not imagine that any generation of American writers has felt so much 'inner unrest inspired ... by the phenomena of the outside world'. It is against this background that I think we can begin to understand the attraction of the spectacle of Nabokov's and Borges's imperturbable assurance on the terra firma of their lexical playfields.

Chapter 2   The Music of Invisibility

> 'Could this compulsion to put invisibility down in black
> and white be thus an urge to make music of invisibility?'
> (*Invisible Man*)

In the Introduction to his essays (*Shadow and Act*), Ralph Ellison,
recalling the circumstances of his youth, stresses the significance of
the fact that while Oklahoman jazz musicians were developing 'a
freer, more complex and driving form of jazz, my friends and I were
exploring an idea of human versatility and possibility which went
against the barbs or over the palings of almost every fence which
those who controlled social and political power had erected to restrict
our roles in the life of the country.' The fact that these musicians
working with 'tradition, imagination and the sounds and emotions
around them', could create something new which was both free yet
recognizably formed (this is the essence of improvisation) was
clearly of the first importance for Ralph Ellison; the ideas of versatility and possibility which he and his friends were exploring provide
the ultimate subject-matter, and nourish the style, of his one novel to
date, *Invisible Man* (1952), a novel which in many ways is seminal
for subsequent American fiction. His title may owe something to
H. G. Wells's novel *The Invisible Man*, for the alienated Griffin in
Wells's novel also comes to realize 'what a helpless absurdity an
Invisible Man was—in a cold and dirty climate and a crowded,
civilized city' and there is a very suggestive scene in which he tries
to assemble an identity, which is at the same time a disguise, from
the wigs, masks, artificial noses, and clothes of Omniums, the large
London Store. It would not be surprising if Wells's potentially very
probing little novel about the ambiguity involved in achieving social
'identity' had stayed in Ellison's extremely literate memory. But if it
did so it would be because Ellison's experience as a Negro had taught
him a profounder sort of invisibility than any chemically induced
vanishing trick. As the narrator says in the opening paragraph, it is
as though he lives surrounded by mirrors of distorting glass, so that
other people do not see him but only his surroundings, or reflections
of themselves, or their fantasies. It is an aspect of recent American
fiction that work coming from members of so-called minority groups

has proved to be relevant and applicable to the situation of people not sharing their immediate racial experience or, as it may be, sexual inclination; and *Invisible Man*, so far from being limited to an expression of an anguish and injustice experienced peculiarly by Negroes, is quite simply the most profound novel about American identity written since the war.

The book begins and ends in a small underground room, situated significantly in a 'border area'. It is there that the unnamed narrator — unnamed because invisible on the social surface — is arranging his memories, structuring his experiences, creating his life. It is important to bear this in mind since the book is not only an account of events but quite as importantly about what the consciousness of the narrator has managed to make of those events, how it has managed to change because of them. His little room is flooded with the light from 1,369 light bulbs, run by free current drained off from the Monopolated Light and Power Company. It is an echo of Hemingway's 'clean, well-lighted place' but with many significant differences. The narrator has had experience of electricity before. As a child he had been engaged in one of those grotesque entertainments in which white Southerners make negro youths fight among themselves for coins which they are then invited to pick up from an electrified rug. The narrator discovers that if he is careful he can contain the electricity, but then he is thrown bodily on to the rug by white men who persist in shouting misleading cues and directions. The agony is intense and it seems that a century will pass before he can roll free.

The whole experience is an early paradigm of the treatment he is to receive all through his adult life. Later in life he is given electric shock 'treatment' which is intended to have the effect of a prefrontal lobotomy without actually cutting into the brain. The white doctor explains his technique, describing how they apply pressure to the centres of nerve control — 'our concept is Gestalt.' This implies that simply by applying the appropriate pressures they can alter the way a man reads reality, another device for that monitoring of consciousness which is so abhorrent to the American hero. And the electricity is important here. It can be seen as the indispensable force by which society warms and lights its way. That power can be also used to make cruel sport of the individual, to condition him, make him jump to the whim of the man at the controls. The question is, can the narrator find a way to 'contain' this power, to use it without being its helpless victim or its ruthless exerciser?

The first time he finds himself in opposition to the existing authorities, Dr Bledsoe, who runs the Uncle Tom-like State College for negroes in the South, tells him, 'This is a power set-up son, and I'm at the controls.' The moral would seem to be—control or be controlled; as when, later in his life, he sees two pictures of bull-fighting in a bar in one of which the matador gracefully dominates the bull while in the second he is being tossed on the black bull's horns. There is a black powerhouse close to the white buildings of the college, and while the notion of black power which has since emerged in America is not entirely irrelevant here, Ellison is making the much more profound point that power is what keeps society going at all levels; the lights in the library and the chapel, the machines in the factory and the hospital all derive from the morally neutral force of electricity. Morality starts when man diverts this power to specific ends. The experience of the narrator is that it is usually used for the more or less cynical manipulation of individuals. Yet electricity is also a source of light, and the achievement of the narrator must be to find a way out of the power set-up altogether (for to be a controller is more pernicious than to be one who is controlled) and tap some of that power for his own private purpose—to 'illuminate the blackness of my invisibility', to become aware of his own form.

The odyssey which the narrator, with the aid of his 1,369 light bulbs, looks back on takes place on many levels. His travelling is geographic, social, historical and philosophical. In an early dream he finds inside his brief-case an envelope which contains an endless recession of smaller envelopes, the last of which contains the simple message 'Keep This Nigger-Boy Running'. It is only at the end when he finally burns all the contents of his real brief-case that he can start to control his own momentum. Up to that point his movements are really controlled from without, just like the people in the New York streets who to him seem to walk as though they were directed by 'some unseen control'. The pattern of his life is one of constraint and eviction; he is alternately cramped and dispossessed. This is true of his experience in the college, the factory, the hospital, the Party. What he discovers is that every institution is bent on processing and programming the individual in a certain way; yet if a man does not have a place in any of the social structures the danger is that he might fall into chaos.

At his college, in the chapel everybody seems to have eyes of robots and faces like frozen masks (i.e. 'fixed' in rigid roles), and the blind preacher telling them 'the way' inaugurates a theme of the blindness or warped vision of all the creatures of the given structures of society, whether leaders or led—a point underlined when Brother Jack's glass eye falls out. References to dolls, actors, masks, dummies, and so on, proliferate throughout, and before the narrator is startled or pushed out of his first given role—at the state college—he too is described, by a man of accredited perceptions, as a ' "mechanical man" '. The speaker is addressing Mr Norton, a trustee of the college, whom he aptly calls ' "a trustee of consciousness" '. He is making the point that such institutions turn out automata, who accept the rigid and restraining role imposed on them as true identity, and defer to the white man's version of reality.

The point about all the representatives of social power that the narrator encounters — teacher, preacher, doctor, factory-owner, Party member, whatever — is that they all seek to control reality and they believe that they can run it according to their plan. To this extent one can say that they have a mechanizing attitude towards reality, and it is no accident that the narrator is constantly getting involved with literal machines (in the factory, the hospital, etc.) as well as with what one might call the mechanizers of consciousness, the servants of church, college or Party. On the other hand there is the point that these institutions, these people at the social controls, do seem to give the individual a role, a place in the scheme of things. At one stage the narrator is enthusiastic about the Party, because it gives the world a meaningful shape and himself an important role in it: 'everything could be controlled by our science. Life was all pattern and discipline.'

The alternative to the servile docility and rigid regulations of the state college would seem to be the utter chaos of The Golden Day Saloon, which with its fighting and drinking and debauchery seems to be in continuous rehearsal for 'the end of the world', as one mad participant proclaims it (see R. W. B. Lewis's fine essay 'Days of Wrath and Laughter'[1] for a discussion of the apocalyptic hints in the novel). It may be more real, more authentic than the fabricated performances in the chapel at the college, but in its utterly shapeless confusion it offers no opportunities for self-development or self-discovery. Society does indeed impose false surfaces on things; a point well made at the paint factory where the narrator has to mix in a black constituent which nevertheless produces a dazzling Optic White paint used for government buildings. It reminds the narrator of the white painted buildings of the campus; it also reminds him that The Golden Day had once been painted white but that now it was all flaking away. The fact that the paint is called Liberty Paint in conjunction with the suggestion that it is at least in part an optical illusion (the narrator can see a grey in the white which his overseer ignores or cannot detect) is a fairly clear irony; we are in fact 'caught' in the official version of reality — the painted surfaces — maintained by the constituted authorities. On the other hand, if you strip all the false paint away you are likely to be confronted with the merely chaotic 'truth' of The Golden Day. In the same way, the mechanizers and controllers of reality turn people into automata and manipulable dummies; but can a man achieve any visible shape or role if he refuses to join any of the existing patterns?

This is indeed the narrator's problem. When he is about to be sent away from the college he feels that he is losing the only identity that he has ever known. At this stage he equates a stable niche in the social structure with an identity, and for a long time his quest is for some defining and recognized employment. The matter of the letters from Bledsoe is instructive; they are supposed to be helping him find a job which might enable him to return to his higher education, whereas in fact they are treacherously advancing Bledsoe's scheme of keeping him as far away from college as possible. He feels all along that he is playing a part in some incomprehensible 'scheme', but it is only when the younger Emerson shows him one of the letters that he begins to understand. 'Everyone seemed to have some plan for me, and beneath that some more secret plan.' It is an essential part of his education that he should come to realize that 'everybody wanted to use you for some purpose' and that the way they recognize you, on and in their own terms, is not to be confused with your identity.

After his accident in the factory he undergoes what is in effect a process of rebirth — not organically but electrically. From his fall into the lake of heavy water and on to his coming to consciousness with a completely blank mind in a small glass-and-nickel box, and his subsequent struggle to get out, it reads like a mechanized parody of the birth process. The electrical treatment has temporarily erased his earlier consciousness and he cannot say who he is or what his name is. His only concern is to get out of the machine without electrocuting himself. 'I wanted freedom, not destruction ... I could no more escape than I could think of my identity. Perhaps, I thought, the two things are involved with each other. When I discover who I am, I'll be free.' This, coming nearly halfway through the book, is a crucial turning-point. The machine is every system by which other people want to manipulate him and regulate his actions. In much the same way the Party gives him a new identity and tries to reprogramme him for its ends. The narrator is not a nihilist — he does not wish to smash the machine, knowing that he will probably be destroyed with it — but he wants to find some sort of freedom from the interlocking systems which make up society, and he realizes that it will have to be mainly an inner freedom. At the end he can look back and see that the individuals from various professions or parties who had sought to direct and use him 'were very much the same, each attempting to force his picture of reality upon me and neither giving a hoot in hell for how things looked to me.' This is why he wants to be free of all parties, all partial pictures, all the imposed and imprisoning constructs of society. This urge will bring him to a second rebirth near the end – this time a private, self-managed one. But before coming to that we should consider some of the advice and examples he has received from figures who are not on the side of the system-makers, not enlisted among the controllers.

His grandfather on his deathbed has given the advice to 'overcome 'em with yeses', and only by the end can the narrator see a possible hidden meaning in this exhortation. Before he leaves for New York, the vet in The Golden Day advises him that, once there, he should play the game without believing it: he explains that he will be 'hidden right out in the open' because 'they' will not expect him to know anything and therefore will not be able to see him. When asked by the narrator who 'they' refers to, he answers, 'Why the same *they* we always mean, the white folks, authority, the gods, fate, circumstances – the force that pulls your strings until you refuse to be pulled any more.' Three further things he says to the narrator are of particular importance. He tells him that much of his freedom will have to be 'symbolic' – a deeper truth perhaps than he knows for the boy who will ultimately find his freedom in the symbols called words. He says, 'Be your own father, young man,' an Oedipal echo (picking up the description we have already had of the narrator standing where three roads converge) and a warning to the boy that he will have to create an identity, not rely on assuming one already waiting for him. Thirdly, he bids him remember that the world is 'possibility'. And this anticipates the narrator's encounter with Rinehart which is perhaps the most important 'epiphany' in the book.

Before this encounter there is the decisive incident connected with Clifton Tod, the narrator's friend who suddenly drops all Party work and makes himself into a sort of parody Negro. Tod becomes a street-hawker in Harlem, mongering self-mocking black dolls. He is duly killed, as his name forwarns us, by a policeman – the cause of his death being described as 'resisting reality'. It is Tod who, after a bitter encounter with the black fanatic Ras, speculates that, 'I suppose sometimes a man *has* to plunge outside history.' History is the temporal dimension of the social structure, its emerging shape, as well as being the accumulation of memories which weigh on us. It is everything that has conditioned society and the individual within it. History we could say is the visible part of society's progress or change, the fraction that shows above the surface. It is worth stressing this because we often see the narrator entering, or falling into, or retreating to, dark subterranean places. It is in a subway, looking at some sharply dressed black boys, that the narrator has his vision of the significance of all those anonymous people who play no part in history, the transitory ones who will never be classified, too silent to be recorded, too ambiguous to be caught in 'the most ambiguous words'. 'What if history was a gambler ... What if history was not a reasonable citizen, but a madman full of paranoid guile and these boys his agents, his big surprise? For they were outside ... running and dodging the forces of history instead of making a dominating stand.' If history is a gambler – and truth tends to come in underground places in this book – then all those people up on the surface who regard it as a manipulable machine are wrong. Up there they 'distort' people in the interests of some abstract 'design'; they force people into tight little boxes, just as Tod is literally trapped in the ultimate confinement of the coffin. Having seen this much the narrator is effectively through with all parties of the surface. It remains for him to see whether there is any alternative mode of life.

This is when he encounters Rinehart, or rather the phenomenon of Rinehart, since Rinehart is not a man to be met so much as a strategy to be made aware of. The narrator comes to 'know' Rinehart by being mistaken for him when he adopts a safety disguise. After being taken for a number of contradictory Rineharts – from gambler to Reverend – the narrator suddenly understands and appreciates the significance of this figure. 'His world was possibility and he knew it. He was years ahead of me and I was a fool ... The world in which we lived was without boundaries. A vast seething, hot world of fluidity, and Rine the rascal was at home. Perhaps *only* Rine the rascal was at home in it.' The realization makes him feel as though he has just been released from a plaster cast; it suggests what life on the surface never suggested: 'new freedom of movement'. 'You could actually make yourself anew. The notion was frightening, for now the world seemed to flow before my eyes. All boundaries down, freedom was not only the recognition of necessity, it was the recognition of possibility.' This is as succinct an expression of the discovery earned in this book as one could wish for. But what follows is also important. 'And sitting there trembling I caught a brief glimpse of the possibilities posed by Rinehart's multiple personalities and turned away.' I stress this because although the narrator learns his most important lesson from the spectacle of Rinehart he does not wish to emulate him.

If we can simplify the structuring of reality implicit in the book for a moment, we could say that just as figures like Norton, Emerson, Bledsoe and Brother Jack are at home on the surface, which is the realm of social rigidification and the mechanistic manipulations of history; just so Rinehart is the figure most at home in the subterranean world, a fluid darkness flowing on underneath history and society, beneath their shaping powers. This lower realm clearly has its potencies and its truths. But a world of no boundaries, a world given over to 'the merging fluidity of forms', which the narrator sees when he puts on his dark glasses, such a world can finally only be a chaos. And Ellison himself has made this point very clear in an interview.[2] Rinehart's middle name is 'Proteus' and Ellison intended something quite specific by his character.

> Rinehart is my name for the personification of chaos. He is also intended to represent America and change. He has lived so long with chaos that he knows how to manipulate it. It is the old theme of *The Confidence Man*. He is a figure in a country with no solid past or stable class lines; therefore he is able to move about easily from one to the other.

To emulate Rinehart would be to submit to chaos. Rinehart, whose heart is in fact all rind, really represents the ultimate diffusion and loss of self; a freedom, indeed, which might easily turn into that nightmare of jelly. The narrator, attempting to discover or create his own identity, does not want to dissolve in fluidity. Yet if he rejects both the life-denying mechanical fixities of the surface operators, and the fluid adaptations and adaptive improvisations of a Rinehart, the question emerges — where can he go, what can he do?

Perhaps we can get nearer the answer if we ask, not where will he go, but how will he move? One thing he learns after all his experiences on different levels is that the prevailing notion that success involved rising *upward* is a lie used by society to dominate its members. 'Not only could you travel upward toward success but you could travel downward as well; up *and* down, in retreat as well as in advance, crabways and crossways and around in a circle, meeting your old selves coming and going and perhaps all at the same time.' This notion of movement is related to that 'running and dodging' of the forces of history he had earlier discerned as a possibility, and is of special importance as it provides the plot lines of many of the novels we will be considering. At the height of the Harlem riots the narrator finds himself running from all parties, but with the new realization that he no longer has to run either for or from the Jacks and Emersons and the Bledsoes and Nortons, 'but only from their confusion, impatience, and refusal to recognize the beautiful absurdity of their American identity and mine.' And just when it seems that he will be killed in the converging forces of that apocalyptic night (which, like the battle royal he was involved in as a child, is in fact engineered by unscrupulous white people so that the rebels and rioters who think they are generating a scheme of their own are in fact fulfilling someone else's) the narrator falls down a hole into the dark chamber of his second rebirth.

First of all he has to burn all the papers in his brief-case to find his way out of the hole: those papers represent all the schemes and treacheries that his various controllers have planned for him. He is in fact burning up his past and all the false roles it has sought to trap him in. With the aid of the light from the flames, (i.e. he has learned something from this past experience) he enters another dimensionless room where he loses all sense of time. He has to go down a long dark passage and then he lies down in a state between waking and dreaming. Subsequently he has a dream of being castrated by a group consisting of all those who had sought to direct and control his previous life. But when he wakes, he is beyond them. 'They were all up there somewhere, making a mess of the world. Well, let them, I was through and, in spite of the dream, I was whole.' At this point he decides to take up residence underground and with this gesture of repudiation – a plague on both your houses – so characteristic of American literature, the book might well have ended. But there is an Epilogue, and in some ways this is the most important part of the book.

As was noted, while writing the book the narrator has been living underground and in a 'border area'. The point is worth remembering because throughout his life he has been striving to avoid being forced into either of the two extremes of life-style exemplified by Emerson's and Jack's surface New York and Rinehart's Harlem. 'I don't belong to anything,' he cries at one point. To be able to exist in a border area is to resist being wholly drawn into one or the other, to secure a bit of private freedom on the edge. And what he has been doing in his refuge of secret illumination is best suggested by a sentence he remembers from his school-teacher, talking about *A Portrait of the Artist as a Young Man*. 'Stephen's problem, like ours, was not actually one of creating the uncreated conscience of his race, but of creating the *uncreated features of his face*.' The narrator has discovered what many American heroes have discovered, that he is not free to reorganize and order the world, but he can at least exercise the freedom to arrange and name his perceptions of the world. He cannot perhaps assert and define himself in action, but sometimes at least he can assert and create himself in some private space not in the grip of historical forces. While running and dodging in the outside world, the hero may be evolving and discovering and defining his true features in his inner world, like this narrator. His most important affirmation may be, not of any pattern in the outside world, but of the patterning power of his own mind. This is not the artist as hero so much as the hero out of dire necessity having to become an artist. For it is only in the 'symbolic' freedom of lexical space that he can both find and be himself. In writing his book the narrator has created his face. He is aware of the paradox involved in the compulsion 'to put invisibility down in black and white' – the phrase pointing nicely both to the black and white which make up the legibility of print, and the patterning of symbolic black and white which in the book itself is one of his main strategies for rendering his experience visible. But in the pursuit of this paradox lies his only freedom. He tells the story of a yokel who beat a prize-fighter against all the odds because he simply stepped 'outside of his opponent's sense of time'. Just so the narrator can step out of other people's times and schemes, but only by creating his own in his writing. He has a memory or dream of asking his mother to define freedom and she answers, 'I guess now it ain't nothing but knowing how to say what I got up in my head.' This is the freedom which the narrator achieves in the act of seeking it in his writing.

But the problem remains of 'the next step'. He had every reason for going underground: 'my problem was that I always tried to go in everyone's way but my own', which meant that he had never been master of his own direction, and 'to lose your direction is to lose your face.' He has gone into hibernation in his cellar to find direction and face. But he makes another discovery there. 'I couldn't be still even in hibernation. Because, damn it, there's the mind, the *mind*. It wouldn't let me rest.' Here indeed we find a conflict of urges shared by many American heroes – the desire to hibernate (celebrated definitively in Washington Irving's tale of Rip Van Winkle – one of the first American 'outsiders'!), and the inability to remain still in hibernation. Ellison's narrator speaks both of his 'craving for tranquillity, for peace and quiet', and of the 'ache' to 'convince yourself that you do exist in the real world'. The difficulty here is that if you remain in hibernation you are likely to stagnate in unseen inertia; but if you rejoin the shared reality of the surface you are going to be forced into role-playing.

Ellison's narrator defends the value of hibernation as a covert preparation for some subsequent action, but after writing his book he is still wrestling with the problem of defining the nature of that ensuing action. 'Yes, but what *is* the next phase?' In hibernation you can become visible to yourself, but to remain in hibernation indefinitely is simply to die. So at the end the narrator says, 'the old fascination with playing a role returns, and I'm drawn upward again', and ends his book with the confession that perhaps 'I've over-stayed my hibernation, since there's a possibility that even an invisible man has a socially responsible role to play.' At the same time there is the recognition that 'up above there's an increasing passion to make men conform to a pattern'. What the narrator seeks is a way of rejoining the reality of the surface without being forced into another man's pattern or made to play a role to fit an alien scheme. In this he is only one of many recent American heroes who seek some other alternative to the twin 'deaths' of total inertia and diffusion into role-playing. It is as though they are bound to oscillate between the reality-starvation involved in complete ego-autonomy, as defined by David Rapaport, and the loss of ego-autonomy involved in the other-directed behaviour of Erving Goffman's hollow role-players (see Appendix Five). Confronting this problem—sometimes an impasse—is one of the main subjects of recent American fiction. No wonder the Invisible Man says he has 'become acquainted with ambivalence'.

We could say then that the Invisible Man, like many after him, is seeking a new way of being in reality. We do not see him rejoin the surface; again like many after him, he leaves us with a verbal definition of the nature of his resolve. He has learned a whole new way of looking at reality and his relation to it. As he now sees it 'my world has become one of infinite possibilities' and 'life is to be lived, not controlled'. What he also recognizes, and this is crucial, is that he too is imposing a pattern on reality by writing the book. Of course, his motive is different and it is the sort of pattern which clarifies and extends his own consciousness rather than one which cramps and limits someone else. But it is important to keep the fact in mind: 'the mind that has conceived a plan of living must never lose sight of the chaos against which that pattern was conceived. That goes for societies as well as for individuals.'

He is including here a recognition of the fact that even to perceive reality is to organize it in a certain way in one's consciousness—that too is a Gestalt principle. This is another reason why the novel is so preoccupied with eyesight and the problems involved in the fact that we live at the intersections of endlessly different paths of vision. Without some patterning we cannot even experience reality, let alone participate in it. What he has learned is that it is always dangerous to start to confuse your own particular patterning with reality itself. From that point of view reality is chaos, and we live only in the patterns we derive from it or impose on it. But if you live too long in any one pattern you are likely to become completely sealed off from all contact with reality—like those people D. H. Lawrence describes as living under an umbrella.[3]

> Man must wrap himself in a vision, make a house of apparent form and stability, fixity. In his terror of chaos he begins by putting up an umbrella between himself and the everlasting whirl. Then he paints the underside of his umbrella like a firmament ... Man fixes some wonderful erection of his own between himself and the wild chaos, and gradually goes bleached and stifled under his parasol. Then comes a poet, enemy of convention, and makes a slit in the umbrella; and lo! the glimpse of chaos is a vision, a window to the sun.

Ellison's narrator has made this discovery in his own way for himself. What he also recognizes is that his book, too, like any work of art, is a 'fixity' of 'apparent form'. A glimpse of chaos is also a glimpse of The Golden Day: to achieve any sense of ongoing identity man needs those houses and umbrellas. Consciousness depends on architecture. What is important is not to forget the fluidity in which it stands.

When he has only been in New York for a short time, the Invisible Man meets a man pushing a cart loaded down with thousands of abandoned blueprints and scrapped plans for houses and buildings. As the man says, 'Folks is always making plans and changing 'em.' The narrator in his naivety says, 'but that's a mistake. You have to stick to the plan,' and the man answers, 'you kinda young, daddy-o.' It is a little parable in passing. Human beings are inveterate planners, but plans are just so many clues for arranging which ultimately go to the scrap heap. What the narrator has to learn is that there are bound to be plans, but that any one plan you get involved in may well involve some falsification or constriction of your essential self. He drops out of all plans for a while to draw up his own. But once drawn up that too has to be left behind, as it were. The highest aspiration would seem to be not to get trapped in any one plan, while recognizing that to achieve any identity is to be involved in plans. One could envisage for the narrator a continuing life of moving in and out of plans; like the rest of us oscillating between chaos and pattern but much more aware of it than most. In that awareness lies a measure of his freedom.

In this connection his final comment that he is sloughing off his old skin is an important metaphor. For 'skin', read 'plan of any kind'. And just as the narrator sheds skins, so Ellison himself 'sheds' styles, an example of what I meant when I said that the activity of the American hero was often an analogue of the activity of his author. Ellison is quite explicit about this. In the interview referred to he describes how he deliberately changed the style of the book as the narrator moved from the South to the North and from thence into a more private territory; at first it is more naturalistic, then expressionistic, and finally surrealistic, each modulation intended to express both the state of mind of the narrator and the society he is involved in. As the hero manages to extract himself from a series of fixed environments, so the author manifests a comparable suppleness by avoiding getting trapped in one style.

Another statement from Ellison makes this very clear and helps to explain the extraordinary proliferation—and sometimes convulsion—of styles which is so especially characteristic of recent American fiction (it is seldom indeed one finds a serious writer committing himself to the sort of naturalism which earlier American writers had helped to develop). Naturalism, Ellison maintains, tends to lead writers to despair, and it fails to confront the diversity of America. Instead, he says,

> I was to dream of a prose which was flexible, and swift, confronting the inequalities and brutalities of our society forthrightly, but yet thrusting forth its images of hope, human fraternity and individual self-realization. It would use the riches of our speech, the idiomatic expression and the rhetorical flourishes from past periods which are still alive among us.

He feels that it must be possible to write a kind of fiction which can arrive at relevant truths 'with all the bright magic of a fairy tale'. Ellison's prose in the novel is heavily foregrounded, demonstrating quite deliberately an ability to draw on sources as disparate as Revelations, the blues, classical literature, Dante, Southern white rhetoric, Harlem slang, and so on. This should not be seen as a wildly eclectic attempt to import significance but rather as a delighted display of the resources of consciousness and imagination which he can bring to bear against the pressures of a changing environment. In such a way the American writer procures some verbal freedom from the conditioning forces which surround him.

Ellison has not at this time published another novel, although one called *And Hickman Comes* has long been promised. Considering the wealth of *Invisible Man* one might wonder whether he had not put all his material into that one book. He has published a book of essays called *Shadow and Act*, however, and in these he is visibly concerned with the same basic themes and problems; whether reviewing books on the Negro question or peering back into his own past, he is always exploring the nature of his American identity and its relations with the reality around him. And like his fictional narrator he particularly resents those who would pre-empt his reality by defining it in their terms.

Both as a novelist and as an essayist, one of his primary aims in writing is to challenge any 'patterning' of life—whether fictional, ideological or sociological—which is a falsification of existence as he has experienced it. Perhaps the best image Ellison has for the American writer is the one he takes from the story of Menelaus and Proteus. Eidothea's advice to Menelaus is to keep a firm hold on Proteus until, after all his changes of shape, he appears as himself, at which point he will reveal the name of the offended god and how they can make their way home without further interruption.

For the novelist, Proteus stands for both America and the inheritance of illusion through which all men must fight to achieve reality. Our task then is always to challenge the apparent forms of reality ... and to struggle with it until it reveals its mad, vari-implicated chaos, its false faces, and on until it surrenders its insight, its truth.

What we should notice is that the Invisible Man does not emulate Proteus Rinehart any more than Ellison envisages the American writer capitulating to the Protean reality around him. In many recent American novels we will find the hero in quest of identity confronting a Protean figure whose quick metamorphoses seem to make him enviably well adapted to reality; but the hero seldom takes him for a model, no matter how much he may learn from him, for that way lies chaos, the nightmare jelly, the ultimate dissolution of self. No fixed patterns, then, but not a reversion to Protean fluidity either; instead a struggle with, a resistance to, both, conducted in some 'border area' where author and hero alike attempt to create themselves and come into the meaning of their experience. In projecting his situation in these terms, or in this 'Gestalt', Ellison was, to take up the last line of his novel, speaking albeit 'on the lower frequencies' for more American writers than he can have realized.

Chapter 3   A Mode of Motion

'There was something in people against sleep and dullness,
together with the caution that led to sleep and dullness.'
(*The Victim*)

Only a year after the publication of *Invisible Man*, Saul Bellow published his third novel, *The Adventures of Augie March* (1953), which shows many radical similarities with Ellison's novel while rooted in Bellow's own experience. More to the point, with this novel Bellow deliberately made a stylistic break with his earlier work. The form of this novel is avowedly 'loose' and in an interview[1] Bellow made it clear that he was consciously reacting against the 'severity and style and devotion to exact form' in many contemporary novels, including perhaps his own. So, he went on, 'I kicked over the traces, wrote catch-as-catch-can, picaresque.' Bellow's first novel is about a man who seldom leaves his own small room (*Dangling Man*) and his brilliant book *The Victim* is claustrophobic in its sense of the immobilizing weights and pressures of modern urban life. Critics had praised the formal control and expertise of these early works, so, when in his next novel Bellow created a fictional hero whose greatest gift, arguably, is his ability to resist all fixed social forms, we may infer that for Bellow this represented an attempt to escape from the cramping constrictions of fixed stylistic forms. For author and character alike, the book is a bid for freedom from external patterning.

Augie's opening words focus on this immediately. 'I ... go at things as I have taught myself, free-style, and will make the record in my own way ... Everybody knows there is no fineness or accuracy of suppression.' He aims at 'free-style' in the writing as he did in the living; this way at least he will avoid getting trapped in someone else's life-style or literary-style. One might take these opening words as a justification in advance for a certain amount of blurring, a refusal to be too exact, to define, qualify or subordinate anything. It sounds like part of a general anxious resolution not to get involved with form and pattern in any way. Bellow himself said, in the interview referred to earlier, the book came easily – 'All I had to do was be there with buckets to catch it. That's why the form is loose';

it seems that the adoption of this first-person narrator enabled him to let everything flow. His image of waiting with the bucket brings to mind Henry James's wariness of 'the terrible *fluidity* of self-revelation' — Henry James being one of those writers too preoccupied with the form of the novel for Bellow's liking. Augie March, with Saul Bellow behind him, prefers being fluid to being fixed. It is in some ways then a novel about suspicion of form and pattern, as Ellison's was. But we may note from the start that there is another side to the problem. At one point Augie is complaining about the unusable excess that assaults the individual mind, and he spends some time itemizing it (too much history, culture, news, too many influences and forces, and so on) — 'all this hugeness, abundance, turbulence, Niagara Falls torrent.' The consideration prompts itself — isn't a fluid style in danger of succumbing to those 'Niagara Falls' which are always threatening to drown the individual consciousness? How to avoid being fixed without surrendering to this sort of dissolution or diffusion is Augie's main problem.

With this in mind one can see that one of the themes of the novel is the tension between stillness and movement. Mintouchian says to Augie sympathetically, 'I know this double poser, that if you make a move you may lose but if you sit still you will decay',* and Augie's two brothers exemplify this double poser. Simon, his elder brother, enters the world, becomes everything he is expected to become according to the codes of success, adopting flashy clothes and cynical mores and abandoning his early dreams of heroism, and as a result of this adaptability he gains a large share of the world's riches. That the price for this is a coarsening, brutalizing, even destruction of self, Augie can see all too clearly. If he does at times try to follow Simon's way he very soon flees or ducks out. His younger brother George is simple-minded, utterly sweet, and utterly helpless. He is a pure spirit, but he is, as Augie finds when he visits the asylum to which George has been committed, utterly terrified of reality. For when Augie takes him for a walk in the outside world, George is frightened and cannot wait to get back. His simple-minded goodness seems to necessitate the protection of the asylum walls; it cannot exist in the world. Simon is an active participator in the world, almost a Rinehart in his ability to adapt to and thereby manipulate the given,

---

* Kierkegaard knew this poser too — so central to the whole problem of movement and inertia. 'So it is too that in the eyes of the world it is dangerous to venture. And why? Because one may lose. But not to venture is shrewd. And yet, by not venturing, it is so dreadfully easy to lose that which it would be difficult to lose in even the most venturesome venture... one's self.' (*The Sickness Unto Death*, Anchor edition.)

but the world has absorbed or erased his true self; George on the other hand because of his mental deficiencies is a passive retreater, effectively in permanent hibernation, almost devoid of self. And between these extreme versions of participation and retreat, Augie, the middle brother, moves and tries to have his being.

He is a travelling man as the book amply demonstrates, yet from the start he admits, 'I had the kind of character that looked for ease and places where I could lie down.' There is a recurrent feeling that movement is inherently abrasive. Basteshaw, one of the most interesting of the theoreticians Augie gets involved with, gives copious examples to prove that 'sitting tight is power'. Describing an aunt who 'while she slept she ruled' he says, 'she had the power achieved by those who lie still.' 'Teach us to sit still,' says T. S. Eliot, and a feeling for that immunity from distraction and manipulation which can be the strength of 'those who lie still' is clear in Bellow's continuing interest in different aspects of immobility. *Herzog* is 'written' by a man lying on a couch in an empty room.

But of course there is a darker aspect to this. After Augie has heard of the death of his grandmother he tries to imagine an end to all that interfering energy. But it is too much for him to picture her in the grave—lying still. An aspiring towards stillness may mask a desire for death. The sense of being alive depends on some kind of motion and friction. As Mintouchian says, 'Some people, if they didn't make it hard for themselves, might fall asleep.' Augie believes in 'an open world, a world of possibilities' yet he often holds back from that world because everybody in it seems to be fixed in the role either of manipulator or victim—'they screwed or were screwed'. He does not believe these are the only alternatives, yet even while he celebrates the possibilities of self and world verbally, he is often seen in a prone position, bereft of any sense of direction. 'You've got more possibilities than you know what to do with,' says Clem Tambow, 'but you lie there in a wicker chair.' All choice may be error, but no choice is death. Augie, it would seem, wants something like movement without choice, something between commitment and inertia.

The difficulty as he sees it or experiences it is that society is like the grave: *both* rob you of your outline. He refers to the 'great social protoplasm' and he resists lasting relationships because you get 'attached to, and then absorbed into, a family'. The old lady in Rome who is offended because he does not sufficiently respect her individuality prompts this reflection. 'Death is going to take the boundaries away from us, that we should be no more persons. That's what death is about. When that is what life also wants to be about, how can you feel except rebellious?' Augie wants his own outline, but at the same time he is suspicious of all patternings and fixities. His problem is to gain and retain his self without advancing as far into the social protoplasm as Simon, and without retreating from it into the irreversible stillness of George's premature grave.

Between these identity-annihilating alternatives the only other available mode of motion is the one described by Ellison's narrator — 'running and dodging'. You make lines of your own not necessarily because they lead anywhere but because they are your lines and no one else's. It is a way of holding on to your self and experiencing it *as* your self and not a self made over by someone else's pattern or manipulated by some external force. I would say that the ideal mode of action for Augie and many other recent American heroes is something between fluidity and fixity: we might call it flexibility. This is what Augie March learns from the little animal in Mexico, the kinkajou 'who roved over his square of cage in every dimension, upside down, backwards. In the depth of accident, you be supple — never sleepy but at sleeping time.' He knows when to stir, when to be still. The kinkajou moves in his cage as Ellison's narrator decides he too will move, and Augie would be far from alone in envying the roving suppleness of that animal who, though encaged in the depth of accident (as man may be said to be), seems continuously to demonstrate his sense of being a free entity just by the manner of his rovings. The fact that that endless roving may also indicate desperation is a risk that has to be faced up to; and the question of whether the energy of evasion can ever give way to anything more positive — the energy of construction, perhaps — is something of a problem for author and character alike.

For Augie is primarily evasive in terms of the action in the book. He seldom if ever initiates any line of action; he responds to suggestions, allows himself to be given momentum by other people's schemes, permits himself to be adopted in any number of ways, and then — slips away. The feeling that, in part, keeps him on the run is a conviction that he is constantly running into or getting involved in versions, visions, fabrications — particular rubricizations of reality, and not reality itself. It is implicitly an almost paranoid sense of the environment consisting of competing image-makers: 'inventors or artists, millions and millions of them, each in his own way trying to recruit other people to play a supporting role and sustain him in his make-believe.' As he sees it, one image may come to dominate the rest and assert that it *is* reality. 'Then a huge invention, which is the invention maybe of the world itself, becomes the actual world ... even the flowers and the moss on the stones become the moss and the flowers of a version.' He says later, 'It's always some version or other.' As in Bellow's other books, there are a lot of powerful and persuasive talkers in the novel; Augie is constantly running into great blocks or swarms and mists of words which seek or threaten to pre-empt his consciousness, replacing his unique subjectivity with an alien 'version'. Part of his constantly renewed movement is an instinctive reaction to avoid all the versions and constructions waiting to take him over, like the French dog-trainer who struggles with his animals in order 'that their conception of a dog should be what his was'. Augie can hear the dogs barking their resistance, and identifies it as 'the protest of chaos coming up against regulation'. Quite a lot of Augie's barking is the protest of diffusion coming up against definition. Yet at some level reality has to be organized before it can be experienced, and in holding back from planning and patterning out of respect for pre-patterned 'reality', Augie comes close to disappearing into the scenes through which he passes. He repudiates or avoids the identities which other people seem eager to thrust upon him; the question remains, does he achieve one of his own? There is, most importantly, the book itself, which is as it were *his* version of the relation between his 'self' and the world. Yet it is, as was noted, a blurred and fluid book.

One of the problems for Augie, as for many American heroes, is this. Where is 'reality' to be found; and who can truly be said to be in it or out of it? He recalls seeing a painting of an old man walking meditatively through some empty fields, perhaps dreaming of God's city, while a thief is deftly robbing him of his purse. The old man is too enwrapped in his dream to notice, but the thief himself is depicted as being enclosed in a glass ball. The satire was directed at both of them while the fields themselves were charmless. It was 'a flat piece'. It would seem that *both* the wise man *and* the thief are cut off from the present reality, for one is locked in a dream while the other is enclosed in a glass ball, the limited sphere of his avarice. They each walk wrapped in their 'version' as it were; and apart from them there are only the empty fields. Augie is also a dreamer: he has a number of Utopian dreams of a more satisfying reality, and at one point insists that 'Reality is also these private hopes the imagination invents.' At the same time there is a prevailing feeling that those people who apply their hands to things with ruthlessness and direction are more 'realistic' or more at home in reality as it is constituted. It is another version of the problem posed by the extreme examples of George and Simon. And if it is not clear who is truly 'in' reality, then the problem of which way to move remains acute. 'Why toward, and not instead run from, the huge drag that threatens to wear out your ribs, rub away your face, splinter your teeth?' But on a map with no fixed locations and no compass we cannot with certainty say what is 'toward' and what is 'from', just as Augie cannot say of another character whether she is confronting a fate or evading it.

He himself follows a characteristic sequence of movements. He will make a temporary commitment (or succumb to one), and attempt to turn this choice into a value; then he will run into some sort of brutal physical encounter, and the commitment will be dissolved while he tries to find a place to lick his wounds. Then the sequence will be repeated with a different commitment and another project or aim. But whether he is nearest to reality while moving in hope towards the physical blow which will end the episode, or away from it in disillusion — or at the moment of the blows themselves — Augie never learns. (A blow at least might waken the dreamer, or break open the glass ball.) The fact that he ends his book with a recollection of himself standing in some 'empty fields', reminiscent of those he saw in the painting, may seem to indicate that he has broken through to the bleak terrain of that reality behind all versions. But no more than Ellison's narrator can he outline 'the next necessary thing'. As with Henderson, in *Henderson the Rain King* (1959), at the end of the book we see Augie in a middle area between society and the void, in some ways fixed, yet at large in the desperate expansiveness of his own rhetoric.

One of the problems revealed by Bellow is that while the American hero may feel a yearning to reconcile himself with the universe he may feel an even stronger reluctance to be reconciled to society. It is a matter of different levels of reality, and the fact that American fiction of recent years has been overwhelmingly urban is a consideration of some importance. The ultimate source of values in American literature up to Hemingway and Faulkner was rural, and whether we think of Emerson contentedly ripening with the melons, Huck Finn drifting on the raft, Whitman's loafing narrator or Faulkner's boy disappearing into the 'markless wilderness' of the forest, we are confronted by a deep conviction of the value of passivity, of abandoning the outlines of the self to the impersonal (perhaps divine) flow of nature. For such writers it was possible to feel that a merging with empirical reality was at the same time a reconciliation with metaphysical reality, and that to make of oneself a 'transparent eyeball', or a sponge soaking up the nourishing impressions, was to gain something more important than a sense of self.

But such attitudes become impossible or dangerous in an urban environment, where survival depends on an ability to reject things, extrude distracting impressions, and take action to avoid the coercive and exploiting forces all around you. Here, then, we find an opposition where there was once a harmony. To be reconciled with the universe you need to lose identity, but to survive in modern urban society (which now equals the given reality) you need to create or acquire an identity. At the end of *Herzog*, Herzog is lying on his couch reconciled to the universe, but not at all reconciled to society. Just so Augie discovers his alignment with his 'axial lines' while he is lying on a couch, and to the end of the book he is not in harmony with the things and schemes and people around him in the given world. You cannot 'loaf' in the city, for you will soon become somebody's victim; nor can you be a sponge there, for you will be inundated with an excess of particulars which can be as searing as they are irrelevant or nauseating to you. Augie, and, more importantly, Herzog both reject any ideological synthesis which would help to contain and take care of all the particulars, for they feel that all such ideological constructs are just 'versions', and as such an impoverishment of reality. Yet it is one thing to allow pastoral reality to lap over the edges of consciousness from all sides, annulling the turmoils of self in a greater peace; and quite another to allow modern urban reality to burst on the passive mind in the unmediated totality of its chaos. One of the problems for Bellow's protagonists is that they seem to arrive at a point where they begin to feel that both to have and to lack a defining, confining identity threatens a form of death.

I want to draw attention to three more implications of the particular mode of motion Augie has worked out for himself. Mintouchian, one of the most knowledgeable of his 'instructors', says that his dominant idea is — 'secrets', 'Complications, lies ... Disguises, vaudevilles, multiple personalities'. He takes the example of Ulysses and says that we all enjoy the story of his returning home in disguise to seek his revenge. But, adds Mintouchian, suppose he forgot what he had come back to do and just sat around in his disguise, increasingly forgetful of the fact that it *is* disguise? This example of Ulysses is one of great importance for Augie, and many other American characters. American heroes have always been particularly sensitive to the fact that all social life is based on certain kinds of dissembling. What it is important for them to recognize is that one can wear disguises for different reasons, and that the motive may justify the mask. And what can be the most nightmarish situation for them is to find themselves surrounded by a society of people who have forgotten 'what the disguises are for'. To such people the only reality is falsity, and in the consequent inversion of values the American hero may find himself having to spend most of his energy simply holding on to his vital knowledge that there should be a face behind the mask and an independent consciousness behind the limited role which it chooses to adopt. Otherwise identity descends to puppetry and only the rigidity of the mask is accorded life.

Under the circumstances it is understandable that the American hero, from the beginning, has been tempted to abandon society altogether since even in the company of one other person he finds he has crossed into that complex realm of dissembling where the tensions between self and disguise begin to be felt. When the Invisible Man describes his disinclination to get involved with a woman, saying, 'they usually think in terms of "we" while I have always tended to think in terms of "me" ', he is voicing a suspicion of relationships which runs very deep in American literature, and at no time more so than now. Augie often seeks out the comforts of 'temporary embraces' but there is, as it were, no principle of adhesion in him, and he relies more on chance contacts than continuities. If anything he seems keener to seek out father-figures than a wife. This is not to deny him his gregarious good humour, his kinder instincts, his genial affections. Rather, it is to suggest that he has a diminished sense of the reality of other people. There are dozens of characters in the book, but they tend to add up to a sort of general presence of the not-Augie as opposed to the Augie. They are registered as voices, faces, threatening or desirable shapes, but not, somehow, as independently functioning consciousnesses with their own dimensions of concern and pain, their own internality as mysterious and problematical to them, perhaps, as Augie's is to himself.

Just as the Invisible Man never meets anyone from a previous phase in his life (except for Norton, and that is for the deliberate purpose of non-recognition), Augie does not really have any developing and deepening relationships. As they both run and dodge in their different ways, other people tend to be reduced to occasions of perception, precipitants of passing thoughts. Even if they are threatening, they are usually experienced as phenomena activating the distant peripheries of the narrator's consciousness. In this, these two figures seem to be prototypical, exemplifying an instinct to withdraw from the kind of relationship which involves the interpenetration of two consciousnesses. In part this is a self-preserving strategy. But the question arises, can you in fact achieve a 'self' by keeping other people out in this way? To what extent is identity possible without relationship? If the 'me' feeling expands unchecked it can lead to a state of solipsism which may prove to be a prison of mirrors in which the self gets drowned in its own reflections. It is not clear that such a state is particularly preferable to the opposite death of vanishing into one's wardrobe of disguises.

Augie shows some awareness of how 'internal' his reality is. Very late in the book he describes his discovery that while he has been in apparent idleness, much hard work has been done.

> It's internally done. It happens because you are powerless and unable to get anywhere ... and therefore in yourself you labor, you wage and combat, settle scores, remember insults, fight, reply, deny, blab, denounce, triumph, outwit, overcome, vindicate, cry, persist, absolve, die and rise again. All by yourself! Where is everybody? Inside your breast and skin, the entire cast.

This is a very relevant passage when you consider the *verbal* belief in the supreme value of 'love' which is affirmed in the book: it goes far to explaining why a book so crowded with people and things ultimately strikes one as so lonely and, in an odd way, insubstantial. It also adumbrates the whole form of the novel *Herzog*. And against that passage one may put this other comment by Augie: 'a man could spend forty, fifty, sixty years like that inside the walls of his own being. And all great experience would only take place within the walls of his own being. This would be only a terrible, hideous dream about existing. It's better to dig ditches and hit other guys with your shovel than die in the walls.' The desire to secure those walls against attack, *and* the need to break out into reality to avoid dying within those walls, constitute the paradox at the heart of the book and point us back to that dilemma we outlined earlier: that too much autonomy involves loss of world, while too little leads to loss of self.

Although *Catch-22* (1961) is ostensibly a war novel, Joseph Heller's brilliant dark comedy is less about the tactical struggle of two armies than the struggle for survival of the individual within his own society. For Yossarian, the hero, though the anonymous flak of the Germans creates a background of death constantly threatening to obliterate him, the real enemy is his own side: American society as it manifests itself in the Air Force. Nearly all the action takes place on the base, or in the hospital, or in occupied Rome, and the drama and double-edged comedy of the book are really precipitated by Yossarian's desperate manoeuvrings to survive this world. An army (or in this case an air force) is based on the complete structuring of life down to the last detail; the intention is to achieve an absolute organization which will eliminate human vagaries and subordinate every individual impulse to a pattern of mechanical efficiency. Such complete rigidification of human life is clearly unnatural and anyone who has experienced being in an army, fighting for no matter what cause, will probably agree that often one finds oneself in the middle of a confusion dressed up as a system. Heller is very aware of this and reveals it in some hilarious scenes, but he also sees that the implications of this can go much deeper. In his novel he shows a society in which, if the forms do not say that a man was in the unit, he is said not to have existed although his corpse is rotting on the ground; a society in which if a man is scheduled to be on a plane and that plane crashes then that man is officially dead even if he is standing there protesting his manifest existence. That is to say, the humanly obvious categories of life and death are utterly confused or inverted, and replaced by a pseudo-reality of forms, papers, rules and regulations.

The man who finally reaches the position of greatest power is the obviously named Scheisskopf whose sole interest in life is the organizing of 'parades'. Like many of the characters in the book he is conceived (and perceived) more as a cartoon-strip grotesque than as a real person. He considers various ways in which his men might be nailed or wired together to produce the perfect parade pattern. The humour in this exaggeration scarcely conceals the horrified sense of what mindless authorities are willing to do to the individual in order to secure those fixed arrangements and monolithic organizations which are the essence of their authority. This elevation of form over substance, of abstract pattern over living process, shows up at its most sinister when, for instance, Aarfy murders a girl and the military police arrive, only to ignore the *corpse* and to arrest Yossarian for not having the correct *identification papers*; or when the men are ordered to obliterate a village which has not the slightest strategic significance because the general wants a 'neat aerial photograph' recording an elegant 'bomb pattern'—a phrase which he himself readily admits 'means nothing'. This is a society in which 'identity' is a matter of papers rather than flesh and blood, where people may pointlessly die to satisfy the authorities' desire for a meaningless pattern. It is little wonder that Yossarian should claim that all those who subscribe to this world are mad, and only he is sane. He seems to be caught up in a vast conspiracy to accept the unreal as real.

The world of *Catch-22* offers more menaces to the self than the world in *Invisible Man* and *Augie March*, though the novel seems to me to be about essentially the same dreads and apprehensions. In a time of war Yossarian's paranoia and death-hauntedness are entirely understandable. Starting with Hitler, he goes on to enumerate all the known and unknown people in the world who want him dead. As his list compulsively extends itself it envisages a universe of omnipresent hostility to the precious and precarious self. Yossarian sees other threats as well, and he goes on to list some of the ways the body can let you down, and the various diseases to which it is vulnerable. No wonder he sees every day as a 'dangerous mission against mortality'. What is particularly disconcerting is that the superior powers on his own side seem to be more hostile than the enemy or the processes of nature. It is this experience of the intense gratuitous hatred directed at the individual from within his own society, the willing subversion and distortion of all values, logic, reason, principle and language in the interest of reducing the individual to a manipulable and disposable thing (which *is* Catch-22), that provides the special black humour of this book.

There is an underlying feeling that those people responsible for inventing and imposing the patterns have a loathing for life *per se* and that their mission is not the prevention of the Germans but the annihilation of anything that seeks to resist the inexorable clamps of their system. This produces a situation where Yossarian finds himself moving between the threat of a chaotic death in the air and another kind of death among the sinister parodies of pattern on the base. In such a world, why not have nightmares every night, as Hungry Joe asks. The gentle chaplain's dreams teem with violence and imagined disasters and atrocities, induced by the world around him. In the world of this book the individual wakens from one nightmare into another, and the ensuing strains on consciousness are registered by the style in which an almost hysterical acceptance of the incomprehensible barely conceals a sobbing incredulity. When Yossarian wakes up to open his eyes 'upon a world boiling in chaos in which everything was in proper order' he is registering the paradoxical nature of the reality into which he has been plunged, a reality administered by the 'spinning reasonableness' of the a-logic of Catch-22 itself.

In this world the problem of identity is unusually acute. A figure in hospital graphically demonstrates one kind of threat. He cannot be seen for bandages; the only evidence of 'life' is the liquid waste which drips out of him into a jar from which it is then fed back into him. This soldier 'was constructed entirely of gauze, plaster and a thermometer'. ' "Maybe there's no one inside," ' suggests Dunbar. This image of a completely hollow figure, a moulding of gauze over a void through which some waste endlessly circulates, represents a vision of the emptied or pre-empted self, a dread of one's identity being reduced to an arrangement of surfaces which is to be found in many different American writers (see Burroughs and Purdy, for example). It is another example of society's ability to take your living body and visible identity and replace them with a 'construction' of its own making. In terms of the atmosphere of the book, this aspect is more important than the fact that the bandages may represent an attempt to heal. This scooped-out figure represents one fate of the self.

Milo Minderbender represents another. Milo Minderbender is the Rinehart figure in this novel; he makes himself completely at home in the chaos of a world at war by constant metamorphosis. He is Major Sir Milo Minderbender in Malta, Vice-Shah in Oran, Caliph of Baghdad, the Imam of Damascus and the Sheik of Araby; he is looked up to by the Allies and the Germans; he is even a corn god, a rain god and a rice god in primitive regions. He is paid by both sides, by all sides. He runs a 'syndicate' which transcends all petty impediments like loyalty and principle and reaches into every country in the world; he is in on every deal. If the price is right he will arrange the bombing of his own men. He is the idol of every society, the profit principle in all its forms, the exploiter, and thus the slave, of every base human greed. In a more naturalistic novel he would be entirely improbable. He is another cartoon-strip figure who, in the particular atmosphere of this book, is all too convincing as a presence, a spirit which can appear and dissolve at will. As descriptions of his behaviour make clear ('in the grip of a blind fixation') he is in his way as much an automaton as anyone, a robot which responds automatically to the summonings of commercial opportunity. To have adapted to the reality situation in this way is the ultimate loss of self. For Milo, April is the 'best month'.

Another character who is at home in this intolerable world is Aarfy. He is literally like the figure in a dream who will neither hear you nor disappear, and he terrifies Yossarian. He is the human shape devoid of all human responses; unmoved by the flak and the ruins, impervious to all distinctly human communication, indifferent to human pain. He is another zombie — indestructible because inhuman, at rest within the current system, at home in nightmare. These two figures show ways of enduring within the present state of affairs, but both represent for Yossarian particularly chilling examples of lost human identity. Clevinger on the other hand is a decent man who accepts all the imposed terms and claims of the system, trying to reason other people into justice and fairness; he and people like him are the easiest victims and are effortlessly annihilated. Idealism, or even a belief in reason, in the world of this book, lays one helplessly bare to the manipulators. So the question for Yossarian is, what to be to hold on to his self?

At the start, as censoring officer, he plays with various names and in the hospital there is some revealing confusion caused by changed temperature cards. Once again officials tend to ascribe identity on the basis of paper evidence. When the nurse accuses Yossarian of not caring if he loses a leg, he replies that it's his leg. She answers, ' "It certainly is not your leg! ... That leg belongs to the U.S. Government." ' In this system it is hard for a man to say which parts of the self are his own. Certainly when the system denies you your self, the effect may be as close to death as is conformable with the retained powers of motion. The doctor who is declared dead because he was scheduled to be on a plane which crashed is gradually stripped of his identity, until his wife no longer answers his letters and he is not recognized on the base. He becomes a pathetic ghost figure, gradually wasting away, until he is indeed to all intents and purposes dead. For Yossarian, looking for some way to survive and retain his own authentic self, the available models seem to offer intolerable alternatives—how to stay in this world without being like Minderbender; how to draw out of it without becoming a bandaged void?

Yossarian may be Assyrian but he is entirely American in his dislike of conditioning forces. 'That men would die was a matter of necessity; *which* men would die, though, was a matter of circumstance, and Yossarian was willing to be the victim of anything but circumstance.' To get beyond the reach of 'circumstance' is his impossible dream just as it has been for many American figures. But in this book the margin of refuge offered by a nature as yet undominated by man is so thin as to be non-existent. The sea offers a cleansing experience, but one boy standing on the beach is cut in half by a plane. The chaplain finds some pleasant peace in his clearing in the woods to which, like one or two other oddities regarded as superfluous on the base, he is banished. But there can be no emulation of Thoreau in this world, and he is soon submitted to further harassment. Yossarian takes off his clothes and climbs a tree, only to be followed by Minderbender and his schemes. Paradise is not so easily regained. In one raid Yossarian takes his plane 'into a calm, diamond-blue sky that was sunny and pure everywhere' but the old American yearning for the freedom of clear space is cut short by the necessary re-entry of the plane into the fields of flak.

Within the man-made or man-controlled environment, the hospital seems to offer him the best hope of peace and safety. Like Augie and the Invisible Man, Yossarian is drawn to places where he can safely lie down, out of the fray, and he specifically says that he enjoys relaxing in hospital. It is only another aspect of this inverted world that a healthy man should have to seek out a hospital as refuge. And it is a very risky refuge since a patient in the hospital is most vulnerable to the decisions of the administrators and upholders of the system. In the hospital 'they' can do anything to you (hence the number of times the image of the hospital recurs, from Ellison, to Burroughs, to Kesey) and it is in the hospital that 'they' decide to 'disappear' Dunbar. Yossarian may complain that ' "It doesn't make sense. It isn't even good grammar," ' but this is precisely a world in which sense is not made but destroyed, and deeds outpace language's ability to contain them within orthodox grammar. The hospital is the place where the self may vanish without trace, as dangerous in its way as the flak-filled sky. Once again we find that the American hero, in his attempt to hold on to his self, cannot find any one safe place but has to have recourse to a mode of motion. He runs and dodges, or rather—he spins.

Yossarian's unique way of moving is perfectly demonstrated by the way he leads the other planes on a bombing mission. The men like flying behind him because he does not adhere to the orthodox formation. He comes 'barreling in over the target from all directions and every height, climbing and diving and twisting and turning, weaving his way through the flak with every sort of extreme manoeuvre.' His only mission is to come down alive. When it comes to getting away from the target area 'Yossarian was the best man in the group at evasive action.' Here again we see the American hero breaking out of the fixed formation prescribed by the system, making his own lines of movement in order, simply, to hold on to his life. When he finally decides he has had enough flying he has recourse to somewhat similar self-preserving motions on the base. 'He marched backward because he was continuously spinning around as he walked to make certain no one was sneaking up on him from behind.' He is forced to remain within the system, but by his way of moving he can refuse to be of the system, ignoring or negating its rigid patterns. His nickname is 'Yo-yo', pointing to the sort of to-and-fro movement which has as its only goal the indefinite postponement of stillness and arrest (a notion which will turn up in the work of Thomas Pynchon).

It is not long after that that Yossarian breaks out of the system altogether. But first he has his nightmare walk through Rome which R. W. B. Lewis has seen as 'the novel's apocalyptic vision'.[2] It is indeed a visionary walk through scenes of destruction, violence, fathomless misery and ruin. Having asked the reason for some particular act of brutality, Yossarian is told, ' "No reason ... Catch-22. Catch-22 says they have a right to do anything we can't stop them from doing." ' Coming from an old woman in the heart of the Eternal

City, it suddenly makes it seem that Catch-22 is the unchangeable law of human history. After such a discovery the appalled American hero might well want to escape out of time and space altogether, jump out of the nightmare of human history. In Rome Yossarian 'walked in lonely torture, feeling estranged', and the estrangement is from *all* the horrors which occur in, perhaps inhere in, existence. Hungry Joe's recurrent nightmare is that a cat is sleeping on his face. One night he dies in his sleep and they find a cat sleeping on his face. Reality is the worst of our bad dreams.

Such a vision may well seem too sweeping and extreme. In many ways the book is a palpable exaggeration, and there remains the problem — what does a society do when confronted by a Hitler? And paradoxically there is something almost sentimental in the walk through Rome; not that the unspeakable doesn't happen every day, but to isolate and assemble a series of vivid examples is to risk a rather theatrical melodramatic exhibition of horror which, without being a falsification of the entire beastliness and lunacy of war, is nevertheless a simplification of the complexity of human experience. When Yossarian later wakes up to the brutal attentions of two 'evil' doctors, in answer to the question of where he was born he says, ' "On a battlefield." ' Asked in which state he was born he says, ' "In a state of innocence." ' Heller, we realize, has re-activated that most basic of American themes, the confrontation of innocence and experience. And as so often, the world of experience is seen to be so umitigatedly horrifying that the innocent hero cannot assimilate the experience, he can only flee from it. Which leads us to the significant ending of *Catch-22*.

Yossarian has reached the point where every alternative seems intolerable. He considers staying and 'vegetating' in his hospital bed; again, the attractions of inertia. But when Major Danby concedes the attraction of the vegetable life, Yossarian turns on him with some relentless questioning. When Danby says he would like to be a good cucumber, Yossarian points out that he would be sliced up for salad. Conceding that he would prefer to be a poor cucumber, Danby is assured by Yossarian that he would then be used for fertilizer. For the human being, already born into a society, there is no safety in vegetable stillness — he will be devoured or dumped. Yossarian does not want to be a vegetable or a jelly-fish. Nor does he want to be a whale, one of the brutes of the system like Scheisskopf, or one of those inhuman automata that thrive in the nightmare, like Minderbender. Is there any alternative model or example? There is one, as it transpires in the last chapter, the cunningly named Orr. Orr is a small ugly man, who awakens Yossarian's pity. When he is missing, pre-

sumed dead, Yossarian is very sorry. But in the last chapter the news
comes that Orr has turned up in Sweden, and, two pages from the
end of the book, Yossarian sees his alternative.

He realizes that Orr has planned everything from the start, and
that so far from being washed ashore in Sweden by chance he 'rowed'
there (hence the possible pun in his name, which could also allude to
the very notion of an alternative—as in Kierkegaard's *Either/Or*).
All the time Yossarian thought of him as the most helpless victim
of the system, Orr was quietly developing his own plan of action. To
effect this plan he had to disguise himself as the most ordinary and
innocent of servicemen, and even Yossarian never read the disguise
properly or saw the planner beneath the role-player. (It is worth
noting that Orr, the canny outsider, is from a border area, 'the
wilderness outside New York City'.) Here we have one of those cases
of justified self-preserving disguises, discussed in *Augie March*: this
kind of role-playing is to be distinguished from the roles unconsciously accepted by society, or adopted for the purpose of exploiting other people. With Orr as an example, Yossarian is energized to
put into practice his own considered alternative, which is: ' "Desert.
Take off. I can turn my back on the whole damn mess and start
running." ' This is of course the primordial gesture of the American
hero, and Yossarian is making it for reasons just as basic; he is
quitting the society in which it is impossible to put his ideals into
action. For, like the majority of American heroes, despite a mask of
cynical self-concern, he is a frustrated idealist at heart. But,
' "between me and every ideal I always find Scheisskopfs, Peckems,
Korns and Cathcarts. And that sort of changes the ideal." ' He
resolves to get away from the interchangeable dangers of a mad
world—flying among the flak, and lying trapped among the
bandages.

Major Danby calls it a negative move, ' "escapist" ', but Yossarian
laughs his disagreement. ' "I'm not running *away* from my responsibilities. I'm running *to* them. There's nothing negative about running away to save my life. You know who the escapists are, don't
you, Danby? Not me and Orr." ' There is a genuine insight here that
it is those people who build and service the system, in this case the
monolithic regimentation of the army (no matter which side), who
are the real escapists, erecting their grotesque patterns between themselves and reality. Yossarian is not alone in American fiction in
asserting the need of the individual to redefine the direction in which
true reality lies, so that what society would see as retreat he maintains is advance. But we notice once again that after disengaging
himself from what is felt to be a bad society, the hero cannot define

the next necessary step. Once again the one value the hero can assert is — life itself (' "What else is there?" ' he asks). But how to use one's life is a question not answered, not often admitted, since the unspoken conclusion is often that you use your life to stay alive. The euphoria of the last scene gets positively strained, and Yossarian's off-the-cuff assertion that he will also try to save the kid sister of Nately's whore — ' "so it isn't all selfish, is it?" ' — is a most unconvincing scrap of sentimentality which does nothing to conceal the fact that the only responsibility he is moving towards is simple self-preservation. At the same time, as Norman Podhoretz pointed out,[3] his last-minute agreement that the war against the Germans had to be fought would undermine the vision of the book if taken seriously.

This is the gesture which closes the book.

"You'll have to jump."
"I'll jump."
"Jump!" Major Danby cried.
Yossarian jumped. Nately's whore was hiding just outside the door. The knife came down, missing him by inches, and he took off.

He takes off, but this time on a personal flight to Sweden. Nately's whore has by the end of the book turned into another of those nightmare figures, constantly metamorphosing and terrifyingly ubiquitous with her ambushes and threats. Yossarian has always been afraid of knives, the edge of the world's hostility, and Nately's whore has become the multiple incarnation of everything that waits with a knife for the Yossarians of the world. Once again the American hero's best exploit is an avoiding leap. Yossarian calls himself a supraman, and shows what he means by jumping clear out of the world of Catch-22, the realm of knives, flak, human history, death. What he jumps into is less certain. His destination is nominally Sweden, but Minderbender's deals extend there and it would be a dream to imagine that the age-old principle embodied in Catch-22 was miraculously excluded from that one society. The Sweden Yossarian is aiming for can perhaps be compared to the Greenland that Augie refers to: ' "I want a place of my own. If it was on Greenland's icy mountain, I'd take and go to Greenland, and I'd never loan myself again to any guy's scheme." ' (It is surely relevant that despite Henderson's intentions to re-enter society, we last see him pounding happily around the bracing spaces of the 'chill Arctic silence'.) Yossarian is looking for his Eden in Sweden, an unpatterned territory where procreation flourishes rather than war. But, like Greenland, Sweden is a cold northern country, and in this novel cold is associated with death for Yossarian. In the context of Yossarian's predicament, Sweden is less a place than an ongoing dream of freedom which provides a motive for momentum, an aspiration towards a realm beyond all the systems imposed on the self by society. In a sense this is a dream of total autonomy of the self, and if achieved it might well prove to be just such an icy, barren landscape as Bellow's image suggests. But in reality such a state cannot be achieved prior to death, and we may assume that Yossarian will have to go on spinning and twisting and evading to the end of his days if he wants to preserve his own Yossarian self. Given the attractive energy of his resilience it is arguably worth it. Like the Invisible Man and Augie March he is driven to put his faith in a mode of motion; all of them making, in their different ways, the discovery succinctly arrived at by Updike's running rabbit, Harry Angstrom: 'Funny, how what makes you move is so simple and the field you must move in is so crowded.'

I have previously suggested that the predicament of the hero in the plot is related to the author's own struggle with language and the existing conventions of the novel. I think this becomes clear if we consider the status of language in this novel. A good deal of the book is indeed about language; it is full of scenes of men in constricted places working on each other or sparring with words — in offices, planes, tents, the hospital, interrogation rooms, and so on. In terms of the book language is another structure in which man can be trapped, as the innocent Clevinger, who still believes in the reality of the available terms, is trapped into speaking self-incriminating nonsense. (' "I always didn't say you couldn't punish me, sir." ') Conventional language is used by 'them', by authority, to imprison and manipulate people. That language contains terms for values and principles which are, however, no longer related to any felt reality. So these terms are astray and have become part of the equipment of the enemy. This means that the normal, accepted language usually relied on for significant communication and definition is treacherous, often being used to implement the pseudo-reality of the system-makers. What Heller does is to show language breaking up under the strain of trying either to keep pace with, or resist, the chaos which results from the inversion of reality and unreality. In this world definitions become very problematical because the normal bases from which you would launch a definition have been subverted. McWatt 'was the craziest combat man ... because he was perfectly sane and still did not mind the war.' Yossarian is 'crazy', but ' "that crazy bastard may be the only sane one left." ' In this world negatives may be required to make positive statements: 'there were many officers' clubs that Yossarian had not helped build, but he was proudest of the one on Pianosa ... he gazed at it and reflected that none of the work that had gone into it was his.' At a time when most structures are used to trap the individual, Yossarian regards it as a definite achievement not to have contributed at all to the building.

In a rather different sphere we read that Major Major's father worked without rest at not growing alfalfa—since then, as now, the government pays people *not* to grow food, in a world full of starving people. Sentences undermine themselves, cause and effect are dislocated, logic goes awry, propositions are negated as soon as advanced and truth comes in strange forms. 'Their only hope was that it would never stop raining, and they had no hope because they all knew it would.' ' "I won't take the valve apart now," he said, and began taking it apart.' ' "I don't want lots of things I want," ' says Yossarian, explaining why he won't accept the deal to let him go home. ' "My sister is an enlisted man, sir," ' explains the cornered chaplain. This is all symptomatic of what happens to language when the dominating people use it, not as a way of discovering truth, but as a tool for manipulating people: it is the language of a world, like Colonel Cathcart, 'impervious to absolutes'. True communication fades and all sense is awash in a nightmare circus of nonmeanings and power-plays. And part of our admiration for Yossarian is for his very considerable nimbleness among the syntactical and terminological absurdities and contradictions which are as thick as flak around him. In the language situation of this book you have to be an evader if you are to tell any sort of truth, and Yossarian is, among other things, a fine linguistic evader. It is part of the inverted state of this world that his evasions often take the form of an unexpected directness. ' "Subconsciously there are many people you hate," ' says the knowing army psychiatrist, eager to classify him. ' "Consciously, sir, consciously," ' Yossarian corrects him, ' "I hate them consciously." '

Yossarian's effort 'to maintain his perspective amid so much madness' is necessarily Heller's, too. For, as the author, he has to use the same language which he shows to be in such a state of disarray in the book. One of the things he does is to make the reader laughingly aware of what is happening to that language (laughter, we will find, is important for many American writers as indicating a partial freedom from the conditioning forces); as though by making the available language reveal all its capacity for perpetrating perverted formulations he is at the same time demonstrating his own freedom from all this false patterning. Another strategy is to behave with his narrative rather as Yossarian does on the base and in the air: he twists and turns and goes backwards at times, straying from the usual formation. Thus chronologically his plot is a spin, as though indicating that Heller is not going to get trapped into the deceptive orderliness and misleading coherence of conventional plot structure. But the spinning has a centre, just as the language of the book is not entirely cut off from the truth. The short declarative sentences of the book often do contain simple truths; as, concerning the plight of the chaplain, 'He had no real friends.' And the shortest sentence in the book is to be found at the real narrative centre; it is the one reiterated by the dying Snowden freezing to death in a patch of sunlight – ' "I'm cold." ' It is the spectacle of Snowden's horrible death that the book circles around, like Yossarian's turning memory, touching on the scene at least six times before finally confronting the full horror just before the end of the book.

The description is detailed and appalling, a scene that can only be fully looked at once – 'Snowden's insides slithered down to the floor in a soggy pile and just kept dripping out ... Here was God's plenty, all right, he thought bitterly as he stared ... It was easy to read the message in his entrails. Man was matter, that was Snowden's secret ... The spirit gone, man is garbage ... Ripeness is all.' Heller the author, like Yossarian the character, does perceive the truth under all the falsifying forms and patterns and paper façades of this world. Just as he cannot understand the mystery of pain, so Yossarian recoils from the terrible absolute truth of death. In aspiration, that jump into Sweden implicitly contains a Platonic leap into some realm beyond a universe of matter doomed to decay, making unerringly for the garbage heap, sometimes slowly, sometimes with explosive rapidity, but always getting there. When the chaplain starts to have doubts he suddenly becomes aware of this bleak irreversible process. 'Where the devil *was* heaven? Was it up? Down? There was no up or down in a finite but expanding universe in which even the vast, burning, dazzling, majestic sun was in a state of progressive decay that would eventually destroy the earth too.' This is that dread of 'entropy' which, as I shall try to show, haunts so many contemporary American writers. What Yossarian is ultimately in flight from is death – his own, and the great sinking to waste and garbage that he sees around him.

Augie March's friend Padilla was particularly fascinated by 'the little individual who tries to have a charge counter to the central magnetic one and dance his own dance on the periphery.' Ultimately that central magnetic charge turns into the gravitational pull towards the level anonymity of death. The counter-movement celebrated differently by Ellison, Bellow and Heller is a sort of private dance of life. Yossarian cannot avoid being involved with the existing structures of reality as it surrounds him, just as Heller cannot help but be involved in the existing structures of language as he inherited it, but at least they can both keep on spinning to avoid being trapped. Like Conrad's Axel Heyst, they aim to be 'invulnerable because elusive'. The dance on the periphery may not be leading anywhere, but at least it celebrates a refusal to sleep, a resistance to arrest; a mode of motion turns out to be a way, perhaps the only way, of life.

Chapter 4 Frames Without Pictures

> 'Everything in Carrie Moore's expression went so blank that
> Zoe had the impression she was looking at a frame that had
> lost the picture.'
>
> *(Cabot Wright Begins)*

The most important story in James Purdy's *Color of Darkness* (1957)
opens with a couple sitting and talking in a darkening room, trying
to recapture the identity, or a sense of the identity, of a youth,
Fenton Riddleway, who had strayed in and out of their lives some
time in the past. Though still alive they regard themselves as 'dead'
and the atmosphere surrounding them in the house is one of desolation and decline. Between them they are trying to conjure up in
words a sense of the reality of something or someone which has
completely eluded them, leaving them as witnesses poised at the edge
of a vacancy, suffering a sense of loss. In this way '63: Dream Palace'
effectively sets the scene for all of Purdy's fiction, an extraordinary
and original body of work which among other things addresses itself
to the problems involved in the very fiction-making process itself. It is
important to stress the way even this early novella is 'framed' by the
conversation between an unsuccessful writer and his ageing lady
friend because one of the underlying feelings in all Purdy is that
while you are constructing the frame you are losing the picture, and
that when you have completed the frame you may find you are holding a blank. This feeling not only affects the whole concept of
'identity' in his work (the reality of a person is precisely not the sum
of all the terms and names externally applied to him to 'frame' him);
it also cuts at the roots of novel-writing itself—all definitions being,
paradoxically, forms of loss. This is why Purdy starts this early
novella with a writer protesting his inability to write, just as he will
end a later novel with a writer refusing to write. In both cases the
existence of the book in front of us produces the strange effect of a
self-negating presence which is characteristic of Purdy's fiction in
which people and things both are and are not there.

At the start of '63: Dream Palace' the woman, Grainger, asks
the ex-writer, Parkhearst Cratty, why he does not write Fenton's
story. Cratty replies that it is impossible because he never found out

85

who Fenton was. The book which follows is, in effect, Parkhearst's story (although scenes are described at which he could not have been present), his attempt to set a frame around the phenomenon called Fenton Riddleway. Fenton is the stray, orphaned young boy of unearthly beauty who appears throughout Purdy's fiction; he seems to come from another world, quite remote from the squalid contemporary American scene of which the writer is an inhabitant. The writer has gone out into the park looking for 'material', a word he tries to forswear, and suddenly he sees Fenton, whose first question is: '"Where do you get out?"' which may be taken to refer to the park, the book or the whole reality situation in which he finds himself trapped.

Fenton, with his brother Claire, after the death of their mother, has taken up residence in a rotting, derelict house, surrounded by a fence of iron spears. Whether one thinks of the boy as innocence, beauty or youth, there is a feeling of something non-material suddenly falling into the hideousness of the material world and finding it a trap. The book records Fenton's adventures in the city and his brief connection with Grainger and Parkhearst. The two most recurrent aspects of his bemused tourings and strayings are the unreality of everything he sees and the way other people constantly seek to use him to expedite their fantasies. He has a strange power—a curse as much as a gift—of being irresistible, so that people are drawn to him as though expecting him to be able to fill the particular gap which blights their existence, or to be the reward they yearn for. Parkhearst wants him for the story he hasn't written. Grainger wants him to be the husband who has died. She makes him wear her dead husband's clothes, and this dressing up of someone to make him fit a required image is a constant theme in Purdy, again suggesting the way the world imposes roles and identities on the undefined human potential as embodied in the beautiful orphan.

Grainger's first husband was a 'blank' who looked good in all kinds of clothes. Fenton is put into some of those clothes, and while they suit him very well there is all the time an expression of pain and anger 'imprinted on his mouth'. The strange use of the word 'imprint' suggests something applied externally, which could imply that the world had put the expression of rage and pain there, but also reminds us that James Purdy is the chief printer. His book too is a dressing up of a character in clothes which both suit him and don't, which change him even while they cover him, which take away his identity even while imposing one. Connected with this are the rapid, unmotivated and seemingly inexplicable changes in expression 'imprinted' on Fenton, from boredom to extreme excitement, from calm quietness to frothing rage, from pain to love, from murderousness to sleep. This is very characteristic of Purdy and it has various effects. It helps to create that dreamlike atmosphere in which people lose all continuity and change without reason; an atmosphere which Purdy establishes to avoid the confident 'realism' of logical cause-and-effect naturalism. It also gives one the feeling that there is no inner consistency to the self, that we are watching a kaleidoscope of reactions and expressions behind which there is — something, nothing? And it reminds us of the ambiguous power of the author who can pull any garment out of the verbal wardrobe, a power which contains the pathos of the recognition that though he may talk about faces what he produces are only and can only ever be masks.

But if Fenton is somehow unapproachably unreal, so too in another way is the 'this', which he recognizes as his unavoidable surroundings. And one characteristic of all 'this' is its bewildering theatricality. Much of Fenton's time is spent in an ALL NIGHT THEATER and he has the feeling that the screen figures are more aware of him than the people slumped around him in the cinema. When he goes to Grainger's house he finds that it is like the ALL NIGHT THEATER (the notion that the modern 'reality' we inhabit is in fact some sort of 'movie' is quite a common one in contemporary American fiction). Fenton can never be sure that he is not simply dreaming. He does not know if and when he is awake. Like many of Purdy's central characters, he falls asleep at odd times, as though lapsing from participation in a reality which is indistinguishable from an illusion.

The very notion of 'reality' is unstable. Once when Parkhearst sees Fenton with Grainger, something about them makes them seem 'more real and less real than anybody living he had ever known'. More *and* less real: this is the effect Purdy achieves by showing that the intersection of two 'realities' — Fenton, and the city with its night-time corruptions — calls both into question, so that the book seems like a silent implosion such as would occur, we are told, when matter meets anti-matter and they cancel each other out. In this case both realities seem about to collapse and vanish into their own emptiness. When Parkhearst stares at Grainger 'with almost real anger' one feels the precariousness of any kind of 'reality' in this book, the radical uncertainty as to where it might be found. Fenton loves his brother Claire and thinks 'how real he was compared to the Parkhearsts and the Brunos and the Graingers', but after a night which brings to a head the various kinds of intoxications and seductions with which the world seeks to take hold of him, Fenton goes back to the house and kills his brother. He later commits him to a private burial in a chest in the attic which appropriately contains one last garment—a wedding veil. The suggestion seems to be that the cost of entering the world—the singularly corrupt and theatrical world projected by Purdy, be it said—is that it gradually forces you to destroy the only reality you have known. You hide the corpse and put on one of the many available veils of which society is composed, on which it depends.

Purdy has taken the outlines of a perennial American theme—the end of innocence, that initiation into experience and fall into time which the American hero so often has to undergo. It seems as though Fenton is leaving one time scheme and entering another, just as I have suggested that the book catches him moving between two kinds of reality. The book ends precisely and abruptly when he has kissed the corpse and shut the lid on the chest. Just when the frame is completed, Fenton vanishes and we are left with a blank. Whether this means that Fenton's initiation is complete and he has vanished into the unreality of the world, or whether he has receded back into Non-Being is beyond the scope of the writer who can only deal with words—those veils that are left long after the bride has gone.

In his next book, *Malcolm* (1959), Purdy returned to the theme of the young boy who seems to embody some sort of rare beauty and potential and yet whose initiation into the 'reality' of the world is at the same time a gradual recession from Being. Once again, the passage from one kind of reality into another is implied from the outset. Malcolm, the boy abandoned by a father who has died or disappeared, sits motionless on a bench in front of a palatial hotel. He looks untouched, stares out with empty detachment and seems to reveal that open acceptance of everything which distinguished Fenton. He is the cypher and blank which he later describes himself to be, and he is waiting with an air of '*expectancy*'. Mr Cox, the astrologer, is the person who finally precipitates Malcolm into movement and away from the bench. He is 'in a sense, *the* city, the hotel, and, in his own mind, civilization', so this initial confrontation is a fairly obvious metaphysical parable. Malcolm is waiting for some identity to be 'imprinted' on him; Mr Cox knows how all bodies, astral and human, move or ought to move. He is the magician-planner behind the city, as it were the secret artist within civilization. He is just the figure to issue Malcolm with directions, in the form of a series of addresses. One piece of deceptively simple advice in particular reveals something of his philosophical status.

'Give yourself up to things.'
'Give myself up to ... things?'

The pause in Malcolm's slightly uncomprehending reply nicely conveys the hint that he is about to embark on a baffled excursion into materiality under the initial instruction of a master of 'things'. Malcolm has already said that '"things are, well, a bit too much for me, you see".' And just as his speech from the start betrays no very sure relations to language, so his movements reveal no very sure relation to the world of things.

His initiation, which is also his search for his father and his quest for identity (Purdy is deliberately and ostentatiously playing with standard American themes), takes him to a variety of buildings. Here he meets a series of different social types – undertaker, artist, magnate, socialite, welfare-worker and author, popular singer, and so on. The sequence itself is a strange sort of recession, since he starts with an undertaker, and ends up in a brothel prior to his marriage with the sexually insatiable Melba. He gets thinner and thinner, increasingly weary, and after his early death which completes his 'short long life' the local coroner and the undertaker insist that there had been no corpse at all, and that 'nobody was buried in the ceremony.' His movement into 'life' – a progress marked by a series of increasingly addictive drinks which he is offered at every house, moving from Spanish chocolate to whisky – proves at the same time to be a gradual vanishing. The range of characters which Purdy has brought into the book in this way allows him to indulge in some extremely amusing and extensive social satire, but I want to concentrate briefly on the relation of these characters to Malcolm, and the relation of Malcolm and society to Purdy's own art.

Most of the characters seek to appropriate him or use him for their own purposes, fantasies, needs, ' "It is to you we all look ... remember, you are ours." ' Asked at one point if Malcolm has any mind at all, Mr Cox answers, ' "Do you think he needs one?" ' – an ambiguous answer which on the one hand might point to the superior virtue or value of innocence (or the capacity for not assimilating knowledge), and on the other hand to the fact that society is always ready to do his thinking for him, imprinting its designs on him, defining him according to its own obsessions. Shortly before his marriage he goes to a tattoo parlour to get 'matured' (he is only fifteen). There some of the standard emblems of masculinity are violently printed on to his skin, and yet he falls asleep under the needle, apparently incapable of any feeling, and once again receding from consciousness precisely while an attempt to imprint some identity on him is in process. At times people recognize him as royalty, a prince; one admirer says he seems to be like 'the spirit of ... life, or something', because he seems to be without 'any pre-judgment about anything.

Your eyes are completely open.' But that complete openness sometimes seems to reveal a complete emptiness, a lack of all defining solidity. There is a rather sad appropriateness in the one habit with which, we gather, he occupies his solitary hours. He puts his ear to shells—listening to the eternal drone of the sea issuing from a void. His true home is not society but the timeless flow.

At the same time, when Malcolm seems ready to capitulate to the possessiveness of anyone who is reaching out after him, the grasp seems curiously to slacken or be withdrawn. It is as though he provokes strong desires, but these ebb away into indifference when the possibility of actual possession arises. Drawn by the images which they imprint on his blank potentiality, his various admirers allow his undefined reality to fall away from them. (For Madame Girard he is 'the idea of her life'—an abstraction not a being.) The undertaker's name is Blanc; Malcolm indeed goes from blank to blank, and his statement, '"I hardly feel I exist,"' adequately covers what happens to him in the short time in between. In one sense he is not allowed to come into existence because of the way everybody seems to seek and abandon him almost simultaneously. Whatever reality Malcolm embodied while he was still on the bench, in entering into the reality we call society he makes no contact with it and fades out of his temporary entanglement with 'things' in a very short time. And indeed, society itself seems to be receding and falling into unreality, as Purdy suggests in a description of a house which is one of the most beautiful 'entropic' descriptions of the many that occur in recent American fiction. It is a house full of late afternoon and twilight, arrested in a permanent autumn which will never give way to winter.

> It will go on being autumn, go on being cool, but slowly, slowly everything will begin to fall piece by piece, the walls will slip down ever so little, the strange pictures will warp, the mythological animals will move their eyes slightly for the last time as they fade into indistinctness, the strings of the bass will loosen and fall, the piano keys wrinkle and disappear into the wood of the instrument, and the beautiful alto sax shrivel into foil.

This suggests that gradual inner collapse of things, that inward vanishing and fading away, which in one form or another seems to haunt Purdy's fiction.

The characters have the discontinuity of dream figures; their 'lightning' changes of mood defy all logic and reveal no conceivable consistency of motive. They are either very assertive or very unassertive, suddenly looming into focus and as suddenly lapsing out of it. Although there is quite a lot of social and sexual contact, there is no inter-subjectivity, indeed no intercommunication. Thomas Lorch made the very pertinent observation that 'the novel contains an extraordinary number of commands and imperatives.'[1] At the same time he noted that 'the word "perhaps" occurs again and again.' The characters oscillate between manic assertiveness and extreme diffidence. It would seem that in the absence of true inter-subjectivity and communication, everyone either tries to imprint an image of his or her own identity on other individuals, or recedes before a more powerful effort aimed at them. A good example of this occurs when Madame Girard, with her husband and Malcolm, goes to Kermit's studio to force him to come out. Kermit is first seen as an 'outline' against the glass door, suggesting that reduction to two dimensions which afflicts all the characters at times. Madame Girard orders him to come out. But at the idea of being 'translated' into their reality Kermit can only retreat farther and farther into the dark interior of his studio, finally secreting himself in a closet, beyond speech. Meanwhile 'his splendid visitors motored off into the void.' Both parties move away from each other in the direction of an emptiness, never breaking through the 'glass door' which separates them.

Madame Girard's comment after the incident says a lot about the attenuation of reality prevalent throughout—'"silhouettes tell all."' It is Madame Girard who reveals most about the dubious nature of 'identity' in this novel. Shortly after the incident at Kermit's she puts on her veil. The paradox of the veil which cuts her off from the world is that it is also 'attention-bringing'. To Malcolm's comment, '"You could be the headless huntsman,"' she replies, '"Texture is all, substance nothing."' Malcolm is finding himself in a world of 'things' which paradoxically is wholly given over to surfaces, outlines, veils and make-up; like Cora Naldi, who dances 'in loose shawls' whose 'substance' and identity Malcolm cannot make out. Identity is the fabrication and assertion of a texture without substance: you assert your name, your veil, your outlines, or you succumb to nothingness. At one point when Madame Girard is asserting her right to have Malcolm, she accidentally knocks down a stuffed owl and it disintegrates into a heap of dust and feathers. At the end of her tirade she is suddenly silenced when Eloisa knocks *her* down, and she lies on the floor like 'the stone queen, asleep through all the ages'. The sudden reversion of the stuffed bird to the heap of dust and feathers and the social actress to the stone queen offers a succinct image of that oscillation between two forms of unreality characteristic of a book which seems to see everything and everyone moving between veils and voids.

The fact that none of the characters seem to use language for authentic personal expression, but rather as a series of available established phrases to be made use of in the power plays of counter-command, has a profound effect on Malcolm. He speaks in elaborate clichés—'"Madame Girard has not taken ill or died?"', '"I am speechless with surprise at your generosity"'—which readily indicate that his words are not emerging out of something within him, but rather that he is simply returning to the world the dead sets of words which the world has fed to him. He will sometimes say things in a voice which 'did not quite sound like his own', or he will suddenly make a remark 'unaware ... what prompted him to say these words'. Just as he is to some extent a blackboard on which other people draw their fantasies, so he is an echoing board from which society gets back its mechanical verbal conventions. Malcolm, who finds himself at the middle of so many voices, remains terribly cut off. This language does not 'fit' on him, and his premature disappearance is related to his failure to establish any vital linguistic connections with the world. The words of this world are as alien to him as the things to which he also has to give himself up if he wants to leave the bench. It almost makes for a Platonic parable concerning some pure idea which can never come to full realization in the realm of matter, except that in Purdy's book there is no hint of the existence of any transcendent realm of pure ideas.

In the world in which Malcolm finds himself, sense is continually dissolving in contradictions. There is nothing stable enough or meaningful enough around him to enable him properly speaking to 'begin'. The word recurs as Malcolm constantly thinks or hopes that this time 'life is actually *beginning*' as a new social situation opens up to him. Yet the feeling we are left with is that he never really does *begin*; it is as though the visible, audible parts of him are not really his own but borrowed for and from the occasion. He passes through changing scenes but, instead of thickening into identity and con-solidating a real self, his life is really a long fading. This paradox of passing through life without, as it were, beginning to live Purdy explores at length in his most searching novel, where the problem is written into the title, *Cabot Wright Begins*. But at this stage we can make the point that if Malcolm never begins neither does his story ever really begin—another way in which Purdy seems to want to remind us that when we have finished the book we only have texture without substance.

Mr Cox, the astrologer, is a figure who seeks to arrange people's lives into aesthetic situations and combinations. But he is constantly discovering the limit of his powers, and the intended groupings fail. Even while he explains all this to Malcolm in a long speech, Malcolm is yawning as though unaffected by the performance. Once again the 'material' seems to recede from the man who seeks to organize it into certain patterns. This failure of art to contain or ordain any reality is symptomatic of an aesthetic scepticism which prevails throughout the book. The persistently 'empty frames' in Kermit's studio offer one hint. Another comes from Mr Cox's warning that, although Eloisa says she is determined to paint Malcolm's portrait, all her portraits turn out to look just like Eloisa. The implication seems to be that art must either be vacuous or solipsistic – the empty frame or the endless self-portrait.

The paradox, and Purdy is clearly aware of it, is that Purdy himself is doing a 'portrait' of Malcolm; it is as though he has written into the book proofs of the futility of his own undertaking. This of course is one reason why he violates, or undermines through parody, every vestigial convention of naturalistic writing, because writing based on that aesthetic seems completely confident of its ability to contain substantial reality, and such a confidence Purdy sees as a self-deception. It is also, I think, why his novel seems to cancel itself out as it goes along, and why at times the writing descends to a deliberate banality and clichéd flatness, although his prose is clearly capable of magical effects and all sorts of subtle and economic registrations. The result of this is a paradox in the status of the book itself which makes its effect at once so rich and so elusive. From one point of view it does seem to contain a statement about contemporary society: 'a beautiful but terrifying portrait of man on the brink of non-being, or perhaps having already passed over the edge' as Thomas Lorch suggests in the article referred to earlier. Yet at the same time the ability of art to establish any contact with reality is so constantly queried or mocked that the book can become, like one of those optical illusions which you suddenly 'read' in reversed perspective, a statement about the artist's foredoomed inability to produce anything but veils, silhouettes, outlines, a schematized unreality unable to hold the drowsy prince of the promise of life.

In his next book, *The Nephew* (1960), Purdy again brings the writer into the novel, but this time the beautiful boy who is once again the focus of the writer's intentions never appears in the novel at all – the effect being of a novel about a story which never gets started. Cliff is the nephew of the title, an orphan brought up by a spinster aunt and her brother, who at the time of the novel is away fighting in Korea. His absence seems to leave a void in the melancholy suburbia in which the novel is set, and where Alma and Boyd Mason (the aunt and uncle) sit reminiscing in their house at twilight — growing deafer while the rooms grow darker. What emerges from the start is that while he had actually been in the house, Alma and Boyd had been away most of the time, but 'once he had gone away, they talked of nothing but him.' Once again we find the image of someone being cherished when the reality has been allowed to disappear. Indeed the novel is not about Cliff at all but about various versions of him, and residual documents connected with his brief life. The book starts with the last letter to arrive from him, and although Alma concedes that Cliff doesn't say much in a letter, she thinks his letters could be made up into a diary. '"How could they form a diary then, if they tell nothing?"' asks Boyd, and the idea of documents without contents continues throughout the book.

Cliff, like Malcolm, was practically 'non-verbal'; he was never at home in language and could only repeat what was said to him. And, like Malcolm, he was the focal point of many people's fantasies. They each had their version of him, just as Alma has *her* photograph of him (it looks 'retouched' as of course it is, by her dream projections), while a near-by neighbour, Vernon, has *his* photographs of Cliff, which he keeps hung up in a private room. At about the time when Alma and Boyd hear from the army that there was nothing left of Cliff to ship home for burial, the photographs in Vernon's room are destroyed in a fire. The reality and the image have both dissolved back into non-being. Nevertheless the pursuit of the image continues; the flickering pictures on the screens of the ubiquitous TV sets in the background of the book suggest the general compulsion to live in a substitute fantasy world which prevails. It becomes quite clear that in spite of all her seeking for 'information' Alma will never write her memorial to Cliff. But other people feel that it is essential that she be helped to keep alive the illusion that she will write it, as though one has to evoke images to keep out the void, invent consoling pictures in the inexorable twilight.

But the photographs were burnt, and there does seem to be a new kind of recognition at the end of the book. Alma realizes that she cannot write the book, and emerges from her self-delusion: '"I never knew him Boyd, I only loved him."' His answer that, '"We none of us, I'm afraid, know anybody or know one another,"' suggests a new ability to face the void of their present condition. The last chapter bears the strange title 'Threshold of Assent' and it opens with an emphasis on protections being stripped away and coveted symbols falling apart. Mrs Barrington's garden, which helped her to forget that her dead husband had never loved her, succumbs to the inevitable winter. Alma watches with dismay and pity as the storms strip the estate of all its beautiful landmarks, laying it waste. Just so has the cultivated garden of her memory been harshly denuded. And then, as it is Memorial Day, Boyd gets the flag out of the attic, but slips and tears it. Alma thinks she can easily repair it, but when she begins working on it she sees that 'what she held was a tissue of rotted cloth, impossible to mend.' The book starts with an emphasis on flags – 'All the flags were out' – and this late disintegration of such an established and relied-on symbol once again suggests what Yeats called a withering into truth: for Alma, as for us, the unmendable flag is only another reminder of the unwritable book.

At the same time caring is recognized as a reality, even if the caring and the cared-for lack the gift to say it or write it. This perhaps is the threshold of assent at which Alma and Boyd have arrived at the end of the book. It is another threshold as well, as the last scene makes clear. The gathering darkness, the late hour, the lapses in their conversation, their failing hearing, all this, with the muted economy of which Purdy is a master, takes us to the edge of that final blank where Alma and Boyd (or Soul and Body) now stand.

Cabot Wright Begins, written five years later (1965), gathers together all the themes opened up or touched on in Purdy's earlier work and explores them with a subtlety and humour and power which makes this, to my mind, not only Purdy's most profound novel but one of the most important American novels since the war. Cabot Wright is a Yale man who gets bored with Wall Street and his wife and who, after an unusual cure from a strange doctor, becomes a relentless rapist. Put that way the novel might seem to promise the sort of glamorous pornography one associates with a best seller. Yet it contains no detailed sexual scenes at all and it transpires that Cabot Wright can only think of 'boredom' as the motive of his rapes, not lust. More to the point, over a third of the novel is spent in discussing the problems connected with writing a book, the biography of Cabot Wright. Chapter Seven of Purdy's novel is entitled 'Cabot Wright Begins', while the first six chapters are concerned with the people involved in the decision to attempt to make a book out of his life. The frame has never intruded so far into a Purdy novel before.

In those first six chapters we gather that Bernie Gladhart, an unpublished writer, has been goaded and persuaded by his wife Carrie, a semi-retired miniature painter who is also sexually insatiable, to go to New York to find Cabot Wright, recently released from prison, and make a best seller out of his story. Before taking this decision she had enlisted the support of her friend Zoe Bickle, an ex-editor, married to a failed writer who now spends his time annotating Isaiah though he is a Gentile with no knowledge of Hebrew. Altogether they are a rather unsuccessful group of people, all connected with the media that fabricate versions of reality. Appropriately enough, Carrie first comes across Cabot Wright in a newspaper, as a story and a photograph, and she tells Bernie that all he has to do is 'write the truth like fiction', a phrase which seems like an ironic echo of Truman Capote's idea of the non-fiction novel. Bernie comes to New York, does some research, and writes some manuscript before he happens to meet Cabot Wright staying in his own run-down Brooklyn rooming-house. Then the powerful publisher Princeton Keith gets hold of the manuscript, determined to turn it into a best seller. He calls in Zoe Bickle to help with the rewriting. She comes to New York and also meets Cabot Wright and, drawing on some old tape-recordings, other magazine stories, and Bernie's manuscript, she expands the version, at the same time coaxing more material, or at least corroboration, out of Wright.

To remind us that at any one time we are reading a synthesized version of Cabot Wright's life, Purdy will insert ungainly reminders such as: 'The reader, in this case the listener (Cabot Wright eavesdropping on his own story as novelized by Bernie Gladhart and revised by Zoe Bickle) ... ' In addition the constant references to documents, and the equivocal emphasis on words like 'facts', 'news', 'versions', serve to keep it well in the foreground that the novel is about a group of people, including Cabot Wright, who for different motives are trying to construct a written version of his life. When Cabot has occasion to confide in someone that, ' "My life is largely paper work," ' he speaks much truer than he knows. He is, as we learn in the book, a 'supposititious child' and though that word was sometimes used of an illegitimate child, the more general meaning of something counterfeit, established by artifice, 'fraudulently substituted for the genuine thing or person' (as the O.E.D. has it), is one which touches on the central issues of the book.

It is important to remember that Cabot Wright willingly collaborates with Zoe in the effort to write his life, and to note his motives for doing so. These motives point to a major theme in contemporary American literature, the desire to get beyond all versions. Some of his comments after he has read Bernie's initial manuscript are relevant here: ' "I read so many versions of what I did, I can safely affirm that I couldn't remember what I did and what I didn't." ' He gives examples of facts about himself occurring in newspaper descriptions which he had not known himself, and others which were fictitious. "'I've heard my own life so many times, I can say I'm a stranger to the story myself.'" He asks Zoe to 'coax' his story out of him, asking her if she has the time for that necessarily long process: "'If I could see my whole story written straight out, I think I'd be cured ... Cured of being what everybody made me.'" Here, in rather unusual circumstances, we see once again the American 'hero' wanting to shed all the imposed identities and definitions which the image-making media of the world have showered on him, and his method is curiously similar to one recommended by Burroughs—'Get it out of your head and into the machines,' i.e. empty out of yourself all those definitions which have managed to fabricate a completely 'supposititious' life and self around you and within you. Put it all down on tapes and typewriters (into a book) and when it's all down you will be clean, cured and free. At the end of the novel Cabot Wright disappears after one last long letter, a final documentary disburdening.

The strange and paradoxical nature of Cabot Wright's identity is hinted at in the description of him in his room when Zoe finds him in New York. Zoe falls into the room by accident, crashing through a glassed-in aperture—a penetration of some significance as will emerge—where she finds an impeccable man with a hearing-aid, looking 'like the mythical clean-cut American youth out of Coca-Cola ads' who seems neither surprised nor interested in her arrival. A side room is full of clocks and he has a habit of taking his pulse; as he explains, time and his own heartbeat are the only things that 'hold' him; otherwise he seems to have receded almost completely from all contact with external reality, and to have become a set of mobile surfaces drained of all human response. The room is not furnished, but he comments on the wallpaper. "'I have, you see, four or five wallpapers, one under the other. They wear down gradually all of them to the original willow pattern over the calcimine itself, then robin redbreast, scenes at the forge, water lilies, peasants in ancient France.'" For Zoe Bickle the wallpaper reminds her of his unidentifiable accent. 'Though all his speech sounded native American, for Cabot Wright was an American criminal in anybody's book, it was nonetheless, like his wallpaper, composite.' (Note 'in anybody's book', another of Purdy's sly touches, the cliché which turns out to be heavy with secondary meanings.)

This passing incident has many reverberations. What indeed *is* native American, for Cabot Wright is in a sense unmistakably one of its products? The fact that his language seems somehow to have been fed into him from the environment only serves to relate Cabot to those other Purdy figures who are not to be found in the words they use. But the implications go further, pointing to the basic paradox involved both in identity and in art itself. The wallpapers are a heterogeneous set of images imprinted on the wall, in their comic banality representing the apotheosis of convention. Just so, identity is such a series of versions affixed from the outside. But if, in the interests of authenticity, you strip off all the wallpaper, you end up with a blank—it is another instance of veils and voids. Similarly, any literary style is a form of wallpaper, and the book itself reveals the layers which make it up—the newspaper story, Bernie's research, Zoe's revisions and additions, Cabot's comments, and, of course, James Purdy's novel. Take them away in the interests of getting at the 'reality' underneath and you end up with the whiteness of truth, 'the calcimine itself'. By Purdy's own account identity and art alike are both inherently 'supposititious'.

At the end of this particular incident Zoe Bickle leaves, 'convinced there was no story here', and she rightly foretells that whatever they make of the 'subject' will not 'fit' into the publishing lists of a commercial firm. Her last line of all is '"I won't be a writer in a place and time like the present,"' a splendid irony with which Purdy concludes *his* story, and which Charles Newman has described as 'perhaps the most anticipated climax in all post-modern literature'.[2] At the same time, as Newman points out, there is a danger in a novelist's constant mockery of his own activity. The suggestion that there is no alternative between a blank and wallpaper which is a collection of clichés is to reveal a pessimism about the status of contemporary language (a suspicion of the 'word' *per se* which again relates Purdy to other American writers) which, if really acted upon, would result in Purdy's refusal to write novels. Newman's succinct observation is: 'It is but a short step from the constant questioning of form to a mere contempt for it.' '"I feel like the hollow space inside a statue,"' says Princeton Keith— another version of the frame without a picture. But there is more in Purdy's book than in that mere servitor of the commercial media, and something of a portrait of the life of Cabot Wright does emerge.

We gather from the reconstruction of his life that Cabot Wright had a preference for painting and solitary vacations. But it seems that he acquired a set of relations who forced him into Wall Street. As a result of this he felt continuously tired. It is interesting that only when he is walking across the Brooklyn Bridge to work does he feel free and relieved of the weight of his adopted parents and newly acquired wife. The bridge area is equivalent to that marginal place out of reach of various defining social/domestic forces which the American hero longs to find. To seek a cure for his chronic fatigue he visits Dr Bigelow-Martin, one of those strange instructors and doctors, mixtures of charlatan and genius, who appear so frequently in novels by writers as different as Bellow, Barth and Burroughs, and perhaps owe something to the figure of Wilhelm Reich. After his first visit to the doctor Cabot returns to his wife, Cynthia, whose very being, like her speech, seems to be 'borrowed from one of the more intellectual women's magazines'. Cabot starts to look at her with an expression 'between hunger and amnesia' and suggests that she cure him. When she asks, '"Do you love me?"' he answers, '"I adore it."' This little scene is important because it suggests the subsequent progress of the book.

Cabot's exhaustion is something which results from his life among other people, a sort of folding up of consciousness in retreat from the unreality of contemporary society. But at a deeper level there is a very primitive hunger which might emerge while consciousness, deprived of the proper stimuli, lapses into amnesia. This hunger would only see people as sexual objects – 'its' not selves – and, ignoring the charade of personal relations conducted at the level of consciousness, regress to the most primitive abandonment to instinct. This is what happens after Cabot goes to the doctor a second time. The doctor promises, '"We are beginning a new life,"' and slings Cabot over a padded hook telling him to give in to his fatigue – '"let go, Cabot, let go."' He lets go, and after visions of gauchos riding on the pampas, and bullfights, he feels his intestines give, his navel seems to explode like the crust of a pie, and he suddenly sees himself saying *adios* to all his acquired relations from a rapidly receding boat. He is indeed withdrawing from all societal relations, and losing that crust of false, restrictive identity which society imposes on a man (the imagery is very Reichian). Whatever process the doctor used, when he put Cabot on his hook, he fished up his most primordial responses and sympathies.

With the social self sloughed off, those primeval dispositions which the human animal shares with all life begin to emerge. Cabot's first rape takes place in the library, and the whole comic scene is most suggestively arranged. Sitting surrounded by books and inside a typically stuffy piece of social architecture, Cabot starts to read about various methods of pollination and fertilization. A girl comes in who looks as though she has stepped out of a fashion magazine and sits down opposite him. Cabot starts to yawn and sweat profusely and after reading a long passage which ends, 'The stigmas, too, protrude ... winnowing the air for drifting pollen,' he persuades the girl to go outside with him for a cigarette. In the hallway there is a huge hole in the wall which exposes an empty, darkened room into which they go. There Cabot, oozing saliva and sweat, commits his first rape – as always, unresisted. What we are watching here is a man discovering and moving between the different levels of 'reality' which make up human society. The library is the perfect example of man's ability, and compulsion, to turn experience into symbols which may then substitute for that experience. Cabot, in *reading* about the primordial rhythms and fertilization processes of the jungle, is being reminded of a level of reality in nature, to which the very existence of the library (and all it stands for) prevents man from returning. (It is worth noting that Purdy often puts his heroes in just such places where civilization preserves evidence of great evolutionary distances and the jungle. After 'murdering' his brother Fenton goes to a museum and studies the skeletons of prehistoric animals; Malcolm is at one point abandoned in the horticultural gardens where he has been sitting among the tropical plants.) This should not be construed as straightforward atavism, or nostalgia for the jungle. But it does point to the difficulties and deprivations attendant on living in an overwhelmingly literate and verbalizing world. There is a loss in the sensation of engaging with reality and an increased sense of being surrounded by the mechanical fabrications of various symbol-systems, most of these systems, in Purdy's world, being hopelessly cliché-ridden.

In particular this involves a loss of the sense of establishing direct communication with the reality of another individual. This is the point about that hole in the wall which has appeared due to 'extensive alterations' in the building (just as there have been extensive alterations in Cabot's own inner construction). Confronted with women whose appearance and whole consciousness seem to be an assemblage of magazine extracts, Cabot is regressing to a more primitive mode of biological directness in an attempt to make contact on a lower level. To do this, the usual barriers have to be broken through by force: hence that hole in the wall; hence, too, Zoe Bickle's unintentionally breaking through the glass pane into Cabot's room. In each case we have someone breaking through into someone else's reality, or trying to.

This is the drive behind Cabot's repeated rapes, and it is why the setting of his first rape is so important. In a sense it is an emancipation – a stepping out of the stuffy library room full of word-patterns into the refreshing liberation of the empty room and speechless physical contact; at the same time it is a step from a lighted room to a dark one – from definition into invisibility. No doubt something authentic is gained by this return to the mindless flow of the primal drives; but something must be lost too, for whatever else the realm of protruding stigmas and drifting pollen is, it is not human. Just in what sense Cabot Wright does 'begin' when he steps through that hole in the wall is what the book is about. Behind wallpaper, a blank wall; through the wall, a dark emptiness — such at least would seem to be Purdy's demonstration of the impossibility of starting to acquire an identity. All human definition seems to be cliché, and the authenticity of the biological urge is a mechanical activity with all interest in human features obliterated, as Cabot reveals by his almost absent-minded rapes and the way he covers his wife's face with her sleeping mask before submitting her to his new-found sincerity and directness.

Admittedly, his raping is described in terms which suggest that the clichéd surfaces have been sundered to admit some contact with reality, the equivocal reality of 'the flow'. Such brief descriptions of his rapes as occur tend to stress the streams of saliva and sweat that accompany the outflow of his semen. He now prefers to sit staring at the 'confluent waters' of the Hudson and East Rivers to taking part in any social occasion. Indeed whenever he does get involved in such occasions he usually breaks through the tired surface etiquette and becomes 'confluent' with the nearest female. What is clear is that, having stepped out of the constructed unreality of society, Cabot is drawn back into that elemental 'flow' which is both the river of life and of death and in which there is no such thing as identity.

When Mr Warburton, Cabot's Wall Street employer, is sick, he also goes to a doctor who turns out to be Bigelow-Martin now disguised as Dr Bugleford. He takes Warburton into what he calls 'the *beginning* room', makes him lie down on a couch and starts the cure: ' "having realized the hardness of your jaw, let it break, dissolve, flow, vanish, turn to flowing limpid water, flowing, flowing, flowing. Lie back, my good broker, lie back. You are flowing away, out to sea, out to sea, out to the deep ... " ' Suddenly Warburton finds that he has started to drift and relax into a sleep beyond all cares. But when he wakes up he realizes that if he went on like that it would be the end of him — 'deprived of tenseness and anger, his business empire would crumble — he would be calm and happy and *penniless*.' Here again we see impossible alternatives. Dr Bugleford, in his present role, has no interest in identity (he keeps getting Warburton's name wrong), and he urges the casting off of all rigidities in the self, all social 'disguises', to facilitate a return to the primal flow. But Warburton recognizes that his tensions are precisely what hold his social identity together. It seems that there is no alternative for the modern self between being cramped in the 'steel trap' of social identity, and vanishing into the shapeless waters. The 'beginning room' is like the hole in the wall—a very equivocal place to pass through.

Warburton's *Sermons* comprise an outraged indictment of the debased unreality of modern America. Of course, the *Sermons* are just another document in a book of many documents, but it is hard not to feel that Purdy is using them as a vehicle to discharge many of his own feelings. It is stated that Cabot feels in the presence of some 'reality' while reading the *Sermons*, and I think we could say that the document has the same reality as the act of vomiting. There is, as it were, a deep response from the inner man in both. Warburton writes at one point, ' "If I had my way and the strength to do so ... I would open a permanent window on Wall Street and continuously vomit through it for the next 25 years." ' Most of Purdy's central figures have a good vomit (as do characters in many other contemporary American novels), at important moments. I think it is deliberately used as a symbolic, purgative act. It can be seen as a spontaneous repudiation of the environment which has poured its noxious influences into the passive consciousness of the unwary initiate.

In this sense Warburton's desire to vomit out the years is related to Cabot's desire to get all the versions down outside him so he can be free to leave all that part of his life behind him. After he puts all the notes, manuscripts and documents which tell his story into Zoe Bickle's hands, he gives her one last, intent look and 'she had the oddest feeling she might never see him again'. She doesn't, although she does receive a letter in which Cabot writes: 'You listened and you told me. *I saw me all in one piece together like in a movie, and as a result I'm free.*' (My italics.) Free from all the media clichés which defined him and the wallpaper versions imposed on him: the italicized sentence represents an aspiration at the heart of contemporary American fiction. And by the same token it points to one of the central problems: if you do manage to elude the imposed definitions, to get it all down in order to be free of it, how will you participate in the world, where will you go? Often Purdy's characters recede into non-existence without ever having properly existed. But in Cabot's case he adds an interesting P.S. which reveals his awareness of the problem. 'P.S. I am going to take up disguises for a while, I think harmless ones. Think I may be a preacher further South or maybe some kind of a quack healer.' Once again we see the American hero driven to the expediency of disguise and role-playing; but at least, this time—it is often the American hero's sole desperate hope—the role-playing is going to be under *his* control, the wallpaper of his own selection. What is perhaps slightly more ominous is that the two disguises which Cabot is toying with the idea of adopting are precisely the two roles in which Bigelow-Martin/Bugleford appears in this book.

The change that comes over Cabot at the end and constitutes his cure is that he suddenly discovers he can laugh. Up to that point throughout his whole life, 'real and supposititious', he had only been able to giggle. 'Suddenly Cabot Wright could laugh.' It is connected with getting clear of the whole complex of versions brought together by Zoe Bickle, and somehow out of reach of the media which everywhere 'tell you what you are about to do & did'. With the laughter comes perfect solitude.

> Now Cabot was alone again with his non-self. Loneliness feels so good after the mythic contact with the social. Dreams become clear, and nightmares are no longer attention-getting. One sucks eight or nine aspirins and allows his calloused thumb to rest on a quilt. The trauma of birth, life and death pass as shadows on the moon. Mother Nature goes right on keeping house even though nobody is to home.

The interesting thing about this crucial paragraph is that the references to dreams, aspirins and quilt suggest that the state of non-selfhood, which is blessedly out of touch with society, is a sort of revery. Arguably this state is comparable to that dissolution of self advocated by Bugleford's theory of 'flow'.

Just as the Invisible Man conveys the relief of finally dropping out of all 'mythic contact with the social' into his unlocatable refuge in a border area, so in this novel Purdy has demonstrated the need to escape from all the supposititious 'selves' fostered by those illusory contacts. The question again arises — is there a third realm beyond the alternatives of submission to social fabrications or escape by flowing away? Can a 'non-self' have an identity? In rejecting all this non-humanity of society, in what sense does Cabot Wright achieve real humanity? One answer that Purdy clearly intends is — simply by achieving the ability to laugh. He inserts a long rhetorical paragraph on laughter as the supreme consolation; it ends: 'Meaning there is no meaning but the laughter of the moment made it almost worth while. That's all it's about. We was here, finally laughed.' Perhaps you are only human as long as you are laughing; some such desperation is implicit in the sudden unchecked feeling of this paragraph. Cabot continues to laugh until he is 'in erection again'. He goes on laughing until he has an orgasm, and tears are running from his eyes and drivel is coming down from his mouth. It seems as though he has started to 'flow' again! This makes his final remark even more ambiguous than it already is: ' "I thought I'd die but I lived." '

Purdy follows that remark immediately with two lines in italics which are not related to any one voice in the book; indeed perhaps they are the voice of the book itself.

The deadly monotony of the human continuity,
The fog is a sea on earth.

What this rather cryptically suggests is that the same kind of dissolution and perpetual erasing inherent in the endless ebb and flow of the sea is also to be found extending over the land and into the human community. To me it makes the same kind of observation as the one implicit in lines from T. S. Eliot's 'The Dry Salvages', such as:

> The salt is on the briar rose,
> the fog is in the fir trees.

Certainly some of the lines from that poem would not be inappropriate to the underlying mood of Purdy's book and its sense both of the unreality of so-called identity and of nature's endless, inexorable flow.

> The river is within us, the sea is all about us;
> The sea is the land's edge also, the granite
> Into which it reaches ...

One might have thought that Purdy would end his book there, yet the next chapter returns to Chicago to show the final separation of Bernie and Carrie Moore, who has gone through her change of life. The chapter is entitled, obviously enough, 'Mama's Well is Dry' and since we have just left Cabot emitting all kinds of moisture in his unselved solitude one can see that Purdy is intending some sort of connection between sexual aridity and the hollowness of social identity. And then in the last chapter, Zoe Bickle receives what she knows is the 'last' letter from Cabot. It is a very revealing letter from the point of view of our subject. First he describes how he discovered he could laugh; then he reveals that he has got rid of all that he had 'inherited' from Warburton and others; then he mentions that the TV set is broken in his room. TV sets have been booming images from the background of the novel all along, and in connection with his shedding all that society, in the form of Warburton, had sought to pile on him, it clearly indicates an escape from the media and milieu which gave him his supposititious identity. And here is his answer to that most recurrent of American questions – where next?

The thought always on my mind was 'Do you think there's a Chance for Me if I ever Find out who I is?' That's why I've come home to my brownstones in Brooklyn Heights (falling fast), have sold same, and am on my way to extended flight, but this time with myself, and in search of same ... Here I am running out on America, if not myself. That's the funny thing to remember — in case I don't send you more news.

He ends by referring to the clocks that used to line the walls of his room (in the appropriately named 'See River Manor') and says that whereas he used to need to infer his reality from the ticking of those clocks, he can now dispense with such external props. 'WHAT MAKES ME TICK? I don't care about that now, Mrs Bickle, but I do know, hear it any way you want, I am ticking as of this letter, anyhow, and I'll write the symbol for the way I feel now, which is HA!'

It is his last word and in a sense it is a farewell to language, which, along with clocks and buildings, is another form of structuring. Cabot has reached that point at which all structure, *per se*, seems supposititious. 'HA!' is a refusal even to engage in syntactical statements. It amounts to a repudiation by laughter of everything that seeks to condition, control and shape the self from the outside. A stray coloured man appears briefly in the novel and is described as 'obviously not impressed by anything except what was inside him'. This would seem to be the state the American hero is striving for, but it remains a question what internal reality Cabot will establish. At the end of the novel he is left in that state of paradox so common to American heroes: running out on himself to find himself, in extended flight which is also unending search, attempting to find some way of being in the world without being of the world. Perhaps it could be said that his true 'beginning' coincides with his escape from the novel itself. At one point Cabot is looking through a key-hole into a room where his wife has locked herself away from him. We are told that at Yale he was often invited to look through key-holes by snooping friends, but that while they claimed to see a lot 'all he ever saw was a fuzzy portion of wallpaper.' A novel is another sort of keyhole and Purdy seems to have demonstrated that if we peer into his book for a glimpse of the 'real' Cabot Wright all we can ever see is a fuzzy portion of wallpaper. To the extent that Cabot really escapes from the novel, Purdy is in danger of excluding himself from his own genre.

There is a profound pessimism implicit in this unusual novel, and in his next work, *Eustace Chisholm and the Works* (1967), it seems as though Purdy has allowed that pessimism to emerge. He still retains the situation of having a writer within the novel whose final refutation of writing coincides with Purdy's conclusion of his novel. Eustace Chisholm is a run-down writer living in squalor in the Chicago of the Depression years. Like Mr Cox in *Malcolm* he knows what people are and which places they should occupy in relation to each other; in addition he picks up the power of prophecy from a negro fortune-teller. But people do not act according to the patterns he holds up for them; and what he can foresee makes the power of prophecy not a gift but a dreadful curse from which he longs to escape. He calls his apartment 'the clearing house for busted dreams' and by extension it applies to his tormented vision of the way life's reality is constantly disappointing and failing the ideal forms that can be dreamed for it. If the terms seem unduly portentous I think this is perhaps appropriate for a novel which, despite the seedy and oppressive 'realism' of its settings, is also a very abstract work with references to Plato's transcendent reality and Dante's hell coming together in modern America. Despite the failure of Eustace Chisholm, Purdy seems to be projecting a version of reality which this time the novel does not call into question.

References to the futility of art still remain as reminders. Nevertheless a story does get told, the story of Amos (who in the Bible foretold the destruction of Israel) and Daniel (who entered the lions' den). Amos is another version of the boy of unearthly beauty who undergoes dazed initiations into a dirty society which never really touches him. His parentage is uncertain and his early death is really the vanishing back into non-being of an apparition which, however much it is dressed up in rich clothes by admirers, has never been real. The fleeting appearance of an image of such beauty in a world of such foulness and dirt as Purdy depicts in this book suggests that Platonic strain which as we noted before is detectable in Purdy's work. A clue is offered by the fact that Amos is, rather surprisingly, a Greek scholar (he is seen holding the works of Xenophon, who was a contemporary of Plato's and also studied under Socrates).

Daniel is also described as having a kind of perfection but of rather different origins. It is established that he is of American Indian descent. He has Old Glory tattooed on his forearms, and at one point when he asks Amos why he is staring at him, Amos answers that he likes to look at an American face. He almost seems like a representative of a kind of physical 'perfection' which can emerge from the American land. Yet, as he complains, 'somebody is always hounding and deviling me', all through his life, and Purdy asserts that his physical perfection was a 'target attracting destruction'. Daniel is a sleepwalker. Awake, he violently repudiates the idea of his homosexual love for Amos. But asleep he walks into Amos's room and touches him in a protective, but unsexual, manner. In his sleepwalking another level of character, another kind of vision come into action as he gazes at Amos 'with unseeing eyes'. Amos, who never seems wholly to belong to the physical realm, responds to Daniel's strange kind of love as he does to nothing else; he lives only for his evening visits when 'they met together on the borderline of slumber.' It is an impossible love, in the sense that they can never 'connect' in their waking bodies; they can only make contact at the far edges of consciousness between daytime identity and the oblivion of night. Amos himself has almost no sexual drive at all. Explaining this he says, ' "I'll never be ready. I don't belong anywhere ... I'm just real enough for a sleepwalker to love, I guess. That's all Daniel could ever do too, so we were two of a kind." ' Inevitably, in a book with Platonic overtones, the question of what is 'real' remains ambiguous.

Daniel's deepest emotion is not concern at some social taboo, but a loathing of his own body. The fact that he comes from a long line of coal-miners not only anticipates his final descent into a modern inferno, but also points to his inescapably carthy origins. He is compulsive about cleanliness, scrubbing and scouring himself, 'as only a man who hates himself can'. (Amos is always filthy but simply seems unaware of the dirt he has collected; this suggests his celestial, as opposed to Daniel's subterranean, origins.) When Daniel does first confront the fact of his homosexual love with full consciousness, he vomits horribly 'as if now he would part with his guts'. This is what he will literally do when Captain Stadger has finished working on him with his last nameless instrument of torture, and this yearning to be rid of his body is a nausea that goes deeper than any shame at discovering his homosexuality. This nausea is at the root of his liking for the army and his decision to re-enlist. 'The word "re-enlistment" came over him like a wave of sea water ... His excitement became so intense he had an erection.' With a daring reversal of image-associations, Purdy here equates the army with the sea. It is as though he sees that a complete capitulation to routine, pattern, scaffolding (as represented by army life) is simply another way of seeking out the shapelessness of the sea. There is an intensification of structure which achieves the same end as no structure at all, i.e. the annihilation of identity. Daniel's sexual excitement at the thought of rejoining the army reveals him as a man yearning for death, and the far-seeing Eustace writes to him, ' "The army is not going to be a Mother to you, but your dark bridegroom." '

This leads to the last section of the book which bears the Dantesque title 'Under Earth's Deepest Stream' and implies that the ex-miner is returning to his origins. (The first section of this beautifully choreographed book is entitled 'The Sun at Noon' and is concerned with the celestial Amos. In between comes the middle section, 'In Distortion-free Mirrors'. This contains a sickening abortion scene, a direct confrontation of the horror and curse of the original discharge from the womb into the middle realm of human existence.) Daniel knows that once he is with Captain Stadger he is already 'in death's kingdom'. The captain is a figure motivated by an annihilating sadistic fury which is unexplained psychologically, and is indeed inexplicable outside the abstract allegorical pattern which subtends the book. The scenes in which the captain does proceed to break down and scour out that self which Daniel is so eager to be rid of make up the last infernal section of the book. Stadger is welcomed as the anaesthetist who will bring him release. The pessimism implicit in all this is revealed in some of Daniel's late sentiments. He takes satisfaction in the pointless pain inflicted on him by Captain Stadger because it confirms his belief in the inherent vileness of man and life. 'He had never wanted to be alive.'

The Dantesque allusions of the concluding section and the Platonic ones of the first combine to suggest the juxtaposition of opposed realms which is the background for the book (a juxtaposition reinforced by flickering references to snakes and moths). Since Amos and Daniel both go to early and effectively voluntary deaths, there is a suggestion that life between the infernal and celestial regions – i.e. human life – has become impossible or intolerable. Perhaps this is because of the failure of modern society, or that failure of modern feeling which is everywhere evident in Purdy's work; in which case the book contains a prophecy. After the deaths of Amos and Daniel we are told that Eustace Chisholm never wrote again; but Purdy has abandoned his undermining scepticism towards his own medium sufficiently to write the story of Amos and Daniel and offer a pattern of the 'hell and destruction' which the convergence and divergence of their lives perhaps foretells. In view of the legible philosophic aspect of the book, we may remark a further implicit suggestion. The material and physical potentialities of the North American Continent (Daniel), unable to consummate a loving union with the Ideal (Amos, or the American dream), may embark on a course of ghastly self-annihilation.

Chapter 5 Rub Out the Word

'WHAT SCARED YOU INTO TIME? INTO BODY? INTO SHIT? I WILL TELL YOU. THE WORD.'
Letter to Allen Ginsberg from William Burroughs

'Whatever you feed into the machine on subliminal level the machine will process — So we feed in "dismantle thyself" ...'
(*Berserk Machine*)

Most of the American heroes we have studied so far share one dread — of being 'taken over' by some external force, of being assimilated to an alien pattern not of their choosing, of being 'fixed' in someone else's 'reality-picture'. Purdy goes so far as to explore the extreme proposition that the hero's identity may be entirely 'supposititious', an invention of the media. What it might mean to move beyond all conditioning forces and how such a freedom might be achieved and maintained could be said to be an abiding preoccupation of recent American writers; most of whom seem to agree that those forces are too powerful to confront directly.

'And always remember that you are operating under conditions of guerilla war — Never attempt to hold a position under massive counter-attack — "Enemy advance we retreat" — Where?' This cryptic instruction from one of William Burroughs's novels exactly poses the problem for the American hero and his author. And the intention of this chapter is to suggest that William Burroughs, too often seen as a peripheral figure mongering his own obscene nightmares and eccentric experiments, in a profound way is an important writer, concerning himself precisely with many of those themes and problems which are central to recent American fiction. As he himself recognized in an interview,[1] he has been creating a mythology appropriate to the new age and environment which has been brought about by modern inventions.*

---

* It is a private mythology and in its way it could be compared to that powerful yet not always comprehensible private mythology of Blake's, 'The Four Zoas'. Burroughs himself is something of a mystic, while Blake's mythology concerns itself with bad authority, destructive control and 'the blind world-rulers of this life', which are topics explored at length by Burroughs in his necessarily very different, but still very original, way.

In *Naked Lunch* and *The Soft Machine* I have diagnosed an illness, and in *The Ticket That Exploded* and *Nova Express* is suggested a remedy. In this work I am attempting to create a new mythology for the space age. I feel that the old mythologies are definitely broken down and not adequate at the present time. In this mythology, I have Nova conspiracies, Nova police, Nova criminals. I do definitely have heroes and villains with respect to overall intentions with regard to this planet. Love plays little part in my mythology, which is a mythology of a war and conflict. . . . Heaven and Hell exist in my mythology. Hell consists of falling into enemy hands, into the hands of the virus power, and heaven consists of freeing oneself from this power, of achieving inner freedom, freedom from conditioning. I may add that none of the characters in my mythology are free. If they were free they would not still be in the mythological system, that is, in the cycle of conditioned action.

Starting from his own experiences with drug addiction – in which one is 'fixed' by an alien power which enters and takes over one's autonomous consciousness – Burroughs has developed a whole mythology dramatizing all those malign pressures which seem bent on absorbing or exploiting the unique identity of the distinctively human individual. And instead of drawing on classical references, he has availed himself, as he said in another interview,[2] of modern American materials and forms: films, cartoon-strips, science-fiction, fragmented and permeated by a 'carny world ... a kind of mid-western, small-town, cracker-barrel, pratfall type of folklore, very much my own background'. Out of such home-products he has produced a unique version of that cycle of conditioned action which is the American hero's hell, and although his later books do suggest ways in which those enemy hands might be evaded or resisted, we may note from the beginning his insight that any freedom which may be achieved will be 'inner'.

Burroughs is an addict turned diagnostician, a victim of sickness now devoted to the analysis of diseases. That is why so many of his scenes revolve around doctors, surgeons, hospitals, sanitoriums, etc.; an image near the heart of his work is an operating-table from which the patient may perhaps one day escape. There is no question that he is concerned to issue warnings and explore the possibilities of healing, and so far from being a sensationalist writer, despite the nauseating nature of many of his scenes, he is one of the coolest, most cerebral and analytic of American writers. Eventually his scenes are not visual, and one finds oneself in a realm of abstraction close to that thin air

to which he directs his readers, far removed from the terminal sewer
where he is commonly supposed to have taken up permanent
residence. However, his experiences of the horrors of the drug world
were obviously real enough, and in the attempt to explore the nature
of his vision it helps to start with his uncharacteristically traditional
first novel, *Junkie*, published in 1953 under the pseudonym of
William Lee (a persona he retains in later work).

Burroughs now speaks disparagingly of this early work, yet its
autobiographical candour and its uncomplicated narrative simplicity
provide many clues for the seemingly surreal and scrambled works
which were to follow. For here we get some arresting glimpses of
the real events and people later to be metamorphosed by his imagination; here is the actual in which his vision is grounded. Later, he
made the business of drug addiction into a vast encompassing metaphor; in this book he looks at it, with a cool lucidity, simply as the
dominant fact of his life. His childhood was spent in a suburban
vacuum which only served to make city life seem more real and vital;
while the dull respectability of his milieu seems to have engendered
a predilection for the outlaw, the deviant. At the same time, in this
empty environment he sensed hidden antagonists, and had bad
dreams (a recurrent nightmare concerned animals in the wall). It
would seem that a disposition to horrific hallucination was there
from the start. Describing the actual sequence of events leading to
addiction, he stressed that it was mainly a matter of 'not having
strong motivations in any other direction'. In his aimless wandering
he drifted into it. In the Burroughs world evil is not something you
seek out or create — it is always there, waiting. And if you get involved
with it, it takes you over.

This idea of dope (or any other vice, or virus) as a malevolent
power which can move in on you recurs on an increasing scale in his
work until, in *Nova Express* (1964), it is a matter of a cosmic take-
over. From the semi-hoodlum underworld of drug-trafficking which
Junkie describes, Burroughs goes on to a war of the worlds. But if the
scale has changed, the image of take-over has been there from the
start. For instance, he describes a 'fag bar' as being full of puppets
and ventriloquists' dummies. 'The live human being has moved out
of these bodies long ago. But something moved in when the original
tenant moved out.' In a similar way he describes one drug addict as
having two selves: an alert, active, conscious mind, plus the other
self composed of all the cells in his body inhabited by the need for
junk. Need, as an all-else devouring state of body and mind,
Burroughs was also to explore in later works. For need creates
a shameless subservience which allows an alien substance to enter

one of the many vulnerable channels of which the individual is composed. It can then drain the life out of that individual. 'Program empty body,' is the order issued by the alien invaders of his later work; 'junk takes everything and gives nothing,' he observes in *Junkie*. And the people who live off other people's needs and addictions, even in the comparatively naturalistic world of this early novel, are described as being peculiarly monstrous—animals in the walls of his prose. The world into which Burroughs wandered in his flight from suburban unreality provided him not only with the sensations and sufferings connected with addiction and withdrawal; it introduced him to a whole gallery of living grotesques, and examples of the unspeakable degradations that can afflict the human form. He compares such figures to predatory animals, or even to proto-plasmic creatures of the sea floor. Either they are negative, invisible, or they seem to have returned to some lower form of life. The respectable upholders of ordinary society are inhuman in another way, having the unreality of façades, or acting in mindless hostility to the individual who does not conform—faceless bureaucrats, stupid and bullying policemen, a lethal bore, lifeless hospital patients, and a moribund psychiatrist who was 'ready to take down my psyche and reassemble it in eight days'. Ordinary human reality seems to have disappeared from both levels of society.

Particularly important are the hallucinations incident to his life as an addict. 'One afternoon, I closed my eyes and saw New York in ruins. Huge centipedes and scorpions crawled in and out of empty bars and cafeterias and drugstores on Forty-Second Street.' And, as well as the breakdown of the city, the breakdown of the human shape appears to him. For instance, he has a vision of a face being eaten away by disease. The disease spreads 'melting the face into an amoeboid mass in which the eyes floated, dull crustacean eyes. Slowly, a new face formed around the eyes. A series of faces, hieroglyphs, distorted and leading to the final place where the human road ends, where the human form can no longer contain the crusta-cean horror that has grown inside it.' Junk can induce an utter indifference to reality, an inertia, a flatness; at the same time it gave Burroughs horrific images of apocalypse, disintegration, and unspeakable human metamorphoses which provide part of a basic vocabulary for his later work.

Burroughs's earlier work drifts with little sense of continuity and this is a reflection of his own compulsive, seemingly purposeless travelling. Yet it was not quite purposeless. There was always the element of flight and evasion, the feeling of having to get out of the way of some gathering threat (the first words of *Naked Lunch* — 'I can feel the heat closing in' — not only tell us a great deal about the rest of the book; they could have come from the mouth of nearly any of the other American protagonists we have considered). And there was also the sort of inverted Holy Grail search for 'the final fix'. The last words of *Junkie* show Lee heading into South America in search of yage, in the hope that yage may be the final fix. If we look at the Yage Letters written to Allen Ginsberg in 1953, we can see once again how the necessity of moving through strange, alien territories in search of this new fix affected Burroughs's imagination. For one thing, it is inevitable that someone travelling with rather dubious motives through remote places in South America will run into a lot of trouble with all sorts of hostile bureaucracy. From these letters, it would seem that Burroughs often found himself suddenly confronted by the unpredictable powers of what he calls 'cancerous control' (another metaphor he was to develop later). This fugitive, paranoid sense of being at the mercy of malevolent powers becomes part of the larger vision of the later books. And in turn it induces what he calls a 'nightmare fear of stasis', revealed most clearly in the conclusion to his last letter in the series, from Lima.

> Everybody has gone and I am alone in a nowhere place. Every night the people will be uglier and stupider, the fixtures more hideous, the waiters ruder, the music more grating on and on like a speedup movie into a nightmare vortex of mechanical disintegration and meaningless change ... Where am I going in such a hurry? ... I don't know. Suddenly I have to leave right now.

The dread of inertia and arrest, the compulsion always to move on to new places, goes deeper than the surface drama of police-dodging and drug-hunting. It is significant that when he wrote that last letter he had in fact found his yage, which proved no more of a final fix than the others. Burroughs's 'stasis horror' is really a vivid name for that common American preference for a life which is not arrested and crystallized in a pattern. The special details of Burroughs's situation should not disguise how deeply American his particular set of responses is. What makes him unusual is where his particular movement-hunger took him. For whereas we often find the American hero vanishing or left suspended at the end of his novel, Burroughs came to a very definite halt — 'at the end of the junk line'. He describes how he lived in one room in Tangier, without washing or moving — except to inject himself as he approached terminal addiction. The 'stasis horror', ironically, brought him to the horror of total stasis; the 'nightmare fear' of being 'stuck in one place' has been realized;

and all that urgent evasive-questing movement has led to the dreaded state of absolute immobility. Unawares, he had been pursuing the inertia he sought to flee. And it was there, I think, that Burroughs made an important discovery. In a later interview he said, 'I suddenly realized I was not doing *anything*. I was dying. I was just apt to be finished.'[3] And it was at this point at the end of the line that everything that had been gathering in his memory and imagination throughout his fifteen years of addiction was discharged in *Naked Lunch*. Burroughs's realization that his long roving search for junk was ultimately a death quest or 'death route' — 'If all pleasure is relief from tension, junk affords relief from the whole life process' — lends an extra dimension to his use of addiction as a general metaphor for the various diseases afflicting contemporary civilization. The incredible panorama of his book reflects a world to a large extent addicted to death. Death is the final fix.

Naked Lunch (1959) is a book with no narrative continuity, and no sustained point of view; the separate episodes are not interrelated, they co-exist in a particular field of force brought together by the mind of Burroughs which then abandons them. Slapstick scenes from some dark carnival and what could be frames from a strip-cartoon alternate with passages of cool scientific analysis; horrific images of material vileness are distanced by their proximity to discursive and abstract explanations. Burroughs describes his book as a blueprint which ranges from insects to planetary landscapes, from abstractions to turds, and this suggests the sort of expansions and contractions of episode which in this book replace linear narrative. And the episodes themselves are experienced as a distribution of fragments rather than as internally organized structures: the most common form of punctuation is simply a row of dots separating image from image, voice from voice, and the book gives us a world beneath or beyond syntax and all that that implies. Burroughs says that his book shows 'How-To-extend levels of experience by opening the door at the end of a long hall ... Doors that only open in Silence' and that door, among other things, is the barrier of conventional language.

The title, says Burroughs, means just what the words say — 'a frozen moment when everyone sees what is on the end of every fork'. To produce such frozen moments is the intention, and indeed the achievement, of the book. In one small episode Burroughs describes a lunch served to him consisting of a shelled egg with a nasty object inside it, and an orange which contains only a huge worm. And the book itself offers just such fare — the egg with the shell off, the skinned orange. The cruelties and corruptions of civilization are laid

bare, served up without the covering of a conventional plot. Since
the ordering of the different units is not part of his intention he
insists that one can cut into *Naked Lunch* at any intersection point.
Not for Joyce's reason, that his book, like *Ulysses* or *Finnegan's Wake*,
is organized according to the great cyclical rhythms of existence. But
because by going through the act of breaking through the shell of
plot, the reader will begin to see the lunch in its nakedness. At the
beginning, inviting people to enter Bill's Naked Lunch Room, he
asks, 'Which side are you on? Fro-Zen Hydraulic? Or do you want
to take a look around with Honest Bill?' The reference to Fro-Zen
Hydraulic is part of an image sequence which compares the spine of
the junkie to a frozen hydraulic jack when his metabolism has
nearly reached Absolute ZERO. Life among the addicts is referred
to as life in The Old Ice House, and the idea of life being frozen into
eternal inertness is the entropic nightmare at the heart of the book.
As Burroughs sees it, most people, particularly the established
powers, work on the side of this process, accelerating and spreading
it. The alternative he offers is 'a look around with Honest Bill' — to
see what is really being offered under the comforting rubrics of the
standard menus.

The feeding metaphor is an appropriate one since Burroughs is
really writing about all the different ways human identity is devoured
in the modern world, how the self is dissolved or pre-empted by
nameless forces radically antipathetic to the human image. Just what
the origin of this malign enemy is Burroughs cannot immediately
say. But he can produce a whole range of images to make us perceive
its agencies and its modes of operation. In the first section, which is
about the sub-world of drug addicts, what stands out most vividly
is the encroaching presence of informers and pushers who are seen
as literal devourers of their victims. Willy the Informer, for instance,
'that blind, seeking mouth', who would suck the juice out of every
junkie he found; and Bradley the Buyer who has a 'contact habit', a
yen to assimilate other people into his foulness which 'comes on him
like a great black wind', and in whose presence people disappear;
the Shoe Store Kid who feels for his victim with fingers of 'rotten
ectoplasm'; a pimp who degrades women into non-existence; and all
the shuffling living-dead involved in junk ('Where do they go when
they walk out and leave the body behind?') — these are just some
of the eaters and eaten drifting in and out of the early pages. From
such monsters William Lee flees across those rancid, dying wastelands which appear so often in Burroughs's work, and which are
sometimes America and sometimes anywhere in the world. This
opening section is the world of *Junkie* turned into a nightmare

comic-strip (' "Only thing I read is Little Abner," ' says Lee). It offers a kaleidoscope of glimpses of the disintegrating human image.

The next section introduces Dr Benway, a figure who appeared in the first piece Burroughs ever wrote (in 1938). He is one of those charlatan doctors who appear quite often in recent American fiction, a comically grotesque version of something very sinister. Benway is a master of all methods of assault on the subject's personal identity, and his doings in Annexia and the Freeland Republic offer satiric comment on contemporary society. He is 'a manipulator and co-ordinator of symbol systems', an expert on all forms of control. As such he represents all that the American hero most dreads. The fact that he conducts some of those parody operations which obsess Burroughs indicates his larger interest in all ways of altering and programming the individual with all available instruments. He runs a 'Reconditioning Center' and works on 'Automatic Obedience Processing'. Quoting the case of a female agent who forgot her real identity and merged with her cover story he suggests that there is a useful example here: since an agent is trained to 'deny his agent identity by asserting his cover story' you could use 'psychic jiu-jitsu' and 'suggest that his cover story is his identity and that he has no other. His agent identity becomes unconscious, that is, out of his control ... ' (In just such a way Cabot Wright had been turned into his cover story; and Kurt Vonnegut explores this possibility in *Mother Night*.) Burroughs's use of agents does not apply to any one special war but is a projection of the general feeling that the individual is everywhere getting involved in conspiracies of one kind or another, often without his knowledge. ('We are all agents,' is one of Burroughs's sayings.) Benway is a comic version of a master conspirator, working on the side of the forces of manipulation and control. The chaos which erupts in scenes of sexual madness and violence, when his subjects are accidentally released, conveys Burroughs's sense of the direction to which all addiction and external control is finally leading.

Shortly after the Benway episode there emerges a vision of the City. It is described in such a way as to make it seem like the intestinal interior of a sick human body, given over to addictions and 'unspeakable mutilations of the spirit'. It is populated by more nightmare beasts, whose human originals may be found in *Junkie*. An unexplained force known as the Dream Police occasionally make valiant attempts to storm the City, but they rapidly 'disintegrate in globs of rotten ectoplasm'. It is, however, the first hint of the existence of a force attempting to take issue with the inhuman predators of the slime. For most of the rest of the book the scenes come from Interzone, an explicit enough location, and here again the dominating theme is the dissolution of the human form to jelly or dust. There is another grotesque doctor, Dr Shafer, the Lobotomy Kid, who produces ' "*The Complete All American De-anxietized Man*" ' who turns out to be made of a viscid, transparent jelly which drifts away revealing a giant black centipede. The City of Interzone is the place where all human potentials are spread out in a market, and here all possible agencies of human degradation and all evil diseases congregate and lie in wait – 'Larval entities waiting for a Live One'.

These worms waiting for a human host point to that parasitology which is a crucial part of Burroughs's vision. It is worth noting that it places the source of evil outside man. In his Introduction Burroughs says that 'Junk yields a basic formula of "evil" virus: *The Algebra of Need*. The face of "evil" is always the face of total need.' The inverted commas reveal a certain uneasiness in handling the concept of "evil", and while the book is full of images of the effects and workings of this "evil" there is little said about the source of it. One passage states with abrupt clarity: 'America is not a young land: it is old and dirty and evil before the settlers, before the Indians. The evil is there waiting.' The effects of this notion of an unseen waiting evil on Burroughs's vision are very clear. 'And the U.S. drag closes around us like no other drag in the world ... there is no drag like the U.S. drag. You can't see it, you don't know where it comes from.' In Burroughs's world you cannot 'locate' the evil that seems to be closing in or waiting; instead you register his sense of it, and dread of it, in the series of images, drawn from so many different sources, which make up the book. It is yet another version of that American paranoia which senses a host of waiting evils in the landscape around the self.

In Interzone we overhear many voices – indeed much of the book is made up of voices, soliloquizing rather than conversing, of which we hear occasional scraps. Burroughs is particularly sensitive to the streams of words which people send out into the world in an effort to control it or resist it, and one of the unmistakable achievements of the book is his catching of a wide variety of accents and rhetorics: the professor, the prophet, the party leader, some 'ordinary' men and women complaining of a variety of attempted take-overs – the housewife who thinks she is being sexually accosted by her kitchen gadgets, the hustler who complains that his customers want to take over his life, and so on. In general the world of Interzone is best summed up by the story of the man who was taken over by his anus, which is a parable of matter in a state of hideous revolt. The man is gradually covered by a jelly of Undifferentiated Tissue which seals off everything but, for a time, the eyes. But 'finally the brain must have died, because the eyes *went out.*' Images of dead eyes, cancelled eyes, blank eyes, recur throughout the book. The eye reveals the state of consciousness behind it; that responsive alertness which should be the source of human identity – or that deadness which reveals the successful take-over. And the take-over is always of a higher form by a lower – mere jelly reclaiming the human eye. This is the world in which doctors talk about replacing the complexity of the human body with 'one all-purpose blob'.

This idea of matter returning to lower forms of organization is at the heart of Burroughs's vision – his version of that entropy which is such a common dread among American writers (see next chapter). Dead landscapes and stagnant waters recur throughout, and interpolations like, 'The Planet drifts to random insect doom ... Thermodynamics has won at a crawl,' carry a more specific reference to the second law of thermodynamics. All the various addictions in the book break life down to a lower level, hence the constant references to ectoplasm and liquefaction. The brain taken over by the anus is only a paradigm for all the low forms of life which devour higher forms. So, humans become animals, then vegetables, and finally minerals: warm blood reverts to frozen metal – it is as though there was a continuous reclamation process being conducted by that evil in the land.

In between the various wild episodes which exemplify life in Interzone, Burroughs includes a straight description of 'the parties of Interzone' which constitutes a piece of diagnosis of general relevance, but is especially helpful in making clear the vision of his own work. On one side there are Liquefactionists, Senders, and Divisionists; all in their various ways hostile and threatening to spontaneous individual life. The Liquefactionists and their dissolving and absorbing activities are self-explanatory. Senders believe in dominating people's minds by various methods of control. They have no interest in communicating any significant information, and of course they cannot 'receive' because that would involve a worrying acknowledgment of other independent consciousnesses in the world. They are the masters of the modern media taken to the logical conclusion of their profession, offering a threat of meaningless control for its own sake. To Burroughs, control can never be a means to any practical end: '*It can never be a means to anything but more control...Like junk.*' The Divisionists, on the other hand, are a force making for that homogeneity which Ralph Ellison equates with the death of America, with their practice of making replicas of themselves in embryo jelly. The nightmare conclusion to their activities is suggested as being 'one person in the world with millions of separate bodies'. Again, this party is a threat to all independent, differentiated forms of life.

In opposition to these forces there is only one party — the Factualists, who are against all the rest, especially the Senders. 'Sending *is* evil,' irrespective of what is sent, since its aim is the obliteration of consciousness, not the sharing of it, which is the intention of authentic two-way communication. 'The Sender is not a human individual ....It is The Human Virus....The broken image of Man moves in minute by minute and cell by cell....Poverty, hatred, war, police-criminals, bureaucracy, insanity, all symptoms of The Human Virus. *The Human Virus can now be isolated and treated.*' The opposition is clear enough, and Burroughs's allegiance to the Factualists is that of a man who has experienced the other parties at close hand and now feels that the only way to combat them is to cultivate a dispassionate ability to recognize and apprehend the facts of things as they are. Just how the virus can be treated he explores in another book, but among other things *Naked Lunch* clearly represents a Factualist's attempt to isolate it.

Early in the book Burroughs describes how junk is surrounded by magic and taboos, and he refers elsewhere to the feeling of the yage-taking Indians that their own self-destructive tendencies are due to 'the manipulation of alien and hostile wills'. One can well imagine that to live in the world of junk is to feel oneself surrounded by powers to whom one is in a state of thraldom and powerless subservience (e.g. the pushers), or of whose punitive powers one is afraid (e.g. the police). And as we have said, to take a drug is to cede your consciousness to something which comes in from the outside and mysteriously takes you over. It seems that the experienced addict may well come to be very superstitious, and share that primitive feeling that he is being manipulated by 'alien and hostile wills'. This may be called demonology, and however much he shares it Burroughs certainly makes use of this demonology in writing his books. For although he uses the phrase 'self-destructive trends', in his visionary world the virus comes from without, not within. People do not destroy themselves; they are taken over. There is no psychology; the evil is external — waiting in the land. In a recent interview he went out of his way to assert that he believes there is an unseen power at work behind every seen event — nothing happens of itself. '*Certainly forces operating through human consciousness control events.*' (My italics.)

We should finally consider whether *Naked Lunch* discloses any possibility of escaping from these malign destructive forces. It starts with Lee almost trapped in a subway with the heat closing in. At the end a voice says, '"They are rebuilding the City,"' and Lee answers, ' "Yes....Always...." ' The City is the structure of society, and although it constantly produces 'junk' (which may serve to stand for every kind of rubbish and dead waste), it is also constantly self-perpetuating. Burroughs here seems to have an eye on the circular paradox that man builds the City but the City determines man's consciousness. And how can you destroy a 'rubbish heap'? All that would emerge would be a random redistribution of dead refuse which is what the City seems to offer already. There seems hardly any scope for freedom in all this. Yet in connection with Lee there is a strange episode in which he does make an important gesture of escape. The two policemen O'Brien and Hauser come to arrest him and Lee shoots them and makes his getaway. Expecting increased pursuit he feels the pressure on him is diminishing, and when he finally telephones the police station he is told that there is neither an O'Brien nor a Hauser there. Then Lee realizes: 'I had been occluded from space-time....The Heat was off me from here on out.' He is on 'the far side of the world's mirror' (as far as one can gather from the ambiguous floating syntax), and this ends the central part of the book – the remainder is a preface.

Getting beyond the reach of the conditioning forces has various implications. On one level it is Burroughs's metaphor for being cured of drug addiction. But the notion of breaking through the world's mirror and being 'occluded' from space-time goes further (it is perhaps relevant to add that defenestration, or jumping through a window, is a motif which interests Burroughs). It is pertinent to recall that the only historical figure mentioned in the book is Einstein – who was saved by the Factualists from the Senders. Einstein is the man who 'released' man from fixed patterns and concepts of space-time inside which he had been 'imprisoned'. The world's mirror we could see as everything which gives us back a fixed and fixing image and definition of the self, locked inside his environment. To break through that mirror would be in one sense to liberate the self from the rigid structures by which consciousness is determined, as Einstein did in the realm of physics. Telling of a friend who jumped to freedom through a window from a room full of murderous Arabs, Burroughs adds, 'Cure is always; *Let go! Jump!*' – a cure which has been followed by innumerable American heroes in their efforts to escape from a constricting and threatening environment. The freedom thus gained will be more a mental than a physical freedom; 'The way OUT is the way IN,' Burroughs says, and as we saw he was careful to specify that 'inner' freedom was all that could be aimed for. This aspiration and cure seems to me quite comparable to the Invisible Man's strategy of dropping out of the reach of all parties, or Yossarian's jump – a jump which, if successful, will land him not in Sweden but on 'the far side of the world's mirror', beyond false patternings to a vantage point from which he can see the naked reality, beyond imprisonment in 'the City' to a freedom at least of inner space.

The City is also a City of language, as Burroughs makes clear in an entry in his next book, *The Exterminator*. 'They are rebuilding The City Lee Knows in Four Letter Words..Vibrating Air Hammers The Code Write.' If Burroughs started his writing out of a sense of the danger of man's vulnerability to literal drug-addiction, the emphasis soon shifted to a stress on the danger of man's vulnerability to word-addiction. Agents, alien microphones, the pervasive presence of codes, not connected with a specific plot-line but sensed as being an ever-present part of the surrounding atmosphere: such phenomena recur increasingly in Burroughs's work, with the added confusion that it is seldom possible to identify the Senders and what they are sending. There is more of a general feeling of the possibility of consciousness being clogged with conspiracies which enter while the victim is unaware – codes and messages slipping in like the candiru fish, a creature often cited by Burroughs as being particularly expert at finding and entering unprotected human orifices. As a response to this situation there are three possibilities: a writer may try to jam or foil the codes; he may try to crack them; and he may try to put himself in a position where no codes can reach him – beyond language and into the silence on the far side of the world's mirror. I think we can see Burroughs trying something of all three in his ensuing work which shows a resistance to all forms of entrapment within word-systems. It may be said to share the aim that Wittgenstein outlined for philosophy (Wittgenstein is mentioned by Burroughs in the Introduction) – 'To show the fly the way out of the fly-bottle'.

We must at this point take note of a potential paradox of which Burroughs is himself well aware. He knows that a writer is, like Dr Benway, a manipulator and co-ordinator of symbol-systems, and he has no desire to emulate the very thing he condemns in the book, i.e. sending out a manufactured version of reality which takes over the reader's or hearer's mind. But the fact remains that from one point of view a book is bound to be some sort of 'sending', for we have the block of words and they add up to a legible vision. Burroughs himself once worked in an advertising agency and he is aware of the necessity to differentiate the activity of the writer from that of the copy-writer. This he does by discriminating between different intentions. He is manipulating words and images, not to make people accept and purchase existing products and artefacts, but to 'create an alteration in the reader's consciousness'. If Burroughs himself had really reached the far side of the world's mirror he would be unable to write at all; as he himself notes in the book, he would be 'locked out', exclusion from the present world being the ambiguous other aspect of freedom from it. 'Never again would I have a Key, a Point of Intersection,' he adds after his occlusion from space-time, which means that while he cannot be reached, he cannot reach back. Since the book is there and it is manifestly a reaching back, we realize that we are dealing with a metaphor for some sort of achieved distance and immunity from the threats the book has isolated. Language *is* the Point of Intersection and Burroughs is still involved with it.

The paradox of using language to release people from language is one which we will be examining shortly. Here two points should be made about the style and narration of *Naked Lunch*. The fragmentation of episode and the invitation to enter and leave the book as you like does offer a kind of liberation from the serial continuity of the unbroken unilinear plot. (John Cage does something similar with the traditional melodic line in music in his particular aspiration towards 'silence'.) All tendencies towards a fixed form in the book are countered by a tendency towards atomization. In a sense the book destroys itself as it goes along; there are too many breaks, jumps, unexplained shifts to different places, people, orderings of reality, etc., for us ever to feel so controlled by his vision that we forget we are reading a book. There is no consistent narrator, indeed no narrative principle. We are aware of a stream of evidence but we are not aware of any definitive arranging of it, nor do we know where it is coming from—it is too often unrelated to a participating witness. It is almost as though Burroughs was trying to produce pictures without frames, and he describes his book as spilling off the page in all directions. That this might result in an appearance of a mass of random fragments is a risk he takes. Clearly, for Burroughs to *appear* to abandon responsibility for the framing of his novel, to *appear* not to be controlling his material, is to cut himself off from many of the traditional ways in which the novel authenticates its existence and the impressions of reality it offers. However, I think Burroughs could justify his technique in this book by saying that each reader is invited to put all the bits together in his own way, i.e. to enjoy experiencing the spontaneity and independence of constructing one's own system. And to show language itself constantly falling to bits or fading off into dots might be a way of pointing us on to that precious silence on the other side of the world's mirror where we might be 'free'.

The second stylistic aspect of the book is related to this. It has been remarked what a wide variety of voices, speeches, types of rhetoric, etc., Burroughs introduces, and also that an element of carnival and circus pervades the book (Mary McCarthy was perhaps the first to stress this). I think this crowding and sporting is an important strategy. If one voice prevailed then one version of reality would prevail. By playing with so many different language habits, Burroughs constantly frees himself from the potential trap of any one of them. It is as though he has constantly to destroy the prevailing languages, and as constantly to reconstitute the fragments to make his own book. This sport, this play, goes along with the importance of laughter for Burroughs. It is a great weapon against being programmed and controlled from without; what we can laugh *at* we are at least partially free *from* (this was Cabot Wright's discovery). Every kind of abuse of language may be found in the book, and in an entropic world with everything returning to protoplasmic shapelessness, it is fitting that the very last words are pidgin English: ' "No glot....C'lom Fliday." ' Language itself, as exemplified by the voice of the junk pusher, like the characters, is disintegrating, losing its edge and becoming a blur, a blob. But Burroughs himself is not trapped in this language, he is juggling with it.

All this is related to the problem I mentioned at the outset: that of finding enough form not to be mere jelly; but not so much form that one is fixed once and for all within its defining shape. I suggested that the American hero and writer sometimes find their solution in a mode of motion, between fluidity and fixity, aiming at flexibility. So it is entirely fitting that one of the bulletins of the Factualists reads: ' "We must not project or deny our protoplasmic core, striving at all times to maintain a maximum of flexibility without falling into the morass of liquefaction." ' This seems to me to be exactly what a large number of recent American heroes aim at. And, in this aim, there is no one safe place, no Sweden, no terminal freedom which can be achieved once and for all. Instead there must be a series of constant acts of liberation. The realization seems to be that you cannot *be* free; instead you must continually be freeing yourself.

Around the time of completing *Naked Lunch* for publication, Burroughs was introduced to the idea of collages and cut-ups by his friend Brion Gysin, and together they prepared a small book called *The Exterminator* (1960). Some of the bits that Burroughs put together in this book afford clear hints of his subsequent stylistic experiments. He makes direct statements, and then he cuts them and rearranges them; this has two effects—one is to turn language into nonsense, the other is to make stable units of language yield new meanings, not as propositions exactly, but as suggestive word groups. The main point is to cut the Word Lines which predetermine your response to reality. 'The Word Lines keep Thee in Slots ... Cut the Word Lines with scissors or switch blade as preferred The Word Lines keep you in Time..Cut the in lines..Make out lines to Space.' Anything can be cut up—newspapers or great literature. This stress on cutting up existing word-patterns has an added meaning from the biological metaphor of the genetic language of life. For Burroughs, the body, like the City, is built of four-letter words; the codes at work around us are related to the genetic code which determines our life.

Having quoted various pieces of prose to advance these ideas, Burroughs then cuts them up as if to crack the coded message they contain. Eventually it seems that the attack is aimed at all word-patterns. It is as though a last-ditch stand against determinism and conditioning has taken the form of an all-out attack on the word. 'Word lines keep you in Time Sections....CUT OUT AND SPRAY BACK....'

Burroughs's thinking around this time is perhaps best summed up in a letter he wrote to Allen Ginsberg in 1960. He tells Ginsberg not to worry about returning to 'normal consciousness' and then he tells him to cut up an enclosed letter into four and then rearrange the parts. The enclosed letter, before rearrangement, seems to outline the concerns in evidence in the dark sport of *The Exterminator*. For example:

LISTEN TO MY LAST WORDS ANY WORLD.... WHAT SCARED YOU INTO TIME? INTO BODY? INTO SHIT? I WILL TELL YOU. THE WORD. THE-THEE WORD. IN THEE BEGINNING WAS THE WORD. SCARED YOU ALL INTO SHIT FOREVER. COME OUT FOREVER.... ALL OUT OF TIME AND INTO SPACE. FOREVER. THERE IS NO THING TO FEAR. THERE IS NO THING IN SPACE.... THERE IS NO WORD TO FEAR. THERE IS NO WORD. THAT IS ALL ALL ALL HASSAN SABBAH. IF YOU I CANCEL ALL YOUR WORDS FOREVER. AND THE WORDS OF HASSAN SABBAH I AS ALSO CANCEL. ACROSS ALL YOUR SKIES SEE THE SILENT WRITING OF BRION GYSIN HASSAN SABBAH. THE WRITING OF SPACE. THE WRITING OF SILENCE.

Allowing for certain characteristics of Burroughs's particular vocabulary, this is a very American letter; the hatred of being trapped in time and matter ('shit' being an emotive reference to the foulness of the modern wastelands and sewers which for Burroughs make up man's material limitations), and the desire to escape into clean, silent space is discernible in American literature at least as early as Thoreau, who yearned to 'sport in fields of air alone'. The emphasis which must concern us is the insistence that the ultimate force which keeps us cowering in these temporal and physical dimensions is THE WORD. It is because we inhabit bodies living in time that the virus word can penetrate and work on us. The invitation is — come out of matter into space, out of language into silence. To this end it becomes part of Burroughs's intent to use arrangements of words that cancel arrangements of words, deploying language to destroy language. Where a writer like Pope, seeing civilization in a state of entropic decline, chooses the tactic of using language with ever more precision and embattled incisiveness, Burroughs with a similar apprehension writes to make us immune from language altogether, a paradox which he clearly grasps in the formulation 'the writing of silence'. To understand this stylistic strategy we must try to understand why Burroughs sees 'the word' as the great threat, and why he who projected a nightmare vision of 'random events in a dying universe' (*Junkie*) should turn to the use of random arrangements of words as a weapon against death, inertia and decay.

Clearly Burroughs thinks that one of the main ways the alien forces take over people is by addicting them to 'images' — i.e. by sending false but enslaving configurations of images which prevent the receiver from establishing contact with any genuine reality either inside or outside him. In this connection Burroughs has increasingly interested himself in films with the ultimate implication that for a lot of people 'reality is actually a movie'.* ('Will Hollywood never leave?' *The Exterminator*.) But 'the word' remains as the most powerful way in which consciousness is pre-empted by the encircling media. The question we should examine is, why does Burroughs think that the cut-up method of writing is a major way to combat the dangerous human subservience to 'the word'? We could put it this way. Burroughs found that apomorphine ended his drug addiction and consequently made it into a general metaphor for the cure from all external control; can cut-ups similarly 'cure' us of our addiction to the images and words which are beamed at us continually?

For an answer we can turn to an essay he wrote on 'The Cut Up Method',[4] and two points emerge clearly. First: 'You can not will

* For a different exploration of a similar idea, *see* Walker Percy's *The Movie-Goer* (1961).

spontaneity. But you can introduce the unpredictable spontaneous factor with a pair of scissors.' Since the evil in Burroughs's world is always aimed against individual spontaneity, we can see the cut-up method as a paradigmatic act of spontaneity in an increasingly manipulated world. He values it as action—'*something to do*'. Secondly he says that the method can be applied to fields other than writing. He alludes to the principle of random action in game and military strategy: 'assume that the worst has happened and act accordingly. If your strategy is at some point determined ... by random factors your opponent will gain no advantage from knowing your strategy since he can not predict the move.' Since Burroughs brings in the military analogy we can perhaps suggest how he sees the cut-up method as working. If an army is planning to take you over, by adopting the principle of random action you make yourself less vulnerable and more elusive. Armies move in organized routines; saboteurs can strike at random. If we regard normal linguistic habits as bridges and roads into the human consciousness (Marshall McLuhan sees a direct connection between the spread of roads and words), we can see what Burroughs is trying to do. He is sabotaging the main lines of communication which the occupying army will otherwise use.

A comment by Norman Mailer can be brought in here.

So long as it grows, a civilization depends upon the elaboration of meaning, its health is maintained by an awareness of its state; as it dies, a civilization opens itself to the fury of those betrayed by its meaning, precisely because that meaning was finally not sufficiently true to offer a life adequately large. The aesthetic act shifts from the creation of meaning to the destruction of it.

Up to a point Burroughs would seem to be dedicated to a 'destruction of meaning' for something like the complex of motives outlined by Mailer. In the realm of language Burroughs is acting rather like an underground resistance group in a country occupied by foreign powers. Appropriately he refers to all those people who are combating the virus invasion as 'partisans'. If the invaders have taken over the language of the world, retaliate by blowing it up: the 'ticket' issued to us is to be 'exploded'. Of course, the partisans will also lack roads and bridges; but at least the enemy cannot use them and meanwhile the partisans can, it is to be hoped, survive in an impenetrable territory of their own. Better no pattern than an alien pattern.

What makes for a certain amount of perplexity in this case is that Burroughs recommends that you cut up anything and every-

thing—great writing and junk writing. He has cut up (or folded in—
another version of the same tactic only bringing an indefinite number
of different bits of writing into one new assemblage) Shakespeare,
Conrad, Rimbaud, Eliot, Joyce, Paul Bowles and many others, and
folded selected bits into his own writing. The feeling seems to be that
whereas cutting up a newspaper will render you immune from its
mind-numbing and artificial clichés, cutting up a great writer will
release new potency from his work since his greatness permeates
every part and it can be fed into your own work. It is true that
T. S. Eliot and Pound also used to juxtapose fragments from past
literatures with their own words, but the effect was calculated and
planned: it was a way of bringing past imaginations into dynamic
proximity with present realities. But in Burroughs these fragments
are not really clearly juxtaposed, they are scrambled. As he honestly
admits, his predecessors are really Tristan Tzara and the Surrealists,
whose play with arbitrary sequences of words was more clearly
anarchic.

Yet Burroughs maintains there is a purpose in his methods. As
well as Tzara he refers to 'The Camera Eye' sequences in Dos
Passos's *U.S.A.* as being an influence, and, as he clearly states, the
result of his cut-ups and fold-ins is only apparently random. 'What
is any writing but a cut-up?' And again, 'What does any writer do but
choose, edit and rearrange materials at his disposal?' The reason his
later work offers continual rebuttal to the conscious mind seeking
for familiar orderings and sequences is that he is consciously trying
to simulate the way the unconscious works. To do this he amasses
vast amounts of newspaper, notebooks, photographs, tapes, etc.,
which he takes with him wherever he travels, constantly working on
new conjunctions or collisions between the unceasing accumulation
of images (the weight involved makes it necessary for him to travel
by ship). There is of course a paradox here. Burroughs regards the
magazine group *Time*, *Life* and *Fortune* as 'a control system. ... some
sort of police organisation' drawing on a vast 'word and image
bank' to dupe the readers. Yet Burroughs himself is accumulating
just such a word and image bank. An interviewer put the paradox
to Burroughs. 'You deplore the accumulation of images and at the
same time you seem to be looking for new ones.'[5] The reply was:
'Yes, it's part of the paradox of anyone who is working with word
and image,' but Burroughs goes on to maintain that his way of
arranging (or disarranging) images effects a liberation rather than a
control of consciousness. 'Cut-ups establish new connections
between images, and one's range of vision consequently expands.'
(To those who find minor inconsistencies irritating I might mention

that Burroughs sometimes hyphenates 'cut-ups' and sometimes does not.)

It would certainly be arguable that any writer of merit expands our vision, without necessarily having recourse to Burroughs's experiments. But clearly Burroughs is intending an attack on the usual way of constructing meanings in the Western world. He thinks the straight declarative sentence has been 'one of the great errors of Western thought'; he defines it as the either-or proposition. 'Either-or thinking is just not accurate thinking. That's not the way things occur, and I feel the Aristotelian construct is one of the great shackles of Western civilization. Cut-ups are a movement toward breaking this down.' We perhaps have to look at it this way. Cut-ups destroy old false constructs and models of reality. In addition they help to restore us to a more inclusive sort of response which has more in common with Buddhist epistemology, the Chinese ideograph, hieroglyph systems, and even photographs of street-scenes, than with the selecting and separating habits of the Western mind and eye. Burroughs wants to aim more for 'blocks of associations' than lines of thought (a notion not so dissimilar to the ideas of Fenellosa and Pound). His attack then is mainly on the old use of words. 'Words, at least the way we use them, can stand in the way of what I call non-body experience. It's time we thought about leaving the body behind.'

I think one can usefully compare some of John Cage's ideas about music.[8] Cage considers that the established norms of musical composition simply produce Frankenstein monsters. What he dislikes is the fact that 'the notation of the parts is in all respects determinate, and that, moreover, a score provides a fixed relation of these parts.' To combat this he prescribes the use of random numbers to produce 'indeterminacy' in the performance of music. This is yet another version of that suspicion of imposed forms and fixed versions. Instead of having an overall form he suggests that in the new music the unit will be 'the "frame" or fraction of a second, following established film technique' which is similar to Burroughs's concentration on moments, episodes, images, rather than overall structure. Cage describes how first he made structure indeterminate by bringing freedom of method into the order of structure, and then 'it became apparent that structure was not necessary.' The deliberate use of randomness and chance advocated by Cage to release the performer and allow the sounds of reality immediate access into music, is, as we have seen, precisely the strategy advocated by Burroughs. And Burroughs's apparent abandonment of an overall frame to concentrate on fragments which we can assemble as we wish, is exactly comparable to Cage's stress on 'parts but not scores'; 'the score, the requiring that many parts be played in a particular togetherness, is not an accurate representation of how things are.' Composers who realize this 'now compose parts but not scores, and the parts may be combined in any unthought ways.'

Cage advocates making 'attention ... inclusive rather than exclusive', one of the basic propositions in Burroughs's experiments, and his stress on the value of silences echoes Burroughs in many details. The paradox about the silence that both men value so much is that on the one hand it frees one from the old structures and scores which are felt to be like monsters or dictators; at the same time it makes one open to everything that is going on in the total environment. Bearing in mind George Eliot's reminder that if we heard everything going on around us we would rapidly go deaf or mad, one can still take the point that silence can lead to 'new listening' as well as new looking. However, that one may be enslaved by randomness as much as by form is not a possibility that either man explores. What Cage values about deliberate uncertainty in composition is precisely what Burroughs values in the cut-up: 'It introduces the unknown with such sharp clarity that anyone has the opportunity of having his habits blown away like dust.' Indeed 'word dust' is an image Burroughs uses himself.

In explanation of his whole approach to music, Cage offers the following very clear statement:

> the answer must take the form of paradox: a purposeful pur-
> poselessness or a purposeless play. This play, however, is an
> affirmation of life — not an attempt to bring order out of chaos
> nor to suggest improvements in creation, but simply a way of
> waking up to the very life we're living, which is so excellent
> once one gets one's mind and one's desires out of its way and
> lets it act of its own accord.

Cage's stress on 'play' reminds us of the carnival aspect of Burroughs's work, and that more general sport on lexical playfields we can find in many contemporary American writers. At the same time his statement leaves us with another paradox. Burroughs is avowedly pessimistic about the contemporary environment, to the extent that he wants to effect some sort of release from the body and the threatening matter that surrounds it. Yet he seems to have arrived at similar techniques to those advocated by a man so sure of the inherent excellence of 'the life we are living' that he will dissolve the structure of his work in order to facilitate the unimpeded penetration of environment into art. It is a paradox which is responsible for some of the distinctive counter-tensions in Burroughs's work.

Burroughs's ideas are serious and interesting, and on the basis of the long interview in *Paris Review* (Fall 1965) one can see that he is one of the most intelligent and articulate writers in America today. And his experiments do produce some distinctive effects. Many passages in his books can catch something of the atmosphere of dreams in which vivid fragments of hallucinatory vividness rise and fade in utter silence, leaving one with the curiously abstract experience of witnessing concretions which do not impinge. Echoes, portents, disturbing details, flicker out at us, not as parts of legible propositions but as parts of a drifting turbulence with intensities and intermittences beyond the grasp of syntax. In real dreams, however, one is completely at the mercy of the images which stream out of the unconscious and, since dreaming tends to perpetual dissolution, if one could achieve the state of living among realities as one lives among dream images one might well find oneself in the thrall of a formless terror. If one had, to take a wild hypothesis, a world in which writing was given over entirely to cut-ups, the 'cure' might prove to be worse than the disease. As a limited strategy for disturbing our complacent patternings of reality it can be effective and, given a bit of contrivance, it can produce wonderful incongruities which vividly reveal the endless ability of language to proliferate new formulations and orderings. This in turn can have the entirely salutary effect of reminding the reader how arbitrary any verbal model is. But to what extent it can secure genuinely new ways of 'reading' reality I am not sure.

In this connection I am reminded of an experiment conducted by the late A. P. Rossiter. It involved the presentation of purely nonsensical arrangements of words to children and a study of their reactions. What was notable was that they all tried to extract a meaning from the meaningless cluster. In a way bearing out gestalt theories, they sought for a pattern in the conglomeration of isolated units they were confronted with. And I find that this is very often my experience in reading Burroughs. One is constantly on the lookout for glimpses of significant images; one scans the field of words for hints of planned intent; one listens for signals in the sounds. Old habits die hard, Burroughs might reply, and occasionally one does experience a release from one's usual patterns of awareness. But it remains true that we must understand his warning if we are to heed it, as he himself implicitly reveals in his splendidly factual and clear-lined statements about his own intentions. How can we grasp the drama unless we perceive and interpret the significance of the opposing forces? How can we prefer the Factualists to the Senders unless we distinguish between them? And what is it to distinguish alternatives if not to be indebted to 'either-or' modes of thought?

It is the possibility of counter-tactics that has preoccupied Burroughs in his more recent work. He has become interested in methods of *deconditioning* and *decontrol*. In one sense the world of *Nova Express* (1964) is like the world of the earlier books, but there is a more positive appearance of a force attempting to counter the virus which is attacking man. The Nova Mob is made up of various criminals much like the liquefying, devouring, assimilating beasts of his earlier work. But there are also the Nova Police who are moving in on the criminals in order to arrest them. Good enough, one might think, except that when they are called in to rectify the dangerous situation caused by the criminals they are by no means reliable in their activities. In his *Paris Review* interview Burroughs made the point quite clearly: 'you've got a bad situation in which the Nova Mob is about to blow up the planet. So the Heavy Metal Kid calls in the Nova Police. Once you get them in there, by God, they begin acting like any police. They're always an ambivalent agency ... For Nova Police, read technology, if you wish.' He clearly concedes that his unique brand of science-fiction contains an allegory. And there is a large amount of direct statement in the book. In fact it starts with a long letter full of explicit warnings and admonitions – including the familiar call to '*rub out the word forever*'.

Where Burroughs achieves some of his most striking effects is in the merging of biology and contemporary communication media, just as he merges science and science-fiction, nightmare and comic-strip, carnival, satire and sexual aberration. Word and image can penetrate us like a virus because, to take another of the cryptic lines from *The Exterminator*, 'Only Live Animals have Write Door,' and just as the virus literally empties the body and fills it with its own replicas, so word and image eat out consciousness, replacing mind with junk. In this book Burroughs has developed his use of metaphors drawn from film to amplify his vision. There are constant references to screen, scanning pattern, dark room, and related terms, which are explained by his own statement that, 'Implicit in *Nova Express* is a theory that what we call reality is actually a movie. It's a film, what I call a biologic film.' The idea is not new: Joyce for instance described modern reality as an 'all nights newsery reel'. But the way it feeds into Burroughs's overall concerns is effective and in particular it provides him with something specific to resist. It locates, meta-phorically at least, the implementors of the virus conspiracy. 'There is no true or "real" reality—"Reality" is simply a more or less constant scanning pattern—The scanning pattern we accept as "reality" has been imposed by the controlling power on this planet, a power primarily oriented towards total control.' The power remains anonymous; the word is a gesture towards all the manipulators who put out the false film of modern society. And one of the demands that Burroughs is making is for the restoration of an untouched, unsynthesized reality. The inhabitants of the City in his story no longer know what is film and what is not. To combat the manufacturers of the enslaving film we are taught to call reality, man has to develop immunity from the image virus and then attack the place where the film is made. Much of the action of the book, as far as it can be followed, is concerned with a concerted effort to invade the various centres where the alien powers process the kind of false reality with which they narcoticize and dominate the human race. 'Storm The Reality Studio. And retake the universe.' The recurring cry, 'Break through in Grey Room,' suggests the possibility that the dark room has been penetrated.

The need to 'retake the universe' is made very urgent by the usual graphic images—the metal junkies, the scorpion men, the fish people, the prisoners being broken down into insect forms, the monster crab, the communal immersion tanks which 'melt whole peoples into one concentrate',* the Controllers, the Lemurs, the Mongolian Archers 'with black metal flesh', as well as the mobsters themselves, all convey a vision of a world very nearly completely taken over already. But of course the trouble with metaphors and analogies is that it is not always easy to establish the terms of application. Is there literally an alien force from another planet taking us over? If not then we have to work out what forces on earth the metaphor applies to. The science-fiction plot and the idea of a virus eating out the independent life of a human host convey an authentic dread. But the potential limitation of such analogies is that as well as vivifying a process or phenomenon in another realm, they may simplify it. The malicious appropriation and exploitation of other people's vitality and individuality of mind and body is a major theme in American literature, for instance in the work of Henry James and Nathaniel Hawthorne, and arguably one learns more about the nature of manipulative evil from the studies of Roger Chillingworth and Gilbert Osmond (for example) than from

---

* Oddly enough Henry James referred to American society as the 'terrible tank' in *The American Scene*, to make a not-dissimilar point about its power to erase individual distinctions. (See the Conclusion.) Both terms are probably jokes at the expense of the Melting Pot.

Burroughs's inter-galactic warfare.* However, what we do get is a
ruthless vision of the ultimate implications of the tenets of our society.
To say that the individual is 'free' is dangerously untrue in a society
in which so much is done to shape our tastes, appetites and fantasies.
Eric Mottram makes the point well when he remarks that Burroughs
shows that, 'Ultimate freedom means a society constructed of sadist
and masochist relationships, fantasy living through pleasure-pain
situations of inflicting and receiving ... The helplessness of the drug
addict is the image of free enterprise and its effects.' Writing at a
moment when scientists have put men on the moon at the same time
as they are cracking the code of life, one can find in Burroughs's
fused analogies from disparate realms a disturbing relevance.

Burroughs himself has said that he is interested in suggesting a
remedy and perhaps the clearest evidence of this comes in a later
section entitled 'One More Chance?' The question mark reveals the
tentative nature of what follows. The notion that man is vulnerable
to damaging instructions fed into him as on a tape recorder is
countered with the idea that the tape can be wiped clean. Taking
some terms from Scientology, a young man explains that in childhood or while unconscious the individual can be imprinted with
engrams, words or impressions which store pain that may later be
reactivated. This stored pain is called 'basic' and basic can be wiped
off the tape. 'Oh sir *then* that person becomes what they call a *clear*
sir.' The terms are taken from L. Ron Hubbard, who founded
Scientology, which is itself considered by many to be a piece of
science-fiction. Just how much of Hubbard Burroughs takes
seriously it is impossible to say, although the rather effeminate
over-deferential accents and 'programmed' diction of the speaker
suggest that Burroughs is not a true believer.†

* Of course from one point of view, the energy and vitality of art lies in its
ability to suggest new analogies. In his *Speculations* T. E. Hulme makes the point
that there are no ultimate principles on which all knowledge can be established.
'But there are an infinity of analogues, which help us along, and give us a feeling
of power over the chaos when we perceive them. The field is infinite and herein
lies the chance for originality. Here there are some new things under the sun.'
(Routledge and Kegan Paul paperback, London, 1960.) In America it may be that
the pressures are too great, the encompassing realities are too confused, too
massed and mobile, to permit of any calm analysis or stable identification of what
was behind this threat or that exploitation, or trace to their source the forces of
dissolution and misappropriation. The need, then, for new analogues and
allegories to give some feeling of 'power over the chaos' may be particularly great.
From this point of view, William Burroughs's highly original 'demonizing' of
reality is the most valuable contribution of his fiction.
† He discusses his attitude to Scientology in *The Job* (1970), which appeared
after the completion of this manuscript.

On the other hand he does seem genuinely interested in the man's account of how they can process a person's responses by beaming words and images at him—'vary the tape sir … switch the tape sir … ' —and the way of ending this subservient state is very much in line with Burroughs's own ideas. 'Now all together *laugh laugh laugh* … Oh sir we *laugh* it right off the tape sir … We *forget* it right off the tape sir.' The concluding words of this section—'Do you begin to see there is no patient there on the table?'—suggest a sort of release into invisibility explored in different ways by the other novels we have considered. It seems like a way of referring to that state of being finally 'clear' which, whatever the merit of Scientological beliefs, is certainly an abiding American aspiration.

To escape from words into silence and from mud and metal into space is Burroughs's version of a well-established American dream of freedom from conditioning forces. It would perhaps be obtuse to ask what mode of life would be adopted in silent space. We are being given the morphology of an emotion as much as a literal prescription, when Burroughs exhorts us to shed all verbalizations and leave the body behind. But it may be pointed out that escaping into empty space would seem to entail leaving behind that genuinely real nature and that spontaneous free-moving individual life which Burroughs is so keen to protect and warn. Indeed from a remark in the interview it seems as though he is willing to consider changing the human form as we know it. 'Mankind will have to undergo biologic alterations ultimately, if we are to survive at all … We will simply have to use our intelligence to plan mutations, rather than letting them occur at random.' In line with the ambiguity surrounding 'randomness', which clearly has its dangers as well as its uses, there is a more problematical ambiguity over the need for 'controlling' the individual, a phenomenon which his whole work is written to protest against. Whose intelligence is to plan the mutations? Supposing Dr Benway is put in charge of biologic alterations!

The point is worth stressing because it draws attention to a basic problem posed by his work. Are the forces of evil and good somehow external to man in their origins? Can white magic (technology) counter black magic (entropy)? Do we need a superhuman doctor to ward off the threat of a superhuman virus? If so, what is the status of the merely human: is he a pawn of embattled demons (or cops and mobs), some benevolent, some malign? This schematization of forces is reminiscent of the old morality play (and Burroughs promises us a Western—which is the American version of the morality play). The morality play was often a graphic medium for showing the bemused situation of man, his vulnerability and plight;

but it was, after all, the later dramatists who placed the contending forces deep inside the human individual, who gave us the more penetrating insights into the problems and mysteries of conscious life. It is ultimately harder to write about people than demons. It is easier to plot ways of combating a virus from another planet than to follow a character grappling with a dark impulse welling up from the depths of the individual self.

In terms of Burroughs's developing vision such observations may well seem positively archaic, for in *The Ticket that Exploded* (1967) there is a strong suggestion that the notion of the individual's identity may be another 'gimmick' by which man is entrapped by the various virus powers which require fleshly hosts. Two juxtaposed quotations suggest one of the central propositions of the book: 'Sex and pain *form* flesh identity'; 'sex and pain price of a ticket'. The ticket of admission into the exhibition or amusement park or garden of delights or cinema or vaudeville show or penny arcade or circus or game, which are some of the various images in the book for contemporary reality (turnstiles are constantly mentioned), is fleshly identity. This immediately involves one in sexuality and pain, which in turn render one helplessly vulnerable to parasitic take-over and control by all kinds of image- and symbol-systems. The only way out of this trap is to explode the ticket, which also can mean blowing up the fair. The ticket also incorporates the idea that we are all programmed by a pre-recorded tape which is fed into the self like a virus punch-card so that the self is never free. We are simply the message typed on to the jelly of flesh by some biological typewriter referred to as the soft machine. To counter this there is a recurrent exhortation, 'Why not take over ticket?' 'Operation rewrite' is one of the projects of the familiar Inspector Lee and one of the concerns of the book is to suggest how it might be possible to counter the controlling tape messages being fed into the self, by a special use of tape recorders as defensive machines. The book seems then to embrace two possibilities – the dissolving or exploding of the amusement park of pseudo-reality put out by the familiar virus enemy which controls the media to which the state of 'flesh identity' is so helplessly open and vulnerable; and also the attainment of the desirable state in which identity is erased and, let us say, 'occluded' from the exhibition, a state which can only be reached by passing out of the turnstiles of the fair, getting out of the film.

Modern communications and sexuality are equated as forms of 'vampirism'. Devourers and parasites abound in the book – like the figure of 'Genial', a voice who splices himself in with his lovers on a tape recorder. His words contain a sub-audible directive to commit suicide and this way his victims always end their lives. He himself has no identity but is a virus, who may or may not be part of a carefully worked out blueprint for invasion of the planet. There is a good deal of reference to 'copy planet', which neatly refers to the repetitive abilities of both literal viruses and the media images, whose intent to enter and discharge themselves in some suitable victim/host is paralleled by the aggressive penetrations and vampirisms of the sexual act. 'There are no good relationships – There are no good words – I wrote silences.' This is a succinct formulation of a defensive paranoia concerning all forms of communication which is discernible in a large number of recent American novels. (See Appendix Seven.)

Somewhere at the heart of the book is a feeling that no genuine reality is accessible in present time: ' "There is no real thing – Maya – Maya – It's all show business." ' Images crowd in on all sides and from the past, predetermining the present and pre-empting it of its own reality. Whatever genuine life might appear is moulded by old fabrications or sucked out by living corpses. The general atmosphere is a curious combination of desolate wasteland and fading film – reality is rotting or dissolving, a mixture of entropy and evaporation. There is a hint of apocalypse here. 'I mean what kind of show is it after everything has been sucked out?' The parasite process has produced a 'dead land' and the only solution seems to be to blow up all the existing structures which have been erected to seduce the pliant flesh identity. Burroughs describes modern civilization as a precarious iron city suspended over a void, a city of Ferris wheels and scenic railways as well as planes and cars all in constant motion. This is the whole circus of modern society which takes men in and empties them out. It can be resisted by turning its own weapons on it; camera guns and tape recorders vomit back the destructive input, attacking the source of all the control systems until all control symbols are pounded down to image dust. 'The whole structure of reality went up in silent explosions under the whining sirens.' This is the success of the combat troops. What people have taken to be reality proves to be a rotting film, a false cover which will disintegrate at a touch.

In Burroughs's view the majority welcome the protected unreality of the film in which they live; but as he sees it, the 'reality film' has now become an instrument of monopoly. He notes that anyone who calls the film in question is subjected to punitive pressures by the film-makers. The punishment the film-makers threaten is to be forced to live 'outside the film', but Burroughs, or Inspector Lee, can see that 'The film bank is empty'. For those American writers who refuse to accept the fixed reality pictures, 'outside the film' is exactly where they feel they want to be. (See Chapter Sixteen.) This is why the end of the book once again constitutes a notional abdication from all scripts and structures—a quitting of the exhibition. 'So the best minds coolly shut off a switch and went away down a tunnel of flash bulbs and last words ... The Not There Kid was not *there*. Empty turnstile marks the spot—So disinterest yourself in my words. Disinterest yourself in anybody's words ... ' This gesture of disengagement from the fouling entanglements of language is part of a larger goodbye to the sort of word-body identity which has been shown to be so vulnerable to assault in the shifting panorama of the book.

'Fading' is one of the most recurrent words in the book and phrases like 'Identity fades in empty space' sound a constant leitmotiv. I find a deep, though provocative, ambiguity in the apparent attitude of the author towards the fading of identity. In one sense it is a manifestly desirable thing: it is the escape from the amusement park, the disengagement from the tape and the film versions which are everywhere advocated. In this sense it is analogous to Cabot Wright's escape from media definitions. On the other hand the constant references to the dissolving, disintegrating effects of the agents of decay indicate that they also secure a 'fading', in the sense of a melting or sinking of identity. Reducing it to a crude formula it seems that it is a good thing to fade away from identity up into space, but a terrible fate to fade from it downwards into mud. There is, of course, no question of adopting another identity: 'the offer of another image identity is always on virus terms.' I think we can see again evidence of a profound ambivalence about the very basis of identity. It is manifestly dreadful to be 'milked of identity' ('Face sucked into other apparatus'); on the other hand, the body itself (which is the indispensable condition of identity) is at times referred to as an old 'overcoat' to be free of which is the highest bliss. In this context it is interesting to note that once again we have a scene connecting the act of vomiting with the experience of release. 'Almost immediately i vomited so violently that my body seemed to crack open ... and i was free of my body.' It is also possible that Burroughs intends the suggestion that the sexual fusion to which the flesh identity seems bound to submit might of itself precipitate the fission which will explode all the tickets and release individuals back into air—like Prospero's actors, to whom the book refers.

There is no question of reshaping or reforming the existing moulds —only of breaking them wide open to permit the escape and flight of those trapped within. ' "So come out of those ugly molds and remember good is better than evil because its nicer to have around you. Its just as simple as that." ' One responds to the directness of the appeal, but it would be fair to make the reservation that the freedom beyond all forms and the goodness which is outside of definitions suggest a degree of disengagement, which, like the peace which passeth all understanding, presages a state approximating to death. Since Burroughs is manifestly not writing as a direct advocate of suicide, it seems to be that once again we are confronted by an American writer seeking to establish some third realm—beyond the entrapments and degradations of form and flesh-identity, yet not totally reabsorbed into the unmoulding void.

One of the ways in which the image-onslaught is to be resisted is by the tape recorder itself, an apparent paradox which is summed up in the resolution—'Communication must be made total. Only way to stop it.' The idea is: 'Get it out of your head and into the machines.' If life is a pre-recording, then the one way of introducing a disturbing or fouling factor is to record that pre-recording and then play it back, for that play-back is the one thing that cannot be allowed for on the pre-recording. The book ends by emphasizing the need for the demolition of the play-back, which is the world we are subjected to. The strategy is that you record all the ugliness around and then with counter-recording and play-back you gradually diminish its power. In a sense this points to a basic paradox in Burroughs's own work. For a writer who finds decay and disintegration so horrific he is unusually immersed in its extremest occasions, just as the interviewer saw the paradox of the writer fighting the word while buried in newspapers. But this is his method. The ugliness has to be recorded, then the recorder (author) can play with it at will, exerting *his* control over *it*. By constantly regurgitating all the foul material, replaying it at his tempo, with his splicings and 'inchings', as it were, he is accelerating its disappearance: 'the more you run the tapes through and cut them up the less power they will have   cut the pre-recordings into air into thin air   ' And there, with no full stop, but the cleanness of a blank page to follow, Burroughs ends the book.

Something of the ambiguity in Burroughs's attitudes may be demonstrated by fragments suggesting the directions in which his recent work has been going. In the *Paris Review* interview he gave a lucid definition of the sort of work he now wants to write. 'What I want to do is to learn to see more of what's out there, to look outside, to achieve as far as possible a complete awareness of surroundings. Beckett wants to go inward. First he was in a bottle and now he is in the mud. I am aimed in the other direction—outward.' He describes his new, somewhat cumbersome, techniques—writing in three columns what he is doing, thinking and reading; collecting vast amounts of local data; taking hundreds of random photographs of places. Sounding a different note from the cartoon horrors of his earlier work, this intent seems to hark back to a deliberate sort of inclusiveness of attention to his surroundings reminiscent of Sherwood Anderson or even Whitman. What is different is that much of what he opens out to is the detritus of modern city life. In a short piece called 'St. Louis Return', published in the same issue of *Paris Review*, in which he writes about coming back to his birthplace after his years abroad, there is manifest almost a nostalgia, not exactly for the mud, but for the urban desolations of the American land-scape. He walks contentedly around the town letting it all flow into his eyes, and his camera.

> 'Ash pits — an alley — a rat in sunlight — It's all here,' I tapped my camera, 'all the magic of past times like the song says right under your eyes back in your own back yard. Why are people bored? Because they can't see what is right under their eyes right in their own back yard. And why can't they see what is right under their eyes? — (Between the eye and the object falls the shadow) — And that shadow, B.J., is the pre-recorded word.'

In just such a way Whitman wanted to sweep back the curtains of old literary styles which he said prevented a direct exposure to reality. Burroughs, with his camera and notebook, and his silent recombinations of fragments, is manifestly a more modern bard, but the underlying affinities are there. He is at least half in love with the tumbling material settings from which he elsewhere exhorts us to extricate ourselves. The end of this short and oddly lyrical piece reveals the author walking back through a setting as haunting as a painting by de Chirico: 'back through the ruins of Market Street to the Union Station nudes waiting there in the dry fountain of an empty square — I have returned to pick up a few pieces of sunlight and shadow-silver paper in the wind — frayed sounds of a distant city.' The tone is almost elegiac. It is a long way from the nightmares of that room in Tangier in which he himself experienced that going down-wards into mud which he repudiates in Beckett but which is every-where dramatized in his own diagnostic works. Burroughs now can walk through 'the City' without being of it or trapped in it. One senses the liberation, and it is to be hoped that he will do some more extended writing on the American landscapes which he so thoroughly knows.

Another recent fragment, published in the *International Times* (August 31st, 1967), is called '23 Skidoo Eristic Elite'. It dramatizes yet another battle between the powers who control by sending out false images, and the powers who know how to resist and annihilate the image. It ends with the successful capture and destruction of all the tape recordings and films by which the Controlling Board have kept society cowering within a fixed and false fabrication of reality. At the end a vast tapeworm covered with newsprint twists its way out of a lot of microphones set up in the middle of the city square. The watching crowd cheers and tears the worm to pieces. This is their liberation, and the story ends with '*silence...et pas de commissions*'. Compressed into this short piece are so many images and figures from his earlier work that it reveals that Burroughs has now created a vocabulary—diagnostic and therapeutic—which can engender a theoretically indefinite number of episodes or versions of conflict and victory. This is one of the things that produces that curiously abstract feeling in his prose even when the images are most vivid; one feels the presence of the schematic parable behind the dream images of science-fiction, or the shorthand outlines of the strip cartoon. Scanning the apparently turbulent and broken surface one finds a persistent pattern of curious purity.

The end of the piece I have just described points to the underlying theme of all his important work—a dream of being freed from the conditioning forces, of seeing all the tickets explode, of re-taking the reality studio. This liberation is envisaged as a liberation into space; at the same time, as demonstrated in such pieces as 'St. Louis Return', it is a space from which a sort of total and impregnable perception of 'what is really there' is made possible. We should perhaps think in terms of some inner space, remembering that Burroughs himself indicated that the most one could strive for was 'inner freedom'. This two-way movement—out into reality, up or back into space—is responsible for the strange and unique constitution of his writing which is both deeply immersed in the lowest forms of materiality and serenely withdrawn from them. Using his own term we can call it 'sky writing', fading even at the moment of articulation, leaving us with an almost subliminal yet persistent message and dream—*pas de commissions*.

Chapter 6 Everything Running Down

'Everything running down ... This deliquescent running-down of everything becomes co-existent with Diddy's entire span of consciousness, undermines his most minimal acts.'
(*Death Kit,* Susan Sontag)

On several occasions now the word 'entropy' has occurred in our consideration of recent American writers and at this point I wish to consider the word directly. First we may consult a dictionary definition (from the *American Standard College Dictionary*):

Entropy: a. Physics. A mathematical expression of the degree in which the energy of a thermodynamic system is so distributed as to be unavailable for conversion into work ...

The irreversible tendency of a system, including the universe, toward increasing disorder and inertness; also, the final state predictable from this tendency.

It is my impression that the term, taken from its context of the second law of thermodynamics, is used now with a looseness which any scientist would deplore and is in any case regarded as a rather old-fashioned scientific idea (John Hollander once expressed the opinion that C. P. Snow could hardly have made a less felicitous choice when he cited the second law of thermodynamics as an example of the sort of science an arts man should know, since, as Hollander said, it is the one bit of 'science' which every American schoolboy knows). But the frequency with which 'entropy' occurs, as a word or as a tendency, is in itself a phenomenon pointing to a disposition of the American imagination which we should take notice of.

Among the writers who use the actual word in their work are Norman Mailer, Saul Bellow, John Updike, John Barth, Walker Percy, Stanley Elkin, Donald Barthelme. Without using the word, Burroughs shows in his work a world in the throes of entropy (with human regressing to animal, thence to vegetable, then to mineral, and everything finally ending in a stagnant lake of mud or a vast rubbish heap). More generally, the feeling of 'everything running down', described by Susan Sontag, is to be found in a very large number of novels. The even more widespread fear of the tendency of all things towards eventual homogeneity is another manifestation of the ubiquitous dread of 'entropy'. Just two examples of its use may be given here. When Mailer is advancing his idea that the victory of God over the Devil is by no means certain, he states that either may win, or they might exhaust each other 'until Being ceases to exist or sinks through seas of entropy into a Being less various, less articulated, less organic, more like plastic than the Nature we know.' In Stanley Elkin's impressive novel about guilt called *A Bad Man*, Feldman says to an adviser, ' "I won't have it. Fuck your virgin land … We're in the home-stretch of a race: your energy against my entropy. The universe is running down, Mr Developer. It's bucking and filling. It's yawing and pitching and rolling and falling. The smart money's in vaults." ' Thomas Pynchon's first short story was called 'Entropy' and it provides the preface to his subsequent novels. I want to examine his work in some detail, but before doing so, I think it might be helpful to consider some of the implications of this general interest in 'entropy' manifest among American writers.

Taken in its broadest sense as meaning the increasing disorder of energy moving at random within a closed system, finally arriving at total inertia, the term could be applied to works of literature of the past. It seems particularly appropriate to those works which foretell the doom of a present civilization or society. Thus 'The Dunciad' shows ever more frenzied destructive movement bringing everything down to mud, sleep and universal darkness, the ultimate triumph of Dullness and 'gravity' being Pope's version of the triumph of entropy. (See Thomas Edwards's fine book on Pope, *This Dark Estate*,[1] where he suggests this analogy.) Or if we examine that massive indictment of Victorian London, *Bleak House*, we can see an increasing madness of movement among the atomized inhabitants struggling in darkness and fog (with the muddy Thames as a permanent reminder of more primordial conditions) threatening to bring about a state of total entropy, or what Dickens himself called 'perpetual stoppage'. Obviously it is not to his purpose to show the whole of London actually in that state, he is bound by certain naturalistic conventions of verisimilitude; but he does show the country house of the aptly named aristocrats, the Dedlocks, as having reached a condition one might fairly discern as total entropy.

Thus Chesney Wold. With so much of itself abandoned to darkness and vacancy; with so little change under the summer shining or the wintry lowering; so sombre and motionless always — no flag flying now by day, no rows of lights sparkling by night; with no family to come and go, no visitors to be the souls of pale cold shapes of rooms, no stir of life about it; — passion and pride, even to the stranger's eye, have died away from the place in Lincolnshire, and yielded it to dull repose.

Apart from a final happy note from Esther, this is the real end of the novel, and one notices again the combination of dullness and sleep ('dull repose') which Dickens, like Pope, envisages as signifying the conclusion or consummation of the entropic tendency.*

One of the apparent paradoxes of this tendency is that of movement leading to stillness. But there is a difference between the organic, constructive movement of something (or someone) burgeoning into a full realization of its inherent potential development and the sort of mindless repetitive motions — of Pope's dunces, of Dickens's automata, of Burroughs's addicts — that denote a gradual collapsing towards inertia and death. And one of the reasons why the notion of entropy has become so attractive to recent American writers is that the advanced stages of an industrial, even a post-industrial, society necessarily proliferate processes and actions based on mechanized movement. Some eloquent remarks by the late R. P. Blackmur[2] are in place here.

> Society takes on the aspect of uniform motion. The artist is the hero who struggles against uniform motion, a struggle in marmalade. For the artist regards uniform motion as the last torpor of life. Torpor is the spread of momentum, but we prefer to believe it is the running down of things. For three generations we have heroized the second law of thermodynamics, which is the law of the dissipation or gradual unavailability of energy within any system — which is the law of entropy or the incapacity for fresh idiom, time and perception going backwards. Entropy, from the point of view of the rational imagination, is disorder and is indeed its field. Actually, we have been as busy, as violent, and as concentrated as the ant-heap. We are torpid only because we are glutted with energy and feel it only as trouble. The strains are out of phase with each other and we have techniques only for the troubles.

One thing that follows from these insights is that 'order', if it is dedicated to the procuring of 'uniform motion', may in fact accelerate

---

* There are, of course, entropic hints in earlier American literature — the 'valley of ashes' in *The Great Gatsby*, Tod Hackett's interest in 'the painters of Decay and Mystery' in *The Day of the Locust*, for example.

entropy and not counter it; the disorder (and destruction) produced by the 'order' of the army and air force in *Catch 22* and *Eustace Chisholm and the Works* are examples of this phenomenon. This is why 'flexibility', which may be translated as the continuous resistance to any imposed uniformities of motion, rather than 'order', is the key word for the American hero. Like his creator he wants to be a small counter force to the prevailing entropic tendencies. The difficulty lies in the fact that 'organization' is the phenomenon which resists entropy. The problem of differentiating between that sort of organization which procures and protects intelligible life, and that sort of mechanical 'order' which induces anaesthesia and ultimately irreversible torpor, is one which may be said often to prove too difficult for the American hero.

In the most general terms entropy is concerned with the fate of energy — the individual's, society's, the world's — and as such is well calculated to interest the novelist trying to discern what patterns the released powers and vitalities of his age and society are establishing. In addition entropy has been shown to have a relevance in connection with the transmitting of information, and clearly this is specially calculated to interest the writer, not only as a communicator himself, but as someone who writes about people in their various efforts to establish communications. To attempt to offer any adequate summary of the ideas in this area would be well outside the range of my competence. I prefer to cite some passages from the admirably lucid work of the late Norbert Wiener, whose book *The Human Use of Human Beings* (1954)[3] is something of a modern American classic and may well have been read by many of the writers we are considering. Professor Wiener's particular interest in this book is cybernetics, but some of his comments are clearly applicable to a sphere large enough to contain the work of the contemporary novelist.

He starts by describing how Gibbs introduced the notion of probability into physics, to supplant Newtonian certainties, and how he took into account contingency instead of asserting the eternal applicability and adequacy of fixed causal laws. He compares Gibbs's recognition of an element of incomplete determinism in the world to Freud's discoveries of the irrationality deep inside the self, and relates both to the tradition of St Augustine in their recognition of an ineradicable element of chance in the texture of the universe. 'For this random element, this organic incompleteness, is one which without too violent a figure of speech we may consider evil; the negative evil which St Augustine characterizes as incompleteness, rather than the positive malicious evil of the Manichaeans.' He concludes his introductory remarks with a passage which needs to be quoted in full.

> As entropy increases, the universe, and all closed systems in the universe, tend naturally to deteriorate and lose their distinctiveness, to move from the least to the most probable state, from a state of organization and differentiation in which distinctions and forms exist, to a state of chaos and sameness. In Gibbs' universe order is least probable, chaos most probable. But while the universe as a whole, if indeed there is a whole universe, tends to run down, there are local enclaves whose direction seems opposed to that of the universe at large and in which there is a limited and temporary tendency for organization to increase. Life finds its home in some of these enclaves.

Clearly it will make a big difference in an author's work whether he concentrates on 'the universe at large' or whether he shortens his perspective and focuses on those enclaves of life which show a contrary tendency to the overall decline of things. For a neo-classic writer like Pope, to hold up his beautifully organized and clearly formed poem against the forces of dullness and disorder was in itself an act of resistance, of negative entropy. But the contemporary American writer and his heroes are seldom so neo-classical; and their additional problem, as I have tried to suggest, is that for them 'organization' suggests a rigid patterning of life which is as deathly as the total biological disorganization implied by that recurrent metaphor of jelly (or mud): fixity and fluidity alike imply entropy.

This has implications for the act of writing itself which emerge from another passage in Wiener.

> Messages are themselves a form of pattern and organization. Indeed, it is possible to treat sets of messages as having an entropy like sets of states of the external world. Just as entropy is a measure of disorganization, the information carried by a set of messages is a measure of organization. In fact, it is possible to interpret the information carried by a message as essentially the negative of its entropy, and the negative logarithm of its probability. That is, the more probable the message, the less information it gives. Clichés, for example, are less illuminating than great poems.

There are many implications here for contemporary American writing, some too obvious to need spelling out. In particular, the decay and decline in significant information, which is a necessary consequence of the increasing probability of mass-media messages, has affected the American writer's feelings about the ability of any language to transmit significant information. Hence Purdy's deliberate foregrounding of his style with clichés, hence Burroughs's deliberate demonstration of the entropic disintegration of language itself in *Naked Lunch*. (Hence too, in a different way, McLuhan's flamboyant declaration that there is no more message, that the medium itself is the message. If true this would mean that communications had reached a state of ultimate entropy and there was no more information being transmitted.)

I think this feeling is also evident in the compulsion of the contemporary American writer to go to unusual lengths to assert his own style. Words have to be organized in order to transmit any kind of information, and that organization is in itself a gesture against entropy. To counter entropy they must be organized in such a way as to defy probability; ideally this would mean using words in a way never before encountered. But here there is the danger of simply going beyond all organization, which in the long run is equal to the danger of submitting to probability. Either way the writer may find that the power of his words to transmit any kind of message or vivid information is perpetually in decline. Sometimes I think one can detect a sort of despair about language even in (perhaps particularly in) the most prolific American writers, a feeling about the inescapability of entropy such as is suggested by T. S. Eliot's line about working with 'shabby equipment always deteriorating'.

Obviously, to stress the triumph of the entropic tendencies in the world, or worlds, about which you are writing is to make available almost unlimited effects of pessimism. But as Wiener goes on to show, the existence of 'anti-entropic processes' is an equally important part of the truth. In particular, it has to be remembered that a human being is not a closed system:

> nature's statistical tendency to disorder, the tendency for entropy to increase in isolated systems, is expressed by the second law of thermodynamics. We, as human beings, are not isolated systems. We take in food, which generates energy ... But even more important is the fact that we take in information through our sense organs, and we act on information received.

One notable characteristic of many of the books we have considered or will be considering is that they concentrate on people who precisely *are* turning themselves into 'isolated systems' (or being turned into isolated systems by the world around them); they take in a decreasing amount of information, sensory data, even food, with the result that the sense of their own personal entropy is heightened and this sense is then projected over the world around them. (Susan Sontag's *Death Kit* is a perfect example of this, but it can be found in writers as different as Sylvia Plath and John Barth.) American writers themselves at times also show a tendency to turn themselves into 'isolated systems'.

The important point here for fiction is that as long as an individual is not a closed system he need not, and often cannot, be in a state of equilibrium. 'In a system which is not in equilibrium, or in part of such a system, entropy need not increase. It may, in fact, decrease locally.' Many writers show that for a figure to be in a state of 'equilibrium' (or perfect adjustment to the prevailing ethos of the world) involves the loss of any distinct inner reality he might have had. To that extent such a figure has succumbed to the entropic forces. For the self to hold out against the drift of the surrounding environment and society may thus become an act of life, a counter-entropic gesture. The risk involved in this gesture is that to secure the self against the coercions and intrusive persuasions of society, the individual may inadvertently turn himself into an 'isolated system', and entropy then increases inside him. As Norbert Wiener says, it is highly probable that the world will one day be reduced to a vast 'equilibrium' in which nothing happens because all has been reduced to a 'drab uniformity'. The dread of being reduced to such a uniformity is particularly intense in American fiction, suggesting perhaps that many writers feel that the powers working against variety, diversity, distinction, individuality, are being ominously successful in their own contemporary society. The feeling that, whatever the individual may do, he cannot help but contribute to the entropic process is responsible for a great deal of pessimism in this fiction. It is not always easy for the American hero, or author, to remember Norbert Wiener's reminder that, since it is impossible that any man can be a witness of the world's death, we do well to turn our minds to the positive possibilities of locally decreasing entropy.

We noted, when studying Burroughs, that although the agents of evil were ubiquitous, all of them working to accelerate entropy, the origin of it was vague. The evil was waiting in the land. For any novelist who has been touched by the vision of the gathering triumphs of entropy, the question of evil will be related to the problem of who or what is behind the entropic tendency, working for its ultimate victory. I defined this as Burroughs's 'demonism' and again, Wiener's words are strikingly relevant.

The scientist is always working to discover the order and organization of the universe, and is thus playing a game against the arch enemy, disorganization. Is this devil Manichaean or Augustinian? Is it a contrary force opposed to order or is it the very absence of order itself? The difference between these two sorts of demons will make itself apparent in the tactics to be used against them. The Manichaean devil is an opponent, like any other opponent, who is determined on victory and will use any trick of craftiness or dissimulation to obtain this victory. In particular, he will keep his policy of confusion secret, and if we show any signs of beginning to discover his policy, he will change it in order to keep us in the dark. On the other hand, the Augustinian devil, which is not a power in itself, but the measure of our own weakness, may require our full resources to uncover, but when we have uncovered it, we have in a certain sense exorcised it, and it will not alter its policy on a matter already decided with the mere intention of confounding us further.

The obsession with plots, agents, codes, often accompanied by a general uncertainty of who is working for whom or towards what ends, which is I think a discernible characteristic of much of the fiction we are considering, is not only a measure of the paranoia induced by American life. It is also, I think, connected to a larger uncertainty about the big plot being hatched out by nature. Final information on this matter is of course unavailable to any of us, but it seems to press far more insistently on the consciousness and imagination of the American writer. Demons and conspiracies are to the fore. The work of, for example, Burroughs, Mailer and Pynchon suggests that entropy may be seen as evidence of a Manichaean demon at work in the land.

The most famous application of the law of entropy to society and human history was made by Henry Adams, and although this is not the place to embark on any comprehensive summary of his theories, or hypotheses, some quotations from his work may give an indication of what a later American writer might have found there.

In Chapter Twenty-five of his *Education*, in which he sets up the polar symbols of the Virgin and the Dynamo to suggest the different forces behind medieval unity and modern multiplicity, Adams offers a definition of his historian's business which could well cover the novelist's as well: 'the historian's business was to follow the track of the energy; to find where it came from and where it went to; its complex source and shifting channels; its values, equivalents, conversions.' Surveying the lines of thought which had accompanied the discoveries (and the release) of the energies in nature, Adams finds that 'in 1900, the continuity snapped'. The nightmare that Adams confronts is the discovery that, 'As Nature developed her hidden energies, they tended to become destructive,' and he detected a tremendous acceleration in the rate at which these energies were being released in the twentieth century.

In his 'Letter to American Teachers of History' (1909) Adams starts by referring directly to the second law of thermodynamics and quotes from Clausius, ' "The Entropy of the Universe tends toward a maximum." ' This, says Adams, 'to the vulgar and ignorant historian meant only that the ash-heap was constantly increasing in size.' He cites the work of such new physicists as Kelvin demonstrating 'that all nature's energies were slowly converting themselves into heat and vanishing in space, until, at the last, nothing would be left except a dead ocean of energy at its lowest possible level.' He also takes from the physicists their insistence that the law by no means excludes human existence: 'they are positive that the law of Entropy applies to all vital processes even more rigidly than to mechanical.' In fact he is putting forward the suggestion that the 'great generalization that would reduce all history under a law' may well be found in the law of entropy. For the pessimist historian whose favourite book was *The Decline and Full of the Roman Empire*, there was clearly a sort of melancholy satisfaction to be derived from the existence of this law, particularly as it coincided with his vision of modern man releasing energy at an ever accelerating rate and thus hastening the final stasis: 'man is a bottomless sink of waste unparalleled in the cosmos, and can already see the end of the immense economies which his mother Nature stored for his support.'

Where Wiener would describe conscious man as an enclave of anti-entropy, Adams prefers to stress that 'the law of Entropy imposes a servitude on all energies, including the mental. The degree of freedom steadily and rapidly diminishes.' He even posits a physicist saying, ' "The psychologists have already told you that Consciousness is only a phase in the decline of vital energy," ' and going on to argue that, ' "As an energy he [man] has but one dominant function: — that of accelerating the operation of the second law of thermodynamics." ' The fastidious humour and cool, almost hidden, wit with which Adams conducts his speculations, even when his rhetoric is at its most apocalyptic, may be said to constitute a counter-entropic gesture; although at times the air of cultivated ennui and lassitude seems perhaps to be his contribution to the hastening of the operations of the law which seemed to fit his mood so well. Certainly his vision of 'terrestial shrinkage' and his unfading sense of that 'ultimate ocean of entropy' represent a point of view which needs to be put with William James's more positive sense of the opening possibilities of life if we wish to appreciate the cosmic pessimism which is always latent in the American imagination. This pessimism comes to the surface in a modern writer like Pynchon in a way which shows how deeply Henry Adams can influence subsequent generations.

It is clearly not surprising that a country which has produced such an unprecedented amount of force and witnessed such a unique diffusion of energies into such an unparallelled amount of available space should produce writers who are obsessed with the basic mystery of force and energy. 'Nature is full of rival energies; and, – for any-thing we know, – may once have been full of hostile energies': that is still Henry Adams, but it could be Norman Mailer or William Burroughs. In another essay, 'The Rule of Phase applied to History' (1909), Adams poses the question, 'must all motion merge at last into ultimate static energy existing only as potential force in absolute space?' In a literature so profoundly preoccupied with movement such a question must obviously influence novelists as well.

Adams's use of an image of Rudolph Goldscheid's to the effect that 'order ... was but Direction regarded as Stationary, like a frozen waterfall' points succinctly to the reasons for that dread of arrest and suspicion of 'order' so perceptible in many American novels: form is a freezing, only that which runs is alive. Adams's explorations into the lessons of physics point to the problem confronted by the American hero of which way to move, where to aim his personal energy. 'Lines of force go on vibrating, rotating, moving in waves, up and down, forward and back, indifferent to control and pure waste of energy, – forms of repulsion, – until their motion becomes guided by motive, as an electric current is induced by a dynamo.' It is not too much of an exaggeration to say that the sort of random, uncontrolled movement described here is comparable to that of many American figures in fiction. One way to describe a lot of recent American novels would be to say that they are really about the search for the appropriate motive which will transform motion into direction. And Adams's late reminder – 'Always and everywhere the mind creates its own universe, and pursues its own phantoms; but the force behind the image is always a reality, – the attractions of occult power' – is equally appropriate. It suggests not only the specific work of writers like Burroughs, but also the more pervasive sense in recent American fiction that the phantoms and images by which, and within which, we live are fragile and transitory fictions and projections, and that behind them there is the one mystery under all mysteries – the initiations and cessations of movement, the fate of all energy, 'the attractions of occult power'.

I think this sense of mysterious powers at work behind the visible concretions of the everyday world is unusually strong in American writing, for reasons which have been noted before now. The American writer has much less sense of a stable society which his hero encounters and enters—the process by which the European hero usually gains an identity. The institutions, even the buildings, of American society have never had this stability, and the American writer is more likely to express through his hero his own sense of their bewildering fluidity. Putting it rather extremely, I think we could say that for the English novelist, when his hero comes up against the prevailing structure of society, he considers this to be an encounter with some reality (sometimes with the most meaningful reality). Whereas for the American writer such an encounter is more likely to be experienced as an entanglement with misleading apparitions, hence the perpetually dissolving cityscapes, and the sense of moving among insubstantial ephemera, to be found throughout contemporary American fiction. This is one reason, I think, why there is so much less interest in conventional character study and analysis in it than in contemporary English fiction.

Instead there is a feeling that the true reality is whatever it is that works *through* the characters and conventions of the social foreground; an evil waiting in the land, the attractions of occult power, the coming triumph of entropy. Reality is ultimately made up of those mysterious forces which are so vast, so elemental, and perhaps so timeless, that any prolonged sense of them, or quest for them, inevitably has a reductive effect on the human image, and for some writers a trivializing one. It can make man appear such a futile and pathetic speck, participating in such desperately transient episodes, that some writers now avail themselves of formal devices like the cartoon-strip to project their vision. It is an appropriate form for a fiction which does not consider the presence and appearance of people to constitute a primary level of reality. Emerson and other Transcendentalists also saw the social surface as a transparent flow, of quite secondary importance to the wonders that could be discerned through it—this was a positive, more Oriental vision. The modern American writer, looking at, and then looking through, the chaos of waste and human mutilation so much in evidence in his contemporary urban landscapes, is more likely to see horrors.*

* Characteristically, Buckminster Fuller has shown how it might be possible to take up an entirely different and more positive attitude to the waste and rubbish which seems to accumulate at an accelerating rate in modern society, giving rise to entropic forebodings. In his essay 'I Figure' (in *The Buckminster Fuller Reader* [Jonathan Cape, London, 1970]) he outlines a series of positive

Indeed, his concern could well become fastened on the problem of whether there is anything to be seen at all. Faced with the evidence of an ever more rapid release of power, and the concomitant hastening of processes of disintegration and accumulations of rubbish in the foreground of human activity, he may wonder what sort of conspiracy might be behind this accelerated levelling of things, what might be, in Conrad's phrase, 'the plot of plots'.† This, above all, is what the work of Thomas Pynchon is about.

---

speculations addressed in general to American designers and producers. Admittedly, this piece was written in the very special context of the Second World War, eleven months after Pearl Harbour. Nevertheless, I will quote three of his predictions to show how it is possible for an American to take a different attitude to waste by concentrating on what Buckminster Fuller calls 'scrap recycling':

> ... that the custodians will, however, finally get the picture straight regarding the advantage in wealth gains accruing through accelerated velocity of scrap recycling, in which each cycle represents an impress of sun-free energy into the cumulative commonwealth standard of efficiency advance.
> ... that once the scrap is really recycling on an efficient basis, new design will be constantly in demand to warrant a new cycle and that the world-wide industrial wheels will turn as never before.
> ... that in either case of planned or bomb-wrought demolition, evolution will be demonstrating the large-scale incorporation into popularly comprehended industrial phenomena of the recycling of material elements into progressively more efficient use forms.

† In the conclusion to *Tristes Tropiques*, Lévi-Strauss made this comment:

> Man has never—save only when he reproduces himself—done other than cheerfully dismantle million upon million of structures and reduce their elements to a state in which they can be no longer integrated ... Taken as a whole, therefore, civilization can be described as a prodigiously complicated mechanism: tempting as it would be to regard it as our universe's best hope of survival, its true function is to produce what physicists call entropy: ... 'Entropology', not anthropology, should be the word for that discipline that devotes itself to the study of this process of disintegration in its most highly evolved forms.

Adopting Lévi-Strauss's word we may say that American novelists of the past two decades have shown themselves to be diligent and concerned entropologists.

Chapter 7   Caries and Cabals

> 'Cavities in the teeth occur for good reason, Eigenvalue reflected. But even if there are several per tooth, there's no conscious organization there against the life of the pulp, no conspiracy. Yet we have men like Stencil, who must go about grouping the world's random caries into cabals.'
>
> *(V)*
>
> *'Shall I project a world?'*
>
> *(The Crying of Lot 49)*

Thomas Pynchon made his intentions clear from the outset. The title of his first important short story is 'Entropy'[1] and it contains specific references to Henry Adams. Whereas some novelists would prefer to cover the philosophic tracks which gave them decisive shaping hints for their novels, Pynchon puts those tracks on the surface of his writing. Indeed his work is about those tracks and, more largely, the whole human instinct and need to make tracks. Adams wanted a theory which would act as a 'trail' in 'the thickset forests of history' and even if we change that metaphor of the forest to that of the urban wasteland, thick with the rubble and dead of our century of total wars, the need for a trail or a track may still remain. A philosophy, a theory of history, a law of thermodynamics — any one of these may be a 'trail' and their significance may reside not so much in their verifiable applicability as in the human compulsion to formulate them. Pynchon sees all this quite clearly, and while his work is certainly about a world succumbing to entropy, it is also about the subtler human phenomena — the need to see patterns which may easily turn into the tendency to suspect plots.

The situation in 'Entropy' is simply and deliberately schematic. There is a downstairs and an upstairs apartment. Downstairs, Meatball Mulligan is holding a lease-breaking party which tends increasingly towards destructive chaos and ensuing torpor. This is a recurrent motif in all Pynchon's work, no doubt exemplifying the entropic process (the party is a relatively closed system of people, no one seems able to leave, and the only terminating point is sleep). The entropic process applies to the decline of information as well: two people discuss communication theory and how noise messes up significant signals. Upstairs, an intellectual called Callisto is trying to warm a freezing bird back to life. In his room he maintains a little

153

hothouse jungle, specifically referred to as a 'Rousseau-like fantasy'. 'Hermetically sealed, it was a tiny enclave of regularity in the city's chaos, alien to the vagaries of the weather, national politics, of any civil disorder.' His room is his fantasy, a dream of order in which he has 'perfected its ecological balance'. But the story follows the Adams formulation, 'Chaos was the law of nature; Order was the dream of man.' Callisto and his girl have effectively sealed themselves up in the room, never going out, living a life like a perfectly executed piece of music. Downstairs the jazz gets ever more raucous and the party noises constantly reach up into the 'music' of Callisto's domain.

The house, then, is some sort of paradigm for modern consciousness; the lower part immersed in the noise of modern distractions and sensing the failing of significant communication, while the upper part strives to remain at the level of music, yet feels the gathering strain as dream is encroached on by life. Life, in this context, is not only the party downstairs, but the weather. Callisto finds that the temperature has remained at 37 degrees Fahrenheit for a number of days, and he is by nature quick to detect omens of apocalypse. 'Henry Adams, three generations before his own, had stared aghast at Power; Callisto found himself in much the same state over Thermodynamics, the inner life of that power.' What Pynchon puts before us is the effort of the man in his upstairs sanctuary, with life-destroying weather outside, and sense-destroying noise downstairs, to articulate his theory of what is going on. Callisto finds Adams's ideas relevant to his idea of the situation. At one point he starts to dictate to his girl, using—like Adams in *Education*—the third person.

As a young man at Princeton ... Callisto had learned a mnemonic device for remembering the Laws of Thermodynamics: you can't win, things are going to get worse before they get better, who says they're going to get better ... he found in entropy or the measure of disorganization for a closed system an adequate metaphor to apply to certain phenomena in his own world ... in American 'consumerism' discovered a similar tendency from the least to the most probable, from differentiation to sameness, from ordered individuality to a kind of chaos. He found himself, in short, restating Gibbs' prediction in social terms, and envisioned a heat-death for his culture in which ideas, like heat-energy, would no longer be transferred, since each point in it would ultimately have the same quantity of energy; and intellectual motion would, accordingly, cease.

This is a man drawing on various ideas or laws which he has

learned, to project adequate analogies for the cosmic processes in which man is so helplessly caught up. It is an attempt to make some intellectual music; a music to harmonize the increasing noise.

The story has in effect two different endings: downstairs Meatball is feeling the temptation to crawl off to sleep somewhere. But he resolves to do what he can to keep the party from 'deteriorating into total chaos'. He acts; he starts to tidy up, gets people calmed down, gets things mended. Upstairs however, Callisto is 'helpless in the past', and the bird he had been trying to save dies in his hands. His girl realizes that his obsession with that constant 37 degrees has brought him to a state of paralysed terror. Her act is a symbolic one—she smashes the window of their hermetically-sealed retreat with her own bare hands. It is tantamount to the breaking of the shell round their whole fantasy life of perfect harmonies and maintained ecological balances.

In that composite image of the pragmatic man actively doing what he can with the specific scene, and the theorizing man passively attempting to formulate the cosmic process, Pynchon offers us a shorthand picture of the human alternatives of working inside the noisy chaos to mitigate it or standing outside, constructing patterns to account for it. Man is just such a two-storied house of consciousness, and in the configuration of that shattered window and Callisto's paralysis, Pynchon suggests the potential peril of all pattern-making, or plot-detecting. Callisto cannot save the bird— he cannot transfer his heat energy to it, presaging the time when there is no more energy available to be transformed into work. But where Callisto is in the grip of the hothouse of the past, Meatball is engulfed in the riotous present. Pynchon would return to these two figures in the characters of Stencil and Benny Profane in *V* (1963).

Norbert Wiener said that it is always likely to be a problem whether we interpret whatever it is that makes for disorganization in nature as merely a neutral absence of order (the Augustinian view, he calls this), or as a positively malign force dedicated to the annihilation of order. He adds, 'The Augustinian position has always been difficult to maintain. It tends under the slightest perturbation to break down into a covert Manichaeanism.' This is crucial for an understanding of many contemporary American writers who are either sufficiently perturbed themselves, or are aware of the perturbations in the characters they write about, to have made the tendency to begin to see the world in Manichaean terms a recurrent motif in recent novels, Pynchon's above all. The temptation to regard all signs of entropy in the world as the work of hostile agents is like the demonism in the work of William Burroughs. Both represent attempts to 'give destruction a name or face' (to take a phrase from Pynchon's short story 'Mercy and Mortality in Venice'), and both those reactions to the world reveal themselves in the individual as a continuous leaning towards paranoia.

One aspect of paranoia is the tendency to imagine plots around you; this is also the novelist's occupation and there is clearly a relationship between making fictions and imagining conspiracies. The difference is between consciousness in control of its own inventions, and consciousness succumbing to its inventions until they present themselves as perceptions. But the line between these two states of mind is inevitably a narrow one and a great deal of oscillation and overlap is common. Adopting Wiener's terms we can say that for a novelist looking back over the first half of the twentieth century the 'Augustinian' vision of a world deprived of order in some parts more than in others could easily shade into the 'Manichaean' vision of something demonically at work to annihilate all order, with phenomena such as Hitler and the atom bomb only among its more obvious agents.

Pynchon, I think, understands this very well and, while his novel V contains a variety of plot-makers, he is in no sense committed to the plots they might make. It would be too glib to say that his is an 'Augustinian' novel about 'Manichaean' people; it would also be misleading, since the novelist is clearly inwardly affected by the Manichaeanism of his characters, just as he is by the pessimistic theories of Henry Adams. But he manages to preserve his distance, particularly by locating the main plotting instinct in one character, Stencil. He is the man who is trying to make the connections and links, and put together the story which might well have been Pynchon's novel. By standing back from this dedicated pursuer and collector of notes towards a supreme fiction, Pynchon is able to explore the plot-making instinct itself. To this end his own novel has to appear to be relatively unplotted — leaving chunks of data around, as it were, for Stencil to try to interrelate. Inevitably this is only an illusion and we need not belabour the point that when a strange bit of Maltese history turns up, Pynchon put it there, and when Stencil finds a clue it is only because his author laid it for him. The point is that by taking bits of history from different countries at different times during this century and putting them in the novel with no linear or causal relationship, Pynchon is able to explore the possibility that the plots men see may be their own inventions. The further implication of this — that such things as the concentration camps may be simply meaningless accidents — is responsible for the sudden depths of horror in the book.

The narrative material consists of episodes from history since 1899, and episodes in the lives of various people living in contemporary America called, as a group, the Whole Sick Crew. Just as the historical episodes tend to focus on various sieges, and chaotic violent events preceding or involved in the two world wars, so the episodes connected with modern America tend to focus on wild parties sinking into chaos and exhaustion which seem to reveal morphological similarities with the historical events not otherwise directly related to them. The character most concerned with the historical dimension is Stencil, while the character who experiences most of the modern extension is Benny Profane. The two characters come together and finally travel to Malta at the time of the Suez crisis. Chronological linking is avoided. Of the sixteen chapters, ten are about Profane and the Whole Sick Crew. Five interpolate accounts gathered from various sources or documents of historical episodes, starting with some espionage connected with the Fashoda incident, going on to disturbances in Florence connected with a Venezuelan rebellion and more international plotting and spying, then to a native uprising in German South-West Africa in 1922 which results in a long siege-party, then to an account of the siege of Malta during the Second World War, then back to Paris in 1913 on the brink of the outbreak of the First. The last chapter brings past and present together on Malta, while an Epilogue goes back to 1919 when there were riots on the island. The presence of these apparently random episodes from twentieth-century history is largely due to the research work of Stencil. His father was a British agent who died off the coast of Malta in 1919; he was in some way involved with a woman referred to as V. and in pursuing this figure through her various incarnations, or differing roles and disguises, Stencil finds that he is astray in the history of our century, as Benny, looking for no one, wanders up and down the streets of the present.

We may start by noting that while the endlessly ramifying and superimposed plots of the book defy summary, the general theme of the operation of entropy on every level serves to relate the disparate temporal and geographic material the book contains. Every situation reveals some new aspect of decay and decline, some move further into chaos or nearer death. The book is full of dead landscapes of every kind—from the garbage heaps of the modern world to the lunar barrenness of the actual desert. On every side there is evidence of the 'assertion of the Inanimate'. Renaissance cities seem to lose their glow and become leaden; great buildings progress towards dust; a man's car is disintegrating under tons of garage rubble. Benny Profane's late feeling that 'things never should have come this far' is appropriately ominous if you allow the first word sufficient emphasis. For the proliferation of inert things is another way of hastening the entropic process. On all sides the environment is full of hints of exhaustion, extinction, dehumanization; and *V.* is a very American novel in as much as one feels that instead of the characters living *in* their environment, environment lives *through* the characters, who thereby tend to become figures illustrating a process. At one point Benny Profane is having an imaginary conversation with an automaton named SHROUD (synthetic human, radiation output determined). Such automata, composed entirely of inanimate materials, not only offer a worrying parody of human identity, but seem to embody a prophecy that they represent the condition to which human identity is moving in this century. Benny tells SHROUD that he ought to be junked like an old car. SHROUD willingly concedes that such will be his graveyard, but counters with reference to the pictures of the corpses stacked like junk that came out of the German concentration camps. Benny objects that Hitler was crazy. SHROUD asks, '"Has it occurred to you there may be no more standards for crazy or sane, now that it's started?"' And Benny answers, '"What, for Christ's sake?"' What the 'it' is that has started (if there is an 'it'), what common process links remote imperialist incidents with contemporary automation, tourism, Hitler, and the Whole Sick Crew (if there is any linking common process) — this is what the whole book is about.

One common background is the accelerating release of power which Adams spoke of and foresaw. Man's ingenuity in this respect is kept in view by references to trains, planes, ships, all kinds of mechanical appliances and weapons of war. At the same time all these inventions are often more productive of destruction than anything else. At one point Pynchon simply lists the disasters recorded for a short period of time in an almanac, prefacing it with the generalization that at this time 'the world started to run more and more afoul of the inanimate.' This points to perhaps the most inclusive theme of the book: not that man returns to the inanimate, since that is the oldest of truths, but that twentieth-century man seems to be dedicating himself to the annihilation of all animateness on a quite unprecedented scale, and with quite unanticipated inventiveness. If the 'it' is anything, it is entropy turned Manichaean and working through a whole spectrum of agents; most spectacularly through figures like Hitler who turned millions of people into junk, but also through many minor figures, such as a doctor who favours the introduction of inert substances into the living face.

But Pynchon would scarcely have needed to write so intricate a

novel if his only intention was to show a graph of increasing destructiveness manifest in recent history. As he indicates, you can cull
that from an almanac. What he shows — and here the juxtaposition
of the historical and the personal dimensions is vital — is a growing
tendency, discernible on all levels and in the most out-of-the-way
pockets of modern history, for people to regard or use other people
as objects, and, perhaps even more worryingly, for people to regard
themselves as objects. There is in evidence a systematic and assi-
duously cultivated dehumanization of the human *by* the human. Just
as the tourists in the book cut themselves off from the reality of the
lands they pass through by burying themselves in Baedeker versions,
so do most of the characters avoid confronting the human reality
of other people, and of themselves, by all manner of depersonalizing
strategies. If one theme of the book is the acceleration of entropy,
another is the avoidance of human relationships based on reciprocal
recognition of the reality of the partner. Instead of the recognitions
of love, there are only the projected fantasies of lust. These two
phenomena — entropy and the dread of love — may well be linked in
some way, for they show a parallel movement towards the state of
lasting inanimateness, and share an aspiration to eradicate consciousness and revert to thing-status.

One agent in the book is killed because of a fatal lapse into
humanity, an act of recognition. The description of his death points
to a threshold which is a crucial one for the figures in the book.
'Vision must be the last to go. There must be a nearly imperceptible
line between an eye that reflects and an eye that receives.' Death is
the moment when that line is irrevocably crossed, but the book shows
innumerable ways in which that line is crossed while the body is
still technically alive, thus producing a mobile object which reflects
but does not receive. That this is related to the narcissistic habit of
turning people into reflectors of one's own fantasies and obsessions
is alluded to by a series of references to mirrors, culminating in the
episode called 'V. in love' which describes a Lesbian affair conducted
entirely by mirrors. What unspeakable cruelties are made possible
when that line is crossed and both self and others are experienced as
inanimate objects, the various unpleasant scenes of sadism and sado-
masochism, which recur throughout the book, serve to dramatize.
The general falling away from the human which is under way is
underlined by the transformations in the lady V. In her appearances
she becomes gradually less human and more composed of dead
matter. When she is finally dismantled, it is suggested that she was
found to be composed of entirely artificial objects. Imagining V. as
she might be at the present moment, Stencil envisages a completely

plastic figure, triggered into action by miracles of technology. This is in line with the more general tendency towards fetishism and away from humanity detectable throughout.

The way in which people avoid their own reality (or are refused it) is paralleled in the book by the way in which events are experienced as staged episodes in a meaninglessly repetitious masquerade. On the political, as on the personal, level role-playing has pre-empted the possibility of real experience, leaving only symbols and games. History is as 'stencillized' as the people who compose it, and the result is the theatricalization of reality on a massive scale. Thus history becomes a scenario which the participants are unable to rewrite or avoid. Once again, we find a vision of people being trapped inside an unreality which seems to be the result of some nameless conspiratorial fabrication; humans are akin to props in a cruel and dehumanizing play by author or authors unknown. (Of course Pynchon is aware of the additional irony that these characters are also caught up in a play arranged by *him* — the affliction of his characters is the condition of his form.)

In this world there is very little chance of any genuine communication. Language has suffered an inevitable decline in the mouths of these stencillized and objectified figures. Rachel Owlglass, the figure who more than any other seems to harbour a genuine capacity for love, is reduced to speaking to her car in 'MG words'; while Benny Profane, who seems to want to love, feels his vocabulary is made up of nothing but wrong words. A foreign girl called Paola is presented as a person who has retained her capacity for direct emotion, and she seems to speak 'Nothing but proper nouns. The girl lived proper nouns. Persons, places. No things. Had anyone told her about things?' In a world in which the human is rapidly being replaced by things, this quaint linguistic limitation offers the possibility of an enviable immunity from the tendency towards a reification of people which is inherent in the prevailing language. At the same time, this kind of restricted language may be put to a very different purpose, as the Whole Sick Crew reveals. They play at verbalizing endless possible versions of things. They use mainly proper nouns, literary allusions, philosophical abstractions, and they put them together like building-blocks. 'This sort of arranging and rearranging was Decadence, but the exhaustion of all possible permutations was death.' There is an heretical sect in a Borges story which seeks to hasten the advent of God's rule on earth by trying to exhaust all the possible permutations of sins; there are similar attempts to cover all permutations in the lexical sphere, in his Library at Babel. Just so, the Whole Sick Crew seems to be hastening the entropic decline of language as a vehicle for the transmission of significant information, by playing with all its permutations irrespective of what reference any of the permutations may or may not have to reality. One result of this decline in language is that people scarcely manage to converse in this book, and if they do they fail to establish any real contact.

But if the characters in the book seldom truly talk to each other, they often look at each other. As might be expected, various forms of voyeurism are part of the normal behaviour patterns of a world where any attempt at human inter-subjectivity has been replaced by the disposition to regard people as objects—inside the field of vision but outside the range of sympathy, if indeed any such range exists. Eyes, straining or blank and dead, are emphasized throughout. The sailor whose main joy is to photograph his friends while they are having sexual intercourse is only one of many whose most intense relationships to reality are detached and impotent stares. Another reason why so many characters live in, and by, mirrors, and indeed at one point are said to be living in 'mirror time', is that they experience life only as spectacle. Voyeurism is another way of evading true selfhood and denying or avoiding the possibility of love. Most of the characters 'retreat' from the threat of love when it presents itself, and even the sympathetic Benny wastes himself in avoiding dependencies, and disengaging himself from any field of gathering emotional force. It might be added that Pynchon finds it difficult to suggest what genuine love would be like in this world. Some characters from older civilizations and cultures seem to have retained an ability to love. But the guarded maxim of the black jazz musician, McClintic Sphere, 'Keep cool, but care,' is about as much genuine emotion as the book seems to allow. As such it is unconvincing. This may be part of the vision of the book: in this world people have lost contact with the forms and modes of loving. At the same time it is in part a result of Pynchon's stylistic and formal decisions. You cannot render great emotions in a comic-strip, and 'Keep cool, but care,' is just such bubble talk or the sort of slogan-jargon mongered by advertisements. In proximity to the multiple parodic references which the book contains, any potentially serious emotion is bound to turn into its own caricature and join the masquerade as a costumed sentimentality.

Moreover, in the main, people seek to avoid caring. One girl specifically yearns to become like a rock, and a state of emotional impermeability is sought by many others. Just as the main characters move towards the rock of Malta, so more generally the human race seems to be hastening to return to 'rockhood'. Indeed in Malta we read that manhood is increasingly defined in terms of rockhood. It is part of the basic ambiguity of Malta as described in this book that while on the one level it is an image of an island of life under siege, attacked by the levelling bombs of the Germans, and constantly eroded by the sea, on another level it is an image of a central point of inanimate rock and death drawing people back to that inert state. The Epilogue describes how the ship carrying Stencil's father was suddenly sucked under by a freak waterspout just off Malta, leaving a dead level sea which gave no sign of what now lies beneath the flat surface – this concludes the book.

One way and another, then, everything is sinking. Mehemet, a sage friend of Stencil's father, points out cheerfully, '"The only change is towards death ... Early and late we are in decay."' To Stencil's suggestion that the world recently contracted a fatal disease leading to the First World War, Mehemet replies with more Oriental largeness of perspective, ' "Is old age a disease ... The body slows down, machines wear out, planets falter and loop, sun and stars gutter and smoke. Why say a disease? Only to bring it down to a size you can look at and feel comfortable."' We are always in decay: the question is, is there a plot in the universal rot? Stencil, son of Stencil, is, like his father, inclined to detect plots. A dentist in the book named Eigenvalue regards Stencil's belief in a plot as being like an amalgam to fill 'a breach in the protective enamel'. He reflects that teeth do indeed decay, but that is no reason to conceive of some conscious organization conspiring against the life of the pulp. 'Yet we have men like Stencil who must go about grouping the world's random caries into cabals.' It is precisely Stencil's compulsion to group caries into cabals which makes him one of the central figures in the book, and we should now consider his dominant obsession.

This obsession is the quest for V. V. is an elusive female spy/ anarchist who appears in one of her multiple identities in all these episodes; she once seduced Stencil's father, thus becoming, it seems, Stencil's mother. Her names have varied – Virginia, Victoria, Veronica Manganese, Vera Meroving – and at the end Stencil leaves for Sweden to follow up a remote clue connected with one Mme Viola. Stencil's quest is thus linear through time; but as the book shows – and indeed as Stencil realizes as he turns this way and that, following up peripheral clues – there are innumerable Vs, a point made on the first page of the book which shows a V-shaped cluster of innumerable smaller Vs. There is the jazz club called the V-note, patronized by the Whole Sick Crew; Veronica the sewer rat, so named by Father Fairing during his efforts to convert the rats of New York to Roman Catholicism, and chosen by him as his first saint and mistress; Queen Victoria, Venezuela, Valetta, the strange land of Vheissu and volcanoes like Vesuvius; it is the shape of spread thighs, the initial of Venus but also the initial for Vergeltungswaffe (retaliation weapons).* So from one point of view Stencil has far too much to go on, since he is bound to find clues everywhere—a fact he recognizes near the end: 'V. by this time was a remarkably scattered concept.' Indeed, as this 'concept' expands to include ever more manifestations of V., and as opposites such as love and death, the political right and left, start to converge in this inclusiveness, it points to that ultimate disappearance of differences and loss of distinctions which is the terminal state of the entropic process. If V. can mean everything it means nothing.

On the other hand Stencil really has very little to go on. Most of what he has is inference. 'He doesn't know who she is, nor what she is.' Near the end the suspicion is strengthened that all it adds up to is 'the recurrence of an initial and a few dead objects'. Stencil himself is aware that although he pursues V. as a libertine pursues spread thighs (the comparison is explicit), his quest may all be 'an adventure of the mind, in the tradition of *The Golden Bough*, or *The White Goddess*'. Stencil's father had strange fever dreams of exploring for something in his own brain. Stencil is the copy of his father; the quest is his legacy. The historical melodrama of international interconnections which he puts together may be only the map of his own obsessions. At the same time, the sieges and wars were real enough, with or without mysterious links, and Stencil is representative enough to be called 'the century's child'.

He is also representative of many American heroes in as much as he was powerfully attracted to sleep and inertia, wandering around in a slothful directionlessness, before he came across references to V. in his father's papers. In the suggestiveness of this entirely documentary stimulus, Stencil finds his motive for motion. Out of a few cryptic clues he maps the quest he needs to keep him awake; his terror is that the quest may succeed, returning him again to 'half-consciousness'. 'Funking out, finding V., he didn't know which he was most afraid of, V. or sleep. Or whether they were two versions of the same thing.' The point at which all versions merge into the same thing signifies the final entropic stillness: Stencil's strategy is, 'Approach

---

* As Dan Hausdorff suggests in his helpful article 'Thomas Pynchon's Multiple Absurdities' (*Wisconsin Studies in Contemporary Literature*, vii 1966) Pynchon's *V.* undoubtedly owes something to Henry Adams's interest in the Virgin-Venus symbols, just as his using the name of Yoyodyne for the company run by Bloody Chiclitz is probably an intentional echo of Adams's use of the dynamo to symbolize the amoral power being released in the modern world.

and avoid.' He suspects that he needs 'a mystery, any sense of pursuit to keep active a borderline metabolism', but such self-knowledge does not obviate the need to pursue the phantom he has at least half-created. The book recognizes that such fantasies may be necessary to maintaining consciousness and purposive motion; yet it reveals the solipsism that is implicit in them as well, for one of the subjects of Pynchon's book is the inability of people to love anyone outside their own fantasy projections.

Stencil is the key figure — one can hardly speak of characters — in the book. The O.E.D. defines a stencil as 'a hole in a card which when washed over with colour leaves a figure'; 'stencilling' is defined as 'a process by which you can produce patterns and designs'. Like the lady V. who shows inexhaustible dexterity in handling her different appearances, Stencil is pluralistic in his projection of himself. He also goes in for disguises, finding some relief from the pain of his dilemma in 'impersonation'. Like children and like Henry Adams in the *Education* (Pynchon again makes the comparison explicit) Stencil always refers to himself in the third person. This helps 'Stencil' appear as only one among a repertoire of identities, thus he turns himself into an object, possibly out of some regressive instinct, a dread of taking on full self-hood. He thinks of himself as 'quite purely He who looks for V. (and whatever impersonations that might involve)'. This definition may mean that he is in fact a vacancy, filled in with the colours of his obsession, not a self, but in truth a stencil. And all his techniques of self-duplication and self-extension may be construed as protective screens for avoiding direct engagement with reality.

Stencil's obsession is with a structure of inferences based on an old dossier, cold clues, scraps and fragments from history's littoral which he has transformed into the strange flowers of his fantasy. One character believes, 'that V. was an obsession after all, and that such an obsession is a hothouse: constant temperature, windless, too crowded with particoloured sports, unnatural blooms.' Like Callisto in 'Entropy', Stencil lives in a hothouse of hermetically-sealed fantasy where the past is arrested, as in a museum, immobilized in memory pictures to create an inner climate impervious to the inclemency of outer weather. Paradoxically, those objects which fed Stencil's obsession and gave him an illusory sense of vitality sealed him off as well, turning him into a stencil with a hothouse mind. Like a stencil he will admit no configurations of experience that cannot be shaped into the pattern of his fantasy. Like a hothouse, his identity is a protected enclosure, given definition by the exotic growths artificially fostered within it.

If Stencil is trapped in the hothouse of the past, Benny Profane is astray in the streets of the present. The book opens with him walking down a street and we last see him running down a street in Malta. The street is his natural domain, for he is a rootless wanderer, as unaware of clues and indifferent to patterns as Stencil is obsessed by them. He says expressly that he has learned nothing from his peregrinations up and down the streets of the world, except perhaps to fear them. They fuse into a 'single abstracted street' which causes him nightmares without yielding him insights. The only job he can do – and that not well – is street repair work. Devoid of all sense of positive direction he reacts passively to any puff of momentum that happens to touch him; by himself he cannot initiate or construct anything – no projects, no relationships, no dreams. His movement is a long flight from nowhere in particular to nowhere in particular.

Himself rather a faded copy of the traditional *picaro* and *schlemiel* figures combined, he is almost a cartoon reduction of another of the century's children, for if Stencil is he who searches for V., Profane is he who experiences the street; 'The street of the 20th Century, at whose far end or turning – we hope – is some sense of home or safety. But no guarantees ... But a street we must walk.' Benny seems at the start to be a lonely seeker, hungering for some human authenticity in an inanimate world; he emerges, however, as a participator in the very process he seemed to oppose. He belongs with the Whole Sick Crew, and, despite his *schlemiel* status, his Buster Keaton-like inability to avoid running foul of a world full of things, he can scarcely be considered a victim. If anything, he simply is, as Dickens said of one of his characters, 'of the street, streety'.

It is in the street that the various destructive energies involved in the history of this century erupt – from riots in Florence or Malta to a gang fight in contemporary New York. Throughout the various street episodes, historical and contemporary, there is the sustained feeling that the walls, buildings and shopfronts are an insubstantial façade, that the street itself and all man-made structures are temporary illusions. ('The city is only the desert in disguise,' thinks one character in Cairo. 'Nothing was coming. Nothing was already here.') The last account of violent mob action in the book is situated in Strada Reale, but the idea of a royal street is a very ironic one by this time.

The fact that it is in the street that revolutionary mobs pursue their demands for change prompts Stencil's father to write in his journal: 'we carry on the business of this century with an intolerable double vision. Right and Left; the hothouse and the street. The Right can only live and work hermetically, in the hothouse of the past, while outside the Left prosecute their affairs in the streets by manipulated mob violence. And cannot live but in the dreamscape of the future.' The implication of this is that all political thinking—and by extension all man's mental projections—is either a dream of the past or a dream of the future. By this account man himself can never properly occupy present time. The street and the hothouse are the dreams by which man avoids confronting that nothingness which is the shapeless truth behind the structured fantasy of human history. As with so many apparent opposites, the street and the hothouse meet and merge in V. She is equally at home in both of them. And almost her last reported words are: '"How pleasant to watch Nothing."'

An important part of the intricate spatial geography of the book is that area which lies under the street—the sewers in which Benny Profane hunts alligators under New York, in which Father Fairing converts and seduces his rats. References to channels and tunnels occur in the description of the strange land of Vheissu and the subway travel in modern New York. Hints at the possible existence of an inherited reservoir of primordial knowledge suggest that a deliberate Jungian dimension has been added. The notion that the unconscious nourishes art, even if the unconscious is comparable to a sort of primeval sewer, and that there is much to be gained by descending into our dreams, is so customary by now that one can see that Pynchon has gone some way to turning it into dark farce— Benny and the alligators. At the same time he seems to want to preserve the notion that somehow it is more 'real' under the street than in it. When Benny finally has to end his job we read: 'What peace there had been was over. He had to come back to the surface, the dream-street.'

The far-ranging geography of the book provides a composite image of the various areas of human consciousness. The street is the zone of the waking, planning consciousness which, unable to endure the meaninglessness of the absolute present, projects plans into the future or finds plans in the past. The hothouse is the realm of memory where the mind is sealed up in the secretions of its reveries over the past. The sewer or under-the-street (also compared to under the sea) is that area of dream, the unconscious, perhaps the ancestral memory, in which one may find a temporary peace or oblivion, and into which the artist must descend, but where fantasy can run so rampant that you may start seeing rats as saints and lovers if you remain down there too long. Indeed all three areas suggest the human compulsion or need to construct fantasies, as though each level of consciousness was another form of dreaming.

The modes of motion which prevail in the street are yo-yoing (in the present) and tourism (in the past). The historical episodes are full of references to people living in a 'Baedeker world'. Tourists are 'the Street's own'. The north European tourists who create a *bierhalle* in Egypt 'in their own image' which results in 'a parody of home', are only revealing the tourists' flight from reality even while in the act of travelling; they too live among illusions, inhabitants of their own stencillings, or the stencillings put out by Baedeker. The particular futility of that sort of 'touring' movement is echoed in the activity of yo-yoing practised by various members of the Whole Sick Crew, and particularly by Benny Profane. It consists of shuttling back and forth on the subway for long periods, the ultimate expression of movement without destination — a parody of purpose, we might say. Less literally it covers all the meaningless movements of their parties and hectic, reversible driftings. (More cosmically, the planets are said to yo-yo around the sun.) When Stencil (super-tourist) and Profane (super yo-yo) converge on Malta without quite understanding their motives for doing so, we read: 'Malta alone drew them, a clenched fist around a yo-yo string.' The illusory purposiveness of Stencil's travels, and the manifest purposelessness of Profane's meanderings, both serve to illuminate the condition of movement bereft of all significance except the elemental one of post-poning inanimateness. Both modes of motion, in fact, accelerate entropy, just as they both serve to bring Stencil and Benny Profane to the rock of Malta.

As well as writing about a quester and a drifter, Pynchon writes about all kinds of spies and agents. Their epistemological stance — looking for possible clues to possible plots — is only a projection of that of the novelist himself. Perhaps, indeed, they create the patterns of hostility they set out to trace; perhaps, too, does the novelist. Stencil's ingenious linked detections spread back in time and across space. Is this creative vision which sees a truth beneath the drifting contingencies of life; or is it a paranoid fantasy, an obsession akin to an oblivion? If the latter, then is Benny Profane's unco-ordinated empiricism of the eye, which looks out and sees no plots and learns nothing, true vision? We can hardly expect to adjudicate finally between them.

The preoccupation with signs, codes, signals, patterns, plots, etc., permeates the book so thoroughly that it — the preoccupation, not just the signals and patterns themselves — could be said to be the subject of the book, tying up with the central question, is entropy neutral or malign? From the opening scene in the bar when drunken feet move about in the damp sawdust 'scribbling it into alien hiero-glyphics' to the final barely uttered question as to whether there is a 'third force' manipulating V. and her opponents alike, we are never far away from the feeling that there is something afoot, something going on 'beneath', a code or clue to be deciphered, a plot or portent to be dreaded. Maps abound, whether of the New York sewers or Florence and the Uffizi, or German South-West Africa, and mapping is of course only another form of plotting. It is suggested that for a brief space of time when two of the characters are young and in love 'they seemed to give up external plans, theories and codes ... to indulge in being simply and purely young,' but this idyll of un-patterned emotional directness is momentary, and most of the people at one time or another are involved rather in constructing a plot or a myth.

The various agents and plotters in the historical episodes while planning their own cabals are always worried that they may in fact be taking part in a larger cabal of which they have no knowledge. Stencil always finds some form of V. connected with some kind of conspiracy, if not a plotter then the cause of plots. Whatever V. might be, Stencil affirms 'that his quarry fitted in with The Big One, the century's master cabal'. Stencil's father had found that if people cannot find some sort of explanation for 'this abstract entity The Situation' they 'simply run amok'. He is implying that for most people, worse than the idea of a master cabal is the notion of no plots at all. One character writes that life really has only one single lesson to teach: 'that there is more accident to it than a man can ever admit to in a lifetime and stay sane.' That is why Stencil sees planned cabals in random caries—paradoxically it might be his paranoia that keeps him sane. It is suitable that the last clue he picks up, which will keep him moving on (approaching and avoiding), this time to Stockholm, is about a certain Mme Viola, who is an 'oneiro-mancer and hypnotist'. She will not only be able to divine his dreams, but also induce and prolong them.

In one of the incidents set in South-West Africa there is a character named Mondaugen who has the job of studying 'sferic' signals. At first they come through as mere noise, but then he thinks he detects a regularity of patterning which might be 'a kind of code'. Out of some instinctive wariness he holds back from trying to break the code, but someone else works out a solution. Extracting certain signals from the overall noise, he demonstrates that they add up to Mondaugen's own name, plus the statement DIE WELT IST ALLES DAS DER FALL IST. This of course is the opening proposition in Wittgen-stein's *Tractatus* (a proposition, incidentally, which seems to haunt contemporary American writers). As a coded message it would be the supreme irony, like discovering that the secret is that there is no secret. The assertion that the world is everything that is the case repudiates the very notion of plots, and arguably leaves things and events standing in precisely describable inexplicability. As the book shows, human instinct pulls in the other direction: towards cabalism, or demonism, or projected fantasies, and away from the rarified objective clarities attainable through linguistic analysis. People would rather detect an 'ominous logic' in things than no omens at all. In this book, even the most jumbled atmospheric noises must contain some kind of signal, even if it is only your own name and a bleak tautology. What kind of world it might be to live in if we could love other people instead of our own fantasies, the book does not pretend to say.

The question of whether or not there are meaningful shapes to be detected is also raised by a number of references to geometric shapes and calculations. In a Robbe-Grillet type of episode, a barmaid named Hanne is uncertain whether or not there is a triangular stain on the plate she is washing. She is experiencing as a temporary puzzle what for Stencil is a lifelong dilemma. According to how she focuses her eyes or tilts the plate, the stain changes its shape— crescent, trapezoid—and sometimes fades away altogether. 'Was the stain real? She didn't like its color. The color of her headache ... ' The problem of the book is here in miniature. Perhaps the changing shapes we see on the external blankness are the shifting projections of our own 'headaches' or subjective pressures; on the other hand there might actually be a stain on the plate. The description of the shape in geometric terms is of course deliberate; throughout the book we constantly come across specific angles, intersections, details of linear arrangements and numerically charted positions. It is one of the most enduring of all human dreams (or needs) to feel that we live among geometry. Rather than confront shapeless space, we introduce lines and angles into it. Surrounded by the desert, man builds a pyramid. That would be another way of saying what *V.* is all about.

Related to references to geometry (and chess) are numerous references to the aesthetic patternings of music and painting. The notion of painting being a compensatory activity for the general decline of things is taken up overtly when Mehemet tells a rather unlikely tale of coming across a strange sight in the middle of the sea—a man 'alone on the sea at nightfall, painting the side of a sink-ing ship'. The implication is made explicit. We do cover the blank surfaces of our sinking world, and then live within our paintings; as D. H. Lawrence said, we live in the paintings we put on the under-side of our umbrellas. For Lawrence this was a suffocation, a deprivation, and he considered it the artist's job to come along and slash a gap in the protective umbrella and let in reality. But in Pynchon's world there is a more ominous feeling that if you did cut through the painting a something or a nothing more frightening might be revealed. In one of the historical episodes there is a plot to steal Botticelli's 'Birth of Venus'. The thief is entranced by the 'gorgeous surface' of the painting, but as he starts to cut it out of the frame a great horror grows in him and he abandons the project. This horror at stripping away the coloured surface is connected with something that a character named Hugh Godolphin told him about the strange land of Vheissu, and we should now consider that unmapped country.

Hugh Godolphin found Vheissu on one of his surveying trips for the British Army; his description of the journey and the land itself reads like a mixture of Borges and Conrad. There are no maps to Vheissu, but it is the country which is really at the heart of the book. As Godolphin describes it to Victoria, it might seem like any other remote region except for the changing colours which are ' "its raiment, perhaps its skin" '. When Victoria asks what is beneath, he admits that he wondered whether the place had a soul. What this meant for Hugh Godolphin apparently was a determination somehow to return to Vheissu and find ' "what was beneath her skin" '. Making his way to the pole he digs for his answer, and when he does penetrate the surface what he finds is — ' "Nothing ... It was Nothing I saw." ' He continues his account: ' "If Eden was the creation of God, God only knows what evil created Vheissu. The skin which had wrinkled through my nightmares was all there had ever been. Vheissu itself, a gaudy dream. Of what the Antarctic in this world is closest to: a dream of annihilation." ' That last definition is suitably vague as to whether the whole place is Godolphin's dream, or whether in itself it is a dream of annihilation. What we are given is a notional place with a dazzlingly coloured surface covering Nothing, or perhaps worse, a void of icy negation. The status of Vheissu as a sort of dream is underlined when Godolphin later on in the century complains that Vheissu is gone and impossible to bring back. He means his own particular kind of Vheissu, his private dream: ' "our Vheissus are no longer our own, or even confined to a circle of friends; they're public property." ' It is part of the intention of the book to suggest that the world may now be engaged in making actual a mass dream of annihilation, submitting reality to a nihilistic fantasy.

In Malta, in a final talk with Godolphin, V. reveals her similarity to Vheissu further; for, having expressed her delight at watching Nothing, she goes on to say how much she would like to have a whole wardrobe of different shaped feet in a rainbow range of colours. V. *is* all those constantly changing coloured shapes which make up the dazzling and enchanting surface of Vheissu. She is also the void beneath the decoration, the Nothing at the heart of the dream. We need all those coloured dreams to get us along the street — which may also be a dream. At the start we see Benny walking down East Main Street, underneath a row of lamps 'receding in an asymmetric V to the east where it's dark and there are no more bars'. We last see Benny apparently making a bid to leave the street for the last time, this time in Malta. 'Presently, sudden and in silence, all illumination in Valletta, houselight and streetlight, was extinguished. Profane and Brenda continued to run through the abruptly absolute night, momentum alone carrying them towards the edge of Malta, and the Mediterranean beyond.' V. is whatever lights you *to* the end of the street: she is also the dark annihilation waiting *at* the end of the street.

What Pynchon manages to suggest is that the fantasies we build to help us to live represent, in fact, an infiltration of that death we think we are so eager to postpone. They represent an avoidance of reality, by substituting for it a fetishistic construction. One man in the book has a private planetarium which is a highly complex mechanism of moons and planets, pulleys and chains, and yet which is, after all, 'a parody of space'. If our constructed fantasies are effectively parodies of reality, then this has certain implications for the self-conscious author of the overall fiction of the book. For a particular literary style is a construction analogous to that private planetarium, a personal way of organizing things in space, and thus to some extent a parody of it. Of course there need not be any deliberate attempt to burlesque and ridicule reality present in the construction, and one does not readily think of Tolstoy or George Eliot as 'parodying' reality. The matter of attitude comes up here, and it is a distinctive trait of many contemporary American writers that they are very quick to be suspicious of any one stylistic version of reality and regard it as inescapably parodic.

In this connection we should note Pynchon's systematic stylistic evocation (often parodic) of previous writers as he deals with different episodes in different times and places. Conrad, Evelyn Waugh and Lawrence Durrell are in evidence in many of the historical and colonial episodes; Melville, Henry Adams, Nathanael West, Djuna Barnes, Faulkner and Dashiell Hammett are among the American writers whose work is in some way detectable; Joyce and Nabokov are clearly present in the way the book is organized; and there is one of Borges's mysterious kingdoms at the heart of the

172 CITY OF WORDS

book. This is not to suggest that the book is merely a pastiche, a collage of scrambled sources. Pynchon's point seems to be to remind the reader that there is no one writable 'truth' about history and experience, only a series of versions: it always comes to us 'stencillized'. In such a way he can indicate that he is well aware of the ambiguities of his own position, constructing another fiction and at the same time underlining the fallacies involved in all formal plottings and organizations of space.

In addition I think it is part of Pynchon's intention to demonstrate that the various styles of writers of this century who, in a sense, have imposed their private dreams on us are like those iridescent surfaces with which we adorn the walls of our galleries and cover the countries of our dreams. The attendant implication is that under all this decorative sheen there lies the cold truth of the void. One result of this is, I think, that Pynchon himself has written, no doubt deliberately, what amounts to a 'hollow' book. He brilliantly shows how man produces the painting on the side of the sinking ship; at the same time the detectable element of near-compulsive parody serves to call into question the value and validity of any one style—indeed of style itself. What is felt to be true is the emptiness under the coloured surface, the ice at the pole, the rock to which we all return, the final stillness of the level sea. The book itself is a 'dream of annihilation': it is Pynchon's Vheissu.

This rather ambiguous relationship to the multiple styles made available to the modern artist seems to be a very American preoccupation. As I have tried to suggest, the American writer at times seems to want to shed a style even while he is using it; this is perhaps indicative of a suspicious unwillingness to get too involved in anyone else's particular dream of reality. There is a passage in Nathanael West's *The Day of the Locust* which is instructive here. Tod Hackett is an artist working in Hollywood. The following is a meditation he has when he looks out at the great dumping ground for old sets and props from finished films.

This was the final dumping ground. He thought of Janvier's 'Sargasso Sea'. Just as that imaginary body of water was a history of civilization in the form of a marine junkyard, the studio lot was one in the form of a dream dump. A Sargasso of the imagination! And the dump grew continually, for there wasn't a dream afloat somewhere which wouldn't sooner or later turn up on it, having first been made photographic by plaster, canvas, lath and paint. Many boats sink and never reach Sargasso, but no dream ever entirely disappears. Somewhere it troubles some unfortunate person and some day, when that person has been sufficiently troubled, it will be reproduced on the lot.

Hollywood as the American dream factory is of course a well-known image by now; but this image of a great vista of discarded fantasies—a dream dump—seems to have a more than usual relevance and vividness for the American artist, particularly one like Pynchon who writes both to demonstrate the need for fictions and to impugn or revoke their validity. This attitude he mimes out in the process of writing his book, for, apparently at home in many styles, he finally trusts none. From one point of view both in content and form his book is a dream dump too.

It is worth pointing out here the connection between problems of narration and problems of identity in the contemporary American novel. In *V.* there is a character called Fausto, a man of letters who indeed writes his own book within the book. It is a sort of apologia, and he says this about his activity: 'We can justify any apologia simply by calling life a successive rejection of personalities.' Where Fausto divides himself up into 'successive identities' which he has taken on and then rejected, Pynchon takes on and rejects successive styles in his book. For both, this is a way of seeing past all the fictions which fix the world and the word in particular patterns and styles, and as such it is an activity very common among contemporary American writers. But whether man can live beyond all fictions, whether, even when faced by the pathos and mockery of the dream dump, it would be desirable, let alone possible, to put an end to man's addiction to fantasy, is not explored. Perhaps the advice of Mark Twain's Satan to mankind is the relevant consideration here— ' "Dream other dreams, and better!" '

> 'Americans start with the assumption that they are working with a *synthesized* system. We are driven by our own way of looking at things to synthesize almost everything.'
> (*The Silent Language*, Edward T. Hall)

The synthesizing instinct that Hall refers to in these words is obviously not limited to America. But in stressing what he sees as a peculiarly American compulsion to synthesize environmental data into a system—a need perhaps related to the fact that in America the many patterns, visible and invisible, which constitute the determinants of a culture, are less familiar and less established and articulated than elsewhere—Hall provides a good point of departure for a consideration of Pynchon's second novel, *The Crying of Lot 49* (1965). It is a short, curiously lyrical novel which forms what amounts to an addendum to *V*. Oedipa Maas is a girl like Rachel Owlglass, willing to try to sustain at least the illusion of love, but finding herself in a world where people will not share in this attempt. Indeed they evade it in a variety of ways. At the same time she is involved in a quest like Stencil's, a compulsive and widening effort of 'synthesizing' which may be hallucination and may be discovery. The novel starts when she learns that she has been named as an executrix of the will of an old lover, Pierce Inverarity, a tycoon whose holdings and enterprises in California turn out to be almost limitless. Before he died he had the habit of calling her up from unknown distances and places and speaking to her in a range of assumed and bewilderingly differing voices—from comic tones to simulated Fascistic threats. His will, as it transpires, 'speaks' in comparably multiple ambiguities, and as Oedipa tries to discover the meaning of the will, in a sense her inheritnce, she enacts, by analogy, a quest into the meaning of that larger heritage called America.

The strangeness of the will leads her to become a cryptologist, in an unending effort to discover whether the will itself contains a code which she has to interpret; or whether in fact the will has been tampered with and a false code inserted in order to distract her from discovering the revelations of the will and the truth about Inverarity Holdings. What she discovers, or seems to discover, is an elaborate series of scattered clues which when 'synthesized' all point to the existence of a strange secret system called The Tristero. This she traces back to sixteenth-century Europe when it started as a rival group to the Thurn and Taxis Postal System, later coming over to America at the time of the Civil War and ever since then working secretly against the public communications system through an organization called W.A.S.T.E. (We Await Silent Tristero's Empire). She discovers a great deal of evidence, but it is possible that it has all been planted for her to discover. Her quest involves the scrutiny of many documents, including editions, revisions, variants, textual corruptions and obvious counterfeits; but she cannot, and at one point will not, attempt to verify the status and source of the documents, for they too may have been put in her way through bookshops and university people all somehow connected to Inverarity Holdings.

It is clear that Oedipa has something of the instinct to discern, or suspect, the presence of patterns of revelation in the local landscape before she comes into contact with the estate and The Tristero clues. Driving into San Narcisco, the layout of streets and houses reminds her of a radio circuit—'there were to both outward patterns a hieroglyphic sense of concealed meaning, of an intent to communicate.' Similarly a map of one of Inverarity's housing developments flashed on to the TV screen seems to contain 'some promise of hierophany'. San Narcisco is where the whole possibility of The Tristero System begins to confront her, and bearing in mind that the good duke in a Jacobean play she sees, called *The Courier's Tragedy*, meets his death by kissing the feet of an image of Saint Narcissus which have been secretly poisoned, we may be alerted to the possible presence of a deathly narcissism such as we encountered in *V*.

One form of narcissism is to regard one's particular fantasy of the world as the definitive reality, and it is part of Oedipa's growing agony that she cannot be sure to what extent she herself is guilty of this. In the past she had, we gather, seen herself rather in the role of the maiden imprisoned in the tower, waiting for the knight who would invite her to let down her hair and so deliver her. She had let down her hair for Pierce 'but all that had then gone on between them had really never escaped the confinement of that tower.' Then follows a long and crucial passage based, once again, on a painting. The painting was entitled 'Borando el Manto Terrestre' and showed a number of girls imprisoned in a tower where they were working on an endless tapestry which they allowed to flow out of the windows, 'seeking hopelessly to fill the void'. In the painting 'the tapestry was the world': it contained all you could see outside the tower. The picture makes Oedipa cry. It makes her feel that although she may travel to Mexico she will never really escape from the tower of her lonely self.

The implications of this are worth pondering. The painting of the 'Embroiderers of the Terrestial Blanket' (no doubt owing something to Homer's Penelope, the Three Fates, and perhaps to Tennyson's Lady of Shalott) is of course a lyrical reflection of Oedipa's own embroidery work, those self-spun versions of reality with which she tries to fill the void. The fact that other creatures accept the embroidery as reality is an indication that many people live unquestioningly inside other people's versions or pictures. The sadness that overcomes Oedipa seems to stem from the sudden recognition that she will never escape from her own tapestries. We may take it as a psychological truth that perhaps the only way to escape from one's 'tower' is through the act of love. But then the passage goes on to describe Oedipa's recognition that the tower is incidental and that what keeps her where she is is 'formless magic, anonymous and malignant'. Here again we encounter that suspicion of a demonized reality, with evil as an inexplicable and anonymous force beaming in on people for no discoverable reason. Oedipa's need (and compulsion) is to give a face and a form to the power which she suspects is at work. But she has to work alone; there is no knight of deliverance in her story. She finds no love, or willingness to be loved.

The theme is picked up when we are given at least the suggestion that one object behind her discovery of what she comes to call The Tristero System was 'to bring to an end her encapsulation in her tower'. She comes to be haunted by 'the way it fitted, logically, together. As if ... there were revelation in progress all around her.' We learn that a lot of the revelation comes from Pierce's stamp collection which was often his substitute for her — 'thousands of little coloured windows into deep vistas of space and time'. This stamp collection is one of the central objects in the novel. It is this collection which is to be sold at the auction which ends the book, as Lot 49. As a 'lot' it is related to the used car lots which are an important part of the background of the book; as representing postage, and the whole idea of communication and information, the stamps are related to The Tristero System. As forming a series of little coloured windows on to exotic landscapes and designs which Pierce used as a substitute for his relationship with Oedipa, they are samples of all those dreams and substitute objects by which people avoid love and human relationships. The connection between rubbish and fantasy is close in this book, as the code cryptogram W.A.S.T.E. indicates.

What the book raises as the central and insoluble problem is whether Oedipa has discovered or hallucinated her synthesization which adds up to The Tristero System. Twice she goes into a ladies' toilet: once there is a mysterious message and sign on the wall, which adds fuel to her sensitized, inquiring mind; the second time there is a totally blank wall and she is somewhat unsettled at the absence of any calligraphy or drawing. Both the presence and the absence of signs is disturbing: which is almost the epistemological or metaphysical verdict of the book. As Oedipa gets deeper into her quest (which is, to repeat it, an attempt to find the real meaning of the estate) she finds she is losing all the men who might have loved or helped her — one to suicide, one to LSD, one to a depraved nymphet (three ways of evading reality, however one wants to appraise them). At the same time, the stimulus to fantasy, or synthesizing perception, grows in the form of proliferating clues.

At this point we should consider the nature of The Tristero System — whether it is real, or a staged hoax, or a private hallucination. It may be a genuine conspiracy, a second and hidden America; it may be a simulated conspiracy made up of genuinely perceptible clues and put on by real plotters for the bewilderment of Oedipa; or it may be a conspiracy of the imagination, which cannot stand too much nothingness or loneliness. When Oedipa first goes to see

Genghis Cohen, the eminent philatelist who helps to extract a lot of suggestive hints from the stamp collection, she sees him framed in a long succession of doorways, at the end of a seemingly endless series of receding rooms. It is an appropriate spatial metaphor for the way the Tristero plot looms at the terminal point of endlessly receding possible interpretations. Something of its ambiguity is suggested by its different spellings – Trystero/Tristero. But whatever its ultimate source and status, as a plot with its sources deep in history (real or imagined), it has certain recognizable features (or attributes ascribed to it).

It had its beginning in an attempt to rival the official mail which became a conspiracy to subvert the public systems of communication flow. According to clues and inferences provided by various characters, it was often connected with rebellions and wars – perhaps responsible for the French Revolution, perhaps linked in some way to Nazism, perhaps, coming nearer home, perpetuated through some of the extreme right-wing secret societies of California. One scholar tells Oedipa about a seventeenth-century sect called the Scurvhamites who held somewhat Manichaean beliefs. They became too fascinated with the negative forces of death working against God's creation: 'the glamorous prospect of annihilation coaxed them over.' The scholar suggests that this sect felt that Tristero could well symbolize 'the Other'. The secrecy and subversive acts of The Tristero System may have led people to regard it as representing some 'blind, automatic anti-God'. There is a strong suggestion that The Tristero System represents the process of entropy-turned-Manichaean, stealthily at work bringing disorder and death to the human community. (D.E.A.T.H. is another cryptogram discovered by Oedipa on her night wanderings – Don't Ever Antagonize The Horn.)

However, it is one of the ambiguities of the book which a reader may find as worrying and confusing as Oedipa, that The Tristero System might represent some secret, second America, which in many ways may be preferable or more genuine than the surface society. It is at night and away from the main highways that Oedipa really discovers the Tristero sign everywhere, 'Decorating each alienation, each species of withdrawal'. The Tristero System in its present-day manifestation is that underground America made up of all the 'disinherited' – racial minorities, homosexuals, the poor, the mad, the lonely and the frightened. It also contains revolutionaries from both extremes of the political spectrum who are crazily dedicated to the overthrow of the present society. These inhabitants of the night are both pathetic and frightening; as the concealed pun in Tristero suggests – it represents both the sadness and the terror of America.

But, as Oedipa comes to put it to herself, since the surface society and official communications system are so spiritually impoverished and dedicated to lies, since indeed so much of the visible America seems given over to denying human variety and turning people into objects, perhaps The Tristero is a network by which an unknown number of Americans are truly communicating, perhaps it represents a 'real alternative'. Walking along some rail tracks laid over a cinderbed, as she has throughout looked to find and follow lines and connections in the wasted landscapes of her surroundings, Oedipa meditates on the possibility that 'it was all true'. She imagines all the disinherited squatters by the rail lines, and wonders if perhaps they keep in touch with each other through Tristero. She starts to think of all those others who make up a different America, *in* the great industrial superstructure erected by Inverarity and his kind, but not *of* it: like the squatters who dare to sleep up a telegraph pole in the lineman's tent — 'swung among a web of telephone wires, living in the very copper rigging and secular miracle of communication, untroubled by the dumb voltages flickering their miles.' Here indeed is the nub of the book. Is there another America; can entirely different universes co-habit?

If Tristero is indeed a world of waiting outcasts, keeping themselves aloof from contemporary society, then Oedipa feels she may be drawn to join it. Particularly if they are waiting for 'another set of possibilities' or at least for the current rigid 'symmetry of choices to break down': for Oedipa too, like so many American protagonists, feels that something has gone wrong with the choices offered by America, a country in which the chances were 'once so good for diversity'. Her meditations bring her to the point of envisaging extreme alternatives. 'Behind the hieroglyphic streets there would either be a transcendent meaning, or only the earth … Another mode of meaning behind the obvious, or none. Either Oedipa in the orbiting ecstasy of a true paranoia, or a real Tristero.' The possible existence of The Tristero is now associated with the possible existence of 'transcendent' meaning, almost equivalent to a redemptive vision of another America behind the material concretions of the land. The Tristero is also associated with that yearning for diversity, a world of unprogrammed possibilities, so persistent in American literature.

The 'silence' of The Tristero has hitherto been dedicated to disrupting the customary flow of information. As such it was on the side of entropy, making for loss of order, increase of waste, and death. However, in contemporary America when the public world seems to be on the side of entropy, the silence of The Tristero starts to appear as something positive, a pregnant withdrawal and waiting which may yet hold hopes of another America, another legacy. The confusion for Oedipa, and perhaps to some extent for Pynchon, is that the hidden plot seems to range from that dream of annihilation familiar from V. and Vheissu, to those hopes for Transcendence, a better America one day to be made manifest, which have formed the optimistic (and, arguably, counter-entropic) side of American thought at least since Emerson. If The Tristero does exist, who can be sure, from this range of possibilities, what the true legacy of America will finally turn out to be? If it does not exist then the only legacy of America is a paranoid fantasy. If this seems like a confused and ultimately pessimistic range of alternatives, then one can only say that at the time of writing they exactly catch the mood of contemporary America, for which Oedipa's baffled attempts at deciphering, synthesizing and prognosis are an accurate paradigm.

What makes this deceptively slight book finally so moving is the aching sense of loss and waste which pervades the failing human relationships and the declining landscape alike. There is, for instance, a very poignant meditation on an old car lot which itemizes, in a Whitmanesque way, all the wretched detritus gathering there, and goes on to ponder how saturated the old cars and wrecks must be with human feelings of all kinds. It is as though man is putting his passions into his objects as never before: 'things' have come this far, and we have come this far into things. Or again, Oedipa engages in a related meditation on the old mattress of a down-and-out, drunk sailor. She conceives of the mattress as a 'stuffed memory' and imagines how one day it will inevitably go up in flames as the dozing sailor drops his cigarette on it. It is a vision òf what entropy really means. 'She stared at it in wonder. It was as if she had just discovered the irreversible process. It astonished her to think that so much could be lost, even the quantity of hallucination belonging just to the sailor that the world would bear no further trace of.'

This sense of whole constructed mental worlds of dream and memory — she groups those of the saint, the clairvoyant, the paranoid, and she could have added the artist — vanishing irreversibly away, just as the mattress we lie on will rot or burn or somehow decay, is another linking of rubbish and fantasies suggested by the sign W.A.S.T.E. Do we live in fantasy because things have usurped too much of the human domain; or is the visible accumulation of junk around us only the result of our proclivity for fantasy-life? Either way, the result is an increase in entropy, though the process does not pass unnoticed, for here is Oedipa, and her author, to witness and lament the great sadness and awesome mystery of its unpreventable successes. To this extent, at least, the book is counter-entropic, yet it also adumbrates the final entropic victory even in its very structure. The uncertainties in the structure and overall tone of the book are radical and distinctive. Just as Oedipa doesn't know whether she is discovering another America or simply developing the intricacies of a paranoia, so Pynchon himself is ambivalent about his own fiction-making. The tone of the book oscillates between crude farce and passages of poignant and serious lyrical lament. It is as if the book itself does not know whether, of the available genres, it is trash or tragedy. This is part of that new anxiety in fiction which reveals itself as a nervous compulsion to undermine the fiction in the act of erecting it—the verbal equivalent of auto-destructive art. Needless to say this can become as much of a gimmick as any other convention in fiction writing. But in Pynchon it seems to me that the anxiety about the status of *all* plots is so deeply a part of the subject of the book that the uncertainties infecting the structure of the book are a genuine part of his whole vision.

The blank wall and the encoded wall are both finally disturbing; just so, in the case of a plotted or a plotless universe. By balancing between the two possibilities, it seems to me that Pynchon does produce a serious study of the state of consciousness in contemporary America, while a writer like Barth, who opts to emphasize his mockery of plots at an extreme, excessively plotted length, seems to me to fall away from seriousness without discovering any compensating new sources of interest or beguilement. There comes a point beyond which the mockery of fictions and plots becomes sterile and boring, whether or not one holds to the view that we do after all live by fictions. The joy of pure invention is perhaps the main spur for the writer, but this does not have to be dissociated from a conviction of relevance which makes some fictions more valuable than others. Pynchon did, after all, have a story to tell—how Oedipa Maas inherited America and came to the edge of madness and despair. It is a fiction we learn from by not disbelieving. We are all of us 'synthesizing' one way or another, sensitively or crudely, to our liberation or to our confusion as the case may be, and Oedipa's plight is only an extension of our own. If Pynchon's books are confusing, then it is because he is charting and evoking a state of affairs in which authentic inter-subjectivity has all but vanished. He communicates an increasing failure in communication, and is the plotter of a growing disarray. If there is tension and uncertainty in his tone it is because his style is taking issue with the entropy to which it knows it must, like all styles, succumb.

Chapter 8 The Uncertain Messenger

'Constant pined for just one thing—a single message that was sufficiently dignified and important to merit his carrying it humbly between two points.'

(The Sirens of Titan)

'They were offered the choice between becoming kings or the couriers of kings. The way children would, they all wanted to be couriers. Therefore there are only couriers who hurry about the world, shouting to each other—since there are no kings—messages that have become meaningless. They would like to put an end to this miserable life of theirs but they dare not because of their oaths of service.'

('Couriers', Franz Kafka)

'Peace comes of communication ... '

(Essays, Ezra Pound)

Another writer concerned with the relationship between the proliferation of plots and fantasies, and the decline in significant information — indeed the decline in life itself — is Kurt Vonnegut, Jr. Ilium, Titan, Tralfamadore, Nazi Germany, San Lorenzo, Rosewater County, Dresden at the time of the devastating Allied air-raid — these are some of the settings for Vonnegut's six novels to date, and the juxtaposition of the actual and the imaginary in that list gives a clue as to one of his main preoccupations. What is the relation between the facts we encounter and the fictions we invent? Given the terrible historical actuality of the Second World War, what are we to make of the ambiguous role of fantasy in men's lives? And how does all this affect the writer, who longs to communicate and does so by telling lies? It is a growing awareness of the seriousness of Vonnegut's inquiries which has made people realize that he is not only the science-fiction writer he first appeared to be.

His first novel, *Player Piano* (1952), was, to be sure, a fairly orthodox futuristic satire on the dire effects on human individuality of the fully mechanized society which technology could make possible. A piano player is a man consciously using a machine to produce aesthetically pleasing patterns of his own making. A player piano is a machine which has been programmed to produce music on its own, thus making the human presence redundant. This undesirable inversion of the relationship between man and machine, suggested by the title, is at the heart of the novel. In this society of the future there is one part for the machines and the managers, and another part ('the Homestead') into which have been herded all the unnecessary people. Paul Proteus (whose initials suggest his relation to the theme of the title, and whose second name suggests a predisposition to change) is a top manager who believes in the system. But he starts to feel a 'nameless, aching need', which indicates a nascent dissatisfaction with the very social structures he has helped to erect. He realizes that he is trapped in the system he serves. A friend of his, Finnerty, defects from the world of the managers and goes over to the Homestead to start a revolution aimed at destroying all machines. Paul also finds he wants to leave the world of the managers, but not to join the opposing side. He wants to be released from sides altogether, 'to quit, to stop being the instrument of any set of beliefs or any whim of history that might raise hell with somebody's life. To live in a house by the side of the road ... ' What happens is that the managers insist that Paul should become a spy and infiltrate the revolutionary society to send back information to them; while the revolutionaries get hold of him and insist that he acts as a fake 'Messiah', who will send out to the simple-minded people the messages they will dictate to him. Refusal in either case means death. Here is a basic dilemma in Vonnegut's work. Both sides want to *use* the hero; both sides want to impose a particular role on him and make him into a special sort of messenger or conveyor of information. And, as Paul discovers, between the two sides 'there was no middle ground for him'. Paul is a typical American hero in wanting to find a place beyond all plots and systems, some private space, or 'border area' – a house by the side of the road of history and society. He would like not to be used, not to be part of someone else's plan. But the book shows this to be an impossible dream.

Vonnegut's next novel, *The Sirens of Titan* (1959), is also about people being used, this time on the sort of inter-galactic scale permissible in science-fiction. Malachi Constant (or Faithful Messenger) would like to be an authentic courier with an important message (preferably from God) to deliver. Instead he finds that he is being used in some interplanetary plot which is being controlled by a strange being called Winston Niles Rumfoord. This is a man who now exists as 'wave phenomena' as a result of having run his space ship into an 'uncharted chrono-synclastic infundibulum'. He is '*scattered far and wide, not just through space, but through time, too*', and with his new-found power to arrange things as he wishes, free to handle time and space as he pleases and put people where he wants them, he is a suitably fantastic analogue of Vonnegut himself who is doing just that in his book. But if he is the user, he is also the used. As he cries out, '"Some day on Titan, it will be revealed to you just how ruthlessly I've been used, and by whom, and to what disgustingly paltry ends."' The idea that every pattern may in fact be part of a larger pattern outside its control, and the spectacle of the plotter plotted, are alike very common in contemporary American fiction. In this book Vonnegut takes the idea to its most extreme form: it turns out that our whole galaxy is being used by another one.

As Malachi travels from planet to planet, playing his part in the various adventures all planned by Rumfoord, he comes to a crucial perception — 'that he was not only a victim of outrageous fortune, but one of outrageous fortune's cruelest agents as well.' Himself used and abused, he uses and abuses others. It is man's status as agent-victim which preoccupies Vonnegut; once one of his characters comes to see this double aspect of human life and action he usually, like Malachi, becomes 'hopelessly engrossed in the intricate tactics of causing less rather than more pain'. And once again the desire to be beyond other people's schemes is voiced. '"If anybody ever expects to use me again in some tremendous scheme of his ... he is in for one big disappointment."' This is his protest to Rumfoord; but Rumfoord in turn reveals that the remote planet Tralfamadore '"reached into the Solar System, picked me up, and used me like a handy-dandy potato peeler!"' And with mention of Tralfamadore we come to the joke of the book, a joke at the expense of all human messages and plans.

Many thousands of years ago in Earth time, Tralfamadore sent a messenger (Salo) to convey a sealed message from one rim of the universe to the other. Salo's destination was a galaxy that begins eighteen million light-years beyond Titan, but a slight mechanical failing in his space ship caused him to land on Titan and he sent a message back asking for a replacement. While waiting on Titan for a few thousand years, he studied Earth and discovered that Tralfamadore was using that planet to send messages to him. Thus what we humans think of as Stonehenge is to Salo a Tralfamadorian sign meaning 'Replacement part being rushed with all possible speed'. Other famous structures from different periods of human history — e.g. the Great Wall of China, the Palace of the League of Nations — also spell out Tralfamadorian messages. In sum, human history has been a Tralfamadorian communications system, with the rise and fall of each civilization adding up to a completed or aborted

Tralfamadorian message. Rumfoord explains what he knows before he vanishes.

> '*Everything that every Earthling has ever done has been warped by creatures on a planet one-hundred-and-fifty thousand light years away.* The name of the planet is Tralfamadore. How the Tralfamadorians controlled us, I don't know. But I know to what end they controlled us. *They controlled us in such a way as to make us deliver a replacement part to a Tralfamadorian messenger who was grounded right here on Titan.*'

It is a fantasy of total cosmic control, and the comic futility of the centuries of human effort and suffering that have gone to effect this trivial act of delivery is underlined by the fact that the message which Salo is carrying from one side of the universe to the other is simply a dot — which means 'Greetings'. The human race has been ludicrously 'used' indeed. However, another possible attitude to the discovery of this fate is implied in Beatrice Rumfoord's conclusion that: ' "The worst thing that could possibly happen to anybody would be not to be used for anything by anybody." ' A corollary of this is Malachi's late decision that one purpose of human life ' "no matter who is controlling it, is to love whoever is around to be loved." ' This formulation, albeit very sympathetic, points to a detectable strain of sentimental sententiousness which recurs in Vonnegut's work.

Vonnegut depicts man as an inveterate pattern-maker, as other writers like Thomas Pynchon do. At the end, Mrs Rumfoord is 'spinning arguments' to refute her husband's account of the Tralfamadorian domination of human life. Malachi's son Chrono spends a lot of time making shrines with various stones representing the planets and 'moving the elements of his system about', and at times, gazing at these shrines, Malachi 'moved the elements of his own life about experimentally'. This is what Mr Rumfoord did with people and planets in space and time, and what Vonnegut does as a writer. There are patterns and patterns of course. On Mars human beings are brainwashed and turned into programmed automata to fit into the military patterns of the Martian army: it is a rather Burroughs-like world. On Mercury, on the other hand, there are small wall-clinging creatures who spend their time listening to a constant music which is in the air and 'like to arrange themselves in striking patterns on the phosphorescent walls'. They are called 'harmoniums' (which could be a jocular reference to Wallace Stevens's first book of poems). One takes the point: some orderings are dedicated to death, some are productive of beauty and harmony — conflicting patterns are open to man who is himself such a compulsive perceiver and maker of patterns. The plurality of patterns and messages in the book undermines the notion of any final truth: at the same time it suggests that Salo (whose mission is only to 'say hello' to the other side of the universe), when he stares down at Stonehenge and reads it as a message addressed to him, may be as solipsistic and bemused a messenger as any in the whole galaxy. If that were so he would find himself among friends, as indeed he did when he met his first human beings on Titan.

With *Mother Night* (1961) we are back into the bleakest years of contemporary history. In this book too one may discern a shift in Vonnegut's style. There is less attempt at narrative fullness, and a greater use of short chapters which give the sense of the intermittencies and incompletenesses inevitable in any written version. The impression is of compressed selections suspended in an encompassing silence. The novel is also cast in the form of the 'confessions' of Howard Campbell and here, as elsewhere, Vonnegut makes use of all kinds of documents (books, letters, magazines, recordings, etc.) to increase that sense of dealing with potentially innumerable versions which seems such an important part of the epistemology of contemporary American writers. Because of all this, certain vestigial uncertainties about the moral status of the central figure remain, and this must be entirely deliberate. For Howard Campbell is a quintessential Vonnegut hero: *the* agent-victim, the most uncertain and perhaps the most hapless of all Vonnegut's bemused messengers.

Howard Campbell is an American writer living in Germany when war breaks out. Like other Vonnegut figures he has tried to ignore what has been going on in society around him, in this case Nazi Germany during the 'thirties. ('"It isn't anything I can control ... so I don't think about it."') He feels he can withdraw from history into art, into love. The play he is working on just before the war is called *Nation of Two*, and it is intended to show how a couple in love can stay sane in a world gone mad by being loyal to a nation just made up of themselves. Campbell's play, as described by an American Intelligence Officer, reveals that he loves good, hates evil and believes in romance and heroes. Obviously this is admirable from one point of view; at the same time a serene belief in those things in 1939 might perhaps indicate that the artist's benevolent fantasies are becoming somewhat impervious to contemporary facts.

Because he is so popular in Germany, he is asked to become a secret agent for the Americans and, for motives unfathomable to himself, he agrees. His job is to broadcast to the Germans throughout the war. These broadcasts, which he composes himself, are virulent Nazi propaganda, full of the crudest and wildest anti-Semitic fantasies and accusations, and throughout a treasonable attack on America and the Allies. At the same time, following secret instructions, he inserts coughs, pauses, mannerisms, etc., which form the coded answers to questions the Americans want answering. Any speech, then, was two speeches: the surface message, pandering to the vilest German fixations and justifying their cruellest acts; and a hidden message to the Allies, conveying accurate information which was necessary if the German evil was to be defeated. As this latter information is always coded, Campbell admits, 'I do not know to this day what information went out through me.' This is a truth which goes deeper than perhaps he thinks. For the surface messages, even though they were only simulated speeches to enable Campbell to do the brave work of helping the Allies, did reach the German listeners as real information. Campbell's German father-in-law expresses his gratitude to Campbell because he says that if it hadn't been for listening to his broadcasts he would have been convinced that Germany had gone insane. It is thus conceivable that the simulated message, by giving comfort and justification to the Germans, did as much or more damage than the 'real' message did good. As an artist who knows what it is to construct a fiction to project a value, Campbell is perhaps peculiarly well suited for the position of having to invent a lie (the Jewish plot) to pass a truth (about German military resources, etc.). He later claims it as a virtue that at least he always knew when he was telling a lie, unlike an Eichmann who deceived himself into believing his own vicious nonsense.

But to know when you are consciously lying is not the same as knowing just what information is going out through you, or to what effects your truths or lies are heard. After the war Campbell learns that once he announced the death of his wife without being aware of it. 'One part of me told the world of the tragedy in code. The rest of me did not even know that the announcement was being made.' Campbell is a special 'agent'; but in Vonnegut's vision we are all agents, and the perception that we can never be sure of the full content and effect of what we communicate to the world, by word or deed, is at the moral centre of this novel. It also carries the implicit warning that our lies may be more influential than our truths, a consideration which writers in particular must ponder. (It is worth suggesting that the book may well have been inspired by the case of Ezra Pound, who of course gave treasonable and anti-Semitic broadcasts for the Fascists from Italy during the war. He was finally released from St Elizabeth's Hospital in 1958, and in 1960 Charles

Norman's biography appeared.[1] This contained the rather interesting bit of information that apparently the Italian Government 'mistrusted the broadcasts, even suspecting that they hid a code language'. There is no suggestion of course that Pound *was* transmitting information by code, but the idea might have struck Vonnegut. It is certainly possible that he was drawn to the figure and plight of Pound. Here was one of the greatest of all American writers, languishing in an insane asylum and threatened with prison. Here indeed were some warnings for other American writers — one of them being, perhaps, that in dreams begin irresponsibilities as well. Whether in fact his responsibilities were outweighed by, or even distinguishable from, his irresponsibilities is a major problem for Howard Campbell.)

The uncertain relation between surface message and hidden content is directly related to a comparable uncertainty about the relationship between different parts of the self. The book is full of people with some sort of split between their apparent and concealed selves (just as a magazine that Campbell picks up has a lying photograph of a war incident on the cover, but a surprisingly truthful account of it inside). One of the points of the book is that the schizophrenia which enabled Campbell to be a fervent Nazi and a loyal American at the same time is a device of survival much more in use at the present time than we realize. But it is not just a matter of the vulnerable self having to protect itself against a cruel world with a false cover-self. Two Russian spies (Kraft and Resi) turn out to be better at their disguise roles of painter and lover than they are at their initially real commitments as spies. The intimation is that we may become our own cover-stories and there may be a more authentic self in the invented one than in the given one. One moral of the book is that 'We are what we pretend to be, so we must be careful about what we pretend to be.' Campbell was one of the most effective agents of the war 'at personal sacrifices that proved total'. After the war he has no life to live, no self left to be, no motive to move. Yet, it is implied, anyone who could simulate the Nazi position and temperament so well must have at least a potential Nazi among his real selves.

Campbell is of course as much victim as agent, perhaps more so. He is used by the Germans, by the Americans, and after the war it appears that the Russians now have a 'scheme' for him. At one point he has a renewal of that old dream of slipping quietly out of history, 'out of the trap' to some 'secret village' (interestingly enough it is once again envisaged as a border area, 'on the rim of the Pacific'). As this book remorselessly shows, this is again an impossible dream. The only way out of other people's schemes is death: on the last page it is intimated that Campbell will hang himself. Campbell's attempt to escape into art is, in retrospect, made to appear rather equivocal. His propagandist fabrications were of course dangerous: they strengthened the fantasies of the types who ran the concentration camps. His actual creative writing, however, was intended to nourish much more fruitful fantasies – the superiority of good over evil, the beauty of love. Yet there is an ambiguity even here. An American soldier called O'Hare compensates for a tedious and squalid suburban life by regarding himself as the man picked to be Campbell's nemesis. He does indeed track Campbell down, but it turns out that he is as much a pathetic fool as a dangerous lunatic, drugged, as Campbell says, 'by booze and fantasies of good triumphing over evil'. Such fantasies permit him to 'hate without limit', which is pure evil. Since Campbell's art attempted to promulgate just such fantasies, even his benevolent fictions may be called into question when their effects are assessed.

The book presents, almost in shorthand, a whole spectrum of fiction-making, from the vilest propaganda to the most idealistic art. There is no cynical attempt to identify these two extreme ends of the spectrum, but it is part of Vonnegut's meaning to suggest that the artist cannot rest in confidence as to the harmlessness of his inventions. Campbell, who subsequently discovers that even his early authentic writings have been distorted and 'used', complains, 'The part of me that wanted to tell the truth got turned into an expert liar! The lover in me got turned into a pornographer! The artist in me got turned into ugliness such as the world has rarely seen before.' In one way it comes down to that suspicion of all communication which seems to go so deep in contemporary American fiction. As no one can be fully aware of the 'information' that goes out through him (just as you cannot control the information that is fed into you), the artist as a professional inventor and sender of messages must be very careful about what he puts out. He may think that, in Sidney's terms, he is delivering a golden world from our brazen one. But he might, all unawares, be contributing to the restoration of the ancient reign of Mother Night.

The war features again as a background to *Cat's Cradle* (1963), for the narrator of that book tells us that his adventures started when he set out to write a book about the exploding of the first atom bomb, and the life of its inventor Dr Felix Hoeniker. The book was to be called *The Day the World Ended*, but so potent are the workings of fantasy in this novel that instead of writing his book about the end of the world in America, the narrator lives to see it actually happen from the imaginary island of San Lorenzo. Thus the facts displace the fiction, or the fiction becomes the fact, in a neatly inextricable way. Vonnegut is playing, of course—he has seldom been more comically inventive—but then the whole novel is an exploration of the ambiguities of man's disposition to play and invent, and the various forms it may take. It turns out that Felix Hoeniker was only 'playing' when he invented the atom bomb, and he later said that he learned everything from the real games that nature plays. There are games and games. The narrator discovers that all the Hoenikers are playful in their own way. Angela, the daughter, plays the clarinet, producing melodies expressive of authentic pain. Newt, the midget son, paints nihilistic pictures which reveal the bleakness of accurate perception. It even turns out that Felix had a twin brother who made music boxes rather than bombs. The third son of Felix, Franklin, has a genius for building microcosms. While still a youth, Frank built 'a fantastic little country' in plywood. The narrator, in the course of his research, is shown this model and finds every detail so compelling he says he could easily believe it was a real country. In time he will. For in a book in which invention displaces fact, it is not surprising that the narrator, along with most of the other figures in the book, should find himself in the country of Franklin's fantasy—for that model effectively turns into the island of San Lorenzo.

On that island (which is Vonnegut's invention as well, for he gives it a history, language, religion, etc., quite in the manner of Swift or Borges) all the 'players' converge (except for Felix who is dead). The narrator goes on with his writing, Newt with his painting, Angela with her clarinet playing, and Franklin with his 'building' (he is the person really in charge of the island). In addition there is an Albert Schweitzer figure called Julian Castle who has gone in for the madness of absolute unselfishness and devoted himself to a jungle hospital which is as futile in fact, as the dream behind it is Utopian. Each one is following his dream, creating his fiction. And it is from this island that the process which will end the world is unwittingly launched. This may be Vonnegut's mordant way of predicting the possible final outcome of the human instinct to play. When this island of invention contains both the dreaded compound invented by Felix Hoeniker which can end the world by freezing it (ice-nine) *and* representatives of the artistic and Utopian dreams which console and dignify the race, one can see that Vonnegut is pushing quite hard for a recognition of the deeply ambiguous creative/destructive aspects of the innate human instinct to play. Just as we cannot be sure what information passes through us, so we cannot know how our games will end.

The narrator was going to write one book but ended up writing another. In the course of his research he has consulted many letters, documents, books, and so on, and the very multiplicity of accounts is another reminder that we live among versions. This is apt enough in a book in which fiction pre-empts fact and the characters live and die in and by their own inventions. Vonnegut's own contribution is the history of San Lorenzo, its language and the elaborate beliefs of the dominant religion, Bokonism. In inventing a whole religion Vonnegut exemplifies that human ability to produce a coherent fabrication which the book is, in part, about. And some of the tenets of Bokonism are surprisingly relevant to any consideration of attitudes in contemporary American fiction. There are, in particular, some interesting propositions in connection with that familiar problem—are we part of someone, or something, else's pattern or plot? Consulting the *Books of Bokonon* the narrator discovers that Bokonon maintains that if you do find your life entangled with somebody else's in some inexplicable way, that person may be a member of your *karass*. The narrator quotes Bokonon and glosses: '"Man created the checkerboard; God created the *karass*." By that he meant that a *karass* ignores national, institutional, occupational, familial, and class boundaries. It is as free-form as an amoeba.' Where man imposes his own patterns on existence and divides men, countries, ethical issues and much else, into rigid black-and-white units, Bokonism accepts that there no doubt are subtle arrangings and mysterious configurations in life, but exactly what they are and how they operate will always be, finally, a mystery. And the idea of a pattern which is free form—something between utter shapelessness and absolute rigidity—exactly echoes that desire for some sort of flexible form which we can find in so many American novels. The idea of the *karass* is made clearer by the related Bokonist term, *granfaloon*. This is the word for a false *karass*, 'a seeming team that was meaningless in terms of the ways God gets things done'. Examples given include the Communist Party, Daughters of the American Revolution and any nation at all.

Bokonism allows that we may indeed be pawns or agents in some unseen plot, but suggests that the plot may be God's. Instead of saying 'As it happened', the true Bokonist says, 'As it was *supposed* to happen', deferring to the possibility of plan behind the most random-seeming event. Clearly it is preferable to believe in God's inscrutable plans than in man's more scrutable, and often rather appalling, ones. Yet Vonnegut is hardly proselytizing for a return to the traditional pieties and confidences. For a basic tenet of Bokonism is that it is a religion based on invention, its cosmogony a pack of lies. What the founder Bokonon understood, like many before him, is that mankind needs some lies to live by because it cannot stand very much reality. Conditions on the island are so bad in material terms that Bokonon and his friend McCabe invented a distracting fiction. McCabe would play the cruel tyrant, and Bokonon, along with his invented religion, would be outlawed and become a holy man living in the jungle. People were much happier for believing themselves to be participating in a legendary struggle between principles of good and evil. '"They were all employed full time as actors in a play they understood ... "' The narrator understands. '"So life became a work of art."' Bokonon's word for this theory of holding an equilibrium between good and evil is the old Charles Atlas phrase—'Dynamic Tension'. (The joke has some point—man has to build himself up by the exercise of his own powers.) It is the same principle whereby if you hold your hands apart, pulling in opposite directions, you can string a cat's cradle on them; with no tension, of course, you would just have a muddle of string.

The title is explained in the book. Newt recalls that the one game his father played with him on the day the first atom bomb was exploded was to make a cat's cradle and push it jeeringly into his face. On the island Newt makes a painting of the ancient game of cat's cradle, and adds, '"For maybe a hundred thousand years or more, grown-ups have been waving tangles of string in their children's faces."' In Newt's view it is no wonder that children should grow up crazy, because when they look at the criss-crossed string, what do they see? '"*No damn cat, and no damn cradle.*"' A chapter in *Mother Night* is entitled 'No Dove, No Covenant'. It alludes to the same discovery, which any child is likely to make: namely, that the religions or legends taught to him by adults are just fictions. There is no cat there; nor does God make a sign. On the other hand it is an axiom of Bokonism that man has to tell himself that he understands life even when he knows he doesn't. This is the justification for constructing fictions, for the necessity of art. It does, after all, take skill to weave the string, and something more again to imagine the cat. Still, one must confront the fact that the string *is* only string. The matter is summed up in what the narrator calls 'the cruel paradox of Bokonist thought, the heartbreaking necessity of lying about reality, and the heartbreaking impossibility of lying about it'. That, certainly, is what Vonnegut contrives to suggest in his own brilliant little fiction.

The distinctive tone of Vonnegut's work is very likeable and sympathetic; it obviously bespeaks a compassionate humane spirit. The economy and laconic wit prevent this from issuing in much overt sentimentality, though the tendency is there. However, at times it does seem as though he is using his fiction to issue short sermons on the state of contemporary America, or the world, and this can at times endanger the poise of his work. I think that some of the weaker aspects of his writing show up in *God Bless You Mr Rosewater* (1965), despite the wit and moral feeling with which the book is conceived and executed. Eliot Rosewater is the inheritor of the indescribably wealthy Rosewater Foundation, and with its annual profits he is in a position to do virtually what he likes. He is also insane, and one of the points of the book is to consider the exact nature and implications of that insanity. He is, as he describes himself, a 'Utopian dreamer'. A doctor explains that whereas a lot of unbalanced people have diverted their sexual energies into some perversion or other, Eliot has brought his sexual energies '"To Utopia"'. His Utopia — a not unfamiliar one in Vonnegut's work — would be one in which people are kind to each other, do not go in for destruction, get the love as well as the food they need, in general, a world in which people *matter* and are felt to matter.

The only literature that interests Eliot is science-fiction, because at least it really cares about the future of the human race and tries to explore the implications of the inventions and developments of the present. Perhaps Vonnegut is ironically congratulating himself on his first book. In particular, Eliot likes the work of Kilgore Trout because it contains 'fantasies of an impossibly hospitable world'. Eliot too has such a fantasy and tries to bring some of that impossible hospitality into the present world. To be more precise, he tries to bring it to Rosewater County which is in the 'dead center' of the country, and is 'deathly flat', and full of people who are 'deadly dull'. In effect, Eliot Rosewater brings his fantasy of all-inclusive love to Entropyville, U.S.A. He feels that this is his mission, and, making a connection we have seen before, he identifies his dream as his art. '"I'm going to love those discarded Americans, even though they're useless and unattractive. *That* is going to be my work of art."' He duly sets up a building which carries the notice ROSE-WATER FOUNDATION HOW CAN WE HELP YOU?, and much of the book documents his attempts to respond to the varying needs of the pathetic human specimens who have, as it were, been abandoned for the trash heap while the more powerful and ruthless members of American society forge blindly ahead. It is part of the rather Stein-beckian sentimentality which touches the book that we learn that these people have a secret quality. '"The secret is that they're human,"' explains Eliot's wife.

From one point of view Eliot's behaviour is insane. More than that, as his father the Senator complains, his uncritical love may demoralize people who come to rely on it rather than explore their own capacity for independent action. It also devalues the notion of love as something special that develops between two individuals. And his good works can have bad results. The justification for his behaviour comes from Trout who says that Eliot has conducted perhaps the most important social experiment of our time, namely, '"How to love people who have no use?"' Vonnegut obviously has some sympathy with the authentic reactionary sentiments of the Senator who, albeit he is depicted as a ruthless man, speaks with conviction for the individualist values of an older America. And while Vonnegut obviously feels very close to the benevolent anarchy implicit in Eliot's dream of uncritical love and non-competitive sharing of everything, he has a clear enough eye to see that it is an unworkable dream, remaining more of a private obsession than a public solution.

But to find a moral position in between is difficult. Eliot's wife tries to go along with Eliot as far as she can but finally has a breakdown. She leaves Rosewater County and returns to the high life of the social world. Then she has a relapse, suffering from what is diagnosed as 'Samaritrophia' or 'hysterical indifference to the troubles of those less fortunate than oneself'. This occurs when an overactive conscience is finally suppressed by the mind when it sees that the world is not improved by its worrying or its efforts. The only way to cure a person suffering in this way is to turn his mind towards Enlightened Self-Interest. Sylvia can only be 'cured' by being turned from a deep person with profound sympathies to a shallow one deprived of conscience. She cannot really apply herself to the life of dedicated selfishness and finally enters a nunnery. The problem is clear enough. Can one indeed operate with any authenticity and wholeness of self anywhere between the convinced selfishness of the Senator's sincere *laissez-faire* and authoritarian beliefs, and the uncritical unselfishness of Eliot's anarchic dream of universal kindness and help? Any verdict of insanity passed on Eliot Rosewater may well appear to rebound on the society that makes it. And it is another implication of the book that it is better to be 'crazy' in some way than to drift on in the almost catatonic moral stupor and calm of the majority.

One of the aspects of the book which prevents it from being a thinly veiled sermon against contemporary America is the account of the source of Eliot's 'fantasy'. Part of his obsession is the tireless, indeed fanatical, support of volunteer fire-departments. It turns out that during the war he had to lead an assault on a building supposedly containing S.S. troops. Eliot killed three of them before realizing that they were 'unarmed firemen ... engaged in the brave and uncontroversial business of trying to keep a building from combining with oxygen'. Memory of this terrible mistake causes subsequent breakdowns, and a preoccupation with the fact that we live in a planet with an atmosphere 'that was eager to combine violently with almost everything the inhabitants held dear'. This is his way of referring to the role played by oxygen in combustion, and the rapidity with which this can cause our landscape to change – as at Hiroshima, or at Dresden. In as much as firemen are totally dedicated to preventing this process they are a singular group of people, wholly given over to trying to prevent death. They are a counter-entropic force. Having once unwittingly fired on the firemen, Eliot's expiating fantasy is that he should devote all his time and money to the furthering, consoling and protecting of life. Seen against the background of a room full of corpses, it is the simple phenomenon of life – just life, in all its forms – that unqualifiedly matters.

Eliot Rosewater's last breakdown is triggered off by his conviction that he can see Indianapolis in the grip of a fire-storm. This illusion is partly a recapitulation of his own war experiences, and partly a projection of a description of the fire-storm in Dresden which he has re-read repeatedly. This is the vision of sudden and unbelievable annihilation which has been somewhere behind all Vonnegut's work, and which was finally brought into the centre of a novel in *Slaughterhouse-Five or The Children's Crusade* (1969). Here for the first time Vonnegut appears in one of his own novels, juxtaposing and merging the fantasies of his own life in a book which seems almost to summarize and conclude the sequence of his previous five novels. Slaughterhouse-Five was the actual address of the place where Vonnegut was working as a prisoner-of-war, and from which he emerged to witness the results of the Dresden air-raid. After seeing that, he tells us, he was sure that the destruction of Dresden would be the subject of his first novel. But he discovered that the spectacle of the Dresden fire-storm was somehow beyond language.

He describes how, over the years, he has tried to put a version together and make a novel, until now, at last, his famous Dresden war novel is finished, 'short and jumbled and jangled, Sam, because there is nothing intelligent to say about a massacre,' he adds apologetically to his publisher. But of course it is jumbled to very effective purpose. For it is not a novel simply about Dresden. It is a novel about a novelist who has been unable to erase the memory of his wartime experience and the Dresden fire-storm, even while he has been inventing stories and fantasies in his role as a writer since the end of that war. This book too will be a mixture of fact and invention ('All this happened, more or less' – so the book starts), for Vonnegut has created a character called Billy Pilgrim, whose progress entails not only undergoing the wartime experiences which Vonnegut remembers, but also getting involved in the fantasies which Vonnegut has invented. The result, among other things, is a moving meditation on the relationship between history and dreaming cast in an appropriately factual/fictional mode.

Summarizing the line of the story that Vonnegut tells, we can say that Billy Pilgrim is an innocent, sensitive man who encounters so much death and so much evidence of hostility to the human individual while he is in the army that he takes refuge in an intense fantasy life, which involves his being captured and sent to a remote planet (while in fact he is being transported by the Germans as a prisoner-of-war). He also comes 'unstuck in time' and present moments during the war may either give way to an intense re-experiencing of moments from the past or unexpected hallucinations of life in the future. Pilgrim ascribes this strange gift of being able to slip around in time to his experience on the planet which has given him an entirely new way of looking at time. We may take Vonnegut's word for it that the wartime scenes are factual, as near as can be attested to by a suffering participant. The source of Pilgrim's dreams and fantasies is more complex. The planet that kidnaps him is Tralfamadore, familiar from Vonnegut's second novel. At the same time it is suggested that the details of his voyage to Tralfamadore may well be based on details from his real experience subjected to fantastical metamorphosis. In his waking life Pilgrim is said to come from Ilium (see *Player Piano*); he later encounters the American Nazi propagandist Howard Campbell (see *Mother Night*); in a mental hospital he has long talks with Eliot Rosewater, who introduces Pilgrim to the works of Kilgore Trout, both familiar from Vonnegut's last novel. Pilgrim is not only slipping backwards and forwards in time; he is also astray in Vonnegut's own fictions. Vonnegut himself enters his own novel from time to time (as Hitchcock does his films) and it becomes very difficult to hold the various fictional planes in perspective, as in a picture by Maurits Escher. But the overall impression is that of a man who has brought the most graphic facts of his life to exist in the same medium with his most important fictions to see what each implies about the other. (A relevant comparison may be found in Herman Hesse's *Journey to the East* in which the narrator describes how, on the pilgrimage he took part in, 'we creatively brought the past, the future and the fictitious into the present moment.' It might seem pointless to bring in this reference from a remote European novel; but as it happens the pilgrimage is also described as 'the Children's Crusade' which is the subtitle of Vonnegut's novel. This suggests that Vonnegut may well have read and been influenced by Hesse's book.)*

On the one hand the book is obsessed with death. This obsession is noticeable in Vonnegut's earlier works, but *Slaughterhouse-Five* is packed with corpses. It is the force which rigidifies life that holds Vonnegut's attention. He mentions Lot's wife, turned to a pillar of salt; this foreshadows the uncountable rigidified corpses which resulted from the Dresden air-raid. At one point a trainload of American prisoners is described as 'flowing' as it unloads like a river of human life. The last man of all on the train, a tramp, is dead. 'The hobo could not flow, could not plop. He wasn't liquid any more. He was stone. So it goes.' As we have seen, the opposition between the fixed and the flowing is very common in contemporary American fiction. (The property of ice-nine, in *Cat's Cradle*, is to turn everything liquid as hard and fixed as crystal on contact – accidentally dropped into the ocean it starts the end of the world.) At one point Vonnegut recalls a passage in a book by Céline in which he wants to stop everyone moving in a crowded street: '*There make them freeze ... So that they won't disappear anymore!*' When it comes to freezing people, ice-nine and the Dresden fire-storm are about equally effective. One infers that Vonnegut prefers to see the crowds flowing.

On the other hand, as well as a lot of corpses there are a lot of books in this novel. They range from low fiction (*Valley of the Dolls*), to criticism (*Céline and His Vision*), to documentary studies (*The Bombing of Dresden, The Execution of Private Slovik, Extraordinary Delusions and the Madness of Crowds*), to high-level realistic fiction (*The Red Badge of Courage*), to poetry (Blake is mentioned, Roethke is quoted). One science-fiction book is mentioned, *Maniacs in the Fourth Dimension* by Kilgore Trout. Corpses exist in three dimensions; everything produced by the human imagination (extraordinary delusions, cheap wish-fulfilments or great art) exists in a fourth. Some of the books mentioned, like Crane's *Red Badge of Courage*, are intended to be accurate accounts of the cruel and pathetic maniacs who live in three dimensions; science-fiction goes directly into a fourth. But all the books mentioned form a spectrum

---

* This suggestion of the relevance of Hesse is reinforced by the fact that Vonnegut published an article entitled 'Why They Read Hesse'—'they' referring to the American young—in *Horizon* XII, Spring 1970. At the time of going to press I have not been able to get hold of this article and I am indebted to Mathew Winston of Harvard for informing me of its appearance.

which throws light on Vonnegut's own mixed genre (he could be said to be trying to combine Crane and Trout!).

Taken in sum the books have a general significance. They not only serve to extend the setting for Vonnegut's own tale, they are all symptomatic of that human will to communicate which is of central interest to Vonnegut. In this novel he goes out of his way to describe his days as a reporter and the intricate network of pneumatic tubes through which he had to transmit the news. At the time of writing he calls himself a 'telephoner', because he likes to call people late at night and try to get through to them. This in turn ties up with the curious way in which Tralfamadorian novels are written. Billy Pilgrim cannot read them, but looking at the script which is arranged in brief clusters of symbols he guesses that they might be like 'telegrams'. A Tralfamadorian voice tells him he is correct: '"each clump of symbols is a brief, urgent message—describing a situation, a scene."' These are apparently read all at once, not in sequence. ' "There isn't any particular relationship between all the messages, except that the author has chosen them carefully, so that, when seen all at once, they produce an image of life that is beautiful and surprising and deep ... What we love in our books are the depths of many marvellous moments seen at one time."' This would seem to be an indirect statement of Vonnegut's own aesthetic, for although, not being from Tralfamadore, one necessarily reads in sequence the many compressed fragments or messages which make up his novels, one nevertheless gets the impression of arrested moments suspended in time. In reading Billy Pilgrim's adventures we too become unstuck in time. As a result we are left with something approaching the impression of seeing all the marvellous and horrific moments, all at the same time. Vonnegut, the telephoner, has condensed and arranged his telegrams to good effect. He starts his account of the adventures of Pilgrim with the single word—'Listen'. This is to alert us. We are being messaged.

Billy Pilgrim moves around in time rather as Winston Niles Rumfoord did, and, as was the case with Rumfoord, this gives him an entirely new attitude to the significance and tragedies of those people who still live in an irreversible, linear-temporal sequence. From the Tralfamadorians he learns that all things from the beginning to the end of the universe exist in a sort of eternal present. They can look at time rather as one can scan a wide geographic panorama. Everything always *is*. 'There is no why.' This being the case everything that happens is exactly what has to happen. To use the Tralfamadorian image, we are all like bugs 'trapped in the amber of this moment'. The moment always exists; it is structured exactly as it had to be structured. For the Tralfamadorians the strangest thing they have encountered among Earthlings is the meaningless concept of 'free will'. Clearly this very lofty temporal perspective, like a heightened Oriental view of time, is, from our Occidental point of view, totally deterministic. More than that, it countenances a complete quietism as well. A motto which Billy brings from his life into his fantasy, or vice versa, reads: 'God grant me the serenity to accept the things I cannot change, courage to change the things I can, and wisdom always to tell the difference.' In itself this is an open-ended programme. But immediately afterwards we read: 'Among the things Billy Pilgrim could not change were the past, the present, and the future.' Billy becomes completely quiescent, calmly accepting everything that happens as happening exactly as it ought to (including his own death). He abandons the worried ethical, tragical point of view of Western man and adopts a serene conscienceless passivity. If anything, he views the world aesthetically: every moment is a marvellous moment, and at times he beams at scenes in the war. Yet he does have breakdowns and is prone to fits of irrational weeping.

Here I think is the crucial moral issue in the book. Billy Pilgrim is a professional optometrist. He spends his life on earth prescribing corrective lenses for people suffering from defects of vision. It is entirely in keeping with his calling, then, when he has learned to see time in an entirely new Tralfamadorian way, that he should try to correct the whole erroneous Western view of time, and explain to everyone the meaninglessness of individual death. Like most of Vonnegut's main characters he wants to communicate his new vision, and he does indeed manage to infiltrate himself into a radio programme to promulgate his message. He is, of course, regarded as mad. The point for us to ponder is, how are *we* to regard his new vision? According to the Tralfamadorians, ordinary human vision is something so narrow and restricted that to convey to themselves what it must be like they have to imagine a creature with a metal sphere round his head who looks down a long, thin pipe seeing only a tiny speck at the end. He cannot turn his head around and he is strapped to a flatcar on rails which goes in one direction. Billy Pilgrim's attempt to free people from that metal sphere, and teach his own widened and liberated vision may thus seem entirely desirable. But is the cost in conscience and concern for the individual life equally desirable? With his new vision, Billy does not protest about the Vietnam war, nor shudder about the effects of the bombing. The Tralfamadorians of his dreams advise him to 'concentrate on the happy moments of his life, and to ignore the unhappy ones — to stare only at pretty things as eternity failed to go by'. The Tralfamadorian response to life is 'guilt-free'. At one point Billy Pilgrim thinks of a marvellous epitaph which, Vonnegut adds, would do for him too. 'Everything was beautiful, and nothing hurt.' Later in life when a man called Rumfoord is trying to justify the bombing of Dresden to him, Billy quietly reassures him, '"It was all right ... *Everything* is all right, and everybody has to do exactly what he does. I learned that on Tralfamadore."' Yet he still weeps quietly to himself from time to time.

Is this a culpable moral indifference? In later life we read that Billy was simply 'unenthusiastic' about living, while stoically enduring it, which may be a sign of the accidie which settles on a man with an atrophied conscience. From one point of view, it is important that man should still be capable of feeling guilt, and not fall into the sleep which Germany and Europe slept as eternity failed to go by in the 'thirties. Can one afford to ignore the ugly moments in life by concentrating on the happy ones? On the other hand, can one afford *not* to? Perhaps the fact of the matter is that conscience simply cannot cope with events like the concentration camps and the Dresden air-raid, and the more general demonstration by the war of the utter valuelessness of human life. Even to try to begin to care adequately would lead to an instant and irrevocable collapse of consciousness. Billy Pilgrim, Everyman, needs his fantasies to offset such facts.

At one point when he slips a bit in time he sees a war movie backwards. The planes have a magnetic power which shrinks the fires from the burning city and wraps them up in steel containers which are then lifted into the planes; the men on the ground have long tubes which suck the damaging fragments from wounded planes. It is a magic vision of restored wholeness – 'everything and everybody as good as new' – and as such it is the best possible justification for wanting to escape from linear time so that events can be read in any direction, and the tragedy of 'before and after' transcended. At the same time we are given some hints about the equivocal nature of Billy's escapsim. No one can bear sleeping near Billy during the war because he creates such a disturbance while he is dreaming. 'Everybody told Billy to keep the hell away.' One man even blames his death on Billy. Later, in the prison hospital, the man watching over him reads *The Red Badge of Courage* while Billy enters a 'morphine paradise'. In *Cat's Cradle* the narrator admitted that there was little difference between a writer and a 'drug salesman', and while there is a kind of fiction which tries to awaken men to the horrors of reality (e.g. Crane's book), it is clear to Vonnegut that there are fantasies, written or dreamed, which serve to drug men to reality.

When the reality is the Dresden fire-storm, then arguably some drugging is essential.

Billy's Tralfamadorian perspective is not unlike that described in Yeats's 'Lapis Lazuli' – 'gaiety transfiguring all that dread' – and it has obvious aesthetic appeal and consolation. At the same time, his sense of the futility of trying to change anything, of regarding history as a great lump of intractable amber from which one can only escape into the fourth dimension of dream and fantasy, was the attitude held by Howard Campbell during the rise of Nazi Germany. Vonnegut has, I think, total sympathy with such quietistic impulses. At the same time his whole work suggests that if man doesn't do something about the conditions and quality of human life on earth, no one and nothing else will. Fantasies of complete determinism, of being held helplessly in the amber of some eternally unexplained plot, justify complete passivity and a supine acceptance of the futility of all action. Given the overall impact of Vonnegut's work I think we are bound to feel that there is at least something equivocal about Billy's habit of fantasy, even if his attitude is the most sympathetic one in the book. At one point Vonnegut announces: 'There are almost no characters in this story, and almost no dramatic confrontation, because most of the people in it are so sick and so much the listless playthings of enormous forces.' It is certainly hard to celebrate the value of the individual self against the background of war, in which the nightmare of being the victim of uncontrollable forces comes compellingly true. In such conditions it is difficult to be much of a constructive 'agent', and Billy Pilgrim doubtless has to dream to survive.

At the end of the novel, spring has come to the ruins of Dresden, and when Billy is released from prison the trees are in leaf. He finds himself in a street which is deserted except for one wagon. 'The wagon was green and coffin-shaped.' That composite image of generation and death summarizes all there is actually to see in the external world, as far as Vonnegut is concerned. The rest is fantasy, cat's cradles, lies. In this masterly novel, Vonnegut has put together both his war novel and reminders of the fantasies which made up his previous novels. The facts which defy explanation are brought into the same frame with fictions beyond verification. The point at which fact and fiction intersect is Vonnegut himself, the experiencing, dreaming man who wrote the book. He is a lying messenger, but he acts on the assumption that the telegrams must continue to be sent. Eliot Rosewater's cry to his psychiatrist, overheard by Billy Pilgrim, applies more particularly to the artist. '"I think you guys are going to have to come up with a lot of wonderful *new* lies, or people just aren't going to want to go on living."' Of course, they must also tell the truth, whatever that may be. Kafka's couriers could hardly be more confused. What Vonnegut has done, particularly in *Slaughterhouse-Five*, is to define with clarity and economy—and compassion—the nature and composition of that confusion.

Chapter 9 Necessary Landscapes and Luminous Deteriorations

An ambiguous attitude towards landscape pervades contemporary American writing. On the one hand, a scrupulous attention to the given terrain has long been felt to be a valid stabilizing strategy in the midst of any personal or social confusion (as for example in the work of Hemingway and William Carlos Williams). On the other hand, there has arisen a deep suspicion about the intentions and potencies of the landscapes which surround the modern self. Behaviorism, particularly if not properly understood, offers an immediate nightmare to the imaginative person cherishing dreams of authentic independent action. Popular books like Edward T. Hall's *The Hidden Dimension* seek to demonstrate that our environment controls and circumscribes our actions and responses much more than we think; that there are more 'imperatives' at work on us than we can ever hope to grasp. All this can induce a frame of mind in which sense of territory is undermined by suspicion of territory. This can affect writers in different ways: one reaction is to create what might be called imperative, fictional territories to counter the environmental imperatives from without. This response can be seen most vividly, I think, in the work of John Hawkes.

Looking at that work, we may note straight away that his novels have settings as various as post-war Germany, post-war and Renaissance Italy, post-war England, the American West and islands in the Atlantic and the South Seas: at the same time each is, as Hawkes put it in an interview, 'a totally new and necessary fictional landscape.'[1] They are like dreams, often dreams fractured by appalling violence, and it is not surprising that Hawkes names Faulkner as the American writer whom he admires, and has been influenced by, the most. The violence in his work is as vivid and inaudible as violence under glass. Such effects, and in general the baroque — mannerist is perhaps better — foregrounding of his prose, are recognizably in the Faulknerian mode. But the landscapes are all his own. In the interview he said that he got the ideas for two of his novels from items in newspapers.

In each case what appealed to me was a landscape or world, and in each case I began with something immediately and

intensely visual—a room, a few figures, an object, something
prompted by the initial idea and then literally seen, like the
visual images that come to us just before sleep. However, here
I ought to stress that my fiction has nothing to do with automatic writing. Despite these vague originations and the dream-
like quality of some of these envisioned worlds, my own writing
process involves a constant effort to shape and control my
materials as well as an effort to liberate fictional energy.

The latter point was worth making, if only to make the distinction
between the sort of careful shaping and structuring of material
emerging from the unconscious, exemplified by Hawkes, and the
cultivated unedited spontaneity of a writer like the late Jack
Kerouac.

Hawkes's careful sculpting serves to fix and hold things: one of his
favourite words is 'wax', as in 'waxen tableau'. Hawkes also said
that he started writing by refusing to think in terms of plot, character,
setting and theme, and that, having abandoned these familiar ways
of thinking about fiction, 'totality of vision or structure was really
all that remained. And structure—verbal and psychological coherence
—is still my largest concern as a writer. Related or corresponding
events, recurring image and recurring action, these constitute the
essential substance or meaningful density of my writing.' As a matter
of fact, the plotting of his books—which is the temporal dimension
of their structure—is extremely important, and he is doubtless over-
stating when he gives the idea that he abandoned plot at the outset.
But his comments do point to the essential endeavour in his work:
to build and fix a landscape—a necessary landscape. As he went on
to say, 'my writing depends on absolute detachment, and the
unfamiliar or invented landscape helps me to achieve and maintain
this detachment ... I want to try to create a world, not represent
it.'

The majority of his novels are related to war in some way, and as
a result often centre on landscapes of desolation and decline which
point to the progress of entropy quite as graphically as the landscapes
of Burroughs and Pynchon. Hawkes's private nightmares of violence
and evil are at the same time probings of our common world. For
Hawkes the purpose of the novel is 'to objectify the terrifying
similarity between the unconscious desires of the solitary man and
the disruptive needs of the visible world', so, in his own novels, he
seeks to achieve 'a formalizing of our deepest urgencies'. One may be
inclined to ask why the fictional landscape is 'necessary'; why
re-rehearse in carefully arranged words the horrors of history, the

terror of the mind astray in the night? And it is true that people find some of his passages hard to take – descriptions of a man cutting up a child, a thug truncheoning a girl to death, for example. Here perhaps it helps to cite his own very clear definition of his own literary lineage, which he sees as including Lautréamont, Céline, Nathanael West, Flannery O'Connor, James Purdy and Joseph Heller. What these writers have in common is

> a quality of coldness, detachment, ruthless determination to face up to the enormities of ugliness and potential failure within ourselves and in the world around us, and to bring to this exposure a savage or saving comic spirit and the saving beauties of language. The need is to maintain the truth of the fractured picture; to expose, ridicule, attack, but always to create and to throw into new light our potential for violence and absurdity as well as for graceful action.

The belief that sustains this aesthetic is that 'the product of extreme fictive detachment is extreme fictive sympathy.'

Style itself becomes the saving assertion, a notion of verbal liberation with which we are becoming familiar among contemporary American writers. Hawkes admires Nabokov greatly as a person who 'sustains' American writers, and we have considered the importance Nabokov attaches to a sort of absolute of stylistic finesse and performance. Hawkes's own style owes a lot, also, to Faulkner and Djuna Barnes, the latter in particularly having the ability to depict figures traversing, almost somnambulistically, landscapes of evil and decay in a prose of an intricate brilliance which prompted T. S. Eliot to praise *Nightwood* (1936) for 'the great achievement of a style'. One fairly typical example from *Nightwood* may serve to illustrate how carefully wrought each sentence is.

> Her flesh was the texture of plant life, and beneath it one sensed a frame, broad, porous and sleep-worn, as if sleep were a decay fishing her beneath the visible surface. About her head there was an effulgence as of phosphorus glowing about the circumference of a body of water – as if her life lay through her in ungainly luminous deteriorations – the troubling structure of the born somnambule, who lives in two worlds – meet of child and desperado.

'Luminous deteriorations' is a perfect phrase for something central to Hawkes's vision, and where these are ungainly in life they are made almost choreographically elegant in prose. The creation of fictional landscapes is necessary precisely because of the opportunity it provides to experience, and demonstrate, just such possibilities of stylistic compensation and control.

Hawkes's first novel, *The Cannibal* (1949), begins, as Hawkes has said in another interview,[2] with Germany coming out of an insane asylum into a devastated landscape. It reaches back to 1914, comes up to date through the Second World War, and anticipates a future repetition of Nazi domination, which will ironically involve the return of the whole country to an insane asylum. Such is the nominal historical scope of the book, and by interweaving various figures and their deeds and situations, sometimes bringing them together in a series of juxtaposed images which make up a simultaneous panorama, Hawkes manages to suggest how deep are the seeds of repetitious violence and madness in the Germany of his book. The characters include Madame Snow, an earth mother turned destructive, who ends up by dining off her own nephew; her husband Ernie, a weak man who goes from duelling to religious fanaticism; her son, a cripple who projects pictures at a local cinema with no audience; a Signalman who has 'nothing to eat and nothing to say'; a frightened Mayor who 'had witnessed executions with his eyes closed' and who is burned to death in his own house; a drunken Census-Taker; a Duke who pursues a young boy throughout the whole book, finally cutting him to pieces prior to turning him into the main dish of a cannibalistic ritual; and an American motor-cyclist, in charge of one-third of the country, murdered by the neo-Nazi conspirators. The dominating presence is Zizendorf, the leader of the Nazi group, the narrator of the book: a figure of ruthless sexual and political power. At the other extreme is a small girl called Selvaggia, who stands at the window with open eyes of innocence and terror seeing the deeds of darkness which go on; by the end she is 'wild-eyed from watching the night and the birth of the Nation'. She is ordered by Zizendorf to close the blinds and go back to sleep. 'She did as she was told.' This is the last sentence of the book and it suggests the effortless repression of a new generation and true vision by the authoritarian power of Zizendorf, who is ordering a whole nation back to sleep, back into the asylum.

As far as conventional plot is concerned, the story concerns the history of Stella Snow's family, and the triumph of Zizendorf and his party. Certain narrative lacunae and temporal conflations, in addition to a refusal of any narrative directness, obscure the plot and help to precipitate those surreal and dream-like effects which every commentator on the book has noted. But the progression of plot is there, as surely as the Duke gradually catches up with his human prey. What has happened is that, by rearranging the fragments so that the temporal dimension often seems to be dissolved into the spatial patterning of detail, Hawkes achieves an 'interlocking structure' which we seem to experience as one unbroken landscape, time becoming subordinate to topography. It is above all what we see, like Selvaggia at the window, like Hawkes himself, which carries the impact. Again from that second interview: 'I write out of a series of pictures that literally and actually do come to mind, but I've never seen before.' It is these 'pictures' – in which human figures become part of the landscapes, buildings and things they are involved with – which make up the vision of the book. The meaning of the history referred to is indistinguishable from the desolation of the pictures brought before us.

Some of this desolation is due to the continuous use of negatives which conjures up a prevailing atmosphere of emptiness, silence and inertness, even though deeds are performed and words are spoken – no voices sang, nowhere to eat, there was no sound, there was no post, no one came and went, there was no one, there were no clocks, nothing to think of, no one to dislike, no one she needed to love, and so on. Against this background of entropy the many acts of violence are described with a slow meticulousness which makes them too seem part of the 'luminous deterioration' of the world of the book.

But more important than this are the actual landscapes themselves. These may range from a great, stinking, rotting panorama, in which the villagers are burning out pits of excrement, to an isolated detail deprived of specific location, suggesting that merging of usually separate contexts we experience in dreams. 'An oyster shell on the beach far away was shrouded in oil, coming in off the treacherous tide.' Buildings in various stages of ruin are important and the main building is the institution which is just outside the town. It is noticeable that here, as elsewhere, the building, though in decline, seems to be threatening and capable of forceful activity. 'The institution was menacing, piled backwards on itself in chaotic slumber.' In the description of the University, the same words are used, thus suggesting some identity between the two only apparently different kinds of 'institution'. 'The University was ... menacing, piled backwards on itself in chaotic slumber ... it drew the city into its walls with a crushing will ... ' Among other things, the book is about all kinds of incarceration. The figures wandering or pursuing or fleeing through this land of 'lost architecture' are really prisoners, not only of this or that building, but of delusion, fear, brutality, their own and other people's obsessions and fantasies, so that there is little difference between inside and outside the institution. It is small wonder that they return to the asylum at the end, as obediently and docilely as a child sent back to sleep, for they are never free and have no understanding of freedom. They are permanent prisoners of the landscape of the book.

When Stella and Ernie are on their honeymoon in the Alps, it is referred to as 'the upper world', while a friend who comes and tells them about the war is said to come from 'the lower world'. We are then told that Ernie prays 'knowing nothing of the encircling world'. These varying phrases in close proximity suggest the greater power of the lower and the encircling worlds, for the upper world is the illusory refuge of religious fanaticism experienced as transcendence. In fact its purity is a deathly purity of ice, and it is there that Ernie succumbs to the sickness that takes him back down into the horrendous war scenes of the lower world, and to death. The encircling world may be made up of all those things which the environment presses forward: 'She walked amid heaps of soiled nightdresses, rows of enameled pots for the old men, the stale smell of bones and flies.' Thus Stella walks among the oppressive litter of her heritage, in the house where her father has died. Or the encircling world may be like the labyrinthine obstacles of the decaying theatre which hinder the boy and enable the Duke to catch him. The ruined theatre is in addition an apt place for the Duke to secure the human material to implement his vile fantasy, and having seen the conclusion of the chase the crippled projectionist returns to bed in a state of perverse sexual excitement. The total silence of the boy victim throughout suggests not only a child's helplessness when engorged by an adult's obsession, but also the more general human subservience to the tightening grip of the encircling world.

Hawkes's is indeed a death-haunted vision, with drowned corpses resurfacing, and ghosts regathering at the place of their demise like a thickening of fog, while the living commit their slow dismemberments of chicken or child, or submit quietly to a horror which is everywhere. At the same time we should recall what Hawkes affirmed about the 'saving beauties of language', the detachment with which it defines the landscape which defiles and imprisons everything except the words of the book. By making the neo-Nazi leader, Zizendorf, a first-person narrator, Hawkes has included what is effectively a black parody of himself as writer. Such is the state of the Germany of the book that language itself is in near-total decline, while literature is impossible — a fact registered by the devastated newspaper office where Zizendorf sits. The American motor-cyclist, who travels 'along hypothetical lines of communication ... with his sack filled with unintelligible military scrawls', and whose 'only communication was silence' to the Germans, is another example of the general dissolution of the customary means of communication and the loss of information. By the end Zizendorf is spreading what he thinks of as a new order, and to do this he has to create a new voice with print. 'I, the Leader, the compositor, put the characters, the words of the new voice, into the stick. I wrote my message as I went, putting the letters into place with tweezers, preparing my first message, creating on a stick the new word.' This new word is of course sheer propaganda and rhetoric, but Hawkes knows that it reflects on the ambiguities of his own position. For he too is imposing fictions on us, constructing his 'message' with a care for which the planning leader's delicate arrangement of his words with tweezers is a fair metaphor. Hawkes's purpose is of course different – he is trying to arrest horrors in print, while Zizendorf is trying to impose and increase them through print; but they are both experts with the dark yet entrancing word.

The way Hawkes places his words produces the effect of stillness. At the same time there are reminders that the preserving stillness is in the art, while the actuality is a matter of violence and decay. Hawkes uses verbal contrasts to alert the reader not only to the sort of contrasts actually obtaining in the world of the book, but also to the more general paradox of still art grappling with moving life. Watching Jutta, for instance, 'the Duke, in his most precise manner, had noticed her gentle convolvulaceous long legs.' There is a verbal tension, almost opposition, there between the precise scrutiny and the convolvulaceous legs, between those things sharp and hard and those things curved and soft. This is not an isolated verbal felicity. At the end there is a similar opposition between the Duke, 'an orderly man', and 'the slippery carcass' he is trying to cut up 'precisely'. The 'infernal humanness' of the corpse is constantly defeating him – 'It annoyed the Duke to think that because of his lack of neatness the beast was purposely losing its value' – and he ends up with a botched job, leaving behind a 'puddle of waste'. Gruesome enough, containing touches of an appalling comedy, this scene points to an elemental conflict between destructive precision and the slippery products of nature, elusive even in death. Cannibalism is the root metaphor of the book, the primal act of negation. But what the Duke is doing is the blackest possible parody of what Hawkes himself is doing – stalking his 'subject', taking the carcass and trying to cut it up to fit into his notion of neatness and order. That puddle of waste left behind – the bugs making for it – is, in the inverted world of this book, the hallmark of yet another failed artistic venture. By making his own style both precise and convolvulaceous, Hawkes retains an awareness of a radical opposition in experience itself; it may take many forms, of which the Duke's dismembering of the young boy is, we may hope, the most extreme.

One further aspect of Hawkes's style, which results from the tweezer-like selection and placing of words, is a phenomenon which we may call semantic retardation. He presents us with surprisingly sustained sentences, of Faulknerish length and rhythmic complexity, which force us to pause at every word, to ponder and appreciate each 'isolate' in the 'set'. This sometimes has the effect of defeating the usual semantic impact of a sentence: we do not register a unit of sense and information but find ourselves taking the slow impress of vivid fragments, unanticipated phrases, unusual configurations. It is in such ways that Hawkes maintains 'the truth of the fractured picture' and causes the whole book to hang in our minds like a pervading atmosphere, an unforgettable hallucination. The result is, undoubtedly, the 'advent of a certain reality', if not exactly a historical reality, then unchallengeably a verbal reality of great power.

In *The Beetle Leg* (1951) Hawkes creates a world of the American West in a series of ten highly visualized episodes concerning people who in one way or another are connected with the family of the man buried alive in the great dam which was erected some ten years before the novel opens. The relations between these people and the differing times of the chapters are not always clear, and the plot occasionally vanishes into the sand of the great silent desert which is the background of the novel. Since motives and intentions are not rendered, for Hawkes does not treat the psychological inwardness of his characters as something separable from the land they inhabit, the result once again is of not fully explained movements in a landscape which seems to dominate all those who act, or remain inactive, in it. The pathetic little human communities, clustered around the dam and the growing turbine tower, making almost invisible spots on the vast desert, seem oddly insubstantial and ephemeral — a mirage which will fade in a desolate land which will last.

Many of the figures like to gather in the jail, comparable to the institution in *The Cannibal*. The opposition between man-made structures and the level, levelling desert, is kept to the fore throughout. On the one hand there is constant reference to all things connected with building, erecting and mending, indeed all things necessary to surviving in a frontier situation — tools, iron, drills, spikes, nails, buckets, ploughs, lattices, cooking utensils, wheels, knives and equipment in general. Men shape the wood, apply the iron, shovel away the land, build the dam, erect the towers. However, against all this human endeavour and building, the land seems hostile, moving slowly to obliterate it. At the time of the Great Slide, the landscape showed the direction and force of its slow intent.

It moved. The needles, cylinder and ink lines blurring on the heat smeared graph in the slight shade of evening, tended by the old watchman in the power house, detected a creeping, downstream motion in the dam. Leaned against by the weight of water, it was pushing southward on a calendar of branding, brushfires and centuries to come, toward the gulf. Visitors hung their mouths and would not believe, and yet the hill eased down the rotting shale a beetle's leg each several anniversaries, the pride of the men of Gov City who would have to move fast to keep up with it. But if this same machine, teletyping the journey into town, was turned upon the fields, the dry range, the badlands themselves, the same trembling and worry would perhaps be seen in the point of the hapless needle, the same discouraging pulse encountered, the flux, the same activity. It might measure the extinction of the snake or a dry finger widening in erosion.

This central passage — distinguished by containing the title — indicates that the 'Great Slide' was not a freak, isolated occurrence, but part of the great drift towards a levelling erosion on the part of the whole 'miasmal landscape'. In this hostile landscape a man is swallowed up in the earth, equipment declines, tracks disappear and people trying to find the town go astray in the absence of signs. In its way the book offers a vision of entropy close to that which determines the shape of Pynchon's fictional worlds.

The most striking figures who cross this landscape are the Red Devils and Cap Leech. The Red Devils are a motorcycle gang described only in terms of their leather uniforms and their powerful machines. No human features are ever visible. They are extremely sinister, roaring into the little town, and as suddenly vanishing back into the night; yet they are never shown doing violence. Indeed it is a group of townsfolk with the sheriff which at the end of the book creeps up on the gang and shoots at them with buckshot. As they ride out of the town a boy says, ' "They had jewels all over them," ' to which Luke replies, ' "We don't want to hear about it." ' It suggests the ambiguous fascination they exert, the streak of dark poetry they bring to the landscape.

Cap Leech, a sort of itinerant doctor, as his name suggests, travels around in a horse-drawn wagon, and he is the most ambiguous figure in the landscape. One strange passage serves to connect him with the title and suggests, perhaps, that his occupation has a mythic dimension. 'He crawled jerkily across the gumwood floor, stethoscope pressed upon the shell of a beetle sweeping hurriedly on its wire legs.' For a moment this makes him he who attends, reluctantly, clumsily, to a world moving inexorably to its final obliteration, adumbrated in the sliding of the dam. Yet the book serves to make his very activity of healer, operator, extractor, injector, very ambiguous.

Leech's final operation is in fact the extracting of a tooth from a primitive Indian girl, yet it is described in such a way as to make it seem like the definitive onslaught on the human body, combining destructive aggression with rape in a scene of comic-horrific hallucinatory vividness and exaggeration. Afterwards Leech goes out and encounters a rooster, and responds in his role, not of healer, but of pure dissector. 'He was the dismantler of everything that flew or walked or burrowed at the base of the tree.' He pursues and corners the bird, and, 'Down came his two stiff arms as one.' At this moment he is oddly reminiscent of the Duke in *The Cannibal*, the stiff destroyer of a feathered softness, the master of mortal incisions. The ambiguity of his itinerant activity suggests the ambiguity of all our released energies — ephemeral violences in a desolate landscape which moves with infinite slowness towards the final levelling. Rather than any narrative line, it is such scenes as Cap Leech cornering his rooster, or the Red Devils vanishing into the night, 'jewels all over them', that we remember — these, and the landscape of which they form a violent but deteriorating part.

The two short novels which make up *The Goose on the Grave* (1954) are set in Italy: *The Owl* in a medieval citadel called Sasso Fetore, and the title story in the Italy of the Second World War. The narrator of the first is the public hangman who seems also to be the dictator, having absolute power of life and death, to whom food, daughters and victims are offered. He holds the city in his clutches as the owl holds its prey at night with sharp, tenacious talons. The hangman is at times identified with the bird who is his emblem — Il Gufo. The second story concerns the wanderings of a young Italian orphan, Adeppi, who gets involved with various adults, a soldier, an ageing homosexual, a fanatical priest, and in general a whole landscape of corruption, brutality, degradation and death. There are certain tenuous links between the two, topographical echoes of harsh life in rocky landscapes, and a pervasive feeling of brutal impositions and horribly perverted rituals and deeds in which the principles of life and death have become grotesquely confused. The title occurs in the second story, yet in the first story a troop of geese which parades all over the landscape is one night found slaughtered; and the owl which dominates Sasso Fetore still flies about in the night that has settled on twentieth-century Italy at war. Adapting his rhetoric to the different occasions, Hawkes offers us a medieval and a modern landscape which add up, not to a historical continuity, but to two sides of a single dream centering on human violence in a hostile terrain—sudden deaths in still squares.

In the first story, the strange prerogative of the white geese which are allowed to march in their own patterns across the territory belonging to the black owl does suggest the resistance of art to the 'rigid existence' of a society brutally adjusted to the symmetry of the gallows. In the second story Adeppi at one point serenades the wife of the blind man, standing on earth which smells of 'shallow graves'. When he starts the whole family gathers to mock him. He runs away. 'Adeppi left the mandolin floating on a shallow pond, and when the sun touched the upended neck, the sight of it startled the waking ganders.' Bearing in mind that Hawkes prefaced his book with a quotation from Ezra Pound ('One must have resonance, resonance and sonority ... like a goose') this contiguity does reinforce the suggestion that the geese are somehow exemplars of all human instincts to make some sort of music even while standing on the earth which will very surely become their grave.* And Hawkes's art strives to present us both with the music and the mortality—the goose on the grave.

It is noticeable that in his later work Hawkes has moved away from 'pure vision', in which narrative tended to be dissolved in setting, towards novels which appear to have a more conventional narrative line. He himself has recognized this and sees one reason for the shift coming from 'an increasing need to parody the conventional novel'.[3] The result is another example of that sort of ambiguous parody so common in American fiction today, in which a pattern is undermined or ridiculed, yet at the same time some sort of imaginative statement is made.[4] Hawkes's next novel *The Lime Twig* (1961) includes an intention 'to parody the soporific plot of the thriller'. In the same interview Hawkes goes on to describe his growing sense of 'the possibilities for disrupting conventional forms of fiction'. Forms of fiction may be said to reflect forms of feeling, the ways in which sympathies and responses are shaped and distributed; Hawkes's desire to disrupt the more conventional novel forms is

* In an essay written in 1962 on the possibilities open to modern experimental fiction, Hawkes quoted from Rex Warner's *The Wild Goose Chase* and applied the metaphor when he identified himself as speaking for 'those still seeking the high mysterious flights of the Wild Goose, or concerned with that place into which the creative arts have fled.' (From *The Massachusetts Review*, reprinted in *The American Novel Since World War II*, edited by Marcus Klein [Fawcett Publications, New York, 1969]).

a consequence of his belief, asserted in this interview, that the function of a true experimental writer is 'to test in the sharpest way possible the range of our human sympathies and constantly to destroy mere surface morality'.

The manifest or surface story in *The Lime Twig* involves a gambling syndicate's plot to run a great racehorse, disguised as an outsider, in a big race, for obvious financial reasons. A young innocent couple get involved and come, variously to nasty ends. There are killings and beatings, thugs and prostitutes and policemen, a thrilling climax on the day of the race, and so on—all the paraphernalia of the genre. Given that this parodies the usual thriller (the innocent die mutilated; the thugs remain uncaught, etc.: the usual expectations and satisfactions of the genre are denied), we may ask what is the latent, and more serious, subject of the book? Once again we find ourselves concentrating on landscapes of ruin and desolation—London after the war, with all the squalor and misery and crumbling degradation which linger on in wastelands brought about by war. But the book is not simply another occasion for presenting landscapes necessary for the projection of the dreams emanating from the unconscious; there is a more searching subject than that. The book is not only dream-like, as all its critics have noted; it is about dreaming. It is also about that very American subject, the death of innocence in a world of nightmare evil. But pure innocence succumbing to the machinations of pure evil is melodrama, as we all know. The distinction of Hawkes's book is to suggest that the evil is in part summoned up by the dreams of innocence, that it is permitted so many triumphs because there is so much in the unconscious (even of 'innocence') that is on its side. The horses that are really racing in this novel are the horses of unconscious desire.

Michael Banks, living in the cramped suburban dwelling described in the opening section, dreams of a horse:

> knowing that his own worst dream, and best, was of a horse which was itself the flesh of all violent dreams; knowing this dream, that the horse was in their sitting room ... knowing the horse on sight and listening while it raises one shadowed hoof on the end of a silver thread of foreleg and drives down the hoof to splinter in a single crash one plank of that empty Dreary Station floor.

The dream comes true when Michael helps Hencher and Larry's gang to haul the disguised racehorse, Rock Castle, up from a boat on to the quayside. The horse itself is in the 'posture of rigorous sleep' as if made of marble. Lifted up by the crane 'it became the moonlit spectacle of some giant weather vane.' Then very slowly it raises one 'destructive hoof' and now that the gesture has moved out of dream and into reality, it strikes terror into Michael. It is the rise and fall of those destructive hooves which, again in dream-like abstractedness, reduce Hencher to a pulp; and it is under them that Michael will finally cast himself in an equivocal gesture of victory and release. When Michael is waiting in the cargo shed for the horse to be hauled up, he feels the holes in the floorboards, and looks down at all the scum and greasy water underneath – 'filth for a man to fall into'. Just so, he had dreamt of a horse powerful enough to smash the floor of his miserable home. But while dreams seem to aspire to high things – the horse in the air is like a weather-vane – when they are actualized they involve a fall into filth. Waiting for the horse to arrive Michael feels he is in 'a time slipped off its cycle'. He has indeed moved into the time scheme of his dreams, and the novel is brilliantly 'architectured' to reveal his ambiguous progress.

As the conventional narrative moves nearer the denouement at the race, Michael moves deeper into the world of his dreams, culminating in a night of unlimited sex, laid on by the gang for their own purposes but also representing the realization of all Michael's libidinous fantasies. Meanwhile Margaret is moving towards her death by beating – not unrelated, in its turn, to the masochistic fantasies she has; it is a basic condition of this dream world that it separates people, and Michael, having caught one glimpse of Margaret over the heads of an impenetrable crowd, loses her for ever. The theme of dreaming is prepared for in what seems like the meticulous and cold realism of the opening section, a monologue by Hencher all about the conditions in the rooms in lodging-houses he has experienced and observed. He describes his years 'circling' around the aptly named Dreary Station, looking for a room, with all the attendant hungers and needs such roaming can develop. He often looks up at 'gilded cherubim big as horses that fly off the top of the Dreary Station itself'. From the start the cherubim are linked to the horse and offered as a suggestive reminder of those gilded dreams which rise above the suburban desolation and the tiny rooms.

But this is wartime that Hencher is recalling, and there are other things in the air; fires (one of which kills his mother) lighting up the night, and penetrating the dreams of all those living through them. And on one occasion, Hencher watches a lifeless aeroplane float quietly down to settle in the snow, then he climbs into the control cabin and, sitting next to the dead pilot, he acts out a private fantasy. What one retains from these linked references is a sense of dreams flourishing privately in a landscape given over to death and destruction; and inevitably the dreams are influenced by their setting. 'I had my dreams,' says Hencher ('the cherubim are still my monument')' and he is the one who tries to bring 'the vague restless dreams, behind the Banks' faces into reality. Living in actual squalor they all look up at the cherubim to dream, only to see night fires which scorch their memories and falling planes which crash in their minds. Inevitably the consummation of their dreams will involve violence, perhaps death. What else should the children of war dream about? Little Monica dreams her dolls are on fire.

The cherubim occupy an elevated position – the imagination tends to dream upwards. But Michael's progress tends to be downwards to low, and sometimes actually subterranean, places: an underground lavatory where he is given orders by three men with sinister bombs in their possession; some Dantesque Steam Baths which make a fair inferno, and where Michael watches a bloody murder. From the beginning of the enterprise, Michael is constantly entering atmospheres of fog, shadow, mist, steam, a suitable atmospheric medium for the appearance of the strange and metamorphosing figures of his dreams. At the party where his sexual fantasies are unbelievably catered for, the smoke is finally 'opaque as ice'. But at the end of the night he hears a shot and goes out to see that a child has been killed. He recognizes her, ambiguously, as a girl who 'had always been coming over a bridge for him', and we cannot know just what that figure of innocence might have meant. But now 'the mists were drifting off', and the murdered child is lying there, and it is suddenly clear what has really been happening in this night given over to the realization of dreams.

The fact that Michael is moving, to some extent, through the fog of his own dreams leads us to see Larry and his gang in a rather different light, though the deeds of violence they do are cruel and evil enough. At the same time we may consider the role of the policemen in the book, who are curiously inept and impotent. Michael Banks overhears a part of one of Larry's conversations in which he is saying, ' "And I told the Inspector he was making a horrible botch of it. I said it would never do. Who's pulling the strings I told him and he got huffy, huffy, mind you ... You'd best not interfere, I said. There's power in this world you never dreamed of, I told him." ' It suggests a world not run by policemen but by gangsters, and if one reads this as indicating the relative impotence of bungling rationality in competition with the sleek ruthlessness of libidinal energies, one is registering a part of the portent of the book. For Larry is the dark angel of our darkest dreams – the ones we don't admit as ours. He arranges the excesses of sex and violence which men's, and women's, minds secretly crave. He would be powerless without those dark dreams, to the hidden impulses of which he acts as Satanic servitor. When Michael watches Cowles murdered in the Steam Baths, he sees Larry just standing there 'as if he had nothing better to do than direct this stalking through a hundred and ten degrees and great dunes of steam.' The insight is precise. Larry directs all the stalking in the steam which makes up the world of the book. When he strips at the end of the all-night party, in the room where there are appropriate black-and-white paintings of horses on the walls, he stands out like a dark god, with that same 'brutal calm' that Euripides gave to his ruthless Dionysus in *The Bacchae*. He reigns supreme over the dark kingdom of our dreams, from which in turn he derives his power.[5]

The question arises, can man take issue with the potency of his own worst dreams? This is the point of the 'climax' of the book when Michael decides to spoil the gang's plan and runs on to the racecourse to throw himself in front of Rock Castle, thus preventing that horse from winning the race. It is an equivocal act because in one sense it is the final self-destructive abandonment of himself to the horse of his darkest dream; at the same time it is his victorious bid to break the dream, which at the same time renders Larry and his gang completely powerless and ruins all their plans. The actual race is called The Golden Bowl, and Hawkes said he took the title from Henry James, and meant to imply that Michael Banks manages to break the golden bowl of earthly pleasures.[6] This obviously represents some kind of a victory, and Hawkes went on to admit that the ending of the novel is conceivably redemptive. In addition Michael sees 'a dove bursting with air on a bough' as he runs to his death, thus perhaps alluding to another late James novel.

Such infiltrated references do not make a redemption, though in a novel which has as part of its intricate structure the notion of birds being trapped by limed twigs, the sight of a bird breaking free is perhaps a vision which Michael earns by turning against those forces, inner and outer, which trap him. What is more memorable is the human effort to destroy a dream of evil partly of one's own making. Running out on to the track Michael seems to regain some of his innocence ('The child pounded on his heart') as he turns to encounter the 'approaching ball of dust'. The confrontation points to the nature of the victory he will achieve — 'at one end the horses bunching in fateful heat and at the other end himself — small, yet beyond elimination, whose single presence purported a toppling of the day, a violation of that scene at Aldington, wreckage to horses and little crouching men.' For one moment of resolute, undreaming consciousness, Michael becomes the director, the person in charge of events – even though he cannot prevent Margaret from being killed. He turns on the horses he helped to set running, and which by now have gathered a momentum it is fatal to intercept. To wreck the race at this stage is, then, an act of heroism. It is followed by, is indeed inextricable from, the moment of death. In establishing the landscape of his dream England, Hawkes at one point describes a vast graveyard of ships, arrested in mud, secure from tides and storms – 'All won, all lost, all over.' Banks now shares that condition. But he has broken out of the evil and destructive dreams engendered by the desolate world into which he was born. It is a fleeting victory over the compulsions of the encompassing landscape which Hawkes was to study further in his next book.

The novel is terrifying, at least in its material: a terror related to Hawkes's knowledge, to quote Leslie Fiedler, 'that there can be no terror without the hope for love and love's defeat'.[7] At the same time in reading it one is not fully drawn into the terror, to be drowned in it. There is something keeping us away from the actual sensations going on and being felt in the material. What is interposed is the complicated and wrought fabric of his style – a highly foregrounded style. At one point Margaret notices 'a dead wasp suspended between the window's double sheets of glass'; at another, Hencher recalls the spectacle of his mother eating, refracted through a glass of port, and stilled almost to a painting. Hawkes's style is just such a glass, sometimes a coloured glass, which brings things into new highlighted vividness, throws us into startling intimacy with unexplained or ominous details, and which holds things in stillness and distances them as spectacle even when we most feel their hallucinatory presence. By often confronting us with powerful specificity devoid of explanatory context, Hawkes draws us into the bemusing landscapes and conditions of his work. At the same time, by provoking us to scrutinize the actual texture of the prose, looking for echoes, linked images, fragments of pattern, all those linguistic devices which enable him to erect a linguistic order quite in despite of the often appalling disorder of his subject, Hawkes keeps us back from total absorption into the landscape.

There are various kinds of scrutiny in the book. A boy submits his miserable-looking dog to long, loving inspections, finding pictures on its purple tongue and pearls between its claws. The police study the particulars of the given scene with cold, detached eyes, looking for clues. There are all kinds of attention which can be paid to our environment – and to Hawkes's novel. Since he shows the policemen setting off resolutely in the wrong direction, he would seem to imply that they are missing the *real* plot, being led astray by their narrowly empirical notation of the evidence. It would seem that the loving eye is more perceptive than the detecting eye, and Hawkes, I think, wants us to find the pictures and pearls in the unsavoury material which he has found — and formed.

He has himself described how he worked his way towards the use of the first-person narrator 'by a series of semi-conscious impulses and sheer accidents'.[8] *The Cannibal* was, apparently, written in the third person but then Hawkes, by his own account, found himself identifying with the criminal leader of the hallucinated uprising, and so he went through the manuscript and changed the pronouns from third to first person. In this way the authorial consciousness was given definition 'in terms of humor and "black" intelligence'. Hawkes also states that he added the rather sadistic sheriff's first-person prologue to *The Beetle Leg*, and Hencher's prologue to *The Lime Twig*, as afterthoughts. *The Owl* is narrated by the hangman himself. Sidney Slyter, the prurient and inquisitive columnist who reports on the racing scenes in *The Lime Twig* and whose speculations precede each chapter is, in Hawkes's own words, 'one of the most degrading and perversely appealing figures in the novel' and Hawkes admitted that he intended him to be a parody of the novelist himself. If we take all these figures together, a varied group of narrators emerges. Zizendorf, the sheriff, and the Owl in different ways control the communities around them: they can impose the patterns of their black intelligence. Hencher on the other hand is a victim and an aspirant towards love; he understands the plights and needs of all the dreamers in small rooms. He succumbs to Larry's dark ordering of things. Slyter is somewhere in between — the voyeur at the edge who turns events into the patterns of newspaper copy. Clearly Hawkes can, in this way, project his varying sense of the author's relationship with his material — now the aggressive dictator, now the prurient observer, now the rather helpless lover. But there is also a discernible development from the omnipotent narrator to the impotent narrator, which is completed in his most recent novel, *Second Skin*, narrated by a figure called Skipper whom Hawkes has described as having 'his basis in Hencher'.

Second Skin (1964) not only draws together some of Hawkes's central preoccupations; it also represents an advance, with less of the stasis of landscape and more of the motion of narrative. The title points to the central concern of the novel — skin, the vulnerable surface of our 'schizophrenic flesh', the clothes we cover it with, the points which penetrate it. The idea of a second skin can refer to all the clothes we don according to conventions; or it can suggest the recovery of our original nakedness, and thus innocence. It can imply the sloughing off of an old skin and the rebirth into a new one. This fits in, of course, with the desire to slip off old imposed identities which is so prevalent in contemporary American fiction.

The most searching book on the significance of clothes written in the nineteenth century is Carlyle's *Sartor Resartus* – the tailor retailored. It includes a discussion of Teufelsdröckh's 'mad daydream ... of levelling society' by making everyone dress in the same simple leather garment. The editor is sceptical. 'The idea is ridiculous in the extreme. Will Majesty lay aside its robes of state, and Beauty its frills and train-gowns, for a second-skin of tanned hide?' Teufelsdröckh's idea of a 'second-skin' to be worn by everyone was a scheme for obliterating the distinguishing marks which create social roles and positions, and hence the whole proliferation of hierarchical structures which cause social inequality and make the manipulation of other people possible. This does, indeed, correspond to an abiding American dream.

Hawkes's book envisages a movement towards a dream of *almost* complete nakedness (the importance of the qualification should become clear); in the world of this book those clothes cover best which cover least. Skipper gives us his 'naked history', sitting on a tropical island in minimal garb. Yet we should retain the paradox that to give us his 'naked history' he has to stitch together a verbal rendering of the various episodes. All art entails the fabrication of visible (or audible) surfaces, and works of art can be regarded as a form of clothing in which consciousness displays and defines itself. One of the second skins in this novel is, necessarily, the book itself; and Skipper's naked history comes to us in the most intricate verbal garment which Hawkes has yet woven.

As Skipper reconstructs his life from the vantage point of his tropical island, he has to summon up incidents which include the suicides of his father, his wife, and his daughter, Cassandra. He also has to redescribe the finding of his son-in-law, Fernandez, horribly murdered and dismembered. He has to evoke certain incidents from his time spent in the Navy during the war, including a brutal mutiny led by a figure of demonic malice named Tremlow. He remembers his daughter's wedding and the honeymoon trip to Mexico. At the end of his tour of duty he took Cassandra and her child to a bleak Atlantic island which is dominated by an awesome female named Miranda whose capacity for destructive action and heartless malice seems to lie at the centre of a world of evil negation. From this island he removed himself to the tropical island of pastoral bliss. From here he is now looking back on the varieties of evil which he has witnessed, experienced, and been helpless to prevent — and from which he has now escaped, having survived their multiple affronts and attacks. He brings into focus various distinct areas, or geographies, we could call them — a childhood garden; the wartime cities given over to military purposes; two desert journeys; two spells at sea; the sterile black Atlantic island, hard, cold, and menacing; the colourful and fertile tropical island, warm, welcoming, effortlessly adjusting to the seasonal rhythms.

The patterning of alternating kinds of landscape is what makes up the patchwork fabric of the book, providing a more than narrative meaning for the story we can reconstruct from Skipper's recalled episodes. Again, apart from the tropical island, all the landscapes seem to espouse or nourish some principle of evil, to harbour forces on the side of death. Skipper's father was a mortician and with the frequent deaths of those he loves Skipper is constantly brought to grave-sides and cemeteries. The helplessness of love against death might be said to be one of the themes of the book, and although at the end he is celebrating the birth of a child amidst the fecund lushness of his tropical island, the last celebration takes place in a cemetery. *Et in Arcadia Ego.*

Deathly landscapes predominate. The background to the violence of the human agents is usually a landscape in a state of apparently accelerating entropy. The black Atlantic island in particular is a place of rotting, rusting, moulding, rank disintegration and harsh rocky ruin. The inexplicable malice and destructive horrors which Skipper continually witnesses or encounters he tends to relate back to the brutal and irrational hatred he met in the figure of Tremlow, who organized the mutiny on his ship and prepared a particularly degrading beating up for Skipper. Where Miranda is 'my monster', Tremlow is 'my devil'. Tremlow tries to take over the ship, by taking hold of the wheel and 'leading us into some forbidden circle'. After this experience Skipper swears off the sea for ever; but on the Atlantic island he again submits himself to 'the uncomfortable drift of a destructive ocean' when he goes on the boat trip organized specifically to bring about the enforced seduction of Cassandra. Once again Skipper is beaten by the conspirators, and, as usual, he is entirely helpless to prevent the implementation of all their dark designs.

The destructive ocean, the arid desert, the alien and brutal cityscapes of Pacific wartime, the lifeless rock of the black island, overlooked by the blind stone lighthouse from which Cassandra throws herself on to the sharp black boulders of the shore — these form some of the landscapes traversed by Skipper before he arrives at his blue island of fertility and peace. What all these areas have in common is the presence in them (or on them) of sharp, hard things, sometimes natural, more often man-made, forming a continuum of stony and metallic objects, places and people, most of them with dangerous points and edges. Skipper, with his hypersensitive skin, suffers unusual cuts and woundings. He has trouble with all edged or pointed things, and hostility assails him in a variety of metallic forms. He is constantly liable to abrasions and puncturings, as is brought out in one of the most vivid scenes in the book when he is tattooed at his daughter's request with her dead husband's name. We are made to feel 'every puncture of the needle – fast as the stinging of bees', and this series of atrociously painful pin-pricks marching across his bare chest is a compressed analogue for what he seems to undergo in the book. Despite the pain, he survives. 'Marked and naked as I was, I smiled. I managed to stand.' This too, summarizes what he sees as his essential effort in the whole book. At the end of the tattooing ordeal he refers to 'this green lizard that lay exposed and crawling on my chest' and this points forward to an incident on the blue island when an iguana settles on Kate's back and sticks its claws in. Kate is Skipper's pregnant native mistress, and she has been lying at the edge of a swamp where she intends to have her baby; it is in this position that the great iguana ('twenty or thirty pounds of sprawling bright green putty') fastens on to her naked back. Skipper, despite the nauseous feeling of the reptilian skin on his own, tries to pull the iguana off; but the claws grip like steel. He has to be patient, waiting for the iguana to release its grip and move off of its own accord. There is a clear echo here of the tattooing scene, for both the needle and the claws impose their green pain on the helpless human skin; at the same time there are differences important to the meaning of the book. The iguana is loathsome enough, but it is a part of nature, while the needle is a man-made instrument. Throughout his life Skipper has tried to forestall evil and protect those he loves – his interference has never managed to deflect the evil coming their way, however, and conceivably it has hastened its victory. Now he learns patience, and in time the claws are retracted leaving no unnatural marking. There is horror in nature, but not that particular, destructive malice that Skipper has found in the human world.

There are many harsh collisions between bodies in the book, culminating in a grotesque belly-bumping tournament on the black island. It is perhaps symptomatic of this world that nearly all the contacts between skins – from rubbings and bumpings to more lethal lacerations – are acts of aggression. The fact that love also depends on the contact of skins is less prominent. The prevailing feeling is of the body as an obstacle and the skin as a target. This underlying sense of the flesh itself being a hindrance, something that traps man, runs quite deeply through American literature, producing a dream of an existence beyond the limitations and impositions of physical life which persists today (as in Burroughs) and is subtly at work deep in this novel.

More obvious, however, is the feeling of the imposition of all kinds of clothes. As might be expected in wartime, there are many details of the putting on of uniforms, sometimes too tight, so that one registers the uniformed state as part of generally constrained condition. The group of A.W.O.L. soldiers who accost Skipper and Cassandra in the desert are heavy with uniform and accessories, and the scene describing how they strip off until they are almost naked obviously has a ritual significance – not only in connection with their own determination to discard their military identities, but with Skipper's own burgeoning desire to pass beyond the uniformed condition altogether. On the black island, not only is Miranda dressed in powerful, strident colours, but she mocks Skipper's impotence by putting his uniform on a female dummy. Her own clothes have a sinister potency; a large black brassière in particular comes to seem increasingly menacing until, at the end of the boat-trip on which Cassandra's fate is sealed, Skipper wakes up to see 'the black brassière was circling above my head and lashing its tail'. The power of this negative earth mother, goddess of death, is present in her gross accoutrements. It is on this final boat-trip that the novel's title is uttered, by Skipper when he is given some oilskins to wear: ' "My second skin," I said, because I had gone out once before in oilskins ... ' The oilskin is a protection from the sea, but it is also an imposition to constrict his movements when the boys want to concentrate on Cassandra. In this dual capacity it perhaps points to the ambiguous status of our first skin. Certainly when at the end of the trip Skipper looks at the oilskins piled up on the boat and adds 'Our wretched skins,' we register it as a comment with multiple references.

The blue island is different from the black island in every way; indeed it is so completely the reverse of the Atlantic island of death that the very schematization of opposites attracts our attention. Just as Skipper considers he has somewhat 'redeemed' his father's morbid profession by becoming an artificial inseminator, so more generally the blue island seems to redeem the harsh and evil aspects of the world he has previously experienced. The cows were 'dead and gone' from the black island, but here the herd participates in the heady atmosphere of fertility and sensuality. Where Skipper was the victim of other people's plans and purposes and incapable of taking any efficient initiative against evil designs, he is now in charge of the rituals and movements of his small group of loving friends; where Miranda led one kind of destructive procession down to the beach, he leads his procreative procession into the fields for the ceremonies of insemination. Instead of the sinister tolling of a metallic bell, there is the rich lowing of cattle; instead of the rankness of decay, the sweet smell of wind-blown spices. In place of the harsh edges of metallic things and the repugnant stone of dead architecture, a voluptuous softness and the rhythmic ease of organic growth pervades the atmosphere; from malice, to love; from the island of death to an island of life. If at first this looks like a proto-Gauguin-esque escapism and wish-fulfilment and we think that the consolations of the blue island make up all too neatly for the atrocities and negations of the black one, we should consider that this may have been part of Hawkes's intention. To explain what I mean, I want first to point to a suggestive repetition of image.

When Skipper leaves the Navy after his tour of duty is completed, he sets out on the cross-desert journey which will finally take him to both islands. We may consider that this journey is an attempt to get out of the world of war altogether, a search for a haven not unlike Yossarian's search for Sweden/Eden. The bus station from which he leaves is 'The terminal. Our point of departure.' This suggests the point where one world ends and another one begins. His journeying, I would suggest, is directed towards finding another kind of reality—away from the facts of war to a dream of peace, a very American quest. The different realities he passes through are subtly linked by the presence in each of a starfish shape or a star-shaped hole. In the order in which they appear, this is the pattern. On his first day on the Atlantic island Skipper thinks he sees a naked woman on the beach 'as white as a starfish and inert, naked, caught amongst the boulders'. This is a premonition of Cassandra's coming suicide. Then on his tropical island he mentions the 'star-shaped hole in the roof' which he specifically declines to repair, preferring a roofless barn. We then discover that the ship on which Tremlow mutinied was the U.S.S. *Starfish*. At the peak of Tremlow's brutality to him, Skipper falls down into a lifeboat, breaking through the canvas into the hands of a group of mutineers who start to beat him up. He looks up and sees 'a star-shaped hole in the tarpaulin overhead' and it is through that hole that he escapes, thanks to a rope lowered by a friend. One feels that the hole in the tarpaulin and the hole in the barn are somehow connected – perhaps marking the spot through which Skipper escaped from the dark world of brutality into the dream of peace. Perhaps indeed betokening a second birth – up through the canvas, down through the roof on to the island. Similarly the fatal ship *Starfish* and the starfish corpse suggest a continuity of evil and death. Just as the starfish and the star are linked by a shape, and a name, in common, and yet together point to the extreme distance between one of the lowest forms of life and the highest tokens of our aspiration; just so Skipper falls among starfish yet reaches up to the stars, as buffoons and dreamers are wont to do. This contact between (or experience of) opposite extremes is part of the subject, as a brief consideration of the nature of the two islands quickly reveals.

In addition I think it hints at one of the more interesting possibilities of the book: namely, Skipper's ability to transform one extreme into another – to turn the starfish corpse into the star-shaped hole of escape. Or perhaps it would be better to say that he has the power to metamorphose the forms and shapes of evil, not denying them but transmuting them so that they can be subsumed into his dream island. Thus one could see the iguana as summarizing the green pain inflicted on the human skin in the other world; under his new dispensation this has been transformed into an animal which in time goes away. Another example would be the mysterious water-wheel which is on the tropical island, a useless and inexplicable remnant. It is now thick with green growth, and as such it seems to echo 'the little iron wheel' which was on the ship on which Skipper and Cassandra are taken for that last, evil voyage. More generally it seems to be related somehow to Miranda's sinister spinning-wheel, and then further back to Tremlow's attempt to subvert the ship's course by swinging the wheel over as far as it would go. In turn we may be reminded of all the steering-wheels of the many destructive vehicles Skipper has recalled. One gets the feeling that Skipper has, as it were, subsumed all these hostile wheels into this one enigmatic water-wheel, but on his island the wheel is 'robbed of its power'. It is another example of a predominantly hostile or dangerous shape being transformed, and losing its power for evil, on the magical blue island. In such ways Skipper makes the negative yield a positive, in the specifically photographic sense. This is why the blue island is indeed effectively a direct opposite of the black island. The same outlines can occur in both, but whereas on one they are usually connected with things that crush, on the other Skipper is likely to have extracted a sweetness from them.

The tropical island is as gentle as Skipper could imagine – it is, indeed, the island of his imagination. And as such it represents that release from conditioning which is an American dream: 'it *is* a wandering island, of course, unlocated in space and quite out of time.' It represents a terrain liberated from both the rocky landscapes and the destructive ocean of his earlier experience; here 'I float timelessly in my baby-blue sea'. Where everything was fixed and frozen on the black island, here everything flows. Clothes are shed, uniforms allowed to rot, and with the move towards nudity, identity starts to fade away. Both the sexes and the races tend to merge together. Individual sexual role is less important, and no one is quite sure who is the father of Kate's child. The warm fluidity of the atmosphere and the suggestion of a continuum of unindividuated sexual activity perhaps hint at a return to the 'polymorphous perverse' state of infancy. Whereas the Atlantic island is described as being in the claws of the monster time, the Pacific island is, for Skipper, his 'time of no time' (like infancy). It is also his place of no place. The fact that a passing ship is unaware of its proximity to them indicates to Skipper that 'apparently our wandering island has become quite invisible.'

Skipper opens the book by identifying himself as a 'lover of the hummingbird' and later describes how he watches the hummingbird 'destroying his little body' among the flowers. Birds have always provided a leitmotiv, if not more, in Hawkes's novels, and the hummingbird, with its incredible metabolism which seems to be constantly on the point of annihilating the flesh altogether, and its apparent ability to deny the laws of gravity and remain suspended in the air, is a singularly appropriate bird for Skipper's magic island, suspended mysteriously in no time and no place, this 'mythic rock' on which he conducts his own slow pastorals and supervises peaceful idylls and gentle rituals of love.* This island is the ultimate refuge and triumph — the place where the imagination reigns supreme, free from the iron brutalities and impingements of the other world. It is not fixed but floating, not rigidly plotted on a map but wandering. It represents a mode of motion transformed into a location, and as such could be described as the sought-for destination of many recent American heroes. In a profound sense it is an American dream.

At this point we should consider the narrator himself a little more closely. He is another American idealist, humiliated by the world to

---

* The hummingbird, feeding delicately and deliberately on sweet, rich things, offers a fair analogue for the writer, who is determined to extract sweetness from his garden of experience. Emily Dickinson has two poems about the hummingbird — numbers 500 and 1,463 in the *Collected Poems* — and conceivably Hawkes intends an oblique reference.

a comic degree. If we take him at his own valuation, he is a lover, a man of peace whose endless good intentions and protective attempts are endlessly thwarted in a wicked world. He sees himself as a 'courageous victim' and while he never puts up much of a fight in his fleshly encounters with determined aggression—'in the stuffed interior of my brain I was resisting', as he says of the tattooing ordeal. Confronted with the mess made by Miranda when she empties all the baby bottles and cuts off the tops of the rubber nipples, he says 'I could make nothing of this sad vehement litter,' and the confession could be extended to his experience of all the landscapes of vehement litter that he passes through. The given world is nauseating to him. He has three bouts of vomiting when the foul nourishment—literal and perceptual—thrust upon him by these landscapes is no longer assimilable. On one occasion Skipper adds, 'Anyone who has gotten down on his knees to vomit has discovered, if only by accident, the position of prayer.' Thus his vomiting becomes a symbolic act of reverent repudiation. His helplessness is underlined by the number of people he claims to love who commit suicide or who are killed; yet he insists that his story is not only of 'helplessness' and 'collapse' but rather 'the chronicle of recovery, the history of courage'.

But against this relatively exuberant self-evaluation we could put our dawning realization that he is, after all, very impotent indeed. His role of artificial inseminator seems to suggest that his desire to be a lover is not matched by a comparable energy of performance—Kate's child may well not be his. It is quite clear that one reason his wife committed suicide was his inability to afford her any sexual satisfaction; indeed, there are some fairly strong suggestions that if anything he is homosexual. In many ways he is the 'old maid' he is accused of being. His desire to protect could be seen as an interfering possessiveness, and it is possible to see his very tolerance and affection as having disastrous results in the real world. He is comically smug about his own virtue—'how satisfying that virtue always wins'—and one tends to forget that the only person he finally does take out his anger on is a boy, Bub. We never hear what Cassandra thinks of her father, though she does impose the humiliating tattoo on him, and usually seems eager to avoid his extreme solicitousness. What was he doing on her honeymoon, anyway? He announces at the start that he is most of all 'lover of my harmless and sanguine self' and one could see the whole account as an egoistical attempt to impose on the reader a self-justificatory and delusional version of events which might well have afforded a different reading.

Hawkes himself said that he found something 'affirmative' in this novel, and he stated that he intended Skipper to be seen as a 'survivor' in the struggle of 'life-force versus death' no matter how 'ineffectual' he has been in his relationships with other people. What is clear is that Skipper is finding and exercising a freedom and flamboyant mastery in his verbal patterning of events which he never enjoyed in the events themselves. The last chapter of his account is called 'The Golden Fleas', a possible pun which could refer to the mythical golden fleece of magical potency, which in turn offers a joking comparison with the golden hairs he is growing on his chest to cover the scar of his tattoo. The magic of art is covering over the wounds of life. He can summon up the horrifying events of the past in all their harsh outline — 'brutal silhouette', 'frozen bacchanal', 'waxen tableau' and other such phrases reveal how sharply the painful details are fixed in his mind. But they are now transmuted, in and by his art. He calls his history 'my evocation through a golden glass', thus referring not only to his sunny, island detachment but also to the golden glass of his prose. He is now his own mythographer, and just as he has undisputed authority on the island, so he can do what he likes in his writing. He is transposing his life by describing it in his chosen way. Thus he is able to make whatever was negative in the past into something more healing and affirmative by submitting it to his own stylistic and rhetorical translations. People and places are often introduced preceded by the word 'my'; the reiterated possessive pronoun reminds us that *he* is now doing the arranging and the placing. This is very much *his* version.

It is part of this process that he should feel at liberty to avail himself of a whole range of mythological references, applying them as he pleases. He refers more than once to 'my kingdom' as he surveys the terrain he has traversed, and he seems to see himself both as Priam, the last king of Troy, and Prospero, ruler of Shakespeare's last magic island. If he is both Priam and Prospero, then of course he has *two* daughters — Cassandra *and* Miranda. The fact that in the book they have turned out so ironically different from their prototypes serves to indicate how free Skipper feels he can be in his mythologizing. More importantly, if they are both his daughters, then *both* islands are part of his kingdom. Both islands are fantasy islands, the Atlantic purgatory as well as the Pacific paradise, as Skipper himself comes to realize. His dreaming has two sides to it.

The overall implication of the book, then, is this. Skipper's experience as a child, and as a man in wartime America, was 'real', not fabricated. This experience was then submitted to two dream versions, resulting in the two islands which define the antipodal extremes of Skipper's imaginative universe. The first is a paranoid and self-pitying projection of a world totally given over to the forces of negation and death. The second is a compensating and self-congratulatory version in which those forces are subsumed, rendered impotent, or transformed, and everything is in the sway of the peaceful rhythms of life. One is a nightmare of utter powerlessness; the other is a dream of pure freedom. In the first, Skipper is completely controlled; the second he controls. The two islands are the two necessary landscapes by which Skipper can chart the meaning of his experience, and through which Hawkes can explore the limits of his art. A student in one of my seminars pointed out that there are two different sets of images which recur in connection with Skipper's experience and which derive from his memories of his father and mother respectively. The first chapter contains these early memories. His father is for ever associated, in Skipper's mind, with a hearse-like black car, the bullet with which he committed suicide, the lavatory where he killed himself. From him Skipper learns about 'death as a lurid truth'. His mother, on the other hand, is associated with pastoral and religious memories. Skipper remembers her gardening as if she was praying, and he thinks of her standing veiled and innocent in front of their white house. From her he gathered 'a promise of mystery'. This basic parental polarity establishes a pattern of different orders of experience and truth which can be detected in all the subsequent episodes. The black island can be seen as a vision of the complete triumph of his father's kind of truth in which all the images connected with him are dominant. The blue island, by contrast, sees the full flowering of his mother's promise of mystery, with innocence and reverence recovered in a perpetual pastoral. More than that, the mother's imagery proves ultimately more potent than the father's, because it can subsume and transform it. The final scene is indeed in a cemetery: his father's domain; but it is now experienced as a fruitful garden: his mother's magic.

All this makes the status of any particular narrative event problematical. We cannot be sure how much external reality and history has been annexed by Skipper's imagination or transformed by his fantasies; 'history is a dream already dreamt and destroyed,' he says. Clearly Skipper has had some actual experience: fragments of his naval garments and vestiges of scars remain with him on the blue island, just as memories linger on in his mind. He speaks of himself at one point as one of those good, pathetic men of imagination who, 'are destined to live out our fantasies, to live out even the sadistic fantasies of friends, children and possessive lovers'. The suggestion, perhaps, is that the reality we encounter tends to be fashioned by our own and other people's fantasies, some sadistic, others more Utopian. Where Skipper triumphs is in extricating himself from the evil fantasies by which men (including, perhaps, himself) shape and pervert reality—these too are ugly 'wretched skins' to be sloughed off. Skipper's island freedom is the measure of his ability to dream a better dream.

But we return to the fact that the book itself is a type of skin. In describing his father's suicide, Skipper reveals that he tried to dissuade his father from the fatal shot by playing to him on his cello —'wood that was only a shell, a thin wooden skin'. Just so, the intricately interwoven prose of his book is a skin, an instrument. The cello cannot prevent his father from killing himself—art is helpless against death—yet there may be a goose on the grave. His book is the life retailored, restitched. In the first sentence he describes himself as 'lover of bright needlepoint and the bright stitching fingers of humorless old ladies bent to their sweet and infamous designs', and there is indeed more than a little needlework in the book. Miranda works endlessly at her midnight sewing-machine, and the tattooist is a cruel 'skin stitcher' who imposes a piece of 'needlework' on his skin which is a long time healing. Skipper describes him as a 'brute artist' and once again we can see that Hawkes has included more than one degrading parody of his own position as artist—old lady and brute tattooist. For Skipper is, as we have noted, stitching together his life in his own 'hectic needlework'—to borrow his description of the waves. Turning the sea into needlework is indeed the ultimately fixing art, and some people find Hawkes's intricate needlework so dense and tortuously convoluted that they dislike its airless brilliance. But the book is a garment of real beauty, a comedy of survival which has great relevance for contemporary American fiction. For Hawkes has grasped a central paradox and incorporated it into his book—namely, that the character and author in search of some brave new world, be it Sweden, the other side of the world's mirror, or any other nominal location of a dream of freedom, will ultimately have to find it in the second skin of his art. That is the only island on which he can be at liberty and go almost naked. As Hester Prynne discovered, that is the fine needlework which is the best defence against the needles of the world's dark designs.

Chapter 10 What is the Case?

> 'Nothing for me was simply *the case* forever and aye, only "this case".'
>
> *(Giles Goat-Boy)*

John Barth is a writer capable of an authoritative stylistic idiosyncrasy quite as original and recognizable as that of John Hawkes. But where Hawkes concentrates on necessary landscapes, Barth addresses himself to the problem of arbitrary readings, and this shift of emphasis from necessity to arbitrariness produces a very different body of fiction. To appreciate the significance of this difference is important for an understanding of contemporary American fiction; for where Hawkes transforms horrors into a kind of verbal play, Barth starts with a sense that verbal play precedes existence and experience, and this has led him, if not into horrors, certainly into some problematical areas. The achievement of his remarkable work is in part related to his willingness and ability to explore those areas. In a sense John Barth's fiction takes its point of departure from Wittgenstein's proposition that 'the world is all that is the case.' This sentence recurs in varying forms throughout his work and often serves to pose basic problems for many of his main characters who, in one way or another, are fairly saturated with the author's own thinking. What is the case that is the world, and what clues does it provide for significant action within it? Is the case definitive or provisional, fixed or variable? Several of his characters are aware of the power of the mind to originate a whole range of things which are *not* the case, or to provide such a variety of versions of what the case is that the very notion of any stable meaning or permanent value inhering in the actual given world is denied. This produces a mood or atmosphere of ambiguous freedom, both for the character in his situation and the author in his fiction-making.

If there is no one fixed 'reality' then the self can improvise a theoretically endless succession of roles to play *in* the world, just as the author can invent an 'endless succession of names' *for* the world. John Barth has said in an interview: 'ontology and cosmology are funny subjects to improvise. If you are a novelist of a certain type of temperament, then what you really want to do is re-invent the world. God wasn't too bad a novelist, except he was a Realist ... a certain kind of sensibility can be made very uncomfortable by the recognition of the *arbitrariness* of physical facts and the inability to accept their *finality*.'[1] This impulse to 'imagine alternatives to the world' and his very American disinclination to accept any shapes as fixed and final, involves Barth in a formal problem: how can you have a provisional form? Just as it involves his characters in those problems of identity which were discussed in earlier chapters, how can you be a self if you are a series of roles?

Barth's first novel, *The Floating Opera* (1956, 1967), is the account of a man trying to establish the explanation of a day in 1937 when he changed his mind. This was the day when Todd Andrews decided to commit suicide and then did not. The date was June 21st or 22nd and his refusal to pinpoint the exact day is symptomatic of his inclination to preserve a certain amount of uncertainty in his account and not commit himself to the absoluteness of historical chronology. This is related to his own perception that no explanation can be final and conclusive. He found this out when he tried to explain the apparently inexplicable fact of his father's suicide in an *Inquiry*, a copious amassing of all the details of his father's life. It is an endless task since all the potentially relevant information can never be gathered in, and ultimately it is impossible to see causes, you can only infer them. The feeling here is similar to Tristram Shandy's discovery that to give a truly full account of his own origin would involve him in a history of the universe. The resultant arbitrariness and incompleteness of form which Sterne built into the novel as a lexical dramatization of this realization undoubtedly influenced Barth and, by extension, his character Todd Andrews as he casts around for the facts which led up to and surrounded his own resolution, and failure, to commit suicide. Author and character alike are unusually aware of the arbitrariness of the fiction-making process and the problems that beset any narrative orderings or explanations of those waves of accidents which make up a person's life.

But Todd Andrews is a particular kind of narrator. Barth has said that his early works were intended as studies in nihilism, and the focus here is on a mind cut adrift from the matter and life around it, an intelligent consciousness which lacks any sense of the value of the context it finds itself operating in. In this the narrator is like the emotionally dead narrator of *The Epitaph of a Small Winner*, and we know that Barth has a great admiration for Machado de Assis (who was in turn influenced by Sterne). Andrews reveals himself as a man in whom the usual affective connections to the given world have been corroded, leaving him trapped inside his passionless cerebrations. He may take a detached interest in the case that is the world, or the cases that are the world, just as he retains sufficient curiosity to work out what can be made of the various bizarre legal cases which he handles in his role of lawyer. But he has no belief in justice and regards the law as purely a game. He is entirely indifferent to what finally results from any one case, and in this his attitude to the law is a projection of his view of the world. His attitude to his routine existence is cynical, a parody of purposiveness built on the premise that, 'for me at least, goals and objectives are without value.' Living in the shadow of the great fact of his life — his weak heart — he has come to feel that nothing matters, that *nothing* is intrinsically valuable.' Given that he has cornered himself in the adroit negations of his lonely mind, just as he resides in solitude in an hotel room, the question must be — how did he act, what did he do to occupy his conscious hours?

Lacking any sense of any kind of imperative, and having a purely conditional view of all action, insisting that every 'should' should be preceded by an 'if', Andrews reveals that he has only been able to move and act at all by adopting a series of masks. 'It is a matter of attitudes, of stances — of masks, if you wish, though the term has a pejorativeness that I won't accept.' His heightened self-consciousness makes him unusually aware of the 'wardrobe of masks' which other people draw on for their apparent emotions and reactions, and this sense of the theatrical elements in supposedly genuine living is only heightened by the comically exaggerated and parodically conventional acts, performances and imitations of the literally Floating Opera, a river-boat show which he attends on the day he intends to commit suicide. Having stared into the void behind all the masks and experienced complete despair, he realizes that, *'There is no way to master the fact with which I live,'* and suddenly arrives at the stance to end all stances — suicide.

Andrews has reached a point at which he approximates to a closed system which, as Wiener described, runs down for lack of any input; he has attained an extreme autonomy of inner self from environment, being immune to all emotional stimuli. He has come to this point by insisting on bringing to bear a pure rationality on those less than rational drives and impulses which connect a man to his environment. (Todd is always looking in mirrors, and mirror-gazing, in Barth's work, usually indicates excessive and disabling habits of reflection.) One of the problems he is trying to track down in his *Inquiry* is the grounds for the *'imperfect communication'* between

himself and his father; by extension between himself and the world
that he was born into. But this attempt to work out everything on
paper is a part of his malaise. The little girl who asks 'why' of every
statement made to her, reveals to Todd how quickly 'inquiring' will
bring you to the end of the road—where, if you want to be purely
rational, you find the hemlock of Socrates waiting. Questioners tend
not to be able to enter life with any assurance in Barth's world.
Hamlet's famous speech of reflexive inquiry is spoken by the most
inept performer on the stage of the Floating Opera, and used as a
would-be suicide note by the most inept character in the hotel where
Andrews lives. Hamlet types, it seems, are bad at acting and at living.
Since Todd fails in his suicide attempt it would appear that they are
equally inept at dying. Todd only desists from another suicide attempt because he decides that if there is no reason for any action that
extends to suicide as well. He puts Hamlet's famous question behind
him as meaningless. However, the fact remains that Todd Andrews
himself is, throughout, the most compulsive inquirer, constantly
trying to erect verbal and mental constructs.

In this connection it is directly relevant that he spends much of his
time building boats, an activity which he himself equates with the
writing of his *Inquiry*. He also gives us some direct hints to see his
novel as yet another kind of boat-building. From his childhood the
idea of building a boat and sailing away has been the very image of
his yearning: 'the intensity of this longing to escape must be accounted
for by the attractiveness of the thing itself, not by any unattractive-
ness of my surroundings. In short, I was running *to*, not running
from, or so I believe.' It is hardly necessary to point out that this is
another version of a very recognizable American dream. Even the
reinterpretation of apparent flight as real quest is one we have
encountered before (in *Catch—22*). Andrews's desire was to build a
completely private craft. 'Left to myself, absolutely to myself, I was
certain I could build one and surprise everybody with the finished
product.' It is a perfect metaphor for that wish to create one's own
unique form or structure which we have had occasion to comment on.
In the midst of one of the worst episodes in his life, when he is being
beaten up in a brothel, he remembers thinking, '*Why isn't the whole
thing a sailboat?*' It is a poetic way of saying, I wish I could escape
from the impositions of the given world into the liberation of a
privately created one.

But Todd Andrews never finishes his boats, and here the implications of the metaphor become important. For just as he works on
boats which never actually get him on to the water, so he labours
at systems of thought which never serve to propel him into life.

Indeed it is his preoccupation with system-building which serves to exclude him from the element in which he should live. The attempt to reproduce existence in patterns of rational thought is doomed to incompletion. For one thing, he can inevitably see multiple possible significances in every single fact—there is no end to the possible readings or versions of life. More seriously, as he realizes when he works out a new philosophic position, it is only 'a matter of the rearrangement of abstractions'—just as when he has to use a new ploy in one of his law suits it only involves a shift of rhetoric. It is all a matter of word play, and none of it makes the slightest difference to the fact of his weak heart. On the day he decided to commit suicide he did indeed think that he had completed a vessel of thought, just as he thought he had finished his *Inquiry*. This 'new philosophical position, like a new rowboat', as he explicitly says, is his conclusion that there is no final reason for living. And when he experiences a moment of hesitation about putting it into practice, he reproaches himself in this way: 'Can he be called a builder who shies at launching the finished hull? For what other purpose was it finished?' This is the one boat he does attempt to set sail in—to death.

But even this one doesn't float. By one of the nicest ironies of the book, while the real Floating Opera is indeed floating, Todd's private boat is sinking—i.e. his plan to commit suicide by blowing up the Opera is being thwarted by an accident. The show on board is a very old one, very corny, full of the same old gags, the same old roles, the same old acts—like life itself. But that's the show that goes on. As the captain—of course called Adam—says, that boat was built to last. The posters which spring up all over town to advertise its advent on the day Todd intends to commit suicide describe it as 'original and unparalleled', which is of course quite true. For one of the things Todd learns that day is that he cannot parallel the original. He will never complete any of his own boats.

Except for the novel. This boat—and he himself uses the metaphor—he completes, and he knocks it together in just the way he pleases, according to his own plan. 'It's a floating opera, friend, fraught with curiosities, melodrama, spectacle, instruction and entertainment, but it floats willy-nilly on the tide of my vagrant prose,' he says of his book near the beginning; and near the end: 'Say what you wish about the formal requirements of story-telling; this is my opera, and I'll lead you out of it as gently as I led you in.' We might compare his floating opera to Hawkes's floating island, for both provide a free space in which the writer can order things as he will, and at the same time both are the results of this assertion of personal patterning.

Todd claims that: 'It seems to me that any arrangement of things at all is an order,' the implication being that one man's mess may be another man's pattern. Todd tells us that he lives his life 'in much the same manner as I'm writing this first chapter', and it is of course important that Todd is both character and author – like the Invisible Man and Augie March for instance – demonstrating his freedom to arrange his own life by the way he writes about it. This way is 'after my fashion – which, remember, is not unsystematic, but simply coherent in terms of my own, perhaps unorthodox, system.' As I have tried to show, this is a very characteristic feeling in contemporary American fiction. If there has to be a system, so the feeling goes, then I will make very sure that it is a system of my own choosing and making.

One postscript to this account of his first book is of interest here. Barth subsequently explained that he could only get *The Floating Opera* published by agreeing to change the ending. This he did, and the first published edition is in fact a revised version in which Todd is brought out of his paralysis and suicide attempt at the sound of Jeanine's voice (who is probably his daughter). With the shuffling of a few paragraphs – more mere rearranging – he puts aside his negativity as 'distasteful' and shows signs of turning into an American affirmative. 'Quite suddenly I grew very excited ... It is one thing to say "Values are *only* relative"; quite another, and more thrilling, to remove the pejorative adverb and assert "There *are* relative values!"' This volte-face towards wholesomeness did not fool anybody and most critics found this ending unconvincing and sentimental. Gestures of affirmation are not so easily fabricated. But what is interesting is Barth's willingness to alter the whole shape of his book – to tack, as it were, another stern on to his home-made boat. It provides another demonstration of how arbitrary he sees the whole fiction-making process, how free he feels to chop and change his own design; just as his character/author feels that there is a theoretically infinite number of possible versions and arrangements of things, and later characters feel that the self may adopt an endless succession of roles. That 'infinity of possible directions' is faced by author and character alike, and arbitrariness itself can be seen as a quixotic gesture of life. Whether the sense of this open field of endless possibilities is unequivocal in its effect on author and character is a matter which Barth felt obliged to confront in subsequent books.

In his next novel, *End of the Road* (1958), Jacob Horner (who sat in a corner) has an ineradicable sense of the plural possibilities of movement both in the physical and mental spheres, 'a recognition of the fact that when one is faced with such a multitude of desirable choices, no one choice seems satisfactory for very long by comparison with the aggregate desirability of all the rest, though compared to any *one* of the others it would not be found inferior.' He can find plenty of reasons for doing and *not* doing anything but finds it correspondingly difficult to fix on any one line of action, just as he finds it impossible to view the world as one definitive set of cases. This has narrative implications — 'the same life lends itself to any number of stories.' The immobilization — physical, emotional, mental — which can result from the sense of living in a completely open field of possible lines and multiple versions, is the main focus of the book. Like the previous novel, the book involves a triangular affair and it concentrates almost exclusively on the relationships between Horner and Joe and Rennie Morgan. The end of the road is the same end of the same road travelled by Todd Andrews, though this time the girl dies after a peculiarly repellent abortion scene. Once again Barth is concentrating on a mind which has thought itself into a state approaching terminal arrest. Horner is able to maintain, without any committing enthusiasm, completely polarized opinions on any given subject. 'I did it too easily, perhaps, for my own ultimate mobility.' He has days of catatonic immobility which he describes as weatherless; he succumbs to periodic inertia; and on one occasion, as he recalls, he simply came to a complete halt in a railway station, unable to fix on any particular destination because he found himself without any reason to move. 'I simply ran out of motives, as a car runs out of gas.'

This is an extreme case of an immobility which we have seen descending on other American heroes. The fact that he is not quite physically immobile enough to avoid committing adultery with Rennie — an act mentally inexplicable to both of them — precipitates the tragedy of the book. At the same time it points to one of Barth's recurrent assertions that, in disregard of, and indifferent to, the presence or absence of any formulable motives, the human animal will copulate. At the more conscious level, Horner receives two pieces of medical advice from two rather different doctors as to how to remedy his tendency to motiveless motionlessness — teach rules, and take roles. As suggested cures for inaction these offered solutions are of central relevance.

His first doctor advises him to take up a job teaching prescriptive grammar. '"No description at all. No optional situations. Teach the rules."' And that is what he does. His own mind swamped with notions of arbitrariness and multiple options, he lays down the rules in class.

"You're free to break the rules, but not if you're after intelligibility. If you *do* want intelligibility, then the only way to get 'free' of the rules is to master them so thoroughly that they're second nature to you. That's the paradox: in any kind of complicated society a man is usually free only to the extent that he embraces all the rules of that society."

Horner goes on to another paradox. "'Rebels and radicals at all times are people who see that the rules are often arbitrary—always ultimately arbitrary—and who can't abide arbitrary rules.'" We could rephrase that to say that the rebellious hero and his author both recognize the arbitrariness of the forms in which they are supposed to cast their lives, their words. At the same time they come to see that some form is necessary—for definition, for communication. It is another version of having to avoid both the prison and the jelly.

Everybody seems to need some kind of rules, since with no guiding lines there are no directives for action. Horner calls his speech 'non-directive' precisely because when he speaks from his own convictions he inevitably undermines any one set of rules, consequently taking away those clues for definite actions which any set of rules provides. This is the disastrous effect he has on the Morgans, who are trying to run a relationship based on rules derived from pure reason and logic. Horner, just by his negating presence and his motiveless non-commitment threatens, and breaks, the pure geometry of their life. The vulnerability of the Morgans is just their belief that you can contain life in a single version of it, and they cannot assimilate the incoherencies of existence which surround all coherent patternings of life. The fact of the adultery shatters them metaphysically. "'According to my version of Rennie, what happened couldn't have happened. According to her version of herself, it couldn't have happened. And yet it happened.'" They cannot understand that there are aspects of people, of life, which lie outside any one version of them. At the end since Joe still believes that there must be one version which will contain the facts, he seems to be doomed to lasting torment. Horner, who doesn't seem able to believe in any version of things, seems headed for a paralysis which will be 'terminal' (the last word of the book). Between them Rennie dies in a beastly mess. What this book does, in the figures of Joe and Jake, is to explore some of the limitations or dangers both in the compulsion to systematize (in the sense of making one coherent version of life), and in the inability to adhere to any fragment of system at all.

The other doctor who attempts to cure Horner's proneness to paralysis recommends a strategy with which we are by now familiar — role playing, or 'Mythotherapy' as he calls it. This involves both assuming and assigning roles, with as many changes as are necessary to maintain that motion and momentum which are essential to life. Rather than allowing the self to be defined by the situation it happens to be in, the individual, according to the doctor, should dramatize the situation in his own terms, defining his own and everybody else's roles. He should become, that is to say, his own mythologizer, and always be ready to adapt his myths and roles to cope with a new situation. It is a line of argument we have encountered in one form or another before, and at times the doctor sounds like Erving Goffman. (See Appendix Five.) The reasons he gives for role-playing — '"Move! Take a role!"' — would be understood by many American heroes who are often unable to find a mode or a motive for participating in the world around them. At the same time we should recognize that the doctor is a very ambivalent figure in this book — like those doctors in Purdy and Burroughs, for instance, whose 'truths' have very ambiguous results when applied. It is the doctor who performs the fatal abortion, and his advice must be seen as both helpful yet very equivocal. He is, as it were, a Rinehart with the gift of theorizing, and while much of what he says is pertinent — some people *do* get stuck and rigidify in one role — his prescription is one from which the American hero tends to draw back, as the Invisible Man drew back from the example of Rinehart. Horner does try applying the doctor's Mythotherapeutic methods. But such participating ventures as he does make into reality tend to cause misery and bring about destruction. Once again both stagnating inertia and role-playing movement seem equally intolerable as options for the self.

The question is really whether there is such a thing as self aside from those organized appearances made possible by rules and roles. Horner scarcely feels that he exists. This is why he starts his book with the tentative statement — 'In a sense, I am Jacob Horner.' His identity is provisional. He feels he only exists intermittently when he is coloured by a certain mood. Rennie thinks Jake is all masks and no centre — like Peer Gynt and the onion. The question that the book can hardly settle — given that Jake is the narrator — is just what there is to the human self under all the masks. By the end Jake is not a little tired of himself and in a state of desperation. 'I could not even decide what I should *feel:* all I found in me was anguish, abstract and without focus.' At this point one can hardly infer the distance between Barth and Horner, the importance of this being

that one could take Horner's particular version of the whole affair
(i.e. the book) as one long symptom of the disease and disability
from which he suffers; or one may feel that Barth endorses Horner's
particular vocabulary and descriptions as being those which come
closest to facing up to the problems of selfhood and behaviour in our
modern age. Then the agonizing immobility he comes to might be
seen as part of the torment of honest vision.

The importance of the connection between author and character
is made particularly clear in one passage. The problems of the book
arise from that—scarcely new—sense of the relativity of all values,
and the different ways people react to this. Jake enjoys talking to
Joe about values, not because he is interested in establishing any,
but because he likes talking, producing verbal shapes.

> Articulation! There, by Jove, was *my* absolute, if I could be said
> to have one ... To turn experience into speech—that is, to
> classify, to categorize, to conceptualize, to grammarize, to
> syntactify it—is always a betrayal of experience, a falsification
> of it; but only so betrayed can it be dealt with at all, and only
> in so dealing with it did I ever feel a man, alive and kicking. It
> is therefore that, when I had cause to think about it at all, I
> responded to this precise falsification, this adroit, careful myth-
> making, with all the upsetting exhilaration of any artist at his
> work. When my mythoplastic razors were sharply honed,
> it was unparalleled sport to lay about with them, to have at
> reality.
> In another sense, of course, I don't believe this at all.

The last qualifier is meant to typify the inability of his mind to
rest in any one assertion or position beyond the terms and duration
of its utterance. But the statement has implications important for
the whole book—one of which is that Jacob Horner only exists
while verbalizing. His attitude seems to reverse the normal relationship between language and environment, or at least to distort it.
The motives and momentum for verbalizing are within language
itself; words are not formed by Horner into patterns in an attempt
to arrive at some stabilizing notions about the conditions of the
world around him. They are formed into patterns because he finds
he has the capacity and inclination to form them into patterns, and
because he finds that he prefers this activity to any form of committed
participation in the outer world. Playing with all patterns (systems,
versions, ideas, etc.) and believing in none, Horner celebrates something approaching the autonomy of language. Because he finds his
first order of reality in language it is not surprising that his account

of the people and events in the book is marked by what one feels to be a very nominal sense of concrete reality. It is as though the dialectic between life and mind has broken down and the dissociated consciousness drifts along in sterile isolation, sealed off in its circular musings.

What it comes to is that in Barth's early work we find something approaching an absence or attenuation of environment: those things which usually circumscribe consciousness and with the direct pressure of their presence help to condition thought have receded or been excluded and in the resultant cleared ground the mind runs free. This is why it is of some importance whether we take that mind to be only Horner's — or Barth's as well. Not because one is interested in knowing whether there is anything autobiographical in the book, but because it influences our assessment of Barth's own attitude to that ambiguous licence enjoyed by a mind for which words are no longer answerable to things.

The matter is fairly central to any consideration of contemporary American fiction in which the release of character and author from the moulding and limiting powers of environment are explored, celebrated, or deplored, in a variety of forms. We have had occasion to note that in American literature dreams of pure freedom from environment alternate with nightmares of inexorable forces of control. Barth's early narrators demonstrate an independence of mind from the omnipotence of environment which in one sense is a state much to be desired. On the other hand they are presented as suffering from a nihilism which excludes them from confident participation in life, and which is to be seen as a curse or a blight. At the same time that equivocal mental and verbal freedom which they 'enjoy', and which allows them to be completely arbitrary in the patterns they choose, is the freedom increasingly exercised by Barth himself. His tendency to sport on lexical playfields increases in his following books. In these 'floating operas' signs tend to become more important than their referents, and the impresario of fictions, John Barth, plays with them in such a way that any established notions of the relationship between word and world are lost or called in doubt. Barth is indeed one of the great sportsmen of contemporary fiction. At the same time he is liable to a version of the trouble that Henry James ascribed to America — an 'inability to convince that she is serious, serious about any form whatever, or about anything but that perpetual passionate pecuniary purpose which plays with all forms, which derides and devours them.' If you take out the word 'pecuniary' and make the appropriate changes in the personal pronouns, that seems to me to point to a danger, or a temptation,

confronted by many American writers. They may play with forms
to demonstrate their freedom from any one of them, but taken beyond
a certain point this activity may incur the charge of not being serious
'about any form whatever'. Certainly the question of the nature of
Barth's commitment to the forms he habitually works with has been
raised by his later novels in which 'arbitrariness' is not only an
existential dilemma but an ordering, or disordering, aesthetic
principle.

The hazards of mental play uncorrected by the limitations of the
world are conceded, somewhat ruefully, in Barth's latest book,
Lost in the Funhouse (1968). 'Alas: for where Fancy's springs are
unlevee'd by hard Experience they run too free, flooding every
situation with possibilities until Prudence and even Common Sense
are drowned.' In much the same way, the 'innocent' young poet in
Barth's next novel, *The Sot-Weed Factor* (1960), is upbraided for
knowing nothing of '"the *entire great real world*! Your senses fail
ye; your busy fancy plays ye false and fills your head with foolish
pictures."' It might seem that it was in order to immerse his characters in a very specific 'real' environment that Barth turned to
American history for the setting of *The Sot-Weed Factor*, and rever-
ted to what looks like an eighteenth-century style of epic-historical
narration. There *was* an Ebenezer Cooke and he did write a poem
called 'The Sot-Weed Factor' in 1708: his complete works are
available in a volume called *Early Maryland Poetry*. Moreover
Alan Holder has pointed out[2] that Barth has drawn heavily on
material preserved in the Archives of Maryland, and he has written
an interesting article showing just where Barth seems to deviate
from the records, both in his depiction of figures like Cooke and
Baltimore, and in his plotting of incidents. Yet the result is far from
an historical novel as we understand the term, despite the presence
in the book of a wealth of authenticated material and the number of
mordant morals about America's early history that can legitimately
be drawn from it.

Barth has more than once said that if someone built Chartres
Cathedral now it would be embarrassing unless he did it ironically.
Just so, the available facts of eighteenth-century Maryland history
have been dissolved and re-erected in an ironic form by the un-
sleeping presence of Barth's twentieth-century American mind. Barth
has said that 'the use of historical or legendary material, especially
in a farcical spirit, has a number of technical virtues, among which
are aesthetic distance and the opportunity for counter-realism,'
and the spirit of farcical counter-realism is strong in the book. This
is of course quite deliberate. Having embarked on an 'historical'

novel Barth loses no opportunity to promote the question: how can we tell 'history' from the various and multiple 'fictions' or versions of it which are available and which have been promulgated from time to time? In doing so he is effectively applying the suggestion contained in Carlyle's question in *Sartor Resartus*: 'What if many a so-called Fact were little better than a Fiction?'

Much of the historical incident in the book is concerned with plotting, as Holder notes, and to all their plots Barth, in his capacity of novelist, has added *his* plotting; and if, at least initially, we have no means of telling where history shades off into fiction (the device is, probably, derived from Borges), by implication we cannot place too much unquestioning confidence in the documents that have come down to us. For they too are versions, and as such dependent on the limitations of the particular categories that the particular historian or commentator used. There is a great deal of story-telling in the book, resulting in a multiplicity of versions which is one source of confusion to the poet Cooke; just as one important sub-plot is concerned with tracking down fragments of a document which has different versions written on each side, suggesting that history is, at the very least, two-faced. All documents are to some extent fictions, and Barth reveals an almost obsessive need to point out time and time again that we cannot be sure when we are in touch with facts, as opposed to fictionalized versions of facts. Such an attitude is, needless to say, inimical to the very idea of history as the establishment of an authoritative veridical account.

The notion of history as something to play with, or play at, is introduced from the first when we read how the enigmatic Burlingame teaches young Ebenezer and his sister Anna. 'To teach them history he directed their play-acting to historical events.' Philosophy and the search for truth he similarly teaches as a game; and Ebenezer's later confusion about the topography of reality and unreality may perhaps be traced to the fact that Burlingame 'made little or no distinction between, say, the geography of the atlases and that of fairy-stories'. Their young minds are thus inseminated with notions of the arbitrariness of all divisions between fact and fiction. In terms of the events of the story the results of this sportive pedagogy are far from being wholly desirable, yet Barth writes as Burlingame teaches and clearly there is a considerable overlap of the author's and the character's views. The notion of any serious historical inquiry is undermined and all systems or theories are mocked. At the end Barth offers his own defence of playing fast and loose with the chronicler's muse. 'In the first place be it remembered, as Burlingame himself observed, that we all invent our own pasts, more or less, as times are a clay in the present moment that will-we, nill-we, the lot of us must sculpt.' We may remark Barth quoting his character Burlingame with approval.

This I think justifies us in singling out one or two of Burlingame's statements for the light they shed on Barth's own approach to history. It is said of Burlingame that he can 'play this world like a harpsichord' and 'manipulate its folk like puppeteers'. In many ways he shows himself to be the supreme 'plotter' in a world of plots, because of his manipulating abilities, both with self and world. Some of his advice to Cooke reflects quite directly on the author: '"If you'd live in the world, my friend, you must dance to some other fellow's tune or call your own and try to make the whole world step to't."' This is a very American statement, containing a notion which on one side looks back to Thoreau. What gives it its modern flavour is the idea that a man must impose his version on the world if he is to avoid the world imposing its scheme on him. We can see this as an assertion once again of the potency of thought and fiction-making against the possibility of dominance from without, and as such the book constitutes a gesture of freedom from imposed historical patternings. Speaking of the liberty of America, Burlingame makes another central point: '"'Tis philosophic liberty I speak of, that comes from want of history. It throws one on his own resources, that freedom—makes every man an orphan like myself and can as well demoralize as elevate."' Burlingame is aware that this freedom is both a blessing and a curse, '"for't means both liberty and lawlessness."' What Burlingame does *in* the book, Barth does *with* the book—in their American freedom each makes the world dance to his tune. And, like Burlingame, Barth is to find such freedom both a blessing and a curse: when liberty threatens to become indistinguishable from lawlessness, problems of identity arise for the character and problems of form arise for the author.

As a child Ebenezer is already 'dizzy with the beauty of the possible' and unable to select any one line of activity because, as he sees it, '"*All Roads are fine Roads.*"' This produces those bouts of complete immobility which we have come to recognize as part of the peculiar fate of the American hero. His reasons for being unable to choose echo those of Robert Musil's Ulrich—'"The moment I grow sensible that I must choose, I see such virtues in each alternative that none outshines the rest,"' and 'he felt full to bursting with ill-defined potentialities.' Definition necessitates choice, but to choose is to exchange an open field of possibilities for the relative constriction of the single, limited set of conditions. This is the familiar dilemma of the American hero who for a variety of motives is unwilling to commit himself to the given world that is the case.

Burlingame, the tutor who sets out to correct Ebenezer's apathy and 'crippling indecision', prescribes the mythotherapy familiar from the last novel, providing a defence of role-playing that in one form or another, implicit or explicit, has occurred in many of the novels we have considered. Arguing from the perception of the world as flux, and the rejection of the notion of a fixed and stable self, Burlingame maintains that the only way to be in the world is to adopt multiple roles and rapidly changing short-term goals. He is the chameleon Rinehart whose relativity enables him to be at home in any given situation in the actual world. Unlike Ebenezer, Burlingame is extremely capable in the given world of things and politics and people, and this capacity is related to his ability and willingness to assume an extremely fluid series of provisional identities. The existentialist wardrobe is all before him to choose from, and the emphasis given to dressing up in various kinds of clothes in the book is a way of underlining the idea that a man is only the robes he chooses, the mask he dons. Burlingame turns up in every situation, on all sides of the political struggle, in different roles in different countries, even with a shifting racial identity. His constant metamorphoses—and he is protean to a degree—are a literal illustration of his conviction that a man may make himself over as many times as he chooses, and that only by this willingness to choose roles can a man get into the world at all.

Being so fluid, Burlingame can elude all the categories and divisions—of identity, political party, race—that other men live by. He lives in a pre-conceptual continuum. The all-inclusive range of Burlingame's sexual aspirations is a reflection of his disregard for the dividing categories and classifications men impose on the world. ' "I am a Suitor of Totality, Embracer of Contradictories, Husband to all Creation, the Cosmic Lover!" ' But obviously if this programme were really to be lived out, the human self would have to be reabsorbed into the amorphous, flowing totality of things. It is pertinent that until late in the book Burlingame is impotent. It seems that he would stop short of total dissolution. As he tells Ebenezer, ' "One must needs make and seize his soul, and then cleave fast to't ... and declare ' 'Tis *I*, and the world stands such-a-way.' One must *assert*, assert, assert, or go screaming mad." ' It is the old cry of having to give shape, if arbitrarily chosen shape, to the jelly of the uncommitted and undefined self. Burlingame's advice is necessarily made partly ironic by his own jelly-like malleability, and the many 'I's he temporarily asserts for short-term reasons.

(The one 'I' he does assert consistently is the self who is searching for information about the identity and fate of his father, and of course this fact of his orphanage puts all Burlingame's theories of fluidity and role-playing in a very special perspective. A father, argues Burlingame, is a man's link with the past; therefore to be rid of all trace and knowledge of one's father is to be left ' "free and unencumbered" '. At the same time it is an ambiguous freedom in that he will never have any identity if he establishes no links, no continuities with the past. In this one figure Barth has summarized an age-old debate about America's relation to history and the old world, and related it to contemporary American preoccupations with identity problems.)

In saying this we should recognize that Burlingame is different from characters like Rinehart and Minderbender in two crucial ways. He never forgets what the disguises are for; and in fact he always turns out finally to act on behalf of man rather than to exploit him — his last act being to prevent an Indian uprising and the ensuing massacre that is planned. In some ways he embodies that flexibility which is what saves the American hero. On the other hand, Ebenezer has that suspicion of multiple role-playing evinced by the Invisible Man, and he hopes that there might be some more stable 'house of Identity' than seems possible in Burlingame's fluid and relativistic vision of things. In voicing his weariness with roles and plots, Ebenezer is at the same time passing judgment on a world in which such roles and plots seem necessary. The men who are completely at home in this world and who ruthlessly compete in their attempts to run it as they will impress him, or oppress him, with 'their strange and terrible energy'. His virginity, his dream of value, his idealism are comparatively his impotence; and he shares with other American heroes a familiar dismay that it seems impossible to relate any idealism to any energy of construction in the given world. Burlingame has abandoned his innocence and fallen into the world, as he says, and he can spin plot for plot; yet even he seems most adroit at counter-plotting, preventing and amending rather than initiating a new society, a new America. Ebenezer's final adjustment to the world takes the form of some soured, disillusioned poetry and a long silence of bitter knowledge.

The historical dimension of the book is important. What produces an uneasiness is the uncontrolled parodic element, which suggests that the author does not believe in such a thing as history even while his narrative pretends to evoke it. The suggestion that Coode and Baltimore may not have existed at all, which Mr Holder sees as a particularly arbitrary piece of obscurantism, is a case in point.

Ebenezer reflects at one point on how much more powerful, and even substantial, fictions seem in comparison with his own shadowy self, and in doing so he reveals a bias of his author for whom fictions are much more potent than facts. Since fictions can be proliferated endlessly, it is hard to see what formal checks his historical novel needs, or can respond to. At one point in the book two women exchange terms of sexual abuse for seven pages. Ludicrous as a piece of history, this minor verbal gesture reflects a major mood of the book, namely the dominance of words over things, the potency and independence of sheer language. Like these good ladies, or rather the author behind them, you can call each fact a hundred names — indeed you can proliferate names quite independently of facts. Supposedly dealing with history, Barth is actually at sport on lexical playfields, and the substantiality of fact melts away as we watch him at his brilliant rhetorical play.

The author is primarily rebutting all historical versions and impositions; recognizing the constraints and ravages visited on man by his involvement in the world, the book itself is an assertion of freedom from external conditioning. Just how valuable that freedom is is perhaps left open to some doubt. In an opium dream Ebenezer visits the top of Parnassus, where a rather bored ancient tells him, ' "There's really naught in the world up here but clever music." ' It is only a dream, but it suggests a sense of the futility of all art, the valuelessness of the fiction-making process, which one sometimes feels is at the heart of Barth's own work.

There is certainly something uneasy in the way Barth surrounds his next fiction, *Giles Goat-Boy* (1966), with multiple dubieties. The book itself wears masks and you have to peel off various letters, disclaimers, introductions, and so on, before you reach the narrative proper. A publisher's disclaimer contains four letters from readers of the manuscript; this in turn is followed by a cover-letter from J.B. saying the book is not written by J.B. but is probably by an obscure wizard whose *nom de plume* is Stoker Giles, although there are other possibilities, including the hint that it might have been written by a computer. Just as his historical novel acted as a demonstration of his freedom from history, so the recession of frames to this novel seems like a bid by Barth to liberate himself from any of the available modes of authorship and narration, to create a fictional space into which anything may be admitted and anything done with it, without the author (whoever or whatever he is) being held responsible. In this way the relationship of the author to his material is never clear, and since all these devices for stressing the equivocal status and origin of the fiction only serve to make us more aware of

Barth's own constant presence, we become aware of a writer going to perverse lengths (710 pages) not only to demonstrate what he can invent—and that is prodigious—but to demonstrate how he can equivocate about, trivialize and undermine his own inventions. In a way this is another example of an American writer constantly freeing himself from the frames or forms to which he has to commit himself to get anything written (thus any tendency in the book to congeal into allegory is countered by farce, the temptation to construct a new myth is challenged by corrosive philosophical questioning, and so on).

In one of the letters within letters, Barth, in his adopted role of hypothetical critic of his own work, writes:

> As for *style*, it is everywhere agreed that the best language is that which disappears in the telling, so that nothing stands between the reader and the matter of the book. But this author has maintained (in obscure places understandably) that language *is* the matter of his books, as much as anything else, and for that reason ought to be 'splendrously musicked out'; he turns his back on what *is the case*, rejects the familiar for the amazing, embraces artifice and extravagance ...

Barth's books, like other American novels we have considered, are very much about language that *appears* in the telling, and which proliferates in arbitrary patterns in exuberant disregard for what is the case. This is what I referred to as foregrounding, calling more attention to language than to what is signifies. Of course, language must retain a minimum referential role, but a writer can juxtapose and relate the verbal signs in such a way that the illusion of a single coherent model of reality being erected is constantly negated. We hold one book in our hands but it puts forward not one world but a 'clutch of worlds'.

Thus in *Giles Goat-Boy* references from Greek tragedy, the Bible, Dante, *Don Quixote*, *Ulysses*, and numerous other fictional models, are fed into a version of contemporary American and international politics; in addition, constructs from consciously theoretical books like Lord Raglan's *The Hero*, and Joseph Campbell's *The Hero with a Thousand Faces*, and passages which could come from analytic studies of philosophy and linguistics or from psychological theories, are drawn into the book. What emerges is not a new synthesis but a constantly dissolving plurality of versions and combinations. One is at times tempted to fasten on the notion of the computer-author, taking that as an image of Barth's own mind. For clearly his powers of mental absorption are unusual and, like the best computer, he can do almost anything with the vast amount of material that has been fed into him (via books, college courses, newspapers, the whole modern media onslaught).

To arrive at the overall scheme of the book it is as though he has fed into his mind the instruction to exploit down to the last detail all the possible cross-references, relationships, variations, permutations, ironic parallels to be derived from seeing the world as campus, or universe as university. The giant computer in the book, WESCAC, which perhaps runs the whole campus – a Burroughs-like nightmare of being totally programmed by a power beyond one's control – has the power to EAT people, which means 'they suffered "mental burn-out" ... like overloaded fuses.' If Barth has used his mind as a computer this could be an attempt to remain in charge of his own programming. Rather than let the plethora of the world's information and theory and literature devour you, you devour it. EAT that ye be not EATEN. Barth demonstrates his mastery of – and thus liberation from – the material that besets his contemporary mind, by playing with it. His prolixity thus appears as an essential strategy. It is related to Burroughs's notion of recording everything then reversing the tape recorders and spraying all the fed-in information back out. As long as Barth is getting it out of his head and into the machines (the book is, after all, presented as a series of reels), he is in control. The length of his book is the tenure of his freedom. But occasionally one feels that it is a precarious hold.

Further equivocation about the status of Barth's book occurs in another cover-letter in which J.B. tells how he described the novel he was working on when Stoker Giles came to see him. This was to have been a novel about a Cosmic Amateur, and Barth describes how he outlined to Stoker Giles the sort of character this man would have and what his fate was to be. Giles told him to abandon that book and take on the Revised New Syllabus of his father, George Giles. But of course this too is by John Barth and he in fact went on to write the novel which he started by abandoning. For if Giles Goat-Boy aspires to the heroic role of Grand Tutor, his adventures and changes subsume many of the developments in attitude mapped out for the Cosmic Amateur. Like other Barth characters, he starts life by being unable to accept reality as 'the case' – something final and fixed. He regards natural laws as provisional, the ground rules of only one of many imaginable games. Of course, instead of remaining a spectator of the game, Giles sets out to be a hero and 'save' the campus. (It is worth noting that in recent American fiction 'heroic' action seems most likely to occur in fantasy. Burlingame and Giles contrast with the more realistic figures of Todd and Jacob Horner.

Similarly Bellow's Henderson, heroically active in his dream Africa, contrasts with Tommy Wilhelm and Herzog, immobilized in contemporary America.) Yet what the Cosmic Amateur was to have had to learn—the nature of his, often farcical, involvement in the given world, and the singleness of death—is part of what Giles has to learn. The manuscript that Barth is 'given' turns out to be, at bottom, closely related to the ones he has already written.

For instance, the false Grand Tutor, Harold Bray, has a way with masks and a mastery of metamorphoses which enable him to impose successfully on society. At one point he turns into just about every character in the book. In this he seems to be carrying on Burlingame's gifts, but in fact he is more like Rinehart and Minderbender, his cynical impostures being solely devoted to personal advancement and self-aggrandizement. He is the bad role-player, from whom the American hero always has to turn away, even while he may learn a great deal from his worldly example. Burlingame saw himself as being, throughout all his varied roles, 'Suitor of Totality, Embracer of Contradictories', and this central aspiration is assumed by Giles himself in his strange adventures from goat farm to campus to WESCAC. His elevation (or evolution) from animal to human to hero, then (almost) to martyr and (vaguely) to prophet-philosopher, finally (perhaps) to a tragic pessimist, is a long quest devoted to the basic problem of how to embrace the world—in thought, in word, in deed. Starting from a frisky, uncomplicated animal innocence, he gradually becomes acquainted with the more problematical human emotions, appetites, guilts, regrets and sorrows. His plans to become a hero and Grand Tutor and furnish a new healing philosophy (or revised syllabus) for the whole campus have to be continually modified or abandoned and recommenced as he confronts and tries to absorb the realities of evil, time, death, and the inexplicable phenomenon of love, which makes such a confusion out of sex. The deeper he gets into the labyrinthine complexities of human life, the torments of consciousness, and the problems of nature, the more equivocal he finds everything, and the harder it gets to sort things out. The book itself is that labyrinth as well as an account of Giles's movements through it. Those movements, and the question of whether or not they add up to a progress, form the narrative line in the labyrinth.

It would be folly indeed to attempt any summary of the many episodes and characters beyond acknowledging the amazing parodic and satiric range and reach of the book. Indeed the fact that in places it is scrambled and dense beyond clear summary is an essential part of the experience it offers. However, I think one can isolate the main preoccupation at the heart of it, which is also a concern at the centre of contemporary American literature. I can best suggest this by juxtaposing two phrases from the novel. As George Giles first starts to waken to human consciousness under Max's education he describes it in this way: ' "Then I had known nothing; now my eyes were open to fenceless meadows of information." ' And when he first sees the incredibly complex structures of the New Tammany campus, Max tells him that this is but a fraction of the university which in turn is but one of an infinity of other universities 'whose existence in the fenceless pastures of reality ... had perforce to be assumed.' These metaphorical meadows and pastures connect up ironically, of course, with the actual campus; and the problem suggested by these phrases is – are there fences (categories, divisions, distinctions) in reality, or in our formulations about reality? Or is one, are both, fenceless? Giles overhears a copulating couple discussing whether man can know things directly, or only the 'screen' of conceptual distinctions projected by the mind. This question of whether one can experience unpatterned reality or whether one is doomed to encounter reality mediated through screens is, I have tried to suggest, a profoundly American concern. In a way it is the American version of the old dispute between Nominalists and Realists as to the epistemological status of concepts; Barth, characteristically, transposes it into a farcical situation. But it is the continuing preoccupation of the book, and what Giles tries to discover is whether you can penetrate that screen of distinctions, and if so, what lies on the other side.

As he tries to turn his accumulating experiences into wisdom he first decides that he has learnt the necessity of clear distinction. But this attempt to establish sharper definition turns out badly: he comes to feel that the source of evil and confusion is 'differentiation' and the new wisdom is 'Embrace!' Pondering his earlier attempts to pass judgments on people (Pass or Fail), he later sees his whole effort as misdirected – 'as if the seamless university knew aught of such distinctions'. He denies the existence of any 'boundaries' and asserts that those things that had previously seemed differentiated, such as East and West Campuses, Passage and Failure, and so on, are 'inseparable and ultimately indistinguishable'. He decides that 'studentdom' is 'hobbled by false distinction, crippled by categories' and in his own person as goat-boy (animal and human merged and perhaps sired by a machine), he decides he is 'a walking refutation of such false conceits'. However, the ruinous effects of his perverse insistence that 'All discrimination must go by the board' soon become apparent. Chaos breaks out on campus and he learns the actuality of distinctions, although this brings him no peace of mind. He is approaching the realization that reflection does not necessarily help you to live (mirror-gazing is again used as an analogue for disabling habits of reflection—for instance in the story of Peter Greene).

What happens is that, in trying to juggle and relate the complex concepts and logical arguments by which humans seek to comprehend and evaluate nature and experience, 'paradoxes become paroxysms'. One example of his mental turmoil: 'Passage *was* Failure, and Failure Passage; yet Passage was Passage, Failure Failure! Equally true, none was the Answer; the two were not different, neither were they the same; and *true* and *false*, and *same* and *different*—Unspeakable! Unnamable! Unimaginable! Surely my mind must crack!' He has reached that breaking-point of realizing that the full mystery of life and reality cannot be spoken or named, cannot be confined within no matter what arrangement of linguistic fences. When the paroxysms become unbearable, he breaks through and lets go—'I let go, I let all go.' (In another context this is what Herzog does, and—odd company though this may seem—it is what Burroughs's William Lee does: 'I sat back letting my mind work without pushing it. Push your mind too hard, and it will fuck up like an overloaded switch-board, or turn on you with sabotage.' Cabot Wright 'lets go', and of course *Letting Go* is the title of one of Philip Roth's novels. In general, letting go seems to be one way of attempting to drop out of all patterns.)

Giles seems now to move into a state of indifference and acceptance—things are distinguishable, but they are interdependent, like love-hate, male-female, life-death. He seems to regard all categories as 'names of neutral instrumentalities'. The final sanctuary beyond all harrowing divisions, categorizations and discriminations of existence is found through love, with his lady friend Anastasia in the belly of the giant computer. Here he has a blissful experience of unified totality of being. Since the belly of the computer is probably related to the place of his own conception, one can see this as a return to the preconscious uncomplication of infantile or foetal responses and feelings, as well as being a breakthrough to a mental realm beyond philosophy: 'in Anastasia I discovered the University whole and clear ... In the sweet place that contained me there was no East, no West, but an entire, single, seamless campus.' The difference between this and his earlier notion of the seamless university seems to be that then he tried to insist on the identity of opposites, whereas after his night in the computer he seems to have passed beyond the whole problem of meaning. 'For me, Sense and Nonsense lost their meaning on a night twelve years four months ago, in WESCAC's Belly — as did every such distinction, including that between Same and Different.' It seems that he has become indifferent to his own teachings, indeed to all verbalizations of life. He now prefers the company of the mulatto boy Tombo — they see 'termless Truth in each other's eyes'. It is perhaps another of Barth's ironies that it has taken over 700 pages to bring his hero to a realization that truth lies beyond terms. Giles's own last words — if they are his — suggest that he expects to die like Oedipus at Colonus. He has presumably passed beyond all the fences of language and experience.

There is certainly no more moving drama than the journeyings of Oedipus, nothing more perennially relevant than the lesson he has to learn so painfully concerning the limits of human modes of cognition, and the odyssey of Giles Goat-Boy, from the fields before knowledge through the massed complexities of human thought and human experience on to the fields beyond knowledge, is capable of stirring deep responses and recognitions. Barth clearly intends a certain amount of parallel reference. There are a great many references to eyes, problems of vision, myopia, blindness, and so on. In addition there is a good deal of play with mirrors, microscopes, fluoroscopes, telescopes, and lenses of all kinds. The not unfamiliar point is made that what we think are perceptions often turn out to be projections; a warning of the limitations of our instruments and the solipsistic streak in any scientific — or fictional — model of the world. The need which Giles feels to get beyond all versions is in part a desire to transcend the narcissism implicit to some degree in all our structurings of reality. Oedipus starts to approach true vision and genuine knowledge when he has put out his eyes and moved away from the city of his ambiguous cognitive triumphs.

References to Oedipus — or Taliped as he becomes in the university of the book — occur throughout. But the seriousness with which these references might reflect on Giles's own quest has been undermined from the start by the purely farcical and frivolous version of *Oedipus Rex* which Barth has included. This raises one of the main problems in dealing with this work. If a writer chooses a form which undermines the status of all forms, a fiction which questions the validity of all literary genres and modes, then that writer has excluded the possibility that *any* particular section of his rhetoric can be taken seriously. If the dilemma and drama of Oedipus is trivialized into farce, then Giles's own quest for knowledge can never be other than farcical. It may be Barth's intention to portray all the activities of the human mind as farcical, thus making his book another of those bitter attacks on the fall into consciousness which has been lamented by American writers from at least the time of Emerson. But such a position would seem to be belied by the extraordinary energy and resourcefulness of his prose and the manifest mental ingenuity and inventiveness which is behind it and keeps it moving. What Barth seems to have lost is a sense of the value of fictions and any conviction that they may be significantly related to our experience of reality.

It is of course possible to combine farce, fantasy and deep seriousness, but it requires a control of tensions and intentions which does not seem to me to be apparent in this book. A large number of potentially serious issues are indeed entertained, but they are caught up in the prevailing atmosphere of anarchy, ridicule and farce, giving an overall impression of brilliant frivolity. (Among other books, it reminded me of *The Wizard of Oz*, with various odd characters capering through fantastic landscapes in quest of wholeness, and WESCAC replacing the old fake magician.) It might well be a comic parable of the state of contemporary knowledge, although since everything is called into question, dissolved, turned into its opposite, arbitrarily made over by Barth's all-dominating mind, the main source of interest becomes a sort of uninvolved curiosity as to what Barth will choose to play around with next and how he will do it. I think Barth might be saying—look what a scrambled unusable wealth of mixed ideas, religions, philosophies, psychologies, moralities, political systems, etc., beset the modern mind, and what a comic confusion of coping is the result: the most salutary thing to do is to put yourself beyond their reach by making your own sport out of them, committing yourself to nothing. Seen this way the book represents a recognizable American gesture, its tone and 'structure' of frolicsome evasion distinguishing it very markedly from the work of such learned modern European parodists and ironists as Thomas Mann and James Joyce. Nevertheless, this novel does pose the problem of whether there is not a point at which the arbitrary unimpeded sport of sheer mind damages rather than nourishes a novel—particularly a mind which is continuously sceptical about the point of the inventiveness it continuously delights in; and if so, whether John Barth has not, in one of the most elaborate fictions written in America since the war, sailed determinedly clear past it.*

Barth's next book sufficiently indicates the impasse to which his sense of the arbitrariness of invention, and the futility of fictions, has brought him. This sense had previously prompted him to abandon

---

* I might point out that Richard Poirier (in the *Washington Post*, August 7th, 1966) and Robert Scholes (in *The Fabulators*) both give cogent reasons for rating the achievement of this book more highly than I do.

anything one might recognize as a conventional 'realistic' novel. As he said, in an interview, with obvious comic exaggeration (or perhaps it was boredom): 'What the hell, reality is a nice place to visit but you wouldn't want to live there, and literature never did, very long ... Reality is a drag.' What seems to have happened by the time of *Lost in the Funhouse* (1968) is that he can no longer get hold of any 'reality' at all; everything he touches turns into fictions and yet more fictions. There is no reason for his words to follow in any one direction; as a matter of fact there is no reason why he should go on writing except that there seems to be an underlying feeling that identity is conterminous with articulation. The 'I' is only ascertainable as that which speaks: self is voice, but voice speaking unnecessary and arbitrary and untrue words. The torment of this book is that of a man who cannot really find any sanction for writing either in world or self, yet feels that it is his one distinguishing ability, the one activity which gives him any sense of self. In 'Autobiography', intended for tape recording, voice turns on voice in a void. 'I hope I'm a fiction without real hope. Where there's a voice there's a speaker ... I must compose myself ... I'll mutter to the end, one word after another, string the rascals out, mad or not, heard or not, my last words will be my last words.' (The debt to Beckett is large and obvious.) Words floating free in this way never encounter any necessity, so they can drift on in self-cancelling and self-undermining recessions as long as the voice lasts. If this is what 'identity' is, it is surely in a precarious state.

The corrosive doubt about identity and its relation to language reveals itself in Barth's preoccupation with the relationship between self and name. Ambrose, who figures in three of the stories in the book, knows well 'that I and my sign are neither one nor quite two'. I think this sense of the ambiguous relation between 'I and my sign' is the focal point of a larger dubiety about the relationship between all names and bodies, between words and world. One rather grotesque story called 'Petition' takes up the old Mark Twain 'joke' about incompatible Siamese twins and gives it a philosophical twist. The petitioning brother (very much the writer), is an intelligent, almost mandarin figure who is seeking 'disjunction' from the coarse, brutish, appetitive brother to whose back he is stuck. ' "He's incoherent but vocal; I'm articulate but mute." ' The incoherent brother is life itself, in its headlong noisy energy constantly shrugging off the attempts of language to circumscribe it within particular definitions and renderings. Language, in the form of the articulate brother, would be happy to pursue its inclination to ponder its elegant patternings in pure detachment from the soiling contacts of reality. But they are brothers, divided yet related—neither one nor two. Like Ambrose who cannot work out the relationship between his self and his sign, so Barth seems to have reached a point where he cannot stop troubling himself with his uncertainty about the relationship between the words he invents, and the world he shares.

'Lost in the Funhouse', a story which owes a lot to Beckett and to Robbe-Grillet, approaches this problem again, with Barth never allowing us to forget the foreground presence of the typing man who, lost in the freedom of his inventions, can put down any words he likes in any order. 'This can't go on much longer; it can go on forever.' There is no pressure to keep the words in order, and they can start reversing their tracks and dissolving their statements as easily as they can advance new stages of the account of the family's adventures. 'Is there really such a person as Ambrose, or is he a figment of the author's imagination? ... Are there other errors of fact in this fiction?' In such ways does the story destroy its own sustaining conventions. In addition Ambrose himself is not clear whether what he is experiencing at any one moment is a private fantasy or a public fact, so the uncertainty surrounding any sequence of words is multiplied, leaving us with a sense of fictions within fictions within fictions. At the same time, an anguished sense that meanwhile 'the world was *going on*!' just occasionally intrudes into this lexical paralysis; unvexed by reflection and possibility, in dark corners of the Funhouse, couples wordlessly copulate. One senses Barth's own dissatisfaction with the feelings of exclusion which beset the fiction-maker.

The Funhouse itself seems to represent a variety of structures, evoking associations both of Burroughs's vaudeville and Borges's labyrinth. From one point of view the Funhouse is an analogue of life itself, in which the relatively mindless or unselfconscious merrily and energetically couple, while Ambrose is astray in the mirror-maze, vexed by endlessly receding 'reflections' and unable to disentangle dreaming from doing. But the Funhouse is also that pseudo-world which man invents for his own amusement, the edifice of the fictions with which we distract ourselves. Ambrose in the Funhouse can imagine various endings to his adventure; Barth at his typewriter can imagine various endings to his story. Once again one feels the close connection between the character's situation in the story and the author's position among his words. 'The climax of the story must be its protagonist's discovery of a way to get through the funhouse. But he has found none, may have ceased to search.' Both Ambrose and Barth may be destined to remain confined in their own fictions. 'He died telling stories to himself in the dark.' Thinks Ambrose about himself. Writes Barth about Ambrose. Says Barth about Barth. Unfixed in any one frame and unlocated in any one plane, the words float before us, in multiple perspective, in no perspective at all.

But the closing narrative statement about Ambrose is clearly a refracted statement about the author. 'He dreams of a funhouse vaster by far than any yet constructed; ... he will construct fun-houses for others and be their secret operator — though he would rather be among the lovers for whom funhouses are designed.' *Giles Goat-Boy* was indeed a sort of vast funhouse, with Barth at the controls. Life itself is also a sort of funhouse, but the gift (and curse) of the writer is that he can invent alternatives. The funhouse is not everything that is the case. But what one notices in this most recent book is that it is not a funhouse, but a series of depositions about building, or not building, funhouses. In 'Life Story', which is precisely not the story of a life, the narrator tells of meditating on the 'grandest sailing-vessel ever built'. We recognize the metaphor and the dream it contains of a privately perfected structure. But this narrator can erect nothing because he lacks a 'ground-situation', which is the equivalent of that firm floor which Henry James said was indispensable for any fiction. It is suggested that this lack might in itself constitute a ground-situation, but the idea is not a fructifying one. One conclusion to all this non-progressive muttering is that fiction, having acknowledged its fictitiousness, must establish some new relation between itself, author and reader. Meanwhile, no stories get told, no funhouses get built on their ground of no-ground.

Barth seems to be obsessed with triangular relationships, and there is a particularly interesting triad present in the 'Menelaiad'. For here Barth takes up that image of Menelaus struggling with Proteus which Ralph Ellison used to describe the American artist's relation to American reality. Added to this pair in Barth's story is Helen, 'that faultless form', who figures as a contrast to Proteus whose gift for metamorphosis and multiple temporary forms makes him the epitome of fluidity. Menelaus loses Helen because he keeps asking why she loves him, instead of being content to accept the mystery of love in a wordless embrace. That loss, brought on by a compulsion to understand and verbalize, is also a loss of substantial reality. From then on Menelaus can never be sure what he has hold of, if indeed he has hold of anything. His struggles to hold Proteus extend to a more prolonged effort to catch hold of something in his narrative. Menelaus is telling a story which includes himself telling stories, and so on and so on. There are tales within tales, and the narrator can never be sure what he has hold of, just as Menelaus cannot be sure whether when he is trying to hold Proteus he is grappling with dreams. His lament:

' "When will I reach my goal through its cloaks of story? How many veils to naked Helen?" ' sounds like a projection of Barth's own despair of ever reaching and holding any authentic formed reality through the multiplying layers of fiction in which he feels entangled — the Helenic quest impeded at every turn by the Protean encounter.

Even when he does seem to regain his Helen, he cannot be sure whether it is the real Helen or a dream substitute made of cloud. 'For all I knew I roared what I now gripped was but a further fiction, maybe Proteus himself ... ' The crippling and inhibiting worry that even Helen may be Proteus is a precise analogue of the suspicion that even Reality is a Fiction. At one point Menelaus says, " 'Menelaus! Proteus! Helen! For all we know, we're but stranded figures in Penelope's web, wove up in light to be unwove in darkness." ' Again the triangle, again the ever underlying suspicion that all apparent facts may be part of some larger fiction. Penelope's 'embroidrous art', Menelaus's 'ravelled fabrication', Barth's own 'cloaks of story' — where does it or can it stop? One hope expressed by the story is that one thing will survive all the changing, receding fictions of existence — 'the absurd, unending possibility of love'. But the story itself is a story of loss, a demonstration of how we lose what we don't believe in, how we can never again be sure of the Helen we called into question. Floundering in fictions, we may never regain a firm hold on reality. This I think is the dread of deprivation which is detectable in most of these recent pieces by Barth.

It is evident in the last story of the book called 'Anonymiad', no doubt a nod to the anonymous Homeric story-teller as well as a hint of Barth's own feelings of being just a disembodied voice. It is the first-person account of a minstrel who was not taken to Troy but left behind in the court of Clytemnestra, and then marooned on an island. There he dreams dreams with multiple possible endings, he invents a private Mycenae to substitute for the real city he has been excluded from, and subsequently develops a new mode of writing — which he calls *fiction*. Although excluded from the Trojan war and all knowledge of it, he amuses himself by imagining various versions of its progress and different possible denouements. Lacking an audience he commits his compositions to the sea in bottles. When he later finds a bottle containing an undecipherable parchment on the beach, he does not know whether he is being truly 'messaged' or whether his own work is drifting back to him devoid of meaning. After exhausting various genres he finds he is running out of material and in a new pessimism he imagines his 'opera sinking undiscovered' — a neat retrospective pun. He finds that 'as my craft improved, my interest waned ... Was there any new thing to say, new way to say the old?' He no longer cares what actually happened in the war—i.e. he is indifferent to what is 'the case'.

He outlines his idea for his next work: it would synthesize all genres, merging everything from 'grub fact' to 'pure senseless music'. But of course he does not write it, he only writes about planning to write it. His time is spent in 'considering and rejecting forms', and the notion that the very plurality of available forms and styles can have a paralysing as well as a liberating effect is directly relevant to the situation of the contemporary American writer. The narrator comes to realize that all he has produced is a chronicle of 'minstrel misery'. He then launches the last of his 'opera' – 'my tale's afloat' – and foresees the time when it will perish, 'with all things deciphered and undeciphered: men and women, stars and sky'.

Perhaps in this account of seemingly futile writing in an endless solitude, Barth has constructed an analogue for his own situation as he experiences it—though, as a best-selling novelist, some of his bottled messages must have found an audience. But whereas before he distracted himself with stories, he now seems to be tormenting himself with accounts of stories that failed, that cannot be written, that can never be started. The first piece in his last book is called 'Frame Tale' and it invites the reader to make a circular strip out of a page, which will then read; 'Once upon a time there was a story that began once upon a time … ' and so on *ad infinitum*. And inside that verbal circle, which moves but never progresses, Barth seems temporarily to have trapped himself.

At one point in 'Anonymiad' he says, 'I yearned to be relieved of myself … I'd relapse into numbness, as if, having abandoned song for speech, I meant now to give up language altogether and float voiceless in the wash of time like an amphora in the sea, my vision bottled.' To abandon the difficulties of language is to leave behind the problems of self: Barth is here giving utterance to that American temptation or desire earlier described, to pass beyond all forms and definitions and abandon the contours of self and style to dissolution and silence. But this ultimate solution to the torments of identity and narration—torments amply demonstrated in this volume, hovering and limping obsessively around the arbitrariness of all names and naming, all fictions and their telling—is irreversible. It would mean a final capitulation to some unselving flow or jelly which, quite as much as the dread of getting trapped in fixed patterns, is a nightmare which as we have seen haunts many contemporary American writers. To float voiceless in the wash of time is to die, and even the self-paralysing voice in Barth's latest book resists that particular quietus and quietness—' "I'll mutter to the end." '

Barth is what Robert Musil described as a 'possibilitarian', meaning one who was possessed of a 'sense of possibility'.

Anyone possessing it does not say, for instance: Here this or that has happened, will happen, must happen. He uses his imagination and says: Here such and such might, should or ought to happen. And if he is told that something *is* the way it is, then he thinks: Well, it could probably just as easily be some other way. So the sense of possibility might be defined outright as the capacity to think how everything could 'just as easily' be, and to attach no more importance to what is than to what is not.[3]

Obviously this 'sense of possibility' can be a very liberating thing, an invaluable weapon against an environment eager to impose a single reading of reality on the consciousness of the individual. As Kierkegaard expresses it in *The Sickness Unto Death*, 'When a human existence is brought to the pass that it lacks possibility, it is in despair ... Possibility is the only saving remedy.' But Kierkegaard goes on to warn of a subtler, but no less real, form of despair which seems very relevant to some contemporary American writers. 'Now if possibility outruns necessity, the self runs away from itself, so that it has no necessity whereto it is bound to return – then this is the despair of possibility. The self becomes an abstract possibility which tires itself out with floundering in the possible, but does not budge from the spot ...' That seems to be Barth's position in his latest book pretty exactly, and what follows applies to many other authors, or at least their characters. 'Possibility then appears to the self ever greater and greater, more and more things become possible, because nothing becomes actual. At last it is as if everything were possible – but this is precisely when the abyss has swallowed up the self ... and this is precisely the last moment, when the individual becomes for himself a mirage.' What diminishes, as it diminishes for Menelaus enwrapped with Proteus, and for Barth telling the stories within the stories, is 'the sense of actuality'. It is another ambiguity in the position of the American writer and his hero alike that in seeking to extract themselves from the prison of necessity – the cycle of conditioned action – they may find themselves hopelessly 'astray in possibility'.

Chapter 11 Interior Spaciousness — Car, Bell Jar, Tunnel and House

'It does seem to me, that herein we see the rare virtue of a strong individual vitality, and the rare virtue of thick walls, and the rare virtue of interior spaciousness. Oh, man! admire and model thyself after the whale! ... Do thou, too, live in this world without being of it ... Like the great dome of St Peter's, and like the great whale, retain, O man! in all seasons a temperature of thine own.'

(*Moby Dick*, Melville)

'wherever I sat ... I would be sitting under the same glass bell jar, stewing in my own sour air.'

(*The Bell Jar*, Sylvia Plath)

'I am crawling through the tunnel of myself.'

(*The Benefactor*, Susan Sontag)

'I've fallen as far as the poet, to the sixth sort of body, this house in B, in Indiana, with its blue and gray bewitching windows, holy magical insides. Great thick evergreens protect its entry. And I live *in*.'

(*In the Heart of the Heart of the Country*, William Gass)

A good example of the aptness of Kierkegaard's diagnosis is offered by the central character, Will Barrett, in Walker Percy's second novel, *The Last Gentleman* (1966). Barrett has lived in a state of 'pure possibility' up to the time when the novel starts, when we find him lying down. His general proneness is an indication of the effect of living in this state. 'The vacuum of his own potentiality howled about him.' He is one of the deracinated, the last of the line of an old Southern family, and he has become 'a watcher and a listener and a wanderer'. Most of his life has been 'a gap' and he has a tendency to fall into 'fugue' states which are reminiscent of Jake Horner's 'weatherless' days. At such times it is as though he drops out of the reality shared by everyone around him, into a sort of absent consciousness beyond all identities and names. One result of his inability to remain operative within the given social structure is a condition which besets many other American heroes—'a strange inertia.' When Barrett does move, this movement usually takes the form of purposeless wandering which ends with him suddenly completely estranged from his environment and unable to recognize where he is. He often resolves to integrate himself with society in all the conventional ways, but one scarcely feels that he will get beyond the impasse which he has experienced before. 'He either disappeared into the group or turned his back on it.' Which is a succinct formulation of the classic dilemma of the American hero in his relations to society. At the end of the book we see Barrett, not with his wife and in a home as he resolved, but on the road, running after the philosophically and medically unorthodox Dr Vaught (another of those equivocal doctors) to ask him one more question.

This doctor has a notebook in which Barrett reads the following extracts:

Man who falls victim to transcendence as the spirit of abstraction, i.e., elevates self to posture over and against world which is *pari passu* demoted to immanence and seen as exemplar and specimen and coordinate, and who is not at the same time compensated by beauty of motion of method of science, has no choice but to seek reentry into immanent world *qua* immanence ... But entry doesn't avail: one skids off into transcendence. *There is no reentry from the orbit of transcendence.*

A later extract comments on Barrett: 'he wishes to cling to his transcendence and to locate a fellow transcendence (e.g., me) who will tell him how to traffic with immanence (e.g. "environment," "groups," "experience," etc.) in such a way that he will be happy ... Yes, Barrett has caught a whiff of the transcendent trap and has got the wind up. But what can one tell him?' It is possible to resolve to re-enter ordinary reality, but the actual mode and moment of re-entry may still elude the aspirant to immanence. This is demonstrated in many recent American novels — Saul Bellow's Herzog, for example, is just such an aspirant. Walker Percy's book suggests indirectly that a man may exist between transcendence and immanence as a 'wayfarer', and we can readily recognize how many American heroes have felt forced to adopt the way of life suggested by that designation.

Perhaps the most revealing passage concerning Barrett's relationship with the world around him is the one which describes the Trav-L-Aire car in which he travels around the South. It is completely self-contained with all the conveniences necessary for the owner to be self-sufficient, and it has an observation dome as well. Barrett delights in this way of life: 'mobile yet at home, compacted and not linked up with the crumby carnival linkage of a trailer, in the world yet not of the world, sampling the particularities of place yet cabined off from the sadness of place, curtained away from the ghosts of Malvern Hill, peeping out at the doleful woods of Spotsylvania through the cheerful plexiglass of Sheboygan.' His tone is here clearly somewhat ironic and the attitude expressed is not offered as a final one. Even so, his pleasure at being 'cabined off' from the world, temporarily secure from the coercions of the conditioning forces, is in line with that familiar American delight at feeling free from external control and shaping. At the same time it is precisely such a 'cabined off' feeling, in the world yet not of the world, somehow sealed up in the self, that also presents itself to Barrett as the main problem with which he has to struggle as he wanders without anchorage or definition through the realms of possibility.

Barrett's praise for his car and his position of being in the world without being of it may remind us of Melville's encomium to the 'rare virtue of interior spaciousness' and his image of the dome of St Peter's which suggests a veritable cathedral of consciousness, well able to rebuff the outside world if necessary, and supply its own internal compensations. At the same time the drop from cathedral to car suggests some diminution of that interior spaciousness, and it is this contraction I wish to consider here. The instinct to cultivate and protect an area of inner space is a recurrent one in contemporary American fiction; indeed it is, as I have suggested, often the only area in which a writer and his hero can experience any freedom. The ability to do this is often the salvation of the writer, and the American hero often avails himself of the consolations of unreachable inwardness. At the same time, some American writers have been exploring some of the less happy aspects and effects of cultivated interiority, and their fictional conclusions are an important part of contemporary American literature.

Sylvia Plath's only novel, *The Bell Jar* (1963),[1] is perhaps the most compelling and controlled account of a mental breakdown to have appeared in American fiction. That Sylvia Plath subsequently became famous as a poet, and that the autobiographical basis for her one novel is well-established, should not be allowed to obscure the fact that it is a very distinguished American novel in its own right. The heroine, Esther Greenwood, is beset by feelings of detachment and estrangement from reality which make her a representative contemporary character. Esther has won a fashion magazine contest and visits New York as part of the prize. But though in the crowded clangorous city, she is not of it. She feels like a hole in the ground, like a negative of a person, an absence instead of a presence, a silence instead of a communicant. The things and events of New York press upon her, but without significance. Her numbness and estrangement from reality bring her to a recognizable sort of paralysis – mapless and motiveless.

When she looks at the features of a face in a photograph they melt away, just as the words in a book she reads start to flow past making no impression on the 'glassy surface' of her brain. She finds it difficult to perceive any meaningful patterns in reality, a failure of gestalt which empties perception of significance, reducing vision to mere dots and language to sounds. That glassy surface is really the bell jar inside which she sits, through which she perceives the world. To see the world through glass is to register signs without gathering meanings, and Plath's own style with its clear yet remote documentation of the strangeness of the world outside the glass, is a perfect bell-jar style. After her breakdown and suicide attempt, in the hospital her mind continues to disengage itself from the context of the moment. 'Every time I tried to concentrate, my mind glided off, like a skater, into a large empty space, and pirouetted there, absently.' This is a beautiful image for that inclination to escape into some private space away from the pressure of the moment which is recurrent in American literature. She is the sealed-off spectator, telling herself ' "I am an observer." '

The fact that she is in New York to work for a fashion magazine only heightens her sense of unreality, and it is no idle gesture that one night she climbs to the parapet of her hotel and throws away all the clothes she has been given. A similar inclination to renounce the impositions of the external world is detectable in her use of the hot bath as a cure for her feelings of claustrophobia in New York. It makes her feel that everything is 'dissolving', and that the acquired layers of the day are falling away. (This is another example of the delights and reliefs connected with 'flowing'.) After a hot bath she feels like a new baby, and the whole private ritual is rather like a Reichean dissolving of acquired covers to rediscover the buried child in the self. There are endless references to Esther looking in mirrors and seeing peering out from the prison of the glass an increasingly strange and unrecognizable face in various states of mutilation and deterioration. Finally she can only think that the mirror is a picture of someone else: her alienation from her visible self has become complete.

But the suicide attempt is the prelude to a rediscovery of self expedited by electric-shock treatment in an institution. And this recovery of self is experienced as a lifting of the bell jar. 'I felt surprisingly at peace. The bell jar hung, suspended, a few feet above my head. I was open to the circulating air.' The point is that the person in the bell jar is imprisoned in the airless landscape of his own mind and memory, with no chance of any 'circulating air'. 'To the person in the bell jar, blank and stopped as a dead baby, the world itself is the bad dream.' But the stuffy air inside the bell jar is the air of self not world. (And there is an implication in the book that 'ordinary' people are 'under bell jars of a sort'.) So freedom for Esther consists of getting out of the claustrophobic prison of her own detached self—not just out of the institution, though that may seem to be the most visible prison, but out of the bell jar. The book ends with the experience of a second birth and the hope of a new life. But Esther cannot be sure that, wherever she goes, 'the bell jar, with its stifling distortions, wouldn't descend again.' And the subsequent suicide of her brilliant author all too grimly underlines the fragility of this fictional resolution. Even so it is a resolution very common in recent American fiction—a concluding intention to somehow get out of the bell jar and back into the world.

With the sort of receding of self away from the usual contacts with the external world, which is the beginning of her breakdown, goes a fairly obvious death wish. All the imagery of the book suggests that Esther envisages that death would be an occasion of rebirth at the same time. When she is skiing she plunges down the great slope with reckless delight: 'People and trees receded on either hand like the dark sides of a tunnel as I hurtled on to the still white point at the end of it ... the white sweet baby cradled in its mother's belly.' When she does try to commit suicide, the action is also experienced as a return to a dark, comfortable, womblike retreat — in fact she does creep into a hidden hole in a cellar and takes sleeping-pills. The subsequent experience echoes the precipitous feeling of her skiing—'I was being transported at enormous speed down a tunnel into the earth.' In Esther's case she does finally come out at that white point at the end of the tunnel, so that the almost-death is turned into a kind of second birth. But for other characters in other books who also make their retreats from the world, the tunnel often proves to yield no white light at the end of it.

Hippolyte, the narrator of Susan Sontag's *The Benefactor* (1963) says, 'I am crawling through the tunnel of myself', and both her novels are about the interior journeying suggested by this recurrent metaphor. In his notebook Hippolyte makes a couple of entries which effectively summarize an aim or resolution he shares with many other contemporary American heroes (the fact that he is nominally French cannot disguise the true nationality of his preoccupations). 'Despite the force with which I press myself against the line, I cannot jump outside the circle of my consciousness. But I can step further inside. I can find a smaller circle within the larger circle, and climb into that.' 'If I cannot be outside myself, I will be inside. I will look out at myself as my own landscape.'

The theme is taken up again in *Death Kit* (1967) which starts and ends in a tunnel. The protagonist, Diddy, sells microscopes, and this fact is symptomatic of his alienation from environment. (Walker Barrett is obsessed with his telescope, and John Barth tells of a projected novel about a man addicted to lenses – in each case this implies a loss of unmediated contact with reality.) On the train journey that starts the book he meets a blind girl, Hester. This encounter points to one of the main concerns of the book – the problematics of vision. The seeing person can stand away from his environment and turn it into abstractions, while the blind person is involved in constant contact with particulars thus, in a strange way, coming closer to reality. Diddy starts to worry about the mixed blessing of sight. 'Because he can see, he can perceive the world abstractly. At a distance ... Of course, he can't get rid of his eyes ... Must unlearn old ways of seeing. If it's not too late.' This desire to learn a way of looking that will bring the self into the world, immerse it in concretions, is a long-established American aspiration. Hester cannot lapse from the world into abstractions. She is like the Princess in Hippolyte's fairy-story who is happy because she goes completely blind and is thus relieved of all the problems of perception, assessment, evaluation, interpretation, etc., which are posed by the very act of seeing. At the same time it is clear that Diddy is keen to learn new ways of *not* seeing, for his dominant desire is not really to establish or renew a tangible intimacy with the world, but to get away from it altogether.

At one point he finds himself in an elevator inside the building which comprises the headquarters of the firm he works for. The architecture of this building is marked by a particular eccentricity, a blue-and-gold dome. In Victorian times, this dome was the top of a chapel, but the chapel has been cleared away and the space is now used for 'research and technological development'. The dome is thus an incongruity, the wrong head for the body of the building. But Diddy feels very drawn to the dome and has fantasies of going up into it in an elevator, and nestling there on his own with other people excluded. Specifically, he appreciates 'the fantasy the dome embodies'. I think it is clear that the dome is a projection of human consciousness, once religiously wedded to the actions of the body, but now something of a functionless anachronism in this modern mechanical and technological age. For the detached Diddy, this dome offers the ultimate refuge; the novel concerns the fantasies that are possible, and the nightmares that are unavoidable, in this retreat.

That he is journeying into interior space is made clear throughout, and it is a journey undertaken because exterior space, and all that is contained in it, seems either alien or hostile to Diddy. Even the many, small, man-made spaces he finds himself in – railway carriage, hotel room, hospital ward, TV studio, elevators, etc., are claustrophobic without being comforting: 'however small the space Diddy means to keep free for himself, it won't remain safe.' The outside world is 'running down', another of those entropic nightmares we have had occasion to discuss earlier in the book. In this case it is likely that the entropy is internal to Diddy; for he is trying to cut out the world, thus encouraging that 'running down' which is the fate of any self-isolated and self-sealing organism. But Diddy can see no appropriate or hospitable terrain in the outer world. 'He will have to go further into himself, away from all coherent rational spaces.' The route is signposted at regular intervals. 'Diddy, inside himself. Which for Diddy, doesn't necessarily mean being in his body. In his mind, then?' There it is he wants to nestle, perchance to dream, perchance to find the release and annulment of dreamless sleep. The nominal plot – how he gets off a train to explore a dark tunnel where he thinks he kills a sinister workman; his deteriorating relationship with Hester; their final return to the tunnel to re-enact his murder; their frantic love-making, and Diddy's subsequent exploration of the chambers of death to which the tunnel leads – really presents stages on the long crawl into the tunnel (or shell) of self. As we watch Diddy crawling, or sinking, deeper and deeper into the dome/tunnel/shell, venturing less and less into the world, declining into lassitude, sickness, and that familiar inertia of those who have stepped out of the world, we may recall Miss Sontag's praise for 'Beckett's delicate dramas of the withdrawn consciousness – pared down to essentials, cut off, often represented as physically immobilized.' (For what it's worth, the nickname of Vladimir in Waiting for Godot is Didi).

One might also wonder whether she has been influenced by Elias Canetti's rather nightmarish book, Auto da Fé, with its programmatic schema – 'A Head without a World: Headless World: The World in the Head'. From one point of view Miss Sontag's books are precisely about how the head gets rid of the world, though whether this is diagnosed as something deplorable, or prescribed as something desirable, is left equivocal. But the energies of disburdenment – or the fatigues of relinquishment – are very evident in both her novels; and though there are certainly European models available for this sort of theme, I would suggest that Miss Sontag's novels focus on a mood or disposition which is very common, in a variety of forms, in American novels of recent years. It has to do not only with a dread of environment, a suspicion of material impingements, but also with what happens if you do possess the dome for yourself and keep all others out.

Certainly Diddy's envy of that continuous oblivion to the world (hence its negation) involved in blindness is part of his nauseated repudiation of his surrounding world, and not a measure of his desire to re-establish contact with it. There is a lot of play in the novel not only with eyes and microscopes, but with lamps, torches, glasses, screens, and so on; and the alienating effect of being at once condemned to see, but frightened to touch, is explored in a way which is particularly typical of contemporary American fiction. Relief only comes to Diddy when he turns away from the lighted areas of life and the seen world. He decides or discovers that the tunnel is 'essentially, unilluminable'. Diddy abandons perception, just as he withdraws from communication; he loses weight as he loses world.

It is true that at one point, when he is making a bid for recovery, he thinks he will try to view the world more generously. 'Not only as an arena of contamination, but also as a space to be continually reinvented and reexamined.' But, as so often in American literature, the dream of the world as providing the space in which to be free turns into the nightmare of the world as a force inhibiting freedom. The environment proves to be intractable, closing in on Diddy like the walls on Edgar Allan Poe's prisoner. Diddy 'thinking ... to etch his benign fantasy upon it. (Now) finds the world closing in on him, untransformed and unequivocally menacing.' The ability of consciousness to transform the world in a work, or play, of art, is part of Miss Sontag's own aesthetic, so from one point of view Diddy reveals that vulnerability to environment which threatens the failed artist. Turning away from the world, he sets his face towards the interior of the tunnel with the final words, '"There is another world but it is inside this one."' Leaving behind Hester, and his clothes, '(Now) he's free to go.' But this freedom is equivocal since the rooms he now enters in the recesses of the tunnel prove to comprise 'the house of death'.

The amazing contents of these silent chambers through which he wanders add up to the accumulated debris of the past—words, things, people. It is all random, hodgepodge, 'a wholly eclectic assortment of graphic styles and plastic standards', an accumulating litter on all levels which eventually promises the final entropic stillness. As he passes through these rooms Diddy moves beyond the

ability or need to categorize or pattern his experience. He enters
the silence beyond language with one final formulation. 'Life = the
world. Death = being completely inside one's own head.' So it is
that having penetrated deeply enough down the tunnel he finds
himself among corpses. It is here that Miss Sontag's imagination
shows most signs of life, and it is the main discovery of the book that
at the centre of the house of consciousness is the house of death.
It is perhaps symptomatic of one major change between traditional
and contemporary American literature that the 'stately mansions'
envisaged in Oliver Wendell Holmes's 'Chambered Nautilus' have
given way to the morgue. Make your mind like the dome of St
Peter's, says Melville, but sampling the recurrent contemporary
images for the world within convinces one that there has been a
sharp diminishment in the dimensions of the architecture of consciousness: the dome, in all its forms, is smaller, more imprisoning,
ultimately full of death. It is the achievement of Miss Sontag's
Death Kit to evoke vividly, with one final burst of imagination, what
lies waiting at the dark centre of the tunnel of self. As an 'exemplary'
work her novel has a moral of some moment for American writing
of our time. Namely—what shall it profit a man if he shall gain his
head, and lose the whole world?

To summarize all the different examples of the self withdrawing
from the world in recent American stories and novels would be a
pointlessly lengthy task. It is not, of course, that the emphasis on
interiority is something new in literature. The title of Erich Heller's
The Artist's Journey into the Interior is enough to remind us that art
has been bent on exploring and charting the inner world for some
considerable time, whether you want to go back to Hegel or to
Hamlet, or wherever. Where there does seem to me to be a difference
is that the Romantic and nineteenth-century exploration of the
interior (for example) is intimately connected with the discovery of
the creative powers of the imagination, the immense potential
wealth of memory, the runic codings of the unconscious; in contemporary American writing the retreat into the self seems a more
defensive, less assured and less creative move. 'Solitude a necessary
protection', writes the narrator of Evan Connell's *Diary of a Rapist*
(1966), and similar sentiments can be duplicated from any number
of recent stories and novels. Characters tend to withdraw, not into
art, but into anxiety. It is anxiety, an instinct to retire before the
threatening abrasiveness of the environment, which leads Diddy to
have recourse to that 'organized screening out' that takes him ever
deeper into the tunnel. Ezra Pound wrote in 'The Age Demanded':

> By constant elimination
> The manifest universe
> Yielded an armour
> Against utter consternation.

The contemporary American hero often finds that a too-constant elimination may transform the armour into something more imprisoning than defensive, and precipitate new consternations to replace the old.

Almost Diddy's last sensation in the depths of the tunnel in the rooms full of death is this: 'As though Diddy were living at last in his eyes, only in his eyes. The outward eye that names and itemizes, the inward eye that throbs with thought.' A similar state is achieved by the narrator of William Gass's 'In the Heart of the Heart of the Country' (1967). The title itself suggests an unusual degree of 'withinness', an interior within an interior, and the narrator reveals that he has withdrawn to some very isolated centre, not only of the Midwest but of the self as well. Sitting on a stump alone amid the level fields he says, 'It's as though I were living at last in my eyes, as I have always dreamed of doing, and I think then I know why I've come here: to see, and to go out against new things.' But his contact with the world around him remains almost completely visual, and instead of going out he goes in; living very much *in* his protected house which, with its blue-and-grey bewitching windows and magical insides, is something of an analogue for his own body. Characteristically, it is from within the house that he regards the environment. 'My window is a grave, and all that lies within it's dead ... We meet on this window, the world and I, inelegantly, swimmers of the glass; and swung wrong way round to one another, the world seems in.' The window is the token of his sense of separation, of seeing a world he is not wholly in; meeting at the glass also means parting at the glass. It is this feeling which is behind his subsequent sensuous and evocative panegyric to the swarms of flies in the orchards where he picked fruit as a boy. 'As the pear or apple lit, they would explosively rise, like monads for a moment, windowless, certainly, with respect to one another, sugar their harmony.' The narrator, who is trying to recover from the loss of a girl, feels he has lost the gift for such windowless intimacy.

In some respects, then, the situation in his story is by now a familiar one. But William Gass had previously shown in *Omensetter's Luck* (1966) that he is one of the most original and interesting of the new American writers, and his story is more than another exercise in isolation. Against the emptiness of the outside world the narrator asserts the fullness of his own language; and in his actual apartness, his words swarm like the enviable flies in his memory – they at least windowless to each other. The structure and organization of the story convey the general sense of unrelatedness. It is like a journal, and entries appear under simple headings such as 'a place', 'weather', 'my house', 'people', 'vital data', 'business', with one or two significant groupings such as 'house, my breath and window'. This has the overall effect of an environment not syntactically related, as well as conveying a sense of perceptions bereft of any synthesis, a distinctive phenomenological mood. His itemizing has the effect of desolation rather than of any Whitmanesque celebration. He is like a benumbed topographer who simply lists the things and buildings around him without comprehension. The effect conveyed in such passages is finally one of the pathos of discreet objects somehow astray in a vast vacancy.

The pathos extends to the people who seem to participate in the general atmosphere of bleached lostness; they are, as it were, absent presences, like the figures in Edward Hopper's paintings or George Segal's sculptures. 'Where their consciousness has gone I can't say. It's not in the eyes.' Just by stating the different sorts of weather, putting down the various activities or non-activities of the inhabitants, itemizing all the clubs, listing the range of shops, and so on, Gass manages to convey the atmosphere of a townscape which seems to be entering a state of lasting arrest, full somehow of the fact of its imminent vanishing. The impression is one of accumulating debris, slow disintegration and sudden emptiness. It is as though the whole place abuts on to the void.

The great empty space which surrounds the town is visible in the blank lacunae between the narrator's several entries. He lives *in*; in the house, in the words. In his house he is as inert as many another American protagonist bereft of motive and direction. He keeps telling himself that he must 'resolve, move, do'. But the problem of *what* to do prolongs his passivity. Specifically he is trying to restore himself after losing his girl, but what we might call the convalescent consciousness is so common in contemporary American fiction (think of Herzog and Portnoy, for instance) that if we do regard this narrator as some sort of an invalid, we recognize him as a very representative one.

Physically almost immobile, he is verbally very active, and this is the richness in a story set in declining and denuded landscapes. Envying the cat, for instance, he lets his words start to roam. 'You, not I, live in: in house, in skin, in shrubbery. Yes. I think I shall hat my head with a steeple; turn church; devour people. Mr Tick, though, has a tail he can twitch, he need not fly his Fancy. Claws, not metrical schema, poetry his paws ... ' Thus the world, even this world of deprivation and near-death, bestirs him to language, and where there are words, there is life—that is the feeling. Memories of the girl he himself has lost keep flowing back into his thoughts without warning, their vividness contrasting with the external vacancy and intensifying his sense of loss. At the same time they flower in language, for he is for ever writing them down. 'A bush in the excitement of its roses would not have bloomed so beautifully as you did then. It was a look I'd like to give this page. For that is poetry: to bring within about, to change.' In just such ways he cultivates his language until, amidst the drab aridity of the Midwestern plains, flowers bloom in what we may pardonably call his lexical fields. (A more recent short work by Gass, *Willie Masters' Lonesome Wife*, also concentrates on the comminglings of memories, musings and vagaries of a mind in isolation; and in this case the typography and layout have been wondrously broken up and rearranged in an attempt to offer a typographical miming of the polyphony which goes on in that theatre of simultaneous possibilities, the mind. The pages in the excitement of their words bloom beautifully.)

In his 'retirement' the narrator reveals something of that disburdening instinct we have noted in other American protagonists. For instance, he describes how a figure called Uncle Halley shows him his basement which is stuffed full of fading mementos from the past—papers, letters, photograph albums, maps, posters, and so on. The list extends itself for about a page, registering with something like awed fascination the detritus of the past, assembled randomly but now settled down into a weird synthesis in this basement catafalque. As the narrator goes over the heaped contents —'I saw a birdcage, a tray of butterflies, a bugle, a stiff straw boater', and so on—he captures some of the feeling for both the pathos and terror of waste which characterizes Pynchon's work.

At the same time, his descent into the basement to witness the accumulating sediment deposited by time—in a house, in a mind, in a life—is curiously analogous to Diddy's exploration of the morgues at the heart of the tunnel. But Gass's narrator flees, with the smell of death in his nostrils, and later sets about burning leaves as a conscious rite of purgation. He adds, 'I still wonder if this town —its life, and mine now—isn't really a record like the one of Ramona that I used to crank around on my grandmother's mahogany Victrola through lonely rainy days as a kid.' This is a gesture and a flight which we can recognize now as being another of those familiar attempted repudiations, an attempt to turn one's back on the gathering rubbish—omens of entropy—which seems to threaten the freedom and very existence of the self. In suddenly suggesting that perhaps the reality around him is only a record, the narrator is turning to a Burroughs-like assertion that what we take to be our social environment may just be some mechanical prefabrication.

This, I think, is the point of the end of the story. The narrator is standing in a street during Christmas week. He is alone and there is no one in sight. 'They're all at home, perhaps by their instruments, tuning in on their evenings, and like Ramona, tirelessly playing and replaying themselves.' A speaker in a tower is grinding out barely recognizable tunes in metallic strains. The narrator thinks it is 'Joy to the World'. 'There's no one to hear the music but myself, and though I'm listening, I'm no longer certain. Perhaps the record's playing something else.' It is an appropriately desolate scene with something quintessential in it for recent American fiction. The narrating consciousness is absolutely alone: it stands in a terrain which it can perceive but with which it has no connecting links or contacts. For a moment it seems as if reality is a worn-out record playing tunes which get harder to recognize as distinctions decrease, drowned in the noise of the machinery required to project them. Perhaps the record has changed, but if so the narrator no longer can tell; and, although there is a pervasive sense of loss, perhaps he no longer cares. For although he looks out, he lives *in*.

As an epilogue to this whole chapter, we might consider a little fantasy which Joey tells his stepson Richard, in John Updike's *Of the Farm*. It is about a frog who '"had heard rumours of a wonderful treasure stored deep in the dungeon of his guts, where he had never been."' One day he decides to make an exploratory descent, and sets off down inside himself. '"Down and down, into stranger and darker rooms, and the lower he went, the smaller he got, until finally, just when he was sure he had reached the dungeon where the treasure was, he disappeared!"' Richard asks if the frog died. '"Who said he died? He just became so small he couldn't find himself. He was hibernating."' Joey gives the fantasy a happy conclusion: '"the frog woke up, looked around in the darkness, ran up through the rooms, up the circular stairs, threw open the lids, and looked out. And the sky was blue. End of story."' Whether the American hero can make the return from hibernation to some form of participation is another story, with perhaps a different ending—certainly a more complicated one. We may consider next how Updike explores the problem.

Chapter 12   A Compromised Environment

> 'For ... while each cell is potentially immortal, by volunteering for a specialized function within an organized society of cells, it enters a compromised environment. The strain eventually wears it out and kills it.'
>
> *(The Centaur)*

John Updike seems on first reading to stand quite apart from his contemporary fellow writers. His work reveals no visible need for continually renewed formal experimentation and he seems serenely immune from the paradoxes of the fiction-maker which beset John Barth. For his subject matter he has taken New England suburbia and, at a time when most American novelists seem to regard middle-class life as a desert of unreality, Updike has maintained, and demonstrated, that middle-class existence is more complex than American literature usually allows. Suburbia is the 'compromised environment' in which his characters live and to which, like the majority of the American population, they have committed their lives. Just how people live with and within that compromise, and how they die of it, is Updike's avowed subject; and where many contemporary American novelists tend to see the social environment as a generalized panorama of threatening impositions and falsifying shapes, Updike accepts it as the given world for his characters, the one and only locale in which they will learn what they learn and lose what they lose.

In a short story entitled 'The Blessed Man of Boston, My Grandmother's Thimble, and Fanning Island' Updike seems to give a clear indication of the kind of fiction he aims to write. It is a story about the subjects of three unwritten stories. The blessed old man is a figure he recalls having seen just for a moment at the end of a baseball game. On the strength of this glimpse, Updike (the narrator-novelist) intended to write an immense book about the old man's life, producing pages of detailed but completely imaginary data about his daily routine and surroundings. The thimble is a real object which the narrator comes across one night. It causes him to embark on a lengthy recollection of his grandmother, her place in the family, and how the generations have changed since her time. He

273

wants to write about her because she existed, because she was unique, and because that uniqueness shines out brightly for him now when 'identical faces throng the streets'. The third unwritten story was to be about a remote Pacific island and a crew of men who once drifted there and were never able to sail away again. There was no woman with them. They lived in unprocreative indolence and slowly died off. The narrator-writer says that it could have been a happy story if he had managed to tell it. In effect, it would be a dream of permanent hibernation, an irreversible retirement from the compromised environment of society—with all the peace and sterility that such a state would entail. Similarly, it is worth noting that part of the blessedness of the Man of Boston was his imagined bachelorhood. Clearly the idea of opting out of all the complications attendant on reproduction is an attractive dream. But, as clearly, Updike is more the writer of the second story, concerning marriage, children, the relationship between generations, and the difficulties and satisfactions of familial continuity. (See for instance his excellent novella *Of the Farm* [1965].) All three stories were going to be full of details ('Details are the giant's finger'), and this indeed is the technique which Updike applies in his own work. What this short story seems to be implying is that the narrator may well be drawn to dreaming of existences very unlike his own. He can give a detailed account of a completely imaginary life in contemporary society; or a detailed account of some exotic retreat from society altogether; or a detailed account of the kind of experience he and his family have had within American society. Updike's details fall mainly in the third category.

The perspectives of his books are all from within the society he knows, whereas most American writers take up perspectives very much more from without it. One stylistic result of this is that the things of this society seem to be perceived, named and related as they would be by the inhabitants of that society; whereas most contemporary American writers find it necessary to submit society to their own particular distortions or patternings and to formulate a personal style in which they can recreate it in their own terms. If one adds to this the fact that Updike is one of the very few contemporary American writers to acknowledge that he is a believing Christian, one can begin to understand how he has acquired something of a reputation for being almost too impeccably orthodox and perhaps too well adjusted to the suburban world and minds he writes about. John Barth once described Updike as the Andrew Wyeth of contemporary American writers, adding that he arouses the same admiration and reservations; and one can see the aptness of the comparison. In Updike's books there is that same accumulation and momentary arrest of things, that same effect of lacquered stillness in some of the descriptions, and that heightened sense of topographical detail that one associates with Wyeth. 'Overhead, held motionless against the breeze, its feet tucked up like parallel staples, a gull hung outlined by a black that thickened at the wing-tips. Each pebble, tuft, heelmark, and erosion gully in the mud by the church porch had been assigned its precise noon shadow.' That could be a description of a painting by Wyeth. In both men one finds that same wholesale immersion in the details of a well-known locale which sometimes produces a sense of the wonder and strangeness of a world of objects distributed in space, and at other times gives the impression of a brilliantly tessellated surface over a void. And both men have aroused suspicions of meretriciousness through the amazing facility of their technique.

And yet Updike's work contains more than the recognition that most Americans live and die in suburbia and experience all their joys and fears within its ailing routines and often numbing geometries. Norman Mailer, who predictably dislikes Updike's prose and his 'pietisms', nevertheless sees there is something else in his work. 'The pity is that Updike has instincts for finding the heart of the conventional novel, that still-open no man's land between the surface and the deep, the soft machinery of the world and the subterranean rigors of the dream.' The vocabulary is Mailer's, and it is his own ambition to work that no-man's-land he describes, but he is right in saying that behind the attention lavished on the 'soft machinery of the world' there is another dimension of feeling in Updike's work. He might seem too much at home in suburbia but, after a little reading, his books start to reveal preoccupations and patterns of feeling and apprehension very similar to some of those we have found in his more obviously worried and experimental contemporaries. Updike's prose does give the impression of being a somewhat rococo version of fairly conventional naturalism, but at its best it is edged with dread. This dread stems from related sources: a terror at the sense of the infinite spaces in which the world tumbles, and the horror which attaches to what he thinks of the Darwinian demonstration that 'the organic world, for all its seemingly engineered complexity, might be a self-winnowing chaos.'

These feelings of cosmic vertigo seem to feed the basic dread in Updike's work—the fear of death, the fact of decay and the inevitable collapse into nothingness. This produces what he once called 'a panicked hunger for things' which will stabilize him as it stabilizes his characters. Harry Angstrom in a moment of worry and apprehension reaches out to touch things 'to give himself the small answer of a texture' (*Rabbit, Run*), which is exactly what Updike's prose does as it moves with sometimes hallucinatory alertness among the proliferating objects and surfaces of the suburban landscape. But there are possibilities of dread there as well, for things decay as well as people. What gives a disturbed urgency, characteristic of his best writing, to Updike's apparently suave dealings with things, is a continuous awareness, like an undertow, 'that things do, if not die, certainly change, wiggle, slide, retreat, and ... shuffle out of all identity'. Harry Angstrom has a nightmare about a crying girl 'and to his horror her face begins to slide, the skin to slip slowly from the bone, but there is no bone, just more melting stuff underneath': it is remarkably similar to the Invisible Man's dream of the girl turning into running jelly and it shows that Updike too shares that nightmare of formlessness, of the progressive fading of all identities, which grips so many other contemporary American writers. And it is not only the loss of human identity that produces the moments of metaphysical dread; there is a more embracing sense of the world slowly submerging into the 'melting stuff underneath'. The universal fact of continuous erosion falls like a shadow across Updike's mid-century American suburbia. 'Waste' is a crucial word and obsession in his work, and his sense of the pathos and horror of a wasting world brings him into unexpected relationship with writers like Pynchon. Updike has also had his vision of an entropic world and in his best work it is what prevents both his prose and his characters from feeling too much at home among the soft machinery of the world.

His first novel was *The Poorhouse Fair* (1959), an original little drama of people moving slowly towards their last repose who still retain enough tenacious will to live to put on their annual poorhouse fair. Updike's own acknowledged preoccupation with the fact of death was surely in part responsible for the rather unexpected phenomenon of a brilliant young *New Yorker* writer choosing to write about an old people's home in his first novel. Instead of yet another subjective monologue about the feelings and worries of youth, Updike imagines the thoughts and actions of a group of people very near the edge of all the mysteries. It may be noted from the start that although Updike's work is, as he admits, deeply rooted in his own familial and territorial experience, he never gives the impression of being imprisoned in the self which is so common in many other American writers. No matter how much refracted autobiography gets into his novels, he does make an unusual bid to explore other minds, and the differing pressures of life on people of different ages. He does this, let it be said, with varying success, but it should be recognized that he has avoided the turmoil experienced in the dwindling tunnel of self by other writers. To those to whom this turmoil is the most real experience they know, this avoidance may well look like an evasion; and to see Updike doing so easily what they feel can scarcely be done at all has led many of his contemporaries to regard his work very equivocally. Yet few, I think, would deny the originality and success of much of his early work.

The Poorhouse Fair starts with one of the old people, Gregg, complaining about the name tags that the new prefect of the poorhouse, Conner, has had put on the chairs. It suggests a routinizing and disciplining of the old people which variously offends their still active sense of themselves as individuals; and the whole book is really a struggle between Conner's humanitarian but abstract notions of patterning, and the old people's vital, if sometimes seemingly perverse, instincts to wander free of them. Conner is a man of the future. He has 'lost all sense of omen', and regards existence as something of a vast mess extending backwards through time and across space which is amenable to more or less indefinite clearing up as dictated by the enlightened, scientific human mind. Just noting all the horrible things that can happen to the present human form in its stages of decay makes him assert that '"Life is a maniac in a closed room,"' and the only heaven he can believe in is a future in which cleanliness and order reign, and suffering has been eradicated. '"There will be no waste. No pain and above all no *waste.*"' It should be realized that many of these sentiments overlap with ones which Updike himself has avowed — particularly the fear of nature's endless and indifferent wastings — and it is wrong to see Conner as a totally unsympathetic figure. But in him a dislike of mess and dirt has been taken to the point of an antipathy to life itself. At one point the foul-mouthed rebel Gregg introduces a horribly wounded and mutilated cat into the institution. The motive for this is simply 'a disturbance of accustomed order'. In this cat, Conner sees primarily its disfigurement and probable disease and he orders it to be shot, because 'he wanted things *clean.*' When he hears the gunshot it pleases him, 'anxious to make space for the crystalline erections that in his heart he felt certain would arise, once his old people were gone.' It is Conner who accepts the theory of 'entropia, the tendency of the universe toward eventual homogeneity' which was discussed in a previous chapter. His shortcoming is that he feels no dread, only distaste.

Conner has his office in a remote cupola which affords him a comprehensive 'inclusive' view. The preference for regarding things from a distance is in itself indicative of a disposition to see things in patterns. It is symptomatic of his attitude that when he goes down among the old people setting up their tables in preparation for their annual fair, he notices that the tables are 'poorly aligned', and suggests that they be rearranged. Hook, the most authoritative of the senior inmates, a man of faith representing an older America, says to Conner, ' "I have sometimes thought, had you and your kind arranged the stars, you would have set them geometrically, or had them spell a thought-provoking sentence." ' Hook can still look at nature sensing that there are mysteries beyond the legible regularities of man-made patterns and propositions. And despite various unforeseen accidents and upsets, the fair, in all its harmless disorder, takes place.

From the elevation of Conner's window 'the people in the crowds appear to bumble like brainless insects, bumping into one another, taking random hurried courses across the grass.' The crystalline geometries of Conner's rationalistic dreams have to concede the day to the apparently brainless randomness of life at the fair. Updike has said in an interview[1] that the carnival atmosphere of the last pages of the book, with its merging fragments of multiple conversations, reminds him a little of the opera ending of Barth's *The Floating Opera* — 'a brainless celebration of the fact of existence' — and we may recall that this carnival atmosphere appears in the work of another novelist who has been deeply affected by visions of entropy, William Burroughs. In their different ways these writers share what seems to be a common feeling that the carnival (or funhouse or circus) can serve to stand for some of those instincts in life which resist rigid patternings — of authority, of thought, of some hostile force — with a randomness and sportiveness of motion (though in Burroughs the image is ambiguous as I have tried to show). The fair — any fair — is counter-entropic and counter-crystalline.

At the same time one notes that in what Updike himself has called a latter-day version of the stoning of St Stephen, Conner is the man who is stoned by the rebellious inmates, albeit their throwings are fairly inept and the wound is more psychological than physical. Just how far Updike intends to extend the analogy between Conner and the first Christian martyr is not clear. From one point of view it might seem to suggest a vindication of Conner and a vilification of the old people which Updike can hardly intend. It is perhaps because Stephen was also, in a way, the first Christian administrator that Updike invoked the comparison, suggesting at the very least that it has always been a thankless task to run the necessary institutions of society, particularly the ostensibly benevolent ones. But one of the inmates does seem to speak out for virtues which Conner neglects, and that is Hook. The difference between Conner's and Hook's visions of life is made almost schematically plain (compare the opposition between McMurphy and Big Nurse in Ken Kesey's *One Flew over the Cuckoo's Nest*). Hook speaks out for the better carpentry of fifty years ago, the more dedicated craftsmanship and more authentic building materials of the past. Christ was a carpenter and the profession has symbolic meaning for Hook. But rather than any God-built universe, Conner believes in the laborious and wasteful trials and errors of evolution. Again Hook speaks out for the value of the suffering which Conner would eradicate: ' "Far from opposing the existence of virtue, suffering provides the opportunity for its exercise." ' For Hook, ' "There is no goodness, without belief. There is nothing but busy-ness." ' In his eyes Conner can never be more than a busy man, one whom Hook wants somehow to help and advise. It is Hook's thoughts which conclude the book. It is as though he wants to hand something on to the younger generation of thinkers before going to his final rest. Until then he and Conner cohabit in one world.

The novel then brings together many tensions and themes in a single action, a single day—faith and science, the American past and the world of the future, untidy life and orderly planning, the mangy cat and the crystalline dream. Aspects of all these oppositions are clarified and momentarily vivified in this seemingly simple and economical description of the day of the poorhouse fair, and the voices and dispositions of many generations are brought together as parts of a comprehensive statement, fragments of one containing scene. The simultaneous presence of two apparently opposed human groupings—the institution and the fair—conveys an appropriate, and entirely unforced, sense of the realities and ramifications of a compromised environment.

How an individual cell can rebel against the compromised environment of an organized society is the subject of *Rabbit, Run* (1960). Harry Angstrom who, as a youth, had experienced the joy of unhindered graceful movement in the special space of the basketball court, finds the world thickening around him as marriage and children and the suburban routines bring a weight of responsibility to bear on him. One of his last realizations, just before the book ends, is a succinct formulation of a discovery made by endless American characters before him. 'Funny, how what makes you move is so simple and the field you must move in is so crowded.' How crowded this particular field is, and how Harry Angstrom attempts to find some personally satisfying mode of motion within it or out of it, is the subject of the novel. I cannot imagine that the 'endless

circumstantiality' of this particular kind of suburban world has anywhere been rendered with more 'density of specification' than in
this book. As the prose meticulously itemizes the objects among
which Harry moves, so we can feel the accumulating weight of them
pressing on his eyes and nerves and thoughts to the point of
claustrophobia. Things are observed in minute detail — brands, prices,
foods, cars, household appliances and furniture, all are described
and identified by name. From the toys littered on the carpet to the
gas tanks glimmering in the smoke and the great stretch of brick
which is the town seen from above, Updike fills in the whole
panorama of near and far so that we seem to experience to the full
the total field which is congesting Harry's vision

The narrative itself is fairly simple. Harry leaves his dull wife and
takes up with a tough prostitute; he returns to his wife when she is
having their baby, leaves her again as a result of which she gets
drunk and accidentally drowns the baby; he returns only to flee once
more from the funeral, and on discovering that his mistress is now
pregnant he once more starts to run. In their oscillation Harry's
movements rehearse that pattern of attempted disentanglement from,
and attempted reintegration into, society which has been so marked
in the novels we have considered. More than many novelists Updike
does considerable justice to all the other people who are adversely
affected by Harry's discontinuous manoeuvrings — the women who
suffer, the parents who grieve. He manages to show with a fair degree
of impartiality and insight the damage done to society when the
insurrectionary self refuses the bondage of its undertaken and
imposed responsibilities. At the same time he does communicate the
unfocused urgency and incipient panic felt by Harry as he senses that
something precious and irreplaceable is being drained out of him
while the environment moves to entomb him. Updike produces an
extensive vocabulary of constriction to this end. From the beginning
when he stops to watch some kids playing basketball and realizes
his own displacement, Harry feels 'crowded'. It is a constantly
reiterated word and it is echoed by words and phrases describing
how Harry feels cramped, closed in, weighed down by liabilities,
imprisoned in packed rooms, his energy fading in the constant
negotiation of clutter. In walking out on it all Harry thinks he has
found a 'freedom into which the clutter of the world has been
vaporized by the simple trigger of his decision'. But it is of course
part of the realism of the book that while leaving seems easy, to discover destination is difficult; and decisions which start in simplicity
can end in a renewed thickening of the encircling clutter and
confusion.

The problem is acted out in all its stultifying circularity when Harry takes a premonitory drive. On impulse one evening he decides to transform a simple errand within the suburban routine (fetching the car from mother's house) into a reckless flight from it. At first it is as though the road is drawing him away, hinting at escape to a sunny mythical south; but he cannot find the right roads or work out a route, and he has trouble maintaining direction. At one point for instance, he finds 'he is going east, the worst direction, into unhealth, soot, and stink, a smothering hole where you can't move without killing somebody.' In a sense that is the road he is inevitably on, a graphic version of the road to death, and all his attempts to find a way south are small gestures symptomatic of a larger and more desperate effort of avoidance. But he finds that all roads seem to be 'part of the same trap'. Just as the clutter of the house he has left 'clings to his back like a tightening net' so the roads promising release become a net, a trap (both words are often repeated). Since he does not really know where he is heading for he does not know how to get there, and the problem of mapless movement is experienced in all its frustration.

Like many American figures before him Harry starts to get the feeling that no matter how he moves he cannot get free of some kind of system. 'The further he drives the more he feels some great confused system, Baltimore now instead of Philadelphia, reaching for him.' Looking for some road on which 'he can shake all thoughts of the mess behind him' Harry feels the net thickening and is finally brought to a halt, tangled up in a mess of unknown roads. When he tries to find himself on the map, he finds only a picture of the net in which he is lost. 'There are so many red lines and blue lines, long names, little towns, squares and circles and stars ... The names melt away and he sees the map whole, a net, all those red lines and blue lines and stars, a net he is somewhere caught in.' The stress on the geometrical shapes is worth noting, for when Harry tears up the map he is giving vent to that revulsion against the prospect of fixed and defining forms, that antipathy to crystallization, which is such a constant reaction among American heroes. Ambushed by geometry, he finds that there is nowhere to go. At this point, and more so later on, Harry comes close to that despair of necessity which is as constant in American literature as the despair of possibility, and, of course, intimately related to it.

After enjoying the space of the basketball court, Harry experiences the social field outside him only as an arena of hostile manipulation — a Burroughs world if without any of the Burroughs imagery. And he feels that there is something precious and unnameable, which is the very essence of the self, that has to be guarded against external manipulation, 'He's safe inside his own skin, he doesn't want to come out.' We have encountered the retracted and protected self before, and Harry's claim that, ' "All I know is what's inside *me*. That's all I have," ' is a familiar one. But his moments of confidence when he feels free of all external pressure — 'Funny, the world just can't touch you' — are short-lived; and his often repeated action of suddenly running is a measure of his growing panic that the world cannot *not* touch you, that all fields (in any world knowable to Harry) are crowded fields. What keeps him away from home the night his wife Janice drowns the baby is not really the search for his mistress: it is the idea that somewhere 'he'd find an opening'.

But there are no 'openings' in this sense, no hidden apertures in the soft machinery of the world which will afford the individual sudden release into pure uncluttered freedom. Harry's realization as a child 'that this — these trees, this pavement — was life, the real and only thing' is a moment of enduring truth. Indeed it is one of the truths conveyed by the texture of the book; it can make it suddenly very oppressive so that we share in Harry's panic. The possibility of escaping into spacious edifices erected by the imagination is not here envisaged, and the only moments of temporary illusory escape are provided by authentic sexual experiences. These may, indeed, provide an opening, and on his first night with the prostitute Ruth, Harry feels 'He is out of all dimension'. Or, as we may perhaps put it, out of all maps and nets, beyond the geometries of time and space and a thing-packed world. Since such moments cannot be extended into a programme for everyday living, Harry's movements can have no constructive goal, no destination beyond that of renewed sexual passion. Harry has inchoate religious feelings which lead him to announce vaguely that behind all the visible scenery ' "there's something that wants me to find it" ', but there is some justice in Eccles's reply that ' "all vagrants think they're on a quest. At least at first." ' It is the old problem for the American hero of whether he can transform 'from' into 'towards': like many good men before him Harry cannot get beyond enacting a mode of motion — running, as Augie March and so many others run.

As Harry comes to realize that he has lost that irrecapturable vitality of youth, that 'it' which he feels alone makes life worth living, he approaches a mood of resignation. 'The best he can do is submit to the system ... The fullness ends when we give Nature her ransom, when we make children for her. Then she is through with us, and we become, first inside, and then outside, junk.' Reminders of decay and decline are constantly turning up in the landscapes Harry moves in —

a junk heap, a treeless waste, a derelict house, a roof covered in litter, a heap of dead stalks; and it is quite clear that Harry experiences the dread of suddenly realizing he is in an entropic world which comes to so many of Updike's figures. His particular dismay is to realize how the entropic process also affects him, turning him into an object of junk where once vitality flowered. It is part of his dislike of waste and litter that makes Harry by instinct a tidy man who likes cleanliness, and even at times makes him want to accept the system and be a model maintainer of its order. But we encounter once again the paradox that both the regularities and routines of a rigidly ordered world (geometry) and the waste and litter which accumulate along and across its lines (shapelessness) are productive of death.

At the close of the book Harry finds himself confronted by a 'dense pack of impossible alternatives'. Standing in the streets he imagines a road leading back to his responsibilities and commitments, back into the heart of the city; and 'the other way ... to where the city ends'. Then: 'He tries to picture how it will end, with an empty baseball field, a dark factory, and then over a brook into a dirt road, he doesn't know. He pictures a huge vacant field of cinders and his heart goes hollow.' The field of cinders (almost a Pynchon touch) or the suburban net, it is death either way, and it is death that Harry is really in flight from—unwilling to confront or accept the ancient truth that in the matter of man's relation to death 'away from' and 'toward' are the same thing. He looks around for guide lights away from the darkness. The delicatessen bulb is shining, but shopping means responsibilities; the church window is dark. On impulse Harry turns from both buildings and just follows the street lights—the illusion of an illumined path. ' "I'm on the way," ' is his last communication to Eccles, after he has run from the funeral into the woods, and his inability to announce the terminal point of his movement is the most eloquent part of the message.

There is another aspect to his running as well. Trying to work out and balance all the worries and counter-claims on him inside society induces unusual feelings of heaviness of self; he feels clots of concern, clots of sin, or simply clogged with himself. It is only by running, that is by refusing any location and denying any stasis, that he can gain a sense of inner freedom and the weightlessness of the world. 'Goodness lies inside, there is nothing outside, those things he was trying to balance have no weight. He feels his inside as very real suddenly, a pure blank space in the middle of a dense net.' He remembers the relief on the basketball court when no one could touch you because you had passed the ball and 'in effect there was nobody there'. He is experiencing the emancipation of invisibility. These are his thoughts while running, feelings engendered by the act of running; that paradoxical American dream of being a weightless self, of combining the relish of identity with the purity of unassailable space is momentarily realized. It is almost a flight away from matter — matter being the ultimate trap.

There is a religious aspect to this, and phrases like 'the ideal subsoil to reality' and Harry's questions about ' "the thing behind everything" ' testify to the flickering transcendentalism in Updike's own thinking, as well as Harry's need to believe in something more than the crowded field. But the religious dimension is very tenuous in this book and is in turn part of a much deeper ambiguity in Harry's reaction to the materiality of the world. From one point of view he clings to it, almost like a Hemingway character keeping the void at bay. Sometimes the 'solidity' of things is welcome, sometimes nauseating. It is part of the painful paradox of this sort of experience that Harry can feel as though he has fallen out of the given world at the same time as he realizes he cannot escape from it; at once alienated and trapped. For all his feelings that the world cannot touch him, it is 'a paralyzing sense of reality' which besets him and which starts him running once again at the end of the book. The end is indeed inconclusive, and as far as Mailer is concerned 'Updike does not know how to finish.' It seems that he blames the author for Harry's own cowardly indecision. But this is an indecisiveness and evasiveness which has a long history in American literature, and Harry Angstrom running is simply one of many modern Huck Finns wanting to quit society and avoid growing up but with no 'territory' to light out to. Perhaps Updike is not sufficiently ruthless in tracing out the inexorable end of Harry Angstrom. But he has made the compromised environment real enough to us for us to realize that Harry Angstrom, whatever his decisions or adopted direction, can only run deeper into the trap, closer to the vacant field of cinders.

A great garbage dump stands in the background of Updike's next novel, *The Centaur* (1963). The book concentrates on three days in the life of George Caldwell, an ageing school-teacher who is having to come to terms with his own decline and imminent death. ' "I'm a walking junk heap," ' he says. As a teacher of evolution, Caldwell can think back to the time 'when consciousness was mere pollen drifting in darkness' and on to his own annihilation: zero to zero. At one point he questions a pupil on the subject of 'erosional agents' and, despite his blundering affection for people and capacity for love, his mind is more preoccupied with nature's wasting than with nature's bounty. ' "I hate Nature. It reminds me of death. All Nature means to me is garbage and confusion," ' he cries out, late in the book, and everywhere he looks the lesson is the same: all things, cars and people alike, revert, fold, fall apart. 'Things never fail to fail.' Reminders of waste and death and 'the many visages which this central thing wears' are subtly omnipresent in the texture of the suburban world.

The basic subject of the book is the behaviour and reactions of a man finally accepting, absorbing, the fact of his own death, and the effect that sombre realization has on him.

> Since, five days ago, Caldwell grasped the possibility that he might die ... a curiously variable gravity has entered the fabric of things, that now makes all surfaces leadenly thick with heedless permanence and the next instant makes them dance with inconsequence, giddy as scarves. Nevertheless, among disintegrating surfaces he tries to hold his steadfast course.

This description of his shifting perceptual relationship with the things around him is also a good description of Updike's prose which can register things as being both meaninglessly obdurate and scatteringly ephemeral. In one scene he describes Peter watching with fascination the effect made by the shadows of snowflakes in a pool of lamplight. Directly under the light the shadows seem simply erratic, but away from the centre the shadows seem to repeat endlessly the same patterns of falling. It is another version of an experience central to his work; a dual sense of both the shifting plasticity and the steady geometries of existence.

Moving towards the periphery of the illuminated area 'Peter does seem to arrive at a kind of edge where the speed of the shadows is infinite and a small universe both ends and does not end.' This moment of experience seems to offer an analogue for the more metaphysical concept of the situation of man which underlies the book (Karl Barth's statement that man is 'the creature on the boundary between heaven and earth' stands on the title-page). All Updike's books in one way or another are about moving towards that boundary marked by death, that 'kind of edge' at which the small universe of a single man, say that of a school-teacher in an American suburb, ends and — if religious hopes are answered — does not end. Even without any religious certainty it is clear that we live in a world which is always and never ending, full of things evolving and reverting, growing and wasting in mysterious simultaneity, and it is that world which Updike tries to make us aware of behind the almost trivial familiar details of his foreground scenes.

This reaching for a dimension or realm beyond or behind the visible edges of the given, the compromised environment, is manifest in another way by Peter's sense of the existence of two worlds. As an aspiring artist his feelings cannot be very different from Updike's (himself the son of a schoolmaster), and he spends a good deal of time in an imaginary world to compensate for unaesthetic impositions of the actual. Having spent an evening watching slides illustrating cattle diseases, he returns home to take solace from his book of Vermeer reproductions. Again when his father picks up a hitch-hiker in filthy disarray, Peter is horrified at this affront to his artistic aspirations. 'That my existence at one extremity should be tangent to Vermeer and at the other to the hitchhiker seemed an unendurable strain.' This is another version of the mangy cat and the crystal dream cohabiting in the same world. More pleasantly, when he finds he can buy coughdrops made in Alton when he visits the dream city of New York, the unanticipated fusion delights him: 'The two cities of my life, the imaginary and the actual were superimposed; I had never dreamed that Alton could touch New York. I put a coughdrop in my mouth to complete this delicious confusion and concentric penetration.'

This is a fair hint at the concentric penetrations of the worlds of Greek myth and contemporary suburbia which Updike is attempting in the novel itself. Peter as narrator says, 'I was haunted at that age by the suspicion that a wholly different world, gaudy and momentous, was enacting its myths just around the corners of my eyes;' and Updike as writer has tried to do justice to this feeling by, at times, keeping two narrative strings vibrating (as a violinist can hold two notes), and at other times making the legendary and the contemporary echo each other, or, as at the beginning and end, merge into each other. The Chiron myth is appropriate to his purposes, not only because of the figure of noble Chiron, wounded and finally giving up his immortality to seek the repose of death; but because the Centaur, crossing the usual classifications (cf. *Giles Goat-Boy*) by being part animal and part man, occupies 'a dangerous middle-ground', analogous to that occupied by man in Updike's religious vision. It would be pointless to go through the novel pointing out just where and how Updike has made the mythic and the contemporary echo or interpenetrate. He has in any case added a Mythological Index so that if you cannot always get the clue, you can—as with any published puzzle—look up the answer in the back. What is more interesting to consider is what might be behind this attempt to conflate two worlds, or, as it might more accurately be put, to turn one world into two.

In the interview Updike discussed the different purposes of the mythic parallel in his book: it offers a 'counterpoint of ideality' to the everyday drabness, it allows him to make a 'number of jokes', and it serves as a serious expression of his feeling 'that the people we meet are *guises*, do conceal something mythic, perhaps prototypes or longings in our minds.' One remembers Augie March's feeling that we all catch up with legends more or less, and perhaps part of the particular appeal of Joyce for American writers has been his demonstration of how a mythic dimension can be quite consciously subtended from a segment of contemporary experience. It may be one way of checking that vertiginous feeling of placelessness, or nowhereness, which seems particularly prevalent in America. Asked why he had not done more work in this mode, Updike answered, 'But I have worked elsewhere in a mythic mode ... there is the St. Stephen story underlying *The Poorhouse Fair*, and *Peter Rabbit* under *Rabbit, Run*.' Two observations seem to me to be relevant here. First of all there is the easy grouping of classical myth, biblical history or legend, and a children's story. To view *Peter Rabbit* as a myth seems to me rather quaint: it is a familiar tale of great simplicity and charm with a tiny (bourgeois) moral and a comfortable ending, but to call it a myth is to propose an unhappy dilution of the meaning of the word. What Peter Rabbit, St Stephen and Chiron do have in common is that they all figure in well-known stories, and although these stories exist in very different worlds (or concern different orders of reality), it seems that Updike identifies them as being equally suitable for his purpose. By placing the lineaments of a familiar story beneath the contemporary incidents he suggests the existence of an extra dimension (back through time, down into common archetypes), which will give depth and resonance to what might seem to be the fleeting contingencies of his suburban settings.

His own statement, during the interview, of the function of these hinted parallels is an attractive one. 'I think books should have secrets, like people do. I think they should be there as a bonus for the sensitive reader, or there as a kind of subliminal quavering ... In any case, I feel the need for this recourse to the springs of narrative, and maybe my little buried allusions are admissions of it.' But, and this is the second observation I think one can make, it seems to me that our detection of these allusions has no effect on our reading of the surface story. As was pointed out, the relevance of St Stephen to Conner is rather far to seek, while to push the analogy between Angstrom and the naughty bunny would if anything trivialize the potentially serious problems posed by the book. The more elaborate network of allusions to the Chiron myth, in my experience of reading the book, does nothing to or for the foreground reality which Updike puts before us with his customary meticulous annotations. What I am aware of, in detecting the allusions, is Updike's own delight in his sport and mental agility.

It has been clear from the beginning that it is often in such sport (James's 'fun') that we will find the American writer indulging or exploring his capacities (though what sort of book this can lead to when the capacities are formidable and the sport insecurely grounded, I think *Giles Goat-Boy* demonstrates). The more modest bonus which Updike offers his alert readers puts no such strain on the narrative process. But Updike is also what most other American writers are not, a religious writer. Through the dread and need and hopes of his main characters he seems to want to suggest the existence of another world behind this one, another dimension. But while experiencing his incorporation or interweaving of another *narrative* world (mythic or biblical) as a feat of mental ingenuity, even of fiction-making sport (as in Nabokov whom Updike admires), it is hard to place much credence in the references to another, *religious*, world which Updike surely intends seriously. Paradoxically the effect of most of his work is to leave us feeling that there is only one world, and that the wall of detail with which he confronts us looms all too authentically large. Then we as readers can find ourselves claustrophobically ensnared in that ultimate trap of material clutter which he knows and shows so well.

At one of the many parties in *Couples* (1968) the guests are trying to recall the name of Poe's story about the walls squeezing in on a prisoner. They make their usual compulsive banter about the subject and one suggests that it was by ' "I. M. Flat, a survivor in two dimensions." ' But the wall of matter is indeed squeezing in on the contemporary suburb of Tarbox, and the question of loss or retention of dimension is a crucial one. Updike has never before gone to quite such lengths to itemize the dense tissue of appurtenances which makes up the wealthy contemporary American suburb. Piet Hanema is said to believe that there is, 'behind the screen of couples and houses and days, a Calvinist God Who lifts us up and casts us down in utter freedom, without recourse to our prayers or consultation with our wills'; it is perhaps symbolic of his retention of older virtues and attitudes that he does at one point pull off some screening doors with his bare hands. But despite the awesome burning of the church which concludes the book (based, I am told, on an actual event) and which might seem to portend the anger or indifference of a God, what we are made to feel behind the screen is not God so much as—once again—death.

Although in this prosperous suburbia people live well muffled lives (' "We all rather live under wraps," ' says one character), death and decay are subtly pervasive. The details of Kennedy's assassination filter in from the news media though they are barely registered by the couples busy at their games; the death of all those aboard the submarine *Thresher* which sank beyond trace is made a topic of conversation at a dinner party. Piet himself is however very painfully aware of the reality and imminence of death. At unexpected moments he suffers 'a dizzying impression of waste' or gets a 'sense of unconnection among phenomena and of falling'. He has death panics 'as he felt time sliding, houses, trees, lifetimes dumped like rubble, chances lost, nebulae turning'. Some of the characters seem almost resigned to 'the world's downward skid'. Freddy Thorne, the rather obviously named dentist who takes a perverse pleasure in drilling away at people's weaknesses, can get sexually excited by thinking of the rotting enamel he deals with every day. ' "Death excites me. Death is being screwed by God. It'll be delicious." ' Angela loves the severe elegance of Freud's *Beyond the Pleasure Principle* because it stresses that we all ' "carry our deaths in us" '. But such adjustments to the fact of irreversible decline are not for Piet and he seeks for some footing among the sliding. In all the general decay and waste two human activities at least seem able, temporarily anyway, to hold out against the inevitable dissolution — building and love.

As we have noted, carpentry has been present from the start in Updike's work, usually representing the values of an older America, and Piet who comes from a family of builders is recognized as a genuinely dedicated carpenter. Grappling with materials — and they are given in great detail — helps Piet to fend off that sense of the void: 'he needed to touch a tool. Grab the earth,' an echo of that self-stabilizing pragmatism celebrated by Conrad and Hemingway. The sea reminds him of waste, and he prefers well-made frames. 'All houses, all things that enclosed, pleased Piet.' He draws back from the foaming formlessness of the sea, the shapeless mud of the swamps, and builds inland. He likes the sense of 'space secured'; at the same time he recognizes the rape of 'sacred ground' involved in putting up a housing estate — 'a pampered rectilinear land coaxed from the sea'. There is a realization that man can become too caged in his own constructions, and there is some subtle play with the importance of doors, the point of mediation between architecture and space, form and formlessness. One of his affairs gives him the pleasure of 'going from indoors to outdoors' and since the women in the book are more usually connected with the flow of the sea and the undefined openness of space, it suggests that the carpenter at times feels the need to escape from his own carpenterings. When his wife calls him a caged animal and Piet retorts, ' "But Angel, who made the cage, huh?" ' we surely recall that Piet himself has been shown to be the expert cage-maker (he constructs one for the children's hamster); to some extent the retort recoils on him. For in a larger sense the 'cage' or 'trap' is simply that compromised environment which he himself works to maintain with his well-made frames.

The other act which counters death is love. To quote from Updike's essays: 'A man in love ceases to fear death ... Our fundamental anxiety is that we do not exist – or will cease to exist. Only in being loved do we find external corroboration of the supremely high valuation each ego secretly assigns itself.' And the fact that in the act of love it takes two to do just about everything is felt to be the ultimate defence against entropy. 'She was double everywhere but in her mouths. All things double. Without duality, entropy. The universe God's mirror.' Hence the title *Couples*, and the various references to 'The beauty of duality. A universe of twos'. It is the desire of these twos to take up mirror positions with one another that makes the world go round. 'At the corner two dogs were saying hello. Hello. Olleh.' Man is himself a duality – groin and brain – and the large amount of oral sex described in the book is seen as a response to this condition, a ritual meeting of mind and matter. There is clearly a philosophical or biochemical point in Updike's elaborate detailing of the exhaustive sexual permutations acted out by the wealthy inhabitants of Tarbox. In the interview Updike said, 'I was struck, talking to a biochemist friend of mine, how he emphasized not only the chemical compositions of enzymes but their structure; it matters, among my humans, not only what they're made of, but exactly how they attach to each other. So much for oral-genital contacts.' A concern with structure permeates the book, manifest not only in Piet's carpentry, but Ken Whitman's biochemistry (it is part of Updike's acuteness of observation that he can show how different professions tend to make people think and talk in different ways), and a more general concern about whether matter – from stars to starfish – is chaotic or systematic.

To a man who asks how 'a complex structure' can arise spontaneously out of chaos, Ken replies, ' "Matter isn't chaos ... It has laws, legislated by what can't happen." ' Shortly before he changes his life by marrying Foxy, Piet dreams of ill-fitting frames, structures that will not stay erect. Then he dreams that, 'He was standing beneath the stars trying to change their pattern by an effort of his will.' In combination these dreams seem to suggest that although the individual may make a mess of the particular patterning of his life in the social and domestic sphere, he is ultimately participating in a vaster, deeper, older pattern from which—along with the starfish and the stars—he is helpless to deviate. Early in the book Foxy thinks of Ken working in his laboratory 'down there, where the protons swung from molecule to molecule and elements interlocked in long spiral ladders'. Just so, the book seems to imply, the inhabitants of Tarbox interlock in long spiral ladders. Mirrors are much in evidence in the book and one effect they have is to make a single grouping appear like a symmetrical pattern and repetitive process. ('The sliding glass doors ... doubled their images, so that a symmetrical party seemed in progress.') In all their clumsy, heartless, and often rather cruel and jaded sexual games, the 'couples' are to be seen as acting out a pattern which is rooted 'down there' in the biochemical sources of life. Without abandoning his felicitous notation of contingent details, which give one that illusion of randomness characteristic of changing social scenes, Updike manages to convey the presence of this underlying pattern.

But just here, I think, a problem obtrudes for the novelist. For to the extent that he suggests the dominance of that pattern he is likely to diminish the sense of the importance of differences between the individual agents who maintain it. From the point of view of the pattern, the dogs at the corner are helping to maintain the universe. Of course, they are; but then from this point of view how is one to differentiate among humans who, in their coupling, are also obeying and preserving the structure of life. From one point of view the novel could be showing how, in the 'post-pill paradise', sex, so far from maintaining the universe by leading to procreation, has degenerated into an empty and sterile game. But there are quite a few children scattered around, and when it comes to enjoying fornication divorced from any thoughts of conception Piet is well to the fore. And yet Piet is clearly meant to be in some way the hero of the book, a true lover. Updike surely intends his relationship with Foxy to be a serious love story, but in this world—or the world seen from this point of view—how is sex as love to be differentiated from sex as lust? Nearly all the sexual activity of the book is celebrated lyrically and yet it would seem that a good deal of it is meant morally to be judged adversely, or at least seen as a symptom of some social malaise.

There is a blur in the novel when it comes to this problem, and while the book certainly makes clear the difficulties involved in taking up any definite religious or moral attitudes towards sex in our relativistic age, I think this blur makes the attempt to differentiate Piet as somehow more authentic than the other characters unconvincing. Accused not unjustifiably of weakness by the other couples, there is an attempt to interpret this to mean that his 'strengths weren't sufficiently used'. To romanticize his adulteries by saying things like 'only Piet had brought her word of a world where vegetation was heraldic and every woman was some man's queen,' reads like banal literary exoneration. It is not a question of reintroducing a proto-Victorian abruptness and certainty of censure. It is only that one would like to see an important problem brought into focus. What is it that makes one 'coupling' better, more humane, more authentic, than another, when from one point of view every coupling is an act of participation in, and preservation of, the universal structure? Perhaps, indeed, we are in need of a whole new vocabulary if we are to discuss the problem adequately, and Updike's novel at least goes some way to exploring the whole problem of 'relationships' in contemporary America.

One way in which Updike attempts to give an added dimension to Piet is to suggest his relationship to older prototypical figures. To quote his own words: 'Piet is not only Hanema/anima/ Life, he is Lot, the man with two virgin daughters, who flees Sodom, and leaves his wife behind.' He also says that he was aware of Piet and Foxy as 'being somehow Tristram and Iseult' and accepts that Piet may also be Don Juan. Again, I do not see that these references or analogues operate to any great effect in the book; their very multiplicity in itself suggests something a bit too easy. What does serve to mark Piet out is his capacity for dread and his heightened sense of the compromised environment through which he moves. The ending is thus equivocal. He has broken out of his marriage and the Tarbox trap, but only into another marriage and another suburb, 'where, gradually, among people like themselves, they have been accepted, as another couple.' So the book ends, echoing the first sentence and suggesting the circularity of the whole process.

Updike has stated that he intended the ending to be ambiguous.[2] It is a 'happy' ending, since Piet marries Foxy. But by putting his guilt behind him and becoming just another satisfied person Piet 'in a sense dies'. In elaborating on this Updike made a statement which is relevant for an understanding of all his novels: 'a person who has what he wants, a satisfied person, a content person, ceases to be a person ... I feel that to be a person is to be in a situation of tension, is to be in a dialectical situation. A truly adjusted person is not a person at all.' More than any religious implications, it is this feeling which the book communicates most strongly—that to allow the self to be absorbed into the compromised environment is tantamount to losing one's selfhood (a deeply American feeling); at the same time life *in* that environment, with a well-loved wife and a well-built house, is the best antidote to that great cosmic dread and sense of universal waste which besets Updike's characters. Because this fear can be so intense Updike sometimes seems to write in support of the compromised environment, though not without recognizing the ambiguity of what it offers.

It is this qualified, or intermittent, support for the suburban environment which has sometimes provoked the criticism of writers and critics who feel that the writer's repudiation of American society should be more total, or his attack on it go much deeper. Sometimes Updike's prose does take on a slick sheen which to a hostile eye may seem to partake a little of the suspicious polish of the merchandise which clutters the suburban world he writes about. There is no doubting his brilliance and fluency as a prose writer, and there are certain atmospheres, occasions, moods, which he can evoke with incomparable vividness and authority. At the same time there is something decorative and strained about many of his similes — an air of cultivated 'fine writing' — which can detract from the impact of his work, giving it at times the timbre of a stylistic exercise. He himself has said that he writes fairly rapidly without much revision and he describes the author's deepest pride, as he has experienced it, 'not in his incidental wisdom but in his ability to keep an organized mass of images moving forward, to feel life engendering itself under his hands'. I think one can appreciate much of what is good in his writing if one bears in mind this delight in maintained momentum.

As has been clear from the start Updike shares that vision of entropy so common among contemporary American writers. Those of his characters who 'run' do so, among other things, from the entropic facts of life. To Freddy Thorne, a 'vortex sucking them all down with him', Piet says, ' "I think you're professionally obsessed with decay. Things grow as well as rot." ' This counterbalancing truth is one which it seems unusually hard to hold on to in contemporary American fiction. I would suggest that for Updike writing is a way of holding on to the fact of growth, holding out against entropy. Ken, the biochemist, is trying to approach the mystery of organic life, 'chlorophyll's transformation of visible light into chemical energy. But here, at this ultimate chamber, the lone reaction that counterbalances the vast expenditures of respiration, that reverses decomposition and death, Ken felt himself barred.' He feels himself facing 'an irreversible, constricted future'; the squeezing of the walls of the compromised environment. But Updike in the act of writing is, as it were, overcoming that barrier, and in his own way celebrating or miming that 'lone reaction ... that reverses decomposition and death'. He has said that his first thought about art was 'that the artist brings something into the world that didn't exist before, and that he does it without destroying something else. A kind of refutation of the conservation of matter. That still seems to me its central magic, its core of joy.'[3] Society, as an organized cluster of cells, inevitably shares in the process of entropy; the engendering of a work of art can appear, temporarily, to refute it. In the compromised environment which gradually entraps his characters, it is perhaps Updike himself as the writer who is the most subversive cell. The complaint of some of his critics is that, at times, he is not subversive enough.

Chapter 13 Fictionalized Recall - or 'The Settling of Scores! The Pursuit of Dreams!'

> 'Yes, I might—if I could learn something! If I could be some-how sprung ... from the settling of scores! the pursuit of dreams! from this hopeless, senseless loyalty to the long ago!'
>
> *(Portnoy's Complaint)*

> 'Late in the spring Herzog had been overcome by the need to explain, to have it out, to justify, to put in perspective, to clarify, to make amends.'
>
> *(Herzog)*

In his struggles within a 'compromised environment' the American hero often finds that he has arrived at a condition of prone arrest—Bartleby the Scrivener and Oblomov are relevant ancestors. So much has already been made abundantly clear. But of course it is also true that different characters do different things in their state of stillness, and some of them prove to be amazingly, and irresistibly, articulate. It must be more than a freak coincidence that two of the most remark-able and popular novels of the 'sixties are written by men lying down and conducting, as it were, their own analyses—of self, psyche, family, society, and beyond. I refer to *Herzog* (1964) and *Portnoy's Complaint* (1968). Before considering these crucial novels I want to make a point about an emerging genre which includes other works besides these famous examples. It is no secret that much of Herzog's experience is Bellow's nor that many of Portnoy's complaints are Roth's. I make the observation not in the interests of furthering gossipy speculations or facile reductions. My suggestion is, rather, that for some American writers their experience of life in America is so intense and primary that it seems supererogatory to invent new material. Instead, the craft of the fiction-maker goes into shaping and ordering the overall structure of his recollections. William Carlos Williams called this process 'fictionalized recall' and it is the name I would like to give to the genre that I want to explore in this chapter. The adoption of a different name for the remembering self gives the author the licence to make such distortions and suppres-sions, and indeed additions, as seem to him desirable or necessary for the particular vision and diagnosis he wishes to articulate.

It may be objected that Herzog and Portnoy write their books in very different settings. True, while Herzog is alone on his couch in his run-down country house in the Berkshires, Portnoy is on the couch of Dr Spielvogel in New York. But the doctor is a silent witness and both books amount to amazing monologues by recumbent figures determined finally to 'have it out' at whatever cost to traditional novel plots and patterns, to give reign to their self-obsession at whatever risk of solipsism. Their minds are so freighted with memories and speculations based on retrospection, that they have slowed down or succumbed to a point of arrest in present time. I have written elsewhere of Bellow's difficulty in moving beyond monologue[1] (his first piece of published fiction was entitled 'Two Morning Monologues'). Portnoy's self-disgust at his own state— 'Nothing but *self*! Locked up in *me*!' —reveals at least a comparable discontent with that ego involvement which, in turn, provides both the substance and the narrative voice (retrospective, ruminatory, reproachful) of both books. The fact that these self-absorbed figures 'produced' books which were instantly recognizable as being among the most arresting fictional achievements of the decade is itself a phenomenon of some significance, with some implications for contemporary fiction which are worth exploring.

In 1961 Philip Roth wrote an interesting article[2] in which he discussed the writing of American fiction and by extension the problems facing the contemporary American writer. He started by recounting the sordid and bizarre details of a Chicago murder as reported in the press. The moral, he says, is this: 'that the American writer in the middle of the 20th century has his hands full in trying to understand, and then describe, and then make credible much of the American reality. It stupefies, it sickens, it infuriates, and finally it is even a kind of embarrassment to one's own meager imagination. The actuality is continually outdoing our talents, and the culture tosses up figures almost daily that are the envy of any novelist.' Thus it is that outer reality comes to be experienced as a grotesque invention, which the novelist cannot recognize as his own country. This must certainly seem a serious occupational impediment. For what will be his subject? His landscape? What Roth wishes to draw attention to is 'a loss of subject; or if not a loss ... a voluntary withdrawal of interest by the writer of fiction from some of the grander social and political phenomena of our times.'

Considering some works by his contemporaries, Roth discerns a phenomenon he describes as 'reality taking a backseat to personality' and two of his comments have a relevance beyond the specific works he cites. He speaks of a deliberately mannered style by which 'the real world is in fact veiled from us by this elaborate and self-conscious language-making.' This he thinks represents 'not so much an attempt to understand the self, as to assert it'. All of which, he suggests, may be symptomatic 'of the writer's loss of the community as subject'. Following this loss, says Roth, the writer in his rage, disgust, or impotence, may well turn

> to other worlds; or to the self, which may, in a variety of ways, become his subject, or even the impulse for his technique. What I have tried to point out is that the sheer fact of self, the vision of self as inviolable, powerful, and nervy, self as the only real thing in an unreal environment, that that vision has given to some writers joy, solace, and muscle.

However, 'when the self can only be celebrated as it is excluded from society, as it is exercised and admired in a fantastic one,' then, says Roth, we have little to be cheerful about. Among other things, it means that novelists have lost faith in the idea that the individual can ever realize himself in contemporary social territories.

Roth ends by quoting the concluding plight of Ellison's *Invisible Man*, and one can readily see how pertinent all his remarks are to our discussion of the American fiction which has come after that book. It is perhaps a dramatic confirmation of Roth's whole thesis that he himself, by the end of the decade, should produce a novel in which the narrating hero lies passive and apart, complaining of 'nothing but self'. The phenomenal success of the novel suggests, however, that his diagnosis at the beginning of the decade was perhaps not exactly right. The writer's inability to comprehend the American community in his fiction may be much less important than the need of the community to participate in (imaginatively) or to witness the unabashed expeditions into the self conducted in their different ways by writers like Bellow and Roth. It should also be noted that no very profound analysis of the lower depths of the psyche is undertaken by either writer, nor do they seek to make their compulsive reminiscences yield a lasting verbal artefact as Proust did. If anything they seek a release from the past, an escape from old psychological guilts and intellectual torments. Both Herzog and Portnoy, in their differing ways, have been subjected to too much control, too much information, too many alien patternings of reality – like Burroughs's characters. In company with most American protagonists of the last decade, their main desire is to gain a measure of freedom from the conditioning forces, and some release (even immunity) from those behavioral and intellectual versions of reality which have helped to bring them to their present state of immobility.

In an article written in 1968[3] Saul Bellow summarized the contentions in Roth's article and added his own comments.

The modern writer specialises in grotesque facts, and he cannot compete with the news, with 'life itself'. Perhaps he should begin to think of interesting himself in something other than the grotesque. There is good reason to think that absurdities are travelling in two directions, from art into life and from life into art. We cannot continue to ignore Oscar Wilde's law. "Nature imitates Art." Roth is right if — and only if — fiction cannot leave current events without withering away.

Bellow is here continuing his long-standing criticism of the sort of novel which seems to invoke monstrosities and conjure up grotesque images of evil and visions of apocalypse and doom: his dislike and disapproval of a writer like William Burroughs has been made clear. His answer to Roth — and in this article it is rather an elliptical one — is that fiction ought to be able to turn from current events without withering away. On the other hand it has also been a continuous contention in Bellow's criticism that the sort of 'art' novel which turns away from ordinary life is a sterile and negative model for fiction which he deliberately abandoned after *The Victim*. I am not here attempting to catch Bellow out in a contradiction; rather I am trying to clarify a difficulty of which Bellow is clearly aware and which I think throws some light on his recent fiction. The problem would seem to be, can there be a kind of novel which turns away from 'current events' and yet remains in vitalizing contact with 'ordinary life', a fiction which rejects unwholesome pressures without isolating itself from the ageless and shared truths of human experience? In an earlier article[4] Bellow again gave some indication of his wish to steer between two kinds of American novel: the novel of information, with its exclusive interest in externals, things, process and documentation; and the novel of sensibility in which 'the intent of the writer is to pull us into an all-sufficient consciousness which he, the writer, governs absolutely.'

In another piece of criticism[5] Bellow defines a problem for American writers which sounds very similar to Roth's. 'American novelists are not ungenerous, far from it, but as their view of society is fairly shallow, their moral indignation is non-specific. What seems to be lacking is a firm sense of a common world, a coherent community, a genuine purpose in life. No one can will these things into being and establish them by fiat.' The last observation is important. The modern American writer is most usually a product of an anonymous urban environment which has not provided him with a sense of community. While wishing to adopt the sort of outward-looking assimilative fictional genre which will incorporate the life around him, he may find that as he opens his novel to the world (as it were) what come in are not images of a richly structured community such as he has found in the great European and Russian social novels, but the hideous facts mongered by the mass media, or the torrents of unrelated information which Bellow and Roth, for example, have specifically repudiated as being unsuitable material for a truly serious American fiction. Lacking community, such a writer might well turn back to the self and the experienced authenticity and relevance of its specific responses. There is here an important paradox. Because of what the environment has done to them, both Herzog and Portnoy are trying to disburden themselves of memories and thoughts which weigh too heavily and paralysingly on their present consciousnesses; on the other hand those memories also represent their contacts with 'externals', that experience of ordinary life which, even if it didn't add up to life in a genuine community, is all the reality they know. Both novels, in their different ways, have something of this dual aspect of being at once desperate disencumberings and cherished re-evocations. Memory becomes an ambiguous phenomenon and both Bellow and Roth seem to get rid of something by getting hold of it.

In *Herzog* one could say that Bellow is attempting to combine what he discerned as the separate strands of the American novel, by depicting a sensibility oppressed by too much information. The single sensibility cannot hope to triumph over the waves of incoming information (which includes personal and international news, environmental data and fragments of science, philosophy and culture — all the past and all the present), but it is the effort of the book not to let the information completely annihilate that part of the sensibility which is in fact the core of the self. Thus it is a book about a man breaking down (the possibility of madness is raised in the first line and again near the end) but also seeking to arrive at a new form of integration; the energy of the book is aimed at recomposing the 'decomposing' self. Rather than attempt to rehearse all the merits of the book or assess its overall achievement I intend to single out a few aspects of it which give some indication of how central a novel it is for the whole period under consideration.

In this connection I want to concentrate on the by now familiar preoccupation with systems and versions which obsesses Herzog, and the equally familiar awareness of general dissolution and disintegration which hangs over the book. Herzog's foreground speculation and retrospection take place against a background of entropy, and the fact that the book ends with Herzog having arrived at a state of total inertia (a stasis which is temporary in terms of Herzog's putative 'real life', but terminal in relation to the book) is as equivocal as much else in the novel. It can appear as a capitulation to the entropic forces, or it may be seen as the beginning of a more truly human adjustment to the mysterious processes and rhythms of existence. As in other comedies, the possibilities of dual perspectives are allowed, indeed encouraged, to the end.

Herzog's shifting struggle to establish some coherence amidst the randomness and density which are unavoidable in the modern world is not of course a new one. We can find Matthew Arnold writing to Arthur Hugh Clough in 1849, criticizing Keats and Browning on the grounds that 'they will not be patient neither understand that they must begin with an Idea of the world in order not to be prevailed over by the world's multitudinousness.' Arnold's formulation applies nicely to Herzog's predicament: will an idea of order (a system) enable him to resist being prevailed over by the world's multitudinousness? But there are so very many systems to choose from, and it is entirely possible that this very plurality of 'Ideas' or versions is the most toxic part of the multitudinousness which vexes Herzog's weary and inflamed consciousness. How then can a man gain some immunity from the vast amount of unusable information which besets him, some reprieve from those exhausting bouts of frantic mental gyrations characteristic of the mind which has not found its proper employment? It is perhaps worth noting from the start that whereas Herzog's fragmented speculations tend to be abstract and lead him into wastes of impersonal generalities, his memories are necessarily more concrete and serve to bring his mind back to those specific and personal experiences (no matter how painful) which are unique to him. Fitfully arguing with dead German metaphysicians or running over the cosmic implications of a contemporary physicist's theories or a politician's pronouncement, while jammed in an anonymous crowd in the subway, may easily lead to a drastic attenuation of the sense of self; but to recall to present mind the kitchen details of one's own family is to realize that one is a self indeed, for no generalization or theory can contain quite all the details of that particular home, that particular life. It may be that memory serves as the best antidote to the confusion of varying systems of thought, a way of discovering relevance in the world's distractions.

Herzog's constant grappling with the problems attendant on adopting or rejecting a system of some kind is clear throughout. Something is in his head 'pounding for order'. But then a little later after discussing certain types of people he thinks, '*Foo to all those categories*,' and it would be true to say that that sort of suspicion and rejection of categories which is so much a subject in Barth's fiction is also a part of Herzog's own American temperament. But of course any mental order or system must necessarily depend on patterns and categories. Herzog only arrives at the possibility of orderings beyond language at the end of the book, and one cannot be sure whether it is an assured discovery or a pious hope. He has been a man, he admits, 'in pursuit of a grand synthesis', but consulting his own habits of self-isolation and detached observation he comes to the ironic conclusion—'*what kind of a synthesis is a Separatist likely to come up with?*' Just as Herzog finds himself quarrelling with the different philosophical syntheses which men have attempted, or are attempting, to promulgate in the world, so he resists the differing 'systems' by which other people account for the way reality is, the way people are. His own remembered experiences remind him that 'human life is far subtler than any of its models', an insight which, as he realizes, applies also to his own 'construction' of people and events.

In one of his last letters Herzog 'writes': "*The dream of man's heart, however much we may distrust and resent it, is that life may complete itself in significant pattern. Some incomprehensible way. Before death.*' The dream of pattern is reasserted after a book in which the futility and dangers involved in all sorts of patternings of reality have been explored. But the tone has changed. For it is not now a philosophical or ethical pattern which is being sought; not, certainly, a social pattern (its patterns and organizings are invariably deathly in Bellow), but a significant pattern which will be, precisely, incomprehensible—i.e. beyond the formulations of mind and language. To achieve such an invisible and soundless pattern would be at the same time to escape from the all too visible and audible 'patterns' which make up modern life. Inevitably there is something mystical about the sense of such a pattern, and one could perhaps relate it to the intuitions and beliefs of the Transcendentalists and their sense of wordless rapport with nature. It is apt that the last chapter of *Herzog* is set in a garden.

With the mention of 'death' in that last quotation we come to the one great fact which is for ever at the back of Herzog's mind. Mixed in the swarm of data which assaults Herzog's mind are recurrent reminders of the decline and disintegration of things. In his early recollections Herzog sees himself as a man with 'a fatal attraction to the "City of Destruction" ', and his first reaction to his excited letter-writing is that it 'might be a symptom of disintegration'. Ageing faces, heavy flesh, wrinkling skin, all remind him of the irreversible erosion of the body. Not only does he vividly recall the dying moments of his mother and father, but his imagination pursues them into the earth, thinking of them turning into insignificant soil. One of his early letters starts with a reference to the presumed 'disintegration' of some Russian cosmonauts in space, and this is only one example of Herzog's more general preoccupation with the notion of man disintegrating in space – the individual, the race, then the planet, and the stars, all passing from void to void. The attempt to assert moral realities and individual values against a background which man is turning to waste is Herzog's particular counter-entropic struggle. The urban landscapes he passes through are a constant reminder of the proliferation of waste – junk heaps, demolition projects, the clouds of dust rising from a slum-clearance project. It is, as it were, a constant fact that outside his city window 'they were demolishing and raising buildings'. The whole circular process of turning rubble into forms, forms into rubble, and so on, endlessly, is an important influence on Herzog's thoughts. Again it brings Burroughs to mind – ' "They are rebuilding the City." ... "Yes ... Always ... " ' What both men can see, in their different ways, is that the environments that man constructs, with all the attendant production of dead waste, can be regarded as part of the entropic process – an acceleration of it rather than a resistance to it. To resist entropy is to hold on to one's individual form, but that is precisely what the American urban environment with its contagious indistinctness does not do, nor does it encourage its inhabitants to do so.

The will to deny the universal truth of the law of entropy is what drives Herzog on, even though in his own disintegrating state he is an ambiguous witness against it. He feels the presence of something in the sheer fact of life which is more positive and more important than the bleak though undeniable fact that even in life we are in the midst of death. Life is not only about its own inevitable decline. When he is flying to Chicago, Herzog, typically thinking about what would happen if the plane crashed, looks out at the sky. 'And the sun, like the spot that inoculated us against the whole of disintegrating space.' This is an important sentence.[6] 'The sun is God,' said Turner, and the feeling that by constantly summoning things forth into colour and life and miracles of beauty the sun is a force against entropy (or a temporary inoculation against disintegration), is one which increases in importance for Herzog. Life not only confronts us with junk heaps; there are also 'sudden intrusions of beauty' and these too deserve to be heeded as evidence, signs. Herzog likes to linger over trees and flowers, registering them intensely and gratefully, and the reminder that things blossom as well as decay is a major factor in Herzog's recovery of a degree of equilibrium and calm.

This I think is why the garden setting for the conclusion is so important. His house — 'Herzog's Folly' — rises out of a tangle of weeds, flowers, and blossoms. When he returns, it is in such a mess that he abandons any idea of restoring it to any form of order. In saying 'let be' to the jumbled profusion of his neglected garden, Herzog is beginning to learn to extend a similar attitude of acceptance to the confusion of his mind. Just as he decides that he will not prune the garden nor attempt to put the house in order, so he will not try to re-establish a neat set of categories to contain the dishevelled garden of his mind. One very late meditation contains the realization that *'Everywhere on earth, the model of natural creation seems to be the ocean ... What keeps these red brick houses from collapse on these billows is their inner staleness ... Otherwise the wrinkling of the hills would make them crumble.'* And his last note to himself turns to a mode of passive acceptance based on the example of the non-human world. In terms of the novel, Herzog's last act is to pick some flowers, lie down, and give up his 'letters' for stillness and silence. 'Not a single word', the book ends, and again one cannot help remarking that in its own way this follows the Burroughs prescription, by putting the self beyond language altogether. The anti-social, or non-social, nature of Herzog's last meditations and reconciliations is also notable. He sees the oceanic flow behind the ephemeral human dwellings; he relishes the way the garden has started to reclaim the house; he lies down and turns to 'the radiance of the sun' like a flower. Admittedly he has been thinking about his daughter and he is expecting his girlfriend, Ramona. But the actual novel leaves Herzog at a point when he has found some peace by getting beyond language, outside of society, and accepting a prone passivity — *almost*, as it were, allowing himself to be reclaimed along with his declining house, by the tidal rhythms of nature's processes.

But this lyrical resolution poses some problems if we are to imagine Herzog ever re-entering society. As Leo Marx has so well demonstrated,[7] the pastoral moment cannot be extended into a way of life; what it can do is provide a spiritual refreshment which may strengthen the individual for his renewed encounters with the non-pastoral realities of the city. Certainly we feel that Herzog has achieved such a moment of refreshment and found a temporary peace beyond patterns; but the fact remains that an indefinite sojourn there would amount to a capitulation to the oceanic flow which Herzog, who cherishes the sense of being a self, would hardly wish to accelerate. At the same time he is scarcely eager to re-enter society. Herzog in his garden is in that third area sought for by so many American heroes, not society nor yet quite the flow. The near-by village of Ludeyville is, appropriately, not on the map. When Herzog's brother, Moses, comes to inspect Herzog's location, Herzog knows what he is thinking. '*The edge of nowhere. Out on the lid of hell.*' For Herzog it is closer to being the threshold of heaven. But one thing is certain. He has arrived at the edge.

Bellow himself has spoken about the implications of his hero's plight, and the intended point of the whole novel.[8] He points out that Americans do not expect thought to have results in the moral or political spheres, in the way a Frenchman might. If anything, the American intellectual is likely to feel humiliated by a sense of impotence.

> To me, a significant theme of *Herzog* is the imprisonment of the individual in a shameful and impotent privacy. He feels humiliated by it; he struggles comically with it; and he comes to realize at last that what he considered his intellectual 'privilege' has proved to be another form of bondage ... Any *Bildungsroman* ... concludes with the first step. The first *real* step. Any man who has rid himself of superfluous ideas in order to take that first step has done something significant.

Bellow goes on to admit that he may have let himself off easily. In his attempt to discover a way of resisting the 'controls of this vast society' without falling into nihilism or empty rebellion, he concedes that he may not have followed certain questions 'to the necessary depth'.

One can readily appreciate and be grateful for Bellow's desire to uphold some of the traditional sanities and balances, and one can accept his tentative affirmation that 'There may be truths on the side of life.' At the same time, I think this attempt to establish some middle ground between pessimism and optimism contributes to what Updike called 'the soft focus of Bellow's endings'. Bellow is not alone in disliking the sort of shock tactics exploited by a writer like Burroughs, yet there are times when extreme fictional strategies are necessary if certain questions are to be followed to the 'necessary depth'. For some writers there is something a little too easy, and even self-satisfied, in the way in which Herzog achieves the desired disburdenments and reconciliations in the pastoral moment of the last chapter.

I referred earlier to the ambiguous role of memory in the work of Bellow and Roth. Herzog, like Portnoy, is a great one for settling old scores by going over past events and releasing some retrospective accusations and resentments. From one point of view this is how he gets rid of the burden of these past events, as though by playing them back, as it were, he can erase them from the tape of memory. But in another sense his memories are a source of strength —immobilizing yet nourishing. 'How he doted on his memories!' They are a hidden wealth, not an invisible burden. He often lapses from the confusion of the present into memories of his family and childhood. He warns himself that it is perhaps not wholly healthy to love the dead so much. But the mild self-admonition is not heeded and soon he returns to the past. 'Engrossed, unmoving in his chair, Herzog listened to the dead at their dead quarrels.' It is worth drawing attention to this habit of Herzog's because although this compulsive mental return to childhood memories is itself a symptom of self-preoccupation, it also points to a possible move away from solipsistic tendencies in the self. Roth was quite correct when he predicted that American writers were more and more likely to turn to the self as their subject. At the same time it can be said that there is a certain mode of memory which may serve as an indirect way of re-establishing some contact with things (and people) outside the self. Certainly in two admirable recent short stories, Bellow again focuses on figures with their gaze fixed firmly on the past.

In 'Mosby's Memoirs' (1968) he makes rather an interesting experiment. Mosby, an ageing ex-diplomat, sits in Mexico sipping mescal and writing his memoirs (one senses a remote echo of *Under the Volcano*). Like other Bellow figures he is a lonely thinker — 'he would not cease from mental strife.' It seems that he has been involved in most of the politics and history of his time and has acquired a disenchanted political and human wisdom. He writes of himself in the third person, like Henry Adams in his *Education*, as Bellow points out, and he is clearly the WASP type to whom 'unmastered emotion was abhorrent'. He is a Senecan, a believer in 'the clear classic hardness of honourable control', cool, perhaps cold in the silent retention of his emotions. For some comic relief in his memoirs he conjures up the remembered figure of Lustgarten, a sloppy, emotional, resilient Jew. As emerges from Mosby's recollections, Lustgarten was a man given to wild schemes for whom everything went wrong, who nevertheless has subsequently reached happiness in a state of 'passionate fatherhood'.

In Mosby's eyes Lustgarten is a purely comic spectacle, though in a later, less comfortable recollection he has to resurrect the fact that he once arranged for Lustgarten's absence so that he could seduce his wife. This rather darker memory comes to Mosby when he is touring some local temples and is part of an altogether unpleasant

fantasy. 'It was that he was dead. He had died. He continued, however, to live. His doom was to live life to the end as Mosby.' When
the sightseers finally go down into the tomb, a great claustrophobia
and death-panic overtake him. 'To be shut in here! To be dead
here! ... *Dead*-dead.' He flees back to daylight and air. There the
story ends. The Jew and the WASP: comic, fumbling (and fecund)
life set over against an astringent, cool control which has a great
dread of death at its secret centre; two aspects of America, two kinds
of psychology, with a hint of betrayal in their relationship – summarized that way Bellow's story might seem to be almost schematically simple (and if we were expecting an active man after Herzog's
promising resolutions we have to observe that Mosby, sitting and
sipping his mescal, turning memories into memoirs, is just about as
immobile as Herzog).

Yet it is a most suggestive and probing story, full of rich ambivalence, and there is a particular interest in seeing a Jewish writer
simulate a mandarin, Gentile consciousness, through which to gain
perspective on another Jew. This device gives this short story real
depth and complexity, and it makes possible objectivities and dual
perspectives which were not available in *Herzog*. Through controlled indirection Bellow has found a way of aiming his imagination
back at the world outside the self. At the same time his most basic
subject is still there at the heart of the story – the realization that all
things live in the shadow of their own imminent departure, that
flowers are as transient as they are vivid. 'Mosby felt ill with all this
whirling, these colors, fragrances, ready to topple on him. Liveli-
ness, beauty, seemed very dangerous. Mortal danger ... Behind the
green and red of Nature, dull black seemed to be thickly laid like
mirror backing.' It is no doubt an aspect of Mosby's somewhat
sterile view of life that the highly coloured rage of the vegetation
makes him feel threatened – not for him Herzog's happy garden state
and a face turned gratefully to the sun. At the same time one recognizes that Mosby is another typical Bellow character in his constant
awareness of that endless black behind the green and red.

His other recent story, 'The Old System' (1967), ends in a similar
way. Once again Bellow portrays a man of middle age, caught at a
moment of prolonged pause, lying in bed for much of the day, moving slowly about his lonely house, and giving up his 'afternoon to the
hopeless pleasure of thinking affectionately about his dead'. Unlike
Mosby, Dr Braun is a Jew and, although he is a scientist with an
orderly analytic mind, he soon finds himself hopelessly entangled in
the 'crude circus of feeling' re-enacted in his mind by his now dead
relatives. His emotions are set flowing by his memories, and unlike

Mosby he makes no attempt to keep deep feelings at bay by a maintained tone of ironic disengagement. Braun specifically rejects the contemporary 'unhealthy self-detachment' and succumbs to his 'useless love' for the past, the dead. His 'longing of having known' precipitates vivid detailed memories and scenes, a quite different mood and attitude from the metaphysical fretfulness of some of Bellow's earlier characters. It is as though Braun is bowed down in reverence and silence before the unfathomable mystery of people and things and places that are at once so achingly real and so utterly gone.

He is, as he describes it, 'overthronged', and the word would serve as a good description for the mental state of most of Bellow's previous heroes. But in this case it isn't the junk and unrelated pseudo-ideas of the mass media and the onslaught of urban chaos which are weighing his mind down. He is thronged with more valuable freight, and instead of attempting to 'put the world in rational order', Braun is content to let the past possess his mind in its own way: 'the facts arranged themselves – rose, took a new arrangement. Remained awhile in the settled state and then changed again. We were getting somewhere.' The mixture of flow and focus suggested by this description is more like an organic process than the attempt to arrange things in fixed categories, and it enables Bellow to write some of his most assured and unhindered prose – rich but uncluttered, relaxed and yet evincing a complete grasp of his material. Here Bellow gives the impression of being completely at home with his subject.

This subject, alluded to by the title, is not only his past but the more general question of generational differences among Jewish immigrants into America. Phrases like the old system, the old rules, the old conditions, refer to certain qualities of experience, certain ways of inhabiting reality, certain emotional modalities (good and bad in all cases) which are inevitably vanishing or being drastically altered in the conditions of modern American life. Usually, but not exclusively, Jewish qualities are specifically in question. 'In America, the abuses of the Old World were righted. It was appointed to be the land of historical redress. However, Dr Braun reflected, new uproars filled the soul. Material details were of the greatest importance. But still the largest strokes were made by the spirit. Had to be!' In receding from the new uproar to the passional intensities of his dead relations, Braun is also exploring his own sense of those spiritual realities and mysteries which make man more than the material details which ensnare him, more than the scientific categories which define him.

At the end of the story, after concluding a moving death-bed scene, Braun meditates on the mystery of human emotions—their poignancy, their futility. Recalling the emotional excesses indulged in by some of his dead Jewish relations, Braun feels temporarily attracted to the 'cold eye' which watches the life process dispassionately and unmoved. But then he feels that a cold eye would necessarily involve an internal coldness which he repudiates. Tears may be useless, but a man will weep as he sees his loved ones fade from him into the grave. Tears wept from the heart do seem to justify something, or give you the feeling of understanding something—we may remember the conclusion to *Seize the Day*, where Tommy Wilhelm weeps uncontrollable tears over the dead body of a man he never knew, and sinks towards 'the consummation of his heart's ultimate need'. But what is it that one seems to understand when weeping?

Again, *nothing*. It was only an intimation of understanding. A promise that mankind might—*might*, mind you—eventually, through its gift which might—*might* again!—be a divine gift, comprehend why it lived. Why life, why death.

And again, why these particular forms—these Isaacs and these Tinas? When Dr Braun closed his eyes, he saw, red on black, something like molecular processes—the only true heraldry of being. As later ... he went to the dark kitchen window to have a look at stars. These things cast outward by a great begetting spasm billions of years ago.

Mosby has the cold eye, and he ends up in a vault, breathless from a terrible sense of death. Braun, who to some extent shares Mosby's distant disaffiliation from the excesses of uncontrolled emotion squandered and indulged in by the Jews they have known, nevertheless is not afraid to let his own strong feelings flow, sinking back into the intensely human reality of the people of his past. Like Mosby he is very aware of the void waiting to assimilate the living forms—when they look out at nature they both see red on black. But he ends his day with an almost visionary sense of the awesome mystery of life, his mind turned to the wonder of the 'begetting spasm' rather than the dread cessation of the tomb. It is noticeable that both men can be seen moving, not towards any re-engagement with society (they are both singularly solitary men), but towards a lonely encounter with the ultimate mysteries. This seems, indeed, to be the direction of all Bellow's work, and it is perhaps superfluous to add that such lonely encounters are a recurrent feature in the central tradition of American literature. And by exploring the different ways that two such different kinds of self re-establish relationships with their own and the American past, Bellow has found a particularly rewarding way of approaching his deepest preoccupations.

Mr Sammler's Planet (1969) scarcely represents an advance in Bellow's work. Sammler is a recognizable Bellow character, a more pessimistic Herzog with something of Mosby's European sceptical disinterestedness of vision. He is another lonely thinker ('seven decades of internal consultation'), and perhaps his most important recognition is that he will never be able to 'put together the inorganic, organic, natural, bestial, human, and superhuman in a dependable arrangement, but ... only idiosyncratically, a shaky scheme, mainly decorative or ingenious.' Some of his speculations, precipitated by reading a paper on 'The Future of the Moon', make him sound almost like William Burroughs, for Sammler is beginning to think that his planet Earth has just about had its day. 'Wasn't it the time – the very hour to go?' The Earth is a 'glorious planet'. 'But wasn't everything being done to make it intolerable to abide here, an unconscious collaboration of all souls spreading madness and poison?' There might be a whole new age of hope for man 'once we were emancipated from telluric conditions.' (cf. 'Prisoners of the earth come out' and 'Time to look beyond this rundown radioactive cop-rotten planet' – sentiments from Burroughs's *The Job*.) The most important aspect of the book is its preoccupation with the problem of different kinds of knowledge. In his youth Sammler had admired H. G. Wells and his attempt to explain the world and the future intellectually. But now, as he approaches the end, he reads only the mystic Meister Eckhardt. I think Bellow's characters (and through them Bellow, perhaps), are searching for what I would call the Tolstoyan moment. In *Anna Karenina* Levin spends many frustrating hours of talking and reading, 'searching by the aid of reason to discover the significance of the forces of nature and the purpose of life'. What reason is helpless to provide comes to him in the simple words of the old peasant, Fiodr. Fiodr describes an upright man by saying, ' "He thinks of his soul. He does not forget God." ' Levin asks what it is to live for the soul. ' "Why, that's plain enough: it's living rightly, in God's way. Folks are all different, you see. Take yourself, now, you wouldn't wrong a man either ... ' (Penguin translation.) These words penetrate Levin to the heart as no rational idea has ever done. Just so, under all the farrago of man's changing intellectual explanations, Sammler is convinced that 'we know *what is what*.' It is in the presence of death, 'summoned to the brink of the black', that this deep creatural intuitive knowledge is most likely to be felt. Throughout the action of this book Sammler's nephew Gruner is dying, and in the last scene Sammler makes yet another descent into the realm of death, down into the depths of the hospital to bid goodbye to Gruner's corpse, asserting to any God who may be listening that, 'he did meet the terms of the contract. The terms which, in his inmost heart, each man knows. As I know mine. As all know. For that is the truth of it—that we all know, God, that we know, that we know, we know, we know.'

Herzog by the end of his book had reached a point at which he felt 'a deep, dizzy eagerness to *begin*'. At the end of Portnoy's uninterrupted complaint which makes up his book (Philip Roth's *Portnoy's Complaint*), when in his own way he too has passed beyond articulation, his psychiatrist is allowed the last word—'"Now vee may perhaps to begin. Yes?"' Both these figures, then, have reached the threshold of their particular 'beginning room' (as Purdy called it), and in both cases the novels about them concentrate on arriving at that point and not on how to pass beyond it. One condition for being able even to think about 'beginning' is some degree of liberation from the past, and Roth himself has spoken in an interview of wanting to 'kick a lot of the past'.[9] At the same time, as is the case with Herzog, Portnoy's compulsion to re-evoke the past is so obsessive one wonders about the possibility of his achieving the desired detachment from it. And that is perhaps the most serious aspect of his complaint—that the sense of guilt has been so deeply implanted in him that there is nothing in the resources of rational consciousness or language which can disperse it. He ends his complaint with a paranoid fantasy of the police coming for him, and an abandonment of language, not, as in Herzog's case, to move into a serene if temporary silence, but to collapse into a howl—'A pure howl, without any more words between me and it!'

Just as for Cabot Wright the recovering of the ability to laugh signified the beginning of freedom, so Portnoy has found that only by turning guilt into laughter can he achieve some degree of emancipation from it. As Roth himself has said, 'not until I had got hold of guilt, you see, as a comic idea, did I begin to feel myself lifting free and clear of my last book, and my old concern.'[10] Kafka is a writer who has obsessed Roth, and *Portnoy's Complaint* could be seen as an American version of Kafka's *Letter to His Father*. Roth's novel is undeniably funny, indeed hysterically so; yet it is in some ways as painful as that strange and troubling work by Kafka, and equally fixated on the minute details of the familial and social past and the focal point at the centre of it all—the uncertain, suffering self.

At the end of one of Roth's most impressive early short stories, 'The Conversion of the Jews', the boy Ozzie Freedman, who has been bullied and penalized by his religious teacher, flees to the roof of the synagogue and stands on the edge threatening to jump. In this way he brings his mother, the rabbi and the watching crowd to their knees, and in this situation he can legislate to his legislators. From his dangerous edge he hurls down defiance and extracts concessions from them, making them promise that they will not use their authority to force their version of God on other people. It is another picture of a small American hero going out to a lonely edge to make his complaint against the subtle or brutal imposition of fixed definitions and rules. Waiting beneath him is a large net held out by firemen which looks like 'a sightless eye', while above him is the 'unsympathetic sky'. 'Being on the roof, it turned out, was a serious thing.' For the young boy poised on the edge of so many things – manhood, society, and all the problems of future direction – the alternatives seem bleak. Having made his 'superiors' bow to his will, Ozzie jumps into the net which for a moment glows 'like an overgrown halo'. In some ways the story is a fantasy of revenge, the put-upon little boy finally finding a voice and a stance with which he can dominate the familial and social authorities who exercise such control over him. The jump too must be an exhilaration and relief – a kind of 'letting go'. At the same time the net must be ambiguous, for it is what the guardians of society hold out. It cushions the fall, yet it surely traps the faller. At the end of Roth's subsequent novel, which was actually called *Letting Go* (1962), Gabe Wallach, who has revealed some of the psychologically crippling effects of being brought up in the family net, or trap, writes a letter to a girl he has been involved with, which ends thus: *'It is only kind of you, Libby, to feel that I would want to know that I am off the hook. But I'm not, I can't be, I don't even want to be – not until I make some sense of the larger hook I'm on.'*

When Portnoy 'lets go' and allows himself to fall on to the psychoanalyst's couch – another sort of net waiting for the grown man – he is determined to bring that 'larger hook' into the open. There is no real knowing of the self until it becomes aware of the past it is impaled on. Sartre's observation that introspection is always retrospection can be extended to take in this truth, and for Roth's characters the sense of self and untranquil recollections from the past are inseparable. In the story, 'Defender of the Faith', Nathan Marx, a Jewish sergeant in the army, who resists the way some Jewish soldiers under his command try to exploit and presume on their common racial identity, nevertheless finds that 'one rumor of home and time past, and memory plunged down through all I had anesthetized and came to what I suddenly remembered to be myself.' Portnoy's memory takes such a plunge and he finds that, once started, he cannot desist 'from the settling of scores! the pursuit of dreams! from this hopeless, senseless loyalty to the long ago!' And, as he says from the psychoanalyst's couch – 'My God! the stuff you uncover here!'

As Ozzie Freedman races 'crazily towards the edge of the roof' he finds himself throbbing with the question "Is it me ME ME ME ME! It has to be me – but is it!" At the end of Roth's novella, *Goodbye, Columbus* (1959), Neil Klugman stands staring at his reflection in a library window after the unpleasant conclusion of an affair.

> I was only that substance, I thought, those limbs, that face that I saw in front of me. I looked, but the outside of me gave up little information about the inside of me. I wished I could scoot around to the other side of the window ... to get behind that image and catch whatever it was that looked through those eyes ... I looked hard at the image of me, at that darkening of the glass, and then my gaze pushed through it, over the cool floor, to a broken wall of books, imperfectly shelved.

This shift in vision whereby a scrutiny of the image of the reflected self gives way to a perception of actual external objects is apt to Roth's work. In one form or another, the majority of his work has been preoccupied with the problem – what is this mysterious ME rushing towards the edge, or staring back at me from the glass? At the same time his real talent as a novelist has been for a meticulous observation of the familial and social scenes around him – for the books that are actually there on the other side of the window.

It is perhaps an awareness of having this talent which made him feel that the contemporary novel should stress outer reality more and self less. Yet that desire of Neil Klugman's to 'get behind' and find some 'inside' information about the self is there from the start in Roth's work. It is arguable that this tension between social observation and self-exploration had an effect on his two following novels. There is no mistaking Roth's ability to evoke the abrasions and lacerations of intra-familial rows and discords in *Letting Go* and *When She was Good* (1967), and his social eye is amazingly acute. At the same time there is something rather laboured about these novels, particularly *When She was Good*, in which Roth offers a study of a desperately neurotic woman in the distinctly non-Jewish society of the Protestant Midwest. The prose in which the book is written is uncharacteristic: rather flat, remote, dispassionate, at times somewhat lifeless. It was almost as though in a valiant attempt to write a coolly objective book about an American world removed from the self of the writer, Roth had produced rather a mask of a book.

Portnoy's Complaint (1969) is by contrast unmistakably a face, and the unhindered flow of the book must owe something to the fact that at last Roth's interest in the social scene and his feeling for the obsessed self coalesced in the writing. Everything is allowed to emerge in this monologue of a man who is insatiably avid for sex but incapable of relationships, and who sets out to retrace the steps of his childhood to find out why. This particular type of man—carnal and selfish, guilty yet incorrigible—has been there from the start of Roth's work, but he has never explored himself, or been explored, to any great depth. Nor did he dominate the foreground of the novels to the exclusion of other characters. But in *Portnoy's Complaint*, Portnoy holds the stage, indeed he is the stage. If he is some sort of psychological cripple with all kinds of emotional retardations and 'hang-ups' (Roth's image of the hook prompts one to use the current colloquialism), then all that too is going to be exposed and explored. He is determined to 'let it all hang out', in the terms of another suitable colloquialism. The result is indeed the return of the repressed, and guilt, which is usually employed as an internalized agent of inhibition and retention, is paradoxically forced to promote a degree of uncensored revelation which is unusual even in recent American fiction.

Nothing is treated as sacred or taboo: everything, certainly everything physical, is brought to the level of speech—whether it is his mother's concern about his excrement, his childhood masturbatory practices or the particular forms of sexual gratification he seeks from the *shikse* girls who obsess him. All the doors on all the rooms of his childhood are opened and while this permits us to see the comic-desperate strategies of the sexually maturing child, it also enables us to hear the cacophony of conflicting imperatives which beset him, and to become aware of all the irrational rules and emotional bullyings which were visited on the bewildered child. It is in this way that self-obsession merges with social observation, for what Portnoy does is re-evoke scene after scene and situation after situation from his past so that environment and other characters appear vividly before us even while—and just because—he is conducting an inquiry into the determinants of his present sickness. Even the compulsive recalling of these scenes is part of the 'complaint' (as much disease as reproach); what Portnoy tries to do is to turn the complaint into an exorcism and make the concluding and inevitable howl of pain and need a howl of laughter as well.

'Doctor, maybe other patients dream—with me, everything happens. I have a life without latent content. The dream thing *happens*!' Portnoy's book is also without latent content precisely because he is able and determined to bring everything to the surface. But his unresting consciousness of himself and the resourcefulness of his vocabulary do nothing to mitigate his distress and confusion. At least, not apparently. From one point of view they too are part of the complaint inasmuch as he is constantly demonstrating that competence of terminology cannot do anything to remedy defects of temperament. Unlike Whitman's animal he certainly does moan and whine about his condition, and he knows it. 'Whew! Have I got grievances! Do I harbor hatreds I didn't even know were there! Is it the process, Doctor, or is it what we call "the material"? All I do is complain, the repugnance seems bottomless, and I'm beginning to wonder if maybe enough isn't enough.' Again: 'Is this truth I'm delivering up, or is it just plain kvetching? Or is *kvetching* for people like me a *form* of truth?' One could as readily answer in the affirmative to such questions, or not answer at all, for all the help it is to the man so helplessly launched on the flood of his own rhetoric. The questions are really aimed at himself. 'Oh, why go on? Why be so obsessed like this?' Here indeed is a question which gets to the heart of the complaint. At the same time it seems that only *by* going on like this can he alleviate some of the weight of the past which presses so damagingly on his present life. Everyone has problems in balancing conscience and appetite, but Portnoy has been submitted to so many prohibitions, warnings, taboos and hysterical laws laid down by his family that he has to have recourse to the momentary relief of comic exaggeration. 'I am marked like a road map from head to toe with my repressions. You can travel the length and breadth of my body over superhighways of shame and inhibition and fear.'

There is brilliant comic exaggeration throughout, and the nervous inventiveness of the rhetoric seems to be at once both consolation and symptom. For the complaint is still real. The weight of his family is still heavy upon him — 'fighting off my family, still!' — and he reiterates his appeal to the silent Dr Spielvogel: 'Doctor, get these people off my ass, will you please?' Like the monologist comedian, the late Lenny Bruce, to whom Portnoy has been compared, he gives the impression at times of talking for his life, of fending away continuous threats and pressures by the arresting brilliance of his loquacity. What he really yearns for is some clean, uncluttered space, like most other American heroes. This dream is implicit in his recollection of how much he enjoyed playing 'center field' in baseball games. 'Doctor, you can't imagine how truly glorious it is out there, so alone in all that space … ' 'Center field' is the blissful opposite of home.

While *Portnoy's Complaint* can readily be appreciated and enjoyed by anyone who can recall anything of the awesome mystery and humiliating farce called growing up, it obviously does have a specifically contemporary relevance for American Jews. Portnoy is obsessed with the whole WASP American world, not just WASP girls, and he is bent on full assimilation, away from ghetto identity and towards American identity with its much wider horizons of possibility. Yet if he has left the ghetto he has not yet arrived at a place where he can have a confident new identity. If in some ways he is a 'success' there has been a heavy price to pay, as his moaning presence on the psychoanalyst's couch attests. And, as Dan Yergin pointed out in his review of the book,[11] although there is a general idea in the Jewish family that each son will be more successful, more liberated, than the father, Portnoy's job of mediating between poor minorities and established WASP society (as Assistant Commissioner for Human Opportunity) is basically similar to his father's job of peddling insurance to the poor blacks on behalf of a rich WASP firm. Portnoy is not really 'free', and yet after a visit to Israel he realizes that, in spite of the validity of the Israeli girl's criticism of American Jews, he is nevertheless irremediably American. He is a transitional figure, like so many other Jewish figures in recent American fiction, neither quite in nor wholly out of the established society.

Perhaps it is because of Portnoy's transitional position that Roth really doesn't know how to finish the book. In the last scene that Portnoy recalls, he depicts himself 'whimpering on the floor with MY MEMORIES' after his comic-squalid failure with the Israeli girl. He knows now that he is 'a patriot in another place (where I also don't feel at home!)'. This does not represent any great progress in self-knowledge, nor the achievement of a new state of mind. Any new beginning will have to come after the end of the book — as usual. And although Portnoy recalls a lot he does not delve very deeply; there is no real opening up of hitherto sealed-off areas of the self, no attempt to establish some communication with the unconscious level. One does get the feeling that Roth did not carry his inquiry into the nature and origin of Portnoy's 'complaint' as far as he might have done. The question Portnoy asks near the end of the book is indeed a crucial one. 'How have I come to be such an enemy and flayer of myself? And so alone! Oh, so alone. Nothing but *self*! Locked up in *me*!' The state of self-incarceration which the book reveals is a condition quite prevalent among recent American characters; indeed the tremendous popularity of the book is probably related to the kind of unreachable privacy of self it finally exposes and as such it may well indicate that this is an exceedingly common condition for its readers too. But the question is not answered and the listening Dr Spielvogel opens his mouth only to close the book.

Roth had once considered doing a series of Spielvogel stories, with the mysterious doctor at the centre of a group of New York patients. Only two were published and one, 'The Psychoanalytic Special', has a revealing twist to it. The woman who is the patient is gradually trained to resist her impulses to sexual promiscuity. But the self-restraint is also experienced as a deprivation. 'Truly, it was awful if this was what it was going to be like, being better.' It is a truism by now that to attempt to 'adjust' someone to the prevailing society might be to rob him of his most distinctive individuating qualities, and that one's neuroses might be related to the most valuable energies of the self. It may well be that Portnoy does not really want to be 'cured', nor even 'analysed' in any profound way. What he does want to do is talk without restriction about himself. Roth himself has said 'The book is *about* talking about yourself ... The method is the subject.' [12] He has arranged the book as though it were a series of what he calls 'blocks of consciousness', an arrangement of clusters of associations released with a pace and vitality which make them seem like the direct effusions of stream-of-consciousness; although in fact the blocks of consciousness are of course cunningly arranged in a sequence which leads finally to the point at which the monologue began—the psychoanalyst's couch. Since the book is about monologizing ('the method is the subject'), it was obviously crucial to abandon the idea of writing stories which centred around the doctor, and to allow the first-person voice complete dominion over the whole book and as much verbal space as it requires to fill with its recollections. Part of the liberating feeling in the book comes from the speaker's abandoning all pretence at dialogue: even if the compulsion to monologize is part of Portnoy's 'complaint', the unhindered freedom to do so for the duration of the book is part of Portnoy's delight.

There are, of course, many other contemporary examples of 'fictionalised recall'—*The Bell Jar* is one, for instance; Frederick Exley's *A Fan Notes* (1968) is another. (This rather self-indulgent book is a good example of the genre I am attempting to define. The deceptively simple title points to the whole concern of the book. Exley, the narrator, regards it as his destiny to be merely a fan, one of the anonymous millions who come to rely on a few outstanding public individuals [in this case Frank Gifford] who have the rare ability to give 'syntax' and 'shape' to their fantasies and have thus achieved visible identity. Exley calls his book 'Notes' because in retrospect he finds his life to be simply an agglomeration of fragments. The narrator, an alcoholic who goes in and out of mental institutions, experiences that basic American dread of never achieving any identity at all: 'quite suddenly it occurred to me that it was possible to live not only without fame but without self, to live and die without ever having had one's fellows conscious of the microscopic space one occupies upon this planet.' Like other American heroes, not least Herzog and Portnoy, he spends long periods lying down, turning things over. 'All this I see as time re-lived; I then believed that nothing whatever was at work, that I was drifting quite aimlessly on a davenport, when in fact that davenport was taking me on an unwavering, rousing, and often melancholy journey.' The result of the journey is the book itself, and in the course of writing it Exley records a moment of realization which implicitly defines the motivating energy of 'fictionalized recall'. 'I indulged myself either in memories of my father or in what had become for me an alarmingly elaborate fantasy, about neither of which it occurred to me to write.' Exley stresses that his work is a 'fictional memoir' and asks to be judged as a 'writer of fantasy', while admitting that the book is based on his own life. What he discovered was that that admixture of factual memories and indulged fantasies, which he thought was another symptom of his unproductive inertia, could, precisely, provide him with the subject of his book. The 'fans's notes' yield an individual's form, for in writing the book Exley is defining that self which it was his fear he might never achieve.) But I would like to concentrate briefly on one of the most successful and satisfying works in this vein to have appeared, Frank Conroy's *Stop-time* (1967). It is offered as a clear, unadorned account of Frank Conroy's life—the broken home of his infancy, childhood pleasures and discoveries in Florida, a harsh adolescence in New York with new lessons of survival to be learned, an attempt to run away from home, a visit to Europe, and finally a fresh start at university, at which point the memoir is concluded. What makes the book remarkable is the combination of absolute lucidity in the description of each separate episode, and the feeling of an emerging *forma*, some possible shape which links the apparent randomness of the detached events. Each chapter is itself beautifully and subtly structured without any apparent thematic manipulation of each unique detail of the life under recall.

Conroy describes how once in Paris an artist friend showed him a drawing of some sort of machine and asked him if he knew what it was. Conroy could not at first make out the drawing and the artist told him that it was a drawing of the lock on the Metro door. 'I looked again and recognized it instantly. In a single moment I understood distortion in art ... What he had drawn was the *process*, the way the bar approaches the catch, slides up the angled metal, and drops into the locked position. He had captured movement in a static drawing.' The drawing leaves him speechless; when he finally thanks the painter it is as though he has discovered the principle on which he will attempt to capture the movement of his own life in the static medium of words. In fact many of the chapters of the book end in movement – on foot, on bikes, in cars, on ships, so that the very patternlessness of his family's and his own wanderings begins to take on a pattern (a very American one), which is gradually recognized only after the whole book is read. Just as Conroy himself had to wait to see the overall pattern in the artist's drawing of the lock, in which process and pattern were at one, were indeed indistinguishable.

In addition Conroy frames the book with a car journey taken at the time of writing the book. The Prologue describes how he drives at reckless speed back from London in his Jaguar. The Epilogue takes up the journey to the point where he goes into a skid and is sure he is going to crash and die. This would indeed complete the parabola of a life of movement in the final stillness, the ultimate stopping of time. But as it happens the crash is avoided. 'Everything stopped' – but not with the final arrest of death. Just as in all the chapters in the book, things are temporarily brought to a halt, held in the stillness of his prose, while at the same time we are made aware that the principle of momentum which precipitated each particular episode is still alive within the stillness; so Conroy is still alive in the stillness of the English night beside his stopped car, and will soon precipitate more episodes, more process. Any art can be a way of 'stopping time', in a way which we sense comes somewhere between the pure fluidity of actual experience and the absolute fixity of death; Conroy has availed himself of this fact with an unobtrusive subtlety which is quite beautiful.

At the end of the first chapter he describes his feelings when he wakes up in the middle of the night. It is as though he loses his grasp of chronological time, and simultaneously he starts to doubt his own continuing identity. 'My memories flash like clips of film from unrelated movies ... I look into the memories for reassurance, searching for signs of life. I find someone moving. Is it me?' He goes on to describe how uncomfortable he feels, floating around in this way, and he turns to a memory of waking in an infirmary as a child after he had been unconscious for at least a day. To remember this instant is, for him, to recover the one still point at the centre of his life. 'Waking in a white room filled with sunshine ... I don't know who I am, but it doesn't bother me. The white walls, the sunlight, the voices all exist in absolute purity.' This could be seen as a recapitulation of being born. In any case it sets the tone for the whole ensuing book. He is always to have uncertainties about his identity (movement and 'floating' tend to dissolve such certainties), yet he can find a stabilizing stillness in the film-like 'stills' of his memories. And whatever and whoever he is, he is a perceiving consciousness. When he opened his eyes there were things to be seen. He saw them. And he can only say who he is by defining what he saw.

How he reacted to what he saw can also be remembered and that too can be put down. But the two things are not to be confused or merged. For Conroy, 'Keeping a firm grip on reality was of immense importance,' and in many of his evocations of his youth he achieves an almost uncanny ego-less objectivity. A fine description of the delight of simply sitting watching at a gasoline station ends—'In ten minutes my psyche would be topped up like the tanks of the automobiles.' It is Conroy's ability to recapture this receptivity of the child's psyche, to communicate to us that feeling of the process whereby the individual consciousness gradually takes on definition as it allows its vacancy to be 'topped up' with the images of things, whatever they may be, which are always there. He is aware, too, of how consciousness can sometimes succumb to the intensity of its own perceptions, and he describes moments when he slipped out of the world, driven under by images. Like Bellow and Roth, Conroy is using his past as the very source material for his art even as he wants to leave that past behind. But they do not approach the phenomenological accuracy of his account of the growth of consciousness. Portnoy and Herzog see everything in the light of their obsessions, fantasies, worries, dreams, and so on—and indeed such a light can make things vivid in a way that mere documentation cannot emulate. It is Conroy's special distinction to capture the separation of self and object, both having their strange isolated integrity, even while he can evoke the wonder of how consciousness interpenetrates with things, and has to in order to remain a consciousness.

Literature had a particular lesson for the growing Conroy. 'I could not resist *the clarity of the world* in books ... Books were reality. I hadn't made up my mind about my own life, a vague, dreamy affair, amorphous and dimly perceived, without beginning and end.' In order to see whether he can bring his life to the level of clarity he himself will turn to writing a book, not in order to impose a fiction on the amorphousness of his experience, but to see whether it will yield a clarity which does no violence to the constituent fragments of his experience. The sort of order that does seem to emerge is detectable in the way in which certain qualities echo each other in different experiences. Moments of sudden loneliness in space recur, as do sudden and frightening eruptions of violence, the unpredictable intrusions of adult force into the child's field of vision. A particular aspect of this general pattern is the recurrence of forms of insanity. Conroy describes running in horror from a man who suddenly starts to have a fit in his presence. In his flight he runs into a parked car and knocks himself out, and as he slips to the ground 'it came to me that the world was insane. Not just people. The world.' Later in his youth he finds himself in an institution for the feeble-minded where his parents had taken jobs as wardens. His description of how it felt to be a child suddenly surrounded by all kinds of mentally deranged people is one of the most telling passages in the book. 'All around me were men in a paroxysm of discovery, seeing lands I had never known existed, calling me with a strength I had never known existed ... I stood balanced on the pinpoint of my own sanity, a small, cracked tile on the floor.' The scene is very actual and circumstantial; at the same time one feels that it somehow offers a glimpse of a basic situation in all of Conroy's experience, a configuration which, *mutatis mutandis*, will recur. When his sister Alison shows signs of mental derangement in Paris one experiences it as having its own specific pathos while contributing to a slowly surfacing pattern. We begin to see the lock on the Metro door.

Obviously the very writing of the book is a manifestation of a need on the part of Conroy to detect a kind of non-violating order in his life. Since, with a statement like that, one is in danger of applying the most bland truisms to a remarkable and unusual book, I would juxtapose two of the memories in *Stop-time* and suggest that we can see in them both that delight in the contingency, friction and movement of life, and that need for some containing pattern, which I have tried to show are at work throughout the book. For the first I would select his account of an evening with a friend on the bumper cars at a fair. Just describing them for what they were, and how the boys relished them, makes one realize what an amazing thing an arena of bumper cars is. We may then turn to his memory about discovering his skill with the yo-yo.

The yo-yo represented my first organized attempt to control the outside world. It fascinated me because I could see my progress in clearly defined stages, and because the intimacy of it, the almost spooky closeness I began to feel with the instrument in my hand, seemed to ensure that nothing irrelevant would interfere. I was, in the language of jazz, 'up tight' with my yo-yo, and finally free, in one small area at least, of the paralyzing sloppiness of life in general.

As a reward for having won a competition a yo-yo champion shows him a very special trick called 'The Universe'—' "Because it goes around and around ... like the planets." ' Conroy finally manages to master 'The Universe', but only for private satisfaction, since that particular skill was not called for or recognized in the public tournaments of the time.

The whole chapter about his deep interest in yo-yoing is beautifully fresh and original, and gives the impression of being totally unforced. And yet it is fair to perceive the outlines of the future writer in the boy all absorbed in practising his 'Universe' and delighting in the discovery of the pleasure to be found in things that go 'around and around' in rhythmical patterns. It is a different pleasure from the dizzy delight to be found in things that go bump as they collide and separate in the unplanned confusion of the bumper car arena. Yet they are both pleasures and both registered by the same individual. It could be said that many American artists have to move between the raw energy of the bumper cars and a practised mastery of the yo-yo, but the generalization resists being extracted from Conroy's particular work. The incidents are so very much a part of his life, his book, that one feels that he has made them his own, in all their suggestive specificity. At its best this is how 'fictionalized recall' (which is really applying the skill learned with the yo-yo to the experience had on the bumper cars) can work, and triumphantly justify itself as a genre.

Chapter 14 A New Life

'We have two lives, Roy, the life we learn with and the life
we live with after that. Suffering is what brings us toward
happiness."

(The Natural)

Bernard Malamud's characters, like Herzog and Portnoy, are also
eager to begin. And, like so many other American characters, they
soon find that they are involved in a compromised environment
which offers a wide variety of frustrations to their particular aspirations. What they are keen to begin is usually some form of 'new life';
and one of the effects of their sufferings in the compromised environment is to make them re-define the form and content of that notional
new life. At first glance Malamud might seem to be a realistic writer,
deriving his topics from contemporary or historical actualities. His
first novel is about a baseball hero who succumbs to corrupting
influences at the height of his fame. There followed two novels: in
one of which a man takes over a failing grocery store, while in the
other a young college teacher takes over the wife and children of a
senior but impotent colleague. Then came a novel about a poor Jew
who gets caught up in the virulent anti-Semitism which was rife in
Russia in the early years of this century. His most recent novel
follows an American who is a 'self-confessed failure as a painter'
who goes to Italy to continue painting and failing. All these subjects
offer occasion for studies in social realism, and indeed Malamud can
register the force of historical actualities, the obdurate solidity of the
given world, with mordant clarity. But in fact his novels are far
removed from anything we might understand by social realism.
Speaking of the Jewish characters who figure in Malamud's work,
Philip Roth made a relevant observation.[1] They are not, he said, the
Jews of New York City or Chicago.

> They are a kind of invention, a metaphor to stand for certain
> human possibilities and certain human promises ... Malamud,
> as writer of fiction, has not shown specific interest in the
> anxieties and dilemmas and corruptions of the modern
> American Jew ... rather, his people live in a timeless depression

and a placeless Lower East Side; their society is not affluent, their predicament not cultural.

Roth's point was that Malamud dramatized his moral concerns in isolation from 'the contemporary scene' — another example, for Roth, of an American writer who seemed not to be able to extract his fictional material from contemporary American society.

Obviously this is pertinent, but what I want to suggest in this chapter is that, while Malamud can certainly take cognizance of historical facts, he also resists history with his inventions. The pain experienced in time and place is eased by the timelessness and placelessness conferred by his own style. What Roth once saw as a possible limitation I would see as a distinctive achievement. In Malamud's apparently very different novels we can find a recurring pattern which links them closely together and reveals a profound consistency. The facts change; the pattern endures. All his novels are fables or parables of the painful process from immaturity to maturity — maturity of attitudes, not of years. This is unusual in American literature, which tends to see initiation into manhood as a trauma, a disillusioning shock, a suffocating curtailment of personal potential. Harry Angstrom in Updike's *Rabbit, Run* is a representative voice when he says, ' "If you're telling me I'm not mature, that's one thing I don't cry over since as far as I can make out it's the same thing as being dead." ' Malamud's characters discover that it is only by this 'dying' into maturity that they can find the 'new life' for which, in their various ways, they long.

The continuity of this vision may be suggested by the fact that all his main characters are involved in a quest. Each novel makes a point of emphasizing the searching and travelling of the central figure — characteristically we either see the central figure on a journey or just having completed one. *The Natural* (1952) starts with an account of Roy Hobbs's train ride bringing him from the Pacific Coast to Chicago where he hopes to break into big-time baseball. As Earl Wasserman has pointed out, this journey is described in such a way as to make it echo the whole birth process. And Roy Hobbs is travelling with high hopes and big demands. ' "I feel that I have got it in me — that I am due for something very big." ' Similarly Frank Alpine in *The Assistant* (1957) 'had lately come from the West, looking for a better opportunity', while Sam Levin makes another exhausting trans-continental trip from New York to the West Coast searching for 'a new life' in the novel of that name (1963). And Yakov Bok in *The Fixer* (1966) is moved by very similar yearnings and expectations when he leaves the *shtetl* and sets out for Kiev. ' "The truth of it is I'm a man full of wants I'll never satisfy, at least not here. It's time to get out and take a chance. Change your place, change your luck, people say." ' We may note here that for all these questers the change of luck in *material* terms is usually for the bad. After brief fame Roy Hobbs succumbs to sickness and corruption; Frank Alpine ends up running a sinking little grocery shop which is constantly referred to as a prison; Sam Levin gets involved in marital difficulties which terminate his tenderly cherished hopes of an academic career; while Yakov Bok is soon immured in a very real prison where he is subjected to atrocious indignities and iniquities. The quest for a better life seems always to end in some form of prison. And yet Malamud is far from being a pessimistic determinist. He shows, for one thing, how a man may help to imprison himself; for another, how an imprisoned man can forge a new self in his reaction to the imprisoning forces. In his world the bad luck which nearly breaks a man may also make a man.

Baseball being the national game, the rise and fall of Roy Hobbs readily becomes a parable concerning the fate of those youthful energies and abilities which society needs to revitalize and maintain it. As Earl Wasserman has conclusively demonstrated,[2] while most of the incidents in the book are based on historically accurate facts (the shooting of Eddie Waitkus in 1949, Babe Ruth's stomach illness of 1925, the throwing of a crucial game by the White Sox in 1919), the novel as a whole is organized as a modern version of the Arthurian legend, an up-to-date regeneration myth. Roy Hobbs starts his career by out-pitching the reigning king, the Whammer, in the process effectively killing his father figure, Sam. He is now the new champion. At the end of his career he is himself out-pitched by another boy fresh from the country, Youngberry. The fertility cycle is renewed. Such transforming of history into myth and fable is an essential part of Malamud's art. But the main focus of the book is on Roy's personal moral failure. Although there are evil figures plotting round him, such as Gus the gambler (Merlin) and Memo the temptress (Morgan le Fay), Hobbs betrays *himself*. He does this by being an egotist who thinks only of what *he* wants from the world. From the start there are many indications of his infantile self-preoccupation, and when he is asked about his magic bat, Wonderboy — so clearly phallic — he describes it as something he made 'for himself'. When Harriet Bird asks him what he hopes to accomplish, he says, ' "I'll break every record in the book," ' and boasts of becoming ' "the best there ever was in the game" '. When she answers, ' "Is that all? ... Isn't there something over and above earthly things — some more glorious meaning to one's life and activities?" ' he fails to understand her. In her role of the destructive mother, Harriet shoots him, thus inflicting the symbolic wound which ends his youthful, fatally solipsistic promise.

As a man (at least in years) when he returns to the game after many hardships, he is not totally selfish. For periods he does revitalize the whole team—he serves the community. But at key moments he slumps and loses form. These failures are related to his attitudes to two key women: Memo, who is barren, sick and in love with the dead; and Iris Lemon, the Lady of the Lake, who at one point restores Roy's potency so that he miraculously regains form. Memo is childless and dedicated to destruction, while Iris is so fertile she is already a grandmother and in time bears Roy's child. But Hobbs chooses to pursue Memo and ignore Iris and this reveals his central flaw. He rejects Iris because he cannot stand the thought of her being a grandmother; typically he omits to read her letter informing him of her pregnancy by him. He does not want to know anything about children. Attitude to the role of paternity is crucial in Malamud, and Roy refuses it. His fecundity, his reproductive and regenerative energies are all distorted into a sterile and self-satisfying lust. He is too narcissistic to concern himself with the continuity of generations. At one point he thinks he and Memo have run over a boy in the road —a psychological omen indicating his destruction of his own youth and innocence and also his negation of the children he might have. The self-destructive nature of his self-preoccupation is graphically drama- tized by Roy's insatiable appetite for food. He develops a hunger which cannot be satisfied and it is a night of excessive gorging which brings on his crippling stomach attack. With a pump the doctors 'dredged up unbelievable quantities of bile'. Still hungry, in hospital he thinks he has a prime hunk of beef in his mouth, 'and he found it enormously delicious only to discover it was himself he was chewing.' The procreative energies turned inward become unappeasable appetites which devour the self.

Roy's disinclination to become even a nominal grandfather is allied to his attempt to deny time. On one of his good days he smashes a clock to pieces with one hit. But the image of the loco- motive which he keeps hearing throughout the book indicates the inexorable movement of time which not even his energies can bash to a standstill. When he catches a sense of himself as 'on a train going nowhere' he is close to the truth of the matter. He thinks he is pur- suing his own impatient wants: 'so much more to do, so much of the world *to win for himself*' (my italics), but as long as he has that attitude he will always experience the torment of 'still wanting and not having'. Time is meaningless to the man who lives only for

himself. In a dream Roy has a significant conversation with his old
father figure, Sam.

'Let's go back, Sam, let's now.'
Sam peered out of the window.
'I would like to, kiddo, honest, but we can't go out there now.
Heck it's snowing baseballs.'

Like other Malamud questers and travellers he suddenly wishes to
retrace his steps, to get back to a time before time. But, of course,
you can't go home again. A related discovery, in a similar image, is
made by Yakov Bok. 'Once you leave you're out in the open; it rains
and snows. It snows history, which means what happens to somebody
starts in a web of events outside the personal.' (This is clearly a root
metaphor for Malamud. Morris Bober's last act in *The Assistant* is
the attempt to shovel away the ever-falling snow outside his failing
shop. And in *A New Life* when Levin falls in love with a colleague's
wife and finds his well-protected self-sufficiency shattered, Malamud
adds, 'It snowed heavily.' Of a character in *The Magic Barrel* we
read 'the world had snowed on him' and so on. Snow is everything
that falls on you when you leave the room, or the womb.)

But Roy Hobbs does not face up to the fact that it 'snows history'
and so he fails to come into possession of the meaning of his life. Iris
Lemon, on the other hand, is 'tied to time': although she suffers, her
suffering has meaning because of the children to whom she devotes
herself. It is she who gives Roy the most important lesson in the
book. When, like so many of Malamud's protagonists, he is complaining of his unlucky fate she says:

'We have two lives, Roy, the life we learn with and the life we
live with after that. Suffering is what brings us toward
happiness.'
'I had it up to here.' He ran a finger across his windpipe.
'Had what?'
'What I suffered—and I don't want any more.'
'It teaches us to want the right things.'
'All it taught me is to stay away from it. I am sick of all I have
suffered.'
She shrank away a little.

Roy is far from evil. He repents of the corrupt deal he makes with
the gamblers, but it is too late. His potency has left him and his bat
splits in half. He rejects the dirty money which was his reward for
throwing the match and beats up the dark conspirators. It is his sentiments as he leaves his last baseball game in a mood of intense

'self-hatred' that form the concluding lesson of the book. 'He thought, I never did learn anything out of my past life, now I have to suffer again.' Relevant here is Santayana's insight that those who ignore past history will have to live it through again. The only hope is for man to learn from his suffering, otherwise—'I have to suffer again.' Roy Hobbs has at least learned that much.

Just what a man can learn from his experience and suffering, and what are the possibilities for a second life may be said to be the main preoccupation of Malamud's following three novels. In *The Assistant* Malamud seems to have moved towards realism. The economic facts of Morris Bober's fading attempts to keep his little grocer's shop running are made depressingly accurate. Morris is a poor Jew, a consistently good man who has unfailingly bad luck. History has very much happened *to* him. Even his newspaper is 'yesterday's'—he is floundering and sinking in time. He is effectively 'entombed' in his store, which is just one of the many dark, constricted spaces in which so many of Malamud's characters have to live out their suffering. But although the plight of the Bober family is real enough, the novel moves effortlessly towards fable. Morris Bober is the dying father who has already lost his only son. Frank Alpine, who stumbles so strangely into his life, replaces that lost son. First of all he joins in a squalid hold-up of Bober's shop in which Morris is literally felled—a ritual 'killing', followed quite shortly afterwards by actual death. Out of remorse, and some more complicated feelings, Frank returns to the shop and gradually takes over all the work. In view of the fading energies of the sick old man he becomes the indispensable 'assistant'. When Morris is being buried, Frank accidentally slips into the grave, thus inadvertently dancing on the dead father's coffin. From now on he takes on the role and responsibilities of the father—provider, protector, living for others where he had previously lived only for himself.

This transformation of Frank does not happen easily. Like Roy Hobbs he has a lot of selfish hungers in him; but he also has a quality of moral aspiration revealed by his growing desire 'to change his life before the smell of it suffocated him'. 'He stared at the window, thinking thoughts about his past, and wanting a new life. Would he ever get what he wanted?' What kind of 'new life' does he want? Is it to help himself to more of the goods of life, as he helps himself to the cash register even while working for the store, and as, in a moment of desperate frustration, he helps himself to the daughter Helen? But that would not be a 'new' life, only an extension of the old. A really new life involves a radical change of attitude towards the self and other people. The painful emergence of selflessness from selfishness is the real drama of the book. We learn that he has always been attracted to St Francis of Assisi since he heard about him in the orphanage where he was brought up; and since he likes to feed birds, and has a talent for carving wooden flowers, we are not surprised to find certain saintly inclinations in Francis Alpine which finally prove stronger than his merely appetitive self. In particular his attitude to the Jews changes. At first he is often disgusted with what seems to be Morris Bober's cowed resignation. 'What kind of man did you have to be born to shut yourself up in an overgrown coffin? ... The answer wasn't hard to say – you had to be a Jew. They were born prisoners.' Yet he is increasingly drawn towards something in the Jewish attitude to life. He asks Morris for his definition of a Jew. Dismissing details of orthodoxy Morris says that the only important thing for a Jew is that he believes in 'the Law'. ' "This means to do what is right, to be honest, to be good." ' Frank complains that Jews seem to 'suffer more than they have to'. Morris answers, ' "If you live you suffer. Some people suffer more, but not because they want. But I think if a Jew don't suffer for the Law, he will suffer for nothing ... " ' Frank asks Morris what he suffers for and receives the answer: ' "I suffer for you." ' Asked for more clarification Morris only adds ' "I mean you suffer for me." '

It sounds like a simple lesson, but it is one which Malamud's characters learn only through pain and anguish, and after much resistance to commitments and responsibilities which override the clamouring hungers of the self. Morris Bober is a Jew because, as the rabbi says at his funeral, ' "he lived in the Jewish experience ... He followed the Law ... He suffered, he endured, but with hope ... He asked for himself little – nothing ... " ' It is this kind of Jew which Frank Alpine finally becomes. Paradoxically it is by identifying himself with these figures of imprisonment and suffering that he finds the 'better life' he sought. Helen recognizes the change in him when she discovers that he works all night to keep the family fed and her at school. He is not the hungry man who once raped her. 'It came to her that he had changed. It's true, he's not the same man, she said to herself ... It was a strange thing about people – they could look the same but be different. He had been one thing, low, dirty, but because of something in himself ... he had changed into somebody else, no longer what he had been.' The main focus of the novel is not on the economic misery of the Bobers, but on the moral transformation of Frank Alpine. In taking on the shop, replacing the father, and becoming a Jew, he is really coming to man's estate and putting away childish things. He suffers for others now, not simply for self: in this sense he is the 'new man' he wanted to be. He has learned what Roy Hobbs failed to learn, and he has won his 'new life'. Thus realism becomes parable in Malamud's imagination and vision.

At one point in the novel Frank Alpine is reading *Anna Karenina,* and 'he was moved at the deep change that came over Levin in the woods just after he had thought of hanging himself. At least he wanted to live.' This summarizes fairly exactly what happens to the main character in Malamud's next novel, *A New Life.* The 'woods' which provide the setting for the great transformation are the whole Pacific North-West. Levin, an urban Jew who has been incarcerated in New York for many alcoholic years, moves west to teach at a small college. The fact that he brings with him a large volume called *Western Birds, Trees and Flowers* gives some indication both of his expectations and his 'pastoral' aspirations. More specifically it is in a forest that he encounters Pauline Gilley and they first make love. At this point too we can talk of 'the deep change that came over Levin in the woods'. Here is Levin's reaction to the vernal embrace. 'He was throughout conscious of the marvel of it – in the open forest, nothing less, what triumph!' Inevitably there is a kind of undermining irony here which is absent in Tolstoy, an extracting of humour from a potentially painful sense of personal unfitness and incongruity.

Levin would not be one of Malamud's 'heroes' if he did not attract more than his share of bad luck which is both comic and incommoding – food slopped in his lap by the nervous Pauline, a child urinating on him, a car that breaks down as he drives feverishly towards an erotic tryst, clothes stolen by a jealous friend during his first awkward encounter with one of the 'country copulatives', and so on. (Indeed he has trouble with his trousers throughout, and when Pauline literally thrusts him into a pair of her husband's trousers after the dinner accident of their first meeting, it offers a comic adumbration of the conclusion when he steps into Gilley's trousers more finally by taking over his role of husband.) Malamud's Levin is a *schlemiel* – deracinated, insecure, friendless and powerless to an extent which makes him a very remote echo of Tolstoy's powerful and authoritative figure. And yet Malamud's point is surely that a man may yearn for a new and better life with as much seriousness and anguish in contemporary America as in nineteenth-century Russia. Malamud refers, it is true, to Joyce's Levin, but it is inconceivable that he did not also have Tolstoy's Levin in mind. Malamud's Levin is not a complete *schlemiel* since he, like other Malamud characters, finds reserves of unsuspected strength inside him which he can bring to bear at the crucial moment. To quote some words of Malamud: 'A man who can overcome circumstances and his own weakness is not, to me, a *schlemiel*.' (The name Levin also means, of course, east, the light, and I have it direct from Mr Malamud that by a pun on 'leaven' he is suggesting 'what the marginal Jew may bring in attitude to the American scene'.)

Still in relation to the name, I should like to refer to two of Malamud's short stories where it recurs. In 'The Lady of the Lake' Henry Levin sets out on his travels with a view to satisfying his 'adventurous appetites'. He thinks he will find a new life in Europe by denying his Jewishness. 'With ancient history why bother? ... a man's past was, it could safely be said, expendable.' He pretends his name is Henry Freeman. This attempt to repudiate the identity imposed on him by history, to make an Emersonian bid for the freedom and autonomy of the individual self, is of course very American. But time after time in Malamud's work it is shown to be not only an error but an impossibility; Levin-Freeman feels discontented with his new life — 'he lived too much on himself.' So he is delighted when he meets a mysteriously lovely girl on a slightly magical island. Sensing the possibility of an aristocratic alliance he puts forward his best new self. Thus he is much taken aback when she asks if he is Jewish and is quick and emphatic in his denials. It turns out that she is not a titled lady but a Jewish girl who suffered in Buchenwald. Levin loses the very person who could have brought fulfilment into his life because, where he attempts to deny the past, she accepts it: ' "My past is meaningful to me. I treasure what I suffered for." ' At one point in the story we read 'he felt time descend on him like an intricate trap', and one of the lessons of Malamud's tales is that the man who attempts to deny the past (which is to deny time) may find himself imprisoned and trapped in ways which are worse than the physical impositions of history. Not by any change of name can an individual transform himself into a free man. (In *A New Life* Levin first adopts the name Seymour in his attempt to create 'a new Levin'; at the end he reverts to his real name — Sam.) The penalties for attempting this sort of personal leap out of history into egotistical freedom may be dire. ' "What did he do to deserve his fate?" ' Freeman asks when he is shown a tapestry of a writhing leper in hell. The Lady of the Lake answers him, ' "He falsely said he could fly." '

In 'Angel Levine' Manischevitz, a poor Jewish tailor suffering Job's own tribulations, one night finds a Negro in his house who introduces himself as Alexander Levine. Manischevitz asks with a smile, ' "You are maybe Jewish?" ' and receives the answer, ' "All my life I was willingly." ' The last word is the key one. Levine is now an angel who offers vague aid, but Manischevitz dismisses him as a 'faker'. He now loses all faith in God as his troubles get worse, and complains about his entirely pointless suffering. But one night he does seek out Levine in a dirty Harlem bar, and above the hostile taunts of the crowd he affirms his faith. ' "I think you are an angel from God." ' When he returns home his wife has miraculously recovered her health. His final comment is: ' "A wonderful thing, Fanny ... Believe me, there are Jews everywhere." ' Clearly Malamud is not here concerned with matters of orthodox belief, but with some more general human kind of faith which can transform a life. The miracle is partly a matter of that 'luck', that quixotic turn of events, without which none of his figures would ever find their 'new life'. But it is also indicative, I think, of a change in attitude on the part of Manischevitz. What he learns from Levine is to accept life and its sufferings positively, 'willingly', instead of maintaining an attitude of personal resentment. Such a change of attitude towards the burdens of history can sometimes make those burdens miraculously lighter. Some critics complain of this kind of surrealistic fantasy in Malamud just as they suggest that his reliance on fable and myth indicates a somewhat impoverished appreciation of the actual stuff of the world. It seems to me more profitable to see Malamud as a writer who has an instinctive feeling for the folk-tale, the wry fable with an only half-hidden moral — his best work combines both real and 'fabulous' elements.

I think that *A New Life* is less successful than Malamud's other novels precisely because he strains to maintain uninterrupted continuity of realistic detail. Nevertheless the fable is still clearly present, even if it does give the impression of being uneasily imposed on the close-knit, naturalistic texture of the narrative. Levin is in quest of a 'new life' and wants to slough off a miserable and disastrous past. However, he soon discovers 'how past-drenched present time was', and he makes a note of the discovery that 'The new life hangs on an old soul.' But he makes the mistake of thinking that the new life involves securing himself against all confusing emotions and relationships, just as he thinks he can shut out history by not reading the newspapers. He manifests something of the mixture of solipsism and greedy appetite which was the undoing of Roy Hobbs. However, he is not content to stay submerged in this sealed-off self-preoccupation. Still aspiring to freedom, he has learned enough to know that the crucial problem is 'how to win freedom in and from self'.

But it is one thing to have theories of freedom, and quite another to enact them. (The limitations involved in a purely cerebral solution to the problem of self and freedom are shown up in the figure of

Fabrikant. Fond of quoting Emerson's 'Nothing at last is sacred but the integrity of your mind', he is shown up to be completely impotent — a childless bachelor who is also a coward on the campus.) Levin's test comes when he falls in love with Pauline, the wife of the very man who gave him his job, Gerald Gilley. At first Levin, fearful of any entanglement, sets out to 'harden' himself and 'put on armor against love'. 'He wanted no tying down with ropes, long or short, seen or unseen — had to have room to move so he could fruitfully use freedom.' But he finally abandons this theoretic freedom for the real Pauline and her children, and in doing so he is fulfilling his part in Malamud's favourite regenerative myth — the ritual slaying of the old failing father figure. At first cringingly deferential, Levin finally challenges, eliminates and replaces the arid and by now sterile Gerald, the original father figure who effectively brought him into the western world.

Vengefully Gerald will only let him have the children if he will give up all ideas of a college career, but Levin is up to the sacrifice.

> 'Goodbye to your sweet dreams', Gilley called after him ... 'An older woman than yourself and not dependable, plus two adopted kids, no choice of yours, no job or promise of one, and other assorted headaches. Why take that load on yourself?'
> 'Because I can, you son of a bitch.'

Levin has given up dreams for reality; and has paradoxically found his freedom by willingly taking on the load of family commitments. Suitably, after his final tourney with Gerald, Levin is informed by Pauline that she is pregnant by him. He is the new father; a mature man. Once again the quest for a new life ends in what looks like an imprisoning set of commitments and undertakings, and Levin certainly gets a trapped feeling up to the last moment. But then he realizes: 'The prison was really himself, flawed edifice of failures, each locking up tight the one before.' And so, perhaps with too much manifest contrivance by Malamud, the fable is concluded. Its moral is one with relevance for a large number of contemporary American heroes: the only true freedom is liberation from the prison of self. With a nice final irony Levin discovers that his earlier freedom was in part illusory because Pauline tells him that she had picked out his photograph from the heap of applicants and persuaded Gerald to offer him the job. Levin responds with appropriate Jewish irony. ' "So I was chosen." ' After much painful struggling Levin accepts his predestined role; a role ordained for him not only by Pauline, but by history and nature.

At the risk of not doing justice to the differentiating details of

Malamud's novels, I have been trying to show how a certain patterning of events recurs. The pattern is roughly as follows. The hero
travels somewhere in quest of a new life. He is a figure of some distinct practical ability (on the pitch, in the shop), but he has no faith
in anything beyond the urgencies of his own hungers and appetites.
When he arrives in the world where he is to search for this new
satisfying life, despite his attempts to secure only his own interests
and further his single development, he runs into all kinds of bad luck
and hampering involvements. The search for a new freedom usually
ends in an imprisoning tangle of relationships and commitments and
responsibilities. The attempt to deny time and evade the impingements of history yields reluctantly and painfully to the discovery that
when a man sets out on his travels he is involved willy-nilly in various
processes and large networks of events which the individual can
neither resist nor reshape. To be born is to be born into history; and
various thoughts and theories concerning the freedom and invulner-
ability of the individual self fade before the experienced fact of
involuntary involvement in the lives of other people.

This discovery is either preceded or accompanied by a ritual slaying (or replacing or dispossessing) of a symbolic father figure of
failing powers (never an actual parent). This coming-of-age is
signalled by the fact that the hero has to decide whether or not to
take on the symbolic *role* of father (i.e. before he can have his own
children he has to demonstrate that he *willingly* accepts all the
ramifying responsibilities and limitations on self that the role
involves, by agreeing to be the nominal father of children not his
own). If he refuses, then his suffering — and they all suffer — has been
for nothing, and his life remains devoid of meaning. This is the fate
of Roy Hobbs who, with all the valuable energies necessary for
heroic status, at the end is no hero at all. If the burden and role of
nominal paternity is accepted then the *schlemiel* quester finds his true
freedom, not in further gratifications of self, but in the willing undertaking to live for other people. By changing his attitude to the
respective claims of self and others, he enters on his second life, the
real 'new life'. This is what happens to Frank Alpine and Sam
Levin who achieve the only true heroism in Malamud's work, the
heroism of growing up. To use Bellow's phrase, this is the first *real*
step. And this basic pattern is repeated down to the last detail in *The
Fixer*, in which Malamud demonstrates with singular power and
authority his ability to combine the intransigence of history with the
resilience of fable. By transforming some particularly grim facts of
Russian history into a positive parable, Malamud demonstrates his
own ability to transcend the nightmare of Jewish history without

forgetting it. From the sufferings imposed on one Jew, he has derived a story which is even older than the madness of anti-Semitism—the coming to maturity of a man.

It is well known by now just how closely the fate of Yakov Bok is based on the infamous Mendel Beilis case: the Black Hundred who, in an attempt to start a pogrom, helped to fabricate the charge of ritual murder against the manifestly innocent Beilis when a boy was found horribly murdered; the brick kiln in which Beilis worked; the pathological attempts of the Minister of Justice, Scheglovitov, to secure an indictment no matter how often he had to change the prosecuting officials or solicit transparently false evidence against Beilis; the two years Beilis was kept in prison without a trial—these facts appear all but unchanged in the novel. (Malamud even inserts one corroborative date. Yakov Bok signs a document on 'February 27, 1913' a few months before his trial: Beilis was brought to trial in October 1913.) All this is the kind of history which gives added point to Saul Bellow's remark that history has always been singularly ambivalent for Jews: 'They were divinely designated to be great and yet they were like mice. History was something which happened to them; they did not make it.'³ And yet the book does not read like history. Despite the intense vividness of the local details it seems more like something between a folk-tale and a dream. The environment is not given full specificity; the characters are far from being fully individuated; the time, despite that one date, is any time in human history. And the impersonal tone of the narrator, telling the tale with brooding economy and drawing the various scenes with the firm, incisive contours of a woodcut, suggests that it is a tale which could be told over and over again. The blurb claims that the theme of the book is injustice and man's inhumanity to man. Both are, indeed, vividly dramatized in the book. But so much is history, though admittedly history of the direst sort. And what Malamud has always been more interested in is a man's reaction to the history he finds happening to him. This I take to be the theme of the book.

Yakov Bok comes to Kiev, 'hoping for a better life than I had'. When he sets out from the poverty-stricken *shtetl* he 'didn't look back'. As far as he is concerned 'the past was a wound in the head.' He is attempting to turn his back on his own history and that of his race. He resentfully dismisses the old Jewish God, and adopts instead a sort of free-thinking pragmatism. Instead of faith, he believes in his tools—he loves to fix things—and a few books, like the works of Spinoza. When, on his omen-haunted journey towards the great dark city, he is ferried across the Dnieper by a virulent anti-Semite, he silently drops his phylacteries in the river and conceals his Jewish identity. In Kiev he continues concealing it. When he helps a drunken man who turns out to be a member of the dreaded Black Hundred, he gives a non-Jewish name; and when that man in gratitude offers him a good job in a brickworks in an area which Bok knows is forbidden to Jews, he continues the deception.

And why shouldn't he? He has no faith in the Jewish God, he feels no allegiance to other people and only wants to be allowed to work and live in peace. ' "I am not a political person ... The world's full of it but it's not for me. Politics is not in my nature." ' So he pleads. Of course he is apprehensive about getting involved with rabid anti-Semites but he has appetites crying out for satisfaction, and the anti-Semitic family offers financially rewarding work just as it puts before him great spreads of rich food. He falls on both with the same urgent hunger which was the moral undoing of Roy Hobbs. Bok rationalizes to himself, ' "After all it's only a job. I'm not selling my soul," ' but it transpires that such sophistic distinctions are not made with impunity. His punishment for trying to suppress his given identity and replace it with one of his own making is to be worse than the deprivation imposed on the Levin who wanted to be Freeman. In his office he sometimes writes essays and in one he jots down: ' "I am in history, yet not in it. In a way of speaking I'm far out, it passes me by. Is this good, or is something lacking in my character?" ' When anti-Semitism rises in the area after the discovery of the murdered boy, Bok prepares for discreet and urgent flight. But he walks into a detachment of police who have come to arrest him. Yakov Bok finds himself *in* history with a vengeance. His search for a new freedom of opportunity has brought him to the most literal prison in Malamud's work. And there he stays for most of the book.

Rather than summarize the many physical things that happen to him – the interrogations, the beating up, the starvation and undoctored sicknesses, the near-madness, and so on – I want instead simply to point to a few key steps in his radical change of attitude. One influence on his mind is Spinoza, for Bok, too, sees himself as a free-thinking Jew. But just how valuable are those 'free thoughts' when the unreason of human experience closes in on you? We note that, when he starts to read Spinoza, Bok also studies some books of Russian history, wincing at their accounts of indescribable cruelties. At the time he does not feel the disjunction between the theoretical serenity of free thoughts and the actual horror of accomplished facts, but he is to learn of this discrepancy through his own experience. After some time in prison we read, 'the fixer's thoughts added nothing to his freedom; it was nil ... Necessity freed Spinoza and imprisoned Yakov. Spinoza thought himself into the universe but Yakov's poor thoughts were enclosed in a cell.' The philosphy of Spinoza perhaps has something of the ironic function of Emerson's creed in *A New Life*. Philosophy alone cannot free a man from the literal impositions of history, cannot keep the brute facts at bay. Still, even if Spinoza cannot release him, the very fact that Yakov keeps constructing complex configurations of thought is a partially liberating gesture. It is a way of not totally succumbing. So Spinoza does perhaps help Yakov to tackle the burdens of history, not with applicable precepts, but by the example of resistant mental activity.

These burdens seem to Yakov, even so, monstrously unfair and incomprehensible. In particular he realizes 'being born a Jew meant being vulnerable to history, including its worst errors. Accident and history had involved Yakov Bok as he had never dreamed he could be involved.' He feels entirely devoid of hope. And yet a part of the meaning of the book is that such total pessimism is not finally warranted. There are some friends; there are a few who care for human justice. When Bibikov commits suicide and Bok again feels utterly abandoned, another man convinced of his innocence turns up. Even one of the prison guards, as in *King Lear*, finally rebels against the cruelty meted out by the authority he serves. Bok is indeed a victim; but he is neither as totally innocent nor as totally alone in the web of history as he thinks. (The rebellion of the guard extends the motif of adopted paternity. Kogin has lost his son in Siberia and in effect 'adopts' Yakov, just as Yakov 'adopts' Chaim. The found father himself finds a 'father'.)

The change that comes over him in prison can be seen in his transformed attitude to the authorities. At the start it is abject and conciliatory; but as the conditions get worse his resilience grows, appeasement gives way to anger, and his vigorous contempt for the imprisoning powers is revealed in his refusal to settle for less than full justice (he refuses a *pardon*, which would imply that he was guilty: he wants a free *trial*.) At the same time he seems to discover something of value in the old Jewish religion; he even takes an interest in the sayings of Christ, quoting His words with cutting defiance to his Christian captors. But he refuses to take refuge in religious quietism and pious passivity. When his old father-in-law says, ' "God's justice is for the end of time," ' Bok's wry answer is, ' "I'm not so young any more, I can't wait that long." ' If he is immersed in history, then he wants a timely, not a timeless, justice. He begins to rage against injustice instead of simply trying to avoid it. While his physical freedom is diminished, until he is finally chained to the wall, his attitude to his fate becomes more positive.

At first simply nauseated by his fate and sick of Jewish history

with all its suffering, he later decides, 'if I must suffer let it be for
something.' Offered his freedom if he will denounce the Jews, he
refuses. 'He is against those who are against them. He will protect
them to the extent that he can. This is his covenant with himself.'
Not a covenant with God: Bok is not obeying an imposed rule so
much as willingly creating his own responsibilities. Again we are
witnessing the shift from egotistical self-concern to a sense of an
involvement with others. Bok's suffering is quite disproportionate to
any of his human failings (indeed it is two acts of kindness which
cause most of his trouble). But that is how history can be. The
important thing is that Bok makes something of all this uninvited
history. He has suffered, he has learnt, he has changed. In the blackest
possible circumstances he has found his new life. Unlike Roy Hobbs
he has entered his human maturity.

This conclusion to the fable is emphasized by two events which are
surely interpolations by Malamud. Shortly before his trial, Bok's
wife Raisl, whom he had left because she was childless and unfaith-
ful, comes to him in prison. She is allowed in because she is made to
bring a confession for him to sign. The confession blames the murder
on 'my Jewish compatriots'. On this Bok writes, 'Every word is a
lie.' But she also tells him that she has had an illegitimate son for
whom she needs a nominal father since he is suffering from being a
bastard. Bok surreptitiously writes on an envelope: 'I declare myself
to be the father of Chaim, the infant son of my wife, Raisl Bok.'
This is really the key moment in the book. He refuses to betray
other people in the interests of personal comfort; and he willingly
takes on the role of father to a child not his own. In the Malamud
world this is the heroic moment.

The decisive sequel to this moment is presented in a brilliant
manner when Malamud describes a reverie Bok has when he is
finally being taken to his trial. While he is being driven through the
town someone throws a bomb. Bok survives, but a young Cossack's
leg is now 'shattered and bloody'. This episode continues the subtle
but insistent motif of spilt and dribbling blood which persists
through the book, giving the impression that various forms of
blood-letting are the very essence of history. After the incident, Bok
dreams he is in a 'cell or cellar' with the Tsar, Nicholas the Second.
They talk first of children – and blood: they discuss the murdered
boy, whose blood Bok was supposed to have drained, and the Tsar's
son, a haemophiliac, liable to bleed to death any moment from
natural causes. The Tsar asks Bok, ' "Are you a father?" ' and Bok
makes the significantly worded reply – ' "With all my heart." ' The
Tsar himself is in a very enfeebled state. He is naked, 'his phallus

meagre', he is coughing and smoking; and he is very much on the defensive as he tries to justify his conduct in history. Yakov Bok is very much in the ascendant and refuses to accept the Tsar's insincere evasions and attempts to excuse pogroms. By way of a response to these excuses Bok takes up a revolver and shoots the Tsar.

As if to emphasize the significance of the ritual we are witnessing, Bok addresses the Tsar as 'Little Father' just before he shoots him. The fact that he dreams this ritual killing of the 'father' indicates only that his state of mind has changed—outside him history remains very much the same with the Tsar well out of reach. But Bok's spirit is now that of the grown man who will no longer humbly defer to the ailing and declining power of the authority which is impeding his right to a full human life. In political terms this change of mind means a new militancy on the part of Bok. 'One thing I've learned, he thought, there's no such thing as an unpolitical man, especially a Jew.' But the fable goes even deeper than a call to action; for it shows a representative individual coming to a mature awareness of the limitations and responsibilities of man-in-history.

Whether or not Malamud believes in the possibilities of social progress is not the main issue of the book. I think this is made clear by one last interesting point concerning Malamud's treatment of his historical data. Amazingly enough, despite anti-Semitic judges and ignorant jurymen who believed in the ritual murder legend, Mendel Beilis was acquitted. But Malamud chooses to end his novel with Yakov Bok on his way to the trial, the verdict still in doubt. Why does Malamud not show us the somewhat freakish justice of the original facts? Surely because that would shift the emphasis from the individual attitude to the social fact. It would diminish a parable of universal relevance (the growth of a man) to an account of one a-typical historic moment (for the justice finally meted out to Mendel Beilis is not a justice one could rely on to recur in any repetition of the circumstances). And the inconclusiveness of the fable is surely its most important assertion of superiority over the conclusiveness of history. For any *final* verdict of innocent or guilty is out of our hands. The real trial is not a matter of sentence or acquittal but the imprisoned years which preceded it, during which a man has the chance to derive some meaning from what he is caught up in. It is in the prison, not in the courtroom, that a man must win his freedom and earn a new life. And what the 'judges' will finally say is less important than man's developing attitude as he moves towards his last reckoning.

Any contemporary American writer addressing himself to the

archetypal theme of the American who travels to Europe to become an artist can hardly avoid comedy. And a fine comedy is just what Malamud has produced in his most recent novel, *Pictures of Fidelman: an Exhibition* (1969), in which Fidelman comes to Europe and tries his unlucky hand at art criticism, imitation, forgery, reproduction and original creation. It might be said that he almost shows most powers of invention when it comes to finding different ways of failing in his chosen thing: in quick succession he recapitulates in his own way the varied experiences of a hundred years of American artistic aspirants in Europe. It is a comedy, but not a farce. All the serious issues which have engaged Malamud in his previous fiction are present, but more implicitly, in abbreviated forms. Fidelman is the recognizable Malamud hero. He sets out on his travels with aspirations for some sort of new life. He is after something for himself ('where's mine?'), and is at first excessively protective of his own interests. Surrounded by the vast deposits of history he gets 'quickly and tightly organized'. When an impoverished refugee named Susskind brazenly asks Fidelman to give him a suit, Fidelman repudiates any responsibility for him. He reorganizes his routine to shut Susskind out so that he can devote himself solely to his study of Giotto. It is the first of many incidents in which he fails to make the appropriate adjustments and adjudications between the claims of art and the needs of life. As happens to most of Malamud's heroes, his egotism is chastened the hard way. His tight organization proves to be hopelessly porous to disintegrating and distracting contingencies. He is incarcerated and beaten up by some crooks who make him forge a painting; he is humiliated and rejected for months by a frigid woman; he comes close to starvation. Unlucky in love, he becomes a pimp; insufficiently talented in art, he falls into derivative pastiche. In a dream he is buried alive. As who should say—there's yours.

Yet, the book is a comedy. For one thing, Fidelman does have his resiliences and triumphs. For another, in the last chapter Fidelman finds love (with both sexes), and abandons his pretensions to art for the more modest role of apprentice craftsman. Recognizing that his previous attempts to teach himself have been another aspect of his doomed egotism, he is now happy to be 'instructed'. He becomes an 'assistant' and we recognize the term as honorific in Malamud's moral universe. More than that, he reverses the whole myth and shows that you can go home again. He returns to America where 'he worked as a craftsman in glass and loved men and women'. To Yeats's poetic statement that man is forced to choose 'Perfection of the life, or of the work', Fidelman before setting out on his travels had added his comment—'Both.' To this somewhat greedy demand,

his experiences would seem to offer the harsh rejoinder—'Neither.'
Yet Malamud bestows on him the happy ending he seems to have
earned at last. We leave Fidelman with his dream of inclusive
satisfactions realized (albeit on a humbler level than he initially
expected), the life and the work improbably, felicitously, at one. It is
worth noting that this comic resolution and happiness is achieved
only after Fidelman has finally put behind him his various attempts
at art. His manuscript on Giotto is burned by Susskind, who recognizes that 'the spirit was missing'. The one original work he completes he himself effectively destroys. In the last chapter Beppo,
Fidelman's lover and instructor in glass-blowing, persuades him to
burn all his derivative attempts to emulate contemporary styles.
' "Show who's master of your fate—bad art or you." ' Fidelman thus
finds release from all those formings and framings of the past and
present which have effectively imprisoned him. His return from an
inhospitable Europe is at the same time an escape from unsuitable
artistic ambitions and alien orderings.

The book is also a comedy because all the incidents are suspended
in a medium of lyricism and humour which invites us to respond to
those intimations of reconciliation and hints of magic which take
us beyond the tragic moment. In Malamud's vision, there *is* magic
in the web of it—and for 'it' you can read art and/or life, sometimes
one, sometimes the other, sometimes both. If *The Fixer* had some of
the grimness of Rouault, this book has some of the lift of Chagall.
Comparisons with paintings are apt in connection with this novel.
It is an exhibition, and one which is mounted with unobtrusive
mastery. When you come out you do not at first realize how much
you have seen. Although the first three chapters have been published
previously as short stories (in *The Magic Barrel* [1958] and *Idiots
First* [1965]), the whole novel is beautifully organized. Most of the
chapters are set in a specific city—Rome, Milan, Florence, Naples,
and finally of course, Venice. Each one has some subtle connections
with particular painters or paintings—Giotto, Rembrandt, Titian,
Picasso, Modigliani, Tintoretto. References to art works ranging
from Sicilian mosaics to the productions of Pop Art contribute to the
overall texture, and also help to make us realize the hopeless
plethora of styles Fidelman as artistic aspirant is confronted with.
Faced with such a gallery, what can originality mean, what indeed
can creation mean? Fidelman works in turn from other works, from
real life, from still life, from a photograph, from memory, from
imagination, from devious sexual aspiration, from sheer financial
desperation.

He runs the gamut of the problematics of 'invention' and it is hardly surprising that at one point he should declare ' "I reject originality," ' thus echoing the artist hero of William Gaddis's *The Recognitions*, and, more curiously, Hilda in *The Marble Faun*. Forced to forge an imitation of a Titian Venus, he falls in love with his own copy, a poor thing but his own. As long as he is struggling to become an artist, with insufficient genius to move beyond all extant formulations, such solipsism is understandable and perhaps inevitable. One of Fidelman's failures in art, his most protracted, is his inability to recapture, evoke or invent the image of his mother. At the same time, he can, for much needed money, turn out any number of highly competent and acceptable carvings of the Madonna. One of the first objects that Fidelman notices on his arrival in Italy is a statue of 'the heavy-dugged Etruscan wolf suckling the infants Romulus and Remus'. At the end, Beppo, his instructor, reminds him of his mother. One could say that Fidelman has to find out just which is his real mother, or where the source of true nourishment is to be found. He has to learn to distinguish between what suckles life and what negates it.

While Fidelman fails in different modes, Malamud succeeds. As he modulates his style, changes the pace, brightens his colours or works in chiaroscuro, we have the sensation of watching different pictorial representations. As we have seen, Malamud has always been able to move from economic realistic notations to fable, folk-tale, surrealism and fantasy, and his manifest ability in this book to produce so many different canvases conveys an exhilarating sense of a man in assured control of the resources of his medium. While Fidelman's life is disintegrating. Malamud's style is reorganizing it on a verbal level. I will point to one example of the way in which the different pictures are related to each other. In the comparatively realistic first chapter where Fidelman repudiates Susskind, we have a long account of Fidelman's attempt to trace Susskind after the latter has stolen his manuscript. By the end of his search Fidelman finds himself in a graveyard. He notices an empty grave which commemorates an unretrieved victim of the Nazis. Fidelman also has dreams of catacombs, of cemeterial darkness, of Susskind rising up from a grave. When he does find where Susskind lives, it proves to be no more than a wretched cave. In the strange surrealistic dream which makes up the fifth chapter, or picture, many of these details reappear, having been subjected to the metamorphoses of Malamud's art and Fidelman's life. In very reduced circumstances Fidelman is now concentrating on sculpting perfect holes (as, indeed, Claes Oldenburg has done). He justifies these empty holes as studies in pure form, and charges admission to anyone who wants to see them.

A poor young man is tempted into one of these shows, paying with money which should have been used to buy his children bread. Finding nothing nutritious to the spirit in the exhibition (' "Holes are of no use to me, my life being so full of them" '), he asks for his money back so that he can at least provide bodily nourishment for his children. Fidelman sends him away penniless, and in remorse the man commits suicide. As the dream gathers pace a threatening figure appears at Fidelman's exhibition to revenge the poor young man. He knocks Fidelman into one of his own empty holes (which, unlike the empty grave in Chapter One, has no human significance), and covers him up with earth, adding mordantly – ' "So now we got form but we also got content." ' With his arid aesthetics and indifference to humanity Fidelman has indeed been digging his own grave.

The dream continues with a sermon by Susskind transformed into a Christ figure; and it concludes with an account of a surviving engraving by Fidelman called 'The Cave' from a series entitled 'A Painter's Progress'. It depicts Fidelman working away in a cave, covering its surface with colours and designs, while upstairs his sister is dying alone. Advice can come from strange sources in Malamud, and in this case a light bulb tells Fidelman to go upstairs. That he does finally manage to leave the cave of art for the house of life-and-death perhaps prefigures his success in the next chapter when, in the Venetian daylight, he becomes an assistant and a lover. From the house of his lover(s) he can look out over the island cemetery. Life and death are still close together, but now at last they are in their proper places. And so the theme of the differing claims of art and life is refracted through many different scenes and styles, the spirit being absent or present in unpredictable ways.

Beppo, who initiates Fidelman into homosexual love when he finds Fidelman sleeping with his wife ('Both'), also teaches Fidelman to blow glass. He tells him that it is a wonderfully flexible medium – ' "you can make a form or change it into its opposite." ' Fidelman finds that its plasticity helps you to understand 'the possibilities of life'. From the little hole which you first introduce into the molten glass – 'a sculptured womb' – you can, if you know how, 'blow anything'. This craft has its own mothering powers and can generate 'unexpected forms', new worlds. Fidelman as apprentice is not sufficiently the artist to be in control of the medium. He 'blew forms he had never blown before, or seen blown', evoking huge complicated monstrosities which sometimes crack in mid-air, or fail to stand upright when completed. Free form can lead to mal-form, and the assistant still needs to be instructed. But in the hands of a master, like Malamud, this freedom to produce new and unexpected forms in the flexible medium of the novel/fable does serve to increase our sense of the possibilities both of art and life.

Just before he leaves Italy for America, Fidelman does manage to produce one perfect and pure red glass bowl. After the golden bowl, the glass one: and unlike the bowl in Henry James's last created work, Fidelman's has no crack in it. Instead of being broken and reassembled it simply vanishes, leaving Fidelman free to go home, and leaving us with Malamud's flawless fable clear before us.

Chapter 15 On the Parapet

'Every hundred yards Cummings steps up on the parapet,
and peers cautiously into the gloom of No Man's Land.'
(*The Naked and the Dead*)

' ... and I was up, up on that parapet one foot wide, and
almost broke in both directions, for a desire to dive right on
over swayed me out over the drop, and I nearly fell back to
the terrace from the panic of that.'
(*An American Dream*)

In this chapter I will consider some aspects of the work of Norman
Mailer, and suggest why the image of a man standing on a parapet
which appeared fleetingly in his first novel should become the crucial
situation in a novel he wrote seventeen years later. But before looking at Mailer it is relevant to bring into focus the fact that in considering the fiction written in America during the last twenty years,
we have had few occasions to refer to realism or naturalism — fictional
genres in which American writers of the past have secured some of
their most honourable achievements. Rather than simply attempting
to transcribe the state of affairs which obtains in what Burroughs
called the cycle of conditioned action, the majority of contemporary
American writers try to offset or challenge the realm of conditioned
action with gestures of verbal autonomy of one kind or another. This
is not to say that aspects of contemporary American society are not
admitted into contemporary fiction; of course they are. But even
while recognizing these aspects the style of the writer seems to make
clear its right to break free from them, or transmute them into something more amenable to their lexical organizings.

However, it would be wrong to suggest that attempts at a more
direct kind of transparent, or neutral, realism are no longer made.
What I want to do briefly is to cite three works from the last decade
which in their differing ways attempt to convey fairly directly something of the actual horror of some contemporary American conditions, the violence, the misery, the squalor and the pathos of the
innumerable incomplete and degraded human beings who live and
die beneath the level of most people's attention. Hubert Selby Jr's
Last Exit to Brooklyn (1964) attempts to convey to us the quality of

life in certain parts of Brooklyn in a style which has an anti-elegant harsh-edged directness about it. Selby says that his stories are about 'loss of control', and inevitably he has to transcribe a good deal of brutality and all sorts of lapses from what we like to think of as human modes of conduct. It would not be fair to say that his work itself loses control, though it deliberately excludes some of the customary methods of organization open to fiction writers – perhaps because he feels that too much formal satisfaction would distract attention away from the plight of his hapless characters.

A good way to describe what Selby is doing is to say that he is trying to depict a human version of what the ecologist John Calhoun called a 'behavioral sink'. In a 'behavioral sink' all normal patterns of behaviour are disrupted, and the unusual stress leads to all forms of perversion, violence, and breakdown. This is what happens when too many animals are crowded into too little territory. On the human level that is exactly what is happening in many American cities, and one recognizes the impassioned honesty with which Selby draws our attention to what it can be like in a particularly extreme example of a human behavioral sink. But the comparative absence of any stylistic resistance to such hellish conditions makes Selby's book rather demoralizing. Of course he could argue that it is salutary to be thus demoralized. The countering proposition to that would be, I imagine, that there is enough dire evidence and information coming at us from a whole range of media and, under the circumstances, we want the fiction-maker to assert the independent power of his form. We would like to see the magic in the web of it.

Another and more famous attempt to present some of the horror of contemporary American life in a spirit of pure neutrality was Truman Capote's *In Cold Blood* (1966). On November 15th, 1959, Richard Hickock and Perry Smith shot the four members of the respectable Midwestern Clutter family for no apparent motive, purpose or profit. Brute fact. Starting from the meaningless horror of that night, Capote gathered together groups and clusters of related facts so that the sudden bout of blood-spilling was retrieved from its status as an isolated fact, and provided with a wider context in which it becomes the focal point of converging narratives. Capote worked on the valid assumption that a fact is simply a moment in an ongoing sequence, that it ramifies in all directions, and that to appreciate the full import of any incident you must see as much of the sequence and as many of the ramifications as possible. By juxtaposing and dovetailing the lives and values of the Clutters with those of the killers, Capote produced a schematic picture of the doubleness in American life.

There is no doubt that Capote brought together some very revealing facts, but his technique merits a little consideration. He claimed to have written a 'non-fiction novel', to have presented only facts derived from observation, official records and interviews. He does not comment, he presents; he does not analyse, he arranges. This means, for one thing, that he cannot approach the profound inquiring psychological insights into the psychopath and his victims attained by Musil (in his study of Moosbrugger) or Dostoevsky. As a result, despite some telling details about the lives of the people involved in the case, the respectable citizens tend to be caricatured, and the forlorn, dangerous criminals sentimentalized (particularly Perry Smith). The way Capote juxtaposes his 'facts' reveals his subjective feelings about the world he presents, and this begins to press on our attention. I am not saying that Capote has twisted the facts to make life appear as a Capote novel. But he has manipulated them to produce a particular kind of *frisson*. In the past great novels have been written about criminal acts which were initially provoked by actual reported crimes (e.g. by Stendhal, Dostoevsky). But by making their works frankly fictions, the novelists recognized that to explore the latent significance of such acts the most valuable aid is the human imagination. By pretending not to avail himself of this aid, Capote produces the impression of factitiousness rather than fact. In the absence of a witnessing and controlling ego, the status of the facts is called into doubt. Oddly enough, there is finally something unreal about this true documentary which seems to have been disavowed by its author and assembler.

The Hell's Angels are another violent fact, actually existing in contemporary America. The journalist Hunter Thompson wrote a book[1] about them which the young American novelist Stephen Schneck reviewed very sympathetically.[2] He noted that Thompson's account was 'punctuated with the dreadful unmelodious thud of authenticity', and commended him for writing a sort of stiff, undistinguished reportage which did not sensationalize or romanticize the Hell's Angels. Schneck drew a conclusion: 'In these overwritten times, we cannot expect our authors to waste effort on such affectations as literary style. It is enough to write the facts in a clear hand: it is a mistake to attempt to embellish or improve upon the fantastic actuality.' This would certainly seem to justify both Selby's and Capote's ways of writing. But Schneck went on to derive another consideration from Thompson's book—the problematical nature of just what is 'actuality'. 'Where does the nightmare end, and where does the decent reality, the sanity of daylight, begin? The Hell's Angels, along with everyone else in America, are included in the dreadful confusion.

Much of the Angels' difficulties seem to stem from their inability to distinguish between an act of somnambulism and a dream of sleepwalking.' Access to the reality of people's lives is not perhaps so easy as Selby and Capote implicitly propose.

Schneck certainly seems to suggest as much in his novel, *The Nightclerk* (1966). 'At 3.33 in the morning, there's only people lying wide-eyed in bed, wrongdoers creeping close to the walls, and Nightclerks sitting in haunted lobbies. Why devise elaborate narrations? Why tell everything but the truth?' We note straight away that traditional narrative techniques are equated with a falsification of reality. The feeling is that the old ways of constructing a novel cannot get at the real horrors and actual menaces of modern American life. Schneck's nightclerk is a fat, soiled monster of a man who works in a seedy hotel in downtown San Francisco. (Perhaps there is a debt to O'Neill's *Hughie*.) But Spencer Blight, the nightclerk, is no ordinary man and his role on the twilight edges of society is no ordinary role. For Blight is the obscene dreamer of the modern city; in his grossness he is the repository and expediter of the forbidden vices of society. On him all private perverted yearnings and dirty secrets converge; from him strange and horrific sexual acts mysteriously emanate. When there is a series of ugly sexual assaults (every Wednesday 'something new and savage, with no satisfactory explanations'), Blight is vaguely connected with it all, not so much as a doer of the deeds, but rather as a dreamer of the deeds, a 'fat spider who sat spinning the night away in the rotten core of the haunted hotel'. The book is surrealistic, blackly humorous; but it puts forward the important consideration that in dreams begin realities.

For most of the novel the nightclerk sits in his chair, reading pornography, musing, remembering, his capacious mind permeable to past and present foulness, and generative of more. But, says Schneck, this state is not to be 'mistaken for sleep, but must be respected as a state of magick: a trance into which Blight did withdraw at will, to hold converse with the dark and fearful Wonders whose Wednesday celebrations seemed somehow connected with a Nightclerk, wrapped in silence.' 'Magick' is the key word: it recurs throughout the book. Whatever happens, happens mysteriously, through occult powers which cannot be seen or plotted. This determines the dissolving shape of Schneck's book. It could be said that traditionally a lot of the energy of the novel has been directed against magic. The omniscient author may pose a mystery or uncertainty only to clarify and explain it; his work asserts and explores a universe of cause and effect, even though it may reveal that causes and effects are related to each other in stranger and subtler ways than we usually assume. Obviously one of the reasons why the novel has suffered so many mutations in this century is simply that the old shared assumptions about the nature of reality—the way of things, the why of things—have broken down. In particular this seems to be true in American fiction since the last world war. Book after book gives evidence of people simply bewildered at the workings of the world around them and one result of this is that there is a growing tendency among American novelists to refer to ghosts, demons, occult powers, and all sorts of magic when it comes to offering some account of the forces at work in the real dream, or dreamed reality, of modern life (cf. the extraordinary upsurge of interest in astrology in America during recent years).

The feeling of a world dominated by demons and magic is at work in Schneck's novel. He does not explain the city at night; he makes it vivid. There is no conventional narrative because there are no ordinary doings. There is instead an atmosphere—the city turning in its troubled sleep, and at the centre Spencer Blight in his hotel. This hotel exists 'outside the laws of nature as well as most municipal ordinances'. Sometimes it is the many-roomed home of all the banished perversions of the city. Sometimes something more symbolic: 'The lobby is a world of trinkets, but the floors overhead are the *vacua horribilia*. Suspended over the lobby, over the vast accumulations of trash, are six flights of the void.' In every sense it is a place where reality gives way to fantasy and unreality, the customary world separating out, as in so many recent American novels, into trash and void. Everything is running down and by the end the lobby is empty, the furniture is dead, and the nightclerk is 'like a man all used up'.

Objections may be brought against the three books I have mentioned. Selby's makes reality too crude, Schneck's makes it too grotesque, while Capote's illusory objectivity seems to falsify its evidence by seeking to hide all reportorial bias and disposition. Looking at these books one might speculate that a writer seeking to get at American reality might do well to combine the documentary and the demonic modes, to develop a sense of magic without losing the empirical eye, and to admit his own relationship to the material he is handling and the interpretations he is offering. This, it seems to me, is exactly what Norman Mailer has done, and why, despite varying performances, he is one of the most consistently relevant and revelatory writers about contemporary America. In dealing with grim facts he asserts the force of his own style; engaged in documentary work he reveals the presence of the registering, interpreting ego in the events, thus authenticating whatever version—no matter how idiosyncratic—he offers; and in his fiction he allows himself every form of licence, pushing invention as far as he can. In his various applications and extensions of his own particular genre, which we might call the demonized documentary, Mailer has shown a continuous ability to expose himself to what is going on and respond with some kind of vital lexical performance. In particular when he permits himself to operate in a frankly fictional dimension, where some people find him most outrageous, I think he is most successful.

At the end of Saul Bellow's *The Victim*, Leventhal cries out one last question to Allbee: ' "What's your idea of who runs things?" ' It is an apt question to conclude a book in which the persecutor and the paranoid are never quite sure which role they are playing at any particular moment. But more generally it could be said to be the question which occupies a large number of American novelists who, in one form or another, are obsessed with the problems and mysteries of power. It is certainly Mailer's central concern, and his first three novels can be seen as studies of three different kinds of power and their distinctive manifestations or modes of operation. In each, the geographic setting suggests an extra dimension of power outside the particular human power situation being studied. *The Naked and the Dead* (1948) is about men and war, and the temporary military installations are set in the jungle and surrounded by the sea. *Barbary Shore* (1951) is about men and politics, and the run-down boarding-house in Brooklyn which contains most of the action is surrounded by the unfathomable density of the modern megalopolis. *The Deer Park* (1955) is about men and sex, and it takes place for the most part in an unreal annex of Hollywood called Desert D'Or. More real is the actual desert all around it. When he came to write *An American Dream* (1965), Mailer brought together these different geographies (either as actual settings or as metaphors) to make his most comprehensive exploration of the operations of power on many levels.

An interest in the mysteries of power necessarily involves a curiosity about the presence or absence of patterns and plots. This has been made abundantly clear in the course of this book. It is evident in Mailer's work from the start. In *The Naked and the Dead*, the American soldiers on the Pacific island often experience the feeling that, 'It's a plot,' or, 'It's a trap.' On one level this is an obvious reaction to being caught up in the exacting discipline of their own army, as well as being constantly vulnerable to sudden attacks by the Japanese. But the emotion is a response to something more than the force of contending armies. When the young soldier Hennessey is killed shortly after the beach landing, the reaction is not simply, *c'est la guerre*. One man, Red, has an awed sense that 'someone, *something*' is behind it. 'There was a pattern where there shouldn't be one.' Another man, Croft, whose will to exercise his destructive power over the men is to be so decisive during the campaign, reacts with a strange feeling of omnipotence, since he feels that he controls the fate of his men. The death of Hennessey tantalizes him with 'odd dreams and portents of power'. Later on we are told of the feeling that the detached, cerebral Lieutenant Hearn experienced when he sailed for war. 'Always there was the power that leaped at you, invited you.' Determined to bring a wounded man back to base, another soldier, Brown, addresses his resolve to 'whatever powers had formed him'. The men share the same war, but each has his different experience or sense of the presence of more than human powers.

But the person most preoccupied with power is General Cummings, who is said to 'control everything' on the island. Accused of being a reactionary by Hearn, he dismisses Hearn's narrow political frame of reference, and speaks of the coming 'renaissance of real power'. The war is not fought for ideals, it is simply 'a power concentration'; to attempt to plan for a just society is foolish since ' "the only morality of the future is a power morality," ' and so on – the word is constantly on his lips. Cummings is a somewhat monstrous figure who commands a dark authority and feels himself in touch with the essential powers that run things. He is the first of many such figures, actual and fictional, from boxers to politicians, who are to absorb Mailer's attention in his subsequent work. As Cummings lies awake arranging his plans, he is sure that there is always a pattern if you know how to look for it. When he has ordered an attack he feels the thrill of total control. 'The troops out in the jungle were disposed from the patterns in his mind ... All of it, all the violence, the dark co-ordination had sprung from his mind. In the night, at that moment, he felt such power that it was beyond joy ... ' Later that same night, he tries to write down in his journal a comprehensive theory of how all power operates, to draw the curve which accurately defines the line of force as it rises and falls through human affairs. It is rather like Henry Adams's undertaking. But when it comes to drawing the definitive curve, he finds it is beyond him. 'There was order but he could not reduce it to the form of a single curve. Things eluded him.' This is borne out by what happens in the campaign, which is supposedly being run by him. His men do finally achieve victory, but he has a momentary recognition that he personally has had almost nothing to do with it: 'it had been accomplished by a random play of vulgar good luck larded into a casual net of factors too large, too vague for him to comprehend.' If there is a pattern it is beyond his grasp; the controller of the island is himself controlled in unfathomable ways. The master tactician has no idea who runs things, though he will go on pretending it is himself.

In connection with the delusory nature of man-made patterns, the setting is all important. While men consult the rule book, the moon exerts her mysterious force. The military concept of a 'connected line' vanishes in the impenetrable jungle – 'no army could live or move in it.' The mountain which dominates the island dominates the men with its motionless hostility. The sea around them wears all things down and is full of death. The land itself becomes terrifying in its 'somnolent brooding resistance'. It seems as if there is a cosmic conspiracy against men, as if something working through the various forces of nature is seeking to bring them to a standstill, erase their identities, annihilate them altogether. The heaps of kelp on the beach remind Hearn of a lecture he had once heard on this seaweed. These plants live without movement in murky undersea jungles – 'stationary, absorbed in their own nutriment'. In storms they are heaped up as so much waste on the beaches, useful only as fertilizer. Their presence on the beaches of the island is a constant reminder that all things including men are worn down inexorably to some lowest common denominator of existence. It is the island which strips the men naked, leaving all of them exposed and many of them dead. Everything surrounding the men seems to presage some final immobility. If General Cummings had looked very carefully when he stood on the parapet peering into no-man's-land, this is the entropic pattern he would have discerned, the enemy he should have recognized. At the end of the book a foolish major is planning to lay a co-ordinate grid system over a picture of Betty Grable to 'jazz up' his map-reading class. It is a last farcical reminder of the futility of imposing man-made patterns on the mysterious undulations of life.

The imposition of political patterns on the movements of history is experienced as ultimately futile in *Barbary Shore*. The pessimistic McLeod, who has moved beyond conflicting ideologies and is killed for such individual presumption, outlines a future of increasing chaos and conflict – ' "the deterioration continues until we are faced with mankind in barbary." ' The book contains a lot of political debate, with various ideological points of view advanced in some detail. Yet there seems to be a more mysterious power at work than that which is focused and applied by party conspiracies, and one indication of this is the presence of an unexplained secret object which the parties are trying to gain possession of. It could refer to some atomic secret plans, or more generally stand for that elusive mystery of power which men continually strive to appropriate and use. In the event McLeod hands it on to the narrator, along with the remnants of his socialist heritage, and the narrator is himself a man who will spend his time evading conscription into any particular party.

It is important that the narrator is a man who has lost his memory and hence all his connections with the past. He thus becomes a man who lives existentially, since he starts with no prior commitments or allegiances. He cannot reconstruct his identity, despite all his inquiries and studies of documents; he therefore has to create it anew. He has a recurrent fantasy of a traveller arriving at what he thinks is a familiar city, only to find that the architecture in it is strange, the clothing unfamiliar, the language of the signs indecipherable. He thinks that he must be dreaming, but the narrator imagines shouting to him, 'You are wrong ... this city is the real city, the material city, and your vehicle is history.' It is because the narrator himself has to learn to comprehend what is to him an alien city, and formulate a role for himself in it, that he is attracted to the patterns and clarifications offered by politics. But by the end he has moved beyond all groups, like so many American heroes. He is alone, but his isolation is given meaning by his possession of the mysterious object, a moral act, as McLeod defined it, since as long as a single individual has the object, no party or country can exploit it. At the end, the narrator foresees a life of continual moving on, using flexibility to avoid destructive conscriptions, dodging and weaving from the hostile pre-emptive forces of the modern world. Mailer ends his novel with an inverted echo of the end of *The Great Gatsby*, heavy with pessimistic predictions of the coming chaos and destruction — 'the storm approaches its thunderhead, and it is apparent that the boat drifts ever closer to the shore. So the blind will lead the blind, and the deaf shout warnings to one another until their voices are lost.' The drift is towards Barbary Shore, and the hero's one aim is to resist the drift at least in his own person — politics and parties and countries and armies seem only to hasten it.

The Deer Park is set in the town of Desert D'Or, close to the capital of cinema in Southern California. Hollywood, and California in general, are situated on the edge of the Pacific. Desert D'Or is on the edge of the desert. In the last century it was a shanty town round an oasis from which prospectors set out to look for gold. They called it Desert Door. Now it has been completely rebuilt. It is 'all new'. In giving us these details of the setting on page one, Mailer outlines the main subject of his novel. People come west searching for dream gold; every age will define the dream gold it seeks. The quest brings many people to some kind of extreme edge, where they may be confronted with a door through which they might push to some new dimension of experience. Or they may discover that dream gold is fool's gold, and wake up to the actual mess of their lives which becomes clear as the power of fantasy wanes. Once again, the location of the Hollywood dream factory on the western edge of the continent has struck an American novelist with its irresistible suggestiveness.

On the narrative level, the novel is an account by an ex-serviceman named Sergius O'Shaugnessy who plunges into the life of Desert D'Or. He not only has problems about his own identity, but some temporary blocks in the creative realm — both sexual and literary. After various adventures or entanglements — mainly in the rather unreal area in which sex is inextricable from cinema — he finally leaves Desert D'Or for Mexico where he recovers sufficient potency to learn some of the rudiments of bull-fighting, and sleep with a bull-fighter's mistress. From there he goes to New York where he achieves full literary potency and writes his book — which will be *The Deer Park*.

Another important inhabitant of Desert D'Or is Marion Faye. A pimp and drug addict who seems to go in for deliberate degradation of self and others, he is in his own way a quester. He wants to 'push to the end ... and come out — he did not know where, but there was experience beyond experience, there was something. Of that, he was certain.' The nature of his quest is perhaps best indicated by his deliberate act of not locking his door, thus metaphorically leaving himself open to the dreads which come in from the desert and the more literal threats of his many enemies in town. Most people in Desert D'Or live with their doors locked in every sense. The houses have walls round them to keep out the sight of the real desert. At the same time they have extravagant interior settings and extensive mirrors, so that life achieves the sustained unreality of prolonged narcissism in theatrical conditions. The bars are made to look like jungles, grottos, cinema lounges — life becomes an indefinite extension of the film sets close by. In these conditions people can only play roles and sex becomes a desolate game; where fantasy is everywhere, there is no chance for truly productive relationships. It is not surprising that more than one character, including Sergius, gets locked up sexually, unable to perform the creative act.

Such a world is, to Marion Faye, a world of 'slobs'. He is trying to find the door which opens to some authentic experience which he feels can only be had at the extreme edge of reality. It is one of his

pleasures to drive with great speed out into the desert to a small sum-
mit from which he can look out, not only over the desert, but also to
the gambling city and the atomic testing grounds which are both
situated out there. He feels contempt and distaste for the way politicians and army officers produce verbal justifications for these great
experiments with destructive power — 'for the words belonged to the
slobs, and the slobs hid the world with words.' But Marion Faye
does not regret the coming destruction which he foresees; rather he
longs for it. He yearns for the great explosion which will erase the
rot and stench of civilization as he knows it — 'let it come for all of
everywhere, just so it comes and the world stands clear in the white
dead dawn.' It is an authentic vision, but its purity is nihilistic: it
seems appropriate that Marion Faye should finally involve himself
in a nasty road accident. It is obviously imperative somehow to exit
from the unreality of Desert D'Or, but the book suggests that Marion
Faye has taken the wrong door out. Is there a right one?

This of course is the problem for Sergius O'Shaugnessy. In
Desert D'Or he has rented a house 'on the edge of the desert', and,
like many other American heroes, he has good reason for pitching
his habitation in such a border area, for his experience has taught
him that there are two worlds and he has seen enough of both to
realize that one has to negotiate a perilous existence somewhere
between them. 'I had the idea that there were two worlds. There was
a real world as I called it ... and this real world was a world where
orphans burned orphans. It was better not even to think of this. I
liked the other world in which almost everybody lived. The imaginary
world.' What his experience in Desert D'Or teaches him is that the
imaginary world can have its own ruination and destructiveness. At
the end of the novel, Sergius imagines a friend of his named Eitel (a
film director who has lost his integrity) sending a silent message to
him. In it Eitel confesses that he lost the true drive and desire of the
artist, which is the conviction that whatever happens ' "there still
remains that world we may create, more real to us, more real to
others, than the mummery of what happens, passes, and is gone." '
He then urges Sergius to ' "try for that other world, the real world,
where orphans burn orphans and nothing is more difficult to discover than a simple fact. And with the pride of the artist, you must
blow against the walls of every power that exists, the small trumpet
of your defiance." ' This is potentially ambiguous, but the feeling
that emerges is as follows. From the world of brutal facts — wars and
orphanages — Sergius has moved into the realm of Technicolored air-
conditioned fantasies. But there is a further move to make. The
imaginary world not only covers the world in which people live

isolated in their own dreams and illusions; it also points to the truly creative world of art through which the artist may find a way into the secrets of reality. For Sergius, writing is the right door out of Desert D'Or – and all the puns are functional.

Having touched bottom, Sergius finds the strength to leave Desert D'Or, and his subsequent travels in Mexico and then to New York mark stages in his liberation. At the very end he seems to have arrived at a point beyond all politics and religions to put his trust in sex, for he hears from God that sex is time and time is 'the connection of new circuits'. The important transferences and linkings of power will in future be very private affairs, with the ostensibly important power circuits of society counting for less than the mysterious forces which work behind and through them. This is one of the terminal suggestions of the book.

In the ten years before he published his next novel, Mailer spent much of his time writing the various essays which he gathered together with some fragments of fiction in the two books, *Advertisements for Myself* (1957) and *The Presidential Papers* (1963). One may note in passing that the two titles suggest a range of interest from the self-assertive power of the writer's own ego right up to the most powerful man in America. In a famous essay entitled 'The White Negro' Mailer wrote that no matter how horrifying the twentieth century is, it is very exciting 'for its tendency to reduce all of life to its ultimate alternatives'. When Sergius started to find his feet as a writer he tells us that he started to think in 'couples', such as love and hate, victory and defeat, and so on, and this binary reduction or schematization of life is much in evidence in Mailer's own subsequent journalism and occasional writing. 'Today the enemy is vague,' he also said in an early essay, and one can see that throughout his work he has tried to dissipate that vagueness by postulating pairs of opposed extremes – assassins and victims; conformists and outlaws; the cancerous forces of malign control resisted by the bravery and health of the hero as hipster; the black magician versus the good artist (see his classic account of the Liston-Patterson fight); love and death; being and nothingness; cannibals and Christians – and finally God and the Devil. These are just some of the 'couples' that Mailer has deployed in his essays, and obviously he feels the excitement of going after extreme alternatives.

Looking back at those essays one can detect an increasing preference for images drawn from biology, from diseases and from primitive superstitions. Like Burroughs he sees cancer as an appropriate symbol of the forces of death which are gaining on us. He refers to the 'cancer of the power that governs us'; the F.B.I. is a faceless 'plague-like' evil force; totalitarianism is a spreading disease; the nation is 'collectively sick'. Few people resist this spreading disease, 'the slow deadening of our best possibilities'. There are just a few individuals—Kennedy, Castro, beats, hipsters, Negroes, psychopaths, who can assert their own inner energy and independent vision of reality against the prevailing forces. Such figures are resisting the overall drive towards death which is the dominant conspiracy. Mailer has a 'dynamic view of existence' which sees every individual as 'moving individually through each moment of life forward into growth or backward into death'. And what is going on in the universe as a whole is a battle between an existential God and a principle of Evil 'whose joy is to waste substance'. The confrontation is comparable to that outlined by Burroughs, and we recognize the principle of Evil as entropy turned Manichaean. What Mailer feels is that somehow we have lost the ability to respond to this awesome confrontation. 'The primitive understanding of dread —that one was caught in a dialogue with gods, devils, and spirits, and so was naturally consumed with awe, shame, and terror has been all but forgotten.' Among other things, his next novel was to be about a man who seeks to recapture an adequate sense of dread.

In another coupling, from one of the Presidential Papers, Mailer suggests that Americans have been leading a double life: 'our history has moved on two rivers, one visible, the other underground; there has been the history of politics which is concrete, practical, and unbelievably dull ... and there is the subterranean river of untapped, ferocious, lonely and romantic desires, that concentration of ecstasy and violence which is the dream life of the nation.' The writer must be in touch with both, with all levels of American life, and able to swim in all its rivers: it is almost a direct prescription for Mailer's next novel. Having complained that 'the life of politics and the life of myth had diverged too far' he would create in it a character who experienced their point of convergence—and separation.

The title, *An American Dream* (1965), might suggest that in this novel Mailer decided to leave the surface river of American life and plunge into the subterranean river to explore 'that concentration of ecstasy and violence which is the dream life of the nation'. And it is true that the hero of the book, Stephen Rojack, is twice very close to a literal plunge from lighted rooms in high buildings to dark streets below. Early in the book during the course of a party, he goes to the balcony to vomit out his rising nausea (that familiar act which he performs more than once, well aware of its ritual cleansing significance). The moon seems to be calling to him to jump from the balcony, and he does in fact start to climb over. He is 'half on the balcony, half off' when 'the formal part' of his brain tells him that he cannot die yet as he has work to do. Outside—the moon, strange influences in the darkness, superstitious promptings, the possibility of a descent which confusingly suggests itself as an ascent, an ambiguous summoning to liberation which may be death. Behind—the constricting and debased routines of a society out of love with itself and engaged in petty power plays and empty sexual games. Poised between them—the Mailer hero, caught in the paradox that while the summons from the moon seems more authentic and important than the voices from the party, to obey the moon would be to abandon form for formlessness, consciousness for unconsciousness, life for death. In this little incident Mailer adumbrates the subject of the whole novel, and anticipates the crucial scene when Rojack walks round the parapet of a high balcony, later in the book.

If you regard this novel simply as a narrative of incidents—as some critics did, and found it outrageous*—what happens is this. Stephen Rojack, an ex-war hero, had wanted to get into politics and, partly with this in mind, he had married Deborah Kelly who was socially influential and whose father wielded extraordinary, and nameless, powers. But having had a very intense experience of the mystery of death during the war when he killed some Germans in a desolate moonlit landscape, Rojack finds that the political game comes to seem like an unreal distraction in which the real private self is swallowed up in a fabricated public appearance. Rojack departs from politics to continue his 'secret frightened romance with the phases of the moon'. By the same token he is leaving the mental enclosures of bourgeois society and venturing into a new kind of power area in which the supernatural, the irrational and the demonic hold sway. This step out of society is marked by his murder of Deborah. He manages to make the murder look like suicide, and afterwards he finds that he has dropped out of respectable society and has entered a strange underworld. The geography shifts from fashionable uptown New York to the Village, Harlem, the Lower East Side; the atmosphere becomes darker and more confused; he is pursued by police and criminals and is involved in power manoeuvres which he cannot fathom. He has to fight for his life—psychically with a gang of hoodlums; physically with the Negro Shago Martin. He

---

* The best answer to these critics, and a brilliant comment on the novel as a whole, is to be found in a short piece by Leo Bersani in *Partisan Review* (Fall, 1965), entitled 'The Interpretation of Dreams'. Among other things he reminds us that the telling of the story is Rojack's invention and that its exuberance is a calculated effect—'we should be admiring the power of extravagance in Rojack's tall story instead of upholding the faded banner of verisimilitude.'

has, in effect, taken that plunge to the lower level of American life. On that lower level he also finds true love with a singer named Cherry, an authentic passional relationship which had not been possible in the confines of society. But that lower level is also the place of death, and Cherry is pointlessly and brutally murdered. It is done in error, but there is no clear light at this level and everyone is prey to confusions. After this Rojack leaves New York, first of all going to make a lot of money in Las Vegas, and at the very end of the book heading for the jungles of Guatemala and Yucatan, away from the United States and towards the most primeval area left on the whole American continent. He is by this time well beyond the constituted power of the law, and the unconstituted powers of the lawless inhabitants of the lower level—indeed it might be said that he is beyond the United States of America altogether. It would seem that his apparent escape from the powers of retribution was very upsetting for some reviewers who felt that wife-murderers should not get off so easily. But taken as a vivid exploration of a man's relationship to the different orders of American reality, the novel is much more interesting and complex than any gesture of *épater le bourgeois*—which many reviewers took it to be.

Although the novel takes place in contemporary America, through the use of metaphor it opens on to every kind of pre-social reality—the jungle, the forest, the desert, the swamp, the ocean-bed. This metaphorical activity in the writing is so insistent that it provides a dimension of experience as real as that provided by the very detailed documentation of settings and scenes in contemporary New York. People are described in animal terms throughout. In addition the constant emphasis on all sorts of odours emanating from people, places, things, bespeaking growth or, more usually, decay, suggests a regression to a more primitive mode of perception and orientation. Language is efficient only on one level; elsewhere it is often safer to follow your nose.

In addition to touching on those powers and drives which operate on the many natural levels below society, language and consciousness (the three are obviously linked), the book tries to point inclusively to those supernatural powers which transcend this distinctively human trilogy. Starting with the moon, we encounter a widening range of references to evil spirits, vampires, demons, voodoo, magic, Zen, grace, and all those strange powers which the individual experiences as an '*it*' working *through* him, but not originating within him (this reminds one of Burroughs's universe). The thesis of Rojack's great work—for he is in effect the writer Sergius set out to become—is that 'magic, dread, and the perception of death were the roots of motivation.' As he says, he has come to believe in witches, spirits, demons, devils, warlocks, omens, wizards, fiends, incubi and succubi – 'in grace and the lack of it, in the long finger of God and the swish of the Devil'. One statement imputed to him is that 'God's engaged in a war with the Devil, and God may lose.' The implications of this are potentially pessimistic, for it reduces man to an incidental point of intersection of warring super-natural powers, a helpless pawn in a larger battle, susceptible to voodoo, desperate for grace. Rojack sees civilization itself as a disturbance of two orders. Primitive man had an instinctive sense of dread in his relationship with non-human nature; civilized man has disrupted this by believing himself to be permanently elevated above animals and the jungle. As a result that sense of dread which is requisite for psychic and spiritual health has been greatly attenuated. Related to this is civilization's 'invasion of the supernatural' which takes the form of denying powers which it cannot see. The price of this, he thinks, is to accelerate our sense of some indefinable but imminent disaster. If a man becomes aware of those dimensions of nature and super-nature from which he feels that the rest of society has resolutely closed itself off, where does that leave him standing? By analogy we might say on an edge as precarious as the parapet round a balcony.

I will return to this analogy, but first let us reconsider the plot line of the novel, this time thinking of it as an almost allegorical explora-tion of different levels of mystery, different areas of power, different orderings of reality. One could simply say that Rojack moves through the three different worlds of Mailer's first three novels – war, politics and sexual experience, encountering different forms of death in each world. But a little more detail is called for. The world of Deborah Kelly and her father is centred on Park Avenue and is connected with all kinds of political power. The Kellys are involved in a power web which reaches not only to President Kennedy, but to the C.I.A., the Mafia and unspecified spy rings and international agents. Entering this world in an attempt to gain political power, Rojack finds himself very much its prisoner: he is manipulated and pre-empted by its far-ranging coercive resources, he is in danger of being trapped in its version of reality. When he murders Deborah, he is breaking free not just from a destructive woman, but from the picture of reality imposed by her world. As he is strangling her he feels he is open-ing a door, and he glimpses what lies 'on the other side of the door, and heaven was there, some quiver of jewelled cities shining in the glow of a tropical dusk, and I thrust against the door once more ... and *crack* the door flew open ... and I was through the door ... I was floating. I was as far into myself as I had ever been and universes wheeled in a dream.' The image obviously recalls the attempts of Sergius to find the right door out of Desert D'Or, and among other things Rojack has broken out of the conventional novel into a realm of dream — one should take the hint. The question which interests us is what he finds on the other side of that door. Does Rojack find heaven, the jewelled cities, or is he drawn on by a mirage? Is his journey away from society and down finally to the ancient centre of America an analogue for some deep descent into his own self?

He has the vision of a jewelled city on two further occasions, both times as an accompaniment to sexual orgasm. The first occurs with Ruta, Deborah's maid, with whom Rojack has intercourse immediately after the murder. During intercourse, he alternates between vaginal and anal penetration. The detail of this scene is offensive to some, but for Mailer it is quite clearly an analogue to a more metaphysical ambiguity. For just as one kind of intercourse is procreative, and the other kind quite the reverse, so Rojack cannot be sure whether he has broken through to some of the true mysteries of creativity after the sterile world of politics; or whether he has unwittingly aligned himself with the Satanic forces of waste. With Ruta the resultant vision of the mysterious city is desolate and dead. It seems like a place in the desert or on the moon, and everything in it looks as unreal as plastic.

Having left the political world, Rojack finds himself in a demonized world of invisible powers and strange portents, of rampant super-stition and accurate magics. In moving away from Park Avenue both to Harlem and to the Lower East Side, Rojack is in effect leaving established society and conventional modes of consciousness for darker areas of experience, hidden at the heart or forgotten at the edge — of the city, of the mind. And in this world Rojack experiences a visionary orgasm with Cherry. This time it is purposefully and successfully procreative (he throws away her diaphragm as a signal of his intent). As a reward the vision is not of an arid, plastic place, but one of rich undersea mystery. 'I was passing through a grotto of curious lights, dark lights, like colored lanterns beneath the sea, a glimpse of that quiver of jewelled arrows, that heavenly city which had appeared as Deborah was expiring ... ' It scarcely matters whether we feel this to be Jungian or not. In sinking or plunging down to the depths (the second river of American life), Rojack has re-established contact with the secret source of life. It is as near heaven as he gets.

In the depths, authentic passion is inseparable from authentic violence, for this is the subconscious (or slum area) in which all the basic intensities are freed from the control of the socialized consciousness (or the uptown authorities). Rojack's intensely private moments of happiness with Cherry are foredoomed, and while Shago Martin is being beaten to death in Harlem, Cherry is being murdered in her Lower East Side hideaway. This area is full of its own threats and manipulations, and Rojack does not find it wholly liberating to be in an area in which the older dreads and magics connected both with the jungle and the moon have full play. Here death seems to strike more often than love.

Leaving New York, Rojack comes to Las Vegas and before setting off for Guatemala and Yucatan, he walks out into the desert to look up at the moon and back at the city. 'There was a jewelled city on the horizon, spires rising in the night, but the jewels were diadems of electric and the spires were the neon of signs ten stories high. I was not good enough to climb up and pull them down.' This has various implications. The two kinds of 'jewelled city' he glimpsed while in union with Ruta and Cherry may indicate the two aspects of the creative-destructive dream which man has imposed on the American continent in his continuing loving and raping of the land. Given Rojack's response to Las Vegas it would seem that the destructive element has been realized and the original American 'dream' has turned into this plastic and neon reality in the desert, deceptively brilliant from a distance. In his search for the true heavenly city, Rojack will have to keep on moving. Perhaps it is like Gatsby's green light, the orgiastic future which recedes as it is pursued. Perhaps it can only ever be a private vision, never to be realized but occasionally to be glimpsed in the rich depths of the imagination. In any case, Rojack leaves Las Vegas, which after all is only a distillation of the corruptions and violences he has encountered in New York. After talking to Cherry (in heaven) on a disused rusty phone — for when a man is standing between the desert and the moon, the customary circuits do not obtain and new kinds of communication are possible — Rojack heads south in space and back in time, aiming perhaps to penetrate the secret centre of his own, and America's, identity.

The crucial last chapter is entitled 'At the Lion and the Serpent' (Rojack's exodus from society through Las Vegas and towards South America is contained in an Epilogue, which suggests that the critical and decisive moment is passed). In terms of the plot, the situation in the chapter is as follows. Kelly has summoned Rojack to the Waldorf Towers on Park Avenue to question him about the death of his daughter and other matters. Rojack sets out with the conscious intention of keeping the appointment. But as he is travelling there he is aware of a subconscious voice telling him to ' "Go to

Harlem" ' if he wants to save Cherry. (In addition, Shago Martin's umbrella which Rojack has brought with him seems to be twitching with signals in his lap—telepathy and animism are common in Harlem.) He has earlier referred to the magician who lives in the 'gaming rooms of the unconscious' and who sends messages up to 'the tower of the brain', and the irrational summons to the dark depths of Harlem which challenges his more rational resolve to go to the Towers on Park Avenue obviously comes from that source. Once again, the two parts of New York serve as projections for different levels of consciousness. Rojack's uncertainty as to which part of New York he should head for at this moment of crisis offers an analogue for Mailer's uncertainty as to which part of the psyche he should rely on in trying to cope with the mystery of America — the empirical or the demonic, the formal decisions of reason or the formless promptings of dream.

In the Waldorf everything suggests death; even the real flowers look plastic. In Kelly's room, the ageing mobster Ganucci seems to reek of the cancer which is devouring him: decay is everywhere in the air. At the same time, the room is a centre of political power, with lines reaching to the White House, the C.I.A., the Mafia and other unspecified organizations. Kelly himself, though he works through political agencies, seems like an elemental force or principle to Rojack. He smells of animal power, and, although his furniture is composed of expensive antiques and art works, Rojack has the sense of 'vegetation working in the night' and experiences the civilized apartment as being something between a dark corner of the jungle and an ante-chamber of hell. Kelly tells him, ' "There's nothing but magic at the top," ' and one is made to feel that all the magic he draws on, as he manipulates the political levels of reality so cynically, is black. The forces he commands serve to extend the empire of death, just as his deepest sexual drive is incestuous (with his daughter), his aids and agents are cancerous (Ganucci), and his cities are plastic (he is a big power in Las Vegas). The power passing through Kelly is on the side of entropy.

Early on during this evening encounter Rojack goes out to the parapet of the balcony. Standing half on the edge, strange intuitions and suggestions come to him: to jump would be a cleansing act after the foulness of the room he has just left; it would be for Cherry; God exists, he suddenly feels as he looks down. But he also realizes that the fall to the street would mean a death as sharp and certain as that threatened by Shago Martin's knife—an important connection of ideas because it relates the notion of the jump to the Harlem side of Rojack's experience. At this stage Rojack climbs down from the parapet and returns for his long conversation with Kelly, but he returns to it at the end of the conversation because – ' "I was caught." ' He is caught between the deathly force emanating almost irresistibly from Kelly and the disturbing dreads which seem to be reaching him from Harlem. He is caught up among encircling and opposing demonisms which he cannot control nor clearly understand, or perhaps between the Devil and the Lord who have however lost their consolingly familiar theological identities to become names uncertainly applied to gusts and currents of power which drive unpredictably through the air. And Rojack decides – 'I wanted to be free of magic ... But I could not move.' It is at this point that he decides he must walk round the parapet of the terrace. Once up on the parapet he is poised between 'the chasm of the drop' and 'the tower behind me' or, as we might say, between rigid architecture and formless darkness. The jump into the authentic darkness, down to the street, would be as literally fatal as the return to the room would be symbolically a succumbing to Kelly. Both Park Avenue and Harlem would destroy Rojack, just as we have seen that too much form (fixity) and pure formlessness (flow) alike threaten to obliterate the identity of the American hero. Both rivers of American life promise drowning.

This is why Rojack has to walk round the parapet. He has to prove that he can negotiate that edge where the worlds meet – capitulating neither to a political nor to a demonized ordering of reality, avoiding the traps of social architecture and the chaotic dissolutions of the pre-social or sub-social dark. To be able to keep his balance is to achieve some degree of liberation from the coercive powers of both worlds – and after his walk Rojack strikes down Kelly and then throws Shago Martin's demon-charged umbrella over the parapet. He is temporarily free from both magics, and in terms of the plot it is this symbolic demonstration of his ability to keep that precarious balance on the edge which frees Rojack and effectively allows him to move beyond the two kinds of power exerted by the tower and the chasm. Earlier in the book he had described himself as feeling like a creature locked by fear to the border between earth and water who finally 'took a leap over the edge of mutation so that now and at last it was something new'. Passing through doors, moving across changing terrains, Rojack feels like a 'new breed' of man and is once described as a 'new soul'. Whether or not he actually becomes a new breed of man, and what the novelty consists of, the book may fairly be said to leave ambiguous. But it does make clear that he is a man who has to live at the edge, trying to hold on to his identity between two threatening realms. If he does finally take a leap, it is not from one realm or atmosphere or river into the other, but rather into some third or new area beyond the existing alternatives formulated by North America. Yucatan is, one feels, as temporary a destination as Sweden was for Yossarian. Rojack is really moving out beyond the world's mirror towards some placeless city of his own imagination.

In this connection it is interesting to note the frontispiece of Mailer's next book, *Cannibals and Christians* (1966). It depicts a model of a possible vertical city of the future and was designed by Mailer himself. The whole section in the book devoted to 'Architectural Excerpts' is extremely relevant in considering *An American Dream*, and I will quote a fragment.

> Perhaps we live on the edge of a great divide in history and so are divided ourselves between the desire for a gracious, intimate, detailed and highly particular landscape and an urge less articulate to voyage out on explorations not yet made. Perhaps the blank faceless quality of our modern architecture is a reflection of the anxiety we feel before the void ...

Since man is caught between old architecture and the void of space, as Rojack was caught between the tower and chasm, Mailer has designed a sort of dream city which will rise up into the sky and sway there like a ship in oceans of space. This is obviously again a sort of third area, between old architecture and unknown space. It is really the city of his own style.

With the mention of style, we have come to the last aspect of the book I wish to consider. I have stated previously that I think we can often detect a significantly analogous relationship between the situation of the character in the plot and the author in his language. Just so, when Rojack is moving in the world of politics and policemen, Mailer tends to employ a mainly documentary style, full of empirical notations and transcriptions of recognizably realistic dialogue. But when Rojack has broken out of this world into an area in which both the pre-social and the supernatural seem to hold sway, so that life is experienced more as a jungle full of magics, then Mailer calls on every kind of mythic, religious, superstitious reference, and metaphors drawn from every level of existence, to provide a style which is adequate to Rojack's novel experience. The documentary is extended to incorporate the demonic. A nice example of the confrontation of styles comes when the police are interrogating Rojack about the death of his wife. Rojack, fabricating his version of Deborah's death, explains that she committed suicide because she felt haunted by demons. ' "I don't know how to put demons on a police report," ' says Roberts. The police report is the equivalent of a style which only credits empirically perceived facts, a narrow naturalism. Rojack is quite sure that there are more things in heaven and earth than can be contained in a police report, and his vocabulary (which is Mailer's style) has been enlarged accordingly. One policeman is convinced he knows the facts of the matter. He asserts that Rojack killed her with a silk stocking—that is how it is usually done. Even so-called empirical realism has its own predetermining fantasies which it imposes on the given data. One of Rojack's struggles is against the inadequate fantasy patternings of reality implicit in the policeman's narrow and clichéd terminology; and it reflects Mailer's sense of his own struggle with available, inadequate, literary styles. Rojack's ability to defy the police and to negotiate that haunted violent part of New York connected with his Harlem and Lower East Side experiences is linked to Mailer's ability to break out of an old style and negotiate that new territory linguistically.

But just as Rojack finds that the second level of American life has its own way of trapping people in its version of the world, and he finally gets away from that area too, so Mailer has no wish to exchange naturalism for supernaturalism and commit himself henceforth to a purely demonic mode of writing—for that too is only a version, a fixed reading. He needs his demonology to give some definition to Rojack's confused perceptions of the realities of the dark world of Harlem, dream, chaos and old night. But if he went over to this style exclusively then he would become a prisoner in his own system. Just as Rojack walks the edge of the parapet to signify his intention to remain unclaimed by both sides, so Mailer walks a stylistic edge. He touches continually on two worlds—the inner and the outer, the demonic and the political, the dreaming and the waking, the structured and the flowing—and tries to be stylistically adequate to all without being trapped by any one.

As the plot of the novel thickens, or perhaps one should say multiplies, Rojack experiences that familiar American sense of 'mysteries revolving into mysteries like galaxies forming themselves'. Later, as he is driving through New York, he feels a growing nausea at the realization that although he is aware of plots and mystery revolving around him,

> I did not know if it was a hard precise mystery with a detailed solution, or a mystery fathered by the collision of larger mysteries, something so hopeless to determine as the edge of a cloud, or could it be, was it a mystery even worse, something between the two, some hopeless no-man's land from which nothing could return but exhaustion?

If the mystery is a political, social one then Mailer can meet it with his more naturalistic style and the surface plot—Kelly, C.I.A., Mafia, and so on. If it is a larger mystery then Mailer will try to meet it with his rhetoric of myth, demons and dread. It may be a mystery in between, however. In which case, Mailer shows himself grappling with it, tottering on that vertiginous edge where the two kinds of mystery meet, a no-man's-land (into which General Cummings timidly peered, seeing nothing) which perhaps only the artist can fathom without falling. Unlike Cummings, Rojack has a sense of the powers on both sides of the parapet. Rojack learns that the secret of sanity is 'the ability to hold the maximum of impossible combinations in one's mind', and Mailer's work represents an attempt to show, stylistically, how this may be done.

Ralph Ellison has the narrator of The Invisible Man declare: 'Step outside the narrow borders of what men call reality and you step into chaos ... or imagination.' When Hawthorne's Wakefield stepped out of the 'system' he stepped into a void. Rojack on the parapet is stepping out without stepping over. The parapet constitutes that third area so eagerly sought by American heroes, and using Ellison's terms we can identify it as the area of imagination—a territory not already marked out by contemporary society, but created by a personal energy of style. By asserting his own unique style, the writer on the edge resists imposed patterns (or patternlessness) from both sides. Ellison's Invisible Man, we remember, wrote his book in a 'border area', withdrawn from uptown politics and plots, and from Harlem chaos, creating an identity with the illuminations of his own writing. William Burroughs's figure, Lee, writing from the other side of the world's mirror, and John Hawkes's Skipper, writing on his magic floating island, both seem to me to offer situational metaphors which can be compared with Rojack's parapet and Ellison's border area—all of them indicating a desire to find some third area beyond conditioning, avoiding both fixity and flow (or prison and jelly), where they can create without being controlled. It is an area from which the contemporary world is still intensely visible, but inside which the world's coercions and impositions are transformed into material which can be fashioned on the writer's own terms. It is the City of Words.

In Why are we in Vietnam? (1967) Mailer continued his explorations into the mystery and source of power, trying to find the intersection point where the pure pre-moral force of nonhuman nature enters into, affects, or works through the human agencies of society. The narrative occasion is a hunting expedition into Alaska which takes a group from Texas into the northern wilderness. Vietnam is not mentioned until the last page, but the book is effectively trying to answer the question posed by the title. Is there a force of negation emanating from the northern ice which works through the 'higher' orders of nature (animals and men), causing them to extend its empire of non-being by awakening impulses of destruction in them? Is there something in the American continent itself which touched the men who settled there, transforming creative impulses into periodic dark rages of annihilation which were turned not only on the original inhabitants, the animals, and the land itself, but which also now reach out as far as the jungles of Vietnam? Was the evil there waiting in the land, as Burroughs has said? Burroughs is mentioned by name more than once, and in fact this is Mailer's most Burroughs-like book inasmuch as it tries to examine the operational modes of whatever power it is that seems to be working to bring organic life back to the crystalline fixity of ice. The narrator refers to himself ironically as a Manichee and we could say that the novel is another approach to that nightmare of entropy turned Manichaean which seems to obsess American writers.

The narrator is a voice which identifies itself as D.J. He gives an account of the expedition to shoot bear which was organized by his father, Rusty, a powerful, brutal, Texan business man. D.J. is accompanied by his close friend Tex, and when the bear-shooting is over they take a walk together as far into the northern snow as they can, not to kill but to open themselves up to the mystery and dread of this geographical extreme. The book seems to include a deliberate evocation of Faulkner's classic story 'The Bear'. There a boy is initiated into 'the wilderness' concordant generality' of which the bear is experienced as the ancient presiding spirit. In Faulkner's story the forest of course contains its danger and its violence, and the chilling snake encountered in the closing paragraphs of the story is also part of the spirit of the woods. Even so, it is fair to say that Faulkner allows one to feel that there is an ancient integrity and value and wisdom in untouched nature which the encroachments of civilization are systematically destroying. As a result something precious and irreplaceable is lost. Mailer, writing some twenty-five years later and from an urban background, seems to want to suggest that this traditional dichotomy between nature and civilization which is so dear to American literature and is enshrined in Faulkner's classic tale, needs to be questioned. Man does indeed despoil the beauties of nature, cuts himself off from its prime mysteries, devotes himself to corporations like the Pentagon, collects guns and contracts cancer, invents helicopters to defoliate and decimate, lives inside the deadening impurities of industrial and mental smog, and is curiously attracted to death—all this and more is touched on by Mailer's novel. But it generates the further suggestion that the original prompting for this compulsion to waste substance was not brought by man into the unspoiled realms of nature but rather contracted there—whether in the jungle, the desert, or at the polar ice cap. This is one reason why Mailer's book can be felt to be confusing. Because on the one hand he does make it seem wonderfully purifying to leave all the foul mess of society behind and 'shed' the 'corporation layers' to come into contact with the clean authenticity of the northern wilderness. On the other hand, having experienced this 'purification', D.J. leaves for Vietnam with something approaching exhilaration. It is thus an ambiguous ceremony of initiation.

D.J. believes that we are all agents of Satan and the Lord, and that America is 'run by a mysterious hidden mastermind'—sentiments familiar from Burroughs's work, to go no further afield. In moving out beyond society, D.J. is trying to get at the power anterior to all society. First the hunters move into a special camp, a 'collision area marginated halfway' between civilization and nature. With guns and helicopters, they do their hunting with one foot firmly lodged in the land of technology which they have only half left behind. Thus the encounters with wild nature are usually ugly, messy woundings which maim the animals and shame the hunters. Not until they have left their arms and the rest of the expedition behind can D.J. and Tex experience the pure unrefracted mystery and power of the north, the animals, the lights and the awesome ice peaks. Not surprisingly they pause 'on the edge' of the snow line; once more the American hero has brought himself to an edge. And in stepping over that edge, they make a temporary venture into undifferentiation, the 'wilderness' concordant generality' in Faulkner's terms, 'the endless noncontemplative powers' of pre-conscious nature in Mailer's own words. Significantly, it is also a temporary step beyond language. The narrator's language is throughout usually obscene, as many reviewers noted, but the following statement offers an important clarification. Having recorded their last dialogue, the narrator explains that they were 'in such a haste to get all the mixed glut and sludge out of their systems that they're heating up all the foul talk to get rid of it in a hurry like bad air going up the flue and so be ready to enjoy good air and nature, cause don't forget they up in God's attic.' Cleansed of society's mores, weapons and words, they are ready to receive God's message, and tune into the secret of His power. And in the silence D.J. first experiences Him as a great beast, summoning him up into the darker north to die; then, as he resists this summoning (as Rojack resisted the moon's summons to jump from the parapet),

God becomes a beast whispering, 'Fulfill my will, go forth and kill.' This seems to be the last message from the north.

However, all that I have said about the novel depends on accepting the narrator as a reliable delineator of his own experiences, and treating his account as a coherent version. But this the voice itself continuously, aggressively and mockingly discourages us from doing. It reminds us that we can never really know the identity which lies behind the written or spoken word. The voice tells us that it might belong to a crazed Harlem Negro who is hallucinating that he is a rich white boy in Texas, or precisely the reverse – a shade dreaming of being a spade, as he puts it. We are told that, one, we cannot be sure 'whose consciousness' we are getting, and two, 'there is no security in this consciousness.' Notions of stable narration are dissolved in reminders of the problematical relationship between stream-of-consciousness, memory, imagination, fantasy (plus the possibility of drug-induced hallucination), documentary and the arbitrary fabrications of a processed tape recording. The whole thing could be a sportive programme put out by the self-styled Disc Jockey; or it could be the twitchings of an 'expiring consciousness', the 'unwinding and unravelings of a nervous constellation just now executed'. The voice aims at exploiting all the available speech levels of America, from the obscenities of Harlem slang to the pedantries of academe. We cannot possibly 'fix' the identity of this narrator, and this manically maintained mysteriousness is a demonstration of a larger truth. 'You never know what vision has been humping you through the night.' We have encountered many American protagonists who are exceedingly anxious and uncertain about both the source and the nature of various versions of reality which they feel are being more or less subtly imposed on them. In this novel Mailer transfers that condition to the reader.

In one sense, then, we as readers are beset by the multiple voice of the American dream life made articulate. This voice has internalized so many of America's hidden desires and compulsions and power drives, just as it has assimilated so many of America's languages and sub-languages, that one has the disturbing sensation of tuning into many wavelengths at once. Like the work of Burroughs, this is another book which calls into question many of McLuhan's more sanguine aphorisms, for this voice comes from a consciousness picking up and transmitting a density of mixed messages which cannot be reduced to coherence nor reassembled into verifiable versions. What one can never know from the book is whether the narrative account comes from a victor or a victim. Thus, one could indeed hear the voice as coming from a consciousness which has been so conditioned and dazed by the onslaught of contemporary America that when it does get beyond the Arctic Circle it can never really 'clear' all the static or sludge out of itself, but simply projects on to the god of the northern ice an exhortation to destruction which had in fact been fed into it since childhood by the power circuits of American society. Despite its manic assertiveness, this voice may just be frantic from excessive 'input' which has inflamed rationality to the point of incoherence.

On the other hand one could say that the voice does at least avoid being trapped in any one version of patterning of reality—an abiding American aspiration as we have seen. It calls into question its own theories, it mocks its own metaphors and notions of magic—many of these close to Mailer's own, so there is the incidental possibility of self-parody here. Whatever else it is, this narrating voice is counter-crystalline, since it refuses to be 'fixed' and will never rest in the stasis of a single configuration. In a book which at one level is about ice, the narrative voice itself is constantly melting and refusing terminal forms. Of course, this leaves us with no one version, or interpretation, to hold on to; indeed it calls the whole range of narrating and interpreting activities of consciousness into question. The book removes itself to a plane of pure ambiguity. Perhaps, as Burroughs recommended, the narrator is getting all the accumulated junk of consciousness down on tape and playing it back just to get rid of it: perhaps, like Cabot Wright, he feels that when he has put all the versions down before him he can be free of them all, eluding all patterns to be finally alone with his non-self. Or perhaps he *is* trying to get at some deep truths about the source and nature of power in America, at the same time desperately avoiding the temptation to believe in any one definitive account. There is after all great energy manifested in and through the writing, whereas the sense of the difficulties involved in offering narrative accounts has led a writer like John Barth more in the direction of paralysis. Among these possibilities and others, we can never decide. D.J. does not walk a parapet but the book itself exists on a precarious edge where it is difficult to discriminate the status of winner and loser, just as the operations of Satan and the Lord seem almost indistinguishable. On that edge, however, it manages to communicate with unusual vividness something of what it is like to be a vexed and struggling consciousness in contemporary America. One could perhaps regard the book as being rather like one of Browning's dramatic monologues in which, as Walter Bagehot so admirably remarked, we are confronted by '*mind in difficulties* ... amid the circumstances least favourable to it, just while it is struggling with obstacles, just where it is encumbered with incongruities.'

In some of his more recent journalism, *The Armies of the Night* (1968) and *Miami and the Siege of Chicago* (1968), Mailer's material seems to polarize itself into convenient oppositions in a rather too predictable manner. It suggests that he is beginning to write in accordance with his own established formulae, and the consideration prompts itself that even Norman Mailer must confront the danger of becoming fixed in his own patternings. But it would be unfair and misleading to dwell on the weaknesses of Mailer's most recent work. The main point is that for most of the past two decades he has constantly sought to expose himself to the influences at work in America without capitulating to any of them, and has constantly sought for appropriate modes of utterance to project his responses to those influences and transform reaction into style. We may think back to Rojack walking round the parapet, while the powers around him push and tug at his precarious balance. It is perhaps only a personal dare, a private test of courage, in a way a rather preposterous performance. Yet it is only by this performance that he achieves a 'provisional sanity' and secures at least a temporary freedom from the oppressive magics circulating around him. Some lines from Robert Browning's 'Bishop Blougram's Apology' seem to me relevant here.

> You see lads walk the street
> Sixty the minute; what's to note in that?
> You see one lad o'erstride a chimney-stack;
> Him you must watch—he's sure to fall, yet stands!
> Our interest's on the dangerous edge of things.
> The honest thief, the tender murderer,
> The superstitious atheist ...
> We watch while these in equilibrium keep
> The giddy line midway: one step aside,
> They're classed and done with.

If the boy on the chimney-stack, or Rojack on the parapet, take one step either way, they are 'classed' and, indeed, 'done with'. Mailer's main achievement has been to keep an equilibrium on 'the dangerous edge of things' through the resources of his own style. Norman Mailer on his parapet is doing what many other American writers are doing, or trying to do, in their own way— resisting classification, preserving a tottering freedom by not capitulating to the patterns and powers on either side of him, walking his own line in a bid to defy conditioning. It is perhaps the most characteristic stance of the American writer during the last two decades.

Chapter 16　Edge City

'Because always comes the moment when it's time to take the
Prankster circus further on toward Edge City.'
(The Electric Kool-Aid Acid Test, Tom Wolfe*)*

While Norman Mailer has been defining his own position on the edge
in the eastern part of America, another writer has been moving
towards his own kind of edge on the West Coast. One might think
that it would be hard to find a contemporary American writer more
different from Mailer than Ken Kesey, and certainly Kesey's North-
Western origins and Californian odyssey are quite different from
anything in Mailer's upbringing and subsequent adventures and
explorations. Nevertheless, despite the fact that they seem to derive
their experience from two different Americas, their work reveals
certain shared preoccupations and parallel perceptions which suggest it might be possible to generalize about an American vision
without ever wishing to minimize the rich variety of individual
talents.

At first glance Kesey has all the marks of a peripheral figure, even
an eccentric. Born in Oregon, he attended creative writing classes at
Stanford in the late 'fifties. While he was there he volunteered to be a
guinea-pig in some experiments with psychomimetic drugs. One of
these was LSD; this took Kesey into a realm of consciousness in
which everything was perceived in an entirely new way. With the
proceeds of his successful first novel, *One Flew Over the Cuckoo's
Nest* (1962), he set up an establishment in La Honda, California,
where with a group of like-minded friends he experimented with
LSD (not then illegal). They tried supplementing and extending 'the
experience' with all sorts of audio-visual aids. More people gravi-
tated to the group, and in time they held more public parties and
trips (or 'acid tests'). This in turn led to acid-rock, light shows,
psychedelic posters, and the vast gatherings of young people at
places like the Fillmore Auditorium and Avalon Ballroom in San
Francisco, and later in halls all over America. As the law tightened
up, Kesey duly found himself in trouble with the police and he became
a famous fugitive in Mexico in 1966. He returned to San Francisco
where he was caught and finally sentenced to ninety days in a work

camp. Before serving the sentence he held a strange inconclusive ceremony which was supposed to mark the 'graduation' from acid — to what he did not say. At present Kesey is living quietly in Oregon, while speculation about his doings and intentions is still quite alive on the West Coast. He may thus seem a somewhat odd figure with which to conclude a study of American fiction during the last two decades. Yet the strange thing is that his work and life seem effectively to summarize a number of the issues which have arisen in connection with the other American writers discussed in this book, and to push certain possibilities and paradoxes we have noted to their extreme conclusions. Just how he does this, and what his significance is, I shall attempt to suggest in this chapter.

One Flew Over the Cuckoo's Nest is about a mental hospital (Kesey worked in one while writing it). It is dominated by Big Nurse, a female of dread authority. She is the servant, or rather the high priestess, of what is referred to as the 'Combine' or 'system', another version of the notion that society is run by some secret force which controls and manipulates all its members, which is so common in contemporary American fiction. Big Nurse keeps the patients cowed and docile, either by subtle humiliations or punitive electric shock treatment. In a crude way she embodies the principles of Behaviorism, believing that people can and must be adjusted to the social norms. Into her ward comes a swaggering, apparently incorrigible character called Randle McMurphy. He is outraged to see how Big Nurse has reduced the men to puppets, mechanically obeying her rules. He tries to inculcate by example the possibilities for independent action, for the assertion of self against system. By the end Big Nurse finds an excuse to have him lobotomized, but her authority has been broken and most of the inmates break free of the institution. The opposition is intentionally stark. Big Nurse speaks for the fixed pattern, the unbreakable routine, the submission of individual will to mechanical, humourless control. McMurphy speaks an older American language of freedom, unhindered movement, self-reliance, anarchic humour and a trust in the more animal instincts. His most significant act is to persuade a group of the inmates to accompany him on a one-day sea voyage. Most of the men are frightened to venture outside at first (they are mainly self-committed to the institution). It is this fear which keeps them cowering inside Big Nurse's routines. But McMurphy persuades the men to come with him, and he duly leads them to the edge of the land — where the ocean starts. The voyage they then embark on is one of very unconcealed significance: it affords the various pleasures of sex, drink, fishing, and the authentic joy and dread of trying to cope with the immense power of the sea.

McMurphy has brought them all out of the System, and into — 'Reality'.

It may be objected that such a parabolic simplification of American life is excessively schematic. McMurphy is like a cliché hero in a cartoon-strip, a Captain Marvel or Superman; while Big Nurse is a cartoon horror—like Spider Lady, who drew her victims into an electrified web (cf. the electric shock treatment meted out by Big Nurse). I think this is deliberate. Comparisons with cartoons are made throughout, so Kesey is hardly unaware of his technique. Someone calls McMurphy a TV-cowboy; a girl gives him some underpants with white whales on them because ' "she said I was a symbol." ' He is addicted to comic-strips and TV which have in turn nourished his stances and speeches. You could say that he is acting out one of the most enduring and simple of American fantasies — the will to total freedom, total bravery, total independence. Big Nurse is a projection of the nightmare reverse to that fantasy—the dread of total control. Wolfe in *The Electric Kool-Aid Acid Test* (1968)[1] records Kesey talking about 'the comic-book Superheroes as the honest American myths', and Kesey may be defying us to distinguish comic-book clarity from mythic simplicity. In the contemporary world as he portrays it, to be a hero you have to *act* a hero (it is a discovery in his next novel that while weakness is real, strength has to be simulated: 'you can't ever fake being weak. You can only fake being strong.'). McMurphy has had to base his act on the only models he has encountered, in cartoons and movies. He is, if you like, a fake, a put-together character with all the seams showing. But, the book suggests, such fakery is absolutely necessary, unless you want to succumb to authentic weakness and the mindless routine supervised by Big Nurse. It is McMurphy's fakery and fantasy which lead others out into reality. In time, it would be Kesey's.

What makes the novel more interesting than just another cartoon, or John Wayne film, is that Kesey understands the need or compulsion to fantasize which is prior to the emergence of such apparitions as McMurphy and Big Nurse. As some of the men in the institution realize, they are really driving McMurphy to play out the role of heroic rebel. When he finally moves to attack Big Nurse, the act which gives her the excuse to have him lobotomized, the narrator recalls: 'We couldn't stop him because we were the ones making him do it. It wasn't the nurse that was forcing him, it was our need that was … pushing him up, rising and standing like one of those motion-picture zombies, obeying orders beamed at him from forty masters.' Fantasies of the weak converge upon him; one of the burdens McMurphy is carrying (and he is exhausted by the end) is the number of wish-fulfilment reveries which are secretly, perhaps unconsciously, projected on to him by the inmates. The clichés he acts are the clichés they dream. It is worth remembering that he was committed to the institution as a psychopath: the psychopath as hero is not a new idea in America. Robert Musil, in *The Man Without Qualities,* made a profound study of the psychopath in the figure of Moosbrugger and added the suggestive comment: 'if mankind could dream collectively it would dream Moosbrugger.' The inmates of the asylum in Kesey's novel are American and as such they have a particular popular cul ture determining their most elementary fantasies. If they could dream collectively they would dream McMurphy. From one point of view that is exactly what they do.

We must read McMurphy, then, in two ways. In a sense he is an authentic rebel who steps to the music that he hears; yet there is a sense in which he is marching to the music of the fantasies projected on to him and, as such, in his own way a kind of 'zombie' too, a servitor of the versions imposed on him. Perhaps Kesey intends us to understand that McMurphy's heroism is in realizing this second truth, and nevertheless continuing with the imposed role. He is a singular man inasmuch as not many people would be able to support the fantasies of strength and independence projected on to him; the majority are more likely to submit to the controlling plot and imposed pictures of the Combine and step to the mechanical music of Big Nurse.

But how we react to McMurphy necessarily depends on our sense of the narrator, since his version of things is the only one to which we have access—and he is a giant, schizophrenic Indian called Big Chief.[2] He is a rather notional Indian, a representative of the towering vitality of the original life of the American continent, now tamed to terrified impotence by all the mechanical paraphernalia of the white man's institutions. McMurphy teaches him to regain the use of his strength and at the end of the novel he is running away from the hospital and towards the country of his ancestors. This is all fairly obvious. What is unusual is the brilliant way in which Kesey has recreated the paranoid vision of a schizophrenic in the narrating voice.

Big Chief's vision of the hospital as a great nightmare of hidden machinery, wires, magnets, push-buttons, and so on, is utterly convincing. He is sure that the powers in the institution have fabricated a completely false environment: 'they' can accelerate or decelerate time, the windows are screens on which they can show whatever movie they want to impose as reality, they have fog machines which fill the air with a dense scummy medium in which Big Chief gets utterly cut off from everything and lost. They can do whatever they like with individuals because they have installed automative devices inside them (such as Indwelling Curiosity Cutout). It is a very Burroughs-like vision. This coherent paranoid fantasy extends to the world outside the hospital ward, for that world too is being 'adjusted' by Big Nurse and her like. What others would call factories and suburban housing developments, Big Chief sees as evidence of the spreading power of the Combine, which works to keep people 'jerking around in a pattern'. What the Combine is spreading is another version of entropy—all individual distinctions and differences erased and nature's variety brought down to the deadly uniformity of a mechanically repeated pattern. Some people may want to get 'out', or protest, but any such deviants are sent to the hospital where special machines can adjust them. (One interesting point is that a simple man may escape the Combine—'being simple like that put him out of the clutch of the Combine. They weren't able to mold him into a slot.' This sense of the special value of simplicity is recognizably American, and it is related to the detectable anti-intellectualism in Kesey's work.)

For Big Chief, McMurphy is the man who demonstrates that the Combine is not all-powerful: McMurphy makes the fog go away and enables him to see things clearly; he makes the pictures imposed on the windows vanish, so that when Big Chief looks out he sees the actual world. He gives Big Chief the sense of what it is to be an individual; he restores reality to him, and restores him to reality. At one point Big Chief writes: 'I still had my own notions—how McMurphy was a giant come out of the sky to save us from the Combine that was net-working the land with copper wire and crystal.' The importance of people's 'notions' of other people, and reality, looms large for Kesey.

His second novel, *Sometimes a Great Notion* (1964), concerns a logging family in Oregon. The novel centres on the mainstay of the family, Hank Stamper, a tough and stubborn individualist cast in the same mould as McMurphy, and nourished in his childhood on the same Captain Marvel comics. He is the strongest man in the book when it comes to any physical deed of bravery, effort or endurance. He is a Paul Bunyan type, and, in holding out against the coercive group pressure of a union in a local logging dispute, Hank is asserting a kind of American individualism which Kesey clearly admires. But there are aspects of his relationships with his wife, Viv, and his brother, Lee, which suggest that he suffers from being sealed off in his heroic role. He is more at home confronting the elements, as, for instance, on the dangerous logging run down river on which he has just embarked when the book concludes.

Not that nature in this book is benevolent. There are few pastoral moments in Kesey's sombre Pacific north-west. Through a series of very powerful and evocative descriptions one is made aware of a continual background process of dissolution and erosion: the endless rains, the turbulent rivers, the changing sea, the heavy clouds, the penetrating fog, all make this particular part of America seem like a dream world of endless decay, on which man can never hope to leave any 'permanent mark'. It is a lush and fecund land, but it is also a land 'permeated with dying'. The slow death by drowning of a man trapped in a rising river, described in very poignant detail, serves to focus the more general dread of obliteration, and the absolute certainty of it, which permeates the lives of all who live there. The ubiquitous sense of all things flowing steadily away is responsible for the underlying fear which pervades the community in Kesey's account.

Since logging is the livelihood of the community, some contact with this awesomely flowing nature is inevitable. But there are degrees of removal. Lee Stamper has gone east to study at a university, and has become a neurotic intellectual (much of the plot is concerned with what happens when he returns to Oregon). The union official, Draeger, is a man who believes he has reality neatly contained in his own system of definitions and maxims. He lives in the 'dream of a labeled world', and operates in a verbal world of disputes between workers and management. Hank has little time for this world and prefers to be out in the forests doing the actual cutting. He does not sentimentalize nature. It is something which has to be fought, and fought with machines too. But the direct encounter with nature provides an experience of reality which cannot be had in the protective structures of society. Hank is another American who prefers to move out to the edge. ' "It's the part of the show I like best, this edge, where the cutting stops and the forest starts." ' He likes to get to that point at which the contact with untouched nature has to be resumed. It is shown that life in this area can be very dangerous; but at least it is pure. One is beyond categories and, somehow, into the thing itself. In this connection the location of the Stamper house is very suggestive. It stands nearest to the threatening and ever-widening river from which all the other inhabitants have moved back for fear of being washed away. For all its exposed position, it has nevertheless preserved its identity longer than the other houses — 'a two-storey monument of wood and obstinacy that has neither retreated from the creep of erosion nor surrendered to the terrible pull of the river.' This suggests that perilous point, somewhere between the social edifice (to which the population has 'retreated') and the unselving flow of elemental natural forces, which so many recent American authors and their heroes seem to be seeking. Right at the edge, but not over it. Mailer's parapet makes an obvious comparison.

As a study of a certain mode of heroic individualism the book has surprising power and authority; but it is another aspect of the book which I want to touch on here. The book is framed by an encounter between Draeger and Viv in a bus depot. Draeger has come to ask her to explain her husband Hank to him. She in turn refers him to a photograph album she has with her, covering the family history of the Stampers. At the end Viv gets on a bus, leaving behind the photographs as she is leaving Hank and Lee and the whole area. Throughout this meeting it is raining very heavily. This juxtaposition of the photographs and the rain seems to me to point to a more profound tension in the book between fixed images and flowing forces. At bottom Kesey's novel is a meditation on themes implicit in this conjunction.

Photography can be seen as an activity which treats people as objects, a substitute for conducting a living relationship. In the novels considered in the course of this study there are many figures who find it easier to photograph other people than to try to establish relationships with them. The last words of Malamud's *A New Life* are ' "Got your picture!" ' – the revealing cry of the impotent Gilley who can now only take photographs. As we have seen, the dread of being involved in some imposed film version of reality is pervasive. Photographs and films catch and 'fix' the individual, disregarding the full dimensions of his living uniqueness. This brings me back to Kesey's novel, and Viv, whose name, like her temperament, suggests just the mysterious quality of 'life' itself.

Both Hank and Lee in their differing ways 'love' Viv; at the same time Kesey makes it clear that each tries to impose his own version of her. From the start of their marriage Hank has told her how to cut her hair, what to wear, how to behave, turning her into his idea of a mate without wondering what was going on inside her. Lee's love seems to be more sympathetic and sensitive, but he gives himself away when he asks to be allowed to take away a photograph of her which is, we learn later, an early photograph of his own mother. The implication is that he has never seen the real Viv, but only the image he has projected on to her. Thus in differing ways, Viv has been made to fit into the brothers' reality pictures, while her own reality has remained unperceived and thus unloved. This is not depicted as cruelty; if anything it is one of the sad results of that loss of ability to recognize and communicate with other people's reality which more than one American novelist has portrayed.

Before she marries Hank, Viv takes one last look in her mirror and kisses her reflection goodbye. The meaning of this gesture is brought out by one of her later thoughts. 'It means this is the only way we ever see ourselves; looking out ... ' Viv is the one character who has had the ability to move beyond narcissism and look *out* at other people and really see them, and their needs, and this is the only way that true vision — of self and others — can be reached. In some ways, Hank and Lee are still operating within the images they project. It is appropriate that at the end Viv leaves both brothers, for despite the generosity of her love she cannot devote her whole self simply to being what other people need her to be. She gets on the bus simply to move on, with no destination in mind. It is a bid to escape from the images that have been imposed on her, and leave the photographs behind. Almost her last words are — ' "I'm just going." ' Just so, life itself flows away despite all attempts to hold it.

Photographs are like art and human identity in the one respect that they offer a temporary extrapolation from the flow, a holding of some fragment of the flux of nature in fixed outlines. A novelist has to work with outlines, and Kesey's own novel is the verbal equivalent of a family album. At the same time, the timeless ongoing truth of nature's flow must not be forgotten, and Kesey does what he can to remind us of it: 'the Scenes Gone By and the Scenes to Come flow blending together in the sea-green deep while Now spreads in circles on the surface.' This is what lies behind the narrative strategy of the book which involves a dissolving of chronological time so that past and future events swim into each other, and during the fictional present we move without transitions from place to place, person to person. The intention seems to be to achieve the illusion of temporal and spatial simultaneity in which 'everything is at once'. (As in his first novel, it is possible that Kesey drew on LSD-induced sensations for his narrative strategy.)

The novel suggests that although human perception necessarily deals with particular configurations of reality, we must beware of identifying these temporary arrangements and fixities with the 'whole Truth' — whether we are thinking of reality arrested in photographs or arranged in verbal conceptual systems. We must always be willing to look round the edge of the fixed image to the flow behind it. We must also be aware, as Viv is, that, *'There are bigger forces ... I don't know what they are but they got ours whipped sometimes.'* One chapter has as a heading a little story about a squirrel who lived in a davenport. He knew the inside so well that he could always avoid being sat on. However, the outside got worn out and it was covered with a red blanket. This confused him and undermined all his certainties about the inside. Instead of trying to incorporate this blanket 'into the scheme of his world', he moved to a drainpipe and was drowned in the next fall of rain—'probably still blaming that blanket: damn this world that just won't hold still for us!' It is a neat reminder that we must keep our schemes of reality flexible so that they can be expanded to incorporate any new phenomenon which the outside world may present. Our notions are only our notions, while the flow is more than we can ever know.

Having depicted two fictional heroes who created themselves on the lines of the available archetypes to be found in cartoons and other such repositories of the more vital popular mythologies, Kesey took a step further. His third hero was Ken Kesey. He moved beyond literature into life, and acted out the kind of fantasies he had previously only described. At this point let me summarize one of the basic themes encountered in the American writing considered in this study. We have found a pervasive fear of control and all suspected methods of conditioning; these can range from the brutal manipulative adjustments administered by Big Nurse to the subtler control of consciousness which is exerted over the individual by the social relationships he has to negotiate, the concepts he is taught to think with, the language he is forced to employ. Because he is uncertain of the sources of power, the American hero is as fascinated with it as he is paranoid about its modes of operation. Related to all this is a feeling that we live inside externally imposed versions of reality, somehow cut off from reality itself. We are trapped in roles that have been forced upon us, we are fixed in a falsifying social structure, we are caught up in a vast movie which some unnamed power insists is reality. There is a strong desire to step out of all this into some kind of free space; at the same time, it is not certain what would happen to the individual if he did manage to break out of all these versions, roles, structures. We have found another pervasive dread of ceasing to have an identity and flowing into something as shapeless as protoplasm, jelly or mud. It has been a constant preoccupation among the writers we have examined to see whether some third area can be found, beyond conditioning but not so far into the flux as to mean the end of the individual altogether. All these issues have been confronted by Kesey, partially in the fictions he wrote, but even more in the fiction that he lived. To see how this is so we have now to turn to Tom Wolfe's chronicle of the experiments of Kesey and his friends, the Pranksters,—*The Electric Kool-Aid Acid Test*.

Three of the key words that recur in Wolfe's account of the

adventures of Kesey and the Pranksters are 'games', 'movies' and 'flow'. In Kesey's view, people are always trying to get you into their game or their movie. We have seen how writers as various as Burroughs and Bellow share this idea that other people are always trying to recruit you to their version of what is real; and that apparent reality is only a film has been a recurring proposition. Kesey and the Pranksters explored the implications of this idea and lived out their reactions to it. In their eyes, most people, 'are involved, trapped, in games they aren't even aware of', taking part in other people's movies. For instance, when Kesey was in jail he listened to the prisoners talking, and he says that he realized that ' "it isn't their language, it's the guards', the cops', the D.A.'s, the judge's." ' When you speak someone else's language you are in their movie, playing their game. Kesey was out to resist this. For instance, when he was asked to speak at a Vietnam War Protest he noticed that one of the speakers looked exactly like Mussolini and realized that the pro-testors were in fact using the language of the military. ' "You're playing their game," ' he declared, and, refusing to participate in the dominant rhetoric, played 'Home on the Range' on an old har-monica, introducing deliberate incongruence into the protest 'movie'. A similar motive was behind a lot of the Pranksters' 'pranking'. It became their delight temporarily to foul up other people's movies—hence their far-out clothes, their multi-coloured bus, and their weird antics on the roof of it. As they drove down a suburban street they shocked people because they were not assimil-able into the suburban movie. Kesey knew very well how upset people can become when their reality picture is disturbed, but he acted on the assumption that such a disturbance is beneficial. Another of their words was 'fantasy'. Everybody lives in some kind of fantasy; where a lot of those fantasies coincide there is an agreement to identify the fantasy as reality. To avoid the danger of getting drawn into other people's fantasies Kesey and his followers decided it was essential to create fantasies of their own, just as they played their own games, made their own movies, and created their own roles. This was one of the motives behind all the dressing up they went in for. Choose your fantasy. Kesey in particular could 'rise up from out of the comic books' and become Captain Flag, Captain America, Captain Marvel: when the police were moving in on him he countered by acting the role of Pimpernel. The group fantasy was that they could all be 'Superheroes'.

By driving round America taking an endless movie of everything, as Kesey and the Pranksters did, they were making a gesture of putting America into *their* movie before the more usual reverse process

happened. And because they had room for everything in their movie —
their aim was total unselective assimilation — they were less vulnerable
than the ordinary citizens who live in a rather narrow movie with a great
deal framed out. Later they delighted in drawing other groups — the
Hell's Angels, a Unitarian Church conference — out of their own particular movie and into the Prankster movie. At one point near the end
they felt they had 'got the whole town into their movie by now, cops
and all'. There are indications in this of the possibility of delusions of
grandeur and somewhat megalomaniac dreams of total power. At
the same time we may remember Blake, who built his own system so
that he wouldn't be imprisoned in any other man's.

But clearly there is room for a further step. It is possible to become
trapped in your own movie: the very metaphor is bound to engender
dreams of getting beyond movies altogether. This occurred to Kesey.
He gave his followers a talk on the time lag between perception and
reaction. ' "The present we know is only a movie of the past, and we
will never be able to control the present through ordinary means.
That lag has to be overcome some other way, through some kind of
total breakthrough." ' In seeking for the absolute NOW, the pure
present, Kesey is re-activating a strangely persistent American
aspiration, articulated by writers from Emerson to Norman Mailer.
It is this desire to pass beyond *all* structurings of reality (including
your own movie, though that is preferable to anyone else's) into
reality itself — sheer unmediated participation — which is behind the
LSD experiments Kesey made. LSD gave hints of that breakthrough:
it opened the mind to a world which 'existed only in the moment
itself — *Now!*', a world which consciousness coincided with exactly,
so that subjective and objective ceased to have much meaning. In the
view of Kesey and the Pranksters it was important not to try to
structure and programme the LSD experience — hence their emphasis
on spontaneity, play, improvization: any attempt to plan, or write a
script, 'locked you out of the moment, back in the world of conditioning'. It is quite common to come across the paradox of the writer
who is suspicious of all plots and patterns nevertheless having to plot
and pattern his own novel. Kesey has attempted to explore just how
far beyond planning, composition, orchestration — in a word,
structure — one can go, leaving novel-writing behind and moving
out of all movies and into the flow.

'Go with the flow.' This is one of the key Prankster slogans which
recurs throughout Wolfe's account. It is hardly necessary at this stage
to point out how often the notion of 'flow' has occurred, in novels as
various as *Cabot Wright Begins, Herzog, Slaughterhouse-Five, Sometimes a Great Notion*, and many more. And of course the feeling for

the tidal flow of nature is very deeply rooted in American literature. It is, for instance, ubiquitous in the work of Whitman in which everything is part of an oceanic flow. When the poet looks at the world, says Emerson, he sees 'the flowing or Metamorphosis'. 'The Universe is fluid and volatile'; 'this surface on which we now stand is not fixed but sliding' — such statements by Emerson could be easily supplemented by assertions from other Transcendentalists, and American writers in general have shown less sense of the solidity of the social edifice than European writers, and more sense of some underlying flow. (The music of Charles Ives seems to exemplify this feeling, for there is often an unbroken background stream of sound which flows on, quietly and imperceptibly modulating, while more assertive and distinct foreground noises come and go.) Even Henry James's habitually socialized characters often find themselves, through metaphor, in flowing waters. Whether a writer feels that one should try to go with the flow or hold back from it will obviously depend on his whole world view.

For Kesey the idea of going with the flow expresses, on one level, the fairly traditional longing to escape the imprisoning, limiting structures of society which screen out so much of reality: 'transcending the bullshit' as one of his followers concisely puts it. It also points to the attempt to get out of the subtler entrapments of language. Kesey is quoted as saying that writers are 'trapped in syntax' and artificial rules; more generally it appears that he saw people increasingly living in language as a kind of shadowy substitute for life, distracted by any number of symbols from the thing itself. It is a central belief of the Pranksters that the most important aspects of their experience cannot be labelled. Hence some of their speech habits; for instance the indiscriminate use of 'thing' to refer to anything at all — a return to deliberate imprecision as if to counter the illusion of definitions and distinctions which language propagates.

The flow, then, is all that reality which is felt to lie on the other side of the screens and networks of society and language. There are at least two very different attitudes which can be taken towards this notional flow. The loss of all distinction and differentiation involved in the flow could be a stage in that entropic process which will one day bring life to one great level lake of sameness. It can be the ultimate nightmare, as for instance in the work of Pynchon. But the attainment of such a state from a more Eastern point of view might be called nirvana, that final state of universal quietude which is the goal of existence and which *also* betokens the end of all distinction, differentiation, individuation. So far from being a nightmare this is felt to promise the ultimate bliss. Embarking on the path of spiritual progress which leads to a comprehension of the abiding reality of nirvana, and which transforms 'common people' into 'Saints' is known as 'Entrance into the stream'.[3] The path being explored by Kesey and the Pranksters was intended to turn ordinary American youths into 'Superheroes', and their cry was, 'Go with the flow.' Kesey specifically ruled out any ideas of adopting Buddhist tenets and attitudes; this is where he differs completely from Timothy Leary whom Kesey sees as avoiding the real American present and facing the past. Nevertheless one feels that Kesey's wild bus was headed more for nirvana than Entropyville. It was intended as a joyous ride, and Kesey and his friends aimed to go with 'the whole goddam flow of America', assimilating and 'grooving' with everything, finding everything instantly significant without the interpretative super-structures offered by books or theologies. That this may indeed be too much for some people is indicated in the fate of one mentally unstable girl who broke down while they were making their trip around America. Tom Wolfe's summary is appropriately ominous. 'She had gone with the flow. She had gone stark raving mad.'

There was also a more metaphysical aspect to the flow for Kesey and the Pranksters. They accepted that man may well be caught up in some vast pattern far beyond his power to alter or resist. 'But one could *see* the larger pattern and move with it — *Go with the flow!* — and accept it and rise above one's immediate environment and even alter it by accepting the larger pattern and grooving with it.' Kesey certainly has that common American sense of being controlled. 'We're under cosmic control and have been for a long long time ... And then you find out ... about Cosmo, and you discover he's running the show ... ' Obviously for some people Cosmo might be God or the Devil, as in the work of Mailer. For Kesey he seems to be some sort of Nietzschean power, beyond good and evil, some Shavian life-force. His image for the relation of the individual to Cosmo is a cable containing many intertwined strands of wire; the wires are the individuals, Cosmo vibrates all of them. If you cut across the cable you have the illusion of separately functioning individuals; but if anyone can break through and grasp the total pattern, and tune into it, and go with it, then the power of the whole cable passes through him; more than that, such a person will be able to start to control the flow, or at least wield it and divert its force.

Such a notion could lead to extreme fantasies of power and manipulation. Part of the honesty of Wolfe's book is the way it records a growing feeling that Kesey became obsessed with control, with playing power games, with organizing other people's trips. Some people later came to regard him as a sort of Elmer Gantry, even as a leader with distinct fascist tendencies. Obviously he had the charisma for such a role. However, it could be argued that his interest in control was based on the recognition that the more we can become aware of the forces operating on and through us, the more chance we might have to exert some control over our lives. Kesey's desire to grasp the pattern behind all patterns is in fact very American. Cosmo is the 'main party' which a superhero must try to deal with. (One corollary of believing in Cosmo is that if one's wonder turned to fear it could become a fear of vast proportions. Kesey's paranoia when he was on the run in Mexico was clearly on a cosmic scale. Perhaps a superhero is never far from feeling himself a supervictim. Arguably it might be out of a deep basic paranoia that the need to believe one can control the controller first arises.)

Trying to put the Kesey phenomenon in a larger context, Wolfe points to the visionary experiences recorded by various religious leaders, sect-founders and mystics. In many cases they are similar to the experience described by Kesey on LSD, the barriers between ego and non-ego vanishing, consciousness and environment starting to merge, self and world starting to flow together in a way which releases an intense feeling of enhanced powers. One significant aspect of this is the desire to get beyond individuality, as if personal identity were another of those false structures that have to be left behind if the breakthrough is to be made. Again there are precedents for this feeling in American literature. Emerson's comment on the poet's attraction to all kinds of narcotics, for instance, seems uncannily appropriate. 'These are auxiliaries to the centrifugal tendency of a man, to his passage out into free space, and they help him to escape the custody of that body in which he is pent up, and of that jail-yard of individual relations in which he is enclosed.' And Whitman clearly felt that identity and even individual physiognomy were distractions to be discarded. (See for instance the poem 'To You' which starts:

Whoever you are, I fear you are walking the walks of dreams,
I fear these supposed realities are to melt from under
                                    your feet and hands,
Even now your features, joys, speech, house, trade, manners,
   troubles, follies, costume, crimes, dissipate away from you,
Your true soul and body appear before me ...)

There are also many precedents for this feeling in Buddhism in which the annihilation of individual identity and the voiding of all sense of ego are the objects of prolonged exercises. 'Self' is a fiction which has to be expunged. Now in most contemporary American fiction we find a desperate desire to achieve and protect an individual identity against whatever forces might threaten to dissolve it away; *not* to have or be an authentic self is the great dread for the majority of writers and their heroes. Once again Kesey seems to have turned towards a more Eastern or Transcendentalist mode of vision. At the same time the very active immersion of the Pranksters *into* the material here and now is very different from the passive renunciation of the passing show which is the ideal of the Buddhist. And, as it appears from Wolfe's account, no less important than the merging of 'I' into 'it', was the merging of 'I' into 'we'.

It is quite clear that Kesey and the Pranksters came to feel themselves to be in some ways a group consciousness, 'all one brain'. 'Intersubjectivity' (or 'combinations of mutual consciousness') was cultivated; for instance by 'rapping' which is a group monologue sustained by free associations, not unlike jazz improvisation. The 'all-in-one' feeling became very important and Kesey's statement that, ' "You're either on the bus ... or off the bus," ' refers, among other things, to the fact that the individual had to sink his individuality into the group experiment if he was to stay with them wherever they were going. Anyone drawing back into the protective and defensive armature of his own precious individuality, with all the anxiety and suspicion and guardedness that usually entails, was by definition off the bus. He would have cut himself off from the group consciousness, the 'all-one'. We can find in Edward Conze's description of the Buddhist exercises which consist of 'reducing the boundary lines between oneself and other people',[4] a relevant parallel to what the Pranksters were practising. But once again it would be wrong to detect a specifically religious dimension to Kesey's idea of group consciousness. Although Wolfe describes the vaguely religious atmosphere which was generated by the group, it is clear that Kesey specifically wanted to avoid any programming in the orthodox sense: there were to be no systematic steps of initiation, no laid-down lines of spiritual progress, no body of secret lore gradually to be learned, no fixed rituals, no fore-ordained definition of the state of enlightenment and faith to be achieved. All that was connected with old movies, as it were, behaviour patterns of past religions. Kesey's bus was simply aimed forward, bearing the one-word creed 'FURTHUR' [*sic*], into the absolute now. The only programme was to see how far they could get 'into the pudding'. The light-hearted inadequacy of just such phrases was itself symptomatic of their determination to leave behind the more portentous terminologies of previous religions as they set out to explore a world of new perceptions, new relations. They were to be pranksters, not monks.

Wolfe mentions three books that were of particular interest to Kesey and the Pranksters, and in connection with this desire to leave individual identity behind they have some interesting notions in common. Herman Hesse's *Journey to the East* is about a communal pilgrimage towards the East, the symbolic location of the home of light, everything that the human spirit and imagination have yearned to reach. The narrator describes how, after their leader vanished, the pilgrimage disintegrated and he returned to a prosaic bourgeois life devoid of spiritual aspiration. He subsequently discovers that the pilgrimage did not disintegrate; rather *he* lost faith and so automatically isolated himself from the true questers. In a word, he got off the bus. At the end he is restored into the mysterious sect which maintains the pilgrimage and is received by the lost leader, Leo. One condition of his reacceptance is that he must go and see what the sect's archives say about him. Coming to his name he draws a curtain and sees no words but only a model of two figures joined at the back. Inspecting them he sees that one face is his own in a state of decay and diminution, while the other is that of Leo, strong and radiant. Looking closer he sees that inside the figures there is a 'continuous flowing or melting ... something melted or poured across from my image to that of Leo's.' At the end the narrator lies down and goes to sleep and one feels that his essence has passed into Leo, into the sect; the individual body has been left behind for a larger spiritual existence – the artist has passed into his own work of art. Hesse's novel has many meanings and implications which are not relevant here. The important image is that of the individual fading and merging into something larger, a leader, a corporate group, a visionary pilgrimage.

Turning to the two science-fiction novels favoured by the Pranksters we can find some comparable images. Robert Heinlein's *Stranger in a Strange Land* (1961) has enjoyed an increase in popularity on the West Coast in recent years. It concerns one Mike Smith, a human who was brought up on Mars, and thus initiated into a non-earthly way of regarding reality, gaining at the same time supra-human powers. On returning to Earth he starts a new religion based on more Martian attitudes, a good deal more hedonistic and pacific than most earthly religions. At the end he is torn to pieces by outraged humans: crucified, no doubt Heinlein means us to feel. In our present context the most interesting aspect of this somewhat turgid book is one of the Martian practices that Smith introduces to his human followers. It is called 'grokking' and it is the basis of his new religion. One explanatory gloss is this: 'the mutually merging rapport – the grokking – that should exist between water brothers'.

A more detailed explanation is given by the expert on Martian affairs, Mahmoud. ' " 'Grok' means 'identically equal'. 'Grok' means to understand so thoroughly that the observer becomes a part of the observed – to merge, blend, intermarry, lose identity in group experience." ' 'Grokking' and 'going with the flow' have much in common; the Pranksters adopted the term and Kesey clearly has the charisma to be a leader such as Mike Smith (or Leo).

Arthur Clarke's *Childhood's End* has possibly been even more influential. This is a novel about the end of the world – due not to some humanly caused catastrophe, but because the human race achieves a total breakthrough into pure mind. It happens to all the children under ten, who suddenly cease to be individuals and become a vast group mind endowed with extraordinary powers. Jan, the last man on Earth and spectator of its final hours, watches the children; 'their faces were merging into a common mold.' One of the Overlords (strange creatures from another planet who serve the Overmind) explains that ' "possibly what we have called the Overmind is still training them, molding them into one unit before it can wholly absorb them into its being." ' As an early test of their powers the children strip a landscape bare by a communal act of mental will, a foreshadowing of how they will later return the Earth into Non-Being. Jan watches these last moments, giving an account for the benefit of the Overlords who have withdrawn to their own planet.

'Something's starting to happen. The stars are becoming dimmer ... There's a great burning column, like a tree of fire, reaching above the western horizon. It's a long way off, right round the world. I know where it springs from: they're on their way at last, to become part of the Overmind. Their probation is ended: they're leaving the last remnants of matter behind.'

The notion of the Overmind is distinctly Shavian, to go no further back, and it is appropriate that Clarke should refer to *Back to Methuselah* in the course of his book. For there too it is indicated in Lilith's final speech that matter is the encumbering junk which will have to be left behind so that 'life' can disentangle itself and ' "press on to the goal of redemption from the flesh, to the vortex freed from matter, to the whirlpool of pure intelligence ... " ' What was perhaps of added interest to Kesey was that Clarke's description of the last hours of the Earth reads like an account of the most spectacular light show ever devised, with unbelievable colour combinations and formations following one after the other until the Earth turns transparent and everything starts to dissolve into light. Life on Earth has gone with the cosmic flow, leaving temporary configurations such as human identity and material locations to dissolve behind it. It reads curiously like the ultimate LSD trip.

Some kind of flowing out of self is, then, envisaged in each of these novels, and that is what Kesey and the Pranksters were trying to live out, consciously setting off in 'a fantasy bus in a science fiction movie'. Clearly, just as expanding the mind with LSD might precipitate breakdown in unstable individuals, so also this experiment in group consciousness could interfere seriously with the more orthodox forms of familial relationships. It isn't always clear in Wolfe's account who was minding the children, and no matter how much one might believe in communal mating, instead of hunting in pairs, there are the inevitable risks of unwanted pregnancies and unforeseen jealousies. As Wolfe's account makes clear, there was quite a lot of inter-personal tension as well as inter-subjectivity on the bus. These are some of the risks inevitably incurred in any attempt to leave all the usual forms behind. But, it might still be asked, though it is clear what they were trying to leave behind, just what or where were they trying to reach, once you discount the science-fiction fantasies and metaphors? Kesey and the Pranksters would refuse to define their destination in social, moral or religious terms — indeed, 'terms' were among those things they were leaving behind. Perhaps the most explicit thing they would have said was that they were 'heading out toward ... Edge City', a recurring phrase in their group monologue.

Since it was part of the fantasy they were living out that they should move beyond language, one risks missing the spirit of the whole enterprise by trying to define it. However, we may tentatively surmise that Edge City is where the movies end and the flow begins, or where definitions and versions give way to the thing itself. It points, perhaps, to a point at which the structurings of society, language, accustomed habits of perception, individual identity, begin to fall away. The old Buddhists used trance to reach what Edward Conze describes as 'a station where there is *neither perception nor non-perception*. Consciousness and self-consciousness are here at the very margin of disappearance.'[5] That could also be called Edge City. But whereas within the structure of the Buddhist religion the achievement of such a station was part of a system of enlightenment and so could be experienced as a meaningful ecstasy, Kesey's Edge City stands at the margin of the very idea of 'structure'. There is no guiding theology or creed, and a look over the edge can be 'scary' as Wolfe's account makes clear. It is one thing to slough off notions of self under the guidance of an ancient religion; it is another thing to get in a wildly coloured bus and drive at top speed towards the perimeters of consciousness with no sense of what may lie beyond. Perhaps it would be bliss, 'Freedomland', that final emancipation from all definitions and limits which we have seen is such an abiding American dream: but perhaps it would be insanity, chaos, a nightmare which could not be controlled. Only men who, like Kesey, believe that 'a man should move off his sure center out into the outer edges' and 'test the limits of life' are likely to find out.

If we regard Edge City as being poised between social identity and dissolution, a sort of third area *between* structure and the flow, then it becomes a place many American heroes have sought to find, since few of them are content to remain within given boundaries. Their movements are habitually centrifugal, and we have had plenty of occasion to observe that a large number of American novels are about one sort of approach or another to some kind of edge. But most American authors conduct this venture to the periphery in their imaginative writings; for them Edge City is to be found in the City of Words. Just so, Kesey *imagined* McMurphy leading the inmates out to their adventurous voyage on the ocean, and wrote a book about it. Kesey's singularity lies in his subsequent attempt to 'move beyond writing' and set out for Edge City in person. (Norman Mailer could perhaps be said to have made an attempt to get beyond writing when he ran for the office of Mayor of New York.) You could regard the multicoloured bus as Kesey's third novel, only this time he was inside it and at the wheel. Some people may find it easier to regard him as a deluded maniac in this undertaking; but there is an attractive courage in his willingness to stake himself on his beliefs, to forego writing and risk an approach to the thing itself.

One important aspect of the Kesey adventure which Wolfe brings out very well is that it is very much connected with the actual clutter and appurtenances of modern American life, particularly in the West where there are fewer reminders of history and the past than there are in the East. The gadgets and clutter, the freeways, pylons, lights, and cars, all the modernity and movement which make up the Californian panorama—these are the important setting for Kesey's experiment in moving to the edge; indeed they are partially the source of it. Where Timothy Leary and his followers felt that they could sink solemnly back into the Indian past, Kesey and his Pranksters felt that they were already soaring into the great circus of the American future. There is a significant split between East and West Coast attitudes in America today, and Wolfe helps to clarify this split by distinguishing between the Buddhist direction and 'the Kesey direction ... *beyond catastrophe* ... like, picking up anything that works and moves, every hot wire, every tube, ray, volt,

decibel, beam, floodlight and combustion of American flag-flying
neon Day-Glo America and winding it up to some mystical extreme
carrying to the western-most edge of experience.'
This direction points to a mysticism arising out of modernity, not
in repudiation of it. In this connection the work of Gary Snyder, the
West Coast poet, is very relevant. He is specifically interested in
Buddhism, but he is seeking for a formulation of it which will
embrace life in contemporary America. In his prose book *Earth
House Hold*[6] he too talks about 'breaking through the ego-barrier'
and getting beyond our usual notions of self and society. One idea in
particular that he takes from archaic beliefs is that 'all teach that
beyond transcendence is Great Play, and Transformation.' The
capitalized words could mean many things, of course, but it might
help to understand part of the Kesey experiment if we see him as
someone who, far from turning his back on modern America,
accepts and relishes its most recent productions and manifestations.
But instead of being trapped among all these proliferating things he
makes them part of a game and turns everything to sport. To follow
the Kesey direction out to the western-most edge should mean
deliverance from the stifling world of conditioned action into a realm
where all is Great Play and Transformation. It does not always work
out this way, and the newspapers keep us plentifully informed of the
horrors which may be connected with taking LSD. Nevertheless,
despite what one may think about the use of LSD, and however one
reacts to the inconclusive, even pathetic conclusion to the whole
Kesey venture (' "WE BLEW IT" ' is his own comment as recorded
by Wolfe), I think one should be aware of the significance of his
journey. There is something in the American spirit which has always
tended to move towards that western-most edge, and in retrospect
it may turn out that Ken Kesey is far from being the least memorable
in a great tradition of pioneers.
Obviously to go right over the edge into the flow would mean
death; the point about Edge City is that it is a place, a state of consciousness, an experience, in which one may learn something new
about the relationship of individual identity to the flow—and from
which one can return, perhaps to tell the tale, perhaps to have the
tale told, as Wolfe tells it about Kesey. At one point in Kurt
Vonnegut's novel, *Player Piano*, the rebel Finnerty explains to the
uncertain conformist Proteus why he has given up his job and why he
refuses to see a psychiatrist. ' "He'd pull me back into the center,
and I want to stay as close to the edge as I can without going over.
Out on the edge you see all kinds of things you can't see from the
center ... Big, undreamed-of things—the people on the edge see them

first." ' It was in a similar spirit, perhaps, that the Pranksters put up a large sign reading HAIL TO ALL EDGES, and so many American heroes in the books we have considered have sought out their own particular edge.

Kesey believes that 'our concept of reality is changing' and that a new generation is coming along which will take up different attitudes to life, adopt different priorities and values. Just what these will amount to he can hardly say, just as it is not clear what he envisaged by the idea of going beyond acid and graduating from the 'Garden of Eden' to which acid opens the door. But by aiming to live at the edge he identifies himself as one of those who hope to see more things, and see them first. The garb in which he made his move to the edge may seem strange, or merely eccentric; necessarily any bid to move out of familiar patterns must take an unfamiliar form, and not even Kesey can predict where his own direction will take him. One possibility is that literature and the values of clear utterance would be left behind and one may well feel that such a tendency should be resisted. The attempt to depart from the City of Words once and for all could involve unforeseen deprivations and might well lead to a notable impoverishment of consciousness. Be that as it may, for anyone interested in trying to appreciate what was going on in both American literature and society in the late 'sixties, Kesey is a figure who has to be understood and, it seems to me, respected. Whatever one's verdict on the final value of Kesey's work and example, that sign put up by his Pranksters is a reminder once again of the relevance and truth of Browning's words — 'Our interest's on the dangerous edge of things.'

Conclusion

By way of a Conclusion I wish to say a little about an unusual novel written at the beginning of this period, and then go on to consider some of the work of two young writers who have come into prominence at the end of the 'sixties. The juxtaposition may, I hope, serve to recapitulate some of the main themes of the book and suggest how some of the more recent American writers are reacting to the problems which have been explored by their seniors. The notion that the ordinary individual and the artist alike may be living their lives within an intricate system or pattern of fictions, and the related search for some recognition of non-fictional reality, form a recurrent American theme which no one has explored at greater length than William Gaddis in his novel *The Recognitions*. This amazing one-thousand-page work was written during the late 'forties and early 'fifties (finally published in 1955), and it could be taken as inaugurating a new period of American fiction in which the theme of fictions/recognitions has come to occupy the forefront of the American writer's consciousness. After considering some aspects of this book, I will look at the ways in which Donald Barthelme and Richard Brautigan react to the patterned condition of modern life which has been so variously written about in the last two decades. In the hope that this will convey in a condensed form how American fiction has moved, and is moving, I will conclude with some remarks of my own.

Recognitions

William Gaddis's book remains very underrated.* I am not suggesting that it had a direct influence on many writers of the period (with the possible exception of Thomas Pynchon, whose *V.* seems to me to owe quite a lot to Gaddis); but, while the book in many ways looks back to older writers such as Joyce and Hawthorne, it probes into so many ideas and states of mind and stylistic possibilities which

* The critical neglect of this book is really extraordinary. I know of only one article published on it during the last ten years. This is an excellent piece by Bernard Benstock entitled 'On William Gaddis: In Recognition of James Joyce' (*Wisconsin Studies in Contemporary Literature*, vi, 1965). I suppose Gaddis might have appreciated the irony of this lack of recognition. But the book is immensely rich and funny, and it certainly deserves much more attention.

are peculiarly relevant to the decades which followed it, that it seems surprising more notice was not taken of it. Perhaps one incidental reason is that the book bears the marks of post-war expatriation and prolonged European experience. More recent American writers may indeed be living in exile, but they are exiled within America.

Gaddis takes as his subject one of the oldest aesthetic problems in the world—imitation. The main figure, Wyatt Gwyon, gives up ideas of the priesthood to become an artist, and then gives up attempting to do his own original work to become a fanatical and dedicated copier of Flemish Old Masters. His skill almost inevitably involves him with more mercenary forgers, and the theme of counterfeit creations is explored on all levels. The book is inhabited by every kind of faker and fakery—religious, aesthetic, sexual, social; every sort of fraudulence and façade-making is shown to be at work in the world the book reveals. 'Mask', 'masquerade' and 'reality' are three words which occur in the first sentence, and they form a motif on which variations are to be played for the following one thousand pages. Everybody seems to be questing for something—most of them are susceptible to a fleeting 'sense of something lost'—and we are made aware of the depressing abundance of substitute gratifications put out by modern society: all inadequate of course, the basest kinds of forgery. But 'forgery' is a word which can be extended to cover an almost unlimited number of human activities. Wyatt, an artist of religious seriousness, is the best forger of all; Stanley, a devout composer, wishes to write music like Bach. While Otto, a would-be playwright desperately trying to knock together an original piece of work, is a complete plagiarist who is incapable of moving beyond an absorbing narcissism (he is for ever studying and arranging his image in mirrors). There are innumerable minor figures engaged in their own modes of forgery, and in all this it is scarcely clear where any authentic reality—transcendental or material—is to be found. Wyatt is the central quester, but in attempting to define the relationship of a hero to the other characters in a particular kind of novel, Wyatt defines his own position among the people in *The Recognitions*—'None of them moves, but it reflects him.' And if the best artist is the best forger, what does 'originality' mean?

The artist as counterfeiter is not of course a new notion—Gide, Mann and Joyce all availed themselves of the idea. But Gaddis's hero is a confessed copyist, and so too Gaddis avows his debt to Joyce by some very intricate borrowings or 'copyings' (as described in Bernard Benstock's article). It is as though only through a scrupulous imitation and even parody of the Old Master of modern fiction could Gaddis discover the freedom to register his own personal vision. Like Joyce's Stephen, Wyatt is engaged in a search for his father (human and divine). In fact his intended name was Stephen, but then he was given the name of Wyatt. However, late in the book when he encounters the counterfeiter Sinisterra in Spain, he is given a false Swiss passport bearing the name Stephen Asche. Sinisterra insists on calling him Stephen, and by the end Gaddis also does so. The counterfeit has become the real; Gaddis's 'imitation' of Joyce has resulted in a profoundly 'original' work.

There are clearly opportunities here for an endless recession of uncertainties concerned with reality (?), representations of it (art), copies of the copies (forgery, or ?). Otto tells a story about a man who had a forged Titian painting. When the forgery was scraped away, an original but worthless painting was found underneath. However, under that they found a real Titian which had been there all the time. In a very confused way Otto speculates whether the forger unconsciously knew the original was underneath. Does it mean, more generally, 'that underneath that the original is there, that the real ... thing is there'? Otto's confusion here is of a piece with his confusion as to the source of true art, but more generally it is a kind of confusion the book compounds. Otto himself is spoken of as being 'part of a series of an original that never existed' – a pure fabrication who indeed never manages to find his father. But then, Wyatt gets confused about whether or not a painting he copies is in fact an original, and he experiences a comprehensive dread. 'And if what I've been forging, does not exist?' There are obvious religious implications in all this as well. Thus Gaddis quotes Abraham Lincoln's Treasurer's instruction to the director of the Mint to put on the country's coins a motto expressing the 'national recognition' of 'the trust of our people in God'. What is the status of the coin – and all other value systems dependent on a supreme sanction – when the trust dies away, the recognition fades, and people are left with the suspicion that their signs and images of 'God' may not be based on any original? Wyatt's exclamation of relief when he finds that the picture he copied *was* an original is very much to the point; 'thank God there was the gold to forge!'

The book is really a long religio-aesthetic debate, conducted through the generations of Wyatt's New England family, and across modern America and Europe. This is not the place to analyse it in detail, but some of the ideas about the relationship between recognition and invention are worth examining, in light of the books we have been considering. The word 'recognition' occurs well over twenty times in differing contexts, so it is far from being a simple notion. But there is a growing feeling that a true act of recognition is more profound than any act of invention, and that the greatest achievement of any invention or art work is when it frees you into a recognition of reality. Thus Wyatt, describing his experience on seeing one of Picasso's paintings: 'it was one of those moments of reality, of near-recognition of reality ... When I saw it all of a sudden everything was freed into one recognition, really freed into reality that we never see, you never see it. You don't see it in paintings because most of the time you can't see beyond a painting.' There is a difference, then, between the art which seeks to arrest you within one man's version or fiction, and the art which frees you into true recognition of what is already there. One of Wyatt's sayings, that Otto jots down (to use in his play!), is: 'Orignlty not inventn bt snse of recall, recgntion, pattrns alrdy thr, q.' It is a typical piece of wit that one of the most important ideas behind the whole book should appear in this hurried and clumsy shorthand.

Defending his forgeries, Wyatt maintains that he does much more than simulate a surface likeness: 'the recognitions go much deeper, much further back;' while copying he becomes one with the master painters in ancient Flanders, not only using the same pure materials but re-experiencing the reverence with which they painted. Stanley, the composer who believes more in 'remembering' than 'inventing', has a similar admiration for Bach and some of his great contemporaries, 'for they had touched the origins of design with recognition.' Against these ideas we may set the observation of the perceptive Basil Valentine that, 'Most original people are forced to devote all their time to plagiarizing.' The general feeling seems to be that in their quest for originality, contemporary artists merely synthesize products to vaunt their own egos. Such art works obscure reality. Great art forgets self altogether and contains a recognition of reality. Copying such works to re-experience that recognition may thus become an authentic, selfless mode of access to reality. Gaddis's book keeps returning to the difference between the fictions or fabrications which hinder, and those which facilitate, that recognition of reality which, truly understood, is the most original act of which man is capable.

In all this it is important to remember that Wyatt is an American artist with a New England background. As a child he had felt guilty when he discovered that, when he sketched, 'forms took shape under his pencil' — such an activity was regarded as a potentially blasphemous attempt to recapitulate God's divine ability to create forms out of the void. As an adult that specific guilt is left behind, but his reverence is now directed to the creative acts of the Old Masters. Guilt feelings of blasphemy have been replaced by a sense of the egotistical futility of trying to add to their primal acts of recognition. In taking this theme of the American artist as copyist, Gaddis is specifically relating himself, not only to modern masters of the novel such as Joyce, but to the first great American novelist, Hawthorne. I will run together some of the statements about the New England girl Hilda from Chapter Six of Hawthorne's *The Marble Faun*. They concern the change in her paintings after she comes to Italy.

> Had Hilda remained in her own country, it is not improbable that she might have produced original works ... since her arrival in the pictorial land, Hilda seemed to have entirely lost the impulse of original design which brought her thither. No doubt the girl's early dreams had been of sending forms and hues of beauty into the visible world out of her own mind ... But more and more, as she grew familiar with the miracles of art that enrich so many galleries in Rome, Hilda had ceased to consider herself as an original artist ... the world seemed already rich enough in original designs ... *So Hilda became a copyist* ... Her copies were indeed marvellous ... she wrought religiously, and therefore wrought a miracle. It strikes us that there is something far higher and nobler in all this, in her thus sacrificing herself to the devout *recognition* of the highest excellence in art, than there would have been in cultivating her not inconsiderable share of talent for the production of works from her own ideas. [My italics.]

Here is Gaddis's central theme and even, indeed, his title. (It is worth noting that Chapter Three of *The Scarlet Letter* is entitled 'The Recognition'.) Gaddis too became a copyist, and I am sure he would want us to recognize his own respectful acts of recognition of previous masters. And having read his book twice I would be prepared to affirm that Gaddis, too, 'wrought religiously'.

It is, I think, because Wyatt/Stephen is an American artist that he seems to envisage a further step in his pilgrimage towards reality. Notions of originality give way to copying; by the end this in turn seems as though it is giving way to a desire to get beyond art and artefacts altogether. The last episode concerning Stephen (as he is by now called) takes place in a Spanish monastery where he is staying as a sort of penitent. The monastery is visited by an hilariously phoney American novelist called Ludy, in search of original material and a religious experience. One day he comes across Stephen carefully scraping the paint off one of the great old monastery paintings. Appalled, Ludy asks if he is 'restoring' the paintings, and Stephen ironically agrees that he is. It is quite possible that we are meant to

feel that Stephen is living in a mental world all his own by now –
alcoholism, inanition and a series of extraordinary adventures having taken their toll. Nevertheless I think there are enough signs in
this final episode to indicate that he is pushing on to a more comprehensive idea of restoration – namely, the restoring of reality to itself,
symbolized by his erasing of the interpositions of art, and all the
filterings and fixities which a work of art involves. Previously, before
he left America, he had in fact withdrawn or ruined his forgeries.
Valentine's mocking question – 'Why this sudden attempt to set the
whole world right, by recalling your own falsifications in it?' – has
more truth in it than he realizes. Now, it seems, Stephen is taking the
next step and making a gesture of 'recalling' the 'falsifications' of even
the greatest artists.

I think this next step has implications which go beyond the idea of
erasing artistic fabrications. In his far from coherent mutterings to
Ludy while engaged on his 'restoration' work, Stephen offers a
fragmentary critique of certain kinds of painting which he has
previously copied.

> Separateness, that's what went wrong ... Everything withholding
> itself from everything else ... painters ... cluttering up every
> space with detail everything vain and separate affirming itself for
> fear that ... fear of leaving any space for transition, for forms to
> ... to share with each other ... in the Middle Ages when every-
> thing was in pieces and gilding the pieces, yes to insure their
> separation for fear there was no God ... Everything vain,
> asserting itself ...

At which point Stephen breaks off to eat another of the small
loaves which he has by him. Now, as it happens, his father had left
instructions that his ashes should be sent to this Spanish monastery
after he had been cremated. Due to certain linguistic incapacities the
monks thought the ashes were some kind of wheat germ so they
mixed them in with the next lot of bread they baked. It is this bread
which Stephen is eating, so, in the most engagingly macabre joke in
an exceedingly witty book, Stephen is engaged in eating his own
father. The name on the forged passport, Stephen Asche, could hardly
have been more appropriate! Stephen has finally found his father
and father and son are now consubstantial, albeit unwittingly. No
doubt a religious joke is also implied. But the joke is connected to a
more serious idea, touched on in Stephen's mutterings.

Gaddis shows a world in which people cling to their own separateness, sharing only one thing, 'the fear of belonging to one another'.
People 'exchange forgeries of what the heart dare not surrender',

hence the proliferation of counterfeit images and tokens on every
level. As a man imprisoned for forgery comes to realize, although
'counterfeiting and forging aren't crimes of violence ... they sort of
mean something's wrong somewhere.' What is wrong is the widespread anxious holding on to the apartness of single identity. The
prevailing narcissism indicated by the wealth of mirror-gazing which
goes on in the book reveals a world of people who find it all but
impossible to transcend their preoccupation with self. 'How little of
us ever meets how little of another,' writes one character. Stephen's
last words as he sets out again to continue his quest are revealing in
this context. Ludy is trying to engage him in conversation and says
at one point – 'You and I ... '. Stephen cuts him off. 'No, there's no
more you and I,' and, his very last words, 'Yes, we'll simplify. Hear?'
It suggests that he is going to try to move on to a state beyond
separate identities, as well as beyond the separations of art. He has,
indeed, already started to merge with his father, which suggests not
only a confluence of separate generations but a running together of
those primal divisive categories – life and death.

The girl Esme, who models for Wyatt and is intimately connected
to him, experiences a parallel longing. She likes to write a very personal kind of poetry, but she finds that the available words are in a
state of chaos because they have been debased by constant use in
inane contexts. She tries to move through this 'accumulation of
chaos' because beyond it is perfect simplicity, and originality will
not exist 'because it was origin'. She rebels against the 'damned
accumulations' that bind her in time, and dreams of losing 'the
aggregate of meannesses which compose identity'. Her method is
drugs, which take her into another world which is the 'uncircumscribed, infinitely extended' void, a vastness in which she can soar in
an orgasm of liberation. The words are almost Emersonian, and the
desire – to get beyond language, accumulation, identity itself – is profoundly American, as I have tried to show in the course of this
book.

Related to this is a recurring intimation of the ephemerality of all
kinds of structure. There is an entropic sense of things wearing out,
running down, losing definition and shape. There is, too, an increasing sense of the insubstantiality of the life most of the characters are
living. One minor artist-forger covers a copy of The Idiot to pretend
it is a book by him. When he is exposed he takes consolation by
reading over the last paragraph. ' "And all this, all this life abroad,
and this Europe of yours is all a fantasy, and all of us abroad are
only a fantasy ... " ' These words, coming close to the end of
Gaddis's book, extend back over the whole panorama he has

evoked. In the very last paragraph, Stanley, who has at last completed his composition, comes to a small Italian church to play it on the organ there. The reverberations from the first bass notes he strikes bring the ancient walls crashing down on top of him. It is, in little, as though the structures and façades erected by European art and society and religion have finally collapsed, leaving a silence beyond structuring which William Gaddis himself has not since broken.

If that prefigures the end of all fictions it might be thought to betoken a welcome return to reality. But Stanley himself has had a recognition of the nature of reality as he watched the sea while travelling to Europe: 'Romantic? this heaving senseless actuality? alive? evil? symbolical? ... Boundlessly neither yes or no, good nor evil, hope nor fear, pretending to all these things in the eyes that first beheld it, but unchanged since then, still its own color, heaving with the indifferent hunger of all actuality.' If one does somehow step beyond all systems, fictions, 'forgeries', will it be to merge with the indifferent actuality of the sea, to vanish into that meaningless blank which Melville saw epitomized in the featureless front of Moby Dick? The residual suggestion that the ultimate act of recognition may in fact be death gives a sombre tone to the conclusion of Gaddis's remarkable work. We may recall Borges's reminder that man is sustained by his fictions. Nevertheless, the problems Gaddis raises and the themes he explores seem to me to be at the heart of American literature, and in looking back to Hawthorne while it looks forward to Pynchon, his novel reminds us of continuities which we might otherwise, perhaps, overlook.

Fragments and Fantasies

The 'damned accumulations' only increase over the years. With things and words tending rapidly to proliferate in quantity and diminish in value and meaning, the contemporary writer will be increasingly disinclined to follow the old ways of arranging them. He will move among them warily, looking for new grammars, new semantics. 'Fragments are the only forms I trust,' writes Donald Barthelme, turning the suspicion of conventional patternings into an aesthetic principle. A fragmentary form is an open-ended one that is amenable to the disarrangings and rearrangings of fantasy and, as such, offers Barthelme a way of countering the conditioning forces and expressing his distrust of the 'finished' objects all around him. His writing may be compared to the Watts Towers in Los Angeles. Items of contemporary detritus are extracted from their habitual contexts or heaps and assembled in such a way that improbable

fairy towers arise from the melancholy desolation of the surrounding
trash-strewn urban landscape. Through the resourceful rearranging
of the artist, waste is transformed to magic, environment is redeemed
by play. At the same time Barthelme's work often reveals a distinct
dread of environment and conveys a disquieting unease. It is this
combination of play and dread which makes his odd personal
fantasies seem so appropriate to contemporary America.

In the last story of Barthelme's first book, *Come Back, Dr. Caligari*
(1964), a man appears on a TV programme which pays people to
recount their personal experiences. He starts off, '"My mother was a
royal virgin, and my father a shower of gold,"' and continues in a
similar mythic-heroic-magical vein; and, says Barthelme, 'although
he was, in a sense, lying, in a sense he was not.' This nostalgia for the
terms of the fairy-tale in the age of commercial TV perhaps explains
the basic idea of the novel which followed, *Snow White* (1967). To
attempt to extract a narrative from the book would be rather beside
the point — though there are seven men who live with Snow White,
their occupations being window-washing, and making Chinese baby
food in vats, and there is some detectable villainy and violence which
ends in a death and a hanging. The character who announces that
he gets his nourishment from 'the ongoing circus of the mind in
motion. Give me the odd linguistic trip, stutter and fall, and I will
be content,' offers a better approach to this book. For it is a language
circus, and Barthelme has such sport with the words and things which
make up 'the trash phenomenon' that one registers a spirit of
resilience and carnival countering the deadening accumulations
which make up the materials he handles. One character 'blows his
mind' with the aid of mantras and insect repellent, 'To stop being a
filthy bourgeois for a space ... To gain access to everything in a new
way.' Barthelme does it with words.

To introduce Snow White into the contemporary world is obviously to gain the opportunity for ironies, incongruities, clashes of
genre (the fairy-tale, pornography, the junk catalogue) and indirect
sentimentality — for where will Snow White find her prince in contemporary America? One incident is designated as '*Irruption of the
magical in the life of Snow White*', but arguably she is an irruption of
the magical in the life of all the others. In particular she adds a
dimension of discontent. '"I just don't like your world,"' she cries.
She tells them that she remains in their world because she has not
been able to imagine anything better. '"But my imagination is
stirring ... Be warned."' She feels a sense of 'incompleteness' and
lets down her hair in traditional fashion to see who will seek or save
her. But no one even attempts to climb her hair and she feels that

this must be the 'wrong time' for her if the present world is 'not civilized enough to supply the correct ending to the story'. (By contrast, her seven cohorts have a malevolent fantasy of burning her.) An unidentified voice near the end of the book complains of '"Total disappointment"', and it could well be Snow White's. Before they found her, the seven men lived lives 'stuffed with equanimity', but she has introduced 'confusion and misery' into their lives. If one sees her as embodying the disappointed imagination beginning to bestir itself, then one can see why the men who have lived with her become much less at ease among things. By the end the narrator is turning over the concept of *something better*; 'trying to break out of this bag that we are in'. And on the last page there are just a few headings for unwritten future chapters, the last three being:

SNOW WHITE RISES INTO THE SKY
THE HEROES DEPART IN SEARCH OF
A NEW PRINCIPLE
HEIGH-HO

'Tis off to work they go. Only this time perhaps they will not be content just to tend the vats and wash the windows.

The inclination to play with 'beautiful *dreck*' (as Ludwig Bemelmans once called it) and the countering instinct to get away from matter altogether—a profoundly American combination of feelings —provide the tensions which hold Barthelme's best work together and give it its distinctive vibrant strangeness. An unidentified voice in one chapter of *Snow White* speaks up in defence of his manufacture of an unlikely product, plastic buffalo humps. Revealingly, he bases his defence on the recognition that much of our speech is not communication but a sort of non-semantic stuffing or 'sludge' which we use to fill up the sentences.

The 'sludge' quality is the heaviness that this 'stuff' has, similar to the heavier motor oils, a kind of downward pull but still fluid, if you follow me, and I can't help thinking that this downwardness is valuable ... Now you're probably familiar with the fact that the per-capita production of trash in this country is up from 2.75 pounds per day in 1920 to 4.5 pounds per day in 1965 ... that rate will probably go up, because it's *been* going up, and I hazard that we may very well soon reach a point where it's 100 percent. Now at such a point you will agree, the question turns from a question of disposing of this 'trash' to a question of appreciating its qualities, because, after all, it's 100 percent, right? ... So that's why we're in humps ... They are 'trash', and what in fact could be more useless or trashlike? It's that we want to be on the leading edge of this trash phenomenon, the everted sphere of the future, and that's why we pay particular attention, too, to those aspects of language that may be seen as a model of the trash phenomenon.

We may hardly be surprised that the police band in one of Barthelme's stories is asked to play 'Entropy', for like so many other American writers Barthelme seems to feel that that is the tune to which contemporary society is dancing. The men who live with Snow White

like books that have a lot of *dreck* in them, matter which presents itself as not wholly relevant (or indeed, at all relevant) but which, carefully attended to, can supply a kind of 'sense' of what is going on. This 'sense' is not to be obtained by reading between the lines (for there is nothing there in those white spaces) but by reading the lines themselves ...

Elsewhere in the book a boy, asked by his girlfriend what will become of them both, replies, '"Our becoming is done. We are what we are. Now it is just a question of rocking along with things as they are until we are dead."' The message seems to be—go with the trash flow.

To some extent this sounds like a justification of Pop Art, in which the things that are filling up our environment are moved into our museums having first been enlarged, made more solid or multiplied. You are not asked to read between the soup cans. Just so, Barthelme's work is packed with the detritus of modern life; it seems like an unbroken stream of the accumulations and appurtenances which we see around us. But Barthelme turns it all to strangeness by omitting or deliberately fragmenting the habitual arrangings and separations by which we seek to retain a sense of control over the slowly filling environment. He fractures the syntax and the taxonomies which we hope will keep us sane. His prose seeks to simulate the strange confluence of words and things which is our actual experience, so that the commonest objects from kitchen, bathroom or street are mixed up with the commonest clichés of contemporary intellectual talk; reminders of TV, radio, film, science-fiction, are added to the mix, while sudden moments of intense sexuality or violence alternate with long periods of deprivation and boredom—the whole *dreck* consort dancing or sinking, together. Returning to Barthelme's own phrases we could say that his prose seems to want to be all 'filling' or 'sludge', rocking along with things as they are with a richer sense of fantasy than our habitual modes of attention allow us to enjoy.

But the mood that most often comes across is finally very different from the sort of trash-happiness which Barthelme's work seems at times to be purveying. *'I want to go to some other country ... I want to go somewhere where everything is different,'* says a character in the first story of Barthelme's first book ('Florence Green is 81'), and although the idea is mocked, like every other idea offered as idea in Barthelme, this note of yearning for an unknown somewhere else sounds throughout his work. There is a strong feeling of being distinctly not at home in the trash age; though, since all the usual modes of complaint, dissatisfaction, nostalgia, etc., are registered as being part of the very trash continuum they seek to repudiate, themselves helping to top up the contemporary plenum, this feeling of not-at-homeness necessarily comes through in indirect ways. Thus, for instance, a thirty-five-year-old man is made to attend school with eleven-year-olds. He is told that since the desk-size (social environment) is correct, the pupil-size (uncomfortable individual consciousness) must be incorrect ('Me and Miss Mandible'). He is surrounded by people who read all the signs around them as promises (the American dream); but he has learned a bleaker wisdom – 'that signs are signs, and that some of them are lies.' But Barthelme usually avoids all allegorical portentousness with his antic, and sometimes manic, humour which refuses to allow his material ever to settle in recognizable narrative patterns.

The result is a curious kind of prose, sometimes feeling rather hard and shellacked, like plastic, at other times fluttering like gay ribbons over the contemporary landscape, like the bunting over used car lots. It can be by turns engaging and ominous. One could take two stories from his most recent collection, *Unspeakable Practices, Unnatural Acts* (1968), to suggest the kind of alternation of mood in his work. In 'The Balloon' an enormous balloon suddenly appears over the city. It has no meaning and is apparently purposeless; it is simply a thing which has been mysteriously inserted into the environment. Everyone has a different theory or fantasy about the balloon. Mainly what people enjoy about it is 'that it was not limited or defined', and they come to play on its yielding amorphousness.

This ability of the balloon to shift its shape, to change, was very pleasing, especially to people whose lives were rather rigidly patterned, persons to whom change, although desired, was not available. The balloon ... offered the possibility, in its randomness, of mislocation of the self, in contradistinction to the grid of precise, rectangular pathways under our feet.

In terms of the story the balloon is explained as a 'spontaneous autobiographical disclosure' connected with sexual deprivation. But take it as a kind of free-form artistic product, flexible, plastic and ephemeral, and it exemplifies the sort of art which Barthelme and many other American writers are increasingly interested in. It represents an invitation to play, a gesture against patterning, a sportive fantasy floating free above the rigidities of environment; and the invitation and gesture are more important than the actual material of which the balloon is composed.

Against the delights of 'The Balloon' we may put the anxieties of 'Indian Uprising'. 'We defended the city as best we could'; so it starts, and though we can never be sure just who or what the Indians are, by the end they have padded 'into the mouth of the mayor' and occupied the end of Barthelme's story, dominating the narrator's concluding perspective. The defence has been conducted with familiar things. 'I analyzed the composition of the barricade nearest me and found two ashtrays, ceramic ... a tin frying pan; two-litre bottles of red wine,' the list continues for half a page and ends, 'a Yugoslavian carved flute, wood, dark brown; and other items. I decided I knew nothing.' Things, singly or in accumulation, may not prove much of a defence. The narrator seeks love from a girl who flees from him down streets running with a filthy stream suggesting 'excrement, or nervousness'. He asks his girl, '"Do you think this is a good life?" The table held apples, books, long-playing records. She looked up. "No."' We cannot exactly follow the syntax of the story, but as we experience the modulations and shifts in situations and sentences the unease increases and we begin to feel that this is not a good life and realize that the city cannot hold. When an officer reports by radio that the garbage dump has begun to move, we believe him. There is one rather disturbing character who keeps turning up, a teacher named Miss R. It is not clear which side she is on, but she is suspiciously efficient in handling steel shutters and tends to favour clinically bare rooms. She believes that the litany is the only acceptable form of discourse, and prefers the 'vertical organization' of words in lists. The narrator, on the other hand, prefers 'strings of language extended in every direction to bind the world into a rushing, ribald whole'. But it seems that Miss R.'s impersonal methods of organization and control are destined to prevail over his sense of play. For at the end of the story, the narrator is being stripped and interrogated by a group which consists of Miss R. and the Indians. The enemy is, then, uncertain, but real; threat and coercion come in many forms, from many quarters. Defeat is spreading through the city.

In the last story of *Unspeakable Practices, Unnatural Acts*, 'See the Moon', Barthelme seems to offer a fairly specific account of his art as being a sort of collage activity appropriate to the times. The narrator is awaiting the birth of his child. Meanwhile he is conducting what he calls his lunar hostility studies (for he believes that the moon hates us). Both 'lightminded' and 'insecure' (like Barthelme's prose) he explains his method. 'You've noticed the wall? I pin things on it, souvenirs ... It's my hope that these ... souvenirs ... will someday merge, blur—cohere is the word, maybe—into something meaningful.' With this assemblage on the wall he intends to act as a kind of Distant Early Warning System to his unborn child.

Here is the world and here are the knowledgeable knowers knowing. What can I tell you? What has been pieced together from the reports of travellers.

Fragments are the only forms I trust.

Look at my wall, it's all there.

A comparable use of fragment and fantasy may be found in the work of Richard Brautigan, though his writing seems to float more easily away from the *dreck* of the contemporary environment than Barthelme's—like clouds over the Pacific. Brautigan offers far more than the easy surrealism of unmotivated juxtapositions and associations. Although his work is indeed extremely funny, there is a pervasive sense of loss, desolation and death in it which amounts to an implicit formulation of an attitude towards contemporary America. The first word of his first novel, *A Confederate General from Big Sur* (1964), is 'attrition', and the book manages to combine fleeting reminiscences of the obvious attritions of the Civil War with the less obvious attritions of life on the Californian coast today. The book is the reverse of didactic, and one would be missing the whole point to look for a specific moral to it. In appearance indeed it is very carefree. It offers a series of fragmentary little chapters depicting episodes in the life of the narrator and his friend Lee Mellon. They lead a rather vagrant, shiftless existence in San Francisco and in Big Sur, for the most part in the company of two girls. They exhibit some of the manic improvization of those who are poor in cash and rich in imagination, and the tempo of their life comes across as relaxed and unneurotic. Their one visitor from conformist America, a businessman in flight from his family, is insane, made mad and inhuman through the horrors of his way of life. The day-to-day casualness of the drop-outs, with its erotic and euphoric moments and its odd humour, obviously seems preferable. And yet one feels that the engaging humour, naive and fantastic, is being maintained on the edge of a great emptiness. Lee Mellon is a wild scavenger quite capable of ruthless brutality. He claims his great-grandfather Augustus Mellon was a Confederate general, but when they go to check up in the library his name does not appear. With a series of interposed imaginary glimpses from the past, Brautigan suggests that Augustus Mellon was just another private, another scavenger picking his fearful way across the fields full of corpses, during what Brautigan refers to as 'the last good time this country ever had'. By the end of the book a mood of great desolation and sadness has settled on the group in Big Sur. The narrator describes how he feels 'a sudden wave of vacancy go over me'. In the last scene they are all standing by the Pacific, high on marijuana, just watching the waves hit the land. The narrator's girlfriend undresses him but he feels no desire at all – for anything. It is not contentment, but emptiness. The mad businessman comes back looking for a pomegranate he had left behind, and they agree to help him. 'There was nothing else to do, for after all this was the destiny of our lives. A long time ago this was our future, looking now for a lost pomegranate at Big Sur.' The narrator offers multiple endings for his novel, but the dominant sense is of things thinning away into air, drawn back into the sea, fading away to the silent stillness of an old photograph. There are indeed a lot of 'ends' in the novel. Lee Mellon, drunk and wrapped up in cardboard, is seen as 'the end product of American spirit, pride and the old know-how'. Lee himself has a fantasy of walking along an endless highway looking for a cigarette butt but never finding one – 'the end of an American dream'. In the last fragment the narrator says that 'there are more and more endings ... faster and faster until this book is having 186,000 endings per second.' This most insubstantial of worlds is being rapidly reabsorbed into an immense vacancy.

What the narrator has to sustain him is a gentle gaiety among words and a habit of instant fantasy. He fills some of his evenings reading Ecclesiastes over and over until at last he only counts the punctuation marks. He compares this to counting the rivets of a ship. 'I was curious about the number of rivets and the sizes of those rivets in Ecclesiastes, a dark and beautiful ship sailing on our waters.' The sun coming in through a window makes some motorcycle parts begin to smell like roast meat. The narrator instantly floats along with his simile.

I'd like a slice of motorcycle on dark rye, please.
Anything to drink sir; gasoline?
No. No, I don't think so.

Disturbed at night, he and his girlfriend have to go out and explore the darkness. 'I found our way along the road like a spoon probing carefully through a blindman's soup, looking for alphabets.' With such sporting with language he can keep himself going. But even games have to come to an end. Visiting a friend, the narrator and his companions look into the deserted garden. It is perfectly still and empty except for some dirt and shells and deer antlers which had perhaps been composed in the course of some indecipherable children's game. Or—'Perhaps it wasn't a game at all, only the grave of a game.'

Trout Fishing in America (1967) brought together games and the graves of games in one of the most original and pleasing books to appear during the decade. If there is any narrative line in the book it concerns the author's recollections of his various attempts to find good trout fishing. But Trout Fishing in America becomes a person, a place, an hotel, a cripple, a pen nib, and of course a book. Protean and amorphous, it is a dream to be pursued, a sense of something lost, a quality of life, a spirit that is present or absent in many forms. Because Brautigan has freedom with his words he can sit Trout Fishing in America down with Maria Callas for a meal, or produce a letter from him/it saying he/it is leaving for Alaska, or start a chapter 'This is the autopsy of Trout Fishing in America ... ' and leave us thinking that perhaps that is indeed what the whole book is intended to be.

Certainly the book is full of death. There are endless references to graveyards, mortuaries, cemeteries, wreaths, memorials. A bookshop is 'a parking lot for used graveyards'; an abandoned outdoor lavatory, a decaying mansion, a loft full of ancient 'stuff' ('Everything that's old in this world was up there') offer various reminders of the decline and passing of things. Dead fish are constantly referred to; and a man who goes camping has a human corpse leant against his tent. The narrator tells of making love in a lake coated with dead fish and green slime. Releasing his sperm in the water he watches it instantly become a stringy mess into which a dead fish floats. The feeling of fertility gone sour, of a once beautiful land given over to deadness, hangs over the book. There are specific references to great criminals like John Dillinger and 'Pretty Boy' Floyd, adding to a general sense of the destructive violence which has entered into America's heritage. There is the repulsive legless wino called Trout Fishing in America Shorty who is 'the cold turning of the earth; the bad wind that blows off sugar'. Children run away from him—for instance, the narrator's own little girl who backs away from Shorty when he tries to entice her to him. He 'stared after her as if the space between them were a river growing larger and larger.' Which is perhaps too near to being explicit about how an America grown ugly is constantly receding away from its early innocence. A shepherd who looks like Adolf Hitler, 'but friendly', offers perhaps an oblique comment on the conformist sheep of contemporary society. More savage is the portrait of 'The Mayor of the Twentieth Century'. No one sees him except his victims. He dresses in a costume of trout fishing in America ('Deep water flowed through the lilies that were entwined about his shoelaces'). His weapons are a razor, a knife, and a ukelele—the last being his own special idea. 'Nobody else would have thought of it, pulled like a plow through the intestines.' This comes very close to being a frontal attack on an America which uses its original beauty only as a disguise to cover its murderous violence. Out fishing one day, the narrator's thoughts turn to the gas chamber at San Quentin.

The narrator's quest for Trout Fishing in America is a series of disappointments. Once, when he was a child, what in the distance looked like a beautiful waterfall turned out to be a flight of white wooden stairs. At school he and some friends wrote 'Trout Fishing in America' in chalk on the backs of the other children. They thought it looked good, but they were forced to wipe it off and gradually the vestigial outlines of the words faded away: 'after a few more days trout fishing in America disappeared altogether as it was destined to from its very beginning, and a kind of autumn fell over the first grade.' Later, when he is clearing out an old loft, he finds the Trout Fishing Diary of Alonso Hagen, in which the fisherman had kept a detailed record over the years of all the trout he failed to catch and all the ways in which he had lost them. Hagen's written comment on his seven years of complete failure concludes with the following pregnant words:

> For all its frustration,
> I believe it was an interesting experiment
>   in total loss
> but next year somebody else
> will have to go trout fishing.
> Somebody else will have to go
>   out there.

This could be read as an abiding exhortation to the artist in search of America which is, as the narrator comments, 'often only a place in the mind'.

The narrator's quest brings him finally to the Cleveland Wrecking Yard, another version of that terminal dump of waste and used things which for so many writers seems to loom up as a possible end to the American dream. The Wrecking Yard is offering a used trout stream for sale. The narrator makes inquiries and finds that it is being sold by the foot; the waterfalls, animals and trees are being sold separately, while the insects are being given away. Making his way through the yard, the narrator finds the trout stream stacked up in a room also containing piles of toilets and lumber; an old waterfall in two lengths is gathering dust. He also finds that they are practically out of animals, though there are lots of mice and insects. The whole episode is conducted as a gentle fantasy with no bitterness or anger; nevertheless one cannot fail to respond to the poignant sense of 'loss' it conveys.

One could call Brautigan's book an idyll, a satire, a quest, an exercise in nostalgia, a lament for America, or a joke — but it is a book which floats effortlessly free of all categories, and it is just this experience of floating free which is communicated while one is reading the book. There is certainly a feeling for a pastoral America which has vanished or been despoiled by mechanization, crime, accumulating garbage, and various kinds of poison and violence. In addition there is a sense that the original reality of America has been replaced by fabricated dreams of which the movies are the clearest example. In a chapter entitled 'The Last Time I Saw Trout Fishing in America' the narrator recalls telling this mysterious character about his days in Great Falls. He remembers seeing a Deanna Durbin movie seven times and he describes how he used to think that he would one day walk down to the Missouri River to find that it had begun to look like a Deanna Durbin movie. Trout Fishing in America replies pensively, '"I've been to Great Falls many times. I remember Indians and fur traders. I remember Lewis and Clark, but I don't remember ever seeing a Deanna Durbin movie in Great Falls ... I don't think Lewis would have understood it if the Missouri River had suddenly begun to look like a Deanna Durbin movie ... "' The reproach that reality is giving way to movie is one with which we are familiar by now.

But the book is nothing like a polemic: Brautigan, it is clear, would not engage in anything so formulaic and recognizable as an established genre. That, after all, is someone else's movie. He has found himself a place beyond society and has exempted himself from all the usual modes and conventions. His novel is like no other novel and is one only because he says so, since it flouts all the usual prescriptions for the writing of fiction. The list of contents, the chapter divisions, the 'characters', the narrative episodes, all mock the forms of conventional fiction by pretending to add up to a recognizable structure which is not there when you come to look for it. He retains the illusion of orthodox syntax and grammar, but the sentences are continually turning off into unexpectedness in ways which pleasantly dissolve our habitual semantic expectations. At the same time Brautigan is constantly, cunningly, deviating into sense; there is enough linguistic coherence left for us to experience the book as communication, and enough linguistic sport for Brautigan to demonstrate his own freedom from control.

Among other things the book is a typographical playfield. On the title-page, the words of the title are arranged to simulate a trout jumping. In the course of the text we find blocks of words from signs and monuments, signatures, recipes, a square from a map, addresses, labels, quotations, notes, words from headstones, underlinings, and —'4/17 OF A HAIKU'. With such good-humoured caprices Brautigan shows how free he feels to make his own patterns, and how uncircumscribed he is by the traditional ones. Each chapter is a separate fragment, unpredictable because unrelated in any of the usual ways. Each one engages us for a moment with its humour, or strangeness, or unusual evocation, and then fades away. The writing is like sky-writing; even while articulating it is receding back into silence, dissolving its own patternings before it gets fixed in them. Jack Kerouac once said that he wanted a kind of writing which encouraged the reader to throw it away immediately on reading it, so that the reader should not feel the writer was trying to trap him in his version.* This is one reaction to the paradox of wanting to be a writer without wanting to be a sender or controller, and I think that this search for a self-dissolving or self-cancelling writing is a very American phenomenon. It is one of Brautigan's distinctive achievements that his magically delicate verbal ephemera seem to accomplish their own vanishings.†

Clearly this might all add up to a recipe for whimsy, and a style

---

* 'When you've understood this scripture, throw it away. If you can't understand this scripture, throw it away. I insist on your freedom.' (Verse 45 of *Scripture of the Golden Eternity*, Totem Press, New York, 1960.)

† This concern to work out a more ephemeral mode of writing could be related to a more widespread American interest in 'ephemeralization'. Buckminster Fuller wrote an essay with that title which concluded flamboyantly and, as it seemed, unanswerably: 'Efficiency means doing more with less ... EFFICIENCY EPHEMERALIZES.' (In *The Buckminster Fuller Reader*).

with such a light touch cannot always hope to avoid coyness, false naivety and sentimentality. These are certainly to be found in Brautigan's work, but hardly at all in this novel. The evanescent quality of the writing, the elusive metamorphoses of sense and form (like clouds) nevertheless leave one in possession of something extremely haunting, evocative, and capable of making subtle solicitations to a whole range of authentic feelings. Unhysterical, unegotistical, often magical, Brautigan's work contains some of the most original and refreshing prose to appear in the 'sixties.

With the melancholy conclusion to his seeking in the Wrecking Yard, the narrator could well have ended the book, but there are in fact four very interesting fragmentary chapters after that. In the first, the narrator dreams of a modern American-born Leonardo da Vinci who will invent a new 'lure' for Trout Fishing in America; as if to imply that it will take the artist to entice back that ideal or dream America. In the next chapter, the narrator is given a golden nib with the following admonitions. '"Write with this, but don't write hard because this pen has got a gold nib, and a gold nib is very impressionable. After a while it takes on the personality of the writer. Nobody else can write with it ... It's the only pen to have. But be careful."' To which the narrator adds, 'I thought to myself what a lovely nib trout fishing in America would make with a stroke of cool green trees along the river's shore, wild flowers and dark fins pressed against the shore.' The dream will enter the writer's pen, with the characteristic instruction to write simply and individually, avoiding other people's versions, and not leaning too heavily on his own. While Trout Fishing in America is foundering in the Cleveland Wrecking Yard, it is flourishing in the writer's imagination. It is perhaps one of the most pervasive themes of this critical work that those two realms —the Wrecking Yard and the Imagination—are in a permanent struggle for possession of 'America', but I doubt if any writer has posed the opposition so delicately.

The opposition appears again in Brautigan's next novel, *In Watermelon Sugar* (1968). The narrator lives in a happy commune in an unlocated realm called, mysteriously, iDEATH. The prevailing material there is watermelon sugar—'Our lives we have carefully constructed from watermelon sugar'—which may be food, furniture or fuel. More generally it is the sweet secretion of the imagination. There is still death in iDEATH but it has been made into something mysterious and almost beautiful: the dead are buried in glass coffins which are laid on the riverbed. Foxfire is put inside 'so they glow at night and we can appreciate what comes next.' There was once a more violent time—the time of the tigers—but they have been killed off. More recently there has been a defection from iDEATH by a drunken foul-mouthed figure called inBOIL [reminiscent of Trout Fishing in America Shorty]. He and his gang have gone back to live in an ugly place called the Forgotten Works. This is the ultimate wrecking yard and waste dump, an endless panorama of all the machines and things which made up a vanished way of life—'the big piles of forgotten things were mountains that went on for at least a million miles.' It is the realm of dead trash which the imagination has insisted on leaving behind. But inBOIL returns to the commune insisting that the tigers were the real meaning of iDEATH and that without the tigers [and their terrible violence] there is no true iDEATH. He and his followers say that they will bring back the real iDEATH. They do this by gradually cutting themselves to pieces in front of the disgusted members of the community. Afterwards their bodies are taken down to the Forgotten Works, burned up, and forgotten. Everyone is relieved. Except for one girl called Margaret who had started to show an acquisitive interest in the things heaped up in the Forgotten Works. This interest in 'things' is, in turn, symptomatic of her inability to love in the free and gentle manner of the other members of iDEATH. She commits suicide (Brautigan is almost as obsessed with death as Hemingway). But after the funeral, the community gathers together for a dance, and the musicians are poised with their instruments. 'It would only be a few seconds now, I wrote.' So the book ends (again with a little lexical caprice in the last words). It is a charming and original work with touches of magic, but is perhaps too obvious in its parabolic form. It suggests a commitment to a rather *too* simple-minded version of things which the previous novels avoid. It is a pastoral dream in which the dominance of fantasy and imagination over the Forgotten Works and the wrecking yard is perhaps too effortlessly achieved.

To return to the last two chapters of *Trout Fishing in America* is almost to return to where we started, for they are about language. Brautigan first quotes passages from three books concerning the origin of culture and more particularly the mystery of the origin and evolution of language. He then adds that he himself, 'expressing a human need', has always wanted to write a book that ended with the word mayonnaise. The final chapter he calls 'The Mayonnaise Chapter'. It turns out to be a letter of condolence sent to some people on the passing away of Mr Good. The letter has a P.S. which reads, 'Sorry I forgot to give you the mayonnaise.' Master of his own verbal terrain, Brautigan has satisfied his need, indulged his whim, exercised his freedom—there are any number of ways of expressing the possibilities open to a writer in the City of Words. But this final gesture is not merely frivolous. In an earlier chapter while walking through one of the many graveyards in the book, the narrator takes note of the pathetic improvised markers on the graves of the poor. On one of them is a mayonnaise jar containing wilted flowers commemorating, so he gathers from the inscription, an eighteen-year-old boy who was murdered in a bar; it was left there by his sister who is now in 'the Crazy Place'.* The mayonnaise jar rests on one of the graves of the American dream; similarly Brautigan's lexical games rest lightly, but distinctly, on the panorama of violence, decay and death which is recognized as the real world. A gift for play and a sense of annihilation come together in the placing of the last word of his book, just as they do in his work as a whole. Borrowing a phrase from Gary Snyder, we may say that Brautigan's writing

* It was my intention for a long time to start this book with some comments on *Moby Dick* and conclude it with a consideration of *Trout Fishing in America* which is like a miniature postscript to the earlier novel, different in tone and treatment as befits the changed conditions of America, but nevertheless still about an American quest (Brautigan wrote a short poem called 'The Symbol' in which he imagines Moby Dick now transformed into a truckdriver). Thus it was interesting to learn during a conversation with the author of a deliberate echo in connection with this gravestone. Brautigan's marker reads:

Sacred
To the Memory
of
John Talbot
Who at the Age of Eighteen
Had His Ass Shot Off
In a Honky-Tonk
November 1, 1936

and goes on to refer to the sister, now crazy, who left the jar on the grave. In Chapter VII of *Moby Dick*, Ishmael reads a tablet in the New Bedford chapel:

SACRED
TO THE MEMORY
OF
JOHN TALBOT
Who, at the age of eighteen, was lost overboard,
Near the Isle of Desolation, off Patagonia,
November 1st, 1836.
THIS TABLET
Is erected to his Memory
BY HIS SISTER

Brautigan's echo is typically quiet and unobtrusive, yet indicative of how carefully his deceptively slight book is put together. One hardly needs make the point that a hundred years later young people are still being lost near the Isle of Desolation though the modes of violence and insanity have changed and perhaps intensified.

offers 'Flowers for the Void'. In it we can feel his disengagement from a malign reality—not by ignoring it (for it haunts him), but by moving to that realm where all is Great Play and Transformation, the liberations of fantasy once again triumphing over the constrictions of environment.

The Wide Wings of the Language

Melville started *Moby Dick* with etymology; Brautigan ends *Trout Fishing in America* with references to the history of the language and some sport with words. Allowing for manifest differences in scope and mood and the times, we can still see some continuity. Both writers have a wondering sense of the ultimate elusiveness of the mysterious reality or spirit of America, while both are very conscious of the rich and rare things that can be 'lured' into language by the imagination. The dream may be held while the thing itself may be lost. Both have a sense of the preserving and consoling fantasies and play which are possible in the City of Words, though both have that American wariness about accepting any fantasy (or fiction or version) as the true reality. Both operate from a sense of the radical disjunction between words and things. As I have tried to show in the course of this book, I believe these to be characteristic attributes of a large number of American writers.

This book has made abundant reference to the ambiguous nature of all fantasy (or the unique self-generated version of things) and the fact that it may imprison as well as liberate. It is arguably a limitation in recent American fiction that it has shown so little inclination to develop the mimetic potentialities of the novel while relying so heavily on fantasy in one form or another.* There is no real social novel writing in America today at a time when, I have heard Americans say, the sort of analytic and exploratory models of society which fiction makes possible are badly needed. (Some of the reasons why

---

* It is not only writers who have recourse to fantasy as a way of maintaining themselves in modern America. In Tom Wolfe's third book, *The Pump House Gang* (Farrar, Straus and Giroux, New York, 1968), he discusses a number of people and groups who invent their own world, league, 'statusphere'—some kind of private area in which they invent the rules and define the achievable satisfactions and meanings in contra-distinction to the generally accepted social mores. In this area they can indulge their fantasies to the full; they are 'extending their egos way out on the best terms available, namely, their own'. Such people or small societies, like the Californian surfers, 'float right through the real world, but it can't touch them.' This is obviously a very sympathetic way of dealing with the threat of external controlling forces, and as I have tried to suggest it seems indispensable to the American writer. Whether it is unequivocally beneficial in its effect on a society much in need of some very specific alterations is of course another matter.

this might be so, and what American novelists have achieved in other ways, I have tried to suggest in this book.) This is not to say that the American writer and his hero are unaware of society. Indeed they are; but society is usually seen by them as a metamorphosing range of generalized hostilities. The tendency is to posit society as a vast hostile mass, with specific threatening things and people looming up into brief focus without contributing to an emerging model of the constitution of American society. Society is regarded almost without exception as unequivocally malevolent to the self. All control is regarded as bad control; any authority is immediately interpreted as a part of a malign authoritarianism stalking through the land seeking what further individual freedoms it may devour. Without any doubt there is plenty of ground for such suspicions; at the same time, it might be a valuable gesture if some novelists re-examined the premises underlying this age-old suspicion and repudiation of society by the American writer and his hero. (J. D. Salinger was perhaps moving towards this, but it seems that he lacked an appropriate fictional vocabulary. Charles Newman goes some way towards doing this in his interesting first novel, *New Axis* [1966].[1])

While the inherent instability of American society poses one difficulty for the American writer, his attitude towards his own craft often produces another, since the American writer seems to find it unusually difficult to discover an enabling form to which he is willing to commit himself and his words. Need for forms and suspicion of forms seem to be problematically linked emotions. In an attempt to negotiate all the possible paradoxes and problems inherent in the 'forming' processes of literature, some American writers, while at times producing exciting experiments, seem at other times to get themselves involved in near-disabling contortions which thinly conceal something approaching a despair about all forms. (In this connection I do not think the example of Nabokov has been a wholly unequivocal asset.) All this can be seen as an aspect of the larger problem of whether America itself can find its form, or whether a freedom from all forms will be the abiding American dream?

This was the question which posed itself most urgently to Henry James when he returned to America in 1904, and in *The American Scene* he arrived at some formulations which still seem penetratingly relevant. One of the paradoxes which struck James was that this modern emerging America seemed at once increasingly crowded and radically empty. 'Void' and 'vacancy' are perhaps the words used most frequently in James's account. 'It is the vacancy that is a thing by itself, a thing that makes us endlessly wonder.' This radical emptiness or blankness is not concealed for James by 'the mere modern thickness' nor is it filled by the incoming stream of 'aliens'. To James, people and places seemed to be 'monotonized'. He was struck by the strange homogenization of the population; the way, for instance, an immigrant would lose the distinguishing qualities of his native identity without acquiring any coloration from his new neighbours – 'we surely fail to observe that the property washed out of the new subject begins to tint with its pink or azure his fellow-soakers in the terrible tank.' The modern American novelist would be more likely to use an image based on entropy for 'the terrible tank', but he would surely recognize the perception. James was everywhere struck by the power of the 'terrible tank' to dissolve distinctions, producing mere mass without meaning. Looking into 'the too formidable future' he is haunted by visions of fluidity:

> the so much vaster lake of the materially possible ... differences are submerged in the immense fluidity; they lurk confused, disengaged, in the mere looming mass of the *more*, the more and more to come. And as yet nothing makes definite the probable preponderance of particular forms of the more. The one all positive appearance is of the perpetual increase of everything, the growth of the immeasurable muchness that shall constitute the deep sea ... '

It is just such conditions which the contemporary American novelist is dealing with, and only one has tried the extreme prescription – forget forms and go with the flow.

As well as being appalled by the formless monstrosities (as he saw it), which were being erected, James was shocked at the constant obliterations and effacements of forms from the past. His shock was not simply a conservative's preference for the old familiar forms. He knew that he had to put to himself the question – 'Do certain impressions there represent the absolute extinction of old sensibilities, or do they represent only new forms of them?' At the same time he was unwilling 'to read mere freshness of form into some of the more rank failures of observance'. What worried him was that the new America did not seem to care enough for any of its new structures to wish to preserve them – 'the very sign of its energy is that it doesn't believe in itself.' It was America's 'inability to convince ... that she is serious, serious about any form whatever, or about anything but that perpetual passionate pecuniary purpose which plays with all forms, which derides and devours them,' that depressed James. The basic reason he gives for the ugliness of the new America is 'the so complete abolition of *forms*', and the production of new forms which were so 'plastic' and so 'perpetually provisional' as to constitute a committed formlessness.

As we have seen, plasticity and the flexibility to accept provisional forms have become strategies of survival for many American writers and their heroes. While James's point of view has great authority and validity, it needs to be supplemented by alternative perspectives. We can perhaps bring the story up to date by turning to Tom Wolfe's visit to the Las Vegas sign-makers (in *The Kandy-Kolored Tangerine-Flake Streamline Baby* [1965][2]), who produce the 'new guideposts, the new way Americans get their bearings'. One of them was making a strange boomerang-shaped sign and Wolfe asked him what he called it. '"Well, that's what we call — what we sort of call—'free form'."' Tom Wolfe's reaction is— 'Free form! Marvellous!' Between them James and Wolfe point to the great fascination of the whole American adventure which has always to some extent been a tension between the abolition of fixed forms, and the improvisation of free forms. And while one may respond sympathetically to James's shock at all the brutal obliterations and contemporary ugliness which seem to be an inherent part of the development of modern America, one has to hold on to the truth pointed to in a line by Wallace Stevens—'the vegetation still abounds in forms.'

Just as James despaired specifically of American architectural forms (wrongly in many ways, one may now think), so he experienced a more general doubt whether America would nourish other art forms—'the monstrous phenomena themselves, meanwhile, strike me as having, with their immense momentum, got the start, got ahead of, in proper parlance, any possibility of poetic, of dramatic capture,' he remarked of New York. This pessimism has scarcely been borne out, and I prefer the more hopeful, or open-ended, predictions he made in a couple of earlier essays. Writing about 'American Letters—The Question of the Opportunities' (1898), James is not sanguine about the sort of literature which may be produced by the vast America coming into being, but he does not deny it any possibilities. 'It is impossible not to entertain with patience and curiosity the presumption that life so colossal must break into expression at points of proportionate frequency. These places, these moments will be the chances.' Again in 1898, writing about 'American Democracy and American Education', James formulates a stance of positive expectancy which offers an appropriate model to keep before us. 'There will be much to wait for. The prospect, for the man of letters, certainly for a man of imagination, can scarcely fail to come back to the most constant of his secret

passions, the idea of the great things that, from quarters so inter-
spaced, may more and more find themselves gathered together under
the wide wings of the language.'

At the end of a book of this nature it perhaps falls to the critic
to say just a few words in anticipation of charges of indiscriminating
inclusiveness, and a slack refusal to submit manifestly different
kinds of novels to some sort of hierarchical evaluation which might
tidy up the field. I would say first of all that I value and enjoy the
very multiplicity of versions which literature permits to coexist. I
do not believe, for instance, that if you like writer A then you must
necessarily not like writer B because their world pictures seem to be
mutually exclusive. On the contrary, I believe that the very variety
of available 'pictures' is a valuable and liberating phenomenon. The
word itself points to a famous proposition from Wittgenstein's
Philosophical Investigations (I–115): 'A *picture* held us captive. And
we could not get outside it, for it lay in our language and language
seemed to repeat it to us inexorably.' Different novels, different
selections and arrangings, remind us that the picture can be changed.
The acceptance of, and delight in, a large variety of pictures does
not necessarily mean that one becomes a pure relativist and asserts
that there is no truth to be found. Here the literary critic may align
himself with the philosopher who says that a variety of pictures is
necessary in order to represent the complexity and variety of things
as they are. One of our most common limitations is to get fixed in
established ways of patterning things. Here too, it seems to me that
the very multiplicity of structurings and configurations made
possible by literature has a very real value. It offers us not definitive
verdicts but alternative versions. And to those who are concerned
about the moral status and influence of literary fictions, I would
suggest that a sensitive response to a plurality of fictions inculcates
something between the rigidity of dogma and the fluidity of indifferent acceptance. Let us call it the morality of flexibility, which
accepts Ruskin's admirably succinct definition of our position in
the world — 'you always see something, but you never see all.'

Borges too offers a justification of our necessarily multiple and
incomplete patternings of reality. In 'The Analytical Language of
John Wilkins' he shows how oddly various men's categories can be:
'obviously there is no classification of the universe that is not
arbitrary and conjectural. The reason is very simple: we do not
know what the universe is ... But the impossibility of penetrating
the divine scheme of the universe cannot dissuade us from outlining
human schemes, even though we are aware that they are provisional.'
And in his defence of philosophy as an activity (not of any *one*

philosophy), Borges offers a suitable concluding note to this survey of so many different lexical renderings, for what he says is also very applicable to all literary forms.

> I think that philosophy helps you to live ... I think that philosophy may give the world a kind of haziness, but that haziness is all to the good. If you're a materialist, if you believe in hard and fast things, then you're tied down by reality, or by what you call reality. So that, in a sense, philosophy dissolves reality, but as reality is not always too pleasant, you will be helped by that dissolution.[3]

This liberating feeling of dissolving reality, which can at the same time be an instructive exploration of another aspect of reality, is one of the games which can be played in the City of Words, and all such games, it seems to me, serve to enhance consciousness. Of course some games will strike us as more rewarding, affecting, exhilarating, or morally energizing, than others. But even when the provisional version offered by the writer seems pessimistic and despairing – as has often been the case with the works considered here – we can still be invigorated and extended by the energy of perception and invention which went into the making of the version, and without which there would be no games. Prior to drawing up lists of personal preferences – which may quite appropriately change as oneself and the world grow older – I think it is of more general importance constantly to renew one's sense of the various and wonderful things which may be gathered together under the wide wings of the language.

Appendix One

In his influential book *The Silent Language* (Doubleday, New York, 1959) Edward Hall tries to break some obviously unwelcome news to his American readers. His book was, in part, expressly designed to help Americans going abroad to avoid blunders of etiquette by explaining how many different unspoken rules and conventions operate in foreign cultures. But his American audience apparently needed some persuading when it came to recognizing that their own lives were also 'bound by hidden rules'. He adds that he expects this to come as a shock. What Hall sets out to do is to make people aware of the large number of 'interaction patterns' and systems—most of them non-linguistic—which determine people's behaviour in America. Hall goes out of his way to stress that 'there is a growing accumulation of evidence to indicate that man has no direct contact with experience *per se* but that there is an intervening set of patterns which channel his senses and his thoughts, causing him to react one way when someone else with different underlying patterns will react as his experience dictates.' Confronted with this, American hero and author alike tend to react with a somewhat paranoid worry about who or what implanted those 'underlying patterns' which programme their responses.

After further analysis, Hall offers an expanded definition of pattern. 'A pattern is a meaningful arrangement of sets shared by a group.' The person who disengages himself from *all* the groups available to him—and such acts of disengagement constitute one of the strongest traditions in American literature—is, by the same token, depriving himself of the available patterns which make the details of the environment cohere in a legible, meaningful way. As a result, if he does not join another group and adopt their patternings, he must either generate his own pattern (but is this always possible in solitude?), or face the risk of not being able to relate things to each other in a meaningful way. 'Alienation', a word dead from over-use, could perhaps be redefined to refer to a state of mind resulting from an inability to participate in the available patterns of experience, and an uncertainty as to whether the single self can generate its own patterns. This problematical state is at the heart of contemporary American fiction. And since, as Hall demonstrates, 'it is impossible to participate in two different patterns at the same time,' anyone who finds himself out of sympathy with the dominant patternings of his society may find himself having to choose between foregoing all community to hold on to individuality or giving up the distinct sense of self to conform to the group. Here, too, is a common theme.

Appendix Two

In 1913 in his first paper on Behaviorism,* 'Psychology as the Behaviorist Views it', John B. Watson announced that we could now abandon the old vocabulary of 'consciousness' and write a psychology 'in terms of stimulus and response, in terms of habit formation, habit integrations and the like'. Obviously this is no place to go into the history of Behaviorism and the work done by men like Sechenov, Pavlov, Bekhterev and Thorndike. My point of departure is the fact that Behaviorism became immensely influential in America, and in the 'forties and 'fifties Behaviorist ideas could be said to have dominated American schools of psychology. Since it is my general contention that many American writers who grew up in those years are either instinctively or deliberately challenging, refuting or rebelling against Behaviorist tenets, I want to offer a brief summary of some of the Behaviorist ideas as outlined by John B. Watson in his widely read account of these ideas called, simply, *Behaviorism* (1924: quotations in this Appendix are taken from the 1959 edition [Phoenix Books, University of Chicago Press]). (A slightly fictionalized account of these ideas appeared in B. F. Skinner's *Walden Two* [1948] [Macmillan Paperbacks Edition, New York, 1962]).

He starts by repeating his repudiation of 'introspective psychology' and his hostility to all forms of dualism which posit an independent mind or consciousness (or soul) in the human body. Interested only in 'verifiable conclusions', he will believe only what he can test and see. So much is nothing very new. But Watson affirms that the Behaviorist is not only interested in describing man's doings: 'he wants to control man's reactions as physical scientists want to control and manipulate other natural phenomena. It is the business of behaviorist psychology to be able to predict and control human activity.' If American heroes have shared one basic apprehension during the last two decades, it is the fear of being controlled, manipulated, predictable. Since, in Watson's view, man's emotional life is built up by the effect of the environment on him, by manipulating the environment competent Behaviorists could build into man whatever patterns of emotional response were considered desirable

* I have kept to the American spelling of the word 'Behaviorism' in this book, for the sake of consistency.

423

for the interests of society. Here, then, is good ground for the American hero's suspicion of the designs that his environment might have on him.

In Behaviorist terminology, the individual is composed of certain habit systems which come into operation in response to varying situations: 'personality is made up of dominant habit systems;' there is no such thing as 'ego', only 'organized habit systems'; we should not speak of paying attention as though it were a volitional act, 'Attention is merely ... synonymous with the complete dominance of any one habit system' – these are some of Watson's characteristic assertions. Given this definition of personality, he says, 'it should become clear now that the situation we are in dominates us always and releases one or another of these all-powerful habit systems ... In general, we are what the situation calls for.' People do not decide to change; rather, old habit systems are erased and new ones formed in response to changing conditions. In the view of the Behaviorists, man can be unconditioned and reconditioned at will. All this is anathema to the American hero who will go to some lengths *not* to be what the situation seems to call for, in an attempt to assert his immunity from conditioning. Obviously this can produce a sort of negative determinism in which the non-conformist individual is predictably unpredictable; but we can scarcely overestimate the desire of the American hero to resist, sabotage or avoid the organized patterns of response and habit systems which, in the light of Behaviorist assertions, he may well believe are being subtly imposed on him.

One rather difficult question for the Behaviorist to answer is, given his model of the human being as an entity which responds to stimuli, how is it that this entity is capable of producing novelty and initiating ideas and patterns which have not previously been elicited by the environment? Watson's attempt to answer this involves him in a theory of language which is of particular interest to us. I will summarize it, necessarily somewhat crudely. Verbalizing is one more habit system which a man employs in an instinctive effort to adjust to a situation or solve a problem. He develops verbal substitutes within him for the objects of the outside world. 'Thereafter he carries the world around with him by means of this organization. And he can manipulate this word world in the privacy of his room or when he lies down on his bed in the dark.' This is how Watson accounts for the fact that new things, such as poems, essays (and perhaps psychological theories?) do come into being. 'The answer is that we get them by manipulating words, shifting them about until a new pattern is hit upon.' This concession that a man in the solitude of his own room (which seems to me like Watson's unconscious metaphor for the privacy of man's inner consciousness) can generate new verbal patterns, can play around with new possible arrangings in the absence of direct stimuli (for darkness and bed suggest a zero state of external stimuli), is potentially very damaging to Behaviorist theory. Watson seems to recognize this when he gives his idea of how a poem gets written. It is an amazingly crude attempt to reintroduce the notion of direct external conditioning. The poet's lady friend implies that he is not praising her enough (situational stimulus). He goes to his room and tries various arrangements of words until he arrives at one which he thinks will please her (adjusting response).

But the concession is made again in a much more important form in a passage of crucial importance for any writer. Watson points out that it is not always possible to recondition a man simply by changing his environment. If, he says, you took a spoiled, lazy city man and put him down in the Congo Free States, this should, by the Behaviorist theories, make a frontier individual out of him.

> But he takes with him his own language ... and we saw in studying language that language, when fully developed, really gives us a manipulable replica of the world we live in. Hence, if his present world does not begin to take hold of him, as it may not, he may withdraw from his frontier world and live the rest of his life in the old substitute world of words. Such an individual may become a 'shut-in' — a day dreamer.

'As it may not ... ' — where now is Watson's assertion that 'we are what the situation calls for'? And when he concedes that a man can carry his 'old internal environment with him in the shape of words', is he not conceding that there is an area and an activity of some inner space which is independent of environment? That in addition to the world out there, there is the world elsewhere as Poirier defined it?

The point of particular interest for my study is that in Watson's view language is the culprit. If men could not bring with them this inner world of words, they would automatically adjust to any new situation, for nothing could then stop it from 'taking hold'. Yet as he himself has conceded it is only through the play permitted by language that novelty enters the world. One can see how someone who decidedly did not want the given environment to take hold of him might well, by Watson's own analysis, live more and more in language, inventing anti-environments and counter-situations to keep out of range of that omnipotence of environment and situation asserted by the Behaviorists. Thus a writer might find in his ability to proliferate private lexical patterns a key defence against the social patterns which seek to condition his responses. And if, as a result, he is called a 'shut-in', a day-dreamer, this is hardly likely to worry him. Better that, he might say, than to be a programmed robot, an organization man. In this way, the City of Words might come to seem the last stronghold against Behaviorism.

Appendix Three

There is no doubt that during the last two decades a large number of Americans have come to regard society as some kind of vast conspiracy, plotting to shape individual consciousness to suit its own ends. The great popularity of Herbert Marcuse during the latter 'sixties was to a large extent due to his attempt, as it were, to bring this 'plot' out into the open. Thus, in perhaps his most influential essay, 'Repressive Tolerance' (1965), he claimed that people in the supposedly free societies of the West (above all America) are subtly indoctrinated by the conditions in which they live and think, and which they never transcend. Instead of overt repression, such a society simply makes men immune to preferable human alternatives,

> And when this perversion starts in the mind of the individual, in his consciousness, his needs, when heteronomous interests occupy him before he can experience his servitude, then the efforts to counteract his dehumanization must begin at the place of entrance, there where the false consciousness takes form (or rather: is systematically formed)—it must begin with stopping the words and images which feed this consciousness ... the break through the false consciousness may prove the Archimedean point for a larger emancipation.

Marcuse struck a note of militancy which awakened a response in the younger generations. But American writers, whose work is after all concerned with 'words and images' aimed at other consciousnesses, have been exploring and dramatizing these problems throughout the last two decades.

Marcuse's emphatic reminder of the primary importance of language raises the problem of linguistic patterning. It is an inevitable paradox for the writer that he seeks to control and pattern words which were in fact controlling and patterning his consciousness long before he was aware of the process. In this connection I wish to draw brief attention to some of the ideas of Benjamin Lee Whorf, an American pioneer in linguistics. I will bring together some of his statements from the posthumous collection of papers written during the 'thirties and 'forties, *Language, Thought, and Reality* (M.I.T. Press, Cambridge, Mass., 1956), which have some bearing on the linguistic 'behavior' of many contemporary American writers.

Natural man, whether simpleton or scientist, knows no more of the linguistic forces that bear upon him than the savage knows of gravitational forces. He supposes that talking is an activity in which he is free and untrammeled ... Actually, thinking is most mysterious, and by far the greatest light upon it that we have is thrown by the study of language. This study shows that the forms of a person's thoughts are *controlled by inexorable laws of pattern* of which he is unconscious. These patterns are the unperceived intricate systematizations of his own language — shown readily enough by a candid comparison and contrast with other languages, especially those of a different linguistic family. His thinking itself is in a language — in English, in Sanskrit, in Chinese. And every language is a vast pattern-system, different from others, in which are culturally ordained the forms and categories by which the personality not only communicates, but also analyzes nature, notices or neglects types of relationship and phenomena, channels his reasoning, and builds the house of his consciousness.

Whorf continues with typically emphatic vocabulary.

We saw that ... in linguistic and mental phenomena, significant behaviour (or what is the same, both behaviour and significance, so far as interlinked) are *ruled by a specific system* or organization, a 'geometry' of form principles characteristic of each language. This *organization is imposed from outside* the narrow circle of the personal consciousness, *making of that consciousness a mere puppet* whose linguistic manoeuvrings are held in unsensed and unbreakable bonds of pattern ... human beings are all alike in this respect ... They are as *unaware of the beautiful and inexorable systems that control them* as a cowherd is of cosmic rays. [My italics.]

The 'lexation' or name-giving aspect of language he describes as being completely controlled by the 'patternment' aspect of language, and it is this patternment which without our direct knowledge organizes the reality we live in. 'Each language performs this artificial chopping up of the continuous spread and flow of existence in a different way.' Obviously that 'continuous spread and flow' has to be structured in some way otherwise we would simply drown in unclassifiable, unidentifiable sensations. But Whorf's point is that our consciousness is moulded and determined by the invisible structures which inhere in our particular language. When we think we are speaking, or writing, most freely, we may be as puppets under the control of those patternments and 'inexorable systems'. It is within neither my scope nor my ability to comment on Whorf's work professionally. More to my point is that Whorf, himself an American, describes man's relation to the conditioning powers of language as almost completely passive. The linguistic 'relativity principle' implicit in his work has, needless to say, not gone unquestioned. One critic, Solomon Asch, points out (in *Language in Culture*, edited by Harry Hoijer [University of Chicago Press, 1954]), that Whorf is really implying that the individual is *completely* enculturated, that the specific culture determines all an individual's values, motives, needs and world view through its language, and that the individual is completely 'constrained to certain modes of interpretation even when he thinks himself most free'. Such a theory, says Asch, stresses the diversity and role of cultures, and minimizes the biologic universals as controlling factors in human behaviour. Asch opposes the theory, especially as it applies to the development of ethical values, on the grounds that it assumes 'a dynamically empty organism, lacking directed forces toward nature and society'.

In one phrase, Asch summarizes a deep dread discernible in the fiction under discussion—the vision of the individual as 'dynamically empty': the void under the bandages in *Catch-22*, the blank wall behind the wallpaper in *Cabot Wright Begins*, a hollow construction, an automaton without a soul or thought to call its own. And the phrases of Whorf's which I italicized concur uncannily with the prevalent feeling in contemporary American fiction that all sorts of invisible 'organizations' and 'systems' are manipulating the minds and lives of their unaware puppets. A crucial point of difference is that American novelists and their heroes seldom refer to inexorable systems as 'beautiful'.

Appendix Four

The notion of a tension between rigid forms encrusted on the self and a flowing release from such forms is at the heart of Wilhelm Reich's *Character Analysis* (translated by Theodore P. Wolfe, Vision Press, Peter Nevill, London, 1950). This work was first published in Berlin in 1933, but it has often been reprinted since 1945 in America in response to a continuing demand. A consideration of the influence of Reich's theories and work on American writers would be a fair topic for a separate book. But a few observations about one of his basic ideas are relevant to the tensions we are considering. He starts *Character Analysis* by asserting that society (with the help of the parents) subtly pressures the individual into 'the formation of a psychic structure which corresponds to the existing social order'. 'The character structure, then, is the crystallization of the sociological process of a given epoch.' (A view also held by Erik Erikson, another influential theorist concerned with problems of 'identity'.) What we call 'character' is often, in Reich's view, a defensive 'armor'. 'The individual is "characterologically armored" against the outer world and against his unconscious drives.'

Without reproducing here the steps of his argument, it is fair to say that Reich's response to this character armour or crystallization was to attempt to dissolve it: 'a consistent dissolving of character resistances' provides an avenue of approach to the primal determinants of the self. The stress is always on 'the *dissolution* of the resistance', on '*loosening* the narcissistic protection mechanism, the *freeing* of the anxiety which is bound up in it'. The first of those italics are Reich's and I have added the others to indicate a characteristic vocabulary of release and various forms of de-structuring which Reich opposes to that rigid and rigidifying armour which the self often acquires in the course of its encounters with the external world. We find a similar opposition in many recent novels. And when Reich says that, 'Experience shows that if the character resistance does not *give way* a satisfactory result cannot be expected,' we may be reminded of the importance of the act of 'letting go' for so many American heroes.

At the same time, we noted that the idea of escaping from imprisoning fixities can be attended by a dread of turning to formless jelly. Here again, Reich's observations are relevant. For, having discussed the advantages to be derived from 'the analytic loosening of the character armor', he goes on to admit that this loosening can be dangerous, for that armour might function as an essential 'protective wall' for the self; dissolving it 'temporarily creates a condition which equals a breakdown of personality.' In Reich's view, such breakdowns are an essential pre-condition of structuring a new, more healthy personality. But he admits that it is a risky process. Generalizing from his statements one might speculate that it can be disabling, even destructive, to break down those armatures which, as well as imprisoning the self, may be supporting it. As a result of the complete dissolving advocated by Reich, the self might simply be washed away in the ensuing flow, with no certainty of ever re-achieving any viable identity. As many recent American novels show, 'letting go' in one way or another is seldom if ever the prelude to achieving some more satisfactory reconstruction of the self in its relation with society.

More usually, the self which has 'let go' ends up in an extra-social or isolated situation, often immobilized and impotent. Since, as it has been cogently argued by Erik Erikson (particularly in his book *Identity, Youth and Crisis*), the achieving of a satisfactory identity depends upon interaction, and the participations and recognitions which only some sort of society makes possible, the 'giving way' and dissolving of containing structures suggested by Reich's prescriptions and terms might in practice remove the self from the one area in which it might hope to acquire an identity. (In this connection we might take note of Marcuse's attack on those individuals who rebel against existing society in the name of 'self-actualization':

It isolates the individual from the one dimension where he could 'find himself': from his political existence, which is at the core of his entire existence. Instead, it encourages non-conformity and letting-go in ways which leave the real engines of repression in the society entirely intact, which even strengthen these engines by substituting the satisfactions of private and personal rebellion for a more than private and personal, and therefore more authentic, opposition.

One does not have to share Marcuse's definition of 'authentic opposition' to recognize how singularly a-political the American hero tends to be; how reluctant he is ever to offer any ideas about the kinds of structure which he thinks should replace the structurings in the existing society against which he is rebelling.)

Appendix Five

'The nature of our society is such that we are prevented from knowing who we are': thus, Ralph Ellison. The problem of discovering or creating the self, and the ways in which identity is achieved, imposed, abandoned or lost—these are subjects which permeate many different American disciplines at the moment. While my concern is with fiction, I want to advance some evidence from a sociologist, a social anthropologist, a psychologist and a critic.

The title of Erving Goffman's book, *The Presentation of Self in Everyday Life* (Doubleday Anchor, New York, 1959), could almost stand as a summary of a major area covered by contemporary American fiction. Appropriately enough he takes most of his imagery from the theatre. He sees man as a performer, 'a harried fabricator of impressions' and while he differentiates man as performer from man as character, his conclusion seems to be that character in man is that part of the self in charge of performance on the various stages of society.

A correctly staged and performed scene leads the audience to impute a self to a performed character, but this imputation— this self—is a product of a scene that comes off, and is not a *cause* of it. The self, then, as a performed character ... is a dramatic effect arising diffusely from a scene that is presented.

What is immediately apparent here is that the individual, or whatever the thing is that is capable of entrances and exits, has precious little control over his selfhood which is envisaged as primarily an apparitional phenomenon: 'the performance will come off and the firm self accorded each character will *appear* to emanate intrinsically from its performer.' [My italics.] An important result of this view is that the self is no longer a moral agent but a 'merchant of morality'. The performing self is not concerned with maintaining moral standards 'but with the amoral issue of engineering a convincing impression that these standards are being realized'. This is what used to be called hypocrisy, except that in Goffman's model of the self there may well be no devious schemer behind the studious merchant of morality. Indeed there is very much the feeling in

432

Goffman that behind the performer, adjusting, as it were, his visible surface to the expectations of the surrounding glances, there may not be anything at all.* His vision of society is a fairly stark one in that under the surface there appears to be only a worry about preserving that surface. 'Behind many masks and many characters, each performer tends to wear a single look, a naked unsocialized look, a look of concentration, a look of one who is privately engaged in a difficult, treacherous task.'

Of course the notion that an individual may have many social roles is not new. William James wrote that, 'we may practically say that he has as many different social selves as there are distinct *groups* of persons about whose opinion he cares.' The more modern feeling, of which Goffman's book is a brilliant exposition and example, is that the self is only the sum of the roles it plays – a good or inept role-master, a willing or reluctant impresario of masks. A dread of such a diffusion of self into all the roles it is called on to play is very marked in American fiction, as I try to show. In Goffman's rather nightmarish world the only self you can aspire to become is a role-player capable of the smoothest adjustments to the requirements of a variety of social scenes. For the American hero who might indeed have aspirations of a higher order the problem will certainly occur of what he might do or where he might go to realize his 'true self', a realization which he feels may well lie elsewhere than in becoming one of society's more successful actors. Where Goffman does have an important point is in his perception that often society determines the available reality. It does so by staging a variety of performances which highlight the official values: these performances are like an ongoing ceremony which comes to be taken for reality

* It is not as though this sort of character—or characterless—structure has never been envisaged before. Henry James, for instance, adumbrated the type very perceptively in his depiction of Miriam Rooth in *The Tragic Muse*.

> It came over him suddenly that so far from there being any question of her having the histrionic nature, she simply had it in such perfection that she was always acting; that her existence was a series of parts assumed for the moment, each changed for the next, before the perpetual mirror of some curiosity or admiration or wonder—some spectatorship that she perceived or imagined in the people about her ... It struck him abruptly that a woman ... whose identity resided in the continuity of her personations, so that she had no moral privacy, as he phrased it to himself, but lived in a high wind of exhibition, of figuration—such a woman was a kind of monster, in whom of necessity there would be nothing to like, because there would be nothing to take hold of.

But what for James was perhaps the special case of the artist—certainly the acting artist—now seems to many Americans to be the common condition.

itself. 'To stay in one's room away from the place where the party is given ... is to stay away from where reality is being performed. The world is, in truth, a wedding.' To say that recent American fiction is full of characters who stay in their rooms away from 'where reality is being performed' is to make the general point that a search or a yearning for some reality outside the interlocking charades and pantomimes of modern society is very common. The attempt to find some alternative to the stagnation of a lonely room and the theatricals which society seems to perpetuate is one which tends to be well to the fore in the consciousness of the American hero.

Goffman's 'self' seems to be an anxious void hastily adjusting movable surfaces. Robert Lifton's model in his essay 'Protean Man' (*Partisan Review*, Winter 1968) tends to stress a comparable adaptability. Drawing on the very influential work of Erik Erikson he develops the idea of 'self-process' in preference to older definitions of identity. 'For it is quite possible that even the image of personal identity, in so far as it suggests inner stability and sameness, is derived from a vision of culture in which man's relationship to his institutions and symbols are still relatively intact — hardly the case today.' In place of the idea of a fixed self he posits the image of a flowing one, and suggests the term 'Protean' to describe the most distinctive features of modern identity. The word is of some importance as we shall see and it is important to note that Lifton does not use the term wholly pessimistically.

He describes the protéan style of self-process as 'characterized by an interminable series of experiments and explorations — some shallow, some profound — each of which may be readily abandoned in favor of still new psychological quests.' This, he recognizes, is close to Erikson's observation of 'identity diffusion' or 'identity confusion' but Lifton also maintains that there are positive aspects to modern man's gift for fluent mutations; not least his refusal to foreclose on future possibilities.

As well as protean man, Lifton recognizes a type which he might define as rigidified man, those people who are 'fixed' rather than flowing. They are reacting against the 'protean influences which are always abroad' by opting for a sort of 'one-dimensional' identity, allowing themselves to be held in the 'grip' of the particular reality that society ascribes to them. Reverting to my previous images we can say that such people prefer the 'imprisonment' of fixed outlines to the jelly-like formlessness of protean man; we can find these figures in abundance in contemporary American fiction. But it is part of Lifton's intention to show that protean man is not merely passive and helpless in his flowing; he has a 'strong ideological hunger' and 'is starved for ideas and feelings that can give coherence to his world, but here too his taste is toward new combinations.' The point is that Lifton sees protean man as a quester; he still carries with him Utopian images and expectations, with the result that he is constantly encountering disillusion. He suffers from 'a vague but persistent kind of self-condemnation ... a sense of having no outlet for his loyalties and no symbolic structure for his achievements.' His drifting may contain an exploration, and his mutations may reflect motives hardly conceivable in Goffman's hollow man.

Protean man, then, is as prone to shedding roles as taking them up; he is likely to embrace, alter and abandon 'idea systems', guiding symbols and ideologies with equal ease. And one of the important features of this modern man is what Lifton calls the disappearance of the classical superego, 'the internalization of clearly defined criteria of right and wrong transmitted within a particular culture by parents to their children. Protean man requires freedom from precisely that kind of superego – he requires a symbolic fatherlessness – in order to carry out his explorations.' 'Requires' could in many cases perhaps be replaced by 'suffers from': either way it is surely no accident that the figure of the father is almost totally absent from recent American fiction. This is certainly not new; Jay Gatsby, springing from his Platonic conception of himself, is only one of the more notable American self-parenting heroes. But recent fiction seems to indicate that the problematics of this condition are being more deeply registered and explored. To be fatherless, even if only symbolically, is to be autonomous, yet at the same time it makes one more exposed to the coercions of environment; and one of the problems of the American hero and writer alike is to mediate between an impossible dream of pure autonomy and an intolerable state of total enslavement.

In this connection it is interesting to turn to a psychologist and find the problem being described in almost exactly these terms. David Rapaport, in writing about the 'Theory of Ego Autonomy' (*Bulletin of the Menninger Clinic*, January 1958) starts with an admitted simplification which defines the limits of his discussion. He contrasts what he calls the Berkeleian view of man with the Cartesian. In the Berkeleian view, the outside world is 'the creation of man's imagination'. In this 'solipsistic' view man is completely independent of his environment, and hence dependent solely on 'the forces and images residing within him'. In the Cartesian view, man is a *tabula rasa* on which experience writes with irresistible authority. Such a man is totally dependent on his environment, while there are no forces within him to counter this dependency. Riesman's distinction between the inner-directed and the other-directed seems to indicate a similar basic division. But Rapaport recognizes that neither of the extreme states of his opening contrast are confirmed by observation, and what he sets out to do is to explore the '*relative* autonomy of man from his environment'. (My italics.) He sees two questions as central—'what are the guarantees of the ego's autonomy from the environment? How is the autonomy of the ego from the environment related to the autonomy of the ego from the id?' In his model, man is an organism which must find a point of balance between being completely subservient to the id—drowned in his own desires— and completely created and controlled by his environment. To the extent that one or other of these states preponderates, man is an automaton—a victim of the things about him or the drives within him. His identity is earned by mediating between these two states.

The problem—and it can threaten to be a vicious circle—is that only contact with the external world can keep a man from solipsism, but too much engagement with environment is liable to rob man of his autonomy. The dangers of being what John Cage described as 'omniattentive' or of going into a sort of perceptual retreat from the external world are both clearly envisaged here, just as they are explored and experienced by many American heroes who have to struggle between the twin tendencies to disappear into the self or become diffused into the world. Rapaport describes cases in which those inner drives which are ultimately responsible for the ego's sense of its autonomy are blocked or undermined and 'the result is stimulus slavery'; a danger dramatized by writers as apparently different as Saul Bellow and William Burroughs.* Like a character in an American novel Rapaport finds the self going to and fro between the two extreme alternatives. To the extent that the ego achieves autonomy from the id, it is likely to become enslaved by external stimuli; as this autonomy diminishes, the ego loses touch with reality outside itself. Rapaport himself raises the question of whether either of these autonomies is in fact an autonomy. From one point of view they are alternate forms of enslavement. The world is too much with us, or we are too much without the world.

His conclusion, that the individual has to aim at achieving a point of 'optimal balance' between autonomy from id and autonomy from

---

* Rapaport makes the interesting observation that when the inner drives are repressed 'the drives and their representations, whose access to motility and consciousness was so strenuously barred, invade "objective" reality by infiltrating the very thought processes and logic which were elaborated to curb them, and succeed in filling the person's perception and thought with magic and animism' —a very relevant observation in connection with the perception and prose styles of some of the writers examined in this book.

environment, is of general application. More relevant to this study is his observation that 'the strength which makes a man independent from reality stimulation tends to lead him to build an impenetrable wall around himself.' One could put alongside this the remark of the young American writer, Charles Newman, who pertinently asks in an essay on Henry James and James Baldwin (*Yale Review*, Fall 1966), 'What happens to the rebel who finds that the price of one's resistance is that one has no reality beyond the resistance?' Here could be a problem for both hero and author; that having spent a maximum of energy on keeping out a threatening or swamping environment they both may be left with only gestures of exclusion for their vocabulary of words or deeds. The discovery that one can be trapped in one's own defences is not a new one, perhaps, but it is one being made with a new kind of urgency and poignancy.

Throughout a distinguished career, the literary critic Lionel Trilling has sought to hold on to an idea which he thinks is diminishing: the idea 'that one may live a real life apart from the group, that one may exist as an actual person not only at the center of society but on its margins, that one's values may be none the less real and valuable because they do not prevail and are even rejected and submerged.' It is entirely appropriate that Trilling should have written two of his major critical works on Matthew Arnold (who first formulated the ideal of the intellectual 'alien') and E. M. Forster, whose delicate humane wisdom can only thrive on the margins of society since the clash of ideologies at the centre drowns out all subtler voices. One of the tasks of the recent American hero is to discover whether there are any such margins left.

It is not hard to understand why the figure of Freud has always been an important one for Trilling. In his most recent book, revealingly entitled *Beyond Culture* (Secker and Warburg, London, 1966), Trilling returned to Freud to help him clarify his own deepening ambivalence about 'culture'. Freud, he says, 'does indeed see the self as formed by its culture. But he also sees the self struggling against it.' Trilling seems to have reached an impasse not unlike the dilemma envisaged by Rapaport's version of the ego and its relation to its environment. He acknowledges, indeed emphasizes, that man can only find true fulfilment in a cultural environment; at the same time he has a growing fear that contemporary culture may seduce (where it does not force) the self into total submission. This is why he welcomes Freud's emphasis on the place of biology in human fate. 'It suggests that there is a residue of human quality beyond the reach of cultural control, and that this residue of human quality, elemental as it may be, serves to bring culture itself under criticism and keeps it from being absolute.' This indeed may be said to be the dream or hope of an indefinite number of American heroes and their authors who try to show, in their various ways, that there is a self which does not necessarily 'go awry' if the culture he is in does, that the sense and experience of identity are not wholly at the mercy of the conditioning forces around us.

All these various writers from different disciplines, from whom I have quoted, reveal a shared preoccupation with the problem of just how independent or autonomous the self can be from its given environment, culture, society. How can it indulge in the necessary participations in outer reality on which consciousness depends without becoming only a fluid, protean jelly; how can it retain some sense of its independence and responsibility for its own choice and future without erecting perceptual and psychological walls as arresting as any prison? We might say as another generalization that both author and hero are striving to hold on to, even to celebrate, some principle of 'indeterminism'. Again the words of William James seem relevant:

> Indeterminism thus denies the world to be one unending unit of fact. It says there is a certain ultimate pluralism in it; and, so saying, it corroborates our ordinary unsophisticated view of things. To that view, actualities seem to float in a wider sea of possibilities from out of which they are chosen; and *somewhere*, indeterminism says, such possibilities exist, and form a part of truth.

'Possibilities' is one of the key recurring words in recent American fiction and James makes the connection between a sense of possibilities and a sense of indeterminism clear. Like William James, the American author and his characters can be seen searching for, or maintaining a belief in, a 'universe unfinished, with doors and windows open to possibilities uncontrolled in advance'.

Appendix Six

Perhaps no American writer has enjoyed a greater sense of the creative and sportive potentialities of his own consciousness than Henry James, and unlike Gradus he found his lifelong ventures through the labyrinthine lanes of Lex 'wonderfully amusing'. We are perhaps in danger of forgetting the indispensable values of play and 'fun' in these serious times,* and James's stress on the 'amusement' afforded an inhabitant of the City of Words is worth keeping before us. (The quotations are all from his own Preface to *The Awkward Age*.)

> It comes back to me, the whole 'job', as wonderfully amusing and delightfully difficult from the first; since amusement deeply abides, I think, in any artistic attempt the basis and groundwork of which are conscious of a particular firmness. On that hard fine floor the element of execution feels it may more or less confidently *dance*; in which case puzzling questions, sharp obstacles, dangers of detail, may come up for it by the dozen without breaking its heart or shaking its nerve. It is the difficulty produced by the loose foundation or the vague scheme that breaks the heart — when a luckless fatuity has overpersuaded an author of the 'saving' virtue of treatment. Being 'treated' is never, in a workable idea, a mere passive condition, and I hold no subject ever susceptible of help that isn't, like the embarrassed man of our proverbial wisdom, first of all able to help itself.

There is a salutary emphasis here on the root necessity of a firm subject which will serve as 'that hard fine floor' on which the inventive and playful powers of the writer may confidently amuse themselves and dance. James is pointing out here that there are subjects — loose foundations or vague schemes — which sheer brilliance of treatment are helpless to save, inadequate floors on which the imagination will only dance into disarray. This is valuable because while he recognizes the pre-eminent importance of the

* It is perhaps worth pointing out that James Joyce, who perhaps had more deliberate 'fun' with language than any of the other pioneer modern European novelists, is still a pervasive influence on contemporary American writers.

shaping powers of the mind, he is insisting on the importance of finding appropriate material for that mind to 'play' with. But the statement is also valuable in its recognition of the fact that if the subject is sound enough, there is no limit to the 'amusement' the writer may derive from treating it. Just as, when James is confident of his subject, he can confess his happiness in such statements as 'the more ... I lived in my arrangement and moved about in it, the more I sank into satisfaction', and he will speak of revelling 'while crouching amid the thick arcana of my plan'. It is as though he is saying that once the writer has defined a subject of sufficient bed-rock firmness, he can build on it theatres of possibility, houses of fiction, and indeed any other sort of metaphorical domicile in which his constructive energies and delights can find full play. There is perhaps another implication here—that the creative consciousness will ultimately find most comfort by cradling itself in the cocoon of its own designs. The dangers of solipsism are clearly there, hence the value of his insistence on the need for an appropriate subject which will ensure that preserving contact with otherness.

Appendix Seven

In connection with the defensive, even paranoid, attitude towards all forms of communication, and particularly media communication, so common in contemporary America, the work of Marshall McLuhan is of course extremely relevant. Had not so much been written about him, not to say by him, it would have been desirable to include a chapter on his work. In the circumstances an Appendix should be enough to suggest how oddly similar some of his ideas are to those of Burroughs, and at the same time to point to some basic differences of outlook. McLuhan's first work about communications, *The Mechanical Bride* (1951) (Beacon Paperback, Boston, 1967), is in effect an exemplary Burroughs-type exercise. He starts by alerting the reader to the intentions of the media controllers. 'To get inside in order to manipulate, exploit, control is the object now.' To counter this, says McLuhan, 'it seemed fitting to devise a method for reversing the process.' It would not be too much to call his method a cut-up technique. By extracting a large number of news items and advertisements from their contexts and making us really see how they work on us and influence our perceptions, McLuhan is to some extent freeing us from their thrall. This is also the aim of Burroughs. In particular McLuhan has a section pointing out the pernicious influence of the *Time, Life, Fortune*, group of magazines, which he calls 'The Ballet Luce'. His warning that their 'irresponsible manipulation' of the 'arts of communication and control' could have very sinister results if it moved from the entertainment to the political sphere is precisely what Burroughs has been concerned to stress in his own work. On the other hand another note is sounded in this book which indicates in what way McLuhan's work will diverge from Burroughs's. McLuhan affirms that even the frequent absurdity and unreliability of the news as presented by the new media 'cannot annul the total effect, which is to enforce a deep sense of human solidarity.' Here we can detect that separation of medium from message which formed the basis for his famous slogan. The message may often be absurd or dangerous; but the media may nonetheless have beneficial effects. Burroughs would hardly agree.

The Gutenberg Galaxy (Routledge and Kegan Paul, London, 1962) describes the making of typographic man, or the effects of the alphabet and printing on man and his relation to society. One basic contention in this immensely suggestive book is that the phonetic alphabet had the effect of opening up 'tribal or closed societies' and destroying their 'biological unity'. However, the printing age is now giving way to the 'electronic age' and the effect is, or will be, 'the sealing of the entire human family into a single global village'. The image is an audacious one, though to my mind visibly inappropriate, but what is more to the point is that McLuhan seems constantly to change his ground as to whether this return to a tribal state of mind in a global village is a good or bad thing. His less radical observation that when new technologies and new communications media collide or interpenetrate with older ones people experience all kinds of crises and confusions of perception and judgment is demonstrably true, and his demonstrations of this truth have seemed particularly relevant in America in the second half of the twentieth century.

Just what transformations of consciousness and attitude would result from the new media being introduced into society McLuhan set out to study in *Understanding Media* (1964) (Signet Books, New American Library, New York, 1966). Without wishing to tax McLuhan with a lack of coherence and consistency which his method of improvised speculations never promises, I do think that it is revealing to note a detectable shifting of attitude towards the phenomena he is discussing, and to point out where he seems to differ from a writer like Burroughs. For instance, he says that the movies 'translated us beyond mechanism into the world of growth and organic interrelation'. For many American writers, the movies are the very image of all those powers in society wishing to impose false versions and innutrient fantasies on the population. When McLuhan says that 'subliminal and docile acceptance of media impact has made them prisons without walls for their human users,' he is speaking a language which any American novelist would understand. When shortly after he goes on to say that the new electric technology 'retribalizes' detribalized man, it is less easy to follow him. Since the whole vocabulary of fragmentation used to describe the effects of printing and mechanical technology on man is implicitly critical, the countering vocabulary of organic unity, interrelationship, solidarity and retribalization must be taken to be commendatory and honorific. A sentence like this—'Fragmented, literate, and visual individualism is not possible in an electrically patterned and imploded society'—could be read as offering cause for regret or celebration. Admittedly, McLuhan says that he is only trying to make us 'aware' of the sorts of changes that new media will inexorably effect. Indeed he says that such awareness can bring about an increase in 'human autonomy'. But such autonomy sounds like a resistance to the tribe, a nostalgia for that individualism which McLuhan is seeking to prove is no longer possible.

McLuhan says that the effect of introducing a new technology is to 'numb' conscious procedures. With reference to the subtle effects of electric technology he says that 'once we have surrendered our senses and nervous systems to the private manipulation of those who would try to benefit from taking a lease on our eyes and ears and nerves, we don't really have any rights left.' McLuhan speaks of the phonetic alphabet freeing man from 'the tribal trance'. More emphatically he says that

> Primitive man lived in a much more tyrannical cosmic machine than Western literate man has ever invented. The world of the ear is more embracing and inclusive than that of the eye can ever be. The ear is hypersensitive. The eye is cool and detached. The ear turns man over to universal panic while the eye, extended by literacy and mechanical time, leaves some gaps and some islands free from the unremitting acoustic pressure and reverberation.

One could be forgiven for thinking that here we have the basis of a vision which saw primitive man living in a tribal trance, always liable to panic, and modern man living benumbed in the global village, always vulnerable to media control. The man in the middle would be literate man, isolated and fragmented if you will, but at least enjoying a degree of lucid control and independent consciousness. The only problem with accepting this as McLuhan's vision is that the words used to describe literate man are usually negative, while the tribal and global terms seem more positive.

At one point McLuhan envisages transferring our consciousness to computers, and programming it not to be distracted by the entertainment world—the sort of strategy also envisaged by Burroughs, using good control to combat bad. Then McLuhan goes on to suggest, 'might not our current translation of our entire lives into the spiritual form of information seem to make of the entire globe, and of the human family, a single consciousness?' The honorific words 'spiritual' and 'human family' make this seem a desirable dream; yet the notion of all individual distinction being merged into one universal homogenized blob is a recurrent American nightmare. Another interesting point of similarity and divergence between McLuhan and Burroughs is the attitude they share to moving beyond language. McLuhan says that electricity may point the way to an extension of consciousness which will make verbalization redundant. 'The condition of "weightlessness", that biologists say promises a physical immortality, may be paralleled by the condition of speechlessness that could confer a perpetuity of collective harmony and peace.' Here we have two of Burroughs's ideas — getting beyond body and word into weightlessness and speechlessness. But whereas Burroughs envisages this escape or transcendence as a means of getting beyond all controls into some personal freedom, McLuhan is again thinking of his tribal-global unity. What elsewhere might be seen as group trance now becomes collective harmony, and for a benumbed mindlessness we are invited to read peace. I doubt if Burroughs would allow himself such unstable ambiguity in the application of key terms.

In *The Medium is the Massage* (Bantam Books, New York, 1967) McLuhan hardly said anything new, but one or two of his formulations may be singled out to suggest how easily he accepts phenomena which for the novelist are more problematical. 'Ours is a brand-new world of allatonceness. "Time" has ceased, "space" has vanished. We now live in a *global* village ... a simultaneous happening. We are back in acoustic space. We have begun again to structure the primordial feeling, the tribal emotions from which a few centuries of literacy divorced us.' The tone is purely affirmative. Despite reminders of the dangers of manipulation and control, the book is a celebration. 'Massage' is a pun, but one which suggests the benevolence of the media which 'work us over completely'. Where nineteenth-century man saw himself as detached from the world, to which he then had to relate himself in various patterns, modern man or youth is moving towards a *'participation mystique'*. 'The instantaneous world of electric informational media involves all of us, all at once. No detachment ... is possible.' Again — 'Electric circuitry profoundly involves men with one another. Information pours upon us, instantaneously and continuously.' Indeed it does, but for many American writers and their heroes this is a cause for alarm and even despair. It nearly drives Herzog mad. It is what the mysterious agents for good in Burroughs's work are fighting against. Such writers do not see this pouring stream of information as an *involving* factor which makes man feel responsible for his fellow men. On the contrary, it is experienced as an isolating factor by which the vulnerable individual is drowned in unusable fabrications and versions. (This is not to deny that the sort of far-flung coverage and instant participation made possible by TV, for example, have encouraged a more universal, delocalized concern over matters such as wars and natural disasters.) The use of terms like 'participation mystique', and the euphoric vision of a new communion of the whole human family, united in one world-wide collective consciousness, suggest the presence of a religious dimension to McLuhan's thought, and more specifically a catholic vision of all men being members, if not of one church, at least of one global village and all partaking of the same 'communion'. This of course is not in itself grounds for criticizing McLuhan's ideas, and his willingness to see positive virtues and exciting possibilities in the new media is often stimulating and encouraging. On the other hand it must be admitted that he has really glossed over, or simply chosen to ignore, the sorts of danger which he outlined so tellingly in *The Mechanical Bride*, and we no longer hear much about the tribal trance and the tribal panic. For many American writers I think McLuhan is somewhat too sanguine about the effects of the phenomena he discusses. In his more recent work McLuhan seems to hold out an almost entirely optimistic vision of the happy tribal village to be brought about by mass media, in which individual consciousness is lapped by a sea of images, contentedly accepting the irreversible flow, gradually merging with the mass mind. It is one of the purposes of this book to suggest with what vigour American novelists hold out against such a possible state of affairs.

Notes

PREFATORY NOTE

1. A useful compilation of basic bibliographical and biographical material may be found in *LES USA: à la recherche de leur identité* by Pierre Dommergues (Editions Bernard Grasset, Paris, 1967).
2. Princeton University Press, Princeton, 1961.
3. World Publishing Company, New York, 1962.
4. Oxford University Press, New York, 1967.
5. Jonathan Cape, London, 1965.
6. Oxford University Press, New York, 1966.

INTRODUCTION

1. Princeton University Press, 1965.
2. See Stephen Black's admirable Introduction to *The Scarlet Letter*, Perennial Classic series (Harper and Row, New York, 1967).
3. The Norton Library, W. W. Norton, New York, 1962.

CHAPTER ONE

1. This interview appeared in the *Listener*, October 10th, 1968.
2. Mary McCarthy's article appeared in *Encounter*, October 1962.
3. 'Lolita: The Springboard of Parody' by Alfred Appel, Jr., *Wisconsin Studies in Contemporary Literature*, ii 1967.
4. 'An Interview with Vladimir Nabokov', *Wisconsin Studies in Contemporary Literature*, ii 1967.
5. This interview appeared in *Partisan Review*, Winter 1969.
6. 'The Politics of Self-Parody' by Richard Poirier, *Partisan Review*, Summer 1968.
7. 'The Literature of Exhaustion' by John Barth, *New Society*, May 16th, 1968.
8. *Abstraction and Empathy* by Wilhelm Worringer; translated by Michael Bullock (Routledge and Kegan Paul, London, 1963).

CHAPTER TWO

1. In *Trials of the Word* (Yale University Press, Newhaven, 1965).
2. In *Paris Review*, Spring 1965; reprinted in *Shadow and Act* (Secker and Warburg, London, 1967).
3. 'Chaos in Poetry', reprinted in *Selected Literary Criticism*, edited by Anthony Beal (William Heinemann, London, 1955).

CHAPTER THREE

1. 'Talk with Saul Bellow', *New York Times Book Review*, September 20th, 1953.
2. In the article already referred to, 'Days of Wrath and Laughter': see Chapter Two, Note 1.
3. 'The Best Catch There Is' in *Doings and Undoings* by Norman Podhoretz (Rupert Hart-Davis, London, 1965).

CHAPTER FOUR
1. 'Purdy's *Malcolm*: A Unique Vision of Radical Emptiness' by Thomas Lorch, *Wisconsin Studies in Contemporary Literature*, vi 1965.
2. 'Beyond Omniscience' by Charles Newman, *TriQuarterly*, Fall 1967.

CHAPTER FIVE
1. This was an interview with Eric Mottram for the B.B.C. of which the only printed extracts, to my knowledge, appeared in *Les Langues Modernes*, January-February 1965.
2. In *Paris Review*, Fall 1965.
3. Ibid.
4. See *The Moderns*, edited by LeRoi Jones (MacGibbon and Kee, London, 1965).
5. See Note 2.
6. 'Composition as Process' in *Silence* (Wesleyan University Press, Middletown, 1961).
7. See Note 1.
8. *Silence* by John Cage. See Note 6.

CHAPTER SIX
1. University of California Press, Berkeley, California, 1963.
2. See 'Reason in the Madness of Letters' collected in *A Primer of Ignorance*, (Harcourt, Brace and World, New York, 1967).
3. Eyre and Spottiswoode, London, 1954.

CHAPTER SEVEN
1. *Kenyon Review*, Spring 1960.

CHAPTER EIGHT
1. This biography did not appear in England until 1969 when it was published by Macdonald and Co.

CHAPTER NINE
1. 'John Hawkes: An Interview', *Wisconsin Studies in Contemporary Literature*, Summer 1965.
2. 'John Hawkes On His Novels', *Massachusetts Review*, Summer 1966.
3. See Note 1.
4. See Richard Poirier's article referred to in Chapter One, Note 6.
5. In this connection see the helpful article by Robert Edenbaum entitled 'John Hawkes: *The Lime Twig* and Other Tenuous Horrors', *Massachusetts Review*, Summer 1966.
6. See Note 2.
7. In his Introduction to the New Directions Paperbook edition of *Lime Twig*, 1961.
8. See Note 1.

CHAPTER TEN
1. 'John Barth: An Interview', *Wisconsin Studies in Contemporary Literature*, vi 1965.
2. 'History in Barth's *The Sot-Weed Factor*' by Alan Holder, *American Quarterly*, Fall 1968.
3. *The Man Without Qualities* by Robert Musil, Vol. I (Secker and Warburg, London, 1961).

CHAPTER ELEVEN
1. Published in the United States by Harper & Row (New York, 1971).

CHAPTER TWELVE
1. *Paris Review,* Winter 1968.
2. Ibid.
3. Ibid.

CHAPTER THIRTEEN
1. *Saul Bellow* by Tony Tanner (Oliver and Boyd, London, 1965).
2. Reprinted under the title 'Writing American Fiction' in *The Commentary Reader* (Atheneum, New York, 1966).
3. 'The Perils of Pleasing the Public', *Chicago Sun-Times Book Week*, reprinted in England in the *Observer*, December 8th, 1968.
4. See 'Distractions of a Fiction Writer' in *The Living Novel*, edited by Granville Hicks (Macmillan, New York, 1957).
5. 'Literature', *The Great Ideas Today* (New York: Encyclopaedia Britannica, Inc., 1963).
6. Norman Weinstein makes this the key point of the novel in his interesting essay '*Herzog*, Order and Entropy' which he kindly sent to me in manuscript in 1968. I have not been able to ascertain whether or not this essay has since been published.
7. *The Machine in the Garden* by Leo Marx (Oxford University Press, New York, 1964).
8. In an interview in *Paris Review*, Winter 1966.
9. 'Will This Finally Be Philip Roth's Year?' by Howard Junker, *New York Magazine*, January 13th, 1969.
10. Quoted in 'Portnoy: A Critical Diagnosis' by Dan Yergin, *Granta*, May Week, 1969. See also 'Philip Roth's Exact Intent'. *New York Times Book Review*, February 23rd, 1969.
11. Ibid.
12. See Note 9.

CHAPTER FOURTEEN
1. See Chapter Thirteen, Note 2.
2. 'The Natural: Malamud's World Ceres' by Earl Wasserman, *The Centennial Review*, Fall 1965.
3. 'Laughter in the Ghetto' by Saul Bellow, *Saturday Review of Literature*, May 30th, 1953.

CHAPTER FIFTEEN
1. *The Hell's Angels* (Random House, New York, 1967; Allen Lane The Penguin Press, London, 1967).
2. In *Ramparts*, March 1967.

CHAPTER SIXTEEN
1. Farrar, Straus and Giroux, New York, 1968; Weidenfeld and Nicolson, London, 1969
2. For some suggestions as to the significance of the use of the figure of the Indian in contemporary American fiction see *The Return of the Vanishing American* by Leslie Fiedler (Jonathan Cape, London, 1968).
3. See *Buddhism* by Edward Conze (Harper Torchbooks, New York, 1959).

4. Ibid.
5. Ibid.
6. Jonathan Cape, London, 1970.

CONCLUSION
1. Houghton Mifflin, Boston, 1966; Calder and Boyars, London, 1968.
2. Farrar, Straus and Giroux, Noonday Press, New York, 1966; Jonathan Cape, London, 1966.
3. See *Conversations with Jorge Luis Borges* by Richard Burgin (Holt, Rinehart and Winston, New York, 1969), especially Chapter VII.

Selected Bibliography

This bibliography gives complete details of the books discussed in the text.

BARTH, John
The Floating Opera (Appleton, New York, 1956; Secker and Warburg, London, 1968).
End of the Road (Doubleday, New York, 1958; Secker and Warburg, London, 1962).
The Sot-Weed Factor (Doubleday, New York, 1960; Secker and Warburg, London, 1961).
Giles Goat-Boy (Doubleday, New York, 1966; Secker and Warburg, London, 1967).
Lost in the Funhouse (Doubleday, New York, 1968; Secker and Warburg, London, 1969).

BARTHELME, Donald
Come Back, Dr. Caligari (Atlantic Monthly Press, Little, Brown, New York, 1964; Eyre and Spottiswoode, London, 1966).
Snow White (Atheneum, New York, 1967; Jonathan Cape, London, 1968).
Unspeakable Practices, Unnatural Acts (Farrar, Straus and Giroux, New York, 1968; Jonathan Cape, London, 1969).

BELLOW, Saul
The Victim (Vanguard, New York, 1947; John Lehmann, London, 1948).
The Adventures of Augie March (Viking, New York, 1953; Weidenfeld and Nicolson, London, 1954).
Seize the Day (Viking, New York, 1956; Weidenfeld and Nicolson, 1957).
Henderson the Rain King (Viking, New York, 1959; Weidenfeld and Nicolson, 1959).
Herzog (Viking, New York, 1964; Weidenfeld and Nicolson, London, 1965).
Mosby's Memoirs (Viking, New York, 1968; Weidenfeld and Nicolson, London, 1969).
Mr Sammler's Planet (Viking, New York, 1969; Weidenfeld and Nicolson, London, 1970).

BORGES, Jorge Luis
Ficciones (Grove Press, New York, 1962; Weidenfeld and Nicolson, London, 1962).

BRAUTIGAN, Richard
A Confederate General from Big Sur (Grove Press, New York, 1964; Jonathan Cape, London, 1971).
Trout Fishing in America (Four Seasons Foundation, San Francisco, 1967; Jonathan Cape, London, 1970).
In Watermelon Sugar (Four Seasons Foundation, San Francisco, 1968; Jonathan Cape, London, 1970).

BURROUGHS, William
Junkie (Olympia Press, Paris, 1953; Four Square Books, London, 1966).
Naked Lunch (Olympia Press, Paris, 1959; Calder and Boyars, London, 1964).
The Exterminator (Olympia Press, Paris, 1960; McBride and Broadley, London, 1968).
The Yage Letters (City Lights Books, San Francisco, 1963; McBride and Broadley, London, 1967).
Nova Express (Grove Press, New York, 1964; Jonathan Cape, London, 1966).
The Ticket that Exploded (Grove Press, New York, 1967; Calder and Boyars, London, 1968).
The Job — Interviews with William Burroughs by Daniel Odier (Grove Press, New York, 1970; Jonathan Cape, London, 1970).

CAPOTE, Truman
In Cold Blood (Random House, New York, 1966; Hamish Hamilton, London, 1966).

CONROY, Frank
Stop-Time (Viking, New York, 1967; The Bodley Head, London, 1968).

ELKIN, Stanley
A Bad Man (Random House, New York, 1967; Anthony Blond, London, 1968).

ELLISON, Ralph
Invisible Man (Random House, New York, 1952; Penguin, Harmondsworth, 1965).
Shadow and Act (Random House, New York, 1964; Secker and Warburg, London, 1967).

EXLEY, Frederick
A Fan's Notes (Harper and Row, New York, 1968; Weidenfeld and Nicolson, London, 1970).

GADDIS, William
The Recognitions (Harcourt, Brace and World, New York, 1955; MacGibbon and Kee, London, 1962).

GASS, William
Omensetter's Luck (New American Library, New York, 1966; Collins, London, 1967).
In the Heart of the Heart of the Country (Harper and Row, New York, 1968; Jonathan Cape, London, 1969).
Willie Masters' Lonesome Wife, TriQuarterly Supplement No. 2 (Northwestern University Press, 1968).

HAWKES, John
The Cannibal (New Directions, New York, 1949; Chatto and Windus, London, 1968).
The Beetle Leg (New Directions, New York, 1951; Chatto and Windus, London, 1967).
The Goose on the Grave and *The Owl* (New Directions, New York, 1954).
The Lime Twig (New Directions, New York, 1961; Chatto and Windus, London, 1968).
Second Skin (New Directions, New York, 1964; Chatto and Windus, London, 1966).

HELLER, Joseph
Catch-22 (Simon and Schuster, New York, 1961; Jonathan Cape, London, 1962).

KESEY, Ken
One Flew Over the Cuckoo's Nest (Viking, New York, 1962; Methuen, London, 1962).
Sometimes a Great Notion (Viking, New York, 1963; Methuen, London, 1966).

MAILER, Norman
The Naked and the Dead (Holt, Rinehart and Winston, New York, 1948; André Deutsch, London, 1960).
Barbary Shore (Holt, Rinehart and Winston, New York, 1951; Jonathan Cape, London, 1952).
The Deer Park (Putnam's, New York, 1955; André Deutsch, London, 1969).
Advertisements for Myself (Putnam's, New York, 1959; André Deutsch, London, 1961).
The Presidential Papers (Putnam's, New York, 1963; André Deutsch, London, 1964).
An American Dream (Putnam's, New York, 1965; André Deutsch, London, 1965).

Why Are We in Vietnam? (Putnam's, New York, 1967; Weidenfeld and Nicolson, London, 1969).

MALAMUD, Bernard
The Natural (Harcourt, Brace and World, New York, 1952; Eyre and Spottiswoode, London, 1963).
The Assistant (Farrar, Straus and Cudahy, New York, 1957; Eyre and Spottiswoode, London, 1959).
A New Life (Farrar, Straus and Cudahy, New York, 1961; Eyre and Spottiswoode, London, 1962).
The Fixer (Farrar, Straus and Giroux, New York, 1966; Eyre and Spottiswoode, London, 1967).
Pictures of Fidelman: an Exhibition (Farrar, Straus and Giroux, New York, 1968; Eyre and Spottiswoode, London, 1969).

NABOKOV, Vladimir
Lolita (Putnam's, New York, 1958; Weidenfeld and Nicolson, London, 1959).
Pale Fire (Putnam's, New York, 1962; Weidenfeld and Nicolson, London, 1962).

PERCY, Walker
The Movie-goer (Knopf, New York, 1961; Eyre and Spottiswoode, London, 1963).
The Last Gentleman (Farrar, Straus and Giroux, New York, 1966; Eyre and Spottiswoode, London, 1967).

PLATH, Sylvia
The Bell Jar (First published as *The Bell Jar* by Victoria Lucas [William Heinemann, London, 1943]; Faber and Faber, London, 1966; Harper & Row, New York, 1971).

PURDY, James
'63 Dream Palace' in *Color of Darkness* (New Directions, New York, 1957; Secker and Warburg, London, 1961).
Malcolm (Farrar, Straus and Cudahy, New York, 1959; Secker and Warburg, London, 1960).
The Nephew (Farrar, Straus and Cudahy, New York, 1960; Secker and Warburg, London, 1961).
Cabot Wright Begins (Farrar, Straus and Giroux, New York, 1964; Secker and Warburg, London, 1965).
Eustace Chisholm and the Works (Farrar, Straus and Giroux, New York, 1967; Jonathan Cape, London, 1968).

PYNCHON, Thomas
V. (Lippincott, New York, 1963; Jonathan Cape, London, 1963).
The Crying of Lot 49 (Lippincott, New York, 1966; Jonathan Cape, London, 1967).

ROTH, Philip
Goodbye, Columbus (Houghton Miflin, New York, 1959; Corgi, London, 1964).
Letting Go (Random House, New York, 1962; Corgi, London, 1964).
When She Was Good (Random House, New York, 1967; Jonathan Cape, London, 1967).
Portnoy's Complaint (Random House, New York, 1969; Jonathan Cape, London, 1969).

SCHNECK, Stephen
The Nightclerk (Grove Press, New York, 1965; Weidenfeld and Nicolson, London, 1966).

SELBY, Hubert, Jr
Last Exit to Brooklyn (Grove Press, New York, 1964; Calder and Boyars, London, 1968).

SONTAG, Susan
The Benefactor (Farrar, Straus and Giroux, New York, 1963; Eyre and Spottiswoode, London, 1964).
Death Kit (Farrar, Straus and Giroux, New York, 1968; Secker and Warburg, London, 1968).

UPDIKE, John
The Poorhouse Fair (Knopf, New York, 1959; Gollancz, London, 1959).
Rabbit, Run (Knopf, New York, 1960; André Deutsch, London, 1961).
The Centaur (Knopf, New York, 1963; André Deutsch, London, 1963).
Of the Farm (Knopf, New York, 1965; André Deutsch, London, 1966).
Couples (Knopf, New York, 1968; André Deutsch, London, 1968).

VONNEGUT, Kurt, Jr
Player Piano (Holt, Rinehart and Winston, New York, 1952; Macmillan, London, 1953).
Sirens of Titan (Houghton Miflin, New York, 1959; Gollancz, London, 1962).
Mother Night (Harper and Row, New York, 1961; Jonathan Cape, London, 1968).
Cat's Cradle (Holt, Rinehart and Winston, New York, 1963; Gollancz, London, 1963).
God Bless You, Mr Rosewater (Holt, Rinehart and Winston, New York, 1964; Jonathan Cape, London, 1965).
Slaughterhouse-Five (Delacorte, New York, 1969; Jonathan Cape, London, 1970).

Index

71 72 73 10 9 8 7 6 5 4 3 2 1